Lecture Notes in Computer Science 2911

Edited by G. Goos, J. Hartmanis, and J. van Leeuwen

Springer
Berlin
Heidelberg
New York
Hong Kong
London
Milan
Paris
Tokyo

Tengku Mohd Tengku Sembok
Halimah Badioze Zaman
Hsinchun Chen
Shalini R. Urs
Sung Hyon Myaeng (Eds.)

Digital Libraries: Technology and Management of Indigenous Knowledge for Global Access

6th International Conference on Asian Digital Libraries,
ICADL 2003
Kuala Lumpur, Malaysia, December 8-12, 2003
Proceedings

 Springer

Series Editors

Gerhard Goos, Karlsruhe University, Germany
Juris Hartmanis, Cornell University, NY, USA
Jan van Leeuwen, Utrecht University, The Netherlands

Volume Editors

Tengku Mohd Tengku Sembok
Universiti Kebangsaan Malaysia, Bangi, Malaysia
E-mail: tmts@ftsm.ukm.my

Halimah Badioze Zaman
Universiti Kebangsaan Malaysia, Bangi, Malaysia
E-mail: hbz@ftsm.ukm.my

Hsinchun Chen
University of Arizona, Tucson, AZ, USA
E-mail: hchen@eller.arizona.edu

Shalini R. Urs
University of Mysore, India
E-mail: shalini@vidyanidhi.org.in

Sung Hyon Myaeng
Information & Communications University, Korea
E-mail: myaeng@icu.ac.kr

Cataloging-in-Publication Data applied for

A catalog record for this book is available from the Library of Congress.

Bibliographic information published by Die Deutsche Bibliothek
Die Deutsche Bibliothek lists this publication in the Deutsche Nationalbibliografie;
detailed bibliographic data is available in the Internet at <http://dnb.ddb.de>.

CR Subject Classification (1998): H.3, H.2, H.4.3, H.5, J.7, D.2, J.1, I.7

ISSN 0302-9743
ISBN 3-540-20608-6 Springer-Verlag Berlin Heidelberg New York

Springer-Verlag is a part of Springer Science+Business Media

springeronline.com

© Springer-Verlag Berlin Heidelberg 2003
Printed in Germany

Typesetting: Camera-ready by author, data conversion by PTP-Berlin, Protago-TeX-Production GmbH
Printed on acid-free paper   SPIN: 10972311   06/3142   5 4 3 2 1 0

Preface

The International Conference on Asian Digital Libraries (ICADL) is an annual international forum that provides opportunities for researchers and experts to meet and exchange research results, innovative ideas and state-of-the-art developments in the digital libraries of their respective countries. Building on the success of the first five ICADL conferences, the 6th ICADL conference in Kuala Lumpur, Malaysia aimed to further strengthen the collaboration and strategic alliance between the different researchers and experts from the Asia-Pacific Region in the field of digital libraries.

The theme of the conference, "Digital Libraries: Technology and Management of Indigenous Knowledge for Global Access," reflects the shared belief of the organizers that success in the development and implementation of digital libraries in the k-economy is based on four key areas: the technologies that are employed to create a user-friendly environment, organization, interaction, navigation, and access to content; a knowledge management approach that ensures all types of knowledge (explicit, tacit and implicit) are included; indigenous content, which implies the creation of suitable and specific content to meet the needs of the indigenous community; and global access, which implies that content should be made available across time and space, and also implies that the content should be flexible enough to meet global needs.

The ICADL 2003 began with an opening ceremony and a keynote address. The conference also included 4 tutorials covering: knowledge management systems; the management of indigenous knowledge; Semantic Web metadata; and an overview of digital libraries. There were 6 invited talks and 68 research paper presentations in 18 parallel sessions. These sessions covered discussions on topics such as Information Retrieval Techniques, Digital Libraries Services, Information Retrieval in Asian Languages, Multimedia Digital Libraries, a Digital Library for Community Building, Special Purpose Digital Libraries, Data Mining in Digital Libraries, Building and Using Digital Libraries, Metadata Issues, a Human Computer Interface, Knowledge Management, the Development of Contents, Digital Library Infrastructures, Standards and Conventions, E-Learning and Mobile Learning, Cryptography and Compression, Intellectual Property Rights and Copyright, Data and Communication Protocols, Privacy and Security, Biometrics and Security, Human Resources and Training, Machine Architecture and Organization, and Data Storage and Retrieval. In conjunction with ICADL 2003, the Library and Information Science Education in Asia Seminar (LISEA) was held as a postconference program immediately following the conference.

Despite the fact that the Iraq war and SARS (Severe Acute Respiratory Syndrome) affected world travel, ICADL 2003 still managed to record a good total of 136 papers, with a breakdown of 97 full papers, 36 short papers and 3 poster presentations. The conference had the collaboration of a 69-member program committee composed of well-known digital library experts and researchers from

Pacific Asia, USA and Europe. The large program committee meant that the ICADL managed to reach out to more participants and thus ensured good-quality paper submissions. The reviewing of papers was carried out by reviewers chosen from among the Program Committee members. The reviewing process was managed using the Collaborative Conference Management System (CoMan-Sys) developed by MIMOS Berhad in collaboration with the Department of Information Science, Faculty of Technology and Information Science, Universiti Kebangsaan Malaysia. Forty-five full papers, 23 short papers and 15 poster presentations were finally selected. The increase in the final number of poster presentations was due to the fact that some of the short papers were recommended by the program committee to be accepted as poster presentations.

On behalf of the Organizing and Program Committees of ICADL 2003, we thank all authors for their submissions and camera-ready copies of papers, and all participants for their active participation in the conference. We also acknowledge the sponsors, program committee members, conference support committees, and individuals who gave their continuous help and support in making the conference a success. We fervently hope that the conference will continue to grow from strength to strength as it travels to different host countries in Asia, and will continue to provide a stimulating and enriching platform for innovative ideas, to enable us to design and develop digital libraries that will transcend cultures, races, beliefs and religions to create world citizens who are knowledgeable, tolerant, and understanding, in order to create a world that is harmonious and peaceful for everyone for a long time to come.

November 2003   Tengku Mohd Tengku Sembok (Malaysia)
                                      Halimah Badioze Zaman (Malaysia)
                                             Hsinchun Chen (USA)
                                            Shalini R. Urs (India)
                                       Sung Hyon Myaeng (Korea)

Conference Organization

The 6th International Conference on Asian Digital Libraries (ICADL 2003) was organized by the Perpustakaan Negara Malaysia (PNM) in collaboration with the Department of Information Science, Faculty of Information Science and Technology, Universiti Kebangsaan Malaysia (UKM), the Malaysian Institute of Microelectronic Systems (MIMOS), Multimedia Development Corporation (MDC), and Persatuan Pustakawan Malaysia (PPM).

Honorary General Chair

Chief Secretary, Education Ministry

Advisors

Multimedia Development Corporation (MDC)

General Chair

Dato' Zawiyah Baba (Director-General, National Library of Malaysia)

Program Co-chairs

Tengku Mohd Tengku Sembok (Universiti Kebangsaan Malaysia, Malaysia)
Halimah Badioze Zaman (Universiti Kebangsaan Malaysia, Malaysia)
Hsinchun Chen (University of Arizona, USA)
Shalini Urs (University of Mysore, India)
Sung Hyon Myaeng (Information and Communication University, Korea)

Program Committee

Asia Pacific

Shahrul Azman Mohd Noah (UKM, Malaysia)
Zawiyah Mohd Yusof (UKM, Malaysia)
Juhana Salim (UKM, Malaysia)
Norhayati Abdul Mukti (UKM, Malaysia)
Nazlena Mohamad Ali (UKM, Malaysia)
Aidanismah Yahya (UKM, Malaysia)
Fatimah Ahmad (UPM, Malaysia)
Ahmad Bakeri Abu Bakar (UIA, Malaysia)
Diljit Singh (UM, Malaysia)
Zainab Awang Ngah (UM, Malaysia)
Zaharin Yusoff (USM, Malaysia)
Zulkhairi Mohd Dahalin (UUM, Malaysia)
Peter Charles Woods (MMU, Malaysia)
Zainab Abu Bakar (UiTM, Malaysia)
Raja Abdullah Raja Yaakob (UiTM, Malaysia)
Hwee-Hwa Pang (LIT, Singapore)
Abdus Sattar Chaudhry (NTU, Singapore)
Suliman Hawamdeh (NTU, Singapore)
Schubert Foo (NTU, Singapore)
Min Yen Kan (National University of Singapore)
Ian Witten (Waikato University, New Zealand)
Liddy Nevile (Univ. of Melbourne, Australia)
Li-zhu Zhou (Tsinghua University, China)
Jianzhong Li (Harbin Inst. of Technology, China)
Jianzhong Wu (Shanghai Library, China)
Christopher C. Yang (CUHK, Hong Kong SAR)
Wai Lam (CUHK, Hong Kong SAR)
Jerome Yen (CUHK, Hong Kong SAR)
Vilas Wuwongse (AIT, Thailand)
Shigeo Sugimoto (ULIS, Japan)
Soon J. Hyun (Information Communication University, Korea)
Key-Sun Choi (KAIST, Korea)
Chao-chen Chen (National Taiwan Normal University, Taiwan)
Hsueh-hua Chen (NTU, Taiwan)
San-Yih Hwang (NSYSU, Taiwan)
Jieh Hsiang (National Taiwan University, Taiwan)
K.S. Raghavan (University of Madras, India)
T.B. Rajashekar (Indian Institute of Science, India)
S. Sadagopan (Indian Institute of Information Technology, India)

N. Balakrishnan (Indian Institute of Science, India)
N.V. Sathyanarayana (Informatics India, Bangalore)
S. Ramani (HP Labs India, Bangalore)

Europe

Ingeborg Solvberg (Norwegian University of Science and Technology, Norway)
Norbert Fuhr (University of Duisburg, Germany)
Thomas Baker (Fraunhofer-Gesellschaft (FhG), Germany)
Jose Borbinha (National Library of Portugal, Portugal)
Andreas Rauber (Vienna University of Technology, Austria)
Carol Peters (Italian National Research Council, Italy)
Marc Nanard (LIRMM, France)
Traugott Koch (Lund University Libraries, Sweden)
Erich Neuhold (Darmstadt Univ. of Technology, Germany)
Donatella Castelli (Italian National Research Council, Italy)
Jian Yang (Tilburg University, Netherlands)
Ann Blandford (University College London, UK)
Fabio Crestani (University of Strathclyde, UK)

USA

Christine Borgman (UCLA, USA)
Jim French (Univ. of Virginia, USA)
Edie Rasmussen (Univ. of Pittsburg, USA)
Richard K. Furuta (Texas A&M, USA)
Gary Marchionini (Univ. of North Carolina, USA)
Robert Allen (Univ. of Maryland, USA)
Jerome Yen (Arizona State Univ., USA)
Ching-chih Chen (Simmons College, USA)
Judith Klavans (Columbia University, USA)
Marcia Lei Zeng (Kent State University, USA)
Don Kraft (Louisiana State University, USA)
Edward Fox (Virginia Tech, USA)
Javed Mostafa (Indiana University, USA)
Mirek Riedewald (Cornell University, USA)

Sponsorship Committee

Putri Saniah Megat Abdul Rahman (Persatuan Pustakawan Malaysia)

Workshop Committee

Shahrul Azman Mohd Noah (Universiti Kebangsaan Malaysia)
Nazlena Mohamad Ali (Universiti Kebangsaan Malaysia)

Publicity

Nazlena Mohamad Ali (Universiti Kebangsaan Malaysia)
Aidanismah Yahya (Universiti Kebangsaan Malaysia)

Collaborative Conference Management System Technical Team (CoManSys)

Zaleha Abd. Rahim (MIMOS)
Luke Jing Yuan (MIMOS)
Eng Ngah Looi (MIMOS)
Suit Wai Yeng (MIMOS)

Publication

Abdullah Kadir Bacha (Multimedia Development Corporation)
Mastura Mohamad (Multimedia Development Corporation)

Conference Package

Kamariah Abdul Hamid (Universiti Putra Malaysia)

Social and Hospitality

Siti Zakiah Aman (Persatuan Pustakawan Malaysia)

Exhibition

Hasbullah Atan (Persatuan Pustakawan Malaysia)

Treasurer

Chin Loy Jyoon (Persatuan Pustakawan Malaysia)

Secretary

Saonah Shairi (Perpustakaan Negara Malaysia)

Local Arrangements Committee

Joint Chairman

Tengku Mohd. Tengku Sembok (Universiti Kebangsaan Malaysia)
Halimah Badioze Zaman (Universiti Kebangsaan Malaysia)

Members

Shahrul Azman Mohd. Noah (Universiti Kebangsaan Malaysia)
Nazlena Mohamad Ali (Universiti Kebangsaan Malaysia)
Aidanismah Yahya (Universiti Kebangsaan Malaysia)
Norhayati Abd. Mukti (Universiti Kebangsaan Malaysia)
Zawiyah Mohd. Yusof (Universiti Kebangsaan Malaysia)
Juhana Salim (Universiti Kebangsaan Malaysia)
Ahmad Bakeri Abu Bakar (Universiti Islam Antarabangsa)
Fatimah Ahmad (Universiti Putra Malaysia)
Zaleha Abd. Rahim (MIMOS Berhad)
Mastura Mohamad (Multimedia Development Corporation)
Raja Abdullah Raja Yaakob (Universiti Teknologi MARA)
Zainab Abu Bakar (Universiti Teknologi MARA)
Zamri Mohamed (Universiti Teknologi Malaysia)
Zainab Awang Ngah (Universiti Malaya)
Diljit Singh (Universiti Malaya)

Organizing Institutions

The 6th International Conference on Asian Digital Libraries (ICADL 2003)
wishes to thank the following organizations for their support:

Perpustakaan Negara Malaysia (PNM)
Universiti Kebangsaan Malaysia (UKM)
Malaysian Institute of Microelectronic Systems (MIMOS)
Multimedia Development Corporation (MDC)
Persatuan Pustakawan Malaysia (PPM)

LISEA Committee

Zainab Awang Ngah
Nor Edzan Haji Nasir
Abrizah Abdullah
Noor Harun Abdul Karim
Hasnah Abdul Rahim
Halimah Badioze Zaman
Elizabeth Logan
Abdus Sattar Chaudhry
Sajjad ur Rehman
Ross Harvey
Diljit Singh

Table of Contents

Keynote and Invited Papers

Papers

Information Retrieval Techniques

Multimedia Digital Libraries

Data Mining in Digital Libraries

Machine Architecture and Organization

Human Resource and Training

Human Computer Interfaces

Digital Library Infrastructures

Building and Using Digital Libraries

Knowledge Management

Intellectual Property Rights and Copyright

Cryptography and Compression

Special Purpose Digital Libraries

E-learning and Mobile Learning

Data Storage and Retrieval

Digital Library Services

Development of Contents

Information Retrieval in Asian Languages

Metadata Issues

Posters

Personalization in Digital Libraries – An Extended View

Erich Neuhold, Claudia Niederée, and Avaré Stewart

Fraunhofer-IPSI, Dolivostrasse 15,
64293 Darmstadt, Germany
{neuhold,niederee,stewart}@ipsi.fhg.de

Abstract. Although digital libraries are tailored to the information needs of a specific community, they are large and broad enough in scope to create individual information overload. Digital library personalization reduces the gap between the content offered by the library and individual information needs. Based on an extended view on personalization in digital libraries, this paper discusses various personalization methods for digital libraries. The advantages and challenges of founding personalization on a better understanding of the library user is illustrated by three advanced personalization approaches: Personal Reference Libraries, Collaborative Content Annotation, and modeling and exploitation of Personal Web Context. Each of these approaches focuses on another individual aspect in the interaction between the library and its user. In addition, we also take a closer look at the limitations and challenges of personalization in digital library.

1 Introduction

Personalization dynamically adapts a system's service or content offer in order to better meet or support the preferences and goals of individuals and specific target groups [45]. The goal of personalization is a closer customer relationship by better satisfying the users' needs and, for systems dealing with information and content, like digital libraries, a reduction of individual information overload.

Targeting the information needs of a specific user community, digital libraries play an important role in narrowing the gap between the vast amount of available content and individual task-specific information needs. Quality assured content pre-selection, domain specific content structuring, and enrichment of content with metadata are the central contribution of digital libraries for their mediation role. In addition, a wide spectrum of digital library services enables effective and efficient content access, use, and sharing.

Personalization approaches in digital libraries go a step further in narrowing this gap. In fact, it is becoming increasingly evident that digital libraries must move from being passive, and take a proactive role in offering and tailoring information for individuals and communities, and supporting community efforts to capture, structure and share knowledge. Digital libraries that are not personalized for individuals and group in the community will be seen as defaulting on their obligation to offer the best service possible [8].

T.M.T. Sembok et al. (Eds.): ICADL 2003, LNCS 2911, pp. 1–16, 2003.
© Springer-Verlag Berlin Heidelberg 2003

Prominent examples of personalization services are recommender systems [30], [47], [49] which exploit similarities between users to give advice, and tailor information offers to individual preferences, for example, in personalized newspapers [11], [22]. This paper takes a more comprehensive view on personalization collecting a wide variety of personalization methods affecting the content, metadata, content structuring as well as the services of a digital library.

In addition to this overview, some advanced approaches for personalization are discussed in more detail. *Personal Reference Libraries* follow the idea of personalized information spaces that rely on the paradigm of services of the library, but maintain autonomy with respect to their application. The coexistence of personal reference libraries with other libraries imposes challenging requirements towards balancing autonomy, information exchange, and integration. *Cooperative Annotation* is a complementary form of content personalization putting digital library content into an extended individual context. They are an important medium of discourse in (scientific) communities and assign a more active role to the individuals in the library user community. A large impact on personalization methods is also expected from the Semantic Web Activity. Extended modeling of the user's context-of-use taking into account the *Personal Web Context* includes the semantic annotation of users' profiles to put them into relationships with other entities in the domain like other community members, community events, publications, role assignments, etc. The paper discusses how such approaches can be exploited for improved personalized library services.

The rest of the paper is structured as follows: Section 2 motivates the role of personalization for mediation in a digital library. Section 3 gives an overview of personalization methods and discusses their application in the digital library context. By looking beyond information filtering and recommendation based on user's interests and skills Section 4 presents an extended view on personalization in digital libraries. The paper concludes with a discussion of the limits, caveats and specific challenges of personalization in digital libraries.

2 Personalization in Digital Libraries

2.1 Digital Libraries as Content–to–Community Mediators

A digital library mediates between the information needs of its user community and the globally available content. This is achieved by contributions in four areas [41]:

Content pre-selection: The library selects high-quality content potentially relevant for the members of its user community;

Content structuring: The library structures the content according to the predominant domain understanding of its user community;

Content enrichment: Domain and library experts as well as community members enrich content objects with descriptive and value-adding metadata;

Library services: Services for content retrieval, access, annotation, etc. support the identification of relevant material and facilitate content access;

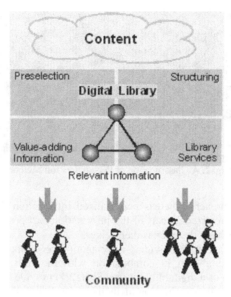

Fig. 1. Digital Libraries as Content-to-Community Mediators

Although these contributions allow a digital library to reduce the gap that exists between the abundant, diverse, globally available content and specific information needs of individuals and small group within its community; there still exists, however, a considerable gap since the content and service offer is tailored towards the community as a whole.

The information needs of individuals and small groups are determined by various factors that can be summarized as the *context-of-use*, like e.g. individual task commitment and goals, personal competences (i.e. expertise and skills) and preferences as well as relationships to other users in the community. Furthermore, individual conceptualization of the information space [15], [50] that differs from user to user, influences individual information access.

Thus, personalization plays an important role in further narrowing the gap by dynamically adapting the community-oriented service and content offer of a library to the preferences and needs of individuals and groups. It generates views onto the digital library and its content that take into account individual context-of-use instead of providing the same view to every member of the community. This personalization goal drives the discussion of personalization methods in the next section

3   Personalization Methods in Digital Libraries

The most popular personalization approaches in digital libraries, or more generally in information and content management, are recommender systems and methods that can be summarized under the term personalized information access. Recommender systems give individual recommendations for information objects following an

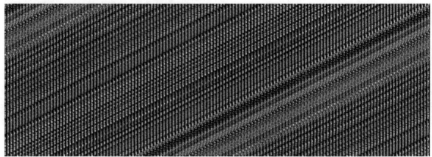

Fig. 2. A Classification of Personalization Methods

information *push* approach, whereas personalized information access (personalized newspapers, etc.) is realized as part of the information *pull* process, e.g. by filtering retrieval results or refining the queries themselves.

Clearly, the various facets of individual information access and use (some of which have been mentioned above) in combination with the four areas of content-to-community mediation of a digital library (see Sect. 2.1) provide several starting points for the development of personalization methods in the digital library context. In order to illustrate the broad range of approaches that can be used to support individual information access, we present a classification of personalization methods applicable in digital libraries followed by a closer look on recommender systems and other popular personalization methods. Three advanced personalization methods, Personal Reference Library, Cooperative Annotation, and Personal Web Context, are discussed in more detail in the next section.

3.1 A Classification of Personalization Methods

Based on the discussed extended view of personalization in digital libraries, personalization methods can be classified as shown in Fig. 2. In the first step, we distinguish personalization methods referring to library services and those referring to library content.

In personalization of library services, we further distinguish services developed to support personalization, like individual notification and personal agents, and the personalization of service properties like e.g. personalized visualization or individual service configuration that also can be found in the personalization of other kinds of systems.

Content personalization is divided into personalization by information enrichment, personalization in content selection, and personalization by individual information content structuring. In personalization by content enrichment additional (meta) is provided to facilitate individual decision making with respect to content selection and content use. These may be comments from domain experts provided for targeted user groups, ratings based on a rating schema, recommendations computed from similarities between user preferences (see Sect. 3.2), and other types of annotations (see Sect. 4.3).

The second content personalization category, content selection, contains methods using information filtering based on user preferences and competences. Most of these personalization methods are based on modeling user characteristics, e.g. user interests, and on explicitly or implicitly collecting data on these characteristics [44], typically by tracking user behavior. These user profiles are used for personalized filtering in information dissemination (*push*) as well as in information access (*pull*) services. An important application area is personalized information retrieval. The information about the user is used for query rewriting [18], for the filtering of query results [9] as well as for a personalized ranking of query results [36]. Further important application areas are decision support in content navigation (see e.g. [42]) and autonomous information agents (see e.g. [31]). An alternative method for personalization in content selection are services that enable the active collection of relevant material e.g. in bookmark lists and other information containers (see also Sect. 4.2).

A simple form of personalization in content structuring is the provision of additional *entry points* to the information offer of a digital library. *Guided Tours* through an information offer (see e.g. [23]) present a user with a manually constructed, personalized superimposed navigation structure that is tailored to a specific task or view on the information space. Another form of personalized structuring computes so-called *Navigation Shortcuts* [2], additional personalized navigation structures based on frequent navigation patterns of the user.

3.2 Recommender Systems

Recommender System can be defined as system that produces individualized recommendations as outputs or has the effect of guiding the user in a personalized way to interesting or useful objects in a large space of possible options. Recommender systems learn about a person's needs and interests and then identify and recommend information that meets those needs. Recommender Systems consist of three major components: 1) background data - the information that the system has before the recommendation begins; 2) input data – information the user must supply to the system in order for a recommendation to be made; and 3) an algorithm that combines the background and input data to arrive at a suggestion [7].

Several types of recommender systems can be distinguished: In content-based recommender systems, (e.g. [29], [39]), recommendations are made for a user based on a profile built up by analyzing the content of information objects the user has seen and rated in the past. Using the features extracted from new information objects, the system tries to recommend new objects which are similar to those the user has liked in the past. Alternatively, knowledge-based recommenders suggest items based on functional knowledge about a user's needs and preferences and how a particular item meets a particular user need. This knowledge is captured via models of both the user of the system and the items being recommended [6], [54]. Knowledge-based systems use adapted quantitative decision support tools or case based reasoning to arrive at a recommendation whereas content-based recommender systems use classifier systems derived from machine learning research. In Fig. 3, a portion of the interface for Entree [6], a knowledge-based system which recommends restaurants to its users, can be seen.

Fig. 3. Entre, a Knowledge-Based Recommender System

Alternatively, rather than compute the similarity of the information objects, as in content-based approach, *collaborative recommenders* (*collaborative information filtering* see e.g. [17]) use the similarity between *users* as the basis of a recommendation. Given the set of ratings on information objects for users with known preferences and a recommendee's ratings on the same objects, users similar to the recommendee are identified and an extrapolation is made from the other's ratings to recommend new objects to the user (see e.g. [4] ,[24]).

In a demographic-based approach (see e.g. [28], [43]), a user is categorized based on personal attributes and a recommendation is made based on the demographic class of the user. Demographic techniques use people-to-people correlations like collaborative approaches, however, it does not base its method on a history of user rating.

The utility-based approach determines a match between a user's need and the set of available options by creating a utility function for each user across all features of the objects under consideration. The function is built by users specifying constraints on an item's features. In Tete-Tete, for example, the user specifies price, delivery time or warranty preferences and the system then employs constraint satisfaction techniques to return prioritized listing of products and merchants filtered to satisfy the constraints [19].

All described recommender system approaches have strengths and weaknesses (i.e. ramp-up, cold start, sparsity and grey sheep problems, portfolio effect, scalability [11], [25], [48]. Therefore, researchers are working on combining approaches, creating hybrid recommenders, in order to overcome the weaknesses associated with individual techniques as well as improve system performance (see e.g. [7], [53]).

In addition to the aforementioned approaches to identify and recommend useful information to users, some recommender systems also consider guiding the users to interesting or relevant objects based on information and community models. These approaches take into account the salient interrelationships and roles of individuals in a cooperation or community context. The systems use, for example, the status of the user (profession, position) or organizational relationship between interacting community members and objects to recommend either relevant documents, other people with whom to collaborate, or alternatively, to support a personalized conceptualization of the environment.

Three prominent examples of this are: 1) Referral Web [21], which uses the co-occurrence of names (i.e. co-authorings, co-citations, personal web pages, organizational charts and news archive exchanges) in documents as evidence of relationships to recommends persons; 2) the Graph-based recommender system [20] that uses an information model based on books-books, users-users, and books-users, to recommend books to its users; and 3) QuickStep, [37], [38] which gathers information such as people, publication, events and research papers from employee databases in order to recommend research papers to academicians.

Recommender systems (particularly those which incorporate community-based models and consider the role of individuals within the community) provide a good contribution for closing the gap between the digital library's ability to target its content and service offer to the information needs of its individual and small group users as well its entire user community as a whole.

4 Next Generation Personalization

To date personalization is restricted by the limited understanding of the users and their interaction with the digital library. Most personalization methods are based on user models, which mainly reflect user interests and skills, i.e. a simplistic representation of users and their information needs that does not take into account other important aspects like tasks, goals, and relationships to other community members. The building and exploitation of more comprehensive user models is one way to improve personalization in digital libraries [8]. Starting from a broader view of personalization we discuss three complementing, fundamentally different ways to improve individual support in digital libraries that operate with an extended understanding of the user:

Personal Web Context takes into consideration the **interrelationship** of users with their neighborhood of entities in the domain. After discovering and representing the (existence and type of) relationships of the user with other entities of the domain this semantically annotated *personal web* of interrelationships is exploited in targeted personalization of a library's information offer.

Personal Reference Libraries take into account the **individual conceptualization** of the information space that differs between users. Following the structuring and service paradigm of a digital library, personal reference libraries are built up for information related projects like artifact construction. Such reference libraries coexist and interact with other digital (reference) libraries in a controlled way balancing autonomy and cooperation.

Cooperative Content Annotation takes into account the **active role** that a user of a digital library can play with respect to library content and metadata. Cooperative content annotation shifts the user from a mere consumer to a contributor to library content and supports discourse and community building.

These three approaches reflect ongoing research efforts at Fraunhofer IPSI. They are discussed in more detail in this section.

4.1 Personal Web Context

The Role of Communities. Studies (see e.g. [27]) have shown that an effective channel for disseminating information and brokering expertise within a community is by exploiting Communities of Practice [56], informal networks of colleagues, friends, and experts. Approaches that explore community modeling for information mediation, like e.g. Social Network Analysis (e.g. [55]), are thus complementing personalization approaches in bridging the gap between the content offered and individual information needs. In essence, they seek to discover and expose the interrelationships among a set of interacting units within the community and exploit these relationships to support the community-based sharing and dissemination of knowledge [35].

Persons, especially professionals, are tied into a manifold network of domain entities. Their connectedness within such a "web" is defined and affected by the work they do, the things and people they know, and the activities they engage in, etc. In our research, we exploit such domain-based relationships to build semantically annotated profiles of users that describes them in terms of their personal web of interrelationships in the domain. A user's Personal Web becomes part of his role-dependent *context-of-use* which is exploited for recommendation and in adapting decision making processes in information and knowledge handling.

In this context, it is not uncommon for people within a community to discover resources (i.e. other persons, documents) via serendipitous means because they are (directly or indirectly) tied into some larger web of social connections by community involvement. After attending a conference, for example, users may discover that the acquaintance they spoke with, mutually associates them with a prominent (and their works) which whom they wish to know personally.

Building the Person Web Context. In order to make use of such personal web contexts, the interrelationships have to be discovered and represented in an adequate way. We do so by harnessing both explicit and implicit knowledge embedded in the structure of domain specific resources and use this as a basis for building models of the user and further, for recommending resources unknown to them.

The concept underlying the Personal Web Context is the resource network of the relevant domain. This is a graph-based information model in which the nodes represent entities in the domain of various types and the directed edges indicate typed relationships between connected entities. Some examples of such domain entities in the network include: information objects (i.e. books, periodicals, recorded presentations), people, organizations, concepts, and events. Typical relationship types in the scientific domain are: a person is *part_of* an organization; an information object *has_focus* with respect to a concept; a person is an *author_of* an information object; or , a concept is the *subject_of* an event .

Fig. 4 illustrates that a user's relationship with the domain entities may be both explicit and implicit. The explicit relationship exists, for example, when two persons, (user_01 and user_02) co_author the same publication or two persons (user_02 and the information seeker) attend the same event. On the other hand, an implicit

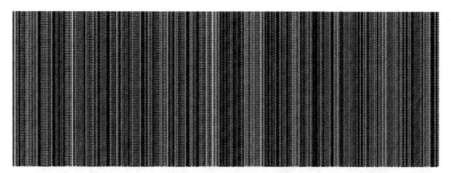

Fig. 4. An example of using the Personal Web Context to derive an impicit relationship

relationship exists because users' context evolve, that is, users engage in activities such as (writing proposals, authoring papers, attending events, being the PhD student of an expert, or editing journals) that subsequently puts them into relationship with unknown resource based on their relationship with known resources. As can been in Fig. 4, based the information seeker's attendance in event_01, the information seeker becomes mutually associated with another resource and we can subsequently infer a relationship between the information seeker and user_01. If for example, the information seeker is looking for a partner in a proposal writing activity and user_01 is a prominent with respect to this activity, we could use this inference a basis for recommending user_01 a resource or possibly other resources in user_01's sphere.

In formulating the typed relationships in the network, we draw upon research conducted in the areas of relational element and classification theories [10], [57]. In these theories, typed relationships are defined in terms of relational primitives – a set of indivisible, underlying properties. The relational primitives are used as the basis for defining operations (i.e. composition and transitivity) that allow particular relationships types to be plausibly combined to infer an implicit resource relationships [1], [12], [21]. The inferences made in our network are then presented to the user in the form of resource recommendations.

One way for a digital library to take into account the role of communities is by modelling, discovering, and exploiting the relationships that effect a community-bound user and then, individually structuring the content accordingly. By understanding users in the context of their communities, more targeted information access and dissemination can be implemented. This ongoing work is one step towards extended user models and considers more comprehensive view of the user. Relationships (explicit or implicit) between users and connected entities are considered as well as changes in a user's sphere of influence and evolving information space.

4.2 Personal Reference Library

Personal reference libraries are a powerful form of project-centered personalization and cooperation in digital libraries. They are based on the idea of reference libraries in the traditional library context, where people collect and structure a collection of information objects like books, papers, and notes according to the needs of a specific

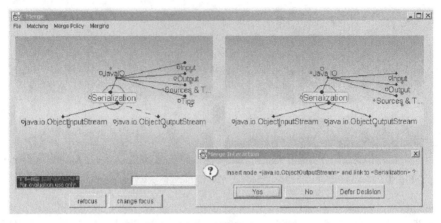

Fig. 5. Merging Personal Reference Library

project like e.g. writing a paper, producing a report, or working on a PhD. A personal reference library (PRL) becomes a subsidiary of the digital library, which uses digital libraries concepts and services to organize and handle a project-specific collection of information objects according to the needs of an individual or a project team.

This form of personalization considerably differs from the ones discussed before. The user takes a much more active part. Furthermore, PRLs give the user a high autonomy with respect to information organization and annotation as it is required for creative work with information and enable the user to adapt the (personal) library structure to his individual conceptualization of the domain.

PRLs can not be considered in isolation. They co-exist and interact with digital libraries and other reference libraries in their context. This imposes challenges with respect to balancing cooperation and autonomy as well as with respect to consistently control the independent evolution of the different coexisting libraries. In building up and extending PRLs, information objects are incrementally taken from digital libraries that act as "master" digital libraries. During their lifetime reference libraries exchange information with other related PRLs. At the end of a project the related PRL can be archived. Much better use is made of the investments, if the findings that developed while working with the PRLs are reused and shared. Therefore, methods for a controlled, semi-automatic integration of PRLs into the master library and for merging different reference libraries have been developed (library merging, see [34]). In Fig. 5, the user interface for merging reference libraries can be seen.

The concept of personal reference libraries is discussed in more detail in [40].

4.3 Cooperative Annotation

Annotations, the enrichment of information object with comments and other forms of meta-information consisting of text, pictures, highlighting, form a clearly separated value-adding information layer above the annotated information object itself [13]. Annotations are a very general concept that takes different forms and is used for various purposes. In [33] annotation forms are, for example, distinguished according

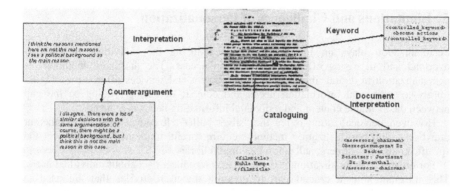

Fig. 6. Cooperative Annotation with COLLATE

to the visibility of the annotation (from private to public annotation), annotation formats (e.g. PostIts, highlighting, comments, etc.), the degree of structuring (from free text to structured data), the purpose, and the relationship to the annotated information object (annotation of the entire information objects vs. annotation of fragments, separate and integrated annotations). Annotations as well as the typed annotation structures can be subject to further processing e.g. for retrieval support.

In digital libraries, annotations are an important method of information enrichment. They enable the user community and domain experts to take a more active part with respect to the content of a digital library by annotating library content. Such annotations can be used for the personalization of content for special user groups and for giving additional context information supporting the interpretation of information objects. As an example, our MediaMime system [51] enables users to superimpose addendums at user-defined temporal, locations within e-Lectures annotating learning content.

Furthermore, annotations are also a valuable medium for collaboration in digital libraries. Advanced forms of annotation services like [46] support the annotation of annotations and the distinction between different types of annotations. This enables the implementation of discussion threats in support of a scientific discourse about content. An example of using annotations for collaboration support is COLLATE [5], an EU funded project at our department. COLLATE is a Web-based systems that facilitates collaboration between distributed end-user groups by providing support for the annotation of a digital multimedia collection consisting of documents describing censorship procedures in the early 1900's in Europe. The COLLATE environment enables historians and domain experts to make evaluations and share valuable knowledge about the cultural, political and social contexts, which in turn allow other end-users to better interpret the historic material in the digital library. The annotation support enables the users and experts to enter into a scientific discourse about the content. As illustrated in Fig. 6, users can make various types of annotations, e.g., interpretations and counterarguments which are annotations to annotation.

Cooperative Annotation approaches thus represent examples of an extended understanding of users – that is the active role they can take while working with multi-format, temporally dependent, digitized multimedia library material.

5 Limitations and Challenges of Personalization

Personalization plays an important role in reducing the individual information overload and in easing effective information access. The discussed methods for personalization in digital libraries tailor the content and services offered by a digital library to individual information needs and context of use. By doing so the gap between the available content and individual information needs is reduced.

However, personalization is not the "silver bullet". It comes with some inherent drawbacks, and personalization methods require careful implementation to meet the specific challenges of personalization in a digital library.

For effective personalization, it is necessarily to collect data about individual users. This information is a crucial part to creating the user profiles that are used in information filtering for personalization. However, given 1) the ability to electronically manage user data 2) today's highly networked systems and 3) the progress in related methods like data mining, user data can easily be collected and exploited, even beyond the boundaries of a single system. The risks of extensive combination of user data even increases with the use of the upcoming Semantic Web technologies [3], which ease semantic interoperability by the use of references to knowledge represented by ontology.

Yet, the collection of data about the user and especially its combination and exploitation is in a certain conflict with the users' rightful wish for privacy and anonymity. The user may feel "spied out" [4], if the system collects data about his interaction for personalization purposes. Careful handling of user data is, thus, an important prerequisite for the acceptance of personalization methods in digital libraries. There are some methods and approaches under development that address this critical point. Services like *Janus* [16] provide the user with an identity that cannot be tracked back to the user, thus assuring anonymity. Since specific identities are created for each visited site, the combination of tracked data from different sites is prevented, without hindering personalization.

The Platform for Privacy Preferences (*P3P*) is another effort in the area of protecting user data. Using this standard [14], which is currently developed by the W3C, the user specifies his privacy preferences, defining which use of his personal data he allows and the content provider commits to a privacy policy stating the intended use of personal data. Since both types of specification are formalized in P3P, privacy negotiation can be automated.

The further class of possible caveats of personalization is connected with the personalized view on the information space that is implemented by personalization in digital libraries. If the personalized view is too narrow this may prevent a broader more comprehensive view on the problem or task under consideration and may hinder occasional, but interesting findings [52].

In cooperative scenarios, a shared view on the information space fosters a shared understanding and supports communication. Tailoring a view to individuals, as it is inherent to personalization, thus can hinder group communication, since not everyone has the same view on the information space. Personalization methods that are targeted towards cooperating teams, rather than individuals, are a possible solution in this situation.

A third principle challenge in personalization, as addressed in [32], is predictability. A view on an information space that is system-computed and dynamically adapting to changing user preferences may be disorienting for the users as they must repeatedly adapt to unpredictable changes of their view.

In summary, for the acceptance of personalization methods it is crucial not only to design useful personalization services but also to inform the user about the personalization and the related collection of user data as well as to enable the user to flexibly control personalization according to his preferences and needs.

References

1. Baker, M., Burstein, M.: Implementing a Model of Human Plausible Reasoning In the Proceedings of the Tenth Annual IJCAI, Milan, Italy, August 1987, (1987) 185–188
2. Barrett, R., Maglio, P.P., Kellem, D.C.: How to Personalize the Web. In Steven Pemberton (eds): Proceedings of the Conference on Human Factors in Computing Systems (CHI'97) March 22–27, 1997, Atlanta, Georgia, USA. ACM Press, (1997)
3. Berners-Lee, T., Hendler, J., Lassila, O.: The Semantic Web, *Scientific American*, May (2001)
4. Bouthors, V., Dedieu, O.: Pharos, a Collaborative Infrastructure for Web Knowledge Sharing. In Serge Abiteboul and Anne-Marie Vercoustre, editors, Research and Advanced Technology for Digital Libraries, Proceedings of the Third European Conference, ECDL'99, Paris, France, September, LNCS 1696 , Springer-Verlag, (1999) 215
5. Brocks H., Dirsch Weigand, A., Keiper, J., Stein, A., Theil, U.: COLLATE - Historische Filmforschung in einem verteilten Annotationssystem im WWW. In R. Schmidt (Eds.): *Information Research & Content Management - Orientierung, Ordnung und Organisation im Wissensmarkt,* Frankfurt am Main: DGI. 183–196 (2001)
6. Burke, R.: Knowledge-based Recommender Systems. In A. Kent (ed.), Encyclopedia of Library and Information Systems. Vol. 69, Supplement 32. New York: Marcel Dekker, (2000)
7. Burke, R.: Hybrid Recommender Systems: Survey and Experiments. User Modeling and User-Adapted Interaction. Vol. 12 No. 4, (2002) 331–370
8. Callan J., Smeaton, A., et. al.: Personalization and Recommender Systems in Digital Libraries DELOS-NSF Workshop on Personalization and Recommender Systems in Digital Libraries http://www.ercim.org/publication/workshop_reports.html June (2003)
9. Casasola, E.: ProFusion PersonalAssistant: An Agent for Personalized Information Filtering on the WWW. Master's thesis, The University of Kansas, Lawrence, KS, (1998)
10. Chaffin, R., Herrmann, D.: Relation Element Theory: A New Account of the Representation and Process of Semantic Relations In D.Gorfein and R. Hoffman, eds,. Memory and Learning: The Ebbinghaus Centennial Conference, Lawrence Erlbaum, Hilsdale, NJ, (1987)
11. Claypool, M., Gokhale, A., Miranda, T., Murnikov, P., Netes, D., Sartin, M.: Combining content-based and collaborative filters in an online newspaper. In Proceedings of ACM SIGIR Workshop on Recommender, August (1999)
12. Cohen, P.R., Loiselle, C.L.: Beyond ISA: Structures for Plausible Inference in Semantic Networks Proceedings AAAI88, St. Paul, MN, August, (1988)
13. Cousins, S.B., Baldonado, M., Paepcke. A.: A Systems View of Annotations. Report P9910022, Xerox Palo Alto Reserch Center, April (2000)
14. Cranor, L., Langheinrich, M., Marchiori, M., Presler-Marshall, M., Reagle, J.: The Platform for Privacy Preferences 1.0 (P3P1.0) Specification, W3C Candidate Recommendation. http://www.w3.org/TR/P3P, December (2000)
15. Fernandez, L., Sanchez, J.A., Garcia, A.: MiBiblio:Personal Spaces in a Digital Library Universe ACM DL 2000, DiSC (2001), 232–233

16. Gabber, E., Gibbons, P. B., Matias, Y., Mayer, A.: How to Make Personalized Web Browsing Simple, Secure, and Anonymous. In Rafael Hirschfeld, editor, Financial Cryptography: First International Conference, FC '97, February 24–28, 1997, Anguilla, British West Indies, LNCS 1318, Springer-Verlag, (1997) 17– 31

17. Goldberg, D., Nichols, D., Oki, B.M., Terry, D.: Using Collaborative Filtering to Weave an Information Tapestry. Communications of the ACM, Vol. 35, No. 12, December (1992) 61–70

18. Gulla, J. A., van der Vos, B., Thiel, U.: An Abductive, Linguistic Approach to Model Retrieval. Data & Knowledge Engineering, Vol. 23 No. 1, June (1997) 17–31

19. Guttmann R.H., Moukas, A.G., Maes, P.: Agent-based Mediated Electronic Commerce. a Survey. Knowledge Engineering Review, 13 Vol 2, (1998) 147–159

20. Huang, Z., Chung, W., Ong, T.H., Chen, H.: A Graph-based Recommender System for Digital Libraries JCDL 2002, July 13–17, Portland Oregon, USA (2002)

21. Huhns, M.N., Stephens, L.M.: Plausible Inferencing Using Extended Composition IJCAI Vol. 2, (1989) 1420–1425

22. Jones G., Quested, D., Thomson, K.: Personalised Delivery of News Articles from Multiple Sources. In Jos´e Borbinha and Thomas Baker, editors, Research and Advanced Technology for Digital Libraries, Proceedings of the Third European Conference, ECDL 2000, Lisbon, Portugal, September, LNCS 1923, Springer-Verlag, (2000), 340–343

23. Jühne, J., Jensen, A.T., Grønbæk, K.: Ariadne: A Java-based Guided Tour System for the World Wide Web. In Proceedings of the 7th International World Wide Web Conference, April 14–18, 1998, Brisbane, Australia, volume 30 of Computer Networks, Elsevier Science, April (1998) 131–139

24. Konstan, J.A., Miller, B.N., Maltz, D. Herlocker, J.L. Gordon, L.R., Reidl, J.: Applying Collaborative Filtering to Usenet News. Communications of the ACM, Vol. 40 No. 4, (1997) 77–87

25. Konstan, J.A., Riedl, J., Borchers, A., Herlocker, J.L.: Recommender Systems: A Group-Lens Perspective. In Recommender Systems: Papers from the 1998 Workshop (AAAI Technical Report WS-98-08) Menlo Park, CA: AAAI Press, (1998) 60–64

26. Kautz, H., Selman, B., Shah, M.: Referral Web: Combining Social Networks and Collaborative Filtering. Communications of the ACM 40(3). (1997)

27. Kraut, H., Galegher, J., Edigo, C.: Intellectual Teamwork: Social and Technological Bases for Cooperative Work Lawrence Erlbaum, Hillsdale, NJ (1990)

28. Krulwich, B,: Lifestlye Finder: Intelligent User Profiling Using Large-Scale Demographic Data Artificial Intelligence Magazine 18, vol. 2. 37–45, 1997

29. Lang, K.: NewsWeedweeder: Learning to Filter News In Proc. ICML 95, (1995) 331–336

30. Lawrence, R.D., Almasi, G.S., Kotlyar, V., Viveros, M.S., Duri, S.: Personalization of supermarket product Recommendations. Data Mining and Knowledge Discovery, Vol. 5 No. 1–2, 11– 32, (2001)

31. Lieberman, H.: Letizia: An Agent That Assists Web Browsing. In Proceedings of the 14th International Joint Conference on Arti.cial Intelligence (IJCAI-95), Montreal, August 1995,. Morgan Kaufmann, August (1995) 924 – 929

32. Manber, U., Patel, A., Robison, J.: Experience with Personalization on Yahoo!. Communications of the ACM, Vol. 43 No. 8, August (2000) 35–39

33. Marshall, C. C.: Toward an Ecology of Hypertext Annotation. In Proceedings of ACM Hypertext '98, June 20–24, Pittsburgh, PA, USA, 40–49, (1998)

34. Matthes, F., Niederée, C., Steffens, U.: C-Merge: A Tool for Policy-Based Merging of Resource Classifications. In P. Constantopoulos, I. Solvberg, editors: Research and Advanced Technology for Digital Libraries, Proceedings of the 5th European Conference, ECDL 2001, Darmstadt, Germany, September 2001. LNCS 2163, Springer-Verlag (2001)

35. McDonald D.W.: Recommending Collaboration with Social Networks: A Comparative Evaluation. Proceedings of the ACM 2003 Conference on Human Factors in Computing Systems (CHI'03), Vol. 5, No.1 (2003) 593–600

36. Meng, X., Chen, Z.: Personalize Web Search using Information on Client's Side. In Proceedings of the Fifth International Conference of Young Computer Scientists, August 17–20, 1999, Nanjing, P.R.China, International Academic Publishers, (1999) 985–992

37. Middleton S., DeRoure, D., Shadbolt, N.: Capturing knowledge of User Preferences: Ontologies in Recommender Systems In Proc. of the ACM K-CAP'Oi. 2001. Victoria, Canada: ACM Press (2001)

38. Middleton S., Alani, H., Shadbolt, N.R., Rource, D.C.: Exploiting Synergy Between Ontologies and Recommender Systems. In Proc. of the Eleventh International World Wide Web Conference Semantic Web Workshop, Hawaii, USA, (2002)

39. Mooney, R.J., Roy, L.: Content-Based Book Recommending Using Learning for Text Categorization Proceedings of the Fifth ACM Conference on Digital Libraries, San Antonio, TX, June (2000) 195–204

40. Niederée, C.: Personalization, Cooperation and Evolution in Digital Libraries. PhD Thesis, Technical University Hamburg-Harburg. dissertion.de, November (2002). (in German)

41. Niederée, C., Steffens,U., Hemmje, M.: Towards Digital Library Mediation for Web Services. In Workshop Proceedings of the First Eurasian Conference on Advances in Information and Communication Technology, Shiraz, Iran, October 29–31, (2002)

42. Pazzani,M., Muramatsu,J., Billsus, D.: Syskill & Webert: Identifying interesting web sites. In Proceedings of the National Conference on Arti.cial Intelligence, Portland, OR, (1996)

43. Pazzani M.: A framework for Collaborative, Content-based and Demographic Filtering, Artificial Intelligence Review, 13 Vol. 5–6, 393–408, (1999)

44. Pretschner, A., Gauch, S.: Personalization on the Web. Technical Report, ITTC-FY2000-TR-13591-01, Information and Telecommunication Technology Center (ITTC), The University of Kansas, Lawrence, KS, December (1999)

45. Riecken, D.: Personalized Views of Personalization. Communications of the ACM, Vol. 43 No. 8, August (2000) 27–28

46. Röscheisen,M., Winograd,T., Paepcke, A.: Content Ratings and other Third-Party Value-Added Information - De.ning an Enabling Platform. D-Lib Magazine, August http://ukoln.bath.ac.uk/dlib/dlib/august95, (1995)

47. Rucker, J., Polanco, M. J.: ACM Special Issue on Recommender Systems Siteseer: Personalized Navigation for the Web," Communications of ACM, Vol. 40, No: 3, (1997) 73–7

48. Sarwar, B., Karypis, G., Konstan, J., Riedl, J.: Application of Dimensionality Reduction in Recommender System A Case Study Technical Report CS-TR 00-043, Computer Science and Engineering Dept., University of Minnesota, July (2000)

49. Schafer, J., Konstan, J., Riedl, J.: Recommender Systems in E-Commerce,Recommender Systems in E-Commerce. In ACM Conference on Electronic Commerce (EC-99), (1999) 158–166

50. Stephanidis, C., Akoumianakis, D., Paramythis, A., Nikolaou, C.: User Interaction in Digital Libraries: coping with diversity through Adaptation International Journal of Digital Libraries Vol. 3 (2000) 185–205

51. Stewart, A., Kermani, P. Mourad, G.: MediaMime: After the fact Authoring Annotation System 7th Annual Conference on Innovations and Technology in Computer Science Education Aarhus Denmark, (2002)

52. Tom, E.G.: Serendipitous Information Retrieval. In Proceedings of the First DELOS Network of Excellence Workshop on Information Seeking, Searching and Querying Digital Libraries, Zurich, Switzerland. ERCIM, December (2000) 11–12

53. Tran,T., Cohen, R.: Hybrid Recommender Systems for Electronic Commerce. In Proceedings of the Seventeenth National Conference on Artificial Intelligence (AAAI-00) Workshop on Knowledge-Based Electronic Markets, July (2000) 78–84

54. Towle, B., Quinn, C.N.: *Knowledge Based Recommender Systems Using Explicit User Models*. Knowledge-Based Electronic Markets Workshop at AAAI 2000, Austin, TX.

55. Wasserman, S., Galaskiewicz, J., Eds.: Advances in Social Network Analysis Sage, Thousand Oaks, California, (1994)

56. Wenger, E., Snyder, W.: Communities of Practice: The Organizational Frontier Harvard Business Review, January-February (2000)
57. Winston, M.E., Chaffin, R., Herrmann, D.: A taxonomy of Part-Whole Relations Cognitive Science Vol. 11. (1987) 417–444

Case Studies in the US National Science Digital Library: DL-in-a-Box, CITIDEL, and OCKHAM

Edward A. Fox

Digital Library Research Laboratory, Virginia Tech
Blacksburg, VA 24061 USA
fox@vt.edu

Abstract. Digital libraries can support education, as is being shown through work on the US National Science Digital Library. We explain this approach, highlighting issues and innovations, by considering three case studies. The Digital Library in a Box project aims to make construction of digital libraries fast, easy, and effective, building upon a suite of powerful components. The Computing and Information Technology Interactive Digital Educational Library (CITIDEL) project supports the community interested in computing-related areas with a large and growing collection of resources and services. The OCKHAM project aims to move the DL field into a next generation, through peer-to-peer services, lightweight reference models, lightweight protocols, and pools of components. Altogether, these parts of NSDL suggest that it is possible for many nations to support teaching and learning with digital libraries, and that it may be time to launch an International Education Digital Library Association.

1 Introduction

One of the most exciting applications of digital libraries is to promote education. UNESCO has recommended that each nation be supported by a Digital Library (DL) for Education (DLE) [1]. In this paper we explore related issues and possibilities by considering as case studies three of the projects that are part of the US National Science Digital Library (a shortened version of National STEM (Science, Technology, Engineering, and Mathematics education) Digital Library – NSDL).

Work in this direction has been enabled by the Open Archives Initiative (OAI) [2]. Launched in 1999, this effort to support harvesting of metadata from around the globe led to a protocol for metadata harvesting (OAI-PMH) [3]. This mechanism supports digital library interoperability [4]. In other words, collections (of any size, from a few records to millions) of descriptive information (metadata) about materials useful for teaching and learning can be hosted by diverse groups, organized along geographic, political, social, discipline, professional, or other lines – and then aggregated into repositories to serve both broad and specialized needs. In particular, a national digital library union catalog may be constructed by harvesting metadata that is in turn assembled by scores of groups, each concerned with different areas, and each assuring quality in their respective domain.

T.M.T. Sembok et al. (Eds.): ICADL 2003, LNCS 2911, pp. 17–25, 2003.

To simplify this effort, most groups involved in OAI make use of the Dublin Core [5]. Indeed, according to OAI, each "data provider" must make available its metadata using this scheme. However, data providers are encouraged to attend to the special needs of the communities they serve, and to provide descriptions of digital objects using other suitable metadata schemes as well. Thus, in the case of the international non-profit educational and charitable organization NDLTD (Networked Digital Library of Theses and Dissertations, http://www.ndltd.org), records also may be made available by members using ETD-MS (the electronic thesis and dissertation metadata standard) [6].

With all the modern advances in the digital library world, and the support of standards such as those established through OAI and Dublin Core, it is indeed feasible for a nation to have a DLE. In the next section we explore efforts in this direction in USA. In sections 3-5 we explore three case studies that are part of the US efforts, but which can support global needs as well. Section 6 concludes this paper and encourages widespread involvement, suggesting some possible steps forward.

2 NSDL

The US National Science Digital Library (NSDL) has largely been funded by the National Science Foundation (NSF) [7]. There have been solicitations in 2000, 2001, 2002, and 2003 [8]; others are planned for at least the next several years. The NSDL program has origins back to the early 1990s when support for work on digital libraries was first proposed [9]. Today, NSDL is visible especially by way of a central system, with hundreds of thousands of resources [10]. That effort is supported by over a hundred project groups, mostly previously or currently funded in part by NSF, which are coordinated in part by a governance scheme, and supported by a communications portal [11]. Most of the funds go into three Tracks: Collections, Services, and Targeted Research. The remaining roughly 20% of the funding goes to the Core Integration (CI) team, which helps with central infrastructure and other types of support, including of standards and planning of the overall architectural [12].

From the early days of NSDL, volunteers interested in governance have worked to develop the vision and plans [13]. There is an Assembly, wherein the principal investigators (PIs) of the various projects serve as members. The Assembly elects a Policy Committee, and the elected chair and vice-chair of the "PC" serve as chair and vice-chair of the Assembly. The PC establishes policies and guidelines, and in other ways helps coordinate the governance system [14]. In particular, the PC established five Standing Committees:

- Community Services
- Content
- Educational Impact
- Sustainability
- Technology

In addition, a number of specialized task forces have been established, to address key concerns such as:

- Accessibility and Diversity
- K-12

- Publishers
- Using Data in the Classroom

Working with the PC, the committees help NSDL as a whole move forward, running an Annual Meeting each fall. In addition, the National Science Foundation provides funding and overall direction, with the advice of a National Visiting Committee, which works closely with CI and the PC.

Some coordination also takes place bottom up. For example, work related to the CITIDEL project (see Section 4) has led to a proposal for an XML log standard [15]. This idea has been refined and deployed in CITIDEL [16], and then passed on to both the Educational Impact and Technology Standing Committees for consideration. It is hoped that it will be generalized and adapted to the needs of a number of NSDL projects.

With all these types of guidance, the teams working on over one hundred projects focus on their mission of advancing education [17]. They function largely autonomously, dealing with a particular type of service (e.g., see Section 3), with a particular content area (e.g., see Section 4), or engaging in research to integrate NSDL with other activities in the nation (e.g., see Section 5).

3 DL-in-a-Box

One of the common needs of NSDL Collection Track projects is to have software to support their efforts. That is the aim of the "Digital Library in a box" (DL-in-a-box) effort [18]. Key to this work is to ensure simplicity, so that the software is easy to use, which has been aided by the help of other groups [19].

DL-in-a-box builds upon Virginia Tech research on Open Digital Libraries [20]. Through his doctoral work, H. Suleman, who serves on the OAI technical committee, explored the problem of providing a framework for more efficient development of digital library software [21]. Taking a cue from software engineering, he recommended building DL systems from distributed components rather than as a monolithic program. Given the success of OAI, he suggested extending it beyond harvesting, resulting in "XOAI" components [22]. That led to a set of small specialized extensions to OAI-PMH, yielding a group of lightweight protocols tailored to particular requirements (e.g., searching) [23]. This combination of small components communicating through lightweight protocols facilitates construction of open digital libraries [24]. H. Suleman carefully studied this approach, demonstrated that it yields systems that perform well, and verified that DL developers can easily deploy the software [25].

Virginia Tech supports this building block approach to the development of digital libraries [26], and is happy to work with any group interesting in applying the software. The number of components keeps growing, and includes a suite of search engines (ranging from a tiny program suitable for a small collection, IRDB, to ESSEX, a sophisticated, largely in-memory, module that should give exceptional performance on large servers when working with hundreds of thousands or millions of records). Many of the DL-in-a-box routines have been tested in the CITIDEL system, discussed in the next section.

4   CITIDEL

CITIDEL [27] is part of the Collections Track activities in the NSDL. In particular, CITIDEL operates and maintains the "computing" content of the digital library that includes information systems, computer science, information science, information technology, software engineering, computer engineering, and other computing-related fields. Led by a team at Virginia Tech, CITIDEL also involves groups at the College of New Jersey, Hofstra, Penn State, and Villanova. The co-PIs have had extensive experience in artificial intelligence, community building, computer history, computing education, digital libraries, human-computer interaction, and multimedia systems. Thus, part of our work involved adding diverse collections.

4.1   CITIDEL Collections

Earlier work by the project team led to development of the Computer Science Teaching Center [28]. This supported teachers uploading resources, editors assigning them to a few reviewers, and free access to accepted items. However, in the computing field there are few rewards for contributing to such collections. Consequently, with the support of ACM (the first computer professional society), a Journal of Educational Resources in Computing (JERIC) was established to collect higher quality materials suitable for archival publication. CSTC and JERIC thus were among the first sources of content for CITIDEL.

Moving beyond full content, to metadata for resources, we were fortunate to arrange with ACM, for the duration of the NSF support for CITIDEL, to get metadata from the entire ACM Digital Library. IEEE-CS, the other leading society in computing, also agreed to a similar arrangement, and we expect to receive their data soon.

In addition to these collections from publishers, we have aimed for materials from the "gray" literature. One helpful genre is that of electronic theses and dissertations (ETDs). Our source for computing-related ETDs is NDLTD (mentioned in Section 1). Another, more voluminous source, is technical reports.

Our work with computing technical reports goes back to the early 1990s. Since the collections are distributed, early efforts used protocols like Dienst [29], a pre-cursor of OAI. The Networked Computer Science Technical Reference Library (http://www.ncstrl.org), at its peak, collected reports from well over one hundred departments and centers [30]. With the unfolding of the WWW, with individuals putting personal papers on their own web sites, and with the aging software base supporting Dienst, in 2001 the decision was made to move to OAI [31].

There are many other sources of content for CITIDEL. With the help of various student project efforts, additional collections have been added [32]. For example, DBLP, a large collection originally focused in the areas of database and logic programming, was mirrored at Virginia Tech, and then records added to CITIDEL. Other somewhat smaller collections are being added now as well.

While there are only a small number of large collections, there are a moderate number of medium-size collections, and many small collections. In order to add collections with minimal effort, we have collaborated with a team in Brazil that works to develop digital libraries from Web content [33]. We plan to deploy their software in a test effort with students to see how much can be added in a short period time by a relatively untrained group.

4.2 CITIDEL Software

In addition to using some of the DL-in-a-box software, the CITIDEL team has developed other tools for a variety of purposes. For example, the ESSEX search engine was developed so that CITIDEL could provide good performance with hundreds of thousands of records, and allow adjustable field weightings to enhance flexibility. We also developed special methods to ensure high-quality filtering of computing-related ETDs from NDLTD (explained in another paper presented at this conference).

The Penn State part of our team runs the eBizSearch and CiteSeer sites, and is working so that this content can be included in CITIDEL. To enhance the quality of the mostly automated gathering process, they have employed sophisticated artificial intelligence methods, and powerful techniques for automatic metadata extraction [35].

A. Krowne, of the Virginia Tech team, launched PlanetMath, for community-based development of a mathematics online encyclopedia (http://www.planetmath.org). His "Noosphere" open source software utilized is available for use in other domains too.

Other special software supports our user base in particular ways. For example, since our aim is to support an international community of users, we adopted a novel approach to employ trusted volunteers to help with translation of the CITIDEL interface, as well as CITIDEL content, into Spanish and other languages.

To support the composition and packaging of sets of resources, in similar fashion to Utah State's Instructional Architect project, we have developed "Active Lists". These allow sequencing, annotation, and special views. The current views supported for active lists are:

- Ordered list
- Unordered list
- Slideshow
- Guided path

To support instructional activities with CITIDEL we developed the Virginia Instructional Architect for Digital Undergraduate Computing Teaching (VIADUCT) system. This supports lesson plans, exercises, laboratory plans, and similar activities. Teachers fill out a template, and to these activities attach resources collected through a CITIDEL binder. This is particularly suited to handling of references, background readings, and additional materials. Further extensions to CITIDEL are likely, but may be shifted to be compatible with the OCKHAM project.

5 OCKHAM

OCKHAM (Open Component-based Knowledge Hypermedia Applications Management) is an initiative [36] that evolved in part out of our research on Open Digital Libraries (see Section 3). We began with the premise that construction of DLs should use components and lightweight protocols, but then added that the architecture should follow the lines of lightweight reference models [37]. In September 2003, NSF funded a collaborative project, led by Emory University, but also involving Notre Dame, University of Arizona, and Virginia Tech [38]. Part of the special appeal of the proposal was our plan to use peer-to-peer (P2P) technologies for education [39]. Another key idea was to expand the use of NSDL by integrating its services into those of university libraries.

In this context, we proposed to develop, using modern Web technologies, a testbed involving at least four universities, and at least the following services:

- Alerting
- Browsing
- Conversion
- Cataloging
- Interoperation
- OAI-PMH-to-Z39.50
- Pathfinding

To guide this effort we are working on suitable reference models, which are relatively lightweight. While many are familiar with the reference model for Open Archival Information Systems [40], we agree with H. Gladney that it may not fit well in our context [41]. We hope to ground our reference model efforts in part on our theory-based work on 5S (Streams, Structures, Spaces, Scenarios, and Societies) [42], which should provide a firm foundation. Our method will be to engage in a variety of focus groups (two scheduled by a Virginia Tech class group this fall) on campuses and in connection with professional meetings. Our aim will be to carefully document our results, and to include the following elements:

- Purpose & scope
- Definitions & vocabularies
- Applicability & scenarios for use (services)
- Rational
- Interoperability & conformance
- Relationships to other standards
- Detailed schematic models
- Road map for development of related standards

Ultimately we hope that OCKHAM will help move NSDL toward a next generation framework with next generation services.

6 Conclusions

This paper has discussed the US National Science Digital Library (NSDL) in general, and provided insights by considering three case studies based on some of the funded projects. We believe that there are many lessons to be learned from NSDL, and that it may help other nations as they work toward goals for a Digital Library for Education. Ultimately, however, we expect that some larger entity will be needed, perhaps an International Education Digital Library Association, and urge that those interested in this concept step forward to further develop the idea.

Acknowledgements. Acknowledgment is given for assistance from DLF (for support of OCKHAM), SUN (for equipment supporting CITIDEL), and NSF (for funding of DUE projects 0121679, 0121741, 0136690, 0333531 and IIS projects 9986089, 0002935, 0080748, 0086227). Thanks also go to members of the Digital Library Research Laboratory and all others involved in the various projects touched upon in this paper.

References

1. Kalinichenko, L. et al.: Analytical Survey on Digital Libraries in Education (DLE) Moscow, Russia: UNESCO Institute for Information Technologies in Education (IITE). (2003)
2. Van de Sompel, H.: Open Archives Initiative. WWW site. Ithaca, NY: Cornell University. (2000) http://www.openarchives.org
3. Lagoze, C., Van de Sompel, H., Nelson, M., Warner, S.: The Open Archives Initiative Protocol for Metadata Harvesting – Version 2.0, Open Archives Initiative. Technical report. Ithaca, NY: Cornell University. (2002)
    http://www.openarchives.org/OAI/2.0/openarchivesprotocol.htm
4. Suleman, H., Fox, E. A.: The Open Archives Initiative: Realizing Simple and Effective Digital Library Interoperability. In special issue on "Libraries and Electronic Resources: New Partnerships, New Practices, New Perspectives" of Journal of Library Automation, 35(1/2): 122–145. (2002)
5. DCMI: Dublin Core Metadata Element Set, Version 1.1: Reference Description. (2002) http://www.dublincore.org/documents/dces/
6. Atkins, A., Fox, E., France, R., Suleman, H.: ETD-ms : An Interoperability Metadata Standard for Electronic Theses and Dissertations. Ch. 16 (pp. 221–232) in Electronic Theses & Dissertations: A Sourcebook for Educators, Students and Librarians, Fox, E., Feizabadi, S., Moxley, J., Weisser, C., eds., New York: Marcel Dekker, in press. (2004)
7. Zia, L.: The NSF National Science, Mathematics, Engineering, and Technology Education Digital Library (NSDL) Program. CACM 44(5):83 (2001)
8. Zia, L., et al.: National Science, Technology, Engineering, and Mathematics Education Digital Library (NSDL) – Program Solicitation NSF 03–530. Arlington, VA: NSF. (2003) http://www.nsf.gov/pubsys/ods/getpub.cfm?nsf03530
9. Lesk, M., Fox, E., McGill, M.: A National Electronic Science, Engineering, and Technology Library, Chapt. 1 Sect. A, in Fox, E., ed.: Sourcebook on Digital Libraries: Report for the National Science Foundation, Virginia Tech Dept. of Computer Science Technical Report TR-93-35, Blacksburg, VA. (1993)
    ftp://fox.cs.vt.edu/pub/DigitalLibrary/
10. NSDL Core Integration Team: NSDL, The National Science Digital Library. WWW site. (2003) http://www.nsdl.org
11. NSDL Core Integration Team: NSDL Communications Portal. WWW site. (2003) http://comm.nsdl.org
12. Lagoze, C., et al.: Core Services in the Architecture of the National Digital Library for Science Education (NSDL). In Proceedings JCDL'2002, 201–209. Portland, OR: ACM Press. (2002)
13. Manduca, C. A., McMartin, F. P., Mogk, D. W.: Pathways to Progress: Vision and Plans for Developing the NSDL: NSDL white paper. March 20, 2001.
    http://doclib.comm.nsdlib.org/PathwaysToProgress.pdf

14. Hoffman, E., Fox, E.: Building Policy, Building Community: An Example from the US National Science, Technology, Engineering, and Mathematics Education Library (NSDL). Short paper in: Ee-Peng Lim, Schubert Foo, Chris Khoo, Hsinchun Chen, Edward Fox, Shalini Urs, Thanos Constantino, eds. Digital Libraries: People, Knowledge, and Technology; Proceedings 5th International Conference on Asian Digital Libraries, ICADL 2002, Singapore, Dec. 2002. Springer, Lecture Notes in Computer Science 2555.
15. Gonçalves, M. A., Luo, M., Shen, R., Ali, M. F., Fox, E. A.: An XML Log Standard and Tool for Digital Library Logging Analysis. In Research and Advanced Technology for Digital Libraries, Proceedings of the 6th European Conference, ECDL 2002, 129–143, Rome, Italy, September 2002.
16. Gonçalves, M., Panchanathan, G., Ravindranathan, U., Krowne, A., Fox, E. A., Jagodzinski, F., Cassel, L.: The XML Log Standard for Digital Libraries: Analysis, Evolution, and Deployment. In Proceedings JCDL 2003, Houston, TX, IEEE-CS, 312–314
17. Fox, E.: Advancing Education through Digital Libraries: NSDL, CITIDEL, and NDLTD. In the Proceedings of Digital Library: IT Opportunities and Challenges in the New Millennium, ed. Sun Jiazheng, Beijing, China: Beijing Library Press, July 9–11, 2002, 107–117.
18. Luo, M., Filippi, G., Suleman, H., Fox, E.: Digital Library in a Box. WWW site. Blacksburg, VA: Virginia Tech. (2003) http://dlbox.nudl.org
19. Luhrs, E.: DL-in-Box. Report for Digital Libraries 553, Rutgers University, New Brunswick, NJ. Available as file LuhrsDL-in-a-Box.pdf from the instructor, Nina Wacholder (nina@scils.rutgers.edu). (2003)
20. Suleman, H., Ming, L., Fox, E.: Open Digital Libraries. WWW site. Blacksburg, VA: Virginia Tech. (2003) http://oai.dlib.vt.edu/odl/
21. Suleman, H., Fox, E. A.: A Framework for Building Open Digital Libraries. D-Lib Magazine, 7(12). (2001) http://www.dlib.org/dlib/december01/suleman/12suleman.html
22. Suleman, H., Fox, E.: Beyond Harvesting: Digital Library Components as OAI Extensions, Virginia Tech Dept. of Computer Science Technical Report TR-02-25, Blacksburg, VA. (2002) http://eprints.cs.vt.edu:8000/archive/00000625/
23. Suleman, H., Fox, E.: Designing Protocols in Support of Digital Library Componentization, Research and Advanced Technology for Digital Technology: Proceedings of the 6th European Conference, ECDL 2002, 568–582, Rome, Italy, September 16–18
24. Fox, E. A., Suleman, H., Luo, M.: Building Digital Libraries Made Easy: Toward Open Digital Libraries. In Proceedings of the 5th International Conference of Asian Digital Libraries, 11–14 December 2002, Singapore.
25. Suleman, H.: Open Digital Libraries, PhD. Dissertation, Virginia Tech. (2002) http://scholar.lib.vt.edu/theses/available/etd-11222002-155624/
26. Suleman, H., Fox, E., Kelapure, R.: Building Digital Libraries from Simple Building Blocks. Online Information Review, 27(5), in press. (2003)
27. Fox, E.A. et al.: Computing and Information Technology Interactive Digital Educational Library (CITIDEL). Web site. Blacksburg, VA: Virginia Tech. (2002) http://www.citidel.org
28. CSTC: Computer Science Teaching Center. (2003) http://www.cstc.org
29. Lagoze, C., & Davis, J. R.: Dienst: An Architecture for Distributed Document Libraries. Communications of the ACM, 38(4): 47. (1995)
30. Davis, J. R., Lagoze, C.: NCSTRL: Design and Deployment of a Globally Distributed Digital Library. J. American Society for Information Science, 51(3), 273–280. (2000)
31. Anan, H., Liu, X., Maly, K., Nelson, M., Zubair, M., French, J., Fox, E., Shivakumar, P.: Preservation and transition of NCSTRL using an OAI-based architecture. In Proceedings JCDL'2002, 181–182. Portland, OR: ACM Press. (2002)
32. Fox, E., Garach, K.: CITIDEL Collection Building. Virginia Tech Dept. of Computer Science Technical Report TR-03-14, Blacksburg, VA. (2003) http://eprints.cs.vt.edu:8000/archive/00000663/

33. Calado, P., Gonçalves, M., Fox, E., Ribeiro-Neto, B., Laender, A., da Silva, A., Reis, D., Roberto, P., Vieira, M., Lage, J.: The Web-DL Environment for Building Digital Libraries from the Web. In Proceedings JCDL 2003, Houston, TX, IEEE-CS, 346–357
34. Krowne, A., Fox, E.: An Architecture for Multischeming in Digital Libraries, Virginia Tech Dept. of Computer Science Technical Report TR-03-25, Blacksburg, VA. (2003) http://eprints.cs.vt.edu:8000/archive/00000692/ (preprint of paper to appear in Proc. ICADL'2003)
35. Han, H., Giles, C., Manavoglu, E., Zha, H., Zhang, Z., Fox, E.: Automatic Document Metadata Extraction using Support Vector Machines. In Proceedings JCDL 2003, Houston, TX, IEEE-CS, 37–48
36. OCKHAM team: OCKHAM (Open Component-based Knowledge Hypermedia Applications Management). WWW site. Atlanta: Emory University. (2003) http://ockham.library.emory.edu/
37. Halbert, M., Fox, E., Dempsey, L., Morgan, E., Frumkin, J.: OCKHAM: Coordinating Digital Library Development with Lightweight Reference Models, panel at ECDL 2002
38. Fox, E.: Collaborative Project: The OCKHAM Library Network, Integrating the NSDL into Traditional Library Services. NSF Award #0333531 Abstract WWW page (with PI Martin D. Halbert, award #0333601, and co-PI Jeremy Frumkin, award #0333497). (2003) https://www.fastlane.nsf.gov/servlet/showaward?award=0333531
39. Koneru, S., Fox, E.: Open Peer to Peer Technologies. Virginia Tech Dept. of Computer Science Technical Report TR-02-19, Blacksburg, VA. (2002) http://eprints.cs.vt.edu:8000/archive/00000613/
40. CCSDS (Consultative Committee for Space Data Systems): Reference Model for an Open Archival Information System (OAIS), CCSDS 650.0-B-1 Blue Book, January 2002. http://wwwclassic.ccsds.org/documents/pdf/CCSDS-650.0-B-1.pdf
41. Gladney, H.: Digital Document Durability. Ch. 14 (pp. 169–210) in Electronic Theses & Dissertations: A Sourcebook for Educators, Students and Librarians, Fox, E., Feizabadi, S., Moxley, J., Weisser, C., eds., New York: Marcel Dekker, in press. (2004)
42. Gonçalves, M., Fox, E., Watson, L., Kipp, N.: Streams, Structures, Spaces, Scenarios, Societies (5S): A Formal Model for Digital Libraries. Virginia Tech Dept. of Computer Science Technical Report TR-03-04, Blacksburg, VA. Preprint of paper to appear in April 2004 ACM TOIS. (2003) http://eprints.cs.vt.edu:8000/archive/00000646/

Character Strings to Natural Language Processing in Information Retrieval

Tengku Mohd Tengku Sembok

Department of Information Science, Universiti Kebangsaan Malaysia,
43600, Bangi, Selangor, Malaysia
tmts@pkrisc.ukm.my

Abstract. The levels-of-processing theory proposes that there are many ways to process and code information. The level of processing adopted will determine the quality of the representation used to store the information in the computer memory or storage. The levels-of-processing applied in information retrieval can be classified as follows: string processing, morphological processing, syntactic processing and semantic processing. These level-of-processing are imbedded into various models of information retrieval. Conventional information retrieval models, such as Boolean and vector space models rely on an extensive use of keywords, as independent strings, and their frequencies in storing and retrieving information. Thus string processing and morphological processing are mainly adopted in these models. It is believed that such an approach has reached its upper limit of retrieval effectiveness, and therefore, new approaches should be investigated for the development of future systems that will be more effective. With current advances in programming languages and techniques, natural language processing and understanding, and generally in the fields of artificial intelligence and cognitive science, there are now attempts made to include knowledge representation and linguistic processing into information retrieval systems. We also focus our research on the application of certain techniques on specific languages. Besides English, we focus the application of certain techniques especially on Malay. In this paper we will highlight some of the research done in the area of information retrieval at the various levels of processing, and also expound the current research we are doing and the future direction that we would like to undertake.

1 Introduction

Information Retrieval (IR) can be defined broadly as the study of how to determine and retrieve from a corpus of stored information the portions which are relevant to particular information needs. Let us assume that there is a store consisting of a large collection of information on some particular topics, or combination of various topics. The information may be stored in a highly structured form or in an unstructured form, depending upon its application. A user of the store, at times, seeks certain information which he may not know to solve a *problem*. He therefore has to express his *information need* as a request for information in one form or another. Thus IR is concerned with the determining and retrieving of information that is relevant to his information need as expressed by his *request* and translated into a *query* which

T.M.T. Sembok et al. (Eds.): ICADL 2003, LNCS 2911, pp. 26–33, 2003.

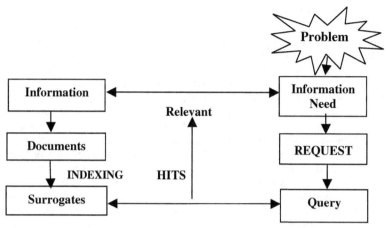

Fig. 1. Surrogates and Relevance

conforms to a specific information retrieval system(IRS) used. An IRS normally stores *surrogates* of the actually *documents* in the system to represent the documents and the *information* stored in them (Mizzaro, 1998), as illustrated in Figure 1.

2 Surrogates and Representation

In conventional document retrieval systems, the surrogates of documents and queries are built by an unstructured collection of simple descriptors, i.e. the keywords. Documents are represented by sets of keywords, or index terms of the form: $Di = (t1,wi1; t2,wi2; \ldots ; tn,win)$, where wij represents the value or weight of term tj which is assigned to document Di. In the Boolean model, the terms are not weighted. Thus, the values of the wij are restricted to either 0 or 1 for terms that are respectively absent from, or present in, a given document. The vector space model give certain value to wij which reflect the importance of the term in the document concern. The basic weights for the terms throughout the document collection are normally calculated using statistical techniques.

In Boolean model, the requests are expressed as Boolean combinations of index terms using logical operators and, or, and not. For example, a query Q might be expressed as:

$$Q = ((ti\ and\ tj)\ or\ tk). \qquad (1)$$

In response to the query given above, all documents indexed either by the combination of ti and tj, or by tk would be retrieved. On the other hand, in vector space model query is represented by the vector: $Q = (t1,q1; t2,q2; \ldots ; tn,qn)$, where wij reflects the present and the importance of the term ti in the query. There are many ways of computing similarity coefficients between a given query and each stored document. For example, one can use the well-known inner-product function, $similarity(Di,Q) = \Sigma_{j=1,n} (qj \cdot wij)$, to do the matching. In these models we need techniques to code and to match strings of keywords that represent the documents and the query.

3 Conflation Methods

One of the main problems encountered in automatic indexing and searching is the variation in semantically related word forms in free text. The differences are mainly caused by the grammatical requirements in a particular language, e.g., COMPUTERISE and COMPUTERISATION in English (or MENG-KOMPUTERKAN and PENGKOMPUTERAN in Malay). The solution to this problem is therefore by reducing the variants of a word to a single canonical form. This process is known as conflation. Conflation can be either manual - using some kind of regular expressions - or automatic, via programs called stemmers. A stemming algorithm is a computational procedure which reduces all words with the same root (or, if prefixes are left untouched, the same *stem*) to a common form, usually by stripping each word of its derivational and inflectional suffixes.

The most commonly used English stemming algorithm is Porter's Algorithm (Porter 1980). For Malay language we have Othman's Algorithm (1993) and Fatimah's Algorithm(1995) which used rule based approach of the forms *prefix+suffix*, *+suffix*, *prefix+*, and *+infix*, as shown in Table 1 below. Stemming algorithms are known to be not perfect. Wrong stems might be derived from a given word. Table 2 shows examples of errors faced in Malay stemmers

Table 1. Stemming Rues

Types	Example of Rules	Word Examples
prefix+suffix	ke+an ke+annya peng+an	kecerdasan keutamaannya pengertian
prefix+	be+ bel+ ber+	bekerja belajar beradik
+suffix	+an +wi +at	makanan duniawi muslimat
+infix	+in+ +em+ +er+	sinambungan gementar gerigi

Table 2. Errors in Malay Stemming

Words	Correct Root	Produced by stemmer	Error Types
kurangkan peringatan sukai mengandung	kurang ingat suka kandung	rang peringat sukai gandung	overstemmed understemmed unchanged spelling
berikanlah	beri	ikan	others

4   Coding Methods

Coding methods are also experimented to match Malay words which are misspelled or having variances in spelling. Four phonetic coding methods and one non-phonetic coding are used in the experiments as in Table 3. Table 4 shows examples of Malay coded words using various coding methods.

Table 3. Coding Methods

Phonetic Coding:
Soundex (Russell 1918): based on sound;
Davidson (Davidson 1962): to handle names spelling variations;
Phonix (Gadd 1988, 1990): online cataloging of PCL;
Hartlib (Rogers & Willett 1991): to handle old spelling.
Non-phonetic coding:
SPEEDCOP (Pollock & Zamora 1983, 1984): to handle spelling errors.

Table 4. Coded Malay Words

Present Malay Words	Phonetic Codes				SPEEDCOP Keys	
	Hartlib	Soundex	Phonix	Davidson	Skeleton	Omission
alam	alm	a45	v45	alm	alma	mla
berpakaian	brp1n	b6125	b125	brpkn	brpkneai	kbpnreai
capaian	cpn	c15	k15	cpn	cpnai	pcnai

5   String Similarity Methods

Conflation methods described above are unable to conflate all possible types of word variants correctly. Thus string-similarity methods, n-gram, are experimented on Malay words. N-gram approach suggested that words that have a high degree of structural similarity tend to be similar in meaning. Each word is represented by a list of its constituent n-grams, where n is the number of adjacent characters in the substrings. Using these lists, similarity measures between pair of words are calculated on shared unique n-grams. Examples of n-grams for Muhamad is (*m,mu,uh,ha,am,ma,ad,d*), and for Mohammad is (*m,mo,oh,ha,am,mm,ma,ad,d*), and their similarity value is twice the ratio of the number of n-grams which are similar over the total number of n-grams in both words which is 2(6/17).

Experiments using various combinations of stemming, coding and n-gram matching were done on a Malay corpur. The results obtained show that the combinations of stemming with other methods performed better, in the following order (Sembok 1995, Zainab et al. 2000): Digram, Soundex,, Davidson, Hartlib, and Phonix.

6 A New Model: Logical–Linguistic Model

Independent keywords indexing scheme used in the Boolean and vector space model is not an ideal document or query content indicator for use in IR systems. Given the following titles of documents:

(1) New curriculum and computer facility for management science students,
(2) The undergraduate curriculum in computer science,
(3) 1989 undergraduate computer science curriculum.

All the three independent terms, *curriculum, computer and science*, characterise all the three titles equally well.

The phrase computer science is only applicable to titles (2) and (3) only.

The representation of a document containing the phrase *computer science* would be more accurate if the phrase can be derived or established from the document's representation itself. This would allow a query containing the same phrase to fully match with documents like (2) and (3), but not with documents like (1). Going a step further, a good content indicator representation would allow a query with a phrase *computer science curriculum* to match documents (2) and (3) equally, but not document (1); even though, only document (3) has exactly the same phrase computer science curriculum. In order to do this the retrieval processor, in one way or another, must be provided with enough information to recognise phrases. In this particular example, a conventional document retrieval system would wrongly match the query containing the phrase computer science curriculum with all the three documents equally well since the information provided by the keyword representation is not informative enough.

The example given above illustrates an obvious shortcoming of the conventional document representation models, such as the vector space model, used in most automatic document retrieval systems. In these systems, a document is represented by an unstructured collection of keywords or terms which are generally assumed to be statistically independent. The representation does not include any information on syntactic or semantic relationships among those terms. We feel that this kind of representations is too simplified to be highly effective. We hold the view that a more accurate representation can be constructed if the method of content analysis takes into account information about the structure of document and query texts, i.e. the information concerning the syntactic and the semantic structure of the texts. The levels-of-processing theory proposes that there are many ways to process and code information and that knowledge representation used in the memory or storage are qualitatively different.

In order to achieve a more accurate representation of documents and queries, the simple keyword representation ought to be replaced by a knowledge representation such as semantic networks, logic, frame or production system (Allen 87). In our experiment we have chosen logic in the form of first order predicate calculus (FOPC) to represent the contents of documents and queries. A sentence *Mary likes her mother* is expressed in FOPC as the proposition LIKES(MARY,mother(MARY)).

6.1   A Simple Document and Query Surrogates

To start with, we have adopted a very simple predicate calculus to represent documents and queries as follows:

```
Di = {
        t1(X),
        t2(Y),
        :
        tn(Z),
        relationship(X,Y),
        relationship(X,Y,Z),
        :
          (t1,wi1; t2,wi2;  . . . ; tn,win)
        }

Q = {
        t1(X),
        t2(Y),
        :
        tn(Z),
        relationship(X,Y),
        relationship(X,Y,Z),
     }
```

We need a natural language processing system to translate documents and queries into knowledge representation. A categorial unification grammar is used in the experiment to do the translation (Sembok, 1999).

For example, a noun phrase "curriculum of computer science" is translated into:

```
comput(X),
scienc(A),
curriculum(C),
r(X,A),
of(A,C).
```

6.2   Benchmark and Experimental Result

A few experimental runs have been performed using the model by changing some parameters to fine tune the system. The test data used is the CACM collection by Fox (1983). The benchmark used to compare the results obtained is based on the traditional keywords approach using the *tf x idf* weighting scheme. Table_5 shows the result obtained using our model as compared to the benchmark. The figures show an improvement of 24.3% over the benchmark.

Table 5. Recall Cutoff Evaluation Result

Recall Levels	Precisions	
	Benchmark	Our Result
10	52.22	58.74
20	38.52	45.64
30	31.90	38.06
40	24.49	28.64
50	21.01	26.00
60	17.59	22.99
70	12.13	17.68
80	10.23	15.62
90	7.04	11.55
100	6.09	10.14
Average	22.12	27.51
% Increase		24.30

7 Conclusion

The level of processing adopted will determine the quality of the representation used to store and retrieve information. The level of processing theory states that the more complicated the level of processing the more effective the storage and the retrieval are. We have experimented to confirm the theory through the application of several methods of strings processing and a natural language processing using the logical-linguistic model. From the results obtained it confirms the theory further.

References

Asim Othman. 1993. Pengakar perkataan melayu untuk sistem capaian dokumen. MSc Thesis. National University of Malaysia.

Allen J. 1987.Natural Language Understanding, The Benjamin/Cummings Publishing Company, Inc.

Davidson, L. 1962. Retrieval of misspelled names in an airline's passenger record system. Communications of the ACM 5:169–171.

Fatimah Ahmad, Mohammed Yusoff, Tengku Mohd. T. Sembok. 1996. "Experiments with A Malay Stemming Algorithm", *Journal of American Society of Information Science*.

Fox E.A. 1983. Characterization of Two New Experimental Collections in Computer and Information Science Containing Textual and Bibliographic Concepts, Technical Report 83–561, Department of Computer Science, Cornell University.

Gadd, T.N. 1988. 'Fisching Fore Werds': phonetic retrieval of written text in information systems. Program 22:222–237.

Gadd, T.N. 1990. PHONIX: the algorithm. Program 24:363–366.

Mizzaro, S. 1997. "Relevance: The Whole History". JASIS, Vol.48, No.9, pp. 810–832.

Pollock, J.J. & Zamora, A. 1983. Correction and characterization of spelling errors in scientific and scholarly text. Journal of the American Society for Information Science 34:51–58.

Pollock, J.J. & Zamora, A. 1984. Automatic spelling correction in scientific and scholarly text. Communications of the ACM 27:358–368.

Porter M.F. 1980. "An Algorithm for suffix stripping", Program, 14(3), pp. 130–137.

Rogers, H.J. & Willett, P. 1991. Searching for historical word forms in text database using spelling-correction methods: reverse error and phonetic coding methods. Journal of Documentation 47:333–353.

Russell, R.C. 1918. U.S. patent 1261167. Washington: United States Patent Office.

Russell, R.C. 1922. U.S. patent 1435663. Washington: United States Patent Office.

Sembok, T.M.T. & Willett, P. 1995. Experiments with n-gram string-similarity measure on malay texts. Technical Report. Universiti Kebangsaan Malaysia.

Sembok, Tengku Mohd Tengku. 1999. Application of Mathematical Functional Decomposition in Document Indexing, *Prosiding : Pengintegrasian Technologi dalam Sains Matematik.* Penang: USM.

Zainab Abu Bakar, Tengku Mohd T. Sembok, Mohamed Yusoff. 2000. "An Evaluation of Retrieval Effectiveness using Spelling-Correction and String Matching Methods on Malay Texts", to appear in: *Journal of American Society of Information Science,* John Wiley.

CMedPort: Intelligent Searching for Chinese Medical Information

Yilu Zhou, Jialun Qin, and Hsinchun Chen

Department of Management Information System, The University of Arizona,
Tucson, Arizona 85721, USA
{yiluz,hchen}@eller.arizona.edu
qin@u.arizona.edu

Abstract. Most information retrieval techniques have been developed for English and other Western languages. As the second largest Internet language, Chinese provides a good setting for study of how search engine techniques developed for English could be generalized for use in other languages to facilitate Internet searching and browsing in a multilingual world. This paper reviews different techniques used in search engines and proposes an integrated approach to development of a Chinese medical portal: CMedPort. The techniques integrated into CMedPort include meta-search engines, cross-regional search, summarization and categorization. A user study was conducted to compare the effectiveness, efficiency and user satisfaction of CMedPort and three major Chinese search engines. Preliminary results from the user study show that CMedPort achieves similar accuracy in searching tasks, and higher effectiveness and efficiency in browsing tasks than Openfind, a Taiwan search engine portal. We believe that the proposed approach can be used to support Chinese information seeking in Web-based digital library applications.

1 Introduction

As the Web is growing exponentially, information on it has become increasingly diverse and comprehensive. Online information in languages other than English is growing even faster. A recent report shows that the non-English online population has exceeded the English online population [Global Internet Statistics. http://www.glreach.com/globstats/]. Globalization has been a major trend of the Internet. However, most research in information retrieval (IR) has involved only English language programs. As non-English speakers wish to access information in their native languages, there is a need to study how to facilitate information seeking in a multilingual world. As the second most popular language online, Chinese occupies 10.8% of Internet languages (China Internet Network Information Center, 2003). It would be desirable to take Chinese as an example to study how techniques used in English IR could facilitate IR in other languages, because Chinese differentiates from English in many aspects.

Medical Web sites are among the most popular Web sites [25]. There are a tremendous amount of medical Web pages provided in Chinese on the Internet, ranging from scientific papers and journals to general health, clinical symposia and

T.M.T. Sembok et al. (Eds.): ICADL 2003, LNCS 2911, pp. 34–45, 2003.

Web pages of widely-varied quality. It is important for Chinese users to find up-to-date and high-quality medical information in Chinese on the Web. Moreover, some medical information might only be available in Chinese Web sites, such as traditional Chinese medicine information. However, Chinese medical information seekers find it difficult to locate desired information, because of the lack of high-performance tools to facilitate medical information seeking. They have to rely on general Chinese search engines, which will bring thousands of unrelated Web sites.

To address these problems, our project aims to developing a Chinese Medical Portal that facilitates medical information seeking. This portal utilizes various techniques such as meta-search, cross-region search, summarization and categorization to benefit searching and browsing.

The rest of the paper is structured as follows. Section 2 reviews related research, including information seeking behavior, technologies that support searching and browsing, and current Chinese search engines and medical portals. In Section 3 the architectural design and major components of CMedPort are illustrated. In section 4 we discuss evaluation methodology and provide some preliminary results. Finally, in Section 5 we suggest some future directions.

2   Related Work

2.1   Internet Searching and Browsing

The sheer volume of information makes it more and more difficult for users to find desired information. This is often referred to as information overload [1]. Search engines are the most popular tools used for information seeking on the Internet. When seeking information on the Web, individuals typically perform two kinds of tasks – Internet searching and browsing [7].

Internet searching is "a process in which an information seeker describes a request via a query and the system must locate the information that matches or satisfies the request." Through searching, individuals want to retrieve specific information on a given topic [7]. Browsing has been defined by Marchionini & Shneiderman as "an exploratory, information seeking strategy that depends upon serendipity" and is "especially appropriate for ill-defined problems and for exploring new task domains." Through browsing, individuals want to explore the information space to gain familiarity with it or to locate something of their interest [7] [20].

2.2   Problems Facing Chinese Medical Information Seekers

A tremendous amount of Web sites have been developed to provide access to Chinese medical information over the Internet. However, various factors contribute to the difficulties of Chinese information retrieval in the medical area. The sheer volume of Chinese medical information causes information overload. A more important problem is the regional differences among mainland China, Hong Kong and Taiwan. Although all three regions speak Chinese, they use different forms of Chinese characters and different encoding standards in computer systems. Simplified Chinese, the official written language in mainland China, is usually encoded using the GB2312 scheme. Traditional Chinese, used in Hong Kong and Taiwan, is often encoded using the Big5 system. Users from mainland China usually find it difficult to read traditional Chinese and vice versa. When searching in systems encoded one way, users are not able to get information in the other encoding. Besides, Chinese medical information providers in mainland China, Hong Kong and Taiwan usually keep information only from their own regions. Users who want to find information from other regions have to use different systems. These factors result in the information gap among mainland China, Hong Kong and Taiwan.

2.3   Techniques Facilitating Searching and Browsing

To address the above problems, we examine techniques that may help information seeking in Internet searching and browsing in this section.

Searching Support Techniques

Domain specific Search Engines. As the amount of information on the World Wide Web grows, it becomes increasingly difficult to find just what we want. General-purpose search engines, such as Google and AltaVista, usually result in thousands of hits, many of them not relevant to the user queries. Domain-specific search engines could alleviate the problem because they offer increased accuracy and extra functionality not possible with the general search engines [5]. A lot of medical domain-specific search engines in English have been built. Examples include MEDConsult (www.medconsult.com), the National Library of Medicine's Gateway (http://gateway.nlm.nih.gov/gw/Cmd), CliniWeb (www.ohsu.edu/cliniweb/), MedTextus (http://ai.bpa.arizona.edu/go/medical/MedTextus.html) [19], HelpfulMed (http://ai.bpa.arizona.edu/helpfulmed) [10], etc. In Section 2.4 we will review the search engines and medical portals in Chinese.

Meta-search. Selberg and Etzioni suggested that by relying solely on one search engine, users could miss over 77% of the references they would find most relevant [24]. Lawrence & Giles also reported that each search engine covers only about 16% of the total Web sites [17]. Meta-search engines can greatly improve search results by sending queries to multiple search engines and collating only the highest-ranking subset of the returns from each [9] [21] [24]. Meta-searching leverages the capabilities of multiple Web search engines and other types of information sources, providing a simple, uniform user interface and relieving the user from the problems of dealing with different search engines and information overload. This technique is also used in domain-specific search engines. For instance, BuildingOnline (www.buildingonline.com) specializes in searching in the building industry domain, and CollegeBot (www.collegebot.com) searches for educational resources [9].

Browsing Support Techniques. In most current search engine systems, returned results are presented as a list of ranked URLs without further analysis. It would be desirable to perform post-retrieval analysis on the returned results for the users.

Categorization—Document Overview. In a browsing scenario, it is highly desirable for an IR system to provide such a feel for an overview of the retrieved document set so that the users can explore a specific topic and gain a general view of a particular area of interest. Categorization has been shown to be a powerful post-retrieval document processing tool that can cluster similar documents into a category and present the resulting clusters to the user in an intuitive and sensible way [9]. Hearst and Pedersen as well as Zamir and Etzioni demonstrated that document clustering has the potential to improve performance in document retrieval [15] [28]. There are two approaches to apply categorization: 1) categorization based on individual document attributes, such as query term frequency, size, source, topic or author of each document. NorthernLight (www.northernlight.com) is an example of this approach. 2) Categorization based on inter-document similarities. This approach usually includes some machine learning techniques.

In Chinese information retrieval, efficient categorization of Chinese documents relies on the extraction of meaningful keywords from text. The mutual information algorithm has been shown to be an effective way to extract keywords from Chinese documents [23].

Summarization–Document Preview. Summarization is another post-retrieval analysis technique that provides a preview of a document [14]. It can reduce the size and complexity of Web documents. There are different approaches to text summarization. Two major approaches are text extraction and text abstraction. While text abstraction is more complex and difficult, text extraction is the most common approach [16] [22]. Text extraction utilizes sentences from the original document to form a summary.

2.4   Current Search Engines and Medical Portals in Three Regions

To better understand the current status of Chinese search engines, especially in the medical domain, we conducted a study on the contents and functionalities of major Chinese search engines and medical portals. Major Chinese search engines in the three regions include Sina (www.sina.com) in mainland China, Yahoo Hong Kong (hk.yahoo.com) in Hong Kong, and Yam (www.yam.com.tw) and Openfind (www.openfind.com.tw) in Taiwan. These general search engines provide basic Boolean search function as well as directory based browsing. Openfind provides term suggestion function, while Yahoo Hong Kong and Yam provide encoding conversion to support cross-region search. However, these general search engines do not provide comprehensive medical content; they mainly keep information for their own region in only one version, either simplified or traditional Chinese; and they do not have comprehensive functionalities such as post-retrieval analysis to address user needs.

Unlike general search engines, medical portals provide focused information in the medical domain. But they do not necessarily include search function. The major Chinese medical portals include www.999.com.cn, www.medcyber.com, www.wsjk.com.cn from mainland China, www.trustmed.com.tw from Taiwan. In terms of content, these portals have quite diverse content, ranging from general health to drugs, industry, research conferences, etc. They act more as a medical content provider and manually maintain their own content. Only www.999.com.cn provides search functions for Chinese medical information on the Internet. Medcyber and Trustmed only provide search functions within their own sites, while WSJK does not incorporate any search ability. Most of these portals maintain a small collection of less than 10,000 pages and only provide one Chinese character version for their own region.

2.5 Summary

In summary, many Internet searching and browsing support techniques have been shown to be effective for English search engines, including meta-search, document categorization, and summarization. However, few of them have been adapted for use in Chinese search engines. In the medical domain, hardly any domain-specific search engines are available in Chinese. Chinese users have to rely on general purpose search engines, such as Sina and Yahoo Hong Kong, to search for medical content in Chinese. There is a need to study how to integrate various techniques into a medical-domain Chinese search engine.

3   Research Prototype – CMedPort

The CMedPort was built to provide medical and health information services to both researchers and the public. It is a prototype for discovering whether integrated techniques can help improve Internet searching and browsing in languages other than English. It uses three-tier architecture (as shown in Figure 1). The main components are: (1) Content Creation; (2) Meta-search Engines; (3) Encoding Converter; (4) Chinese Summarizer; (5) Categorizer; and (6) User Interface. In this section, we discuss each major component in depth.

(1) Content Creation. In order to cover information from mainland China, Hong Kong and Taiwan, three regional Web page collections were created. Containing more than 300,000 indexed Web pages, these were built by the 'SpidersRUs Digital Library Toolkit' from 210 starting URLs and stored in a MS SQL Server database. The 210 starting URLs were manually selected based on suggestions from medical domain experts. They cover a large variety of medical-related topics, from public clinics to professional journals, and from drug information to hospital information.
The 'SpidersRUs Digital Library Toolkit', which was used to spider and index Chinese medical-related information, is a modularized search engine development tool. It uses a character-based indexing approach. Because Chinese has no explicit word boundaries, word-based indexing usually matches text to a Chinese word lexicon. Many valuable words could be missed if they are not included in the matching lexicon. Character-based indexing is known to be more efficient and to achieve higher recall than word-based indexing [12]. The toolkit is able to deal with different encodings of Chinese (GB2312, Big5, and UTF8). It also indexes different document formats, including HTML, SHTML, text, PDF, and MS Word.

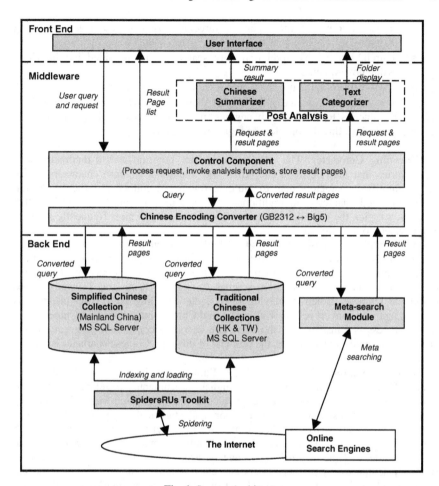

Fig. 1. System Architecture

The indexed files were loaded into a SQL Server database in which the data were separated by the three regions, so that when retrieving, the system could tell which region a webpage had come. Pages from each region were ranked by tf*idf during retrieval. Tf*idf totaled the frequency of occurrence of every word in a document as well as the word's total occurrences in the collection, which indicated the correlation between the documents and a particular keyword. Worthy of mention is that SpiderRUs supports multi languages, including English, Spanish, Arabic, etc.

(2) Meta-search Engines. Besides the regional collections, CMedPort also "meta-searches" six key Chinese search engines. They are:

- www.baidu.com, the biggest Internet search service provider in mainland China;
- www.sina.com.cn, the biggest Web portal in mainland China;

- hk.yahoo.com, the most popular directory-based search engine in Hong Kong;
- search2.info.gov.hk, a high quality search engine provided by the Hong Kong government;
- www.yam.com, the biggest Chinese search engine in Taiwan;
- www.sina.com.tw, one of the biggest Web portals in Taiwan.

By sending queries to these search engines, users could get results from all three regions, thus alleviating the problem of regional variations.

(3) Encoding Converter. The encoding converter program uses a dictionary with 6737 entries that map between simplified and traditional Chinese characters. Since many simplified characters map to multiple traditional equivalents, the conversion from simplified characters to traditional ones is sometimes ambiguous. When that happens, we pick the candidate character that statistically is most frequently selected as equivalent to the original one.

In the simplified Chinese version of CMedPort, when a user enters a query in simplified Chinese, the query will be sent to all mainland China information sources using simplified Chinese. At the same time, the query is converted into traditional Chinese and sent to all information sources from Hong Kong and Taiwan that use traditional Chinese. When displaying results, the encoding conversion program is invoked again to convert results from traditional Chinese into simplified Chinese. The whole process is transparent to the user. The encoding conversion program enables cross-region search and addresses the problem of different Chinese character forms.

(4) Chinese Summarizer. The Chinese Summarizer is a modified version of TXTRACTOR, a summarizer for English documents developed by [22]. TXTRACTOR is based on a sentence extraction approach using linguistic heuristics such as cue phrases and sentence position and statistical analysis such as word frequency. The summarizer can help a user quickly determine whether or not a Web page is of interest. On the summarizer page, summary sentences are displayed on the left-hand side, and the original Web page is displayed on the right-hand side with summary sentences highlighted. Users can click on any summary sentences on the left-hand side and go to the location of that sentence on the original page on the right-hand side. This feature is especially useful for browsing long documents.

(5) Categorizer. Another component of CMedPort is the categorizer. When a user clicks on the 'analyze results' button, all returned results are processed and key phrases are extracted from their titles and summaries. Key phrases with high occurrences are extracted as folder topics. Web pages that contain the folder topic are included in that folder. One Web page may appear in more than one folder if it contains multiple folder topics. We are using only title and summary to extract keywords because it is practical and permits dynamic categorization. Previous research has shown that clustering based on snippets is almost as effective as clustering based on whole document [28].

A Chinese phrase lexicon is used to match and extract key phrases from documents. Existing lexicons do not suit our purpose because they are not up-to-date or are unrelated to the medical domain. To build an up-to-date medical lexicon, we chose to use the Mutual Information program developed by [23], which has been shown to be an effective tool for extracting key phrases from Chinese documents. First, 150,000 pages from medical websites in simplified Chinese and 100,000 pages from medical websites in traditional Chinese were collected. The Mutual Information program then analyzed the two collections and extracted key phrases based on co-occurrence information.

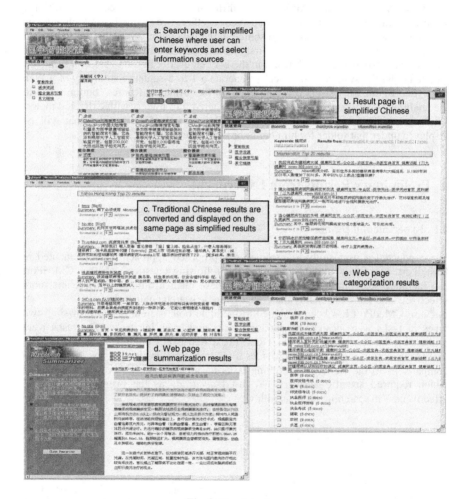

Fig. 2. User Interface

(6) User Interface. CMedPort has two versions of User Interface to accommodate users from different regions: the traditional Chinese version the simplified Chinese version. They look the same and provide the same functionalities, except that they use different encoding and Chinese characters (simplified and traditional). On the search page (See Figure 2.a), users can begin searching by typing keywords in the search box and indicating which local database and meta-search engines to search. Multiple keywords can be entered into the search box at the same time, one keyword per line. Available information sources are organized into three columns by the region to which they belong and can be chosen by choosing the checkbox in front of their names. On the result page, the top 20 results from each information source are displayed as ranked lists. For each result in the lists, the title and a short summary are displayed (See figure 2.b). All results of different encodings are converted into the same encoding as the interface and displayed together (See figure 2.c). By clicking on the name of a particular information source in the navigation bar at the top right-hand side of the page, users can go to the first result from that information source. There is a draw-down box beneath each result in the list that users can use to select a summary length and let the system automatically generate a 1-to-5-sentence summary of a Web page (See figure 2.d). Users can also click on the 'Analyze Results' button to go to the analyzer page where all the results are clustered into folders with extracted topics. Clicking on the folders of interest will produce a list of URL titles that will be displayed under that folder for him/her to browse (See figure 2.e).

4   Preliminary Results from Experiment

4.1 Experimental Design

We conducted a user study to evaluate our proposed approach as implemented in CMedPort. Our study mainly addressed the following question: whether CMedPort can facilitate searching and browsing of Chinese medical information seekers more effectively and more efficiently than other Chinese search engines do.

Because CMedPort has been designed to facilitate both searching and browsing, two types of tasks were designed: searching tasks and browsing tasks. The tasks were designed to be consistent with the TREC (Text Retrieval Conference) standards. The TREC evaluation methodology provides a common task evaluation for cross-system comparisons in the IR field. Searching tasks in our user study were short questions which required specific answers. We used *accuracy* as the primary measure of effectiveness in searching tasks as follow:

$$Accuracy = \frac{number\ of\ correct\ answers\ given\ by\ the\ subject}{total\ number\ of\ questions\ asked} \tag{1}$$

Each browsing task in our user study consisted of a topic that defined an information need accompanied by a short description regarding the task and the related questions In browsing tasks, subjects were expected to summarize the findings of their Web browsing session as a number of themes. Themes were defined as "a short phrase, which describes a certain topic." [9]. Theme identification was used to evaluate performance of browsing tasks. Theme precision and theme recall were used as the primary measures of effectiveness in browsing tasks. They are defined as follows:

$$Theme\ precision = \frac{number\ of\ correct\ themes\ identified\ by\ the\ subject}{number\ of\ all\ themes\ identified\ by\ the\ subject} \quad (2)$$

$$Theme\ recall = \frac{number\ of\ correct\ themes\ identified\ by\ the\ subject}{number\ of\ correct\ themes\ identified\ by\ expert\ judges} \quad (3)$$

A theme is considered correct if it matches with any of the themes identified by experts. Efficiency in both tasks is directly measured by the time subjects spent on the tasks using different systems and post questionnaires were used to study user satisfaction.

4.2 Preliminary Results

In this section, we report the preliminary evaluation results and observations based on the user study of the 15 subjects from Taiwan. They performed searching and browsing tasks using both CMedPort and a commercial Taiwan search engine: Openfind. In Table 1, we can see that CMedPort achieves a comparable accuracy with Openfind in searching tasks. Table 2 summarizes the results from browsing tasks. We find that CMedPort achieves higher theme precision and theme recall than Openfind in browsing tasks. In terms of efficiency, users spent much less time when using CMedPort than when using Openfind in both searching and browsing tasks.

Table 1. Experimental results for searching tasks

	CMedPort	Openfind	P-value
Time spent (Sec)	72.433	114.767	0.04*
Accuracy	0.833333	0.8	0.092

Table 2. Experimental results for browsing task

	CMedPort	Openfind	P-value
Time spent (Sec)	218.1	318.267	0.0006*
Theme Precision	0.789	0.636	0.031*
Theme Recall	0.481	0.215	0.0000*

From subjects' feedback, CMedPort gave more specific answers. "It is easier to find information from CmedPort," one user said. They liked the categorizer feature a lot. Subjects expressed that "the categorizer is really helpful. It allows me to locate the useful information." They also thought showing results from all three regions was more convenient than Openfind. Some of them liked the summarizer, but some complained about the summarization speed. One comment on the summarizer was "It is useful sometimes, but not all the time." In comparing it to CMedPort, they complained about Openfind providing irrelevant URLs.

5 Future Directions

We have reviewed various techniques that could facilitate seeking of Chinese medical information on the Internet. We also have discussed the development of a prototype Chinese medical portal with integrated functionalities including meta-search, cross-regional search, summarization, and categorization. User studies were conducted to evaluate the effectiveness, efficiency and user satisfaction of CMedPort. Through preliminary results from user study, the prototype achieves similar accuracy with Openfind in searching tasks. In browsing tasks, it achieves higher theme precision and recall. In both tasks, it achieves higher efficiency. We are currently analyzing the data from subjects of all three regions and plan to report further results.

Future development includes integrating additional technologies such as self-organizing map (SOM) which categorizes documents retrieved from the Web based on attributes chosen by a user. We also plan to use these searching and browsing support technologies in other languages, such as Spanish and Arabic.

Acknowledgements. The project has been supported in part by a grant from the NSF Digital Library Initiative-2, "High-performance Digital Library Systems: From Information Retrieval to Knowledge Management," IIS-9817473, April 1999-March 2002. We would also like to thank all members in the AI Lab for contributing to various aspects of the project.

References

[1]   D.C. Blair and M.E. Maron.: An evaluation of retrieval effectiveness for a full-text document-retrieval system. Communications of the ACM, 28(3), 289–299, 1985.

[2]   C.M. Bowman, P.B. Danzig, U. Manber, and F. Schwartz: Scalable Internet Resource Discovery: Research Problems and Approaches. Communications of the ACM, 37(8), 98–107, 1994.

[3]   E. Carmel, S. Crawford and H. Chen: Browsing in hypertext: a cognitive study. Systems, Man and Cybernetics. IEEE Transactions on 22(5): 865–884, 1992.

[4]   M. Chau, and H. Chen: Creating Vertical Search Engines Using Spreading Activation. Under Review at IEEE Computer, 2002.

[5]   M. Chau, H. Chen, J. Qin, Y. Zhou, Y. Qin, W. Sung, and D. McDonald: Comparison of two approaches to building a vertical search tool: a case study in the nanotechnology domain. In Proceedings of JCDL'02, Portland, Oregon, USA, ACM Press, 2002.

[6]   M. Chau, D. Zeng, and H. Chen: Personalized Spiders for Web Search and Analysis. In Proceedings of JCDL'01, Roanoke, Virginia, United States, ACM Press, 2001.

[7]   H. Chen, A. L. Houston, R.R Sewell, and B.R. Schatz: Internet Browsing and Searching: User Evaluations of Category Map and Concept Space Techniques. Journal of the American Society for Information Science 49(7): 582–603, 1998.

[8]   H. Chen, C. Schufels, and R. Orwig: Internet Categorization and Search: A Self-Organizing Approach. Journal of Visual Communication and Image Representation 7(1): 88–102, 1996.

[9]   H. Chen, H. Fan, M. Chau, and D. Zeng: MetaSpider: Meta-Searching and Categorization on the Web. Journal of the American Society for Information Science and Technology, 52(13), 1134–1147, 2001.

[10]   H. Chen, A. Lally, B. Zhu, and M. Chau: "HelpfulMed: Intelligent Searching for Medical Information Over the Internet." Journal of the American Society for Information Science and Technology (forthcoming).

[11]   H. Chen, C. Schuffels, and R. Orwig: Internet Categorization and Search: a Self-organizing Approach. Journal of Visual Communication and Image Representation 7,1, 88–102, 1996.

[12]   L. Chien, and H. Pu: Important Issues on Chinese Information Retrieval" Computational Linguistics and Chinese Language Processing. Vol.1, no.1, pp. 205–221,1996.

[13]   J.F. Cove and B.C. Walsh: Online Text Retrieval via Browsing. Information Processing and Management 24, 1, 31–37, 1988.

[14]   S. Greene, G. Marchionini, C. Plaisant, and B. Shneiderman: Previews and overviews in digital libraries: designing surrogates to support visual information seeking. Journal of the American Society for Information Science. 51, 4, 380–393, 2000.

[15]   M. Hearst and J.O. Pedersen: Reexamining the cluster hypothesis: Scatter/gather on retrieval results. In Proceedings of the 19th International ACM SIGIR Conference on Research and Development in Information Retrieval (SIGIR '96) (pp. 76–84). New York: ACM Press.

[16]   E. Hovy, and C.Y. Lin: Automated Text Summarization in SUMMARIST. Advances in Automatic Text Summarization, 81-94, MIT Press 1999.

[17]   S. Lawrence and C.L. Giles: Accessibility of information on the Web. Nature, 400, 107–109, 1999.

[18]   G. Leroy and H. Chen: Meeting Medical Terminology Needs: The Ontology-enhanced Medical Concept Mapper. IEEE Transactions on Information Technology in Biomedicine, vol. 5 (4), pp 261–270, 2001.

[19]   G. Leroy and H. Chen: MedTextus: An Ontology-enhanced Medical Portal," presented at the Workshop on Information Technology and Systems (WITS), BarcelonaMeng,W., W.Zonghuan, et al. (2001). A highly scalable and effective method for metasearch." ACM Transactions on Information Systems (TOIS) 19(3): 31–335, 2002.

[20]   G. Marchionini and B. Shneiderman: Finding facts vs. browsing knowledge in hypertext systems. IEEE Computer 21, 1,70–80, 1988.

[21]   W. Meng and C.Yu, and K. Liu: Building efficient and effective metasearch engines. ACM Computing Surveys (CSUR) 34(1): 48–89,2002.

[22]   D. McDonald and H. Chen: Using sentence selection heuristics to rank text segments in TXTRACTOR. In Proceedings of JCDL'02, Portland, Oregon. ACM/IEEE-CS, 28–35, 2002.

[23]   T. Ong and H. Chen: Updatable PAT-Tree approach to Chinese key phrase extraction using mutual information: a linguistic foundation for knowledge management. In Proceedings of the Second Asian Digital Library Conference. Taipei, Taiwan, 1999.

[24]   E. Selberg and O. Etzioni: Multi-service search and comparison using the MetaCrawler. In Proceedings of the 4th World Wide Web Conference, Boston, Mass, USA, 1995.

[25]   E.H. Shortliffe: The evolution of health-care records in the era of the Internet. Medinfo, vol. 9, pp.8–14,1998.

[26]   C.J. van Rijsbergen: Information Retrieval (2nd ed.) London: Butterworths, 1979.

[27]   E. Voorhees and D. Harman: Overview of the Sixth Text Retrieval Conference (TREC 6). In Proceedings of the Sixth Text Retrieval Conference (TREC-6) (pp. 1–24). Gaithersburg, Maryland: National Institute of Standards and Technology, 1998.

[28]   O. Zamir and O. Etzioni: Grouper: a Dynamic Clustering Interface to Web Search Results. In Proceedings of the Eighth World Wide Web Conference, Toronto, 1999.

Automatic Summarization of Chinese and English Parallel Documents

Fu Lee Wang[1] and Christopher C. Yang[2*]

[1] Department of Computer Science, The City University of Hong Kong
[2] Department of Systems Engineering and Engineering Management
The Chinese University of Hong Kong
yang@se.cuhk.edu.hk

Abstract. As a result of the rapid growth in Internet access, significantly more information has become available online in real time. However, there is not sufficient time for users to read large volumes of information and make decisions accordingly. The problem of information-overloading can be resolved through the application of automatic summarization. Many summarization systems for documents in different languages have been implemented. However, the performance of summarization system on documents in different languages has not yet been investigated. In this paper, we compare the result of fractal summarization technique on parallel documents in Chinese and English. The grammatical and lexical differences between Chinese and English have significant effect on the summarization processes. Their impact on the performances of the summarization for the Chinese and English parallel documents is compared.

1 Introduction

As the information available on the World Wide Web is growing exponentially, the information-overloading problem has become a significant problem. Such problem can be reduced by text summarization, but it is time consuming for human professional to conduct the summarization. Due to the huge volume of information available on line in real time, the research of automatic text summarization becomes very critical.

The information available in languages other than English on the World Wide Web is increasing significantly. In the recognition of the need for summarization systems for languages other than English, summarization systems developed for other languages, such as Korean [21], Japanese [14], and Chinese [3], etc., has been developed recently. Most of these summarization systems are monolingual system, i.e., they can process documents in one single language only. There are some multilingual summarization systems, i.e., they are capable to process document in multiple languages [4, 23]. However, the multilingual documents used for these summarization systems are not in parallel; therefore, the experimental results of these multilingual summarization systems do not reflect the impact of the languages on the results of applying the summarization techniques.

---

[*] Corresponding Author

T.M.T. Sembok et al. (Eds.): ICADL 2003, LNCS 2911, pp. 46–61, 2003.
© Springer-Verlag Berlin Heidelberg 2003

In this paper, we investigate the fractal summarization technique that is proposed based on the fractal theory [26, 27]. In fractal summarization, the important information is captured from the source text by exploring the hierarchical structure and salient features of the document. A condensed version of the document that is informatively close to the original is produced iteratively using the contractive transformation in the fractal theory. User evaluation has been conducted and shown that fractal summarization outperforms the traditional summarization without exploring the hierarchical structure of the documents. The fractal summarization technique is developed based on the statistical approach and can be applied to any languages. In this work, we apply the fractal summarization technique on a parallel corpus in English and Chinese. The summarization results in English and Chinese are compared directly.

The rest of this paper will be organized as following. Section 2 reviews the techniques in automatic text summarization. Section 3 presents the fractal summarization technique. Section 4 analyzes the difference of Chinese and English parallel document. Section 5 compares the results of Chinese and English summarization. Section 6 provides the concluding remarks and suggests some future research directions.

2　Automatic Summarization

Traditional automatic text summarization is the selection of sentences from the source document based on their significance to the document [5, 18] without considering the hierarchical structure of the document. The selection of sentences is conducted based on the salient features of the document. The thematic, location, heading, and cue phrase features are the most widely used summarization features.

- The *thematic feature* is first identified by Luhn [18]. Edmundson proposed to assign the thematic weight to keyword based on term frequency, and the sentence thematic weight as the sum of thematic weight of constituent keywords [5]. The *tfidf* (Term Frequency, Inverse Document Frequency) score is most widely used to calculate the thematic weight [24].
- The significance of sentence is indicated by its *location* [2] based on the hypotheses that topic sentences tend to occur at the beginning or in the end of documents or paragraphs [5]. Edmondson proposed to assign positive weights to sentences according to their ordinal position in the document.
- The *heading feature* is proposed based on the hypothesis that the author conceives the heading as circumscribing the subject matter of the document [5]. A heading glossary is a list consisting of all the words in headings and subheadings with positive weights. The heading weight of sentence is calculated by the sum of heading weight of its constituent words.
- The *cue phrase feature* is proposed by Edmundson [5] based on the hypothesis that the probable relevance of a sentence is affected by the presence of pragmatic words. A pre-stored cue dictionary with cue weight is used to identify the cue phrases. The cue weight of sentence is calculated by the sum of cue weight of its constituent words

Typical summarization systems select a combination of summarization features [5, 16, 17], the total sentence weight *(Wsentence)* is calculated as weighted sum of the weights computed by each sailent features,

$$W_{sentence}=a_1 \times w_{thematic}+a_2 \times w_{location}+a_3 \times w_{heading}+a_4 \times w_{cue}$$ (1)

where $w_{thematic}$, $w_{location}$,. $w_{heading}$ and w_{cue} are thematic weight, location weight, heading weight and cue weight of the sentence respectively; and a_1, a_2, a_3, and a_4 are positive integers to adjust the weighting of four summarization features. The sentences with sentence weight higher than a threshold are selected as part of the summary. It has been proven that the weighting of different summarization features do not have any substantial effect on the average precision [16]. In our experiment, the maximum weight of each feature is normalized to one, and the total weight of sentence is calculated as the sum of scores of all summarization features without weighting. However, the cue phrase feature is disabled for summarization of parallel document, because there is not any parallel cue phrase dictionary defined for Chinese and English currently. Besides, it does affect the performance of the summarization result by adding the cue phrase feature.

3 Fractal Summarization

Many summarization models have been proposed previously. None of the models are entirely developed based on document structure, and they do not take into account of the fact that the human abstractors extract sentences according to the hierarchical document structure. Document structure can be described as fractals. In the past, fractal theory has been widely applied in the area of digital image compression, which is similar to the text summarization in the sense that they both extract the most important information from the source and reduce the complexity of the source. The fractal summarization model is the first effort to apply fractal theory to document summarization. It generates the summary by a recursive deterministic algorithm based on the iterated representation of a document.

3.1 Fractal Theory and Fractal View for Controlling Information Displayed

Fractals are mathematical objects that have high degree of redundancy [19]. These objects are made of transformed copies of themselves or part of themselves. Mandelbrot was the first person who investigated the fractal geometry and developed the fractal theory [19]. In his well known example, the length of the British coastline depends on measurement scale. The larger the scale is, the smaller value of the length of the coastline is and the higher the abstraction level is. The British coastline includes bays and peninsulas. Bays include sub-bays and peninsulas include sub-peninsulas. Using fractals to represent these structures, abstraction of the British coastline can be generated with different abstraction degrees.

A physical tree is one of classical example of fractal objects. A tree is made of a lot of sub-trees; each of them is also tree. By changing the scale, the different levels of abstraction views are obtained (Fig. 1). The idea of fractal tree can be extended to any logical tree. The degree of importance of each node is represented by its fractal value. The fractal value of focus is set to 1. Regarding the focus as a new root, we propagate the fractal value to other nodes with the following expression:

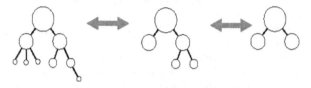

Fig. 1. Fractal View for Logical Tree at Different Abstraction Level

$$Fv_{root} = 1$$
$$Fv_{child\,node\,of\,x} = C\,Fv_x / N_x^{1/D}$$

where F_{v_x} is the fractal value of node x; C is a constant between 0 and 1 to control rate of decade; N_x is the number of child-nodes of node x; and D is the fractal dimension.

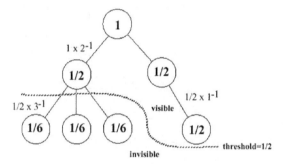

Fig. 2. An Example of the Propagation of Fractal Values

Fractal view is a fractal-based method for controlling information displayed [15]. Fractal view provides an approximation mechanism for the observer to adjust the abstraction level and therefore control the amount of information displayed. At a lower abstraction level, more details of the fractal object can be viewed. A threshold value is chosen to control the amount of information displayed, the nodes with a fractal value less than the threshold value will be hidden (Fig. 2). By changing the threshold value, the user can adjust the amount of information displayed.

3.2 Fractal Summarization

Many studies of human abstraction process has shown that the human abstractors extract the topic sentences according to the document structure from the top level to the low level until they have extracted sufficient information [6, 11]. Advance summarization techniques take the document structure into consideration to compute the probability of a sentence to be included in the summary. However, most traditional automatic summarization models consider the source document as a sequence of sentences but ignoring the structure of document. *Fractal Summarization Model* is proposed to generate summary based on document structure [26].

Fractal summarization is developed based on the fractal theory, the important information is captured from the source document by exploring the hierarchical structure and salient features of the document. A condensed version of the document that is informatively close to the original is produced iteratively using the contractive transformation in the fractal theory. Similar to the fractal geometry applying on the British coastline where the coastline includes bays, peninsulas, sub-bays, and sub-peninsulas, large document has a hierarchical structure with several levels, chapters, sections, subsections, paragraphs, sentences, terms, words and characters. A document can be represented by a hierarchical structure (Fig. 3). However, a document is not a true mathematical fractal object since a document cannot be viewed in an infinite abstraction level. The smallest unit in a document is character; however, neither a character nor a word will convey any meaningful information concerning the overall content of a document. The lowest abstraction level in our consideration is a term. A document is considered as *prefractal* that are fractal structures in their early stage with finite recursion only [7].

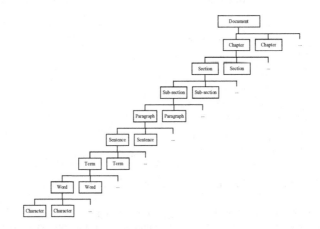

Fig. 3. Prefractal Structure of Document

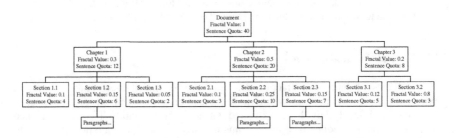

Fig. 4. An Example of Fractal Summarization Model

The Fractal Summarization Model applies a similar technique as fractal view and fractal image compression [1]. An image is regularly segmented into sets of non overlapping square blocks, called range blocks, and then each range block is subdivided into sub range blocks, until a contractive mapping can be found to represent this sub range block. The Fractal Summarization Model generates the summary by a simple recursive deterministic algorithm based on the iterated representation of a document. The original document is represented as fractal tree structure according to its document structure. The weights of sentences under a range block are calculated by the traditional summarization methods described in Section 2. The fractal value of root node is 1 and the fractal values of the child node are propagated according to the sum of sentence weight under the child nodes.

$$Fv_{root} = 1$$

$$Fv_{child\ node\ r\ of\ x} = Fv_x \times \frac{\sum_{sentences\ under\ r} Sentence\ weight}{\sum_{sentences\ under\ x} Sentence\ weight} \tag{2}$$

Given a document, users provide compression ratio to specific the amount of information displayed. The *compression ratio* of summarization is defined as the ratio of number of sentences in the summary to the number of sentences in the source document. The summarization system computes the number of sentences to be extracted as summary accordingly and the system assigns the number of sentences to the root as the quota of sentences. The quota of sentences is allocated to child-nodes by propagation, i.e., the quota of parent node is shared by its child-nodes directly proportional to the fractal value of the child-nodes. The quota is then iteratively allocated to child-nodes of child-nodes until the quota allocated is less than a threshold value and the range-block can be transformed to some key sentences by traditional summarization methods (Fig. 4). A threshold value is the maximum number of sentences can be extracted from a range block. If the quota is larger than the threshold value, the range block must be divided into sub-range block.

Fig. 4 demonstrates an example of fractal summarization model. The fractal value of the root is 1, and the system extract 40 sentences from the root node. The system then allocates the sentence quota to the child nodes directly proportion to the fractal value of child node. The fractal value and sentence quota will be prorogated to the grandchild nodes. For example, the Section 1.2 receives quota of 6 sentences which is higher than threshold value, therefore the system will extend the node in paragraph levels. However, the Section 1.1 and 1.3 receive a quota less than 5 sentences, therefore the system directly extract sentence at section level. The detail of the Fractal Summarization Model is shown as the following algorithm:

Fractal Summarization Algorithm

```
1. Choose a Compression Ratio.
2. Choose a Threshold Value.
3. Calculate the Sentence Number Quota of the summary.
4. Divide the document into range blocks.
5. Transform the document into fractal tree.
6. Set the current node to the root of the fractal tree.
```

```
7. Repeat
7.1 For each child node under current node,
    Calculate the fractal value of child node.
7.2 Allocate Quota to child nodes in proportion
    to fractal values.
7.3 For each child nodes,
         If the quota is less than threshold value
                 Select the sentences in the range block by
                 extraction
         Else
                 Set the current node to the child node
                 Repeat Step 7.1, 7.2, 7.3
8.   Until all the child nodes under current node are
     processed
```

3.3 Experimental Result

It is believed that a full-length text document contains a set of subtopics [12] and a good quality summary should cover as many subtopics as possible. Experiment of fractal summarization and traditional summarization has been conducted on Hong Kong Annual Report 2000 [26], the traditional summarization model without considering the hierarchical structure of the documents extracts most of sentences from few chapters. However, the fractal summarization model extracts the sentences distributively from each chapter. The fractal summarization model produces a summary with a wider coverage of information subtopic than traditional summarization model. A user evaluation has been conducted to compare the performance of the fractal summarization and the traditional summarization without using the hierarchical structure of documents. The results show that all subjects consider the summary generated by fractal summarization method as a better summary. The fractal summarization can achieve up 91.25% precision and 87.125% on average, but the traditional summarization can achieve up to maximum 77.50% precision and 67% on average.

4   Comparison of Chinese and English Parallel Documents

Parallel documents are popular in places with multilingual culture, such as Québec, Hong Kong, Singapore and many other European countries. Hong Kong had its bilingual culture since it was a British colony more than a century ago. The official languages are Chinese and English, therefore a lot of documents are written in Chinese and English using covert translation [26]. For example, most of the documents released by the government have both Chinese and English versions. The documents are written by experienced bilingual linguists, and therefore the quality of the documents can be assured. In this section, we investigate the characteristics in the parallelism of Chinese and English parallel documents.

4.1 Indexing

In informational retrieval and processing, indexing is one of the most important research issues, searching and retrieval of information is impossible without proper indexes. The information content of a document is determined primarily by the frequency of the terms in the document; therefore, the indexing of document is the process to transform a document into a vector of terms with its frequency or other related score. In fact, the process is much complicated since the terms in a document are not properly marked-up. English indexing includes several steps, i.e., lexical analysis, stop-wording, stemming, and index terms selection [8, 13]. The techniques for English indexing are considerably more mature than Chinese indexing. Due to the lack of word delimiters (such as spacing in English), Chinese text segmentation is more difficult. Besides, there are ambiguities in Chinese text segmentation. Different ways of segmenting a Chinese sentence may lead to different meanings [10, 25]. There are three major approaches in Chinese text segmentation: a) statistical approach, b) lexical rule-based approach, and c) hybrid approach based on statistical and lexical information [22].

4.2 Parallelism of Chinese and English Parallel Documents

Parallel Corpus is defined as a set of document pairs that are aligned based on their parallelism. Parallel corpus can be generated by overt translation or covert translation [26]. Due to the grammatical and lexical differences between different languages, words in one language may be translated into one or more words in another language or may not be translated at all. There is probably more than one way to translate a word in one language into another language. However, a pair of parallel documents is always parallel in terms of their information contents.

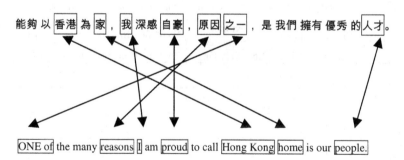

Fig. 5. Reordering of Equivalent Terms in Chinese and English sentences

The sentence structures for a pair of parallel documents in two languages are different due to the grammatical and lexical differences in languages. For example, as shown in Fig. 5, the orderings of terms in two languages are not the same. The structures of sentence can also be changed. Several sentences in one language can be merged into one sentence in another language. It is also possible to mix the content of several sentences in one language together to form a number of sentences in another language. In order to study the alignment of sentences in two languages, we have analyzed the mapping of sentence in Hong Kong Annual Report 2000. 85% of the sentences in two languages are one-to-one mapping. 7.3% of the sentences are one-to-two mapping between Chinese and English and 6.1% of the sentences are two-to-one mapping between Chinese and English. The one-to-one, two-to-one and one-to-two sentence mappings totally yield more than 98%. Most sentences contain tow or less sub-sentences in the other language (Table 1).

Table 1. Mapping of Sentences between Hong Kong Annual Report 2000 Chinese Version andEnglish Version

Number of Mappings (Percentage)		No. of Sentences in HKAR 2000 (English Version)					
		1	2	3	4	5	6
No. of Sentences in HKAR 2000 (Chinese Version)	1	6288 (85.00%)	540 (7.30%)	31 (0.42%)	3 (0.04%)	0	1 (0.01%)
	2	448 (6.06%)	43 (0.58%)	9 (0.12%)	0	0	0
	3	19 (0.26%)	6 (0.08%)	2 (0.03%)	2 (0.03%)	0	0
	4	2 (0.03%)	1 (0.01%)	0	2 (0.03%)	0	0
	5	0	0	0	0	0	0
	6	1 (0.01%)	0	0	0	0	0

Table 2. Statistics of Keyword 'Hong Kong' and '香港 in the Hong Kong Annual Report 2000 and its tfidf score in the first aligned sentence in the Hong Kong Annual Report 2000.

Text Unit	Term frequency		Text block frequency		No of Text Block		*tfidf* Score	
	English	Chinese	English	Chinese	English	Chinese	English	Chinese
Document-Level	1217	1704	1	1	1	1	1217.00	1704.00
Chapter-Level	70	94	23	23	23	23	70.00	94.00
Section-Level	69	93	247	257	358	358	105.95	137.47
Subsection-Level	16	26	405	445	804	804	31.83	48.19
Paragraph-Level	2	3	787	893	2626	2632	5.48	7.68
Sentence-Level	1	1	1113	1357	9098	7976	4.03	3.56

In addition to the alignment of sentence, keywords may or may not appear in both of the aligned English and Chinese sentences and the length of keywords in English and Chinese are not necessary the same. Such problem has significant impact on the thematic weight of keywords utilized in the summarization techniques. Table 2 shows the overall statistics of "Hong Kong" and "香港" in the bilingual Hong Kong Annual Report 2000. The term frequency and text block frequency of "Hong Kong" and "香港" at different levels of the parallel corpus are significantly different. The total frequency of "Hong Kong" is 1217, and the total frequency of "香港" is 1704. The frequency of "香港" is much higher than that of "Hong Kong". In addition, the measurements of the length of keywords in English and Chinese are different. It highly affects the computation of *tfidf* scores of the English and Chinese terms. As a result, the *tfidf* scores for a pair of equivalent keywords in two languages are usually significantly different. However, they are positively correlated. Table 3 shows the correlation of the *tfidf* scores of "Hong Kong" and "香港" at different levels of the Hong Kong Annual Report 2000.

Table 3. Correlation of *tfidf* Scores of "Hong Kong" and "香港" in the Hong Kong Annual Report 2000 at Different Document Levels

Document Levels	Correlation of Keyword 'Hong Kong' and Keyword '香港'
Chapter-Level	0.8456
Section-Level	0.8588
Subsection-Level	0.7574
Paragraph-Level	0.4147

Table 4. Length of Sentences in Hong Kong Annual Report 2000 (English Version and Chinese Version)

	Length of Sentence in Chinese (No. of Characters)	Length of Sentence in English (No. of Words)
Lower Limit	2	2
Lower Quartile	24	15
Median	33	21
Upper Quartile	45	29
Upper Limit	215	128
Mean	36.16	23.14
Standard Deviation	17.30	11.10

The measurements of sentence length in Chinese and English sentences are different. The Chinese text is character based and the sentence length is measured by number of characters. However, the English text is word based and the sentence length is measured by number of words. One English word usually consists of several Chinese characters; therefore the number of characters in Chinese sentences is usually more than the number of words in English sentences. The statistics of sentence lengths of the bilingual Hong Kong Annual Report 2000 in Chinese and English is show in Table 4. There is no significant difference in dispersion of sentence length in two languages, the standard deviation of sentence length in both languages is about half of the arithmetic mean of the sentence length. The difference of sentence length and the sentence alignment in two languages may affect the sum of *tfidf* score of terms in sentences. The sum of *tfidf* score of terms in sentence of two languages is shown in Table 5. It is shown that there is no significant difference in the dispersion of the sum of *tfidf* score of terms in sentences in two languages.

We have also analyzed the sum of *tfidf* score of the constituent terms in a sentence against its sentence length. The correlation coefficient of sentence length and the sum of the *tfidf* score of terms in Chinese sentences is 0.62, which means there is a weak positive correlation. On the other hand, the correlation coefficient of sentence length and the sum of the *tfidf* score of terms in English sentences is 0.52. The correlation in English document is even weaker than Chinese document. Therefore, the relationship between sentence length and the sum of the *tfidf* score of sentences is not strong. However, since a longer sentence tends to have a larger sum of the *tfidf* score, the longer sentence will have a higher probability to be extracted by the summarization techniques as part of a summary.

Table 5. Sum of *tfidf* Score of Terms in Sentences of Hong Kong Annual Report 2000 (Chineseand English Version)

	HKAR 2000 (Chinese Version)	HKAR 2000 (English Version)
Lower Limit	0	0
Lower Quartile	263.74	231.20
Median	464.09	471.09
Upper Quartile	767.16	803.91
Upper Limit	6313.61	8120.42
Mean	584.43	599.10
Standard Deviation	478.57	527.55

5   Comparison of Summarization of Chinese and English Parallel Documents

The comparison of the summaries in two languages produced by the same summarization technique can help us to understand the impact of the grammatical and lexical difference of languages on the summarization result. In our experiment, the fractal summarization has been applied to the Chinese and English parallel documents. In this section, we present the comparison of the intersection of the summaries in two languages, and the precision of the summary generated in two languages.

The comparison of the number of sentences extracted by the fractal summarization technique in each chapter of the Chinese and English version of Hong Kong Annual Report 2000 is shown in Fig. 6. Roughly, the distributions of the number of sentences extracted from chapters in two languages are similar. The correlation of the number of sentence extracted from each chapter in the Chinese and English documents is 0.9353. It shows that they are highly positive correlated.

Although, the number of sentence extracted from chapters in two languages are very similar, they may extract different sets of sentences from the chapters. In order to compare the matching of sentences extracted in the Chinese and English summaries, we define three types of sentence matching:

- A direct match is the case when a one-to-one sentence mapping is identified from the sentences in the Chinese and English summaries.
- A partial match is the case when a one-to-many or many-to-many sentence mapping is identified from the whole sentence or the partial sentence in the Chinese and English summaries.
- An unmatch is the case when a sentence is extracted as the summary in one language, but none of its equivalent sentences is extracted in the summary of the other language.

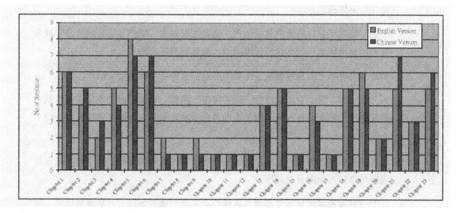

Fig. 6. No. of Sentences Extracted from Hong Kong Annual Report 2000 by Fractal Summarization with 1% Compression Ratio

Table 6. Sentences Matching in Fractal Summaries of HKAR 2000 (Chinese and English Version) with 1% Compression Ratio

Type of Sentence Match	Percentage
Direct Match	16.28%
Partial Match	9.30%
Unmatch	74.42%

As shown in Table 6, the intersection of extracted sentences in Chinese and English summaries is very small. The sum of direct match and partial match only corresponds to 25% of the matching of sentences, and the rest are unmatched. As presented in Table 1, the majority of the sentences in the pair of parallel documents can be aligned by one-to-one, one-to-two, or two-to-one mappings. However, applying the same summarization technique individually on the English and Chinese document produces significantly different set of sentences in the summaries. It reflects that the grammatical and lexical differences of the languages have significant impact on the summarization processes.

Since the percentage of matching sentences in the Chinese and English summaries is low, we have further investigated if there are significant differences in the content of the summaries. It is found that the content of the summaries are very close although the sentences are not exactly matched. Sentences covering similar content are extracted in the Chinese and English summaries. Table 7 presents the summaries extracted from Chapter One of the Hong Kong Annual Report 2000. Six sentences are

Table 7. The Chinese and English Summaries Extracted from Chapter One of the Hong Kong Annual Report 2000

C1. 香港所具備的特質，加上蓬勃的經濟、法治的自由社會、國際商貿和旅遊中心的地位、完善的運輸和電訊基建，以及龐大的國際社會，全都是代表" 國際都會" 的典型標記。
C2. 不過，我們明白，要香港脫穎而出，成為國際都會，我們必須持續改進，提升香港的生活質素，例如積極保護環境、推廣藝術文化等。
C3. 香港是世界第十大貿易體系，主要由於香港是通往中國內地的門戶。
C4. 一九七八年，鄧小平先生推行" 門戶開放" 政策，這個轉變令香港廠商有機會擴展業務，進軍內地市場，間接幫助香港發展為今天全球最重要的商貿金融中心之一。
C5. 其次，我們打算與廣東當局加強合作，推廣香港國際機場和貨櫃港口，促進香港與珠江三角洲的貿易往來。
C6. 我們也會繼續鞏固香港作為亞太區中心和中國門檻的地位，力求實現目標，把香港建設為亞洲國際都會。

E1. "We do, however, recognise that we have to advance further in improving the quality of life in Hong Kong, for example in environmental protection and arts and culture, if we are to compete as a world city."
E2. The change brought about by Deng Xiaoping's 'open-door' policy in 1978 gave Hong Kong manufacturers an opportunity to expand and migrate across the boundary and their success has helped make Hong Kong one of the world's most remarkable trade and financial centres.
E3. "Hence, China's accession to the WTO will mean further enhancement of Hong Kong's position as an international financial and business centre, a transportation and communication hub, a centre for professional services and our traditional role as a gateway to the Mainland."
E4. "Hong Kong's close economic relationship with the Mainland, and in particular with the rest of the Pearl River Delta, puts Hong Kong in a unique position."
E5. "Thirdly, we will encourage Hong Kong companies to co-operate with their Pearl River Delta partners to establish logistics centres and to promote Hong Kong's logistics capabilities."
E6. "In part, the study indicated that Hong Kong's dominant position stems from its political and legal stability, proximity to major markets (Hong Kong is within five hours flying time of half the world's population), excellent infrastructure, its dense network of financial and professional service firms and the quality of its local management."

extracted in the both of the Chinese and English summaries. C2 is a direct match of E1 and C4 is a direct match of E2. However, no matching can be found between C1, C3, C5, C6 and E3, E4, E5, E6. When we pay attention in the content of C1, C3, C5, C6 and E3, E4, E5, and D6, we find that they cover very similar content. They are all conveying similar messages about "Hong Kong as an international financial and business centre", "transportation and communication infrastructure", "the Pearl River Detla", and "Hong Kong relationship with China" .

We further investigate if there is any significance difference in the performance of the fractal summarization technique on different languages in terms of precision. The precision of a summary is computed as follow:

$$\frac{no. \ of \ senetnces \ accepted \ by \ the \ user \ as \ part \ of \ the \ summary}{no. \ of \ sentences \ in \ the \ summary} \tag{3}$$

A user evaluation with ten subjects is conducted The average precision of English summary is 85.125% and the average precision of Chinese summary is 85.25%. The highest precisions of summaries in two languages are both 91.25%. There is no substantial difference in precision of summaries in Chinese and English.

As a conclusion, we find that the sentences extracted in the Chinese and English summaries are significantly. However, the performances of the summaries in terms of precision are very close. In addition, the content of the extracted sentences in the summaries are similar although they are directly matched. These evidences show that the grammatical and lexical differences between languages have significant effect on the extraction of sentences in their summaries. However, the overall performances of the summaries do not have any significant differences.

6   Conclusion

Automatic text summarization is important as the information overloading problem becomes serious on the World Wide Web due to the exponential growth of information in real time. Information available in languages other than English on the World Wide Web is growing significantly. Techniques for processing or summarizing English documents only are not able to satisfy the needs of Internet users. It is desire to determine if the existing techniques can perform in English and other languages. In this paper, we have investigated the impact of the grammatical and lexical differences of English and Chinese on the fractal summarization techniques. The performances of the fractal summarization on English and Chinese parallel documents are also investigated. It is found that the differences of the languages have significant effect on the extraction processes of sentences for summarizing English and Chinese documents. However, the overall performances of the summarization in English and Chinese are similar. The content covered in the summaries is similar although the sentences extracted may not be matched.

References

1. Barnsley M. F., and Jacquin, A. E. Application of Recurrent Iterated Function Systems to Images. In Proceedings of SPIE Visual Communications and Image Processing'88, 1001, 122–131, 1988.
2. Baxendale P. Machine-Made Index for Technical Literature - An Experiment. IBM Journal (October), 354–361, 1958.
3. Chen, H.H. and Huang, S.J. A Summarization System for Chinese News from Multiple Sources. In Proceedings of 4 th International Workshop on Information Retrieval with Asia Languages, 1–7. 1999.
4. Cowie J., Mahesh K., Nirenburg S., and Zajaz R. "MINDS-Multilingual Interactive Document Summarization". In Working Notes of the AAAI Spring Symposium on Intelligent Text Summarization. 131–132. California, USA. AAAI Press, 1998.
5. Edmundson H. P. New Method in Automatic Extraction. Journal of the ACM, 16(2) 264–285, 1968.
6. Endres-Niggemeyer B., Maier E., and Sigel A. How to Implement a Naturalistic Model of Abstracting: Four Core Working Steps of an Expert Abstractor. Information Processing and Management, 31(5) 631–674, 1995.
7. Feder J. Fractals. Plenum, New York, 1988.
8. Frakes W. Stemming Algorithms. In William B. Frakes and Ricardo Baeza-Yates, editors, Information Retrieval: data structures and algorithms, 131–160. Prentice-Hall, Englewood Cliffs, NJ (1992).
9. Gallager R., Information theory and reliable communication, 1968.
10. Gan, K.W., Palmer, M., and Lua, K.T., A Statistically Emergent Approach for Language Processing: Application to Modeling Context effects in Ambiguous Chinese Word Boundary Perception. Computational Linguistics, 531–553, 1996.
11. Glaser B. G., and Strauss A. L. The Discovery of Grounded Theory; Strategies for Qualitative Research. Aldine de Gruyter, New York, 1967.
12. Hearst M. A. Subtopic Structuring for Full-Length Document Access. In Proceedings of the 16th Annual International ACM SIGIR Conference on Research and Development in Information Retrieval, 56–68, 1993.
13. Hull D. Stemming algorithms - a case study for detailed evaluation. Journal of the American Society for Information Science, 47(1):70–84, 1996.
14. Kataoka A., Masuyama S. and Yamamoto K. Summarization by shortening a Japanese Noun Modifier into Expression 'A no B'. In Proceedings of NLPRS'99, 409–414, 1999.
15. Koike, H. Fractal Views: A Fractal-Based Method for Controlling Information Display. ACM Transaction on Information Systems, ACM, 13(3), 305–323, 1995.
16. Lam-Adesina M., and Jones G J. F. Applying Summarization Techniques for Term Selection in Relevance Feedback. In Proceedings of SIGIR 2001, 1-9, 2001.
17. Lin Y., and Hovy E.H. Identifying Topics by Position. In Proceedings of the Applied Natural Language Processing Conference (ANLP-97), Washington, DC, 283–290, 1997.
18. Luhn H. P. The Automatic Creation of Literature Abstracts. IBM Journal of Research and Development, 159–165, 1958.
19. Mandelbrot B. The fractal geometry of nature. W.H. Freeman, New York, 1983.
20. Mani I. Recent Development in Text Summarization. ACM CIKM'01, 529–531, Georgia, USA, 2001.
21. Myaeng S. H., and Jang D. H., 1999. Development and Evaluation of a Statistically-Based Document Summarization System, In Advances in Automatic Text Summarization (ed Inderjeet Mani), MIT Press. 61–70.
22. Nie, J.Y., Hannan, M.L., and Jin, W., Combining Dictionary, Rules and Statistical Information in Segmentation of Chinese. Computer Processing of Chinese and Oriental Languages, 125–143, 1995.

23. Ogden W., Cowie J., Davis M., Ludovik E., Molina-Salgado H., and Shin H. Getting information from documents you cannot read: an interactive cross-language text retrieval and summarization system. Joint ACM DL/SIGIR Workshop on Multilingual Information Discovery and Access: 1999.
24. Salton G., and Buckley C. Term-Weighting Approaches in Automatic Text Retrieval. Information Processing and Management, 24, 513–523, 1988.
25. Yang C. C., Luk J., Yung J., and Yen J. Combination and Boundary Detection Approach for Chinese Indexing. Journal of the American Society for Information Science, Special Topic Issue on Digital Libraries, 51(4), 340–351, March, 2000.
26. Yang, C. C., and K. W. Li, Automatic Construction of English/Chinese Parallel Corpora. Journal of the American Society for Information Science and Technology, 54(8), 2003, pp.730–742.
27. Yang, C. C., and Wang, F. L., Fractal Summarization: Summarization Based on Fractal Theory, Proceedings of the 26th Annual International ACM Conference(SIGIR'03), Toronto, Canada, July 28–August 1, 2003.

Incorporating Virtual Relevant Documents for Learning in Text Categorization

Kyung-Soon Lee and Kyo Kageura

NII (National Institute of Informatics)
2-1-2 Hitotsubashi, Chiyoda-ku, Tokyo, 101-8430, Japan
{kslee,kyo}@nii.ac.jp

Abstract. This paper proposes a *virtual relevant document* technique in the learning phase for text categorization. The method uses a simple transformation of relevant documents, i.e. making virtual documents by combining document pairs in the training set. The virtual document produced by this method has the enriched term vector space, with greater weights for the terms that co-occur in two relevant documents. The experimental results showed a significant improvement over the baseline, which proves the usefulness of the proposed method: 71% improvement on TREC-11 filtering test collection and 11% improvement on Reuters-21578 test set for the topics with less than 100 relevant documents in the micro average F1. The result analysis indicates that the addition of virtual relevant documents contributes to the steady improvement of the performance.

1 Introduction

In this paper, we propose a *virtual relevant document* technique to incorporate prior knowledge into the training set by combining pairs of relevant documents in the task of text categorization. The motivation is that, when the training set consists of only small number of documents, text categorization systems have difficulty in estimating the proper decision boundary. By incorporating virtual documents into the training set, systems can use enlarged document space in learning.

Our method targets for text categorization and batch filtering. Text categorization is defined as assigning a new document to the pre-defined categories. Batch filtering is the task of making a binary decision of accepting or rejecting an incoming document for each profile which represents a user need. Both are a supervised learning task, in which it is required to learn from the training set to make a proper decision about whether a new document belongs to a topic or not.

In these tasks and also in information retrieval, the performance changes depending on term weighting techniques. About the term space itself, we observe that:

- Term space given by the training set is, as it is, restricted and often not sufficient,

- Features (terms) of a new incoming document is also limited.

Thus what is required is to develop a method of producing suitable term space for learning, within the limitation of the training data. In order for that, we made the assumption that the task of text categorization and batch filtering can be regarded as

T.M.T. Sembok et al. (Eds.): ICADL 2003, LNCS 2911, pp. 62–72, 2003.

classifying a document (a discourse unit) to a class of topical discourse, rather than grouping documents under the same category. This view, though rather general, allow us to manipulate the training set more freely, using the information in each document but not restricted to the *existing unit of document*.

The virtual document technique, on the basis of this observation, simply extends a document unit to the combination of two documents. For weighting terms in the combined document, we give more weights to terms that occur in both of the combined documents by multiplying two weights, based on the observation that terms that co-occur in pair-wise documents have stronger relevance to the topical discourse to which the documents belong. To test our method, we used support vector machine.

2 Related Researches

In such tasks as text categorization, routing and information retrieval, some researches try to improve the performance of various machine learning related applications by sampling the training set. All et al. [1] discarded non-relevant documents to make the size of relevant and non-relevant documents equal in the learning phase of a routing query. This is for balancing between the positive and negative evidence in Rocchio learning. Singhal et al [12] selectively used the non-relevant documents that do have some relationship to the user query (query zone) in learning routing queries. Kwok and Grunfeld [5] selected the most effective training subset of relevant documents to create a feedback query based on genetic algorithm. As the sampling techniques basically aim at the reduction of the size of training set, they suffer from the degradation when the number of available training data is small.

On the other hand, many machine learning applications on image recognition, image classification and character recognition incorporated prior knowledge (prior knowledge is the information which is available in addition to the training examples and makes it possible to generalize from the training examples to novel test examples: [2]) about the desired behavior of the system into training data. For instance, image recognition systems use new examples by small distortions of the input image such as translations, rotations, scaling; speech recognition systems produce them by time distortions or pitch shifts. In 3D object recognition, Poggio and Vetter [7] exploited appropriate transformations to generate new views from a single 2D view. In hand-written digit recognition, DeCoste and Schölkopf [2] added virtual examples produced by shifting the images by one pixel in the four principal directions to the training examples. The open issue about the incorporation of prior knowledge is to what extent transformations can be safely applied to the training example, as some distortions can produce worse results.

3 Virtual Examples in Document Space

A document related to a certain topic can be seen as one object in the discourse space of the topic. One sentence can be a unit to describe the topic as well. On the other extreme, the set of document which are judged as relevant to the topic can be regarded as one object/unit of discourse space that dissolves the document boundary.

Likewise, new units in the discourse space are possible on condition that the units preserve relevance to the topic. Intuitively, a virtual document can be generated by concatenating two or more documents which describe the same topic. The virtual document thus created not only is expected to preserve the topic, but even improve the topical representation by exploiting relevant terms that are not given high importance in individual real documents.

The expected effect of virtual documents is illustrated in Fig 1 [11]. The decision boundary (b) made for the limited training documents would lead to the wrong classification of the test document indicated by the question mark. If virtual documents can represent the topic properly, they can help making a better decision boundary, as indicated in (c) in Fig 1.

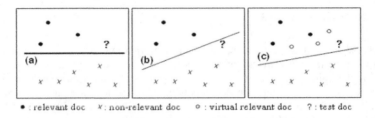

● : relevant doc   ✗ : non-relevant doc   ○ : virtual relevant doc   ? : test doc

Fig. 1. The expected effect by virtual documents on decision boundary: (a) is the true decision boundary. (b) is the decision boundary by a learning method for given limited training documents. (c) is the decision boundary learned by incorporating virtual relevant documents into training set.

4   Incorporating Virtual Relevant Documents into the Training Set

4.1   Generating Virtual Relevant Documents

A virtual relevant document (VRD) is generated by combining two relevant documents. In combining two document vectors, the weight is calculated by multiplying two weights of a term of each vector on the assumption that when terms appear in two relevant documents, they are expected to be strongly related to the topic.

Our hypothesis on generating a VRD is that including all terms in two vectors and differentiating shared terms and non-shared terms in weighting by multiplication would provide new information in learning the decision boundary for classification.

If a VRD is produced by just concatenating two documents, the weight of the VRD will be summation of two documents in weighting scheme by term frequency (TF) and inverse document frequency (IDF). The multiplication operator gives higher differentiation to the weight between shared terms or non-shared terms than summation.

The method of generating VRDs is straightforward as follows:

- Document representation: Each document is represented as a weighted term vector, $d_i = <w_1, w_2, ..., w_k, ..., w_n>$. The weight is calculated by normalized logTF*IDF.

- VRDs generating: For each two documents pair from training relevant set, one virtual relevant document is produced by giving weights for all terms in two documents. For n relevant documents, n(n-1)/2 documents are produced.

- Term weighting for a VRD: The weight of a term in a VRD is calculated as follows:

$$W_{vij_k} = W_{di_k} \cdot W_{dj_k} \qquad (1)$$

where vij_k is the term k of a VRD, di_k and dj_k are the term k of relevant document di and dj, respectively.

If a term k occurs in di and does not occur in dj, the minimum value, 0.005, is assigned for the weight of dj instead of zero ((b) in Fig 2) to keep the term in a virtual vector. To reduce noises by general terms, features are selected by χ^2 for each class.

Though a general term which has the lowest χ^2 value co-occurs in two vectors, it is multiplied with the minimum value. Finally, the weight vector of terms is normalized by cosine normalization.

For the terms of a virtual relevant document, we don't discard non-shared terms since diverse terms can be used to describe the certain topic and two documents can describe the topic using different terminology. For example, when the vector d_1 has one term t_1 and d_2 has one term t_2, in 2-dimensional space, the virtual vector has all the terms as shown in (b) of Fig 3.

The resulting virtual document space is enriched by the method, with weights for the terms that co-occur in two relevant documents.

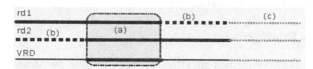

Fig. 2. The terms in two relevant document vectors (rd1 and rd2 vector). Terms in (a) part represents co-occurring terms in two vectors and terms in (b) part do not appear in the vector. In a virtual vector, terms in (a) will have higher weights than those in (b). Terms in (c) do not appear in two vectors, which have zero value in a virtual vector.

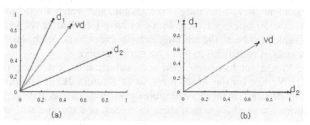

Fig. 3. Examples of virtual relevant documents (vrd) generated from two relevant documents (d_1 and d_2) in 2-dimensional space.

4.2 Virtual Documents and Support Vectors

We use support vector machines [13] for text categorization. A support vector (SV) set is an essential subset of relevant and non-relevant examples, which is learned by a support vector machine (SVM) for the training set. It is this SV set that is used for determining the class in the test phase.

Schölkopf et al. [10] and Vapnik [13] observed that the SV set contains all the information necessary for solving the given classification task. DeCoste and Schölkopf [2] showed that it is sufficient to generate virtual examples only from the SV set in handwritten digit recognition task.

Following these observations, we generate the VRDs from the relevant SV set, and not all the relevant documents in the training set. The procedure to generate the VRDs is as follows:

- training an SVM with all the training documents, thus producing an initial SV set,

- generating VRDs for the relevant support vectors in the SV set, and

- training another SVM with VRDs and the original SV set produced at (a).

Note that two SVM trainings are done, one for obtaining the initial SV set for all the original training documents, and the other for finding the unique separating hyperplane with maximal margin for enlarged training set consisting of the original SV set and VRDs.

5   Experiments and Evaluations

5.1   Set-Up of Experiments

We have evaluated our method on TREC-11 batch filtering and Reuters-21578 test set.

The TREC-11 batch filtering task [8] used the Reuters Corpus Volume 1 [9]. Document collection is divided into training and test set, which consist of 83,650 and 723,141 documents, respectively. The topics are two types: a set of 50 are of the usual TREC type (assessor topic) and a set of 50 have been constructed artificially from intersections of pairs of Reuters categories. The relevance judgements provided indicate which documents have been judged for a topic, and which are judged relevant or not relevant. Of the 50 assessor topics, 48 topics have less than 25 relevant documents among 83,650 documents of the training set (in Fig 4 (a)). With small number of relevant documents, it is difficult to learn for classification.

Reuters-21578 test set has been used for evaluation in text categorization techniques [14][4]. We test on the ModApte split of Reuters-21578 compiled by Lewis [6]. This split leads to a test set of 7770 training documents, and 3019 test documents. The 90 categories are used for which there is at least one training and one test document. The test set also includes the topics which have the small number of relevant documents. Fig 4 (b) shows the distribution of the number of relevant documents for the 90 categories. The 30 categories have less than 10 relevant documents and the 74 categories have less than 100 relevant documents in the training set.

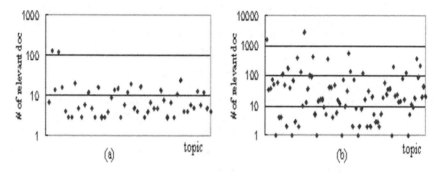

Fig. 4. The distribution of the number of relevant documents (a) for the 50 topics in TREC-11 filtering test collection, (b) the 90 categories in Reuters-21578 test set

125846 terms and 16422 terms are extracted by stemming and removing stop words from TREC-11 batch filtering and Reuters-21578 test set, respectively. For Reuters-21578, terms with above 10 in $\chi 2$ value for a category are applied for multiplication when they co-occur in two vectors to generate a VRD. Terms with the lower value are treated as not co-occurring. To represent a document as a vector, each term is weighted by normalized logTF*IDF. We used SVM^{light} system [3], and trained classifiers via radial-basis function (RBF) kernels and left all SVM^{light} options that affect learning as their default value.

We have compared the effectiveness of proposed virtual relevant documents technique with the base SVM for the training set:

- baseTR: the performance of SVM for the original training set.

- VRDsv: the performance of SVM after incorporating VRDs generated from the relevant SV set into the SV set.

To evaluate the proposed method, we used three measures: the scaled linear utility (T11SU), F-beta measure (T11F) as defined in the TREC-11 filtering task, and the micro average F1. These are defined as follows:

(a) Scaled linear utility (T11SU): The linear utility measure assigns a credit of 2 for a relevant document retrieved and a debit for a non-relevant document retrieved. MeanT11SU is mean T11SU over topics.

$$T11SU = \frac{\max(T11NU, MinNU) - MinNU}{1 - MinNU} \qquad (2)$$

where $T11NU = \frac{T11U}{MaxU}$, $T11U = 2R^+ - N^+$, MaxU = 2 * (total relevant), MinNU = -0.5. R+ is the number of relevant documents retrieved, N+ is the number of non-relevant documents retrieved, and R- is the number of relevant documents not retrieved.

(b) F-beta (T11F): The F-beta is a function of recall and precision, together with a free parameter beta which determines the relative weighting of recall and precision. The beta is 0.5. MeanT11F is mean T11F over topics.

$$T11F = \frac{1.25 * R^+}{0.25 * R^- + N^+ + 1.25 * R^+}$$ (3)

where if $R^+ + N^+$ is not zero.

(c) F1 measure: The F1-value is a harmonic average of precision and recall. Micro average F1 is computed by lumping the all topics together.

$$F_1 = \frac{2 * P * R}{P + R}$$ (4)

where P is precision and R is recall.

5.2   Results and Discussions

On TREC-11 Filtering Test Collection. Table 1 shows the performance for assessor topics in TREC-11 batch filtering task. Table 2 shows the statistics of information in learning process for assessor topics. A lot of relevant SVs included in the new support vectors are taken from VRDs generated artificially, rather than original relevant documents. And the size of SV set learned from VRDsv are similar with that learned from original training set.

Table 1. The performance comparison on TREC-11 filtering test collection

Measure	baseTR	VRDsv	chg %
MeanT11SU	0.359	0.376	4.74%
MeanT11F	0.090	0.190	111.11%
MicroAvg F_1	0.181	0.310	71.27%

Table 2. The statistics of information used in support vector learning (RDs: relevant documents, NDs: non-relevant documents).

	baseTR	VRDsv
Avg # of training docs	861.48	328.24
Avg # of relevant docs	12.78	216.08
Avg # of VRDs	-	(204.92)
Avg # of SV set	123.32	119.44
taken from VRDs	-	(15.32)
taken from RDs in SVset	-	(10.64)
taken from NDs in SVset	-	(93.48)

In the experimental results on TREC-11 batch filtering test set, the proposed method achieved a significant performance improvement on the overall evaluation measures. The proposed method improved 71.3%, 111.1% and 4.7% over the base performance in the micro average F1, MeanT11F and MeanT11SU, respectively. It is 47 topics among the total 50 topics that VRDsv improved performance compared to the base training set.

These results indicate that our VRDs technique provided new information to learn decision boundary in SVMs. However, the base performance of SVMs is low on TREC-11 filtering test collection.

Table 3. Performance comparisons on Reuters-21578 test set for the topics according to the number relevant documents.

Evaluation Measure	67 topics (1<rd<100)			76 topics (1<rd<300)			81 topics (1<rd<1000)		
	baseTR	VRDsv	chg %	baseTR	VRDsv	chg %	baseTR	VRDsv	chg %
MeanT11SU	0.507	0.543	7.14	0.538	0.575	6.97	0.553	0.591	6.87
MeanT11F	0.460	0.503	9.31	0.506	0.550	8.62	0.527	0.566	7.42
microavgF1	0.538	0.596	10.92	0.634	0.681	7.39	0.707	0.748	5.90

On Reuters-21578 Test Set. We evaluated for the topics according to the number of relevant documents in the training set on Reuters-21578 test set: the 67 topics with less than 100, the 76 topics with less than 300, and the 81 topics with less than 500 relevant documents. In comparisons, the total 81 topics are used: The 7 topics with 1 relevant document are excluded since proposed VRDs are generated by two relevant documents pair. The 2 topics with more than 500 relevant documents are excluded since numbers of VRDs are generated. For the 90 topics, the performance of baseTR and VRDsv are 0.8495 and 0.8634, respectively. The proposed method achieved 10.9%, 7.4% and 5.9% improvement over the base performance in the micro average F1 measure for the 67 topics, the 76 topics and the 81 topics, respectively (in Table 3).

We have compared proposed method with other methods in generating VRDs:

- VRDtr: the performance of SVM after incoporating VRDs generated from all the relevant documents in *training set*.

- VRDsum: the performance of SVM after incoporating VRDs generated *by summation of two vectors* from relevant support vector set into support vector set.

As shown Table 4, the result shows that VRDs can be generated from SV set and slightly make better performance than that of generated from training set. The performance of VRDs by summation is similar with that of baseTR. This represents VRDs produced by summation do not provide new information.

Through the comparison with VRDs generated from all training set (VRDtr vs. VRDsv), the result indicates that the virtual relevant documents techniques generating from the SV set is sound. Through the comparison with VRDs generated by summation (VRDsum vs. VRDsv), the results indicates that the proposed method in generating VRDs by product of the co-occurring terms could provide new information in the document space in learning.

Table 4. The comparisons in the methods of generating VRDs for the 67 topics on Reuters-21578 test set.

Evaluation Measure	baseTR	Comparison		VRDsv
		VRDsum	VRDtr	
MeanT11SU	0.507	0.509	0.544	0.543
MeanT11F	0.460	0.464	0.510	0.503
MicroAvg F1	0.538	0.542	0.588	0.596

5.3 Result Analysis

Fig 5 shows the performance changes between performance of baseTR and that of VRDsv VRDsv for the 81 topics in the F1 measure. The performances were improved for most topics.

We have analyzed the performance changes gauged by the F1 measure, according to the number of relevant documents and virtual relevant documents (shown in Fig 6). The performances on the x-axis of 'r1', 'r2' and 'rN' are the performances on the relevant document with 1, 2, and N, respectively. The performances on the x-axis of 'vr2', 'vr3', and 'vrN' are the performance on the all real relevant documents and the virtual relevant documents generated from 2, 3, and N relevant documents, respectively.

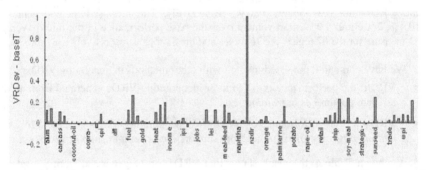

Fig. 5. The performance changes by subtracting the performance of baseTR from that of VRDsv.

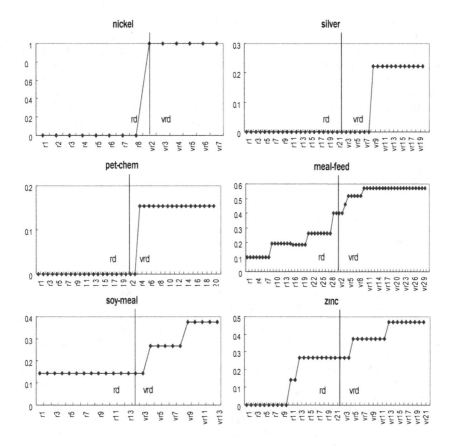

Fig. 6. The performance changes according to the number of relevant document (rd) and virtual relevant document (vrd).

The results show the general pattern that using more training documents in learning produces the better performance. The relative margin of the contribution of VRDs is highly notable, especially for those cases in which the training set consists of the small number of relevant documents (e.g. nickel, silver, pet-chem, soy-meal, and zinc). It is clear that the addition of virtual relevant documents contributes to the steady improvement of the performance.

6   Conclusion

Incorporating virtual relevant documents into the training set in learning phase is effective for text categorization. We suggested the virtual relevant document technique. For the TREC-11 filtering test set, our method achieved 71% improvement in micro average F1 over the baseline. The improvement is 11% for the Reuters-21578 test set for the 67 topics. These improvements are important, especially given the fact that the virtual documents are produced simply and the addition of the virtual relevant documents contributed to the steady improvement of the performance. Our results show that the suitable term space could be manipulated for learning within the limitation of the training set, not restricted to the existing unit of document in the topical discourse space.

We expect that our method will improve other text categorization methods by adding new evidences to the training set, although further researches are needed.

References

1. Allan, J., Ballesteros, L., Callan, J., Croft, W., and Lu, Z. 1996. Recent experiments with INQUERY. In Proc. of the Fourth Text REtrieval Conference (TREC-4).
2. DeCoste, D. and Schölkopf, B. 2002. Training invariant support vector machines. Machine Learning 46(1), pp.161–190.
3. Joachims, T. 1999. Making large-scale support vector machine learning practical. In Advances in Kernel Methods: Support Vector Machines (Schölkopf et al., 1999), MIT Press.
4. Kawatani, T. 2002. Topic Difference Factor Extraction between Two Document Sets and its Application to Text Categorization. In Proc. of 25th ACM-SIGIR Conference on Research and Development in Information Retrieval.
5. Kwok, K. and Grunfeld, L. 1997. TREC-5 English and Chinese retrieval experiments using PIRCS. In the Proc. of the Fifth Text REtrieval Conference (TREC-5).
6. Lewis, D. 1999. Reuters-21578 text categorization test collection distribution 1.0. http://www.daviddlewis.com/
7. Poggio, T. and Vetter, T. 1992. Recognition and structure from one 2D model view: observations on prototypes, object classes and symmetries. A.I. Memo No. 1347, Artificial Intelligence Laboratory, MIT.
8. Robertson, S. and Soboroff, I. 2001. The TREC 2001 Filtering Track Report. In Proc. of the Tenth Text REtrieval Conference (TREC-10).
9. Rose, T.G., Stevenson, M. and Whitehead, M. 2002. The Reuters Corpus Volume 1 - from Yesterday's News to Tomorrow's Language Resources. In Proc. of the Third International Conference on Language Resources and Evaluation.
10. Schölkopf, B. 1997. Support Vector Learning. R. Oldenbourg Verlag, Munchen. Doktorarbeit, TU Berlin.
11. Schölkopf, B., Burges, C., and Vapnik, V. 1995. Extracting support data for a given task. In Proc. of the First International Conference on Knowledge Discovery & Data Mining, Menlo Park. AAAI Press.
12. Singhal, A., Mitra, M., and Buckley, C. 1997. Learning routing queries in a query zone. In Proc. of the Twentieth ACM SIGIR Conference on Research and Development in Information Retrieval, pp. 21–29.
13. Vapnick, V. 1995. The Nature of Statistical Learning Theory, Springer-Verlag, New York.
14. Yang, Y. and Liu, X. 1999. A re-examination of text categorization methods. In Proc. of the 22nd ACM-SIGIR Conference on Research and Development in Information Retrieval.

A Case Study of a Stream-Based Digital Library: Medical Data

Mohamed Kholief[1], Kurt Maly[2], and Stewart Shen[2]

[1] California University of Pennsylvania, California, PA 15419, USA
Kholief@cup.edu
[2] Old Dominion University, Norfolk, VA 23529, USA
{Maly,Shen}@cs.odu.edu

Abstract. A case study of a digital library that contains streams and supports event-based retrieval is described. Medical streams that relate to patients having liver tumors are used in the digital library. 3 types of streams were used: computed tomography (CT) scan, medical text, and audio streams. Events, such as 'Maximum diameter of the tumor', were generated and represented in the user interface to enable doctors to retrieve and playback segments of the streams. This paper presents the details of creating the digital library: the data organization, publishing stream data, generating the bibliographic metadata, using events, relating streams, the search engine, and the playback of the streams.

1 Introduction

A major advantage of using digital libraries over conventional libraries is the ability to store unconventional types of data and use new methods to retrieve these data. A data stream is a sequence of data units produced over a period of time. Video, audio, sensor readings, satellite images, and radar maps are examples of data streams; which are important sources of information for many applications. Saving such streams in digital libraries would add to the value of this information by allowing for new ways for retrieval, besides the other values of using digital libraries such as archival, preservation and access control.

Saving data streams in digital libraries has long been limited to saving audio and video streams. Some projects just preserve audio and video files and allow the retrieval and playback of these files based on bibliographic metadata. An example is the EGARC digital audio library [3]. Current research projects are building video and audio digital libraries that support sophisticated ways of retrieval such as content-based retrieval. Examples are the Informedia project [1] and the VISION project [4].

In [6], we described the architecture of a digital library that contains data streams and supports event-based retrieval (SDL). An event is a noteworthy occurrence that occurred during the stream. There is psychological evidence that people tend to remember by events rather than by their times [9]. To design SDL, our approach was to consider several possible applications, examine the requirements of potential users, list the design considerations, and use these considerations to design the architecture.

T.M.T. Sembok et al. (Eds.): ICADL 2003, LNCS 2911, pp. 73–85, 2003.
© Springer-Verlag Berlin Heidelberg 2003

In this paper, we present a case study of event-based retrieval from a digital library that mainly contains streams of medical content. Actual CT scan streams were stored in the repository along with text and audio streams that relate to the subject of the CT scan data. This paper presents the details of creating the digital library: basic concepts and the data organization, publishing stream data and generating the metadata, representing and generating the events, relating streams, the search engine, and the playback of the streams. Concepts related to event-based retrieval were covered in detail in [6] and a brief overview of the medical application for SDL is given in [5]. Throughout this paper an overview of a concept is presented before proceeding to the actual implementation. Section 2 explains how streams are organized in the digital library and the process of mass-publishing of CT scan streams, event generation, and relating streams. Sections 3, 4, and 5 describe the user interface consisting of the search interfaces, the stream display interface, and the stream playback interface. Conclusions are presented in section 6.

2   Basic Concepts and the Data Organization

Stream Objects. Streams are organized into stream objects; each object contains the stream data and metadata. As can be seen in Fig. 1, the stream object is a file system folder that contains two main subfolders: data and metadata. The data folder contains all the data files of the particular stream, e.g. the image files of a CT scan stream, or the audio clips for a stream of audio clips. The metadata folder contains the corresponding metadata files. The metadata files are usually three files: the temporal metadata file, the standard bibliographic metadata file, and the specific bibliographic metadata file. The temporal metadata file contains a listing of the timing of all the stream frames. The format of this file is simple; it consists of 2-field records, the first field is the offset in milliseconds from the start of the stream and the second field is the relative frame file path. The frame could be an image, an audio clip, a text string, etc depending on the stream type.

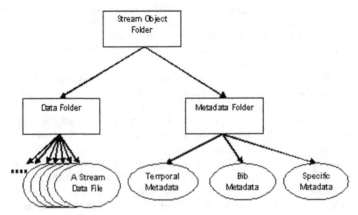

Fig. 1. Structure of the Stream Object. Each (*rectangle*) represents a system folder and each (*oval*) represents a file.

```
BIB-VERSION:: X-streams-1.0
ID:: patients2/p15.2
ENTRY:: 2002-06-06
TITLE: CT scan stream for patient p15 for his visit on 19990608
CREATOR:: Mohamed Kholief
START_DATE: 19990608
END_DATE:: 19990608
TYPE: CT SCAN
FORMAT:: GIF
SOURCE: Station name: CT1X_OC0
DESCRIPTION:: This is the CT scan stream for patient p15 for his visit on: 19990608. The
study reason is: CT CHEST/ABD/PELVIS SCH W/FAITH8-3200-- PREP 0730AM UPMC
HEALTH PLAN. The study description is: CHEST W & ABD W, and the series description
is :
END:: patients2/p15.2
```

Fig. 2. An example of a standard bibliographic metadata file

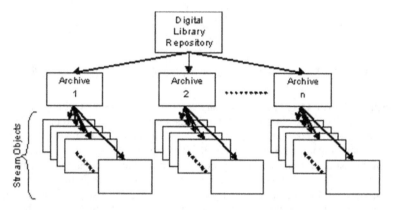

Fig. 3. The digital library repository structure. Each (*rectangle*) represents a system folder

The standard bibliographic metadata file contains general bibliographic metadata about the stream. The metadata fields in this file are standard for all stream types. These fields are: the stream id, the entry date, the title, the creator, the start date, the end date, the stream type, the stream format, the stream source, and the description. Most of these fields are similar to the corresponding Dublin Core fields [2]. The file format, however, follows the syntax of the RFC1807-metadata format [7]. Fig. 2 shows an example of one of the files used in our implementation.

The specific bibliographic metadata file is an optional file that is used to save particular metadata fields that are specific to certain stream types. This makes the system heterogeneous with regard to the type of the streams that could be saved in the digital library.

Stream Archives. The digital library may use different archives to save the stream objects. Streams, coming from different sources, may be saved into different archives. For the core DL engine we use Arc [8], an OpenSource DL system. Fig. 3 shows the digital library repository structure.

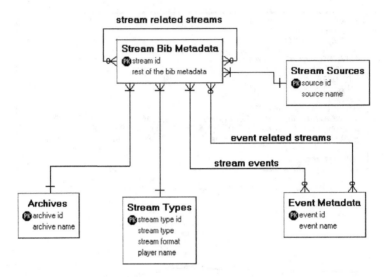

Fig 4. The entity-relationship diagram for the database used in this digital library

Database Server Organization. A database system is used to facilitate the retrieval from the digital library. Using a mature database management system like Oracle or MySQL ensures a fast and reliable search and retrieval of the stream objects.

The following information is kept in the database:
- All the stream standard and specific bibliographic metadata information, thus stream objects could be retrieved based on any bib metadata field.
- All the events information, which enables the retrieval of streams based on events that occurred during these streams which is the main point in this research.
- Information about related streams, those are basically other streams that the user might want to retrieve whenever he retrieves a stream.

The search engine uses the database to retrieve any stream object based on its bibliographic information or based on the events that occur during this stream. Playback scripts use the database to decide on the related streams that will be played back simultaneous to the retrieved stream, and to decide on the playback start time based on the time of any event instance. A simplified entity relationship (ER) diagram is shown in Fig. 4. Because of its availability at out site, we use an Oracle database.

Data Publishing. The functionality to automate the publishing of the CT scan streams is:
- Create the stream object into a specific archive folder, given as a parameter.
- Copy the stream data files from the stream source to the appropriate file system folder, which is the data folder of the stream object created in the last step.
- Create the stream metadata files in the appropriate file system folder, which is the metadata folder of the stream object created in step 1.
- Update the database tables to include the metadata information of this stream.

The main task of the metadata generation process was to map the native metadata fields to the standard and specific bibliographic metadata fields that we decided to use in this system and to add these metadata fields into the appropriate database tables. The selection of these fields and the mapping decisions were all driven by radiologists doing research in the "Liver Tumors" area.

This study was meant as a feasibility project and is not a production system; hence the audio and text streams were created manually. They were actually created "in place", so the publishing process itself was done manually. A future extension to this work is to create a publishing tool that would take the user through a wizard to help her publish the streams without actually having to know the underlying file system or database details.

Event Specification. Searching for data streams based on the events that occurred within the streams is one of the main themes in this research. Event names are specified in the event metadata database table. In this implementation, events were inserted in this table manually. In other words, direct database instructions were used to insert the event names. This table mainly has an event ID and an event name fields. A domain expert is responsible for inserting the new events in this table (via system administrators). In a future extension, an event editor will be used to edit and insert these events in the database without having to know the details of the underlying database design.

Based on the opinions of radiologists who work in the field of Liver Tumors, the following events were used for this particular case study: "Calcification", "Tumor started to appear", "Maximum diameter of the tumor", "Necrosis appearing", and "Maximum necrosis diameter". Adding new events does not require any changes in any implemented software; it only requires changes in the data used by the software. All of those events are related to the liver tumors research topic and are used by doctors to monitor the development of tumors in the patients.

Event Instances Generation. Events may occur in many streams and may occur many times in the same stream. Each of the occurrences of an event is called an event instance. Event generation is mainly applying the event criteria to the streams and generating a list of the times at which the event occurs. This process can be automated for some stream types and has to be done manually for others. Examples were given in [6] on cases for which automatic event-generation could work. In this case study, the event instances' times were manually inserted into the stream events database table. This table has three fields: the stream ID, the event ID, and the event instance time. The event instance time is the offset from the start time of the stream in milliseconds. If the event has more than one instance in the same stream, there will be many rows in this table with the same stream ID and event ID but with different event instance time.

A Prototype Event Generation Tool. In a future extension to this system, an event-generation tool will be used to automate the event generation. The main functionality of this tool will be to:

- Get the event name and the IDs of the streams containing it from the user.
- Apply a suitable ready-made criteria module to the stream to generate the time instances of this event.
- Read the event-related streams from the user, or apply another criteria module to decide which streams relate to this event.
- Insert the event name, time instances, and related streams in the appropriate database tables.

Related Streams Representation. One important feature of SDL is the ability to playback related streams along with the originally retrieved stream. In our implementation, streams can be related to streams or to events that occurred during these streams. Two database tables are used to maintain streams that relate to other streams and streams that relate to events. The fields in the stream-related table are the original stream ID, the related stream ID, why are they related, whether they are synchronous or not, and the time offset in milliseconds between the two streams if they are synchronous, assuming that one of them may start some time after the other. For event-related streams, the event ID and the stream ID are the two fields in the table. Event-related streams are by default non-synchronous with the streams during which this event occurred.

Related Streams Specification. An important question is how to specify the related streams. One alternative is to let a domain expert specify, manually, the streams related to each stream to be published in the library. The more realistic alternative, however, is to use a generation script that applies a certain criteria on all streams for automatic generation of related streams. In this implementation, both ways were used. A generation script was used for one criterion and it can be generalized to accommodate for other criteria. A simple script was used to relate streams of the same patient. Manual specification was used to relate some streams by just inserting the relationship information in the appropriate database tables as described above.

3   The Search Interface

In this case study, a simple search, an event-based search, and a browse interfaces were implemented. The browse interface is just a special case of the simple search where no search terms are specified, thus all streams are returned. A subset of the following figures was used in the short summary [5].

The Simple search interface, as seen in Fig. 5, allows the user to locate data streams in the digital library based on the value of *any* bibliographic field. Users can use the "group by" menu to group the results by archive name, the stream source, or the stream type. The user can also sort the results in the ascending order of the values of either the title, the creator name, the stream start date, or the stream end date using the 'sort results by' menu.

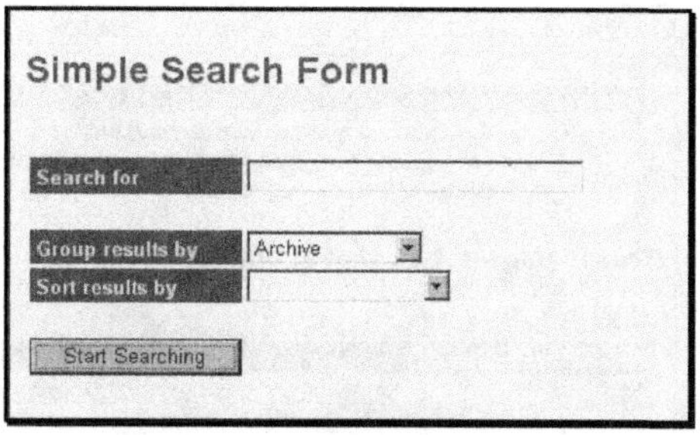

Fig. 5. The simple search interface

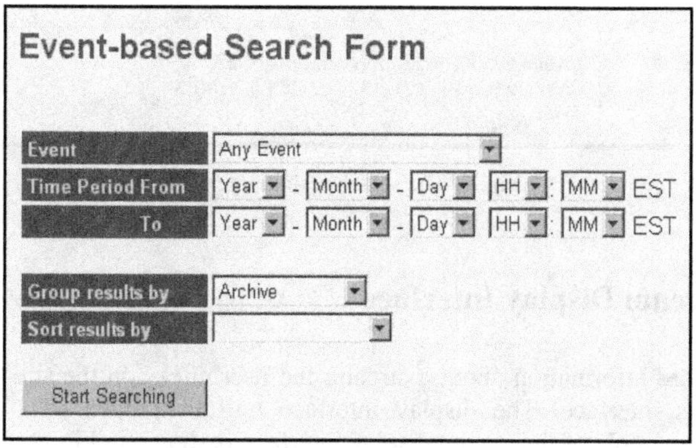

Fig. 6. The event-based search interface

The event-based search interface is seen in Fig. 6. End-users look for events by their names. Currently, all events are read from the events table in the database and displayed in one menu. Users can specify a time period to limit the search. As in the simple search interface, users can specify a group-by value and an ordering value to group and sort the search results.

The search results are organized in the way seen in Fig. 7. The results frame is divided in two columns; the left one contains a list of all the groups that contained results, depending on the grouping field. In the figure, the results are grouped based on the stream type and all results come from one stream type, which is the CT SCAN type. Each group name is followed on the same line by the number of results (hits) from this group. The right column contains the details of the results. It starts with a search summary that specifies the search terms, how results are grouped and how they are sorted. The search summary is then followed by the search results. Results are arranged in pages. Selected metadata information is displayed for each hit.

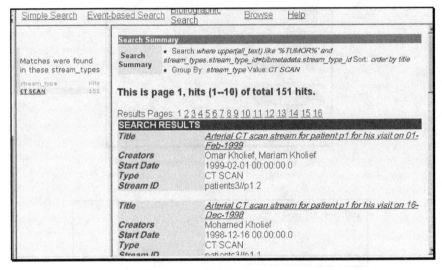

Fig. 7. The search results interface

4   The Stream Display Interface

To obtain more information about a stream, the user clicks on the stream title in the search results interface. The display interface will then open in a new browser window. An example of the stream display interface is shown in Fig. 8.

This interface is divided into two sections. The upper section contains the complete stream bibliographic information and the lower section contains a playback form. The bibliographic information are divided into two columns, one of them contains the standard bibliographic information that are found in any stream object and the other contains the specific information that are optional and differs from one stream type to another. This interface is designed in such a way that automates the display of the bibliographic information regardless of the bib fields being used, which makes it easy for any future changes to the system.

The playback form is used if the user wants to playback this stream. There are two sections in this form. One section is concerned with determining the starting time for the playback and the other one is concerned with determining what other streams, if any, should be played back simultaneously. The user may need to play the stream starting from the time of an event instance. To do so, she can select an event from a menu of all the events that occurred during this stream. Since an event may occur many times during the same stream, the user can then select one time instance of the selected event from the time instances menu. In the case that the user originally was looking for a specific event using the event-based search form explained in the last section, this event will be pre-selected in the events menu and its first time instance will be pre-selected in the time instances menu.

Bibliographic Information			
General:		**Type-specific:**	
Title	Portal Venous CT scan stream for patient p2 for his visit on 02-Feb-1999	Date of Birth	1932071
		Age	066Y
Creator	Kurt Maly	Sex	F
Stream Type	CT SCAN	History	LIVER MA
Stream Source	Global CT Scan	Slice Thickness	7.500000
Start Date	02-FEB-99	Contrast	BARIUM
End Date	02-FEB-99	Reason	CT CHES 8-3200--
Description	This is the CT scan stream for patient p2 for his visit on: 02-Feb-1999. The study reason is: CT CHEST/ABD/PELVIS--PREP 1100AM SCH W/FAITH 8-3200--SLOT OK PER BEV MEDICARE A. The study description is: CH WO&ABD W/WO, and the series description is :		
Stream ID	patients4//p2.1		

Playback Form

(Use this form to playback this stream and, if desired, any streams related to it. The playback starts from the be specified as the starting time.)

Playback Start Time: *(Select an event, and then select one instance of this event to start the playback from the*

Event	-Select an Event-------------------------- ▼	
Event Instances	-Select Time Instance------------------ ▼	Milliseconds from the stream start time.

Related Streams: *(Select zero or more of the related streams to playback along with the original stream. Ctrl+c*

Related Synchronous Streams	--Select Related Synchronous Stream----------- A mini-lecture about CT scans and Lever tumors A mini audio lecture about CT scans and Lever tumors	*(One control pa these streams.*
Related Asynchronous Streams	--Select Related Asynchronous Stream------------------------- ▲ Portal Venous CT scan stream for patient p2 for his visit on 06-Jul-1999 Portal Venous CT scan stream for patient p2 for his visit on 11-Oct-1999 Arterial CT scan stream for patient p2 for his visit on 06-Jul-1999 ▼	*(Each of these playing from its*

For Selected Streams, Display:

Bibliographic information	Relationship details	Play

Fig. 8. An example of the stream display interface

Related streams are divided in two menus, synchronous related streams and asynchronous related streams. Synchronous streams are those streams that can playback synchronously with the original stream and the asynchronous streams are those that have no temporal relation to the original stream. Both types are listed in list boxes that allow multiple selections, so the user can select as many streams as wanted to playback simultaneously with the original stream. The user can check the bibliographic information of the selected related streams by clicking on the "Bibliographic information" button. A window pops up in which the bibliographic information of all selected streams is displayed.

In the stream display interface shown in Fig. 8, the user is also able to see the details of the relationship between the selected related streams and the original stream by clicking on the "Relationship details" button. A window that shows the details of these relationships pops up when this button is clicked, as shown in Fig. 9.

Fig. 9. A popup window showing the relation details between related streams

5 The Playback Interface

In the playback interface, the user can select the starting playback time and other related streams to be played back simultaneous to the original stream and hit the "play" button. Hitting the "play" button starts the playback interface described in this section. As can be seen in Fig. 10, the playback interface consists of two main sections: the upper section contains the players of the related synchronous streams and one control panel to control all these players and the lower section contains the players of the related asynchronous streams with one control panel for each. The leftmost stream player in the upper section is the player for the original stream. The ID and the title of each stream are displayed above its player. If only one stream is to be played back, the player of that stream and a control panel will be displayed in the upper section.

The control panel applet, the rightmost applet in every section in Fig. 10, controls the behavior of the player applets. It contains the following interface elements:

- "Play": starts the playback of the adjacent stream player(s) from the time specified in the current time text field (which shows under the play button in the figure). The label on this button is switched to stop when the stream is playing.

- "Change to Backward": streams start playing back in the forward direction by default. Clicking on this button will reverse the playback direction. The label changes to "Change to forward" when this button is clicked.

- "Set time": the user clicks this button after entering a new time offset in the current time text field that appears to its left. The current time is an offset from the start of the leftmost stream. This button is inactive (dim) when the stream is playing.

- Playback speed slider: this slider bar allows the user to change the playback speed. Sliding the slider toward the "fast" label increases the speed and towards the "slow" label decreases the speed using a simple heuristic.

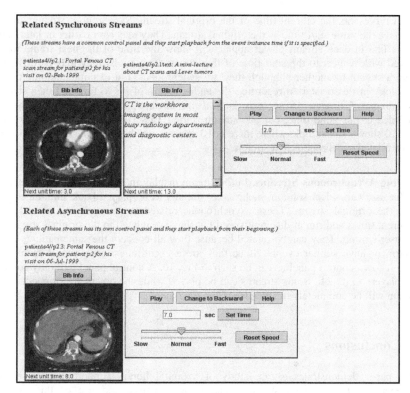

Fig. 10. An example of the playback interface

In our system, there is a common structure for all stream players regardless of the stream type. The player interface consists of three panels. The top panel contains a button "Bib Info", which displays a bib information window for the stream being played. The middle panel shows the stream being played if it is visual as in CT scan and text streams. The bottom panel shows the current status, which is mostly the time of the next frame to be played. The time shown is the offset in seconds from the start of the stream being played. Stream players are controlled by the control panel applet. The main difference between the stream player of a certain type and of another is the way the stream frame will be played. In a CT scan stream, the frame is a GIF image that will be displayed. In a text stream, the frame is a text string that will also be displayed. In an audio stream, the frame is an audio clip that will be played.

Playing Synchronous Streams. In the stream display interface described in section 4, the user can select some synchronous streams to be played back simultaneously with the original stream. Since all of these streams are synchronous, only one control panel will be needed to control all of them. Fig. 10 shows an example of playing back synchronous streams. In the figure, the original stream is a CT scan stream and the related synchronous stream is a stream of text strings. The original stream will play at the leftmost player applet. The time shown in the current time text field in the control panel represents the current time of the original stream. Synchronous streams might not have the same start time as the original stream. They may start earlier or later. The status line in each stream player applet will show the time of the next frame to be played with respect to the start time of that stream, that's why they may be different from a stream to another although they are synchronous. For example, assume that a radiology professor started recording the audio stream of his lecture and then started recording a CT scan 15 seconds later. Both streams are synchronous; they are recorded at the same time, but one stream started 15 seconds earlier than the other. Fig. 10 shows an example where there is 10 seconds gap between the CT scan stream and a related synchronous text stream.

Playing Asynchronous Streams. In the stream display interface described in section 4, the user can select some asynchronous streams to be played back simultaneously with the original stream. These asynchronous related streams may be recorded at different times and run at different speed but they are related to the original stream in the user's mind. They can be related because they all concern the same patient, same doctor, or have similar events. Since they are asynchronous, each one of them will have its own control panel as can be seen in Fig. 10. A control panel will only control the players to its left. Some streams can be played while the others are stopped. Each stream will be completely independent from the others.

6   Conclusions

This paper demonstrates a case study of a digital library supporting event-based retrieval of medical data streams. The implementation and use of this system demonstrated that it is feasible to create a digital library that contains data streams and supports event-based retrieval. We were able to efficiently represent events such that traditional DL services run at a comparable performance. Features specific to the SDL were realized such that retrieval and playback can be done in as few as 3 mouse clicks. The playback interface itself was organized in a way that accommodated synchronous and asynchronous streams and enabled users to control these streams using a set of buttons in a control panel. The ease of use of this library was informally confirmed by a group of radiologists and is yet to be documented. The underlying search engine, Arc, has proven to work efficiently with the data saved in the library, which promises the scalability of this work. The heterogeneity is also emphasized in every aspect of the implementation. In particular, the library can be adapted to support more stream types just by defining a new type in the stream-types database table and defining the player for this new type by implementing a pre-defined Java interface and using an existing template.

Key to the specification of events and what metadata to use were the domain experts (radiologists). In this case study we did not concentrate on fancy editors to publish the streams and events but on the presentation to the resource discovery user. Also, domain experts were used to create the proper wording in the various event and playback menus.

The lessons learned from this study are: one, it is feasible to build a domain specific SDL that is efficient and likely scales to support a production system.

Secondly, we need not only automate the event generation, the publishing process for individual streams, the creation of tools to further automate the process of relating streams, and adding more types but also we need to formally define the processes of tailoring an SDL for a new domain and obtaining the information from the experts.

References

1. Christel, M., et al: Informedia Digital Video Library, Communications of ACM, 38(4) (1997) 57–58.
2. Dublin Core Metadata Initiative, http://dublincore.org/
3. EGARC MP3 Audio Library. http://www.ku.edu/~egarc/diglib/index.htm
4. Gauch, S., Li, W., Gauch, J.: The VISION Digital Video Library System, Information Processing & Management, 33(4) (1997) 413–426.
5. Kholief, M., Maly, K., Shen, S.: Event-Based Retrieval from a Digital Library Containing Medical Streams. JCDL'03, Houston, Texas (2003)
6. Kholief, M., Shen, S., Maly, K.: Architecture for Event-Based Retrieval from Data Streams in Digital Libraries. ECDL'2001, Darmstadt (2001) 300–311.
7. Lasher, R., Cohen, D.: Request for Comments: 1807: A Format for Bibliographic Records. http://www.ietf.org/rfc/rfc1807.txt?number=1807
8. Liu, X., Maly, K., Zubair, M.: Arc. http://sourceforge.net/projects/oaiarc/
9. Wagenaar, W. A.: My memory: a study of autobiographical memory over six years, Cognitive Psychology, 18(1) (1986) 225–252.

Towards Web Mining of Query Translations for Cross-Language Information Retrieval in Digital Libraries

Wen-Hsiang Lu, Jenq-Haur Wang, and Lee-Feng Chien

Institute of Information Science, Academia Sinica, No. 128, Sec. 2,
Academia Rd., Nankang, 115, Taipei, Taiwan
{whlu,jhwang,lfchien}@iis.sinica.edu.tw

Abstract. This paper proposes an efficient client-server-based query translation approach to allowing more feasible implementation of cross-language information retrieval (CLIR) services in digital library (DL) systems. A centralized query translation server is constructed to process the translation requests of cross-lingual queries from connected DL systems. To extract translations not covered by standard dictionaries, the server is developed based on a novel integration of dictionary resources and Web mining methods, including anchor-text and search-result methods, which exploit huge amounts of multilingual and wide-scoped Web resources as live bilingual corpora to alleviate translation difficulties, and have been proven particularly effective for extracting multilingual translation equivalents of query terms containing proper names or new terminologies. The proposed approach was implemented in a query translation engine called *LiveTrans*, which has been shown its feasibility in providing efficient English-Chinese CLIR services for DL.

1 Introduction

With the rapid growth of interests in constructing digital libraries (DL's) in many countries, increasing amounts of library contents are being digitized and accessible from the Web. Such Web-accessible digitized contents may have global use and the demand of cross-language information retrieval (CLIR) [6, 17] services have been increasing. However, practical multilingual search supports in DL systems are still lacking [18, 19].

This paper proposes an efficient client-server-based query translation approach to allowing more feasible implementation of CLIR services in DL systems. Most existing systems provide only monolingual content and search supports in a certain language, which could be cost-ineffective and even impossible to provide multilingual supports for every major language in the world. To facilitate CLIR service in DL systems, it would be critical and challenging to develop a centralized and powerful query translation engine that is able to automatically translate users' queries from multiple source languages to the target language that systems accept. If the engine works well, it will be more flexible for users to formulate queries in their familiar language, and different DL systems only have to deal with queries in their original

T.M.T. Sembok et al. (Eds.): ICADL 2003, LNCS 2911, pp. 86–99, 2003.

languages and need only slight modifications. In our research, we intend to develop such a powerful engine. We will focus on providing translations between English and Chinese at initial stage.

One major bottleneck of CLIR service stems from the lack of up-to-date bilingual dictionaries [10] containing translations of popular query terms, such as proper nouns and new terminologies. Web mining methods that can exploit huge amounts of multilingual and wide-scoped Web resources as live bilingual corpora have received great attentions to alleviate the translation difficulties of query terms not covered by standard dictionaries [3, 16].

The Web is becoming the largest data repository in the world. To utilize rich Web resources for query translation, several Web mining methods have been developed to effectively exploit two kinds of Web resources: anchor texts and search results, where several term similarity estimation techniques, such as probabilistic inference model, context vector analysis, and chi-square test, are employed to extract translation equivalents for "out-of-dictionary" terms.

The primary purpose of this paper is to introduce our experiences obtained in developing two complementary Web mining methods. *Search-result-based* methods can have high coverage of various language pairs, but are especially useful for English-Chinese, due to the fact that the Web consists of rich texts in a mixture of Chinese and English. On the other hand, *anchor-text-based* method can achieve higher precision for high-frequency terms and can extract translations in other language pairs besides English-Chinese. The latter has been proven in our previous work to be particularly effective for extracting translation equivalents of proper names in multiple languages [13, 14, 15].

Next, to facilitate easier support for CLIR service in existing DL systems, a client-server-based architecture is presented where a query translation server (called *LiveTrans*) is designed. The server processes translation requests for cross-lingual queries dynamically from connected clients which are DL systems providing only monolingual search in a certain target language. The server is developed based on a novel integration of the proposed Web mining methods. For out-of-dictionary terms, the Web is searched for the most promising translations which are suggested to users, whose click information on selecting suggested translations is then collected and employed in improving translation accuracy. The proposed approach supports Z39.50 communication protocol between client and server [1]. To add query translation support in existing systems, only a Z39.50-based interface program is needed.

Several preliminary experiments have been conducted to test the performance of the proposed approach. The obtained results have shown its feasibility and great potential especially for creating English-Chinese CLIR services, although there are difficulties to be further investigated.

2 Related Research

Many effective retrieval models have been developed for CLIR. For example, Latent Semantic Indexing (LSI) method [6] has been utilized where inter-term relationships can be modeled instead of exact term matching. Other methods include cross-lingual relevance model [12], which integrates popular techniques of disambiguation and query expansion. However, translation of queries not covered in bilingual dictionary, such as proper nouns and new terminologies, is one of the major challenges in practical CLIR services [10].

To deal with the translation of out-of-dictionary terms, conventional research on machine translation has generally used statistical techniques to automatically extract translations from domain-specific parallel bilingual texts, such as bilingual newspapers [8]. Real queries are often diverse and dynamic where only a certain set of their translations can be extracted through corpora in limited domains. For illustration, our analysis of a query log from real-world search engine *Dreamer* in Taiwan showed that 74% of the top 20,000 popular Web queries in Taiwan, which formed 81% of the search requests in the log, could not be covered by common English-Chinese translation dictionaries. A new potential approach is to perform query translation directly through mining of the Web's multilingual and wide-range resources [3, 16]. Web mining is a new research area concentrating on finding useful information from vast amounts of semi-structured hypertexts and unstructured texts [4, 7]. We have proposed a preliminary approach to extracting translations of Web queries through the mining of anchor texts and link structures and obtained very promising results [13, 15]. In this paper the previous approach is well integrated with search-result-based methods which have been found more effective and especially useful for the English-Chinese language pair.

On the other hand, there is an increasing need for multilingual information access in DL [2, 11, 18, 19, 20]. However, practical multilingual supports in these systems are still lacking. To our knowledge, there is no similar design of query translation server simultaneously supporting many DL's. Federated search engines [20] and meta-search [5, 9] are related systems providing search services for separate DL with different capabilities and retrieval systems. Our work looks more similar to a cross-language meta-search engine for query translation. Federated search that concerns more about integration of information retrieved from different sites is not our focus.

3   The Proposed Approach

In this section, we will describe a design of client-server-based architecture for cross-language query translation in DL.

As shown in Fig. 1, each DL maintains its local dictionary, which is first checked for each query submitted by users. If local translations could be found, normal search process in DL is immediately performed; otherwise a translation request is issued and processed by *LiveTrans* engine where a list of the most promising translations will be returned to client for users to choose.

For the server side, on receiving each query from clients, possible translations are either extracted from a global dictionary or mined from the Web, which are then returned to clients. Since translation candidates might be in a target language unknown to users, displaying some relevant terms in users' familiar language can often help them select suitable translations. The communication protocol between client and server is based on Z39.50 [1], a NISO standard protocol for generic information search and retrieval in databases. The major concern for protocol is the reduction of sever load and client-server communications.

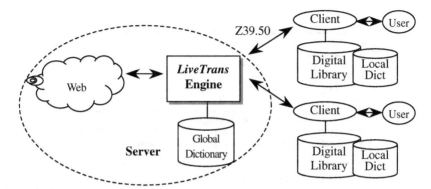

Fig. 1. An abstract diagram showing main components in our architecture of cross-language query translation in digital libraries

Users' responses such as clicks on suggested items can be fed back to adapt *LiveTrans* engine for more accurate translations. Since different users on separate clients may formulate the same queries that need translations, for better performance, queries, translation candidates and clicked information are cached separately on each client. The server periodically integrates clicked information from all clients and re-orders translation candidates by a global ranking function. If users at a client frequently select some translations, the server will inform the client to store the query translations permanently in its local dictionary, which is incrementally enriched with users' preferences and assessments. In real applications, a dictionary management tool can be provided for administrators to directly update query entries.

There are many challenges and issues in developing the proposed approach. The first is how well and in what kinds of domains could Web mining techniques be effective. The second is whether the proposed approach for CLIR services can be accepted in DL. The remaining includes how to reduce server load, whether translation accuracy can be effectively improved with appropriate ranking algorithms, etc. Due to page limitation, investigation on the first two issues will be emphasized in this paper.

4   Web Mining of Query Translations

As shown in Fig. 2, *LiveTrans* server was implemented with a novel combination of the developed anchor-text and search-result mining methods. Since real queries are often short and diverse, search log analysis and bilingual dictionary lookup are also incorporated. The search log records previous queries, extracted translations and clicked information collected from all clients. For each received query, search log is first checked. If the query has been translated and some of the suggested translations have been frequently clicked, the server will return the translations to the client. If no appropriate translations can be found, the Web will be searched for possible translations. Since the major purpose of this paper is to investigate the performance of Web mining methods, in the following discussions and experiments, no dictionary and search log will be considered.

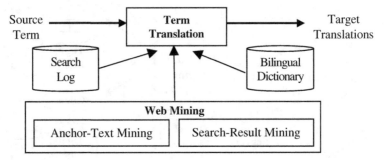

Fig. 2. An abstract diagram showing the system architecture of *LiveTrans* engine

4.1 Anchor-Text-Based Method

An anchor text is the brief description of an out-link in a Web page. There might be many anchor texts linking to the same page, which is collectively called an *anchor-text set*. For a term appearing in an anchor text, its corresponding translations and synonyms are likely to appear in the same anchor-text sets and may be extracted from anchor-text sets as a comparable corpus for a given term.

To determine the most probable target translation *t* for source query term *s*, we have developed an anchor-text-based method to extract query translations through mining of anchor texts and link structures [13, 14]. The method is based on integrating hyperlink structure into probabilistic inference model which is used to estimate the probability between a query and all translation candidates that co-occur in the same anchor-text sets. A translation candidate has a higher chance of being effective if it's written in the target language and frequently co-occurs with query term in the same anchor-text sets. Besides, in the field of Web research, it has been proven that link structures can be effective in estimating the *authority* of Web pages. Therefore, we assume that translation candidates in the anchor-text sets of pages with higher authority may be more reliable.

The similarity estimation function for anchor-text based (AT) method is called model S_{at} for notational consistency as following sections and is defined below:

$$S_{at}(s, t) = P(s \leftrightarrow t) = \frac{P(s \cap t)}{P(s \cup t)}$$

$$= \frac{\sum_{i=1}^{n} P(s \cap t \cap u_i)}{\sum_{i=1}^{n} P((s \cup t) \cap u_i)} = \frac{\sum_{i=1}^{n} P(s \cap t \mid u_i)P(u_i)}{\sum_{i=1}^{n} P(s \cup t \mid u_i)P(u_i)} \quad (1)$$

The above measure is adopted to estimate the similarity between source term *s* and target translation *t* based on their co-occurrence in the anchor-text sets of the concerned Web pages $U = \{u_1, u_2, ... u_n\}$, where $P(u_i)$ is the probability used to measure the authority of page u_i. $P(u_i)$ is estimated with the probability of u_i being linked, and is defined as follows: $P(u_i) = L(u_i)/\Sigma_{j=1,n} L(u_j)$, where $L(u_j)$ indicates the number of in-links of page u_j. In addition, we assume that s and t are independent given u_i; then, $P(s \cap t|u_i) = P(s|u_i) * P(t|u_i)$, and the similarity measure becomes:

$$S_a(s, t) \approx \frac{\displaystyle\sum_{i=1}^{n} P(s \mid u_i) P(t \mid u_i) P(u_i)}{\displaystyle\sum_{i=1}^{n} [P(s \mid u_i) + P(t \mid u_i) - P(s \mid u_i) P(t \mid u_i)] P(u_i)} \tag{2}$$

The values of $P(s|u_i)$ and $P(t|u_i)$ are estimated by calculating the fractions of the number of u_i's in-links containing s and t over $L(u_i)$, respectively.

The estimation process contains three major modules: anchor-text extraction, translation candidate extraction, and translation selection. Anchor-text extraction module collects Web pages and builds up a corpus of anchor-text sets. For each given source term, translation candidate extraction module extracts key terms in the target language as the candidate set from its anchor-text sets. Three different term extraction methods have been tested: *PAT-tree-based*, *query-set-based* and *tagger-based* methods, in which *query-set-based* method has been strongly recommended because it has no problem with term segmentation. A query log in the target language is used as the translation vocabulary set to segment key terms in the anchor-text sets. The precondition for using this method is that the coverage of the query set should be high. Finally, translation selection module extracts the translation that maximizes the similarity measure. For details about anchor-text-based method, readers may refer to our previous work [13, 14].

4.2 Search-Result-Based Method

Although anchor-text-based method has been proven effective for proper nouns in multiple languages, it nevertheless has a drawback that it's not applicable if the size of anchor-text sets is not large enough. Therefore, we present search-result-based approaches to fully exploiting Web resources where search result pages of queries submitted to real search engines are used as the corpus for extracting translations. Search result pages are normally returned in a long ordered list of relevant documents and *snippets* of summaries to help users locate interesting documents. These usually contain a mixture of Chinese and English, where many translation equivalents of query terms may be included. In our research, we seek to find out if the number of effective translations is high enough in the top search result pages for real queries. If that is the case, search-result-based methods can alleviate the difficulty encountered by anchor-text-based method.

The estimation process in search-result-based method also contains three major modules: search result collection, translation candidate extraction, and translation selection. In search result collection module, a given source query is submitted to a real-world search engine to collect the top search result pages. In translation candidate extraction module, the same term extraction method in anchor-text-based method is used. In translation selection module, our idea is to utilize co-occurrence relation and context information between source queries and target translations to estimate their semantic similarity and to determine the most promising translations. Several similarity estimation methods have been investigated based on co-occurrence analysis, including *mutual information*, *DICE coefficient*, and statistical tests such as *chi-square test* and *log-likelihood ratio test*, where chi-square test and context vector analysis achieve the best performance.

Chi-Square Test. Although log-likelihood ratio test is theoretically more suitable for dealing with the data sparseness problem than others, in our experiment, we found that chi-square test performs better. One possible reason is that the required parameters for chi-square test can be effectively computed using the search results pages, which alleviates the data sparseness problem. Therefore, chi-square test (X2) was adopted as the major method of co-occurrence analysis in our study, whose similarity measure is defined as:

$$S_{x2}(s, t) = \frac{N \times (a \times d - b \times c)^2}{(a + b) \times (a + c) \times (b + d) \times (c + d)} \tag{3}$$

where *a, b, c,* and *d* are the numbers in the contingency table for source term *s* and target term *t* in Table 1. These can be obtained from real-world search engines, which accept Boolean queries and can report the number of pages matched.

Table 1. A contingency table

	t	$\sim t$
s	a	b
$\sim s$	c	d

Context Vector Analysis. Co-occurrence analysis is applicable to higher frequency terms since they are more likely to appear with their translation candidates. On the other hand, lower frequency terms have little chance of appearing with candidates in the same pages. The context vector method (CV) is thus adopted to deal with this problem. As translation equivalents may share similar terms, for each query term, we take the co-occurring feature terms as its feature vector. The similarity between query terms and translation candidates can be computed based on their feature vectors. Thus, lower frequency query terms still have a chance of extracting correct translations.

Context-vector-based method has also been used to extract translations from comparable corpora, such as the use of Fung et al.'s seed word [8]; while real users' popular query terms are used as the feature set in our method, which help avoid many inappropriate feature terms. Like Fung et al.'s vector space model, we also use TF-IDF weighting scheme to estimate the significance of context features which is defined as follows:

$$w_{t_i} = \frac{f(t_i, d)}{\max_j f(t_j, d)} \times \log(\frac{N}{n}) , \tag{4}$$

where $f(t_i, d)$ is the frequency of term t_i in search result page d, N is the total number of Web pages in the collection of search engines, and n is the number of pages containing t_i. Given the context vectors of a source query term and each target translation candidate, their similarity is estimated with cosine measure as follows:

$$S_m(s, t) = \frac{\sum_{i=1}^{m} f(w_s, w_t)}{\sqrt{\sum_{i=1}^{m} (w_s)^2 \times \sum_{i=1}^{m} (w_t)^2}} . \tag{5}$$

It is not difficult to construct context vectors for source query terms and their translation candidates. For a source query term, we can use a fixed number of the top search results to extract translation candidates. The co-occurring feature terms of each query can also be extracted, and their weights calculated, which together forms the context vector of the query. The same procedure is used to construct a context vector for each translation candidate.

The Combined Method. Our previous experiments show that anchor-text-based method can achieve a good precision rate for popular queries and can extract longer translations in other languages besides Chinese and English [13, 14], but it has a major drawback of very high cost in collecting sufficient anchor texts from Web pages with the required software (e.g. *spider*).

Benefiting from real-world search engines, search-result-based method using chi-square test can reduce the work of corpus collection but has difficulty in dealing with low-frequency query terms. Although context vector analysis can deal with difficulties encountered by the above two methods, it is not difficult to see that feature selection issue needs to be carefully handled. Intuitively, a more complete solution is to integrate the above three methods. Considering the various ranges of similarity values among the above methods, we use a linear combination weighting scheme to compute similarity measure as follows:

$$S_c(s, t) = \sum_m \frac{\alpha_m}{R_m(s, t)}, \tag{6}$$

where α_m is an assigned weight for each similarity measure S_m, and $R_m(s,t)$, which represents the similarity ranking of each target candidate t with respect to source term s, is assigned to be from 1 to k (number of candidates) in decreasing order of similarity measure $S_m(s,t)$.

5   Experiments

5.1   Performance on Query Translation

The Test Bed. To determine the effectiveness of the proposed methods, several experiments were conducted. We first collected real query terms from the log of a real-world Chinese Web search engine *Dreamer* in Taiwan, which contained 228,566 unique query terms during a period of more than 3 months in 1998. A test set containing 50 query terms in Chinese, called *random-query set*, were randomly selected from the top 20,000 queries in this log, in which 40 of them were out-of-dictionary. Note that the topics of query terms could be very local, and not all of them had target translations.

Performance of the Proposed Methods. To evaluate the performance for random-query set, the *average top-n inclusion rate* was used as a metric, defined as the percentage of queries whose effective translations could be found in the first n extracted candidates. Also, we wished to know if the *coverage rate*, the percentage of queries whose effective translations could be found in the extracted candidate set, was high enough for real queries.

Table 2. Coverage and top 1~5 inclusion rates obtained for random-query set

Method	Top-1	Top-3	Top-5	Coverage
CV	40.0%	54.0%	54.0%	68%
X2	36.0%	50.0%	52.0%	68%
AT	20.0%	32.0%	32.0%	32%
Combined	44.0%	64.0%	66.0%	72%

As shown in Table 2, all methods were reliable, except for AT method where the top-1 inclusion rate was only 20%. The main reason was that many query terms did not appear in the anchor-text-set corpus, not to mention their translations. The merit of search-result-based methods is thus obvious. In fact, we found these two methods are quite complementary, which can be observed from the results in Table 2, where the combined top-1 inclusion rate reached 44% and the coverage rate reached 72%.

Experiments are also conducted to determine the effectiveness of the proposed approaches for other query sets. In testing a set of 430 popular Chinese queries, which are believed to require English translations, we found that 67.4% of the test queries could obtain effective translations with combined approach in the extracted top-1 candidates. Although the achieved performance for real queries looks very promising, we want to know if it is equally effective for common terms. We randomly selected 100 common nouns and 100 common verbs from a general-purpose Chinese dictionary. Table 3 shows the results obtained with the combined approach. It is easy to see that the proposed approach is less reliable in extracting translations of such common terms. One possible reason is that the usages of common terms are diverse on the Web and the retrieved search results as well as anchor-text sets are not highly relevant. Fortunately, many of these common words can be found in general dictionaries.

Table 3. Top 1, 3, 5 inclusion rates obtained with the combined approach for extracting translations of common terms.

Query Type	Top-1	Top-3	Top-5
100 Common Nouns	23.0%	33.0%	43.0%
100 Common Verbs	6.0%	8.0%	10.0%

Discovering useful Web knowledge for CLIR has not been fully explored in our study. In fact, the translation process based on search-result methods might not be very effective for language pairs that do not exhibit the mixed language characteristic on the Web. Therefore, anchor-text method is also attractive, which achieves good precision rates for popular queries in our experience and may extract longer translations in other languages besides English-Chinese.

5.2 Performance on CLIR Services

The proposed approach has been further tested to see if it is feasible to provide real CLIR services in DL systems.

An Application to Scientific Document Retrieval. We tested STICNET database (http://sticnet.stic.gov.tw/), a government-supported Web-accessible online collection of scientific documents in Taiwan, where documents in either English or traditional Chinese are contained, but no cross-language search is provided. The site maintains a list of 410,557 English-Chinese bilingual key terms, which contains many users' queries and indexed terms compiled by indexers.

In our experiment, 100 Chinese and English key terms were randomly selected respectively from this key term set as test queries. We found that 20% of the Chinese key terms could obtain the corresponding English translations in key term set from top-1 candidates, as shown in Table 4. The feasibility and flexibility to create such a CLIR service for scientific document retrieval has been shown. In fact, the service was created only spending several hours writing such a client program. More detailed experimental results are available in Appendix.

Table 4. Top 1, 3, 5 inclusion rates obtained with the combined approach for extracting translations of randomly selected terms from STICNET database

Query Type	Top-1	Top-3	Top-5
100 Chinese terms	20%	27%	31%
100 English terms	17%	37%	52%

To operate a practical query translation service, the response time must be close to real time. However, neither Web mining method can perform in real time, not to mention the combined approach. If online-mode query translations is necessary, *LiveTrans* server normally generates translations using the context vector approach since the required feature terms can be fixed with a predefined query log and their feature vectors can be constructed in advance. In this way, it is possible to execute a query translation process within only a few seconds on a PC server.

Through creating the above CLIR service, several observations regarding the proposed approach follow:

(1) CLIR service can increase recall rate of retrieval, especially in searching for scientific documents with author search. Most Chinese users are not familiar with the English names of local authors, making many English scientific documents unable to be retrieved via Chinese author names. It is interesting that most academic people have homepages on the Web and their English names are

relatively easy to be extracted through Web mining. With the provided service, such a difficult problem can be effectively reduced.

(2) The proposed CLIR service is more helpful to Chinese users. One challenge of CLIR service is that retrieved results are still in languages that might be unknown to users. Since many Chinese users can read English texts, though not as good at formulating English queries, such service was found helpful to Chinese users, especially for academic people.

(3) The flexibility of creating a real CLIR service was shown. For a content site providing a search service, it is not difficult to add an English-Chinese CLIR service with the proposed approach. However, it is not applicable to every content domain. A suitable domain is that translations of many users' queries can be easily found on the Web. Also, domains with rich bilingual translation dictionaries do not show urgent need of such service.

(4) Dictionary lookup is still necessary. Although the proposed approach is very useful in extracting translations of proper nouns, the accuracy is not always reliable. Users' responses to the inappropriate translations, especially for common terms, were not very positive.

(5) The effectiveness on using users' clicked information to improve translation accuracy is expected but still under observation. In scientific document retrieval application, it's not difficult for users to select correct translations from the suggested lists. However, a larger-scale observation in different application domains is necessary to evaluate its real performance.

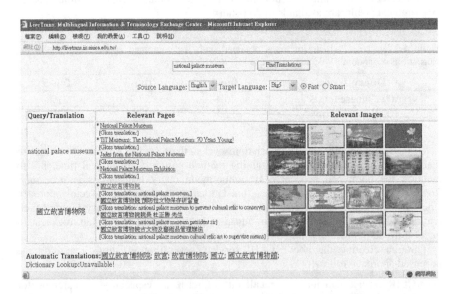

Fig. 3. An example showing an application to Web search, where the given query was "national palace museum" and its extracted translations were "國立故宮博物院", "故宮", and "故宮博物院."

An Application to Web Search. The proposed approach was also applied in providing English-Chinese cross-language Web search as shown in Fig. 3. Users may select backend search engine such as Google or Openfind, and choose either English, traditional Chinese or simplified Chinese as the source/target language. For each query, the system will suggest a list of translation candidates from which users can select the preferred translations, and the server will sort the retrieved Web pages in decreasing order of relevance to the corresponding queries. The titles of retrieved pages are also translated word-by-word to the source language for reference. The system has been tested on some users' queries where most of the obtained translations are really not easy for human indexers to compile.

6   Conclusion

In this paper, we proposed an efficient client-server-based approach to allowing more feasible implementation of cross-language search services in DL systems. A query translation server was constructed to process the translation of source queries dynamically from connected DL's. Several preliminary experiments were conducted to test the performance of the proposed approach. The obtained results have shown its feasibility and great potential especially for English-Chinese CLIR services, even though there exist difficulties to be further investigated.

References

1.   ANSI/NISO Z39.50-1995: Information Retrieval (Z39.50): Application Service Definition and Protocol Specification (1995).
2.   Borgman, C. L.: Multi-Media, Multi-Cultural, and Multi-Lingual Digital Libraries: Or How Do We Exchange Data in 400 Languages? D-Lib Magazine, (June 1997).
3.   Cao, Y. and Li, H.: Base Noun Phrase Translation Using Web Data and the EM Algorithm. Proceedings of the 19th International Conference on Computational Linguistics, (2002) 127–133.
4.   Cooley, R., Mobasher, B., Srivastava, J.: Web Mining: Information and Pattern Discovery on the World Wide Web. Proceedings of the 9th IEEE International Conference on Tools with Artificial Intelligence (1997), 558–567.
5.   Dreilinger, D., and Howe, A.: Experiences with Selecting Search Engines Using Meta-Search. ACM Transactions on Information Systems (1996), 195–222.
6.   Dumais, S. T., Landauer, T. K., Littman, M. L.: Automatic Cross-Linguistic Information Retrieval Using Latent Semantic Indexing. Proceedings of ACM-SIGIR Workshop on Cross-Linguistic Information Retrieval (1996), 16–24.
7.   Feldman, R. and Dagan, I.: KDT - Knowledge Discovery in Texts. Proceedings of the 1st International Conference on Knowledge Discovery and Data Mining (1995).
8.   Fung, P. and Yee, L. Y.: An IR Approach for Translating New Words from Nonparallel, Comparable Texts. Proceedings of the 36th Annual Conference of the Association for Computational Linguistics (1998), 414–420.
9.   Gravano, L., Chang, K., Garcia-Molina, H., and Paepcke, A.: STARTS: Stanford Protocol Proposal for Internet Retrieval and Search. Proceedings of the ACM SIGMOD Conference (1997), 126–137.

10. Kwok, K. L.: NTCIR-2 Chinese, Cross Language Retrieval Experiments Using PIRCS. Proceedings of NTCIR workshop meeting, (2001), 111–118.
11. Larson, R. R., Gey, F., and Chen, A.: Harvesting Translingual Vocabulary Mappings for Multilingual Digital Libraries. Proceedings of ACM/IEEE Joint Conference on Digital Libraries (2002), 185–190.
12. Lavrenko, V., Choquette, M., Croft, W. B.: Cross-Lingual Relevance Models. Proceedings of ACM-SIGIR (2002), 175–182.
13. Lu, W. H., Chien, L. F., Lee, H. J.: Anchor Text Mining for Translation of Web Queries. Proceedings of the IEEE International Conference on Data Mining (2001), 401–408.
14. Lu, W. H., Chien, L. F., Lee, H. J.: Translation of Web Queries using Anchor Text Mining. ACM Transactions on Asian Language Information Processing (2002), 159–172.
15. Lu, W. H., Chien, L. F., Lee, H. J.: A Transitive Model for Extracting Translation Equivalents of Web Queries through Anchor Text Mining. Proceedings of the 19th International Conference on Computational Linguistics (2002), 584–590.
16. Nie, J. Y., Isabelle, P., Simard, M., and Durand, R.: Cross-language Information Retrieval Based on Parallel Texts and Automatic Mining of Parallel Texts from the Web. Proceedings of ACM-SIGIR Conference (1999), 74–81.
17. Oard, D. W.: Cross-language Text Retrieval Research in the USA. Proceedings of the 3rd ERCIM DELOS Workshop, Zurich, Switzerland, (1997).
18. Oard, D. W.: Serving Users in Many Languages: Cross-Language Information Retrieval for Digital Libraries. D-Lib Magazine, (December 1997).
19. Peters, C. and Picchi, E.: Across Languages, Across Cultures: Issues in Multilinguality and Digital Libraries. D-Lib Magazine, (May 1997).
20. Powell, J., and Fox, E. A.: Multilingual Federated Searching Across Heterogeneous Collections. D-Lib Magazine, (September 1998).

Appendix

Table 5 shows an example list of randomly selected Chinese source query terms from STICNET Database and extracted English translations, which are domain-specific terminologies in various fields. Although some translations are not exact, related terms are likely to be extracted in our experiments. For example, acronyms like 'ESWL' are extracted as one translation candidate for '震波碎石 (shock wave lithotripsy)'.

In our analysis, some inexact translations belong to phrases with multiple terms, e.g. 線性二次最佳控制 (linear quadratic optimal control) and 昆蟲病理學 (insect pathology). Cao and Li [3] proposed a technique to determine correct translations of base noun phrase. Basically, multiword translation candidates could be generated by dictionary lookup and the most feasible translation would be picked using the Web as a disambiguation corpus. For example, 'insect pathology' could be created as a translation candidate of '昆蟲病理學' by combining insect (昆蟲) and pathology (病理學) via dictionary lookup.

Table 5. Some examples of randomly selected query terms from scientific documents and their translations extracted using the combined approach

	Source Query Terms in Chinese	Extracted Top-1 English Translations
Exact Translations	腦波圖 (electroencephalogram)	Electroencephalogram
	大腸桿菌 (escherichia coli)	Escherichia coli
	卵白蛋白 (ovalbumin)	Ovalbumin
	機械應變 (mechanical strain)	Mechanical strain
	彈性製造系統 (flexible manufacturing system)	Flexible manufacturing system
	黏滯阻尼 (viscous damping)	Viscous damping
	輕離子 (light ion)	Light ion
	容錯 (fault tolerance)	Fault tolerance
	數值模擬 (numerical simulation)	Numerical simulation
	二氧化碳 (carbon dioxide)	Carbon dioxide
Inexact Translations with Related Terms	震波碎石 (shock wave lithotripsy)	Eswl (acronym, Extracorporeal Shock Wave Lithotripsy)
	共變數 (covariance)	Ancova (acronym, Analysis of Covariance)
	B型肝炎帶原者 (hepatitis B virus carrier)	HBsAg (acronym, Hepatitis B Surface Antigen)
	土壤改良劑 (soil-amending agent)	Pene Turf (a kind of soil-amending agents)
	複合纖維 (bicomponent fiber)	Spandex (a kind of fiber products)
	昆蟲病理學 (insect pathology)	Deacon jw (a plant pathologist)
	老年護理 (geriatric nursing)	Aged care (similar terms)
	前列腺 (prostate)	Prostatic (adjective form)
	線性二次最佳控制 (linear quadratic optimal control)	Advanced digital control
	服務品質 (quality of service)	Service quality

Development of Design Recommender System Using Collaborative Filtering

Kyung-Yong Jung[1], Jun-Hyeog Choi[2], Kee-Wook Rim[3], and Jung-Hyun Lee[1]

[1] Department of Computer Science & Engineering, Inha University, Inchon, Korea
kyjung@gcgc.ac.kr, jhlee@inha.ac.kr
[2] Division of Computer Science, Kimpo College, Kyonggi, Korea
jhchoi@kimpo.ac.kr
[3] Knowledge Information & Industrial Engineering Department, Sunmoon University,
Chung nam, Korea
rim@omega.sunmoon.ac.kr

Abstract. It is an important strategy to investigate customer's sensibility and preference in the merchandise environment changing to the user oriented. We propose the design recommender system, which exposes its collection in a personalized way by the use of collaborative filtering and representative sensibility adjective on textile design. We developed the multi-users interface tool that can suggest designs according to the user's needs in the design industry. In this paper, we adapt collaborative filtering to recommend design to a user who has a similar propensity about designs. And we validate our design recommender system according to three algorithms in off-line experiments. Design merchandizing may meet the consumer's needs more exactly and easily with this system.

1 Introduction

In this research, a Web-based fabric information system has been developed. Recently, the numbers of textile companies that have their own homepages to advertise their product fabrics for apparel through the Web-based E-commerce web site rapidly increase. Unfortunately, traditional fabric information system based on direct meeting and trust cannot give sufficient information to numerous visitors of the Internet sites including fabric buyer for apparel.

In order to develop product with sensibility, it needs to investigate consumer's sensibility for the product. After this investigation, they could develop the system that connects each sensibility to specific designs of product. There had been several studies, such as in the fields of car interior/exterior design, interior design(for example, HULIS) and apparel design(FAIMS, etc.)-especially, those related to school uniform, and wedding dresses [4,12,14]. These systems deal with the various aspects of structure, designs, appearance, structure, shape, color and space. Through these systems, consumers can create the product images on the computer screen simply by entering his/her preferences or needs on the product. The human sensibility on designs was related to their external aspects, such as motif size, motif striking and color as well as the inner aspects of their performance and comfort properties [9-10].

T.M.T. Sembok et al. (Eds.): ICADL 2003, LNCS 2911, pp. 100–110, 2003.

The purpose of this study is to develop design-supporting system based on consumer's sensibility with multi-users interface. Thus we investigated the consumers' sensibility and established databases on sensibility adjectives and on user's attributes. We developed programs connecting database and extracting proper designs according to user's needs. And finally we proposed recommending design system with multi-user interface window. The purpose of our research is to explore the design recommender system using collaborative filtering technique based on server-client.

2 System Overview

We developed the design recommender system because the design industry did not have a system that could coordinate apparel designers and design producers, resulting in an inefficient design development. This system is a project that aims at study how the combined method of collaborative filtering and representative sensibility adjective can be used to build user-adapting design recommender system. Collaborative filtering is a promising technology which predicts user's preference based on other users experience. Collaborative filtering seems to be an appropriate technology to automatically adapt recommender system by presenting a personalized structure to each user. Collaborative filtering systems are generally used for recommender system, which provide personal recommendation based on ratings provided by the user.

Figure 1 shows the design recommender system using collaborative filtering and representative sensibility adjective.

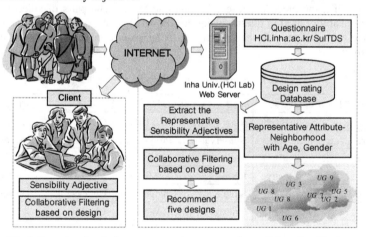

Fig.1. Overview for design recommender system using collaborative filtering

The design recommender system consists of server and client module. The computer uses the PentiumIV, 1.9GHz, 256 MB RAM, and the algorithms use MS-Visual Studio C++ 6.0, MS-SQL Server 2000. We construct the database of design sensibilities and designs made up previously and their connecting modules including collaborative filtering [1-3].

A client is asked to provide multiple preferred sensibilities by using adjectives that describe designs, such as 'feminine, modern and active', as soon as client logs in. After the client enters his/her preferences by using the searching module and the database of representative adjectives of design sensibilities, the system recommends several designs that most closely match the client's sensibility. This is based on the evaluation on the sensibilities of designs in which other users have provided them during previous visits. The database was build by extracting representative sensibility adjectives from the users' evaluations on designs.

If the proper designs are not found, the system goes through filtering technique. The system lets the client evaluate his/her sensibility on a few designs to predict his/her sensibility on the other designs. Also the database on previous users classifies a client into a group according to his/her socio-information. The server regarded the client having similar sensibility with the group with based on representative attributes of neighborhood, such as age, gender. And the degree of similarity of the client with the group was calculated. By sample evaluation and user similarity, collaborative filtering could select the best-fit designs. Filtering techniques recommends the design that the user seeks.

3   Research Methods

3.1   Construction of Database with Sensibility Adjectives on Designs

We decided 18 pairs of the sensibility adjective by extracting them from a dictionary, the magazine, the precedent researches and etc [8,11]. The pairs of adjective about design sensibility used in questionnaire are shown in Table 1. Subjects were asked to evaluate each design with the adjective bi-polar pairs according to 5-point division scale from -2 to +2.

Table 1. The pairs of sensibility adjective on designs

-2 –1 0 +1 +2	-2 –1 0 +1 +2	-2 –1 0 +1 +2
Dark .... Bright	Rural .... Urban	Old .... New
Pure .... Sexy	Conservative ... Progressive	Spaced .... Compact
Dull .... Clear	Curve .... Linear	Female .... Male
Static .... Active	Retro .... Modern	Mechanical .... Natural
Cold .... Hot	Simple .... Complicated	Ungraceful .... Graceful
Soft .... Hard	Oriental .... Western	Childish .... Adult

We selected sixty designs from design books. We tried to choose evenly in the type of design sources, motif size, hue contrast, value contrast, chroma contrast, and the type of motif arrangement, with/without outlines and motif variation as possible. For example, the type of design sources included natural, man-made, imagination, and symbolism and 15 designs were selected from each source. All the designs are classified each 20-design with 4 categorized of Imaginal, Natural, Geometry, and Artificial. After selecting each pair of adjective, which expresses sensibility, we decided 36-sensibility adjective. The questionnaires on Internet web which have 60 designs and sensibility adjectives on each designs are prepared first and open for 3 months, January through April, 2003. The composition of questionnaires based on web follows to 10 phases on 6 designs in one page. During the questionnaire has been online at http://HCI.inha.ac.kr/sulTDS (Figure 2), 512 person(259 males and 253 female) answered the survey. 74926 ratings were collected. The database with sensibility adjective consists of the evaluation rating values and sensibility adjectives, user-attributes, user profile and the design information.

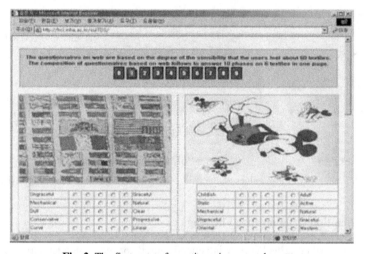

Fig. 2. The first page of questionnaires on web screen

In the design recommender system visitors can express preference by giving ratings to textiles. For textiles that have not been rated by the visitor, the ratings are predicted using other users' ratings and collaborative filtering technology.

Ratings textiles should not be the main occupation of a user. Therefore, the ratings can be conveniently provided while wandering within the recommender system. We noticed in initial trials, that users are hesitant in giving ratings, because giving a rating demands the inconvenience of having to make a decision. Therefore, we provided in the user-interface that the ratings can be provided with very little effort (one mouse click) without disrupting the users chosen tour, if a textile is viewed in detail a rating is mandatory so that the visitor has to provide a rating or otherwise he cannot continues his/her tour.

3.2   Extraction of 5 Representative Sensibility Adjectives on Each Design

It is not easy to evaluate human sensibility objectively because it is vague and non-quantifiable. In addition, it is difficulty to understand it because abstract textile designs are described by limited adjectives. In this paper, we tried to describe the general sensibility of users by looking for representative sensibility adjectives on designs. A rough algorithm, shown below, draws representative sensibility adjectives based on the data collected from users. We used 5 adjectives instead of only one because one is not sufficient to express the sensibility of designs (Figure 3). The results of survey are open on http://HCI.inha.ac.kr/sulTDS/result.htm.

[Setp1] calculating the mean and standard deviation of each sensibility adjective on each design and get its distance from the value of neutral 3.
[Step2] sorting sensibility adjective by its distance in descending.
[Step3] selecting top 5 adjectives and establishing the database.

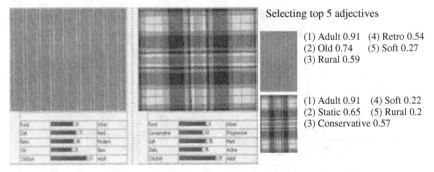

Selecting top 5 adjectives

(1) Adult 0.91   (4) Retro 0.54
(2) Old 0.74   (5) Soft 0.27
(3) Rural 0.59

(1) Adult 0.91   (4) Soft 0.22
(2) Static 0.65   (5) Rural 0.2
(3) Conservative 0.57

Fig. 3. Examples of mean values on the pairs of sensibility adjectives according to designs

3.3   Adapting Collaborative Filtering

Collaborative filtering technology is generally used for recommender services, which provide personal recommendations based on ratings provided by the user. It is currently successfully applied to several content domains: News articles, Grouplens. Music, Ringo. Movie, MovieCritic.[1] Books at Amazon.[2] Collaborative filtering gains more and more popularity in the e-commerce world, since it is excellent technology to improve customer relations by personalizing offers and at the same time increasing sales by targeting products, information and advertisement in a personalized way. Collaborative filtering systems recommend objects for a target user based on the opinions of other users by considering how much the target user and the other users have agreed on other objects in the past. This allows this technique to be used on any type of objects and thus build a large variety of service, since collaborative filtering systems consider only human judgments on the value of objects. These judgments are usually expressed as numerical ratings, revealing the user's preference for objects.

The importance of collaborative filtering is reflected in a growing number of research activities. One of the earliest is the Grouplens project, which focuses in filtering news articles from Usenet, and recently also movie recommendation. Ringo was a collaborative filtering prototype for recommending music, leading to the spin-off company Firefly[3]. Most collaborative filtering systems collect the user opinions as ratings on a numerical scale, leading to a sparse matrix rating (*user*, *item*) in short $r_{u,i}$.

---

[1]   Moviecritic(http://www.moviecritic.com)
[2]   Amazon(http://www.amazon.com)
[3]   Firefly(http://www.firefly.com)

Collaborative filtering technique then uses this rating matrix to predict rating. Several algorithms have been proposed on how to use the rating matrix [6-7]. In our recommender system, we apply a commonly used technique, also used in the Grouplen project and in Ringo, which is based in vector correlation. In the following we describe the underlying formulas in more detail to make the general idea of automatically using other users as expert recommenders understandable.

Usually, the task of a Collaborative filtering system is to predict the rating of a particular user u for an item i. The system compares the user u's ratings with the rating of all other users, who have rated the item i. Then a weighted average of the other users rating is used as a prediction. If I_u is set of items that a user u has rated then we can define the mean rating of user u by Equation (1).

$$\bar{r_u} = \frac{1}{|I_u|}\sum_{i \in I_u} r_{u,i} \tag{1}$$

Collaborative filtering algorithms predict the rating based on the rating of similar users. When *Pearson* correlation coefficient is used, similarity is determined from the correlation of the rating vectors of user u and the other users a by Equation (2).

$$w(u,a) = \frac{\sum_{i \in I_u \cap I_a}(r_{u,i} - \bar{r_u})(r_{a,i} - \bar{r_a})}{\sqrt{\sum_{i \in I_u \cap I_a}(r_{u,i} - \bar{r_u})^2 \bullet \sum_{i \in I_u \cap I_a}(r_{a,i} - \bar{r_a})^2}} \tag{2}$$

It can be noted that $w \in [-1, +1]$. The value of w measures the similarity between the two users' rating vectors. A high value close to +1 signifies high similarity and a low value close to 0 signifies low correlation (not much can be deduced) and a value close to -1 signifies that users are often of opposite opinion. The general prediction formula is based on the assumption that the prediction is a weighted average of the other users' rating. The weights refer to the amount of similarity between the user u and the other users by Equation (3). U_i represents the users who rated item i. The factor k normalizes the weights.

$$p^{collab}(u,i) = \bar{r_u} + k\sum_{a \in U_i} w(u,a)(r_{a,i} - \bar{r_a}) \qquad k = \frac{1}{\sum_{a \in U_i} w(u,a)} \tag{3}$$

Sometimes the correlation coefficient between two users is undefined because they not rated common objects, i.e. $I_u \cap I_a = \emptyset$. In such cased the correlation coefficient is estimated by a default voting ($w_{default} = 2$), which is the measured mean of typically occurring correlation coefficient. The $w_{default}$ is defined as 2 because the sensibility data evaluated on designs has the distribution of bimodal distribution in Figure 6.

3.4   Representative Attribute-Neighborhood

We assumed that the users of a group have similar sensibility on the designs. A group was classified by age and gender of the users. These are the most effective factors on human sensibility so that the recommender system might increase accuracy in the predictions. The algorithm below shows how users are classified according to their gender and age, adapting the Representative Attribute-Neighborhood [6-7]. This study groups users by age, gender through generation gap, discrimination between male and female. For each age, gender grouping from all user profiles, active user who has a profile that is composed of the average of group preference for each Representative

Attribute-Neighborhood is created. We split the users age into 8 age groups (1-14, 15-19, 20-24, 25-29, 30-39, 40-49, 50-59, 60~69). Table 2 shows the data of collected user ratings according to age, gender. This is used in the step determining the number of neighbors used in the prediction [6].

Table 2. The data of collected user ratings according to age, gender (number of users)

Scope	Male	Female	Scope	Male	Female
1~14	12	13	30~39	58	55
15-19	34	25	40~49	35	49
20~24	38	43	50~59	21	30
25~29	59	34	60~69	2	4

Algorithm 1. Representative Attribute-Neighborhood using age and gender of users

```
Num_class ← # of item in ClassID;
Num_gender ← # of item in Gender;
Num_age ← # of item in Age;
For(i=1; i ≤ Num_class; i++){
    For(j=1; j ≤ Num_gender; j++){
      For(k=1; k ≤ Num_age; k++){
          UserGroup(i, j, k) ← satisfying the condition: User Group.
      }
    }
} //Representative Attribute-Neighborhood with gender and age group
Assign(User Group);
```

4   Results and Discussion

We developed the design recommender system to coordinate design sensibility and design products, and enhance the communication efficiency between designers and design merchandisers in design industry. The system has a convenient multi-user interface window, by which the user can input their sensibility on three sample designs into a database for collaborative filtering. The system recommend five designs on screen according to client's preferred sensibility, and he/she can select one of them and also manipulate its image with the control bar. The control bar includes illuminant, flags[none, negative, logarithmic filter, negative & logarithmic filter], basic[contrast, brightness, colorfulness], gamma[red, green, blue], reference[white, black]. This gives the tool controlling in detail on the hue, chroma, value and texture of design. Therefore, this system will become the referencing tool on planning sensibility product to the merchandisers or buyers of design and apparel industry.

Figure 4 shows the design recommender system showing the most suitable design to client's needs. Figure 4(a) is the part that the user enters his/her preferred sensibility in the order and its degree by moving the control bar. The user can select 5 among 18 adjective pairs in drop-down list. The selected 5 adjectives are each given weights: first weight, 100%; second weight, 50%; third weight, 30%; fourth weight, 15%; and fifth weight, 5%. In part Fig. 4(b), the user asked to evaluate 3 designs with sensibility adjectives and these data are used for collaborative filtering with the user's attributes. This evaluation of the client's is referred to predict his/her sensibilities on the rest of 57 designs. Figure 5 shows the results that recommended five designs according to input window with preferred sensibility as shown Fig. 4(a).

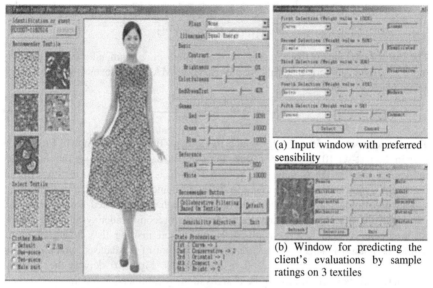

(a) Input window with preferred sensibility

(b) Window for predicting the client's evaluations by sample ratings on 3 textiles

Fig. 4. The 3 windows showing the design recommender system

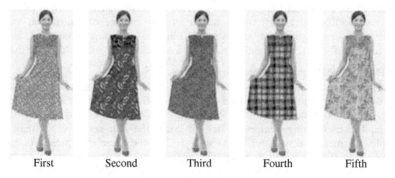

| First | Second | Third | Fourth | Fifth |

Fig. 5. The results of five recommended designs according to 5 adjectives

Prediction accuracy metrics are methods that evaluate the accuracy of recommender system through comparing actual customer ratings with numerical recommendation scores for individual scoring. In order to evaluate various approaches of collaborative filtering, we divided the rating dataset in test-set(r^{test}) and training-set($r^{training}$). The training-set is used to predict ratings in the test-set using a commonly used error measure. We calculate the MAE of three kinds of algorithm recommending the designs. MAE (mean absolute error) between actual ratings and recommender scores is a generally used evaluation measure. MAE treats the absolute error between true customer rating value and predicted score by recommender system. Formally, MAE is calculated as follows:

$$MAE(u) = \frac{\sum_{i \in I_u / r^{test}} |r_{u,i} - p^{collab}(u,i)|}{|I_u / r^{test}|} \tag{4}$$

$$I_u / r^{test} = \{i : r_{u,i} \in r^{test}\}$$

The lower MAE means that the predictive algorithm in recommender system predicts more accurate numerical rating of users. The MAE for several users is then accumulated as follows:

$$MAE = \sum_{u \in U} \frac{MAE(u) |I_u / r^{test}|}{|U|} \tag{5}$$

The test-set contains 50 users for which more than 40 ratings are known. From each user in the test-set 10 ratings are sampled and put aside into the test-set the remaining ratings are used in the training set. We used MAE as an evaluation measure of our prediction experiments in order to report the performance of our prediction approach.

The experiments are based on rating data which we collected from users who participated in our ongoing online trial of the design recommender system. The design recommender system has been advertised in related mailing lists to attract users. While the dataset is still growing, we used a snapshot of the dataset, which contains 74926 ratings by 512 users for 60 textile designs. Figure 6 depicts the bimodal distribution of the user ratings for the designs in the recommender system.

According to the histogram of the user ratings about designs in Figure 6, we can see the fact there are a number of ratings in both -1 and +1. This is considered as the bimodal distribution that expresses the total of the distribution, which is biased to right, and distribution to left. As a matter of convenience of calculation and an economy of memory, this study uses the user ratings as mapping values on 1, 2, 3, 4, and 5 instead of -2, -1, 0, $+1$, and $+2$. This is to expresses the vocabulary pair that has an opposite propensity($[-2, -1, 0, +1, +2] \rightarrow [1, 2, 3, 4, 5] \| [-2, -1, 0, +1, +2] \rightarrow [5, 4, 3, 2, 1]$). The user ratings on both -1 and $+1$ are manifested as mapping value 2. According to the bimodal distribution of the user ratings, we define 2 as the default voting. We found in our experiment that assuming a default value for the correlation between the user rating vectors is helpful when the data-set is very small. For example, we measured in experiments $w_{default} = 2$ as the mean of typically occurring correlation coefficient in out data-set. The application of a default correlation biases the prediction toward the mean, which might stabilize the prediction results for very small datasets. To avoid this bias, we did not use default correlation in our later described experiments, instead, if correlation between a target and a peer user cannot be measured, the peer user is ignored for the prediction for the target users.

We tried the method to recommend the designs by 5 representative sensibility adjectives inputted by a user only (Rep_sen). Other method is to recommend them by collaborative filtering based on design's properties only (TbCF). The last method is the combined method of the two, which use 'Rep_sen' method first and adapt 'TbCF' on the condition that no matching designs exist (Rep_sen_TbCF). Figure 7 shows the MAE according to the number of evaluations. The third method is most effective to predict the evaluation of sensibility on designs. The errors decreased when the number of evaluation increased.

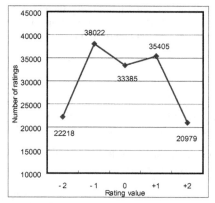
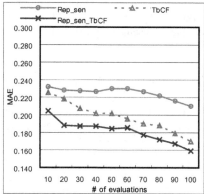

Fig. 6. Histogram of the user ratings

Fig. 7. MAE predicting the evaluation of sensibility

The goal of the prediction is to present users only relevant designs (designs, which they would rate highly), so that the users get the most satisfaction from using our design recommender system. Therefore, a good measure for the comparison of different prediction strategies should be focused on user satisfaction. We believe that the previously uses measure which have been commonly used in the literature, are related to user satisfaction but do not focus on the goals of the user. More appropriate measure should be designed, for example another measure should be designed, for example another measure would monitor the ratings given by the users when they use our recommender system. If the system works well, then only positive ratings should be expected (except for new users). We have not yet investigated further in this direction.

5 Conclusions

We developed the design recommender system to connect the design sensibility and design products, and enhance the communication between designers and design merchandisers in design industry. This system will become the referencing tool on planning sensibility product to the merchandisers or buyers of designs and apparel industry. The system has a convenient multi-user interface window recommending five designs to clients according to the client's preferred sensibility. This system recommends designs to the client after calculating similarity between the attributes of the client and the group members. Representative-Attribute Neighborhood using age and gender for collaborative filtering is used to determine the number of neighbors that will be used for references, and the similarity weights among users use Pearson correlation coefficient.

We tested the performance of this system through three algorithms, manipulating the client's evaluation as well as the database of the other's evaluation. Applied collaborative filtering algorithm was proved to be the most effective to predict the sensibility evaluation. Our design recommender system updates the database and working in Inha University HCI laboratory. This will be made up into set up files and distributed to sensibility researchers to apply in the fashion and design fields.

References

1. Badrul,M., Joseph,A., Herlocker,J., Miller, B. and Riedl,J., "Using filtering agents to improve prediction quality in the grouplens research collaborative filtering system," In Proc. of ACM CSCW, 1998.
2. Breese,J., Heckerman,D. and Kadie,C., "Empirical Analysis of Predictive Algorithms for Collaborative Filtering," Proc. of the 14th Conference on Uncertainty in Artificial Intelligence, 1998.
3. Good,N., Schafer,B., Konstan,J., Borchers,A., Sarwar,B. and Riedl,J., "Combining Collaborative filtering with Personal Agents for Better Recommendation," AAAI/IAAI, 1999.
4. Han,S., Yang,S., Chung,K., Kim,H., Park,J. and Lee,S., "A Study on Design factor Transfer Supporting System based on Sensibility Science,"The Ergonomics Society of Korea, symposium proceedings, 129–135, 1996.
5. Herlocker,J., et al., "An Algorithm Framework for Performing Collaborative Filtering," In Proc. of ACM SIGIR, 1999.
6. Jung,K., Ryu,J. and Lee,J., "A New Collaborative Filtering Method using Representative Attributes-Neighborhood and Bayesian Estimated Value," Proc. of ICAI'02, USA, June, 2002.
7. Jung,K., Lee,J., "Prediction of User Preference in Recommendation System using Association User Clustering and Bayesian Estimated Value," LNAI 2557, 15th Australian Joint Conference on Artificial Intelligence, December 2–6, 2002.
8. Kim,M., "A Study on Sensibility Science Technology of Texture and Colour coordination", Hanyang University, Ph D. Dissertation, 1996.
9. Lee,J., "Case Study on Sensibility Science in the field of Textile Design," Fiber Technology and Industry, 2(4), 433–438, 1998.
10. Na,Y. and Cho,G., "Grouping Preferred sensations of College students Using Sementic Differential Methods of Sensation Words", Kor. Jour. of the Science of Emotion and Sensibility, 5(1), 9–16, 2002.
11. Na,Y. and Kwan,O., "Characteristics of Domestic Textile Designs and Trend Sensibility for Women's Apparel", J. Kor. Soc. Ind., 2(3), 198–204, 2000.
12. Nagamaji,M., "Kanse Kogaku-Sensibility story", Japan standard Association, 1995.
13. Pazzani,M., "A Framework for Collaborative, Content-Based and Demographic Filtering," AI Review, 393–408, 1999.
14. Shinohara, A., Shimizu,Y., Skamoto, K., "Kansei Kogaku e no Shotai", Kumbuk pub., Kyoto, 1996.

Collaborative Querying through a Hybrid Query Clustering Approach

Lin Fu, Dion Hoe-Lian Goh, Schubert Shou-Boon Foo, and Jin-Cheon Na

Division of Information Studies, School of Communication and Information
Nanyang Technological University, Singapore 637718
{p148934363,ashlgoh,assfoo,tjcna}@ntu.edu.sg

Abstract. Harnessing previously issued queries to facilitate collaborative querying is an approach that can help users in digital libraries and other information systems better meet their information needs. Here, the kernel step is to identify and cluster similar queries by mining the query logs. However because of the short lengths of queries, it is relatively difficult to cluster queries effectively using on the terms used since they cannot convey enough information. This paper introduces a hybrid method to cluster queries by utilizing both the query terms and the results returned to queries. Experiments show that this method outperforms existing query clustering techniques.

1   Introduction

People have now come to depend more on the Web or digital libraries (DLs) to search for information. However the amount of information and its growth is a double-edged sword because of the problem of information overload, exacerbated by the fact that not all content on the Web or DLs is relevant nor of acceptable quality to information seekers. Information overload has thus led to a situation where users are swamped with too much information, resulting in difficulty sifting through the material in search of relevant content.

The problem of information overload has been addressed from different perspectives. The study of information seeking behavior has revealed that interaction and collaboration with other people is an important part in the process of information seeking and use [7][8][17]. Given this idea, collaborative search aims to support collaboration among people when they search information on the Web or in DLs [5]. Work in collaborative search falls into several major categories including collaborative browsing, collaborative filtering and collaborative querying [14]. In particular, collaborative querying seeks to help users express their information needs properly in the form of a question to information professionals, or formulate an accurate query to a search engine by sharing expert knowledge or other users' search experiences with each other [14]. Query mining is one of the common techniques used to support collaborative querying. It allows users to make use of other users' search experiences or domain knowledge by analyzing the information stored in query logs (query analysis), grouping (query clustering) and extracting useful related information on a given query. The extracted information can then be used as

T.M.T. Sembok et al. (Eds.): ICADL 2003, LNCS 2911, pp. 111–122, 2003.

recommendation items (used in query recommending systems) or sources for automatic query expansion. An example is given below.

Consider a user A that is interested in novel human computer interfaces for information exploration, and she wants to look for research papers related to this field. Due to her limited domain knowledge, she enters "Human Computer Interface" as the query to her preferred search engine and gets lists of results. However nothing in the top 50 results contains the desired information and she does not know how to modify her query. At the same time, another user B may know that the paper "Reading of electronic documents: the usability of linear, fisheye and overview+detail interface" is a helpful paper that reviews novel interfaces and knows that good search results can be obtained by using "overview detail interface" as the query. Note that B's search history is usually stored in the query logs. Different search engines have query logs in different formats although most contain similar information such as a session ID, address of user, submitted query, etc. Thus, by mining the query logs, clustering similar queries and then recommending them to users, there is an opportunity for the first user to take advantage of previous queries that someone else had entered and use the appropriate ones to meet her information need.

From this example, we can see that the query clustering is one of crucial steps in query mining and the challenge here is to identify the similarities between different queries stored in the query logs. The classical method in information retrieval area suggests a similarity calculation between queries according to query terms (content-based approach) [13]. However the precision of this approach will likely be low due to the short length of queries and the lack of the contextual information in which queries are used [20]. An alternative approach is to use the results (e.g. result URLs in Web search engines) to queries as the criteria to identify similar queries (results-based approach) [5][10]. However one result might cover different topics, and thus queries with different semantic meanings might lead to the same result.

In this paper, we explore query similarity measures query clustering by using a hybrid content-based and results-based approach. The basic principles of this approach are: (1) if different queries share a number of identical keywords in query terms, then these queries are similar; and (2) if different queries share some number of identical query results, then these queries are similar. As discussed, queries are often too short to convey enough information to deduce their semantic meaning. Thus by using the results to queries, our proposed combined method overcomes the lack of contextual information in which the queries are used. However the results-based approach will be affected greatly by the fact that queries representing different information needs might lead to the same results since one result can contain information in several topics. Hence, in order to compensate for this drawback, query terms are considered as complementary information for similarity calculations. Although traditional content-based methods are not suitable for query clustering by themselves, query terms do provide some useful information for query clustering as demonstrated in [20]. Consequently, we assume that a combination of both methods will help us detect similar queries more effectively and thus generate better query clusters. Our experimental results indicate that this hybrid approach generates better clustering results than using content-based or results-based methods separately.

This work will benefit information retrieval systems and DLs in better meeting the information needs of users through collaborative querying. Specifically, the hybrid approach proposed in this paper can be used to improve the performance of the algorithms adopted by query recommending systems to identify high-quality query clusters given a submitted query. Note that cluster quality encompasses coverage, precision and recall, and this will be discussed in detail in Section 4.

The remainder of this paper is organized as follows. In Section 2, we review the literature related to this work. Next, we describe our approach to clustering queries and report experimental results that assesses the effectiveness of this approach. Finally, we discuss the implications of our findings for collaborative querying systems and outline areas for further improvement.

2 Related Work

2.1   Collaborative Search

Collaborative search can be divided into three types according to the ways that users search for information: collaborative browsing, collaborative querying and collaborative filtering [14]. Collaborative browsing can be seen as an extension of Web browsing. Traditional Web browsing is characterized by distributed, isolated users with low interactions between them while collaborative browsing is performed by groups of users who have a mutual consciousness of the group presence and interact with each other during the browsing process [6]. In other words, collaborative browsing aims to offer document access to a group of users where they can communicate through synchronous communication tools [12]. Examples of collaborative browsing applications include "Let's Browse" [6], a system for co-located collaborative browsing using user interests, and "WebEx" [19], a meeting system that allows distributed users to browse a Web pages.

Collaborative filtering is a technique for recommending items to a user based on similarities between the past behavior of the user and that of likeminded people [1]. It assumes that human preferences are correlated and thus if a group of likeminded users prefer an item, then the present user may also prefer it. Collaborative filtering is a beneficial tool in that it harnesses the community for knowledge sharing and is able to select high quality and relevant items from a large information stream [4]. Examples of collaborative filtering applications include Tapestry [4], a system that can filter information according to other users' annotations; GroupLens [12], a recommender system using user ratings of documents read; and PHOAKS [18], a system that recommends items by using newsgroup messages.

Collaborative querying on the other hand, assists users in formulating queries to meet their information needs by utilizing other people's expert knowledge or search experience. There are generally two approaches used. Online live reference services are one such approach, and it refers to a network of expertise, intermediation and resources placed at the disposal of someone seeking answers in an online environment [9]. An example is the Interactive Reference Service at the University of California at Irvine, which offers a video reference service that links librarians at the reference desk at the University's Science Library and students working one-half mile away in a College of Medicine computer lab [16].

Although online live reference services attempt to build a virtual environment to facilitate communication and collaboration, the typical usage scenario involves many users depending only on several "smart librarians". This approach inherently has the limitation of overloading especially if too many users ask questions at the same time. In such cases, users may experience poor service such as long waiting times or answers that are inadequate.

An alternative approach is to mine the query logs of search engines and use these queries as resources for meeting a user's information needs. Historical query logs provide a wealth of information about past search experiences. This method thus tries to detect a user's "interests" through his/her submitted queries and locate similar queries (the query clusters) based on the similarities of the queries in the query logs [5]. The system can then either recommend the similar queries to users (query recommending systems) [5] or use them as expansion term candidates to the original query to augment the quality of the search results (query automatic expansion systems) [10]. Such an approach overcomes the limitation of human involvement and network overloading inherent in online live reference service. Further, the required steps can be performed automatically. Here, calculating the similarity between different queries and clustering them automatically are crucial steps. A clustering algorithm could provide a list of suggestions by offering, in response to a query q, the other member of the cluster containing q. There are some commercial search engines that give users the opportunity to rephrase their queries by suggesting alternate queries. These include Lycos and Google.

2.2   Query Clustering Approaches

Traditional information retrieval research suggests an approach to query clustering by comparing query term vectors (content-based approach). Various similarity functions are available including cosine-similarity, Jaccard-similarity, and Dice-similarity [14]. Using these functions have provided good results in document clustering due to the large number of terms contained in documents. However, the content-based method might not be appropriate for query clustering since most queries submitted to search engines are quite short [20]. A recent study on a billion-entry set of queries to AltaVista has shown that more than 85% queries contain less than three terms and the average length of queries is 2.35 [15]. Thus query terms can neither convey much information nor help to detect the semantics behind them since the same term might represent different semantic meanings, while on the other hand, different terms might refer to the same semantic meaning [10].

Another approach to clustering queries is to utilize a user's selections on the search result listings as the similarity measure [20]. This method analyzes the query session logs which contain the query terms and the corresponding documents users clicked on. It assumes that two queries are similar if they lead to the selection of a similar document. Users' feedback is employed as the contextual information to queries and has been demonstrated to be quite useful clustering. However the drawback is that it may be unreliable if users select too many irrelevant documents [20].

Raghavan and Sever [10] determine similarity between queries by calculating the overlap in documents returned by the queries. This is done by converting documents into term frequency vectors. However this method is time consuming to perform and is not suitable for online search systems [3]. Glance [5] thus uses the overlap of result URLs as the similarity measure instead of the document content, which is quite similar to our approach. However, Glance does not take the query terms themselves into consideration, which can provide useful information for query clustering [20].

3 Calculating Query Similarity

As discussed, our approach is a hybrid method based on the analysis of query terms and query results. There are two principles behind our approach of determining query similarity. That is, two queries are similar when (1) they contain one or more terms in common; or (2) they have results that contain one or more items in common.

3.1 Content-Based Similarity Approach

We borrow concepts from information retrieval [13] and define a set of queries as $D=\{Q_1, Q_2...Q_i, Q_j.... Q_n\}$. A single query Q_j is converted to a term and weight vector shown in (1), where q_i is an index term of Q_j and w_{iQj} represents the weight of the ith term in query Q_j. In order to compute the term weight, we define the term frequency, tf_{iQj}, as the number of occurrences of term i in query Q_j and the query frequency, qf_i, as the number of queries in a collection of n queries that contains the term i. Next, the inverted query frequency, iqf_i, is expressed as (3), in which n represents the total number of queries in the query collection. We then compute w_{iQj} based on (2):

$$Q_j = \{< q_1, w_{1Qj} >;< q_2, w_{2Qj} >;........... < q_i, w_{iQj} >\} \tag{1}$$

$$w_{iQj} = tf_{iQj} * iqf_i \tag{2}$$

$$iqf_i = \log(\frac{n}{qf_i}) \tag{3}$$

Given D, we define C_{ij} as (4) which represents the common term vector of queries Q_i and Q_j. Here, q refers to the terms that belong to both Q_i and Q_j.

$$C_{ij} = \{q : q \in Q_i \cap Q_j\} \tag{4}$$

Given these concepts, we now can provide one definition of query similarity:

Definition I: A query Q_i is similar to query Q_j if $N(C_{ij})>0$, where the $N(C_{ij})$ is the number of common terms in both queries.

A basic similarity measure based on query terms can be computed as follows:

$$Sim\_basic(Q_i, Q_j) = \frac{N(C_{ij})}{Max(N(Q_i), N(Q_j))} \tag{5}$$

where $N(Q_i)$ is the number of the keywords in a query Q_i.

Taking the term weights into consideration, we can use any one of the standard similarity measures [13]. Here, we only present the cosine-similarity measure since it is most frequently used in information retrieval:

$$Sim\_cosine(Q_i, Q_j) = \frac{\sum_{i=1}^{k} cw_{iQi} \times cw_{iQj}}{\sqrt{\sum_{i=1}^{k} cw_{iQ_i}^2} * \sqrt{\sum_{i=1}^{k} cw_{iQ_j}^2}} \qquad (6)$$

where cw_{iQi} refers to the weight of ith common term of C_{ij} in query Qi.

As discussed, the effectiveness of using content-based similarity approaches is questionable due to the short lengths most queries. For example the term "light" can be used in four different ways (noun, verb, adjective and adverb). In such cases, content-based query clustering cannot distinguish the semantic differences behind the terms due to the lack of contextual information and thus cannot provide reasonable cluster results. Thus an alternative approach based on query results is considered.

3.2   Result URLs-Based Similarity Approach

The results returned by search engines usually contain a variety of information such as the title, the abstract, the category, etc. This information can be used to compare the similarity between queries. In our work, we consider the query results' unique identifiers (e.g. URLs) in determining the similarity between queries.

Let $U(Q_j)$ be represented as set of query result URLs to query Q_j:

$$U(Q_j) = \{u_1, u_2 \ldots \ldots \cdot u_i\} \qquad (7)$$

where u_i represents the ith result URL for query Q_j. We then define R_{ij} as (8) which represents the common query results URL vector between Q_i and Q_j. Here u refers to the URLs that belong to both $U(Q_i)$ and $U(Q_j)$.

$$R_{ij} = \{u : u \in U(Q_i) \cap U(Q_j)\} \qquad (8)$$

Next, the similarity definition based on query result URLs can be stated as:

Definition II: A query Q_i is similar to query Q_j if $N(R_{ij}) > 0$, where the $N(R_{ij})$ is the number of common result URLs in both queries.

The similarity measure can then be expressed as (9)

$$Sim\_result(Q_i, Q_j) = \frac{N(R_{ij})}{Max(N(U(Q_i), N(U(Q_j))} \qquad (9)$$

where the $N(U(Q_i))$ is the number of result URLs in $U(Q_i)$. Note that this is only one possible formula of calculating similarity using result URLs. Other measures for determining the similarity can be used. For example, overlaps of result titles or overlaps of the domain names in the result URLs.

3.3   Hybrid Approach

The content-based query clustering method can mine the relationship between different queries with the same or similar keywords. Nevertheless, a single query term without much contextual information can represent different information needs. The results-based method can find the relationship between different queries using the query results returned by a search engine. This method uses more contextual information for a given query that can be used for clustering. However, the same document in the search results listings might contain several topics, and thus queries with different semantic meanings might lead to the same search results.

On the other hand, while content-based methods are not suitable for query clustering by themselves, query terms have been shown to have the ability to provide useful information for clustering [20]. Therefore, we believe that the content-based approach can augment the results-based approaches and compensate for the ambiguity inherent in the latter. Hence, unlike [5], we assume that a combination of both methods will provide more effective clustering results than using each of them individually. Based on this assumption we define a hybrid similarity measure as (10):

$$Sim\_com(Q_i,Q_j) = \alpha * Sim\_result(Q_i,Q_j) + \beta * Sim\_cosine(Q_i,Q_j) \qquad (10)$$

where α and β are parameters assigned to each similarity measure, with $\alpha + \beta = 1$.

3.4   Determining Query Clusters

Given a set of queries $D=\{Q_1, Q_2..... Qn\}$ and a similarity measure between queries, we next construct query clusters. Two queries are in one cluster whenever their similarity is above a certain threshold. We construct a query cluster G for each query in the query set using the definition in (11). Here $Sim(Q_i, Q_j)$ refers to the similarity between Qi and Q_j which can be computed by using various similarity functions discussed previously.

$$G(Q_i) = \{Q : Sim(Q_i,Q_j) \geq threshold\} \qquad (11)$$

where $1 < j < n$; n is the total query number.

4   Query Clustering Experiments

This section provides empirical evidence to demonstrate the viability of the hybrid query clustering method proposed in this paper. The metrics used to determine quality are coverage, precision, recall.

4.1   Data Source and Data Preprocessing

We collected six-month user logs (around two millions queries) from the Nanyang Technological University (Singapore) digital library. The query logs were in text format and were preprocessed (see Table 1 for examples) as follows:
1. The submitted queries were extracted, ignoring other information in the logs.
2. Queries that contained misspellings were removed since such queries will not lead to any results.
3. Due of the large number of queries, 10000 were randomly selected for our experiments.
4. Options embedded in the queries were removed. Examples include options for searching by author and title only.
5. Stop words were removed since they do not convey useful information.

Table 1. Query Samples

cards game	fabrication of CMOS	mobile phone works
communications between people	handbook chemical engineering	NiTi matrix composites
desalination plant costs	intelligence and gene	packaging machinery

Within the 10000 queries selected, 23% of the queries contained one term, 36% contained two terms, and 18% of the queries contained three terms. Approximately 77% of the queries contained no more than three terms. The average length of the queries was 2.73 terms. This observation is similar to previous studies on query characterization in search engines [15].

4.2   Method

We calculated the similarity between queries using the following similarity measures:
- Content-based similarity (sim_cosine) – function (6)
- Results-based similarity (sim_result) – function (9)
- Hybrid similarity (sim_com) – function (10)

Computation for sim_cosine was straightforward using function (6). For sim_result, we posted each query to a reference search engine (Google) and retrieved the corresponding result URLs. By design, search engines rank highly relevant results higher, and therefore, we only considered the top 10 result URLs returned to each query. The result URLs are then be used to compute the similarity between queries according to (9). Note that this approach is similar with [5].

For the hybrid approach (10), the issue was to determine the values for the parameters α and β. Three pairs of values were used, each representing varying levels of contribution a particular method (content-based or results-based) had in determining query clusters. These were: sim_com1 ($\alpha = 0.25$ $\beta = 0.75$), sim_com2 ($\alpha = 0.5$ $\beta = 0.5$), and sim_com3 ($\alpha = 0.75$ $\beta = 0.25$).

In all measures, clustering thresholds (11) were simply set to 0.5. After obtaining the clusters based on the different similarity measures, we first observed the average cluster size and the range of the cluster sizes. This information sheds light on the ability of the different measures to provide recommended queries on a given query. In other words, they can reflect the variety of the queries to a user.

Next, coverage, precision and recall were calculated. Coverage is the ability of the different similarity measures to find similar queries for a given query. It is the percentage of queries for which the similarity function is able to provide a cluster. This value will indicate the probability that the user can obtain recommended queries for his/her issued query.

Precision and recall are used to assess the accuracy of the query clusters generated by different similarity functions. Here, the standard definitions are used:

(1)   Precision: the ratio of the number of similar queries to the total number of queries in a cluster.

(2)   Recall: the ratio of the number of similar queries to the total number of all similar queries for the query set (those in the current cluster and others).

For precision, we randomly selected 100 clusters and checked each query in the cluster manually. Since the actual information needs represented by the queries are not known, the similarity between queries within a cluster was judged by a human evaluator by taking into account the query terms as well as result URLs. The average precision was then computed for the 100 selected clusters.

Recall posed a problem as it was difficult to calculate directly because no standard clusters were available in the query set. Therefore, an alternative measure to reflect recall was used. Recall was defined to be the ratio of the number of correctly clustered queries within the 100 selected clusters to the maximum number of the correctly clustered queries across the test collection [20]. In our work, the maximum number of the clustered queries was 577, which was obtained by sim_com1.

4.3   Results and Discussion

The three similarity functions led to different cluster characteristics as summarized in Table 2. The average cluster sizes of sim_cosine, sim_result, sim_com1, sim_com2 and sim_com3 were 7.86, 4.01, 6.62, 4.10 and 3.96 respectively. The maximum query cluster sizes are 59, 23, 31, 26 and 23 respectively. This indicates that for a query cluster, the content-based approach (sim_cosine) can find a larger number of queries for a given query than the other approaches. Stated differently, the content-based approach can provide a greater variety of queries to a user given his/her submitted query. Here, note that the hybrid approach sim_com1, ranks second in terms of both the average cluster size and the range of cluster sizes.

Further, the results show that sim_cosine ranks highest in coverage (77.63%), demonstrating that the content-based approach has a better ability to find similar queries from a given query. In other words, users have a higher likelihood to obtain a recommendation to a given query than using other approaches. Note again that the hybrid approach, sim_com1, ranks second (65.69%) while the results-based approach, sim_result, ranks last (43.93%).

Table 2 also indicates that the hybrid approach is better able to cluster similar queries correctly than the other approaches. In terms of precision, sim-com3 (99.00%) performs best, indicating that almost all of the queries in the cluster were considered similar. Close behind are sim_com2 (96.97%), sim_result (92.71%) and sim_com1 (87.13%), while sim_cosine's precision is the worst (66.72%). The good precision performance of the hybrid approach can be attributed to the boost given by the search results URLs since sim_result's precision is much better when compared with sim_cosine. For recall, sim_com1 has the best performance at 100%, indicating that all similar queries were contained in query clusters. This time, sim_cosine (90.92%), sim_com2 (68.93%), sim_com3 (67.97%) rank second to fourth respectively, while sim_result ranks last (64.45%). Note that although the recall used in this experiment is not the same with the traditional definition used in information retrieval research, it does provide useful information to indicate the accuracy of clusters generated by the different similarity functions [20]. That is, the modified recall measure reflects the ability to uncover clusters of similar queries generated by different similarity functions on the sample set queries used in the experiments.

Table 2. Cluster Characteristics

Similarity Measure	Sim_cosine	Sim_result	Sim_com1 (α=0.25 β=0.75)	Sim_com2 (α=0.5 β=0.5)	Sim_com3 (α=0.75 β=0.25)
Average Cluster Size	7.86	4.01	6.62	4.10	3.96
Range of Cluster Sizes	2~59	2~23	2~31	2~26	2~23
Coverage	77.63%	43.93%	65.69%	48.19%	43.97%
Precision	66.72%	92.71%	87.13%	96.97%	99.00%
Recall	90.92%	64.45%	100%	68.93%	67.97%

Among the hybrid approaches, the results indicate that sim_com1 is the most promising approach to use because when compared with sim_com2 and sim_com3, its precision and recall performance are only slightly lower than the latter two (87.13% versus 96.97% and 99% respectively) while its coverage performs considerably better than the others (65.69% versus 48.19% and 43.97% respectively). Conversely, although sim_com2 and sim_com3 perform well in terms of precision and recall, they suffer from poor coverage, meaning that if these approaches were used in query recommending systems, users will not be able to get query recommendations in most cases.

Thus taking all three metrics into consideration (coverage, precision and recall), we conclude that sim_com1 provides the best mix of results among the hybrid approaches. Further, when comparing sim_com1 with sim_result and sim_cosine, sim_com1 exhibits the best recall (100%) while ranking second for coverage and precision (65.69% and 87.13% respectively). Hence while sim_cosine and sim_result perform badly either because of the low accuracy of the query clusters (66.72% precision for sim_cosine) or the poor ability to find similar queries from a given query (43.93% coverage for sim_result), sim_com1 provides a balanced set of performance results that suggest its ability to provide query clusters of good overall quality.

Table 3 shows example clusters for the submitted query "computer network" based on sim_com1, with the threshold at 0.5. This example illustrates the usefulness of recommending related queries in that users are given opportunities to explore semantically related areas not explicitly covered in the original query. In the example, queries such as "wireless LAN" and "internet" are suggested as alternate queries that might help meet the current information need.

Table 3. Sample Clusters

computer network, computer networking, network programming, networks, wireless LAN, internet

In summary, our experiments show that users will have a higher chance of obtaining a recommendation using sim_cosine, although the accuracy of the recommended queries will be poor. The sim_result approach improves average precision significantly but suffers from poor coverage and recall. Finally, the hybrid approach, in particular, sim_com1 with $\alpha = 0.25$ and $\beta = 0.75$, outperforms the content-based or results-based approaches since it can provide a balanced set of results in terms of coverage, precision and recall. In other words, the query clusters sim_com1 exhibit good overall quality. Thus, users can benefit from query recommending systems adopting sim_com1 in most cases since they will have a higher chance of obtaining high quality recommendations of related queries.

5   Conclusions and Future Work

In this paper, we compare different query similarity measures. Our experiments show that by using a hybrid content-based and results-based approach, considering both query terms and query result URLs, more balanced query clusters can be generated than using either of them alone.

Our work can contribute to research in collaborative querying systems that mine query logs to harness the domain knowledge and search experiences of other information seekers found in them. The experiment results reported here can be used to develop new systems or further refine existing systems that determine and cluster similar queries in query logs, and augment the information seeking process by recommending related queries to users.

In addition to the initial experiments performed in this research, experiments involving threshold values are also planned. Since the threshold values affect query clustering results, these experiments will determine extent of such effects. Further, alternative approaches to identifying the similarity between queries will also be attempted. For example, the result URLs can be replaced by the domain names of the URLs to improve the coverage of the results-based query clustering approach. In addition, word relationships like hypernyms can be used to replace query terms before computing the similarity between queries. Finally, experiments using other clustering algorithms such as DBSCAN [2] might also be conducted to assess clustering quality.

References

[1]   Chun, I. G., & Hong, I. S. (2001). The implementation of knowledge-based recommender system for electronic commerce using Java expert system library. *Proceedings of IEEE International Symposium on Industrial Electronics*, 1766–1770.

[2]   Ester, M., Kriegel, H., Sander, J., Xu, X., (1996) A density-based algorithm for discovering clusters in large spatial databases with noise. *Proceedings of second International Conference on Knowledge Discovery and Data Mining*, 226–231.

[3]   Fitzpatrick, L. & Dent, M. (1997). Automatic feedback using past queries: Social searching? *Proceedings of SIGIR'97*, 306–313.

[4]   Goldberg, D., Nichols, D., Oki, B. M., & Terry, D. (1992). Using collaborative filtering to weave an information tapestry. *Communications of ACM, 35*(12), 61–70.

[5]   Glance, N. S. (2001). Community search assistant. Proceedings of Sixth ACM International Conference on Intelligent User Interfaces, 91–96.

[6]   Lieberman, H. (1995). An agent for web browsing. Proceedings of International Joint conference on Artificial Intelligence, 924–929.

[7]   Lokman, I. M., & Stephanie, W. H. (2001) Information–seeking behavior and use of social science faculty studying stateless nations: A case study. *Journal of library and Information Science Research, 23*(1), 5–25.

[8]   Marchionini, G. N. (1995). *Information seeking in electronic environments*. Cambridge, England: Cambridge University Press.

[9]   Pomerantz, J., & Lankes, R.D. (2002). Integrating expertise into the NSDL: Putting a human face on the digital library. *Proceedings of the Second Joint Conference on Digital Libraries*, 405.

[10]   Raghavan, V. V., & Sever, H. (1995). On the reuse of past optimal queries. Proceedings of the Eighteenth International ACM SIGIR Conference on Research and Development in Information Retrieval, 344–350.

[11]   Resnick, P., Iacovou, N., Mitesh, S., Bergstron, P., & Riedl, J. (1994). GroupLens: An open architecture for collaborative filtering of Netnews. *Proceedings of the 1994 ACM Conference on CSCW*, 175–186.

[12]   Revera, G.D.J.H., Courtiat, J., & Villemur, T. (2001). A design framework for collaborative browsing. Proceedings of Tenth IEEE International Workshops on Enabling Technologies: Infrastructure for Collaborative Enterprises, 362–374.

[13]   Salton, G. & Mcgill, M.J. (1983). *Introduction to Modern Information retrieval*. McGraw-Hill New York, NY.

[14]   Setten, M.V & Hadidiy, F.M. Collaborative Search and Retrieval: Finding Information Together.
Available at: https://doc.telin.nl/dscgi/ds.py/Get/File-8269/GigaCE-Collaborative_Search_and_Retrieval_Finding_Information_Together.pdf

[15]   Silverstein, C., Henzinger, M., Marais, H., & Moricz, M. (1998) Analysis of a very large Altavista query log. *DEC SRC Technical Note 1998–14.*

[16]   Sloan, B. (1997, December 16). *Service perspectives for the digital library remote reference services*. Available at: http://www.lis.uiuc.edu/~b-sloan/e-ref.html

[17]   Taylor, R. (1968). Question-negotiation and information seeking in libraries. *College and Research Libraries, 29*(3), 178–194.

[18]   Teveen, L., Hill, W., Amento, B., David, M., & Creter, J. (1997). PHOAKS: A system for sharing recommendations. *Communications of the ACM, 40*(3), 59–62.

[19]   WebEx home page. http://www.webex.com

[20]   Wen, J.R., Nie, J.Y., & Zhang, H.J. (2002) Query clustering using user logs. *ACM Transactions on Information Systems, 20*(1), 59–81.

Information Needs in Information Space

Giyeong Kim and Tsai-Youn Hung

SCILS, Rutgers University
4 Huntington St., New Brunswick, NJ 08901, USA
{gkim,tyhung}@scils.rutgers.edu

Abstract. Based on the results of Gregory B. Newby's experiment [1] that an information space of an information system corresponds with the cognitive spaces of its human users, this article further explores the concept of information need. The assumption we explore here is that information needs may appear only when an individual has a partial knowledge of a term. We follow Newby's approach by constructing an information space with term cooccurence and cognitive spaces with term association using twelve terms in the area of Library and Information Science. When the spaces overlap we can get a similarity between term vectors in the information space and in the cognitive space. We assume that such similarity can show how much a human may know about the term. After analyzing the space, information needs are then identified and situated in a moderate similarity group of terms. Discussions about some considerations in methodology and in interpretation of the results are provided.

1 Introduction

Information retrieval can be thought of as matching human information needs to data objects. Traditional information needs and use studies focus on user interaction with systems, and these regard the use of systems as indicators of need, rather than be attributed to internal motivations or other cognitive assessments. After Dervin & Nilan's [2] call for developing theories and cognitive approaches to assessing information needs and uses, the cognitive viewpoint in information science has led to significant advances in the area of user studies and information retrieval. [3] This concern within the information needs literature has now spanned two decades, and many of the gaps in cognitive research have been identified – with ongoing research continuing to fill identified gaps.

Various researchers have investigated the cognitive processes surrounding information seeking behaviors with a goal of designing more responsive IR systems which identify appropriate information to meet users' information needs. Recently, several researchers are trying to reach this goal by studying the concept of information spaces and cognitive spaces. These researchers posit that an act of information seeking behavior to bridge the gap created by information needs involves both the cognitive space of individuals and the information space of systems. An information space is defined as a set of objects and the relations among them held by a system; a cognitive space is defined a set of concepts and relations among them held by an individual. [1]

T.M.T. Sembok et al. (Eds.): ICADL 2003, LNCS 2911, pp. 123–133, 2003.

McKnight [4] was one of the first authors to explore the concept of information space. His research indicates that there are different kinds of information spaces, and like physical spaces, they interact with individuals. More recent research is Newby's [1] study investigating the relationship between cognitive spaces and information spaces. Based on the notion of "exosomatic memory systems," where IR systems are considered as extensions to human memory [5], Newby's quantitative study concluded that for a long-term goal to realize an exosomatic memory system providing high quality information to users, then the information spaces of IR systems need to be tightly coupled to the cognitive spaces of their individual users. The results of Newby's study show that information spaces of systems and human cognitive spaces are consistent with each other and are measurable. The most significant contribution of Newby's study is that he confirmed the importance of understanding the cognitive states of information seekers for designing effective IR systems and used a unique notion of "cognitive space" to define and measure individuals' cognitive state while recognizing that this is a difficult concept to define, to isolate, and especially to measure. We feel that the concept of cognitive space as proposed by Newby might provide an interesting perspective to study information needs. We postulate the following research questions while acknowledging that information needs are a difficult concept to define and measure since this must consider, concurrently, the cognitive processes by which humans attempt to fill a gap in human cognition while recognizing the complexities of an information space.

Research Question: Can individuals' information needs be identified and measured in terms of the information space and cognitive space? If so, how might this be identified and measured?

2 Conceptual Framework

A search usually begins with a problem and a need to solve it. The gap between a problem and answer is called here an information need. Information need is usually taken to be mental states and humans have difficulty in explaining their information needs. An information need implies that the current state is one of incompleteness or inadequacy which makes a person's cognitive state somewhat uncertain. Belkin and colleagues [6] defined this situation as Anomalous State of Knowledge (ASK). ASK hypothesizes that an information need arises when humans confront a problem and recognize that their state of knowledge is inadequate to specify precisely what is needed to resolve that problem. Humans attempt to resolve the anomalies through a database of documents, an IR system. To fill the gap, Belkin and his colleague suggest that an IR system should be a communication system that enable humans and systems to engage in a dialogue in the course of information retrieval. And to have a representative and balanced communication, the IR system should encompass a mechanism for representing information needs and for retrieving texts appropriate to particular information needs. IR system designers do recognize that consideration of cognitive variability influences how users attempting to reach their information goals; however, the problem remains of designing systems able to respond to internally generated information needs of users.

Ingwersen [7] echoes Belkin and his colleagues' viewpoint and argues that the development of a desire for information is a result of a sensing or thinking process. In this cognitive perspective [8], Ingwersen explains the relationship between information needs and human cognitive structure. He proposes that each information processing act is mediated by a system of categories and concepts which is a model of the individual's world. The world model constitutes cognitive space consisting of highly dynamic and cognitive structures which control the perception and further processing of information. An information need then becomes one of the elements constructing and defining the cognitive space[7]. According to Newby's [1] definition of a cognitive space, a set of concepts and relations are held by an individual with the information need itself also defined as a set of concepts or relations. Building on this cognitive framework, this investigation adopts Newby's method to identify participants' cognitive spaces from a set of terms; then, from these cognitive spaces the researchers can further identify participants' information needs from a set of terms about which the participants want to find more information.

3 Methodology

3.1 Definitions

As noted in the previous section, this study purports, first, to discover where precisely the information need is located in a state of knowledge or in a cognitive space of a human being, based theoretically on ASK by Belkin and his colleagues [5], and methodologically on Newby [1]. A brief definition is in order here before we can go on to explain our hypothesis.

First, *information space* (IS) is a multi-dimensional space built by using term cooccurence in a dataset. In our experiment, we have used Library and Information Science Abstracts (LISA) as the dataset. In order to visualize the space, we have decided to construct a three-dimensional space, as Newby did. *Cognitive space* (CS) is another multi-dimensional space, based on individuals' judgments of term associations. In this paper, the CS stands for an individual's cognitive space, and it could be perceived as the individual's state of knowledge. The third and fourth terms are *information space term* (IST) and *cognitive space term* (CST). The concept of each term is the same, but their respective locations differ. This is the reason why we name them differently—IST and CST. Finally, the terms are represented as vectors in both spaces, and the relationships between the terms are represented as *similarity*. To measure the similarity between IST and CST, the cosine coefficient will be used, since it is based on vector space model of IR [9].

3.2 Hypothesis

Figure 1 presents our conceptual framework concisely. Basically, we construct IS and CS with term locations and overlap them into one space. The Newby's study [1] shows that both spaces correspond to each other, even though they are not same as each other. In the overlapped spaces, there are pairs of the same terms, such as *a-a*, *b-b*, and *c-c* in Fig 1. What we measure here are similarities between paired terms. The similarities can be interpreted as follows. The high similarities of *a* means that the individual, whose CS is overlapped with the IS, knows *a* well, and the lower similarity of the term *b* means that the individual knows almost nothing about *b*.

The focus of the research is on the relationship between similarities and information needs. The expected result is that the information needs are mainly located at the terms where similarities are neither very high nor very low. This expectation comes from an assumption that if an individual has a substantial knowledge about a term, s/he might not need information about that term. On the other hand, if an individual knows nothing about a term, s/he might not want to get any information on that term either. Therefore, information needs may appear only when an individual knows something about a term, but not too much, or his knowledge is not sufficient for his needs.

The measured similarities between the paired terms can be categorized into three groups: low similarity group (*low-sim*), moderate similarity group (*mod-sim*), and high similarity group (*hi-sim*). Therefore, a hypothesis can be set for our experiment as follows.

H: terms in *mod-sim* are more likely to fall into the areas where the information need is the strongest than terms in other groups, such as *hi-sim* and *low-sim*.

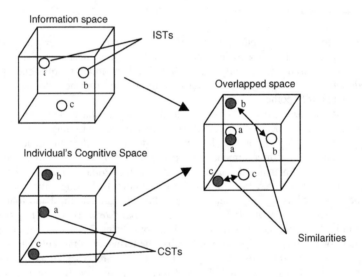

Fig. 1. Conceptual Representation of the experiment

3.3   Experiment Procedure

This research consists of two stages: the construction of IS and CS, and the production and measuring of their similarities. In Fig 2, the first stage is presented from the point of the term selection to the IS & CS construction; as shown, the second stage spans from the overlapping of IS & CS to the analysis. The first stage is very similar to Newby's [1]. First, the 12 terms have been chosen for the construction of cognitive and information spaces. Then, the research is divided in two ways. The first is aimed at examining the term cooccurances of the 12 terms selected from LISA, and then it uses the co-occurance data to construct an information space. The other is employed to survey individuals' judgments on term associations of the 12 terms and to subsequently use the same method to construct the individuals' cognitive spaces. In the second stage, the spaces have been overlapped and the similarities of the term pairs have been measured. Investigating a distribution of the similarities, we have categorized the similarities into 3 groups: *low-sim*, *mod-sim*, and *hi-sim* groups. Finally, we have analyzed the results and identified related issues which merit additional discussion.

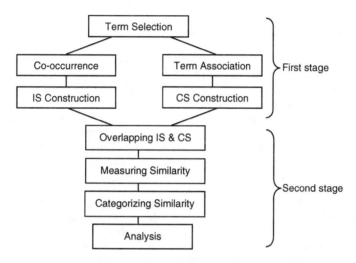

Fig. 2. Experimental Design and Procedure

3.4   Term Selection

Twelve terms in the area of Library and Information Science were selected for constructing the respective spaces. There are 66 term pairs $((12^2-12)/2)$ for the cooccurence and for the term association. The considerations in term selection are that, 1) the terms should be represented in two three-dimensional spaces, IS and CS; and that, 2) the range of frequencies of the terms in a dataset should not be wide.

For the first consideration, the terms are selected in three independent sub-areas in the area of Library and Information Science. The chosen sub-areas are human information behavior, library management, and indexing, which are assumed to be independent to each other. Principal Component Analysis (PCA) was performed in order to identify the latent 3 concepts, which will be 3 axis in IS and CS. We expect that the 3 concepts would be the three sub-areas. The other reason for presetting the areas is the order of the 3 sub-areas by eigenvalues in each IS and CS could be different. That is to say, the highest eigenvalue in each IS and CS is not always same. In the section about overlapping IS with CS covered later, we will describe this situation in more detail.

For the second consideration, each term's frequencies in the dataset should be close to others' in order to maintain the reliability of correlations from the cooccurances. The range of the frequencies has been set from around 1000 to 5000. In addition, the terms should be single-word terms and each term should have only one meaning so as to obtain the homogeneity of the results. If a term has more than one meaning, people might interpret it differently which may cause heterogeneous results. For the truncation, only the singular-plural form has been considered a different form of terms. Finally, 12 terms have been selected as follows: *abstracting, vocabulary, thesauri, keyword, behavior, searcher, intermediary, seeking, circulation, preservation, personnel,* and *inventory.*

3.5   Construction of Information Space

To construct the information space, the term cooccurrences have been investigated, and a correlation-like table of the 12 terms has been produced. The table were not transposed, because the term frequencies differ. Since the table is not transposable, we use a mathematical package, matlab 6.1, to get eigenvalues and eigenvectors for Principal Component Analysis, together with the correlation tables derived from the cooccurrence tables. Three major factors have been identified, which account for 31.6% of the variance. This value is quite low, and actually similar to what Newby achieved in his study [1], but this was expected. Since the variance is accounted for by a large number of terms, the three factors with only 12-term co-occurrences cannot account for a major portion of this variance.

After identifying the factors, we attempted to identify what each factor represents. The first factor (eigenvalue = 1.36) is labeled human information behavior, the second (1.26) is labeled indexing, and the third (1.06) is labeled library management. Using eigenvector results, we achieved coordinates of the term vectors in 3-dimentional IS. Then, the IS with term vectors (locations) has been produced, as shown in Fig. 3.

3.6   Survey

To construct individuals' CSs, we surveyed the individuals' judgments of term associations. Twenty-four masters and doctoral students were recruited from the Library and Information Science department at the School of Communication, Information, and Library Studies at Rutgers University. The aim of the survey was not only to collect data on the term associations, but also on individuals' information needs. Thus, the questionnaire for the survey contains two parts. The first part deals with the individuals' judgment of term associations, and the second part is aimed at discovering the individuals' information needs. As regards the term associations, we have asked the subjects to judge the term associations between the 12 terms with a number from 0 to 10. The higher number means a closer association between two terms.

With regard to the information needs, we have asked the subjects to choose at least two terms about which they would like to obtain more information. Then we have interpreted their selections as the information needs about the terms they picked. Thus, in this research the information need is based only on aboutness.

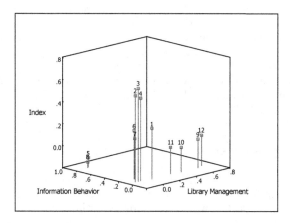

Fig. 3. Information Space with the locations of the 12 terms, *1.abstracting, 2.vocabulary, 3.thesauri, 4.keyword, 5.behavior, 6.searcher, 7.intermediary, 8.seeking, 9.circulation, 10.preservation, 11.personnel, and 12.inventory

3.7   Construction of Cognitive Space and the Overlapping of the Spaces

Using the survey data, we produced each subject's CS. The method to construct the CS is basically the same as to construct the IS. However, in the construction of the CS, more consideration for identifying the factors is needed, because individuals' knowledge about the terms may not be sufficient to specify CS. To do this, we first identified the highest three factors, and then used results obtained from the eigenvectors for these three factors to identify what each factor stands for among the three sub-areas. After identifying the factors, we adjusted the order of factors to that in the IS, and only then could we specify the overlap between the IS and the CS.

Table 1. Eigenvectors for the three factors of the highest eigenvalues in IS and CS, and the identification of the factors

Information Space			An Individual's Cognitive Space		
1st factor	2nd factor	3rdfactor	1st factor	2nd factor	3rd factor
-0.08	**-0.15**	0.12	**0.30**	0.24	0.28
-0.28	**-0.68**	-0.15	**0.36**	0.05	-0.04
-0.18	**-0.47**	-0.08	**0.35**	0.13	-0.02
-0.20	**-0.43**	0.01	**0.36**	0.24	-0.09
-0.54	0.17	-0.04	0.13	**-0.66**	-0.12
-0.18	-0.14	0.08	0.27	**-0.45**	0.08
-0.21	-0.08	0.15	0.29	**-0.17**	0.08
-0.68	0.24	-0.07	0.25	**-0.23**	-0.28
-0.03	-0.02	**0.41**	0.27	0.17	**-0.21**
-0.02	-0.00	**0.21**	0.28	0.13	**-0.60**
-0.06	-0.01	**0.29**	0.21	-0.26	**0.44**
-0.07	-0.03	**0.79**	0.31	0.20	**0.46**
Human Information Behavior	Indexing	Library Management	Indexing	Human Information Behavior	Library Management

Mathematically, the two spaces are not the same, such that we could overlap one space to the other. However, Newby [1] identified that the two spaces correspond to each other. Based on the results, we were able to overlap the spaces with identified axes. An example of adjusting the order of factors in CS is shown in Table1. After adjusting the order of factors, when a three-dimensional space is constructed with 3 axes (x is human information behavior, y is indexing, and z is library management), the coordinate of the first term in Table 1 in IS is (-.08, -.15, .12), and the one of the term in CS is (.24, .30, .28).

3.8   Similarity Measurement

There are 24 overlapped spaces (24 subjects). In each spaces, there are 12-term pairs with terms coming from both the IS and the CS. The cosine coefficient was used to measure the similarity as follows, where a term vector in IS is (x_1, x_2, ... , x_i), and the one in CS is (y_1, y_2, ... , y_i).

$$\frac{\sum x_i y_i}{\sqrt{\sum x_i^2 \sum y_i^2}} \tag{1}$$

3.9   Categorizing the Distances

There are 288 term pairs with their similarity (12 terms $\times$ 24 subjects). Among them, 95 were chosen as the individuals' information needs. The range of the distances is from -1 to +1. We considered two possible ways to categorize the distances into high-similarity, moderate-similarity, and low-similarity groups. One way to categorize the pairs is based on the similarity ranking, but it is not an appropriate way. In this way, each group has 96 pairs, and the ranges of similarity for the groups are not even. Therefore, this way cannot be deemed objective. The other way to categorize the pairs is based on the similarity itself. The range the similarity can be divided into three ranges: $-1 <= sim < -.50$ for *low-sim*, $-.50 <= sim < .50$ for *mod-sim*, and $.50 <= sim <= 1$ for *hi-sim*. This method seems more general than the previous one. We have used this method to categorize the pairs.

4   Results and Discussions

We have 288 term pairs as samples. Among them 4 term pairs have no similarity coefficient. They are rejected, because their numerators are 0. The final number of samples is 284. Among them, 94 are selected as information needs by the subjects. Table 2 shows the statistics about these pairs.

Table 2. Distributions of all term-pairs and term-pairs with information needs

Group	Number of term-pairs	Number of pairs with Information Needs	proportion
low-sim	114	36	.32
mod-sim	77	36	.47
hi-sim	93	22	.24
Total	284	94	

A two-way contingency table analysis was conducted to evaluate whether terms in *mod-sim* are more likely to be terms with information needs than terms in other groups, such as *hi-sim* and *low-sim*. The two variables are similarity with three levels (*low-sim*, *mod-sim*, *hi-sim*) and representative of a manifestation of information need. The similarity and information need were found to be significantly related, Pearson χ^2 $(2, N = 284) = 10.35$, $p < .01$, Cramer's $V = .191$. The proportions of term pairs with information need in *low-sim*, *mod-sim*, and *hi-sim* were .32, .47, and .24, respectively.

Follow-up pairwise comparisons were conducted to evaluate the difference among these proportions. Table 3 shows the results of these analyses. The Holm's sequential Bonferroni Method was used to control for Type I error at the .05 level across all three comparisons. The only significant pairwise difference was between the *hi-sim* and *mod-sim*.

Table 3. Results for pairwise comparisons using Holm's Sequential Bonferroni Method

	Pearson χ^2	*p*-value	Required *p*-value for significance	Significance	Cramer's V
hi-sim vs. *mod-sim*	9.99	.002	.0167	Significant	.243
mod-sim vs. *low-sim*	4.51	.034	.025	Non-sig	-.154
hi-sim vs. *low-sim*	1.54	.207	.050	Non-sig	.207

Even though the follow-up analysis did not allow strict rejection of the null hypothesis of no relationship, we felt we could reasonably conclude that information needs are mainly located in the *mod-sim* group. The results support our assumption that information needs may appear when an individual knows something about a term, but not too much.

Even though the majority of distances with the information needs have appeared in the *mod-sim* group, some distances with the information needs have still been located in the *low-sim* and *hi-sim* groups. This indicates that the aboutness and the individual's state of knowledge are not the only factors determining the information needs. There could be other contextual factors such as situations, tasks, and so on. Other reasons for this inconsistency may be that: 1) the term "information need" may have been misinterpreted. Some subjects, especially doctoral students, seem to have interpreted it as "concerns," "preferences," or "research interests." To be sure, information needs *could* be potentially derived from these. Yet, information needs ought to be more closely related to activities, such as searching. By contrast, the concerns, preferences, or research interests are more an indicative of the individual's cognition. Therefore, they – together with situations and tasks – can be viewed as "other," supporting factors that contribute to information needs. 2) Some subjects might have little knowledge about some terms and thus have just guessed the term associations, or have selected the terms as their information needs arbitrarily.

Using the cosine coefficient to measure the similarity between paired terms from IS and CS, at least one difference in characteristics between the space in the experiment and the space in the vector space model for IR is identified. The document and query vectors of the space in the vector space model have their elements, which are only positive numbers. However, the term vector in our experiment has positive and negative numbers, because of the principal component analysis. A possible problem is how to interpret the negative number as a weight of a term (vector) to a concept (axis). Two possible interpretations are: 1) the negative number would be interpreted as low number, so that a term with -.5 is less similar than a term with +.5 to a concept, and 2) the negative number would be interpreted as reverse relationship, such as an antonym, so that a term with -.5 has the same similarity as +.5. In our experiment, the former has been adopted, because the second interpretation represents a change of the numbers themselves, and we do not have any evidence to support such a change.

Additional implications of these results include that they apparently show that the well-known item by a user is hardly needed information from a cognitive view. Based on such results, we could propose that when a question by a user represents her/his current state of knowledge, a retrieved item, which is most similar to the question, would not be the most needed item. When the retrieved items are ordered by similarity, the most needed items would be located in the middle of the ordered list of the items, because highly ranked items would be already known by the user. This premise could also be applied to a ranking algorithm in IR systems based on the vector space model and similarity ranking system. Results of a number of IR experiments do not reflect this relationship, since the systems have usually included query expansion modules, which would change a user's initial question. Additionally, the retrieved items were ranked not only by similarity but also by related frequencies, such as *tf* and *idf* (refer to the experiment results in TREC at http://trec.nist.gov /pubs.html). To clarify this situation, further study is needed.

What are the characteristics of the "space"? In this study, we have identified that axes, vectors, and the similarity between vectors make up the space. The vectors represent terms; the similarity between terms represents the extent of associations between terms; the axes can be seen as the latent and categorized concepts of terms. Information needs are something which cannot be observed directly. However, in this kind of space, information needs have been identified and located. Even though we do not know the exact meaning of the distance yet, we hope that the result of this study goes one step further in the direction of Newby's [1] long-term goal, namely, the designation of IR systems that could be adjusted for different users in different situations with different information needs.

Acknowledgements. Many thanks to Professor Dan O'Connor for his assistance. Thanks also to Misun Lyu and Muhchyun (Morris) Tang for discussing various aspects of this paper. Note that this paper was originally developed for a project in a class titled Human Information Behavior by Dr. Lisa M. Covi. Thanks to her and to our fellow students in this class. Finally, we thank those who participated in research project for responding to our questions.

References

1. Newby, G.B.: Cognitive Space and Information Space. Journal of the American Society for Information Science and Technology, 52 (2001) 1026–1048.
2. Dervin, B., & Nilan, M.S.: Information needs and uses. In M. , Williams (Ed.), Annual Review of Information Science and Technology, 21 (1986) 3–33.
3. Belkin, N.J.: The cognitive viewpoint in information science. Journal of Information Science, 16 (1990) 11–15.
4. McKnight, C.: The personal construction of information space. Journal of American Society for Information Science, 51 (2000) 730–734.
5. Brooks, B.C.: The fundamental problem of information science. In Horsnell, V. Ed. Informatics 2. London:Aslib (1975)
6. Belkin, N.J., Oddy, R.N., & Brooks, H.M.: ASK for information retrieval: Parts I & II. Journal of Documentation, 38 (1982) 61–71, 145–164.
7. Ingwersen, P.: Cognitive perspectives in information retrieval interaction: Elements of a cognitive IR theory. Journal of Documentation, 52 (1996) 3–50.
8. Ingwersen, P.: The cognitive perspective in information retrieval. International Forum on Information and Documentation, 19(2) (1994) 25–32.
9. Salton, G. & McGill, M.J.: Introduction to Modern Information Retrieval. Singapore: McGraw-Hill Book Company (1983)

An Efficient and Fast Multi Layer Statistical Approach for Colour Based Image Retrieval

Jehad Qubiel Odeh[1], Fatimah Ahmad[2], Mohammad Othman[3], and Rozita Johari[3]

[1] Multimedia University, Faculty of information science and technology,
Malaysia, melaka , Ayer keroh, 75450
jehad.alnihoud@mmu.edu.my
[2] University Putra Malaysia, Multimedia Department, Faculty of Computer Science
and Information Technology, Serdang, Malaysia
fatimah@fsktm.upm.edu.my
[3] University Putra Malaysia, Computer Network Department, Faculty of Computer
Science and Information Technology, Serdang, Malaysia
{mothman,rozita}@fsktm.upm.edu.my

Abstract. In this paper a new efficient and fast technique for colour-based image retrieval is presented. The technique is based on utilizing singular feature in a multi layer system (SFMLSA). The colour features are extracted from image query and images database then distance measure based on city block is used to filter a set of images in each layer. Our approach attempts to overcome the computational complexity of applying bin-to-bin comparison as a multi dimensional feature vectors in the colour histogram approach. Furthermore, the proposed technique eliminate the needs of using the weight matrix, which is usually applied when more than one feature is combined together to judge on the similarity. This needs pre-knowledge of the conditions under which the images are captured. Throughout this paper a comparative study is carried out to examine the performance of the proposed approach with reference to an information theoretic approach using entropy as a discriminator for huge image database. Moreover, we examined the possibility of using the eigenvalues as a discernment feature for colour images, so we developed the necessary algorithms to test this approach. Different database sets has been used and the related algorithms are presented.

Keywords: Entropy, information theory, eigenvalues, content based image retrieval (CBIR).

1   Introduction

Large image databases are usually created and used in many applications, including multimedia encyclopedia, geographical information system and others. The need for an image retrieval system became a challenging research topic [1]. There are several problems associated with the traditional approach using textual information like, the difficulty to describe the image based on content because the same image has different meanings for human and the difficulty in depicting the spatial relationship among the objects. Moreover, the keywords to describe images are subjective and we don't have a unique and standard description to use. Therefore, an efficient and

T.M.T. Sembok et al. (Eds.): ICADL 2003, LNCS 2911, pp. 134–148, 2003.

automatic procedure to retrieve the images based on the content is more desirable, an approach known as content-based image retrieval (CBIR).

In this paper we consider a new approach for colour-based retrieval relies on filtering the whole image through a multi layer system. In the first layer the average pixels value for each band (Red, Green, and Blue) is calculated for both image query and images database. Then a comparison is carried out using a metric distance function. The output of this distance measure is a small set of images considered as the most relevant images and ranked at the top of the retrieval set. In the second layer the accumulative average of the pixels is obtained. Then, distance is measured and compared with a proper threshold value (ε) obtained through the autocorrelation of the distance matrix, to exclude the irrelevant images from being retrieved. The last layer rearrange the retrieved images based on the distance between the standard deviation of the query and the result set, which represent the image contrast. To prove the efficiency of the proposed approach, its performance examined and compared with two other statistical approaches. These are information theoretic approach using entropy and eigenvalues approach. The result demonstrates that the new technique shows higher accuracy in retrieval and more robustness to the varying size of the database.

2   Colour Based Retrieval

Computing the feature signature of an image based on the colour histogram and comparing it with the feature signature of the images in the database, is one of the most widely use technique for image retrieval by contents. The problem with the colour histograms is that they do not provide any information related to shape, texture or location [2].

Colour histogram is a way to represent the distribution of colours in images where each histogram bin represents a colour in a suitable colour space (RGB, Lab, etc). A distance, usually represented by quadratic form, between a query image histogram and a data image histogram can be used to define the similarity match between the two distributions. Typically, 256 colours are adequate to capture the colour distributions of most natural scene [3].

In [4], they presented the problem associated with the original technique using colour histogram for image retrieval. They stated that the original technique, in which the comparison - between the query and the images in the database- using bin-to-bin difference, yield to misleading result in a lot of circumstances because such calculations ignores the relationships between these bins.

In general, there are many problems associated with the original colour histogram approach. The most common problems is the Computational complexity. As presented in [5] there is some research space reduction methods to overcome this problem. The first is to reduce number of bins. The reduction of the number of bins in the colour histogram may cause low retrieval accuracy, that because quite different colours will be classified into the same bin. The second option is to select a subset of the database images for calculating the distances from the query. To select this subset of images is not easy task, since it is difficult to decide which subset to choose. In [6] the problem has been approached through lower bounding the histogram colour with calculating the distance between the average colours of two items. This will reduce the candidate images, then the approach suggests continuing with the original colour histogram approach in the second pass to reduce the false hits, retrieved in the first pass.

The second problem with the colour histogram approach is the perceptual similarity of colour histogram. As stated in [7], incorporating colour similarities into the distance function does not yield to a robust distance function, which corresponds to the perceptual similarity of colour histogram. Methods of non-parametric statistics can be used to determine if two arbitrary distributions are similar. They proposed to store moments representing mean, standard deviation, and skewness for each image, then they calculated the distance between the query and the database by measuring the cumulative distances of these three moments. The problem associated with this approach is that the distance function used is not a metric and the similarity measures based on it may produce false results. They also propose to use the weights for specific applications. The problem with the usage of the weight that it needs pre-knowledge about the conditions under which the images was captured. So, assigning weights may yield to bias the results of the retrieved images.

In his thesis John [8], introduced the entropy as an information theoretic approach to compare and represent colour features in digital images. He stated that the entropy of an image is a measure of the randomness of the colour distribution. The entropy used in this research to augment colour histograms for more efficient image retrieval. A new indexing technique has been introduced to reduce the search space for colour histogram computation. Furthermore, a new similarity measure called the maximum relative entropy has been proposed too.

Eigenvalues has been used in approaches related to feature space reduction and selection, when more than one feature used to register the image. In [9] mentioned that the optimal choice of eigenfeatures is the k eigenvectors associated with the k largest eigenvalues of the image matrix. Eigenfeatures analysis of the images received a lot of attention in applications of image indexing [10], and application to learning and scene analysis [11]. Whenever, we use eigenfeatures analysis we use eigenvalues in indirect way. But upon to our knowledge no researches had done on using the eigenvalues itself as a feature to represent these images. A part of this study we examined using accumulative eigenvalues for image query and images database to be the basis of feature extraction and feature comparison.

3   System Design and Implementation

3.1   The Interface

To construct a visual query the interface should be flexible and allow refinement for the search result. The user may use the query result as a new query. Furthermore, the same interface to construct the image query will show the query result, so the image in a thumbnail will be presented to the user and zooming capabilities should be provided to allow the user to view the image with the original resolution. The user feedback is necessary to refine the searching and to help the system in modifying the retrieving accuracy, this part will be considered to let the user give an informative feedback, which can be exploited by the system. In general there are two scenarios for any image retrieval interface. The user has a sample image to use. So, the user can use the whole image or part of it in searching or the user has a vague idea a bout the image in his mind. We considered the first scenario in designing our interface an approach known as Query by Example (QBE).

3.2 System Architecture

The figure below shows the architecture of the system. The implementation has been done using MATLAB 6.1 on Pentium III PC with 64 RAM, running window 98. MATLAB is an efficient program for vector and matrix data processing. It contains ready functions to manipulate matrix and to visualize image. It also allows modular structure to be used. Based on these facts MATLAB has been chosen as the software prototype to implement our systems.

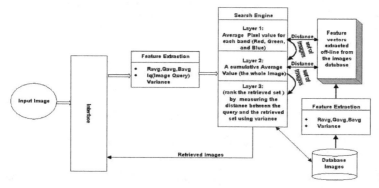

Fig. 1. System overview (SFMLSA)

4 Similarity Measurement and Ranking Technique

There are different methods to measure the similarity or dissimilarity between feature vectors. As shown in previous reference, the difference can be measured by distance measure in the n-dimensional space (the bigger the distance between two vectors, the greater the difference). Given two vectors A and B, where: $A = [a_1 a_2 a_3 \ldots \ldots a_n]$ And $B = [b_1 b_2 b_3 \ldots \ldots b_n]$. Then the distance between A and B can be calculated based on city block as follows:

$$D_{ist} = \sum_{i=1}^{n} |a_i - b_i| \tag{1}$$

City block or absolute value metric is faster compare with other distance measure function like Euclidean distance function at the same time the result will be the same. And since we are looking to increase the speed of retrieval, the city block has gained our selection. The general form representing the similarity between images is defined as follows: An image I is more similar to an image g than another image w if $D_{ist}(I,g) < D_{ist}(I,w)$.

5   Definitions and Algorithms

It is quite important to start with some important definitions before proceeding with our algorithms.

Definition 1: Given that colour image has three bands (Red, green, and blue), the average pixels value of each band for an image I define as:

$$M_r(I) = \frac{\sum\sum_r I_r(r,c)}{S} \qquad (2)$$

$$M_g(I) = \frac{\sum\sum_r I_g(r,c)}{S} \qquad (3)$$

$$M_b(I) = \frac{\sum\sum_r I_b(r,c)}{S} \qquad (4)$$

Where: S is the size of the image in pixels, $M_r(I)$: Mean of the red band of the image I, $M_g(I)$: Mean of the green band of the image I, $M_b(I)$: Mean of the blue band of the image I, r: rows, and c: columns.

Definition 2: Colour histogram is a joint probability distributions of the number of pixels in the image in each band (Red, Green, and Blue), defined as: $P(g) = N(g)/M$, Where M is the number of pixels in the image and $N(g)$ is the number of pixels at gray level g. As with any other joint probability distribution function, the following conditions should be satisfied. $\forall g$, $P(g) \leq 1$ and $\sum_g P(g) = 1$. The standard deviation of $P(g)$ gives a clear idea about the image contrast. In general high standard deviation means high image contrast, while small standard deviation means low image contrast.

Definition 3: Given that x is an input sequence, the autocorrelation of x may define as:

$$A_i = y_{i-(n-1)} \qquad (5)$$

For i=0,1,2,................., 2n-1.Where n is the number of elements in the input sequence x, and y calculated using the following formula.

$$y_j = \sum_{k=0}^{n-1} x_k x_{j+k}$$, For j=-(n-1),-(n-2)....,-2,-1,0,1,2,...,n-1. And $x_j = 0$ for

j<0 or j≥ n.

Definition 4 : Given a vector G of numbers form a set { g_1, g_2, g_3,........., g_n },
where the probability that $g_i \in$ G is p(g_i), the entropy of G is given by:

$$En(G) = -\sum_{g=1}^{n} p(g)\log_2(p(g)) \qquad (6)$$

Definition 5: Any square matrix M has at least one nonzero vector v, which is mapped
as follows: $Mv = \lambda v$, Then v is said to be the eigenvector of M with eigenvalue λ .
Since the image is composed of three bands so for each band there are
{ $\lambda_1, \lambda_2, \lambda_3$,........., λ_n} eigenvalues, and the accumulative eigenvalues representing
each band is the summation of these eigenvalues.

5.1   SFMLSA Algorithms

Within this system we developed two main algorithms, the first (SFMLSA1) to
extract the features from images database off-line and the second (SFMLSA2) to
extract similar features from the image query and compare these features with the
feature vectors extracted from the database. In general (I_q) is used to represent image
query, while (I_d) is used to represent image database, and (D_b) to represent the
database. The two algorithms are developed based on the system architecture shown
in figure 1.

5.2   Entropy Based Algorithms

Within this system two main algorithms for entropy based retrieval have been
developed, the first (ENDA) to extract the values from images database off-line and
the second (ENIQA) to extract entropy value from the image query and compare this
feature with the feature vector extracted from the database.

---

1. For each image $I_d \in D_b$:
- Construct the colour image histogram using 256 bins.
- Compute En(I_d) via Eq. 6.
2. Save the entropy value for each image based on index representing the
   images in a sequence manner.

Fig. 2. ENDA algorithm

1. Apply **ENDA** algorithm to I_q.

2. Compute the distance between I_q and each $I_d \in D_b$ as follows:

   $D(i) = \left| En(I_q) - En(I_d(i)) \right|$, where i=1,.........,n. n represent the number of images in D_b.

3. Sort D in ascending order and maintain the index of the image while sorting.

4. Normalize D such that D= D/max {D(i)}.

5. Get Sz the size of D. For i=1,......,Sz, calculate the autocorrelation of D, $A_{NT}(i)$ via Eq.5.

6. If $A_{NT}(i) < \varepsilon$ then save the value in a new array u. Otherwise excludes the value.

7. Retrieve number of images equivalent to the size of u, based on the indexes obtained in step 3.

Fig. 3. ENIQA algorithm

5.3   Eigenvalues Based Algorithms

Two main algorithms for eigenvalues based retrieval have been developed. The first is EiVAL1 algorithm to extract the accumulative eigenvalues from image database as an off-line process. The second (EiVAL2) to extract accumulative eigenvalues from the image query and compare this feature with the feature vector extracted from the database.

1. For each image $I_d \in D_b$ resize I_d to N x N pixels and convert I_d data type to double.

2. For each image $I_d \in D_b$, compute the Eigenvalues of each band $E(I_{dr})$, $E(I_{dg})$, and $E(I_{db})$.

3. Compute the accumulative eigenvalues of each band as follows:

   $$S1 = \sum_{i=1}^{N} Diag(E(I_{dr})); \quad S2 = \sum_{i=1}^{N} Diag(E(I_{db})); \quad S3 = \sum_{i=1}^{N} Diag(E(I_{db}))$$

4. Save feature extracted from 4 for each I_d.

   Where, I_{dr}, I_{dg}, I_{db} : represent Images database bands (red, green, and blue) respectively.

Fig. 4. EiVAL1 Algorithm

1. Follow step 1,2,3,and 4 in EiVAL1 algorithm to extract features from I_q. Save these features as follows:

   E1: represent the sum of eigenvalues for the red band of I_q; E2: represent the sum of eigenvalues for the green band of I_q; E3: represent the sum of eigenvalues for the blue band of I_q.

2. For each $I_d \in D_b$ Calculate the distance between each band of I_q and the corresponding band of I_d, such that: D1= $\left| E1 - S1 \right|$; D2= $\left| E2 - S2 \right|$; D3= $\left| E3 - S3 \right|$

3. Sort D1, D2, and D3 in ascending order and maintain the actual indexes, which represent all I_d in three arrays as k1, k2 and k3.

4. For i=1,...,n, where n represent the size of D_b. If k1(i)==k2(i)==k3(i) then add the index to an empty array u.

5. Combine the three array of distances in one array as follow: T = D1+D2+D3.

6. Sort T in ascending order and maintain the actual indexes for all I_d.

7. Normalize total by dividing over the maximum value as follow: NT=T/max {T}.

8. Get Sz the size of NT. For i=1,...,Sz, calculate the autocorrelation of NT, $A_{NT}(i)$ via Eq.5.

9. If $A_{NT}(i) < \varepsilon$ then save the value in a new array NT2. Otherwise exclude the value.

10. Get Sz1 the size of NT2. Then, retrieve the corresponding indexes from 6, and save the new indexes in a new array called J.

11. Search u and J for similar indexes. Then exclude the similar indexes from J, and save u1 as u1= u + J.

12. u1 represent the set of candidate images to be retrieved from the D_b. Retrieve and display.

Fig. 5. EiVAL2 Algorithm

6   Evaluation Criteria

Using precision and recall to measure the accuracy of retrieval system still the most prominent technique. Suppose a data set dB and a query q is given. The data set might be divided into two sets: the relevant to the query q, $R(q)$ and its complement, the set of irrelevant images $\overline{R}(q)$. Suppose that the query q is given to a data set and that it returns a set of images A(q) as the answer. Then, the precision of the answer is the fraction of the returned images that is indeed relevant for the query [12].

$$\text{Precision} = \frac{|A(q) \cap R(q)|}{|A(q)|} \qquad (7)$$

And the recall is the fraction of relevant images that is returned by query with respect to the whole set of the relevant images in the database.

$$\text{Recall} = \frac{|A(q) \cap R(q)|}{|R(q)|} \qquad (8)$$

The above technique is valid for a single query. In general retrieval algorithms are evaluated by running them for several queries. So, to evaluate the performance of an algorithm over all test queries, the average precision at each recall level should be considered [13]. The average precision may define as:

$$\overline{P}(r) = \frac{\sum_{i=1}^{N_q} P_i(r)}{N_q} \qquad (9)$$

Where $\overline{P}(r)$ is the average precision at recall level r, N_q is the number of queries, and $P_i(r)$ is the precision at recall level r for the i-th query.

7   Experiments

7.1   Experiments Setup

The total database size is 2000 images chosen from a set of 10,000 images. These images represent different scenes with different colours. The images, which are close in colours or depicting similar events (i.e. swimming, car racing, etc) are grouped together, this was important in reducing the effect of the subjective measurement for precision and recall. The image databases are divided to different sets (200,400,600,800,1000,1200,1400,1600,1800, and 2000) where the higher set contains the lower set of images. From each database a set of 10 images is chosen randomly for testing. The images named in a sequential manner to ease indexing it in the processing stages. Choosing the threshold value has a great effect on the recall and precision. As mentioned before the selection was made based on the autocorrelation of the distance matrix. Autocorrelation values increased dramatically if the gab between two subsequent distance values is high at this point we may choose the threshold value because this give an indication that the distance between the query and that image and the subsequence images is high too. After some trial we used $\varepsilon <= 2$ for SFMLSA and Eigenvalues approach. But for entropy we considered the sensitivity of the Entropy function. It is most likely that if the change in the probability distribution between two images is small then the corresponding distance based on entropy will be small too. So based on this fact we choose $\varepsilon <= 0.5$ for database sets (200,600,1000) and $\varepsilon <= 0.1$ for database set (2000).

7.2   Average Recall and Precision of SFMLS Technique

Within this part of testing, the average recalls and average precision for the 10 images for each database set was calculated. This technique helps in examining the overall precision and recall of the system. It is quite important to be precise in identifying the relevant images with regards to the query, so to remove any perceptual biases of the examiner we used two tools to reduce this effect, these are random sampling and large database size. A large database size ensures that a particular class of images does not affect the method being used and enable to test the scalability of the method. Furthermore, to ensure consistency a record for the relevant images for each query image was maintained in a sequential way to make sure that in the higher database set these images considered as relevant too.The following table shows the average recall and average precision for the different database sets calculated based on equation 7 and 8.

Table 1. Recall and Precision (SFMLIS)

Database size	Average recall	Average precision
200	0.78	0.73
400	0.71	0.78
600	0.80	0.80
800	0.77	0.82
1000	0.77	0.87
1200	0.76	0.87
1400	0.75	0.85
1600	0.77	0.90
1800	0.77	0.90
2000	0.75	0.92
Average	0.76	0.84

Simple analysis of the above table shows that the algorithm is scalable with the different sizes of the databases. The highest precision value (0.92) is obtained through the biggest database size (2000 images), there is a linear relationship between the size of the database and the precision values, while the recall is not affected much by the increasing size of the database. We believe that the recall values may increase through allowing the user to interfere the retrieving process by implementing a suitable relevance feedback technique, which may increase the threshold value to retrieve more relevant images.

7.3   Entropy Experimental Results

The following figure shows the recall and precision calculated based on equation 7 and 8. A total number of 40 images were tested within this system. From each database a set of 10 images was chosen randomly for testing.

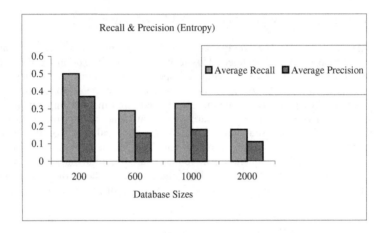

Fig. 6. Recall and Precision (Entropy)

7.4   Eigenvalues Experimental Results

The following figure shows the recall and precision calculated based on equation 7 and 8. A total number of 40 images were tested within this system. From each database a set of 10 images was chosen randomly for testing

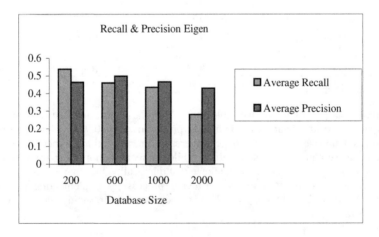

Fig. 7. Recall and Precision (Eigenvalues)

8   Discussion

The following figures show the comparison between the different approaches (SFMLSA versus Entropy and SFMLSA versus Eigenvalues). The comparison was carried out with different database sets (200,600,1000,and 2000) and the same images query is used to test the different approaches based on overall recall and overall precision with respect to different database sizes.

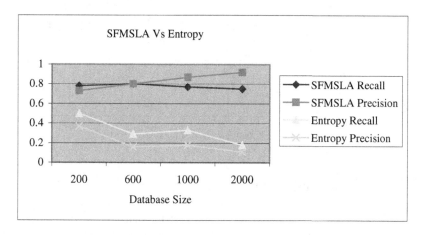

Fig. 8. SFMLSA versus Entropy

As shown in the figure above, the SFMLSA approach given a higher precision and recall compared with the entropy approach. SFMLSA best recall and precision was (80%) and (92%) respectively, while entropy best recall and precision was (50%) and (37%) respectively. Furthermore, the figure shows that the recall in SMLSA starts to decrease slightly with the increasing of the database size, while the precision (accuracy) is increasing all the way. We believe that applying relevance feedback (RF) in this case will allow retrieving more images based on the user interference by increasing the range of the threshold value slightly.

The following figure shows the comparison between SFMLSA and Eigenvalues approach. Eigenvalues best recall and precision was (54%) and (50%) respectively. As a summary, using Eigenvalues as a primary feature to discriminate the images can be more productive and accurate than the information theoretic approach (entropy), at the same time still far away from achieving competitive results compared with our structured approach SFMLSA.

(See the appendix to view samples of the query results for one image using the different approach.)

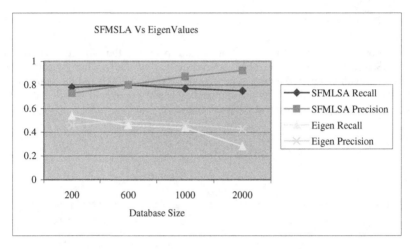

Fig. 9. SFMLSA versus Eigenvalues

9   Conclusions and Future Work

We approached the colour based image retrieval through utilizing the probability theory in a multi layer system. The filtration is carried out in the different layers using single feature at a time calculated based on the distribution of the pixel values. The proposed approach eliminates the need to use the weight matrix, which most of the time bias the results dramatically and need knowledge in the image domain. Moreover, this approach reduces the computational complexity, which associated with comparing multi feature vectors extracted through the colour histogram in the bin-to-bin comparison. In implementing this system two algorithms are developed. SFMLSA1, which is extracted the necessary features from the images database as an off-line process and SFMLSA2, which is extracted the same features from the query image and handling the different layers. Furthermore, a new threshold selection technique based on the autocorrelation of the distance matrix has been introduced. Different database sets is used to evaluate the proposed technique, the results shows high precision rate up to (92%) and reasonable recall rate up to (80%). Also, we found that there is a liner relationship between the size of the database and the precision, which mean by increasing the size of the database we may achieve better precision. We should state that the interpretation of the image as a joint probability density function made it possible to apply the concept of entropy to the images. Through out this research we developed another system with two main algorithms (ENDA and ENIQA) to examine the validity of using entropy in CBIR. We examined a set of images from different database sets in the two systems respectively and the results showed the SFMLSA system achieved better precision and recall compared with the entropy approach. Eigenvalue approach may achieve better result compared with the entropy. We developed two main algorithms (EiVAL1 and EiVAL12) to test the validity of using Eigenvalues as a primary feature to examine the similarity in CBIR. We believe this approach is more promising than the entropy approach and there are rooms for enhancement to achieve better results, especially if the eigenvectors come to the scene. As a future interest in our research we are planning to add one more layer to compare the images based on shape. We will use the result set obtained from the previous three layers – in SFMSLA – to be as input for the last layer using shape. Shape feature will be used as a higher layer since it considered as a slow feature to compute and it is obvious that the fast features should be applied first to reduce the set of candidate images for further processing. The shape retrieval will be based on a modified edge detection technique. This layer will have a major impact on the reducing the size of the result set and on ranking the candidate images. Furthermore, applying relevance feedback is one of our interests in this system to enhance the recall value.

References

[1]   J. Q. Odeh, F. Ahmad, M. Othman, R. Johari. "Image retrieval system based on colour histogram localization and colour pair segmentation". 2nd IASTED conference VIIP 2002, 41–45.

[2]   Apostol Natsev, Rajeev Rastogi, and Kyuseok Shim. " WARLUS: A similarity retrieval algorithm for image database". ACM 1-58113-084-8, 1999.

[3]   James Hafiner, Harpreet S, Sawhney, Will Equitz, Myron Flicker, and Wayne Niblack (1995). "Efficient Colour Histogram Indexing for Quadratic Form Distance Function", IEEE 0162-8828/95.

[4]   Guojun Lu and Jason Philips (1998). "Using perceptually weighted histograms for colour-based image retrieval". In proceeding of ICSP, 1998.

[5]   Guojum Lu . "Techniques and data structure for efficient multimedia retrieval based similarity". IEEE Transactions on Multimedia, Vol.4, No.3. September 2002.

[6]   C. Faloutsos. "Searching multimedia database by content". Norwell, MA: Kluwer, 1996.

[7]   M. Sticker. " Similarity of colour images". SPIE Proceeding series, 1995, San Joes.

[8]   John M. Zachary. An Information theoretic approach to content based image retrieval. Ph.D. dissertation, Louisiana state university, 2000.

[9]   K. Fukunaga. Introduction to Statistical Recognition. Acadmic Press. New York,second edition.

[10]   D.L.Swets and J. Weng. "Using discriminant eigenfeatures for image retrieval".IEEE Transaction on Pattern Analysis and Machine Intelligent, 18(8):831–836,August,1996.

[11]   H. Murase and N. Nayar. "Visual learning and recognition of 3D objects from appearance". International Journal of Computer Vision,14:5–24,1995.

[12]   Arnold W. M. Simeulders, "Content based Image retrieval at the End of the Early Years", IEEE Transaction on Pattern Analysis and Machine Intelligence, vol 22, No. 12, Dec– 2000.

[13]   Baeza Yates. Modern Information Retrieval. Publisher: Addison Wesley, 1999.

Appendix

The following figures shows a sample of the query result of the different approach, the database size is 2000 images, the image query shown at the upper left corner, and the result ranks at (top-down, left-right) sequence.

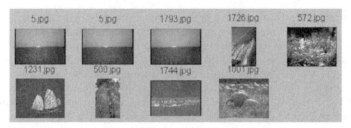

Eigenvalues approach (result set of image query no. 5)

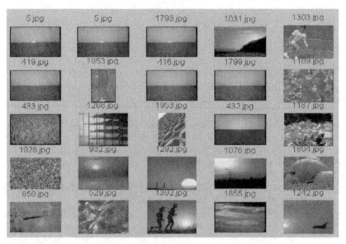

SFMLSA approach (result set of image query no. 5)

Entropy approach (result set of image query no. 5)

Supporting Multilingual Information Retrieval in Web Applications: An English-Chinese Web Portal Experiment[*]

Jialun Qin[1], Yilu Zhou[1], Michael Chau[2], and Hsinchun Chen[1]

[1] Department of Management Information Systems,
The University of Arizona,
Tucson, Arizona 85721, USA
{qin,yilu}@u.arizona.edu
hchen@eller.arizona.edu
[2] School of Business,
The University of Hong Kong,
Pokfulam, Hong Kong
mchau@business.hku.hk

Abstract. Cross-language information retrieval (CLIR) and multilingual information retrieval (MLIR) techniques have been widely studied, but they are not often applied to and evaluated for Web applications. In this paper, we present our research in developing and evaluating a multilingual English-Chinese Web portal in the business domain. A dictionary-based approach has been adopted that combines phrasal translation, co-occurrence analysis, and pre- and post-translation query expansion. The approach was evaluated by domain experts and the results showed that co-occurrence-based phrasal translation achieved a 74.6% improvement in precision when compared with simple word-by-word translation.

1 Introduction

The increasing diversity of the Internet has created a tremendous number of multilingual resources on the Web. Web pages have been written in almost every popular language in the world, including various Asian, European, and Middle East languages. It is difficult for a user to retrieve documents written in a language that is not spoken by him/her. Supporting cross-language information retrieval (CLIR) and multilingual information retrieval (MLIR) for Web applications has become a pressing issue. In this paper, we report our experience in designing and evaluating a Web portal called ECBizPort that supports cross-language retrieval for Web pages in different languages.

---

[*] This project was supported in part by an NSF DLI-2 grant, "High-performance Digital Library Systems: From Information Retrieval to Knowledge Management," IIS-9817473, 1999/4–2002/3.

T.M.T. Sembok et al. (Eds.): ICADL 2003, LNCS 2911, pp. 149–152, 2003.

2 Literature Review

Most reported approaches translate queries into the document language, and then perform monolingual retrieval. There are three main approaches in CLIR and MLIR: using machine translation, a parallel corpus, or a bilingual dictionary. Machine translation-based (MT-based) approach uses existing machine translation techniques to provide automatic translation of queries. The MT-based approach is simple to apply, but the output quality of MT is still not very satisfying, especially for western and oriental language pairs. A corpus-based approach analyzes large document collections (parallel or comparable corpus) to construct a statistical translation model. Although the approach is promising, the performance relied largely on the quality of the corpus. Also, parallel corpus is very difficult to obtain, especially for western and oriental language pairs. In a dictionary-based approach, queries are translated by looking up terms in a bilingual dictionary and using some or all of the translated terms. This is the most popular approach because of its simplicity and the wide availability of machine-readable dictionaries.

By using simple dictionary translations without addressing the problem of translation ambiguity, the effectiveness of CLIR can be 60% lower than that of monolingual retrieval [3]. Various techniques have been proposed to reduce the ambiguity and errors introduced during query translation. Among these techniques, phrasal translation, co-occurrence analysis, and query expansion are the most popular. Phrasal translation techniques are often used to identify multi-word concepts in the query and translate them as phrases [3, 6]. Co-occurrence statistics help select the best translation(s) among all translation candidates by assuming that the correct translations of query terms tend to co-occur more frequently than the incorrect translations do in documents written in the target language [3, 5, 8, 11]. Query expansion assumes that additional terms that are related to the primary concepts in the query are likely to be relevant, and by adding these terms to the query, the impact of incorrect terms generated during the translation can be reduced [1].

Most research discussed has focused on the study of technologies that improve retrieval precision on standard TREC collections rather than real-world, interactive Web retrieval applications. Only a few Web-based CLIR and MLIR systems exist, such as Keizai [9], Arabvista, and MULINEX [4]. However, no evaluation data was available for most of these systems, leaving their effectiveness uncertain.

3 Proposed Approach and System Prototype

To support multilingual retrieval on the Web, we apply an integrated set of CLIR and MLIR techniques in the Web environment and propose an architectural design for multilingual information retrieval on the Web. Our architecture consists of five major components: Web Spider, Pre-translation Query Expansion, Query Translation, Post-translation Query Expansion, and Document Retrieval. The Web Spider component is responsible for building our document collections for the Web portal. These documents are not only the information resources provided to users, but also a comparable corpus that can be used for translation disambiguation and query expansion. The Pre-translation Query Expansion component takes a search query and sends it to the local document collection to perform a search. To achieve higher efficiency, our approach followed the local feedback method [2]. The Query Translation component is responsible for translating search queries in the source language into the target language. The Post-translation Query Expansion component expands the query in the target language in a way similar to Pre-translation expansion. Finally, the Document Retrieval component takes the query in the target language and retrieving the relevant documents from the text collection.

Based on the architecture, we implemented ECBizPort, an English-Chinese Web portal for business intelligence in the information technology (IT) domain. The AI Lab SpidersRUs toolkit (http://ai.bpa.arizona.edu/spidersrus/) is used to build the English and Chinese collections for the Web portal. Each collection consists of about 100,000 IT business Web pages. Query term translations are performed using the LDC (Linguistic Data Consortium) English-Chinese bilingual wordlists as our dictionaries. Phrasal translations [7] and co-occurrence analysis were also implemented.

We built our own lexicon for the IT business domain in both English and Chinese in order to support query expansion using the Arizona Noun Phraser [12] and the Mutual Information technique [10]. The extracted terms were used as the lexicons for both pre- and post-translation query expansion. The last component, Document Retrieval, was supported by the AI Lab SpidersRUs toolkit.

4   System Evaluation

An experiment was designed and conducted to evaluate the performance of our system. Basically, we followed the standard TREC evaluation process in our experiment design. However, because there was no established relevance judgment available for precision and recall calculation, we recruited human judges to determine the relevance of each document. Three business school graduate students, fluent in both English and Chinese, served as the experts. They identified seven Chinese queries of interest in the business IT domain and translated these queries into English as the base queries. The original Chinese queries were used to get monolingual retrieval results. Such monolingual retrieval represents the performance of traditional information retrieval. The English base queries were used to get cross-lingual runs based on five settings: word-by-word translation, phrasal translation with co-occurrence analysis, phrasal translation with co-occurrence analysis and pre-translation expansion, phrasal translation with co-occurrence analysis and post-translation expansion, and phrasal translation with co-occurrence analysis and both pre- and post-translation expansion.

The results were compared with two standard benchmark settings: (1) monolingual retrieval (the best-case scenario), and (2) word-by-word translation (the worst-case scenario). In general, the results are encouraging. All methods except word-by-word translation achieved over 70% of the performance of the monolingual system.

We also observed that all four methods based on phrasal translation and/or query expansions perform significantly better than word-by-word translation, the baseline translation method. Phrasal and co-occurrence disambiguation performed much better than word-by-word translation, achieving a 74.6% improvement. However, pre-translation and post-translation expansion did not greatly improve the performance.

5 Future Directions

This study demonstrated the feasibility of applying CLIR and MLIR techniques in Web applications and the experimental results are encouraging. The proposed approach can be applied in other Web-based applications or digital libraries. In the future, we plan to integrate other CLIR and MLIR techniques into the Web portal to make it more robust. In addition, we plan to expand the Web portal to more languages, such as Spanish and Arabic. Such expansion will allow us to study whether the reported techniques will perform differently for a multilingual Web portal with more than two languages.

References

1. Ballesteros, L. & Croft, B. (1996). "Dictionary Methods for Cross-Lingual Information Retrieval," in *Proc. of the 7th DEXA Conference on Database and Expert Systems Applications*, Zurich, Switzerland, September 1996, pp. 791–801.
2. Ballesteros, L. & Croft, B. (1997). "Phrasal Translation and Query Expansion Techniques for Cross-language Information Retrieval," *SIGIR'97*, Philadelphia, PA, July 1997, pp. 84–91.
3. Ballesteros, L. & Croft, B. (1998). "Resolving Ambiguity for Cross-language Retrieval," *SIGIR'98*, Melbourne, Australia, August 1998, pp. 64–71.
4. Capstick, J., Diagne, A. K., et al. (1998). "MULINEX: Multilingual Web Search and Navigation," in *Proc. of Natural Language Processing and Industrial Applications*, Moncton, Canada, 1998.
5. Gao, J., Nie, J.-Y., et al. (2001). "Improving Query Translation for Cross-language Information Retrieval Using Statistical Models," *SIGIR'01*, New Orleans, Louisiana, 2001, pp. 96–104.
6. Hull, D. A. & Grefenstette, G. (1996). "Querying across Languages: a Dictionary-based Approach to Multilingual Information Retrieval," *SIGIR'96*, Zurich, Switzerland, 1996.
7. Kwok, K. L. (2000). "Exploiting a Chinese-English Bilingual Wordlist for English-Chinese Cross Language Information Retrieval," in *Proc. of the Fifth Int'l Workshop on Information Retrieval with Asian Languages*, Hong Kong, China, 2000, pp. 173–179.
8. Maeda, A., Sadat, F., et al. (2000). "Query Term Disambiguation for Web Cross-Language Information Retrieval using a Search Engine," in *Proc. of the Fifth Int'l Workshop on Info. Retrieval with Asian Languages*, Hong Kong, China, 2000, pp. 173–179.
9. Ogden, W. C., Cowie, J., et al. (1999): "Keizai: An Interactive Cross-Language Text Retrieval System," in *Prco. of Workshop on Machine Translation for Cross Language Info. Retrieval*.
10. Ong, T.-H. & Chen, H. (1999). "Updateable PAT-Tree Approach to Chinese Key Phrase Extraction Using Mutual Information: a Linguistic Foundation for Knowledge Management," in *Proc. of the 2nd Asian Digital Library Conference*, Taipei, Taiwan, 1999.
11. Sadat, F., Maeda, A., et al. (2002). "A Combined Statistical Query Term Disambiguation in Cross-language Information Retrieval," in *Proc. of the 13th Int'l Workshop on Database and Expert Systems Applications*, Aix-en-Provence, France, September 2002, pp. 251–255.
12. Tolle, K. M. & Chen, H. (2000). "Comparing Noun Phrasing Techniques for Use with Medical Digital Library Tools," *Journal of the American Society for Information Science*, 51(4), 352–370.

A Novel Value of Paragraph Content Based PageRank Approach

Jinghao Miao and Suzhen Lin

Department of Electrical and Computer Engineering
Iowa State University, Ames, IA 50011
{jhmiao,linsz}@iastate.edu

Abstract. In this paper, we proposed an novel PageRank algorithm, which segmented each page into several paragraphs. Then we built links between paragraphs by using N-Gram method. The regular PageRank algorithm were applied on paragraphs and score of PageRank for each paragraph was obtained. The average of the paragraph scores of each page, denoted as Value of Paragraph Content, was used to give scores to the pages. In the N-Gram method, we proposed a solution to limit the memory usage through a hash table.

Keywords: PageRank, link structure, web graph, value of paragraph content, N-Gram.

1 Introduction and Related Work

Various link-based ranking strategies have been developed recently for improving Web search query results. Among them, the PageRank algorithm has achieved obvious results. In 12 every page got after a crawl is condensed into a single number, its PageRank. PageRank is a global ranking of all web pages, regardless of their content. The PageRank algorithm precomputes a rank vector that provides a-priori importance estimates for all of the pages on the web based solely on their location in the web's graph structure. The resulting PageRank is independent of any particular search query.

In our paper, we also proposed a page ranking scheme, based on regular PageRank. The scheme that we proposed is actually a finer grain of PageRank, that is, we constructed a finer grain of processing unit. The PageRank algorithm processes pages as its processing units and disregards the internal properties of the page. Our method, however, segments pages into paragraphs and take the linking properties of each paragraph into consideration.

2 Review of PageRank

The PageRank 2 algorithm is based on the link structure of the web. After each crawl of the web, we can get the graph $G(V, E)$ of the web. The nodes in the graph are the pages, and the links in the graph are the links from pages to pages. Each page has some forward links (out-edges) and back links (in-edges). The PageRank algorithm

T.M.T. Sembok et al. (Eds.): ICADL 2003, LNCS 2911, pp. 153–157, 2003.

aims at assigning each page a value called PageRank as the importance or relation with the searched topic. The algorithm is based on the following intuitive description: a page has high rank if the sum of the ranks of its back links is high. This covers both the case when a page has many back links and when a page has a few highly ranked back links.

The definition of a slightly simplified version of PageRank is shown in Equation 1. F_u is the set of pages that page u points to and B_u is the set of pages that point to u. $E(u)$ corresponds to a source of rank. N_u is defined as $N_u = |F_u|$, c is a factor used for normalization.

$$R(u) = c \sum_{v \in B_u} \frac{R(v)}{N_v} + c \times E(u) \tag{1}$$

Equation 1 is recursive and can be computed by starting with any set of ranks and iterating the computation until it converges.

Let A be a square matrix with the rows and columns corresponding to we pages. Let $A_{u,v} = (1 / N_u)$ if there is an edge from u to v and $A_{u,v} = 0$ if not. Treat R as a vector over web pages, then we have $R = cAR + cE = c(AR + E) = c(A + E \times 1) \times R$. It can be proved that the R will converge to the left eigen value of the matrix $A + E \times 1$. Let S be any vector over web pages (for example E), the PageRank may be computed as follows:

$$R_0 \leftarrow S$$
$$loop:$$
$$\{R_{i+1} \leftarrow AR_i$$
$$d \leftarrow \|R_i\|_i - \|R_{i+1}\|_1$$
$$R_{i+1} \leftarrow R_{i+1} + dE$$
$$\delta \leftarrow \|R_{i+1} - R_i\|_i$$
$$\}while(\delta > \varepsilon)$$

3   Proposed Value of Paragraph Content Based Approach

3.1   Document Segmentation

The proposed scheme starts by segmenting the pages into paragraphs of similar sizes. The number of words in a paragraph is preset to be a fix number (i.e. 50 words); however, we allow the following rules and variances in the process of segmentation:

- HTML tags have to be ignored;

- Consecutive carriage returns and spaces are ignored;

- Hyperlinked texts cannot be broken into different paragraphs; after the segmentation, the document set (called D-set) is reformatted into a set of paragraphs (called P-set). In another word, a finer grain of a document set is thus established.

3.2   Establish Links between Paragraphs

New links between paragraphs (called P-links) have to be established in the P-set based on original hyperlinks between pages in the old D-set. We extract hyperlinks in each page and use N-Gram method to generate P-links, which will be explained in detail as follows:

What is N-Gram? An n-gram 34 is n consecutive characters. A document can be represented by the distribution of the n-grams in it. The distributions of n-grams of different pages can be used to compare the similarity among the pages. In more detail, a document can be represented as a vector whose components are the numbers of occurrences of the distinct n-grams. But the problem is that the dimension of the corresponding vector is large. For example, when 5-grams are used and all the 256 one-byte characters are considered, the number of possible 5-grams is 256^5 = 240 which occupies too much memory. So we have to figure out ways to overcome it. Fortunately, most of the possible 5-grams almost never occur in real pages. So we can use a hash table to represent a document vector and this way saves lots of computer resources. If a reasonable hash table is used, the number of collisions introduced by hashing the n-grams that occur is small enough. In our approach, a paragraph is converted to the vector representation by the following steps:

1) Let H be the size of the hash table and W an n-character wide window.
2) Construct an H-dimensional array A and initialize all the components to 0.
3) Move the window W one character along the document.
4) Convert the corresponding n-gram into a number. For example, an n-gram gram can be converted to a number V by Equation 2:

$$V = \sum_{i=0}^{4} gram[i] \times 256^i \tag{2}$$

5) Use a hash function to get the value of this value.
6) Increase the corresponding component of the array A by 1.
7) If the end of the paragraph is not reached, go back to step 3).
8) Return the n-gram vector A.

P-links based on N-Grams. So far we are able to convert paragraphs into N-Gram vectors. These vectors support cosine-based document similarity metric 4. Therefore our tasks is to establish P-links between paragraphs based on N-Grams similarity gauge. Suppose two paragraphs have N-Gram vectors V_1 and V_2 respectively and D is the hash table size. First these two vectors are normalized as shown in Equation 3 and Equation 4.

$$W_i = \frac{V_i[j]}{\sqrt{\sum_{k=1}^{D} V_i^2[k]}} \tag{3}$$

where $0 < j \le D$ and $i = 1, 2$.

$$\sum_{k=1}^{D} W_i^2[k] = 1 \qquad (4)$$

where W_i is the normalized vector. Now all paragraphs (represented by the heads of vectors of N-Gram hash codes) fall on the hypersurface of a hypersphere in the many dimensional space whose axes are the hash codes in our space of possible hash codes. Then a value S is calculated using Equation 5.

$$S = \sum_{k=1}^{D} W_1[k] \times W_2[k] \qquad (5)$$

The more similar the pages, the larger the S. This is known as the cosine measure. S can be used to gauge the similarity of paragraphs; higher values of S indicate greater similarity.

Thus we can establish P-links based on similarity gauge of N-Gram vectors. Suppose page A contains a hyperlink p to page B. After the page segmentation, the hyperlink p belongs to paragraph i in page A. We need to find a paragraph, called j, in page B such that a P-link pl can be built between paragraphs i and j. Therefore the hyperlink p in the old D-set breaks down into p-link pl in the P-set. The algorithm runs as follows:

- Convert paragraph i into an N-Gram vector V_i;
- Convert each paragraph in page B into a set of Vectors SV_B;
- Calculate the similarity between V_i and each vector in SV_B;
- Find a paragraph whose vector is the most similar to V_i according to the cosine measure. If there are multiple candidates, pick one paragraph who as the smallest label (suppose it is j).
- Establish a P-link pl between paragraphs i and j.

3.3   Apply PageRank to P-Set

We apply regular PageRank algorithm to the derived P-set with P-links between paragraphs. It is an iterative process and 2 shows the convergence properties of data. Eventually a PageRank score is calculated for each paragraph. It turns out that a finer grain of PageRank is implemented on the scale of paragraphs.

3.4   Value of Paragraph Contents (VOPC)

We calculate the Values of Paragraph Contents (VOPCs) for each page as the mean value of their paragraph PageRank scores. A page P has d paragraphs whose PageRank scores are $PR(i)$ where $i = 1, 2,..., k$. Then we have Equation 6.

$$VOPC(P) = \frac{\sum_{i=1}^{d} PR(i)}{d} \qquad (6)$$

VOPC combines the PageRank and N-Gram similarity gauge. And we are able to bring orders to web pages according to their VOPCs.

3.5   Analysis

PageRank algorithm has proved to provide higher quality search results to users 2. Paragraph-scale PageRank considers all paragraphs in terms of their outgoing links. We define paragraphs with few outgoing links as poor paragraphs in our approach. On the other hand, paragraphs that have many outgoing links are defined as good paragraphs. Suppose a page contains both good and poor paragraphs. A page is therefore evaluated based on both scores good and poor paragraphs and a more complete and comprehensive evaluation of the page is expected.

Meanwhile, N-Gram based similarity matching to establish P-links helps in a way to cluster paragraphs similar in contents. Consider the following scenario. Suppose three paragraphs i, j and k have a PageRank score of S_i, S_j and S_k respectively with $S_i >$ $S_j = S_k$. Obviously paragraph i is more important than the other two. But it is hard to measure the importance of paragraphs j and k simply based on their PageRank scores. If i has a P-link to j, but has no connections with k. Paragraph j is potentially more important and trustworthy than k because j is more closely related in contents to i who is deemed to be important paragraph. In 5 the proper hash table size has been empirically identified to minimize the collision probability.

4   Conclusion

In this paper, we proposed a novel page ranking algorithm based on regular PageRank. It segments pages paragraphs and builds links between them using N-Gram method to gauge similarity. The regular PageRank algorithm is therefore applied on paragraphs and score of PageRank for each paragraph is calculated. The average of the paragraph scores for each page, denoted as Value of Paragraph Contents, is given as ranking scores.

References

1. Sergey Brin, Larry Page. *"The anatomy of a large-scale hypertextual web search engine."* In Proceedings of the Seventh International World Wide Web Conference, 1998.
2. Larry Page, Sergey Brin, R. Motwani and T. Winograd. *"The PageRank Citation Ranking: Bringing Order to the Web."* Stanford digital library technologies project report, 1998.
3. M. Damashek. *"Gauging similarity with n-grams:Language-independent categorization of text."* Science, 267 (1995), pp. 843–848.
4. W. Cavnar. *"Using An N-Gram-Based Document Representation With A Vector Processing Retrieval Model."* NIST Special Publication 500–226: Overview of the Third Text Retrieval Conference (TREC-3), 1994, 269–278.
5. Daniel Berleant, Jinping Huang, Ji Mu, Rajesh Potti, Xidan Zhou and Zhong Gu. *"Multibrowsers: Reader Interaction with Documents via Direct Multidisplay."* Report, 2001.

Digital Reference Services: Do We Still Need Libraries?

Asimina Margariti[*] and Gobinda G. Chowdhury[**]

Graduate School of Informatics, Department of Computer and Information Sciences
University of Strathclyde, Glasgow gl 1XH, UK
gobinda.chowdhury@cis.strath.ac.uk

1   Introduction

Reference and information services have remained integral parts of traditional library services. However, a quick look at the current state of digital libraries reveals that till date most digital libraries have focused mainly on providing access to diverse digital information resources (Chowdhury and Chowdhury, 2002). While information interactions and human information behaviour have remained a central theme in information retrieval research, human interaction in the digital library is discussed far less frequently. Emphasizing on the need for personalised services in digital libraries, Lombardi (2000) mentions that, "helping clients find resources in a digitally chaotic world is the first priority." In a Delphi study of digital libraries, it was revealed that "the primary roles librarians play in digital libraries include organisation (cataloguing and indexing), selection and acquisition and acting as gateways to the provision of services involving information." (Kochtanek & Hein,1999). Downs & Friedman (1999) also point out that there is a need for end-user instruction on the use of digital libraries.

Arms (2000) argues that since computers can do a lot in performing most of the traditional jobs of reference librarians, their skills may be required only in case of complex information searches. In order to verify the validity of this statement, which will no doubt have a tremendous impact on the future of digital libraries, a number of small-scale studies were conducted by the second author of this paper and his associates at the University of Strathclyde in UK with a view to assessing how far the web-based reference services can meet the user requirements, and thus whether or not we need to go to the libraries – digital or physical – to get answers to different types of general and subject-specific questions.

This paper reports an evaluation of a selected set of web-based reference services. The purpose of this study was to evaluate the ability of the selected reference and information services to provide answers to users in the cyber environment where face to face communication is absent. To achieve this, we assessed the quality of the retrieved results and responses when submitting questions to web-based reference services in a specified domain (Information Technology). In order to assess the overall ability of the services spherically, we selected both types of services available

---

[*] Ms. Asimina Margariti is a former student of the Department of Computer and Information Science, University of Strathclyde, Glasgow, UK.

[**] Dr. Gobinda G. Chowdhury is a Senior Lecturer and Director of the MSc, Information Management Course at the graduate School of Informatics, Department of Computer and Information Science, University of Strathclyde, Glasgow, UK.

T.M.T. Sembok et al. (Eds.): ICADL 2003, LNCS 2911, pp. 158–167, 2003.
© Springer-Verlag Berlin Heidelberg 2003

i.e., Information Services that search for answers automatically and Ask-an-expert Services, where human "experts" reply to the questions. To make the experiment more realistic, we asked only those questions that are most likely to be submitted by people that have no expertise in the IT area and would not use any specialised technology like bulletin boards or forum to find answers to IT related issues.

2   Selection of Services

A number Question Answering Services and other Reference and Information Services are now available (for a detailed list see McKieran, 2001). The following eight web-based reference services were selected for this study.

- Askjeeves (www.askjeeves.com)
- Infoplease (www.infoplease.com)
- Internet Public Library (IPL) (http://www.ipl.org)
- AllExperts (www.allexperts.com)
- Abuzz (www.allexperts.com)
- Xrefer (www.askrefer.com)
- Ask-a-librarian (http://www.ask-a-librarian.org.uk/)
- AskDr.Internet (http://www.nwfusion.com/columnists/blass.html)

3   Policy Review

Firstly, we examined the online policy statements and disclaimers that contain the terms and conditions for service provision. Most sites have a privacy policy to maintain the anonymity of the user and declare that they do not disclose personal information to third parties without the permission of the individual. AskJeeves, Infoplease and IPL have detailed information on their pages regarding privacy protection. IPL respects copyrights and effectively promotes the protection of intellectual property. Abuzz prompts users to fill in short a member agreement form before using the service to agree with its policy. Xrefer regards all information as non-confidential and assumes no obligation to protect such information. Ask-A librarian states that terms apply but it does not list them explicitly. AllExperts and Dr. Internet contain disclaimers that declare that their service can not verify the credentials of the individual volunteers. The sites demonstrate their policies under "terms of use" or "privacy statement" documents that the user can view on the Web. However, some of them state that they might use general traffic data for commercial purposes.

4   Registration

Not all services require registration to use them. From the selected services, only Abuzz, Ask-A librarian and Dr. Internet that provide "expert services" prompt the visitor to fill in a registration form before using the service. The services we selected do not charge for registration. "Cookie" technology is used by some services to record traffic information on their sites.

5   Criteria

Apart from their policies, the selection of the Question Answering services was based on the utilities and features they incorporate. The main prerequisite was for the services to be free of charge and to be addressed to the general public, not to IT professionals. Of course only sites that use the English language were selected. Finally, it was decided that the services should cover a wide range of subjects with the exemption of Dr Internet. From the eight Services selected, three of them (AskJeeves, Infoplease and Internet Public Library (IPL)) are global Services that provide web-based reference services. It was also decided to include UK- based services to add diversity to the study and to gain some insight regarding the state of digital reference in the United Kingdom. For this purpose Xrefer was selected along with Ask-a-librarian, the later provides answers from professional librarians. Finally, the questions were also submitted to an IT related service (Dr. Internet) in order to map the quality of results against the responses received from the general context reference services.

Two other global services(AllExperts, Abuzz)were selected since they provide answers from "experts". It may be noted that the so-called "experts" do not accept responsibility for the validity of their answers in any circumstances and the term "expert" is rather used to describe the service rather than in-depth expertise of an individual. An expert can be a qualified librarian, a volunteer or any other person that feels in his own judgment that can provide an answer to a given question. However, there is a serious question of accuracy. For example, Dr. Internet states that there might be inaccuracies in the answers and they are not responsible for such errors.

6   Selection of Questions

This study was conducted with a set of 10 pre-defined questions in the area information technology. While some of the questions were fairly straight-forward, others were a bit tricky in the sense that they asked for some specific guidelines. The following questions were used for this study.
(A) What is DBMS?
(B) What is an Expert System
(C) What is TCP/IP?
(D) How do I set up a home network?
(E) How do I give IP numbers to my computers?
(F) How does PGP work?
(G) How do I format my computer?
(H) What is packet-switching?
(I) How to design an Access database?
(J) What is client-server architecture in computing?

7   Parameters

Similar experiments (Janes, 2001pp.1107-9) have suggested several parameters for assessing the services. The present study principally examined the:

- time it takes for the user to submit a query. In some cases, the Service used requires the user to register or create an account before asking a question;
- time lag between submitting the query and the time it takes for the services to respond. Alternatively the time it take for the user to look for an answer through matched results (hits);
- number of matches (hits);
- time the user has to spend actually to browse through the suggested results to find a satisfactory answer;
- accuracy and completeness of the best match, scale one- to-five (1-5);
- relevance, the quality of retrieved results, one-to-ten (1-10).

8   Procedure

Five pseudonymous e-mail accounts were used to submit the questions to experts. Retrieved results were accounted taking into account users' common search habits. Users tend to investigate the first page of the retrieved results as they expect to find the required answers there. We therefore selected to view the top ten matches closely. Out of the top ten(occasionally less than ten) matches, we marked with a scale from one to five the response that best answers the question. Also, for the top ten matched results we calculated how many overall would answer the question or part of it.

All the questions were submitted by using the same Internet connection in the University's labs. To eliminate the variables such as changes in a Service's policy, the period for submitting the questions was restricted to two weeks in November 2002.

9   Service Usage

For some services registration is required before the patron can submit a question. This generally does not take a long time. However, given that one might not be a frequent user, or use the service for the first time, registration slows down the search roughly between a two or three minutes. The services that require registration are usually Ask an expert services. In this case, All experts, Abuzz, Ask-A-librarian and Ask Dr Internet require some type of registration. AllExperts provides a list of subject categories to choose from before submitting the query. After choosing the category, the user has to choose from another extensive set of specified subcategories by subject. After that, the user has to decide on the nature of his/her computer problem and pick from yet another list before finally clicking on the name of the expert (s)he wishes to contact. Alternatively, the user can print a keyword for the question (in the search box) and rely on the ability of the engine to match his query. Selection of an expert may be a bit difficult since there are several categories. Nevertheless, next to every expert's name there is a description of the areas (s)he feels most confident in. In many cases we received multiple answers from different experts, so volunteers either route questions between them or they are able to see all questions and respond. After receiving a response, the user has the choice to ask another expert, if he is not satisfied, and to thank/ rate the expert.

Abuzz requires the user to register for the first time, but unlike with AllExperts "cookies" are used and therefore, the user is automatically logged next time he enters the site. Multiple answers might be received in the user's mailbox and personal page. Users are asked to use a screen name and a password to log, in if they are using a different computer. In the same fashion with AllExperts but more concisely, Abuzz offers a few categories to match the type of the query. Abuzz is a designed to give all its registered users the ability to view questions sent by category and add their own responses. Users can rate the quality of responses they receive and can view all the total interactions they have created in their own special page and keep answers for future reference. This service's one step at a time approach and simple interface makes it relatively straightforward to use, with the drawback that if public computers are used visitors have to remember their membership details.

Ask-a-librarian is a UK-based general reference service and does not claim to have the expertise to help with computer problems related to performance that are quite specific. Patrons have to give information every time they use the service but this registration does not support the creation of a personal page where users can view or trace their past queries. Only questions that can not be delivered are stored in a special page. Ask-a-librarian is very simple to use and all answers are delivered to the patron's own e-mail box. Patrons are not asked to classify the type of query they have into a certain category, so sending a question is quite fast.

Ask Dr Internet requires just the e-mail address and the name of the user and delivers responses directly to the user's e-mail box. Users can also download past discussion topics and FAQ's from its ftp site in plain word format. FAQ's are periodically updated and are summarised by topics people ask most frequently. As Dr Internet states in its disclaimer, mistakes are possible and if users do not receive an answer they should assume the query did not reach the receivers and resubmit it. Using this expert service is very simple and the interface has a clear and user friendly lay out.

The rest of services we reviewed do not not require registration. AskJeeves provides a field to type in the question. Along with the retrieved results, it provides some further useful "search term" suggestions. These suggestions can be particularly useful if users are not certain about the terminology to formulate their query. The retrieved results are usually high in number and users might need extra time to search through and find the exact answer to their question. Typically, there is a lot of background, detail and variety provided in the matched results.

Infoplease is a typical reference site and it uses dictionary, encyclopedia, almanac, etc. to find the answers. Therefore, answers tend to be concise or to be confined only to definitions regarding the keywords. Nevertheless, some of the matches might not contain the search term at all.

IPL provides a greater range of results ranging from articles, archives, dictionaries and encyclopedias. The matching entries containing the keywords are traced in its "subject collections" and users have to browse through carefully to find whether there is something relevant in the collections. Depending on the sources, answers may be brief or detailed. The way results are presented might be baffling since the keywords can match a term mentioned in a non relevant category such as "games" instead of "technology". Xrefer is similar to Infoplease and it provides general reference to terms mainly from dictionaries and encyclopedias.

10   Response Statistics

Forty (10 questions x 4 services) questions were submitted to experts and 40 questions (10 questions x 4 services) were tested on the Web. For 80 questions (10 questions x 8 services) submitted, answers to 73.75 % were obtained, i.e., either a answer from an expert (or a reply message saying that the question could not be answered) was received, or we found a match on the Web. Precisely, eleven questions out of forty (27.5%) submitted to experts, received no reply from the expert services. For a further six questions (15%) answers sent by experts were not useful (accuracy = 0). Therefore, only 57.5% of the questions submitted to expert services received an answer (accuracy >0) while 42.5% did not. Out of the forty questions tested on Reference and Information sites on the Web, ten could not be answered (25%).

Further examination indicates that one question was not answered by any of the expert services and none of the four expert services replied three more questions. No expert service could answer all the questions, and one since was unable to answer 80% of the questions. All results can be viewed summarised in Table 1.

11   Response Demographics

As shown in Table 1, the response rate varies from system to system, and from question to question. However, we counted it a positive response if a reply was obtained within a period of two weeks. While for some systems the response rate was 100%, for other it was as low as 50%. Similarly accuracy rate also varied. The best service in terms of response rate and accuracy was found to be Askjeeves, while Dr. Internet was the worst. InfoPlease failed to retrieve any relevant results for 50% of the questions, being very accurate in only one instance, while IPL and AllExperts did not provide any answer to 20% and 30% of the questions respectively. The average time to conduct a search was 5.5' with a range between 1-12 minutes for general reference and information sites and 1.27 days in average for Ask-an expert sites, with a rage from 1 to seven days to receive a response. Nevertheless, most of the expert services answered within one day and for one question only we received a response in seven days.

Askjeeves scored exceptionally good (5/5) in accuracy for all the searches we conducted with 3.7 minutes in average for each search. In IPL we spent the longest (7.2') time for the searches with an average accuracy 3.4/5. Xrefer had the shortest search time (2.1' average), though the accuracy was very low (1.9/5).

Table 1. Overall Performance of the chosen services

Services ------------->

Q	1 t'	1 A	1 R	2 t'	2 A	2 R	3 t'	3 A	3 R	4 t'	4 A	4 R	5 t'	5 A	5 R	6 t'	6 A	6 R	7 t'	7 A	7 R	8 t'	8 A	8 R
A	9	5/5	5/10	3	3/5	2/2	2	5/5	2/10	1d	1/5	n/a	1d	5/5	n/a	1	4/5	2/2	1d	3/5	n/a	1d	0/5	n/a
B	3	5/5	3/10	1	4/5	2/10	7	4/5	1/10	7d	0/5	n/a	1d	3/5	4/4	1	4/5	1/10	2d	0/5	n/a	1d	3/5	n/a
C	5	5/5	5/10	7	0/5	0/10	11	5/5	2/2	1d	5/5	n/a	1d	4/5	1/4	2	1/5	1/5	1d	1/5	n/a	n/r	n/a	n/a
D	2	5/5	7/10	4	0/5	0/10	12	0/5	0/10	1d	3/5	n/a	1d	5/5	3/7	8	0/5	0/10	n/r	0/5	n/a	n/r	n/a	n/a
E	1	5/5	4/10	3	1/5	1/10	4	4/5	1/10	1d	2/5	n/a	n/r	n/a	n/a	1	1/5	1/10	1d	0/5	n/a	n/r	n/a	n/a
F	2	5/5	10/10	2	5/5	1/1	6	5/5	1/1	1d	5/5	3/3	2d	3/5	3/3	1	3/5	1/1	1d	0/5	n/a	1d	0/5	n/a
G	7	5/5	1/10	8	0/5	0/10	11	4/5	2/10	1D	5/5	n/a	1d	5/5	3/3	3	0/5	0/10	1d	5/5	n/a	1d	2/5	n/a
H	2	5/5	4/10	1	2/5	1/10	6	0/5	0/10	n/r	n/a	n/a	1d	4/5	2/8	1	3/5	2/10	1d	5/5	n/a	1d	0/5	n/a
I	4	5/5	2/10	4	0/5	0/10	11	2/5	1/10	1d	5/5	1/2	1d	3/5	2/3	1	0/5	0/10	1d	5/5	½	1d	0/5	n/a
J	2	5/5	6/10	2	0/5	0/10	2	5/5	1/10	n/r	n/a	n/a	n/r	n/a	n/a	2	3/5	4/10	n/r	n/r	n/a	n/r	n/a	n/a

Legend:

services

1: AskJeeves; 2 :Infoplease; 3 :The Internet Public Library; 4 :Allexperts; 5 :Abuzz.; 6 :Xrefer; 7:Ask-a-librarian 8 :Dr Internet

values

n/r: no reply; n/a: not applicable; t': time in minutes; a: accuracy; d: number of days; R-relevance Q: questions from A to J

12   Site Characteristics

Certainly, responses characterise the type of service that is offered by each site. Since Infoplease, IPL and Xrefer are general reference sites we expected to find more concise information that is taken form their databases, encyclopedias and dictionaries they use to match results. AskJeeves performs searches in the Web therefore accessing significantly more resources and providing in some cases more enhanced or complicated answers. Response in expert sites is influenced by the amount of people that are able to see and respond to a question. Abuzz frequently provides more than one answer because all members can see questions asked by category and post an answer. The quality of the answers varies according to the volunteering members who provide answers. However, the quality of the answers is acceptable since the average accuracy score was 3.2/5. AllExperts apparently route questions between them when they can not answer, or suggest that the user tries another expert. In this study where an expert could not answer a question we did not follow up to resubmit the question to another expert. This is because the expert services take time before they return an answer and it was not in the scope of the study to open a communication with the experts by giving a traditional reference interview and becoming more specific for questions that only require general answers. A user could choose to do so for a more specific operational problem that involves taking some technical steps to correct. Abuzz and AllExperts volunteers are more keen to resolve this type of questions rather than general reference questions that might sound like one is asking experts to find theory that could be found elsewhere. General reference sites on the other hand, might not provide enough background to a question. Experts will usually provide links on the Internet along with their answers for the patron to explore more profoundly. In Table 2 we can see a summary of other characteristics by site, such as whether they contain FAQ pages, whether users can resubmit or clarify a question, the submission method, requests for additional personal information and whether sites allow users to conduct category searches.

13   Conclusion

People often turn to the Web to find information about computers and technology. It looks as an ideal place to search for this kind of information but there are clear distinctions among the services we tested. Infoplease, Xrefer and IPL provide mostly concise, authoritative information, similar to using a dictionary or an encyclopedia . If a user is looking for detailed and background information, these services may not be the best choice. AllExperts and Abuzz are probably the best if a user has a specific technical question, problem, or generally a request that involves the explanation of a procedure rather than theoretical aspects. Abuzz uses volunteers as opposed to "experts" to answer questions. However, this services had an average accuracy of 3.25/5. We noted that response rates depend a lot on the phrasing of the questions. If a user wants to find out about networks, he is more likely to get an answer by asking "how can I connect my three computers at home" rather than " information on setting up networks".

Table 2. Summary of service facilities

Service	subjt area requests	submission method	additional information	FAQ pages	resubmit or clarify
AskJ	No	search box	no	no	yes
Infop	Yes	search box	no	no	no
IPL	Yes	search box	no	yes	no
AllEx	Yes	web form	yes	no	yes
Abuzz	Yes	web form	yes	yes	yes
Xref	Yes	search box	no	no	no
Ask-a-L	No	web form	yes	yes	yes
DrInter	No	web form	yes	yes	no

Experts tend to send short answers along with web links that contain more details. The user has to spend some time looking through the sites suggested, and depending on his familiarity with the jargon and terminology, he is likely (or less likely) to find a full answer . On the positive side, usually more than one answer is received from these services which makes it more likely to find a satisfactory answer.

Ask-a-librarian are happy to talk about theory but as they state, they are not computer experts and might not be able to answer to some technical questions. Although AskJeeves performed significantly better than the other services it should be noted that it would probably take little longer to a user with lack of terminology knowledge to select and inspect appropriate documents. However, many of the links it provided on its first page of matches contained some relevant information as 5.3 out of 10 links in average were relevant.

Using Information Services on the web require the user to understand how these services operate. Xrefer, IPL and Infoplease are easy to use while AllExperts require to select exactly where the patron shall be addressing the question and find an appropriate category for the question. Ask-a-librarian does not require the user to make such decisions. All these services require the patron to have a regular access on the Internet. This means that if a user is using public computers the whole process can take days for sending a query, waiting for a reply and then asking for some further explications. Also if a user cannot remember his log in details, he needs to register again since cookies do no work in public computers. In summary, users accessing these services from public computers may find it difficult to use them.

It is hard to ascertain where one could find best answers for IT related questions. If a user is confident in browsing through web pages, AskJeeves is a good choice. For basic information Xrefer, IPL and Infoplease are quick to use and can provide authoritative information where a user can base a second search on. Abuzz and AllExperts are better for specific questions or problems with technology and they encourage users to open communication with the experts and volunteers, by sending clarification messages and feedback. Ask-A-librarian can advice about general questions that involve theory but there is always the danger that a technical question might not be answered. Using these services effectively definitely depends on how experienced is the user. After using this services a couple times each, it becomes easier to know what to expect to find there, or what kind of answer you are likely to be provided with.

Do these findings support the claim made by Arms (200) that we may not need reference librarians in a digital library environment? Probably not, since as we have noted here, and it has been proved by other similar studies conducted by the researchers (to be reported shortly in other journals), that neither the so-called expert and other web-based reference services can answer all the reference questions, nor that they are always very easy to use in terms of the user efforts and time. This proves that despite the availability of these web-based expert services, one still needs to turn to the digital libraries and librarians to get the best possible reference and information services. Nevertheless, as Chowdhury (2002) comments, this is a time when digital library researchers should think of the best ways and means to make the optimum use of the technology and experience and expertise of human intermediaries in improving digital libraries from mere access centres to information service providers. Some library-based digital reference services are now available, but they need to be robust, and technologically more advanced to meet the users increasing demands (Chowdhury, 2002). Current research in the Question-Answering track of TREC (Voorhees, 2002) may be useful in the context of digital reference services.

References

1. Arms, W.Y. (2000), "Automated digital libraries: how effectively can computers be used for the skilled tasks of professional librarianship?", D-Lib magazine, Vol.6 No.7/8, available: www.dlib.org/dlib/july00/armas.html
2. Chowdhury, G.G. (2002), "Digital libraries and reference services: present and future", *Journal of Documentation*, Vol.58, No.3, pp. 258–283
3. Chowdhury, G. and Chowdhury, S. (2002). Introduction to digital libraries. London, Facet Publishing.
4. Janes J. (200?), "Digital reference: services, attitudes, and evaluation", Internet Research, available:
    http://masetto.emeraldinsight.com/v1=9380369/cl=29/nw=1/rpsv/cw/mcb/10662243/v10
5. Janes J., Hill C., Rolfe A. (2001), "Ask-an-Expert Services Analysis", Journal of the American Society for Information Science and Technology, Vol.66, pp. 1106–21.
6. Kengeri R., Seals CD.,Harley HD.,Reddy HP., Fox EA , "Usability study of Digital libraries: ACM, IEEE-CS, NCSTRL,NDLTD", International Journal on Digital Libraries,Vol.2 No.2/3, 1999, pp. 157–162
7. Kresh D.N. (2000),"Offering High Quality Reference Service on the Web: The collaborative Digital Reference Service (CDRS), D-Lib Magazine, Vol.6, No.6
8. Lankes D.,Kasowitz A.S. (2002), "AskA Starter Kit: How to Build and Maintain Digital Reference Service", Library Review, Vol. 51,No.1, pp. 45–59
9. McClennen M., Memmot P. (2001), "Roles in Digital Reference', Information Technology and Libraries, Vol.29, No.3, available: http://www.lita.org/ital/2003_mcclennan.html/
10. McKiernan, G.(2001), "LiveRef(Sm): a registry of real-time digital rference services" available: www.public.iastate.edu/~CYBERSTACKS/LiveRef.htm

Approximate String Matching for Multiple-Attribute, Large-Scale Customer Address Databases

Y.M. Cheong and J.C. Tay

Intelligent Systems and Robotics Lab
Nanyang Technological University
Singapore 639798
asjctay@ntu.edu.sg

Abstract. The default pattern matching capabilities in today's RDBMS are generally unable to cope with errors and variations that may exist in stored textual information. In this paper, we present SKIPPER, a simple search methodology that allows approximate string matching on multiple-attribute, large-scale customer address information for the Credit Collection industry. The proposed solution relies on the edit distance error model and the q-gram string filtering technique. We present an algorithm that integrates the methodology with existing RDBMS through SQL-based stored procedures.

1 Introduction

Efficiently identifying the relationships between multiple accounts to their singular owners amidst a duplicity of possible names and particulars is an important process in Credit Collection (or CC). The discovery of these relationships is crucial to the recovery of assets. The collection company needs to identify how different accounts are related to each other through identification data such as telephone numbers, mailing addresses, names etc. Such identification data often suffer from typographical errors, missing or out-of-order words, and the improper use of nicknames and/or abbreviations. Generally, debtor information used by collection companies are stored in relational databases (or RDBMS). The default exact and wildcard matching capabilities of such databases are limited and insufficient to retrieve information from data that may contain errors and variations. This paper presents the design and implementation of a search methodology that allows approximate string matching of textual information containing errors and variations. The proposed solution can be easily integrated with an existing relational database system using SQL-based stored procedures.

1.1 Problem Description

In CC, the person (known as the *collector*) assigned to locate Customer account holders may use the output of our search application called SKIPPER. The output of SKIPPER is a set of identification data (e.g. names, address and contact number) related to the inputs provided by the user. The collector will use this information to

T.M.T. Sembok et al. (Eds.): ICADL 2003, LNCS 2911, pp. 168–172, 2003.

contact the customer involved. The input information used by the collector to search the database for a debtor's address may include patterns involving name, aliases, the name of his/her spouse, last known addresses, telephone numbers and other identification information such as his/her driver's license number and social security number.

2   The SKIPPER Architecture

SKIPPER uses a three-tiered client/server architecture that consists of web client(s), an application server and a database server. The search engine application and database server will use the approximate string matching (or ASM) module. We now summarized the steps of our proposed methodology to match a pattern against stored strings in the ASM module. SKIPPER's ASM module provides the necessary functions to perform the first two steps.

Step 1: Q-gram Filtering. Discard strings that are not within a certain predefined ED from the input pattern within the database system, thereby reducing the problem size. The *q-gram filtering* technique presented in [1] and [2] was adopted.

Step 2: ED Computation. Compute and store the *ED* between each remaining string and the input pattern. The false positive matches that are not within a pre-defined threshold *ED* are further eliminated.

Step 3: Ranking. Sort the strings according to the computed *ED* in ascending order. This step sorts the strings according to the computed *ED* before displaying the result.

2.1   Single-Attribute Pattern Matching

We use a dynamic programming approach to compute the minimum *ED* between the two given strings. We also adopt a filtering technique that relies on matching short substrings of length *q*, also known as *q*-grams of the string. In [1], *q*-gram properties were used for filtering in a RDBMS. The main advantage of this approach is that it provides approximate string filtering using native capabilities of a RDBMS and can be easily implemented using SQL. The details of this string filtering technique can be found at [1][2].

Let P_i be the input pattern string for string attribute A_i.

1.   Delete all tuples in temporary filtered result table, TA_i

2.   Build *q*-grams of P_i and store into TQ

3.   Threshold distance set as $k = e^*strlen(P_i)$ e is the %error

4.   Filter(P_i, A_i, k)

5.   Store filtered result set into TA_i table.

6.   Foreach string $A_i(t)$ in TA_i, compute $d = edit\_distance(A_i(t), P_i)$

6.1.   If $d <= k$ then insert tuple $(A_o(t), d/strlen(P_i))$ into *Scoreboard*.

Fig. 1. Algorithm to match a single attribute

2.2 Multiple-Attribute Pattern Matching

SKIPPER consists of a search engine that uses the ASM module. The SearchModel will encapsulate database queries to actually perform the queries. The following section elaborates the ASM module, which is used by the SearchModel to match single or multiple fields. The ASM module consists of two classes *EditDistance* and *QgramSQL*. The *EditDistance* class provides two methods to compute the *ED* between two input strings and to verify if two given strings are within a specified threshold. The *QgramSQL* class provides the necessary canned SQL statements to achieve string filtering using positional *q*-grams. The database will be augmented with auxiliary tables to store the *q*-grams of a given column of strings before we can achieve filtering. The details of creating auxiliary tables can be found in [1][2]. The SQL query to perform string filtering with the three filters: *Count, Position* and *Length* are described in [5][6]. The SQL expression prunes out pairs of strings that are not within a specified *ED*.

Matching on a Single Attribute. The algorithm to match a single attribute is shown in Figure 1, Step 1 to 4 are related to string filtering using *q*-grams. The *ED* threshold is set using the parameter *e* in Step 3 of Figure 1. This percentage is a user-defined value.

Matching on Multiple Attributes. Each attribute is filtered sequentially in an ordering defined by the user via the web-based user interface. The algorithm shown in Figure 1 was extended to handle multiple attributes. Due to space constraint, the pseudo-code for matching multiple attributes is not shown here. The extended algorithm will only use all *q*-grams to filter the first attribute. Subsequently, only *q*-grams relevant to the previous attribute are used for filtering.

3   Performance Analysis

This section presents results of an experimental analysis of the parameters *q*-gram length *q* and *ED* *k* and their effects on the resultant number of false positive matches. It was observed that setting *q* to 2 resulted fewer false positive matches. Also, larger values of *q* and *k* resulted poorer performance. This coincides with the observations made in [2].

Data Sets. Two data sets named *S1* & *S2* are provided by a credit collection company. *S1* consists of customers' names, *S2* consists of addresses. Each set contains approximately 90,000 tuples. We randomly select two subsets of 1000 query strings each, *QS1* and *QS2* from *S1* and *S2* respectively.

Filtration Efficiency. The performance measured in this case is the filtration efficiency based on $T / (T + F)$ where T is **total true matches** and F is **total false positives**. For both pairs of query sets and supersets; *QS1, S1* and *QS2, S2,* the results are shown in Figure 2a and 2b. It can be seen that the filtration efficiency decreased with increasing *q* and *k*. This shows that the *q*-gram filtering used in the proposed solution is sensitive to the error threshold and that the filtering is most effective at low error levels.

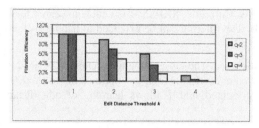

Fig. 2a. Comparison of Filtration Efficiency for S_1

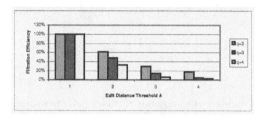

Fig. 2b. Comparison of Filtration Efficiency for S_2

Table 1. Comparison of variation explained

Sum of Squares	Variation Explained (%)	
	Set S_1	Set S_2
SSA (q)	22.1	27.7
SSB (k)	58.7	51.3
SSAB (q & k)	19.1	21.1

Using the data measured from the experiments, we computed the variation of both factors q and k. It was found that for our data sets, k (threshold ED) has dominant effect over the filtering performance. The comparison of variation can be found in Table 1.

4   Conclusion and Further Work

This paper presents a search engine called SKIPPER that is used to match customer addresses. Experiments were carried out to study the effects of the q-gram size and threshold ED on the performance of the q-gram filtering. It was shown that performance degraded with the increase of q-gram size and the threshold ED. This agrees with observations in [2]. The optimal q-gram size is 2. The experimental results were used for computing statistical variations of the factors q and k, and to estimate their relative effects on performance. It was found that the adopted q-gram filtering algorithm was sensitive to the threshold edit distance (ie k). We propose further work in the following areas:

Out-of-order words. Currently, SKIPPER is unable to search for strings that contain out-of-order words. The filtering can be extended to handle such errors by modifying the *ED* algorithm[1][2].

Threshold Edit Distance. The current q-gram technique is sensitive to the threshold edit distance. It would be desirable if an optimal threshold *ED* can be found. A stochastic model presented in [3] allows learning of edit distance from a set of examples.

Computing Record Score. The result is sorted according to the total edit distance of the record computed by the *ED* algorithm that we termed as the "score". The statistical model in record linkage [4] can be applied in the computation of score for more accurate results.

References

1. L. Gravano, P.G. Ipeirotis, H.V. Jagadish, N. Koudas, S. Muthukrishnan, L. Pietarinen, D. Srivastava, Using q-grams in a DBMS for Approximate String Processing, IEEE Data Engineering Bulletin 24(4): 28–34, 2001
2. L. Gravano, P.G. Ipeirotis, H.V. Jagadish, N. Koudas, S. Muthukrishnan, and D.Srivastava, Approximate string joins in a database (almost) for free, In Proceedings of the 27th International Conference on Very Large Databases (VLDB 2001), pages 491–500, 2001.
3. E. S. Ristad and P. Y. Yianilos, Learning String Edit Distance, Research Report CS-TR-532-96, Dept. of Computer Science, Princeton University, 1997.
4. W. E. Winkler, The State of Record Linkage and Current Research Problems, Technical report, Statistical Research Division, U.S. Bureau of the Census, Washington, D.C, 1999.

ISTILAH SAINS: A Malay-English Terminology Retrieval System Experiment Using Stemming and N-grams Approach on Malay Words

Tengku Mohd Tengku Sembok, Kulothunkan Palasundram, Nazlena Mohamad Ali,
Yahya Aidanismah, and Tengku Siti Mariam Tengku Wook

Faculty of Information Science and Technology,
Universiti Kebangsaan Malaysia,
43600, Bangi, Selangor, Malaysia
{tmts,nma,aida,tsmtw}@ftsm.ukm.my

Abstract. The emergence of global information society has increased the
importance of translating articles from Malay to English, and vice-versa, to
assist in the dissemination of information into and from South East Asia, mainly
Malaysia, Indonesia and Brunei where Malay language is widely used. This has
created the need to have computer-aided translation tools to facilitate the
translation process. In this article, the authors describe the design
implementation, and evaluation of a Malay–English and English-Malay
scientific terms retrieving software. The system was designed and implemented
using object-oriented techniques with user friendly interfaces and some basic
facilities. For example, the database maintainer can add, change or delete terms
from the database, and reindex files. The general user can retrieved terms
through the Internet using any browser with JAVA plug-in. The indexing and
retrieving strategies are based on stemming and n-gram methods. The system
was developed using JAVA language and thus Web enabled and can be
accessed at http://www.ftsm.ukm.my/istilah/.

1 Introduction

Research in automatic information retrieval has started since 1940s (Frakes 1991). A
lot of information retrieval systems have been developed since then, such as CONIT
(Marcus 1983), SMART and SIRE (Salton & McGill 1983). However, research in
information retrieval on Malay language is still new (Fatimah 1995). One of the
earliest work in this area is a bilingual information retrieval system called SISDOM
developed by Abu Ata (1995). SISDOM uses a Malay-English and English-Malay
terms translation module called *Istilah*.

The ever growing need to translate articles from English to Malay and Malay to
English has triggered the need to have independent translation software to maintain
and retrieve terms. In this article, the design and implementation of *Istilah Sains UKM*
a bilingual (Malay and English) scientific terms translation package is described.

T.M.T. Sembok et al. (Eds.): ICADL 2003, LNCS 2911, pp. 173–177, 2003.

2 Design Approach

The design of Istilah Sains UKM is based on the object-oriented modeling. Istilah Sains UKM consists of two main modules: the maintenance module and Internet access module. The maintenance module consists of indexing and retrieving modules. The function of indexing module is to update the main data file which keeps the terms and create new index files for the system.

The process of indexing can be divided into two steps: first, clustering of the terms into root words using stemming algorithm; second, clustering of the root words into bigrams (two character subwords). The stemming algorithm used for Malay terms clustering is Fatimah's algorithm (1996). Porters suffix striping stemming algorithm (Porter 1980) is used to cluster the English terms.

The function of the retrieving module is to retrieve words which match the query word. Partial string matching techniques used are stemming and bigram matching which determine whether two words match each other. For bigram matching, Dice coefficient value with threshold 0.6 is used for partial matching. Figure 1 shows an example of the output for the query "solar energy".

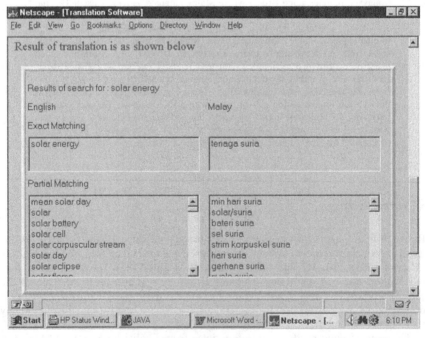

Fig.1. Output Interface

3 Evaluation Procedure

The experiments are performed to evaluate the retrieval effectiveness of various techniques on Malay words employed within the framework of n-gram matching in the contact of automatic query expansion approach as set by Lennon et al. [1981]. Some of the techniques investigated are used in the development of Istilah Sains UKM. The effectiveness of retrieval is evaluated by using recall and precision measures based on the number of words retrieved and relevant (R&R). The recall, R, is defined as proportion of relevant terms actually retrieved from the dictionary with respect to a specified query term. The precision, P, is thus defined as the proportion of retrieved actually relevant. The relevancy of each term in the dictionary to a specified query term is determined manually by exhaustive scanning through the dictionary with the help of the string matching utility "find" in the Microsoft Excel software. Two terms are regarded to be relevant to each other if they share a common root. The measure of van Rijsbergen, E, which is a weighted combination of recall and precision, is also used to calculate the retrieval effectiveness.

For each query term, the terms in the dictionary are ranked based on a similarity matching measure as specified in each experiment. The E values are calculated for cutoff points at 10 to 100, at an interval of 10, top ranking dictionary terms. This is done for all the 84 query terms and the mean values of E is calculated. The average of the mean values of E at the ten cutoff points are calculated and used to evaluate the effectiveness of each technique. Generally the average of the mean values of E at all the cutoff points serve as a good indicator of performance; we used the symbol aE to denote this value. Statistical sign test is used to measure the degree of significance between any two methods [Siegel and Castellan, 1988].

4 The Results

The commonly used similarity coefficients are Dice and Overlap coefficients. We run experiments using both coefficients on digrams and trigrams. Using the E value averages as the basis of comparison, The result shows that Overlap coefficient performed better than Dice coefficient for both the digrams and trigrams. This may be due to the Malay morphology which allows long affixes to be attached to a root word and thus Overlap coefficient performs better in this condition. In digrams matching, the Overlap coefficient gives the value of aE = 72.58 and the Dice coefficient gives aE = 73.27. In trigrams matching, the Overlap coefficient gives aE = 75.07 and Dice coefficient gives aE = 75.41. But the difference between the performance of the Overlap and the Dice coefficients is not significant.

We also tried using both Dice and Overlap coefficient on the digrams matching by taking the average value of the two in order to measure the performance of such fusion of similarity coefficients. Its performance is worst than Overlap coefficient at all the cutoff points accept at the cutoff of 10. But it performs better than the Dice coefficient with aE = 72.64 as compare to 73.27. Generally, we can conclude that the Overlap coefficient performs better than the Dice coefficient and the fusion of the two.

4.1   Digrams and Trigrams Matching

Digrams matching performs better than trigrams at all level of cutoffs and coefficients used. Sign test is performed on the performance of digrams and trigrams matching using the Overlap coefficient. The result obtained indicates that that the digrams performs significantly.

We also tried using the fusion of digrams and trigrams by taking the average value of the two using the Overlap coefficient. The fusion approach performs inferiorly at all the cutoff points except at the cutoff 10. Thus we conclude that the fusion approach is not worth pursuing further.

4.2   Incorporating-Stemming Approach

Stemming process is incorporated into n-gram matching framework in order to investigate it effectiveness. The first approach taken is to stem the query term first before doing the n-grams matching against the unstemmed dictionary. This approach is performed on digrams and trigrams using Overlap similarity coefficient. The results obtained show that the one with digrams matching performs better than the trigrams with the aE = 64.61 as compare to 66.45. It also performs significantly better than the best non-stemmed approach experimented in the last section, i.e. digrams matching with Overlap similarity coefficient with the aE = 72.58.

The second approach taken is to stem both the query term and the dictionary terms.. The one using digrams performs better than the trigrams with aE = 61.04 as compare to 61.35 and obviously better than with the previous approach when only the query terms are stemmed. The results obtained from sign test indicate that the digrams matching using stemmed-query and stemmed-dictionary performs significantly better than with stemmed-query alone.

4.3   Comparison with Stemmed-Boolean Matching

We also run experiments using the conventional stemmed-Boolean matching between the stemmed query and the stemmed dictionary to compare its effectiveness to the approach of incorporating stemming in the n-gram framework. Using variable cutoff points evaluation, stemmed-Boolean approach performs significantly better than the incorporating-stemming approach.

On the other hand, using the cutoff with weighted transformation evaluation the incorporated-stemming approach performs better but not significantly. Thus, we cannot unequivocally say that which performs better. The two methods based on two different approaches, one on the Boolean matching and the other on matching with uncertainty measure and both have their functional purposes.

5   Conclusions

From the experiments performed we can conclude that the Overlap coefficient performs better than the Dice coefficient but not significantly, and the digrams matching performs significantly better than the trigrams. The usage of stemming prior to digrams and trigram matching have significantly enhance the performance. The application of stemming on the query terms and the dictionary performs significantly better than the application of stemming on the query terms alone which in turn performs significantly better than without the application of stemming.

However, we cannot equivocally conclude which is better between the conventional stemmed-Boolean approach and the incorporating-stemming in the n-grams approach. Furthermore, the two approaches are based on different paradigms, one on the Boolean retrieval and the other on the best match ranking retrieval and they having advantages and disadvantages of their own.

References

1. Belal Mustafa, A.A., Tengku Mohd. T.S., & Mohd. Yusoff. 1995. "SISDOM : A Multilingual Document Retrieval System." Asian Libraries, Vol. 4, No.3, MCB University Press Limited, England.
2. Fatimah Ahmad. 1995. Satu Sistem Capaian Dokumen Bahasa Melayu: Satu Pendekatan Eksperimen Dan Analisis. Ph.D Thesis, Universiti Kebangsaan Malaysia..
3. Fatimah Ahmad, Mohammed Yusoff, Tengku Mohd. T. Sembok. 1996. "Experiments with A Malay Stemming Algorithm", Journal of American Society of Information Science.
4. Frakes, W.B. 1992. Stemming Algorithms. In Frakes, W.B. & Baeza-Yates, R. (ed). Information Retrieval: Data Structures & Algorithms: 131–160. Englewood Cliffs: Prentice Hall.
5. Marcus, R.S. 1983. "An Experimental Comparison of the Effectiveness of Computers and Humans as Search Intermediaries." Journal of the American Society for Information Science 34(6):381–404.
6. Porter, M. F. (1980). "An algorithm for suffix stripping". Program, 14, 130–137.
7. Salton, G. & McGill, M.J. 1983. Introduction to Modern Information Retrieval. New York: McGraw-Hill.

THVDM: A Data Model for Video Management in Digital Library*

Yu Wang, Chun-xiao Xing, and Li-zhu Zhou

Department of Computer Science and Technology, Tsinghua University, 100084, Beijing
wangyu02@mails.tsinghua.edu.cn
{xingcx,dcszlz}@mail.tsinghua.edu.cn

Abstract. As an important part of digital library, video library is becoming more and more significant. However, the problem in lacking of appropriate data models prevents the video library from being widely used. In this paper, we first review some existing data models, and then present a new model consisting of three layers: feature layer, semantic layer, and knowledge layer. The model supports non-procedural query language and overcomes the shortcoming of existing models, thus can meet the requirements of new applications.

1 Background

Digital Libraries have emerged as large scale and distributed information and knowledge environment and infrastructure to bring together collections, services, and people in support of the full life cycle of creation, dissemination, use, storage, and preservation of ...... [1]. Video management is an indispensable part of the digital library and is becoming more and more important. The essential reasons for this importance are 1) the features of video of being expressive, intuitive, and easy to use, 2) the extremely rapid increase of the amount of video data. Although video data provide richer information, but finding appropriate information from video database by computer system is a challenging task. And video library is expected to manage the video data, and perform powerful functions just like relational database performs to alphanumeric data. Usually, queries to video data fall into two categories:

- Query by visual Information (Visual Query): queries related to visual features, such as color, texture, shape, motion etc.
- Query by content (Content Query): queries related to the knowledge contained in the video data.

Among these two kinds of queries, content queries are at very high level extraction that allows users to easily express what they want from video database. However, they are much more difficult to evaluate than visual queries. For example, when viewing a video clip about a basketball match, people may ask the following questions:

---

* Supported by the National Natural Science Foundation of China under Grant No.60221120146; the National Grand Fundamental Research 973 Program of China under Grant No.G1999032704.

T.M.T. Sembok et al. (Eds.): ICADL 2003, LNCS 2911, pp. 178–192, 2003.

– How many times did Jordan shoot the basket or foul? Play these shots.
– Play all shots that Jordan's foul causing a foul shot.

In order to answer these content questions, we first need to build a video data model, which can describe the content of the video data precisely and flexibly. Meanwhile it can be applied to different domains to represent domain-specific knowledge. We also need to design a simple but effective query language to retrieve the video data in digital library. However, the complexity of video data imposes great difficulties on the design of video data model.

Firstly, there are various types of video data, thus different representing, retrieving and operating methods are needed. Consider video clips of news and sports. Usually people query news by the main content and the time the news occurs, so the representation of news video may be relatively simple. However, since the sports video contains many players and events which are complicatedly related, it is inappropriate to simply represent sports video using the data model for news.

Secondly, the semantic information in the video data is often implicit, so it is difficult to construct the data model to catch such information. For the traditional relational database, what the alphanumeric data mean and how to represent them are uniform and there is no difficulty in constructing the data model. However, for video data, there is no such a general knowledge and the extraction of semantic information remains unsolved, To catch such information in systems, we have no choice but input it manually. This makes the annotation of semantic information for real applications impossible as the data volume is commonly enormous.

In this paper we emphasize data model's support for video data description and operation, especially for data queries. This paper is organized as follows: section 2 introduces some related works and analyzes their shortcomings. After that, a new video data model named THVDM (TsingHua Video Data Model) will be put forward in section 3 along with its XML Schema description. Section 4 discusses a non-procedural query language for THVDM and analyzes the querying ability of this model. Section 5 introduces a prototype system for proving the validity of THVDM. Section 6 gives the conclusion and future works.

2 Related Works

The research for developing appropriate video data models has lasted for many years, producing a great number of models that can be classified into the following categories.

Although VideoSTAR[2], VideoText[3] and Algebraic Video Model[4,5] describe their content in different logical abstraction level, they all use textual attributes and keywords as the annotation. Different video segments can overlap, thus different users can construct different views over the same video clip. The annotations can be created and updated dynamically and incrementally. However, the using of only textual annotation limited their query ability, making it only possible to query by annotation. Thus whether a query is answerable heavily depends on the completeness of the annotation which, however, can not cover all possibilities. For the first kind of queries given in the previous section, these models can answer it only if every event about Jordan is recorded in the annotation. The second one is beyond theses models' ability.

References [6-8] emphasize on modeling the spatio-temporal relationship among objects. Reference [6] names the interested object as "hot object", which are related to each other by spatio-temporal relationships. The semantic associations among hot objects and other logical video abstractions are represented by video hyperlinks which lead to detail information or another video clip. Paper [7] uses spatio-temporal logic to describe the content of images or image sequences. When performing query, the spatio-temporal of the example is first calculated and then compared with those in the database. [8] can represent not only the intra-clip spatio-temporal relationship but also inter-clip spatio-temporal relationship. These models support the query according to the spatio-temporal relationship, but not those given in the previous section.

Models supporting knowledge (object and event) include AVIS[9], [10], VIMSYS[11], Videx[12], etc.

In AVIS[9], video data falls into two categories: Raw Video Data and set of entities. The whole video sequence is represented by a frame segmented tree. Every node of the tree denotes a frame sequence, related to which is the list of objects and events occurred in the corresponding frame sequence. Events of the same kind are differentiated by different roles. Indices are created for objects, events and event types, thus users can query by object, event or event type. [10] extended the idea of AVIS, adding the ability of querying by spatio-temporal relationship. It views the moving objects in the video as salient objects and records their moving track, thus can answer questions about moving objects.

VIMSYS[11] is one of the earliest data models for the management of images and influenced many succeeding data models. There are four levels in VIMSYS: image presentation level, image object level, domain object level and domain event level. A distinctive idea in VIMSYS is the concept of domain events which connects different domain objects by spatio-temporal relationship.

Videx[12] is a relatively new model put forward in 2000. It integrates the low-level and high-level feature and abstracts the video data into two levels: logical video unit and physical video unit. A physical video unit may be a shot, a scene or a video sequence and can be related to multiple logical video units. A logical video unit contains domain-specific information. Videx can be easily extended for different domains.

These kinds of data models can answer the first question given in the previous section. However, AVIS and the data model in [10] do not support the inter-object and inter-event relation; Videx does not support inter-event relation; VIMSYS's events are very simple, supporting neither time factor nor inter-event relation (for it is a data model for image and image sequence). As the result, neither of them can answer the second question.

3   Video Data Model: THVDM

In order to support as many kinds of queries as possible, we put forward a new video data model THVDM (TsingHua Video Data Model) in this section, the purpose of which is as follows:

– Managing the semantic information of the video data reasonably, supporting multiple kinds of semantic queries;

- Organizing the information flexibly, so as to be applied to different domains;
- Providing friendly interface for users.

To fulfill these purposes, we divide the data model into three layers: feature layer, semantic layer and knowledge layer (as shown in figure 1). The entities in knowledge layer are closest related to people, reflecting the concepts in real life. All activities related to high-level information concentrates in this layer. The feature layer stores the raw video data and the features extracted from it. The semantic layer is a bridge between the feature layer and the knowledge layer and together with the feature layer forming the foundation of the knowledge layer.

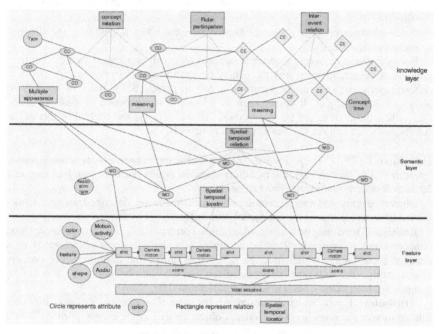

Fig. 1. The architecture of THVDM

3.1   The Knowledge Layer

This layer is the interface between the data model and the user. All the activities related to high-level information are performed in this layer, including schema definition and query. The entities in this layer falls into two categories: concept object and concept event, corresponding to the two kinds of things people interested in: objects and events respectively.

Definition 1 *(CO, Concept object): The concept object represents the things people interested in in specific domain, including the following three kinds:*
- *Concrete concept object: The concrete concept objects can be recognized from a frame of a video sequence and every occurrence has temporal and spatial location.*

- *Abstract concept object: The abstract concept object is the union of a set of video segments. The whole union must be viewed as a single concept.*
- *Composite concept object: The composite concept object comprises of multiple sub-objects while each sub-object can be concrete concept object, abstract concept object or composite concept object.*

The concrete concept object and the abstract concept object are different in the following aspects:

- *The concrete concept object can be recognized from a certain location in a frame of a video sequence;*
- *There are spatio-temporal relationships between different concrete concept objects;*
- *If the abstract concept object is broken into the shots it contains, the original meaning will lose.*

For example, a person is a concrete concept object. It can appear in a certain time point, at a certain location and there may be spatio-temporal relationships between different persons (we can say person A is left to person B). A piece of news is an abstract concept object. It corresponds to a continuous sequence of multiple shots. Only when these shots are taken together, can we retrieval the content of this news. Additionally, we can not say news A is left to news B.

Definition 2 *(CE, Concept event): The concept event represents the events people interested in in specific domain, including common events (such as foul, foul shot in a basketball match) and user defined events.*

Objects, events and the relationships between them are described using a model named ERR which means the ER model plus Rules.

Entities: There are two kinds of entities corresponding to concept object and concept event respectively. That is, an entity is either a concept object entity or a concept event entity, which must be designated during the definition. For concept object entity, the sub-type must be given, which can be concrete, abstract or composing. Every entity has a unique identification (ID).

Attributes: Every entity is described by several attributes. Besides attributes related to specific domain, every concept object entity has an 'events' attribute which contains all the events the concept object participates in. Every concept event entity has a "roles" attribute, a "time" attribute and a "conceptTime" attribute among which the first one contains all the concept objects that participate in this event, the second one show the time the event occurs (e.g. a passing occurs at the 15th minute) and the last one shows the concept time the event happens (e.g. a dunk occurs in the second quarter).

Relationship: concept object entities and concept event entities are connected by some domain specific relationships. These relationships exist between concept object and concept object, concept event and concept event, also concept object and concept event. Besides these relationships, four kinds of relationships are predefined: **composing, temporal relationship, spatial relationship** and **causing relationship** among which the former three are inter-object relationships while the last one is inter-event relationship. A composing object may have multiple component objects through the composing relationship, each of which may be either kind of concept objects. Temporal relationship and spatial relationship considers certain entity instances and

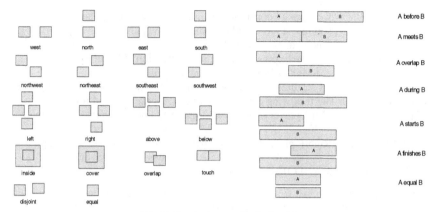

Fig. 2. Spatio-temporal-relationships

need not be defined. They will be extracted from the video data automatically to facilitate the query [13,14] (as shown in figure 2). The causing relationship in defined between two concept events, means that the first event incurs the second one.

Rules: Rules are used to define events by using features or spatio-temporal relationships between concept objects. They can help the construction of the data model, that is, extraction of events. When querying, people should first check whether there is the needed event in the data model, if not, they can then add events they interested in to the model by means of rules. These added events will be stored in the model for future uses. Rules can by named or anonymous. The syntax for defining rules is as follow:

CREATE RULE rule_name logicalExpression;   define a named rule
ATTATCH RULE rule_name | logicalExpression TO event_name; attach a rule (named or anonymous) to an event
where
logicalExpression::= (unitExpression) | (logicalExpression AND logicalExpression)
                    | (logicalExpressiong OR logicalExpression)
unitExpression::= AttributeExpression | TemporalRelationExpression
                    | SpatialRelationExpression | FeatureExpression
AttributeExpression::= AttriIndicator compareOperator AttrIndicator
                    | AttIndicator compareOperator CONST
AttrIndicator::= name((.name)|(->name*))*;   the operator "." means getting the attribute of the current entity; the operator "->" means getting the attribute of the entity to which the relationship before the operator points. If there is no name after the operator "->", it means getting the related entity.
name::= TypeName | AttributeName | RelationName |.*   * means any
compareOperator::= > | < | >= | <= | != | == | like | contains
TemporalRelationExpression::= obj1_name temporalOperator obj2_name
                    | obj_name Occurs TIME_CONST
temporalOperator::= before | meets | overlap | during | starts | finishes | equal
SpatialRelationExpression::= obj1_name spatialOperator obj2_name
                    | obj_name AT SPATIAL_CONST

spatialOperator::= west | east | north | south | northeast | northwest | southeast
                | southwest | left | right | above | below | inside | cover | overlap
                | touch | disjoint | equal
FeatureExpression::=ColorExpression | TextureExpression | ShapeExpression
                | MOtionExpression | AudioExpression

Due to the numerous features and the limited space, we do not list the details of all feature expressions. The following example will illustrate the using of rules.

CREATE RULE JLeftR player1.name == Jordan AND player2.name == Rodman
                                AND player1 left player2
CREATE RULE JRightP player1.name == Jordan AND player2.name == Pippen
                                AND player1 right player2
ATTATCH (JLeftR AND JRightP) TO JBetweenR&P

In the above example, we first defined two rules. The first rule means Jordan is left to Rodman and the second rule means Jordan is right to Pippen. Then we attach the combine of the two rules to the event JBetweenR&P, meaning that both rules being satisfied mean the event JBetweenR&P occur.

Figure 3 is a simple example of applying the data model to basketball match. There are two concept objects (player and coach) and four concept events (dunk, pass, foul and foul shot). The concept event foul may cause the concept event foul shot. The relationship coach between player and coach means the person the coach object represents is the coach of the person the player object represents. The lines between the object player and the events mean that the players can participate in these events.

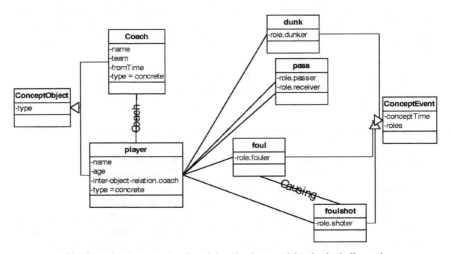

Fig. 3. A simple example of applying the data model to basketball match

3.2   The Semantic Layer

The semantic layer stores all objects in the video sequence extracted by analyzing the features in the feature layer or applying some other technologies (such as face recognition, speaker identification, specific object recognition, story recognition,

OCR etc.) to the raw video data. This layer connects the knowledge layer to the feature layer. The entities in this layer are called semantic objects (SO in short) since they are used to represent the semantic information. Semantic objects also have different types and are used to support concept objects and concept events in the knowledge layer of different types.

1) Single semantic object: The single semantic objects are objects appearing in a certain shot and correspond to something in real life (such as people, object etc.). This kind of semantic objects should be described along two aspects.

− The spatio-temporal location

The spatio-temporal location describes where and when does the semantic object appear. For a moving object, it also contains the moving track which can be represented using interpolation or parametric model.

− The spatio-temporal relationship

During the processing of query, the spatio-temporal relationships between concept objects are actually evaluated using the spatio-temporal relationships between single semantic objects related to the involved concept objects. Since every single semantic object has its own spatio-temporal location, there may be spatio-temporal relationship between any two single semantic objects. However, not all these relationships are meaningful.

The single semantic objects are used to support the concrete concept objects, representing the appearance of certain concrete concept object in the video data. Once a concrete concept object appears in a shot, there will be a single semantic object representing this appearance (multiple appearances in the same shot corresponds to one single semantic object). Through the semantic objects related to a concrete concept object we can find all its appearance in the video sequence.

2) Composing semantic object: The composing semantic object represents the set of continuous or non-continuous shots.

The composing semantic objects are used to support the abstract concept objects. It takes the set of shots as a whole, the meaning of which is provided by the corresponding abstract concept object. For example, in a video of news, a piece of news may last several shots. These shots should be viewed as a composing semantic object and the information related to this news should be illustrated by the abstract concept object related to it.

The utilizing of single semantic object and composing semantic object endows this model with the ability of representing different types of video flexibly, either simple video like news or complex video like sports.

The CE can be supported by either single semantic object or composing semantic object. The decision depends on the property of the CE. If the CE involves spatial location information or only involves time-point-related temporal property (not involving time-duration-related temporal property), it should be related to a single semantic object; otherwise to a composing semantic object.

The composing concept object does not related to semantic objects directly but related to them indirectly through its component objects.

3.3   The Feature Layer

The feature layer stores the raw video data and the features extracted from it. Before the extraction, the video sequence should first be analyzed and separated to a sequence of non-overlap shots. The commonly used features are as follows [15]. However, the features are not limited to these since people can add new features into the model at any moment as long as they think it's necessary.

- Color: color histogram, dominant color, color layout, color structure, GOF/GOP color, etc.
- Texture: texture browsing, edge histogram, etc.
- Shape: region shape, contour shape, shape 3D, etc.
- Motion: motion trajectory, motion activity(intensity, direction, spatial distribution, spatial localization, temporal distribution),etc.
- Audio: spectrum, timber, spoken content, audio classification, etc.

3.4   THVDM Description Based on XML Schema

The structure of THVDM can be described by XML Schema, thus the video content will be described in the form of XML documents that accord with the Schema. When applying the data model to a specific domain, all things defined in the knowledge layer (including entities, attributes, relationships and rules) will be mapped to XML Schema automatically to validate the XML document generated from the video data later. The mapping rules are as follows:

Entity: All concept objects are mapped to subtypes of ConceptObjectType with the sub-element "type" designating the type ("concrete", "abstract" or "composing"). All concept events are mapped to subtypes of ConceptEventType. Every entity has a unique identity (ID).

Attributes: All attributes are mapped to sub-elements of corresponding objects or events. The name of the sub-element is the attribute's name and the value is the attribute's value.

Relationship: The relationships between concept objects are mapped to sub-elements of the "inter-object-relation" sub-element of corresponding concept objects. The relationships between concept events are mapped to sub-elements of the "inter-event-relation" sub-element of corresponding concept event. The relationships between concept object and concept event are mapped to the "participate-in-event" sub-element of the concept object and the "have-role" sub-element of the concept event. The name of the sub-element is the name of the relationship and the value is the ID of the related entity.

Rule: All named rules are mapped to RULE elements whose "name" attribute is the name of the rule. Rules attached to events are mapped to events' "rule" sub-element with the "name" attribute designating the name of the named rule or the value containing the content of the anonymous rule.

For example, the concept object "player" in the example of section 3.1 can be mapped to XML Schema as follows:

```
<xs:complexType name="playerType">
 <xs:complexContent>
  <xs:extension base="ConceptObjectType">
   <xs:sequence>
    <xs:element name="name" type="xs:string"/>
    <xs:element name="age" type="xs:integer"/>
    <xs:element name="inter-concept-object-relation">
     <xs:complexType>
      <xs:sequence>
       <xs:elementname="coach" type="relatedCoachType"/>
      </xs:sequence>
     </xs:complexType>
    </xs:element>
    <xs:element name="participate-in-event"
            minOccurs="0" maxOccurs="unbounded">
     <xs:complexType>
      <xs:sequence>
       <xs:choice>
        <xs:element ref="passing"/>
        <xs:element ref="dunk"/>
        <xs:element ref="foul shot"/>
        <xs:element ref="foul"/>
       </xs:choice>
       <xs:element name="roleName" type="xs:string"/>
      </xs:sequence>
     </xs:complexType>
    </xs:element>
   </xs:sequence>
  </xs:extension>
 </xs:complexContent>
</xs:complexType>
```

4 The Query Language

4.1   The Syntax

In this section we will define a non-procedural query language similar to SQL, which is used in the knowledge layer and has the following syntax:

```
SELECT targetExp
FROM TypeExp(,TypeExp)*
(WHERE  logicalExpression)?
(GROUP BY AttributeExpression)?
where
targetExp ::= SHOT | SHOT OF (TypeExp | alias) | COUNT(TypeExp)
TypeExp ::= (Event | Object).typeName(.typeName)*  (AS alias)?
```

The definitions of logicalExpression and AttributeExpresseion are the same as those in section 3.1.

The FROM clause designates the initial result set. The keyword "Event" shows that the typeName after the "." is a concept event while the keyword "Object" shows that the typeName after the "." is a concept object.

The logicalExpression in the WHERE clause is used to filter the initial result set. The spatio-temporal relationship in the logicalExpression will be converted to the spatio-temporal relationship among related semantic objects and the filtering will result in a set of semantic objects. Visual queries can be achieved by utilizing FeatureExpression in logicalExpression.

The GROUP BY clause group the filtered result set by some designated attributes. Each group will be used to calculate the expressions in the SELECT clause.

The SELECT clause designates how to acquire the final result from the result set acquired after the previous processes. The keyword "SHOT" means the shots that the elements appear are interested in and should be returned. If there are multiple TypeExp in the FROM clause, the keyword "SHOT OF" is needed to specify which TypeExp is wanted. The keyword "COUNT" means take the count of elements.

4.2   The Query Ability

The query ability is one of the most important criterions to measure a data model. In this section, we will analyze the various queries that THVDM supports through which we can draw the conclusion that THVDM has a strong ability for supporting query.

1)   Query by events
     a)   Query by the kind of events
           E.g. get the shots where dunk occurs
           SELECT SHOT
           FROM Event.dunk
     b)   Query by event's instance
           E.g. get the shots of Jordan passing to Rodman
           SELECT SHOT
           FROM Event.pass
           WHERE role.passer->name = "Jordan" AND role.receiver->name =
     "Rodman"
     c)   Query by inter-event relationship
           E.g. get all shots in which Jordan's foul cause a foul shot by Rodman.
           SELECT SHOT OF f
           FROM Event.foul AS f, Event.foulshot As s
           WHERE f.role.fouler->name = "Jordan" AND f.causing-> = s AND
     s.role.shoter ="Rodman"

2)   Query by objects
     a)   Query by concept objects
           E.g. get all shots in which Jordan appears.
           SELECT SHOT
           FROM   Object.player
           WHERE name = "Jordan"

    b)   Query by inter-object spatio-temporal relationship
       E.g. Get all shots in which Jordan appears left to Rodman.
       SELECT SHOT OF p1
       FROM Object.player AS p1, Object.player AS p2
       WHERE p1.name = "Jordan" AND p2.name = "Rodman" AND p1 left p2
    c)   Query by inter-object domain specific relationship
       E.g. Get all shots in which Jordan's coach appears
       SELECT SHOT OF c
       FROM Object.coach AS c, Object.player AS p
       WHERE p.name = "Jordan" AND p.coach-> = t

3)   Query by relationship of object and event

    a)   Query events by objects
       E.g. Get shots of all events that Jordan participates in
       SELECT SHOT
       FROM Event.ConceptEvent
       WHERE role.* ->name = "Jordan"
       E.g. Get all shots of Jordan's dunk.
       SELECT SHOT
       FROM Event.dunk
     WHERE role.dunker-> name = "Jordan"
    b)   Query objects by events
       E.g. Get all shots contains players who participated in the foul occurred at the
  15th minute.
       SELECT SHOT OF p
       FROM Object.player AS p, Event.foul AS f
       WHERE f.role.*->name = p.name AND f.time = "15m"

4)   Statistical query

       E.g. How many dunk occurs in the second quarter?
       SELECT COUNT(d)
       FROM Event.dunk AS d
       WHERE conceptTime = "second quarter"
       E.g. Calculate the number of dunk of each player in the second quarter.
       SELECT COUNT(d)
       FROM Event.dunk AS d
       WHERE conceptTime = "second quarter"
       GROUP BY role.dunk->name

5 The Prototype System

To prove the validity of THVDM, we developed a prototype system the architecture
of which is shown in figure 4. Since we don't bother with the construction of the
model, this process is represented by a single rectangle named "model constructor"
and the data in the data model are collected manually.

From the architecture of the prototype system we can see that it has two main
modules: definition and query.

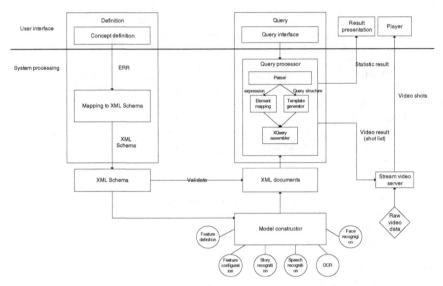

Fig. 4. The architecture of the prototype system

The definition module enables users to define domain-specific concepts. The user-defined, ERR-represented concepts are then converted to XML Schema using the mapping rules mentioned in section 3.4 and stored to validate the XML documents generated by the Model constructor later.

The query module accepts users' queries that conform to the syntax introduced in section 4.1, processes the query and returns the results. The working process and components are as follows:

First, the query is passed to the Parser component where it is separated into two parts: expressions and query structure. The expression includes all the entities, attributes and relationships in the knowledge layer while the query structure includes the remaining.

Second, the expressions are sent to the Element mapping component to be converted to indicators to elements in the XML documents. At the same time, the query structure will be sent to the Template generator component where a XQuery template is generated according to the structure (for example, whether the query is about only concept objects, only concept events or both concept objects and concept events; whether there is a join in the structure etc.).

Third, the element indicators are filled into the XQuery template to form the complete XQuery which can be applied to the XML documents to get the desired results.

Finally, the query expressed using XQuery is executed and the results are returned. If the results are statistical information, they will be returned to users directly through a result presentation component. If some video clips are wanted, the result of performing the XQuery sentences will be a list of shot positions. The list will be passed to the stream video server, which gets the corresponding video clip from raw video data base and invoke appropriate player to play them.

6   Conclusion and Future Works

In this paper, we first analyzed the shortcomings of some existing data model and then presented a new data model THVDM to enhance the ability. THVDM consists of three layers: feature layer, semantic layer and knowledge layer. It supports not only visual query but also content query and can be easily applied to various domains. A simple but expressive query language is developed to query the data represented by the THVDM. All activities related to high level information are performed in the knowledge layer, thus users need not have any idea about the underlying implementation.

Our work will continue along two dimensions. The first aspect will focus on integrating other technologies related to knowledge (e.g. ontology) to the knowledge layer to enhance its reasoning ability, thus serve for more intelligent queries. The second aspect will be concerns with enhancing the semantic layer to acquire more facts from the feature layer and the raw video data to support the knowledge layer.

References

1.   Chunxiao Xing, Lizhu Zhou et al. Developing Tsinghua University Architecture Digital Library for Chinese Architecture Study and University Education. Proceedings of the 5th International Conference on Asian Digital Libraries. Singapore, 2002, pp. 206–217
2.   Hjelsvold R, Midtstraum R. Modeling and querying video data. Proceedings of 20th International conference on Very Large Data Bases. 1994
3.   Jiang H, Montesi D, Elmagarmid AK. "Video Text database systems". In: Georganas ND(ed) Proc. Fourth IEEE Int. Conf. on Multimedia Computing and Systems, 1997, pp. 344–351
4.   Weiss, R., Duda, A., Gifford, D.K.. Composition and search with a video Algebra. IEEE Multimedia, vol 1. 1995
5.   R. Weiss, A. Duda, D. K. Gifford. Content-based Access to Algebraic Video. Proceedings. of Int. Conf. on Multimedia Computing and Systems, 1994, pp. 140–151
6.   Haitao Jiang, Ahmed K. Elmagarmid. Spatial and Temporal Content-Based Access to Hypervideo Databases. VLDB Journal 7(4): pp. 226–238(1998)
7.   Del Bimbo A, Vicario E, Zingoni D. Symbolic description and visual querying of image sequences using spatio-temporal logic. IEEE Trans Knowledge and Data Engine 7: pp. 609–622
8.   Young Francis Day, Ashfaq A. Khokhar, Serhan Dagtas, Arif Ghafoor. A Multi-Level Abstraction and Modeling in Video Databases. Multimedia Systems 7(5): pp. 409–423 (1999)
9.   S. Adali, K.S. Candan, S-S Chen, K. Erol, V.S. Subrahmanian, Advanced video information systems: Data structure and query processing. ACM Multimedia Syst 4: pp. 172–186
10. Li JZ, Özsu MT, Szafron D. Modeling of moving objects in a video database. Proceedings of. IEEE Int. Conf. on Multimedia Computing and Systems, 1997, pp. 336–343
11. Amarnath Gupta, Terry E. Weymouth , Ramesh Jain. Semantic Queries with Pictures: The VIMSYS Model. VLDB 1991, pp. 69–79
12. Roland Tusch, Harald Kosch, Laszlo Böszörmenyi. VIDEX: An Integreated Generic Video Indexing Approach. Proceedings of the ACM Multimedia Conference, 2000, pp. 448–451

13. J.Z. Li, M.T. Ozsu, and D. Szafron. Spatial reasoning rules in multimedia management systems. Proceedings of Int. Conf. on Multimedia Modeling, 1996, pp. 119–133
14. John Z. Li, M. Tamer Özsu, Duane Szafron. Modeling of Video Spatial Relationships in an Object Database Management System. Proceedings of the International Workshop on Multimedia Database Management Systems,1997
15. MPEG7 specification

Yu Wang received the BS and M.S. degree from Xi'an Jiaotong University respectively in 1999 and in 2002. She is a Ph.D student in the Department of Computer Science and Technology of Tsinghua University. Her research interests include database, digital library, and video management.

Chun-xiao Xing received the Ph. D. degree from Northwestern Polytechnical University in 1999, and finished his postdoctor in the Department of Computer Science and Technology of Tsinghua University in 2001. Now he is an associate professor in the Department of Computer Science and Technology of Tsinghua University. His research interests include database, digital library, distributed multimedia systems, and digital rights management. He is the member of IEEE.

Li-zhu Zhou received the M.S degree in Computer Science from University of Toronto in 1983. He is a full professor and chairman of Department of Computer Science and Technology, Tsinghua University. He and his database group has completed dozens of research projects sponsored by the Natural Science Foundation of China and the national high-tech programs in logical databases, multiple databases integration, data warehouses, massive information systems, digital library, geographical information systems etc. His major research interests include database technology, digital library, massive storage systems, data warehouses etc. He is the member of IEEE.

A Multimedia Digital Library System Based on MPEG-7 and XQuery*

Mann-Ho Lee[1], Ji-Hoon Kang[1], Sung Hyon Myaeng[2], Soon Joo Hyun[2],
Jeong-Mok Yoo[1], Eun-Jung Ko[1], Jae-Won Jang[1], and Jae-Hyoung Lim[2]

[1] Dept. of Computer Science, Chungnam National University
220 Gung-Dong, Yuseong-Gu, Daejeon, 305-764, South Korea
{mhlee,jhkang,jmyoo,brain08,jaeback}@cs.cnu.ac.kr
[2] School of Engineering, Information and Communications University
58-4 Hwaam-Dong, Yuseong-Gu, Daejeon, 305-732, South Korea
{myaeng,shyun,theagape}@icu.ac.kr

Abstract. We designed and implemented a digital library system that supports content-based retrieval of multimedia objects based on MPEG-7 and XQuery. MPEG-7, a metadata standard for multimedia objects, can describe various features such as color histograms of images and content descriptors. As such, a multimedia digital library system built with MPEG-7 metadata can provide content-based search for multimedia objects. Since MPEG-7 is defined by XML schema, XQuery is a natural choice as a query language. By adopting the standards, MPEG-7 and XQuery, our system has benefited for interoperability. First, any MPEG-7 metadata instance can be accommodated into the system with no additional effort. Second, any system that can generate a query in XQuery can retrieve necessary information. Third, our system can be easily extended to support any XML documents. Currently we have developed a prototype system for retrieving images of Korean cultural heritage.

1 Introduction

MPEG-7 is a metadata standard for multimedia objects [1]. It allows representing traditional metadata attributes such as title, authors, date, and so on. Moreover, MPEG-7 can also describe various physical features such as color histograms of images and content descriptors. Consider that a query image is give to find similar ones from the set of images with MPEG-7 metadata, especially with color histograms. If we extract the color histogram from the query image, we can search the MPEG-7 metadata set for similar images by comparing the color histograms. As such, a multimedia digital library system built with MPEG-7 metadata can provide content-based search for multimedia objects.

The MPEG-7 metadata schema is defined by XML schema. Each instance of MPEG-7 is an XML data. In order to retrieve MPEG-7 metadata, we need to consider query languages for XML. There have been some XML query languages like as XQL[2], XML-QL[3], Quilt[4], XPath[5], and XQuery[6]. Among them, XQuery,

---

* This research has been supported by Software Research Center, founded by KOSEF.

T.M.T. Sembok et al. (Eds.): ICADL 2003, LNCS 2911, pp. 193–205, 2003.

which has been influenced from most of the previous XML query languages, is a forthcoming standard for querying XML data.

We designed and implemented a digital library system that supports content-based retrieval of multimedia objects based on two important standards, MPEG-7 and XQuery. MPEG-7 enables content-based search. Since MPEG-7 metadata is XML data, XQuery was a natural choice as a query language. Besides we believe that the use of both a standard metadata and a standard query language would be essential for interoperability among multimedia digital library systems.

A user can give a query in the form of an example image or a template filled with values to be used as search keys. The system searches MPEG-7 metadata and returns the metadata that matches the query to a varying extent. The architecture is depicted in Fig. 1. The system consists of five main modules: MPEG-7 Metadata Creator, User Interface, XQuery Engine, Information Retrieval(IR) Engine, and Repository Engine.

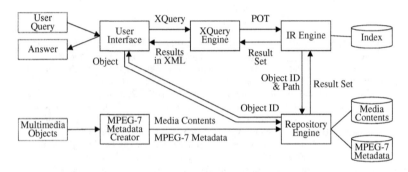

Fig. 1. A Digital Library System based on MPEG-7 and XQuery

The MPEG-7 metadata Creator gets multimedia objects as input and creates their corresponding MPEG-7 metadata. The objects are stored in a multimedia server and their MPEG-7 metadata in a relational DB by the Repository Engine.

The User Interface gives an interactive, easy-to-use, and graphical interface. It translates a user query to its corresponding form in XQuery and passes it to the XQuery Engine. The result in XML from the XQuery Engine, which is an XML fragment of MPEG-7 metadata, is returned to the user.

The XQuery Engine parses the query in XQuery and generates its Primitive Operation Tree (POT), which is defined as a protocol to the IR Engine. The IR Engine takes a POT from the XQuery Engine and searches for the metadata specified by the POT using the pre-configured index. The IR Engine finally finds a list of pairs of an object ID and its path information for the metadata fragment, which is given to the Repository Engine. The engine generates an SQL query to find the XML fragments satisfying the list from the MPEG-7 metadata DB. It executes the query and obtains the result set, which is returned to the XQuery Engine through the IR Engine. The XQuery Engine transforms the result set into an XML form that satisfies the constraint given by the query.

By adapting the standards, MPEG-7 and XQuery, our system benefits for interoperability. First, any MPEG-7 metadata instance can be accommodated into the system with no additional effort. Second, any system that can generate a query in

XQuery can retrieve necessary information. Third, our system can be easily extended to support any XML documents. Currently we have developed a prototype system for retrieving images of Korean cultural heritage.

2 Related Works

Most of the XQuery Engines assumes a storage system such as relational database systems and directly translates a query in XQuery into a storage-dependent query such as an SQL query [7, 8, 9]. Therefore they depend on the storage systems. In our approach, however, the XQuery Engine does not depend on the storage system and only generates POTs, which we consider is a more general data structure than any system-dependant storage.

Retrieving structured documents have been an important issue for information retrieval and database communities. Earlier work emphasized on the principles of ranking when texts are stored in a hierarchically structure document [10, 11]. More recently, researchers have been attempting to extend several query languages for XML data retrieval by inserting similarity-based operations [12]. There has been no approach to using XQuery to deal with MPEG-7 metadata that includes multi-media features such as color layout information in addition to text- and structure-based query constraints.

The MPEG-7 standard focuses on content-based multimedia retrieval and search. The content-based multimedia retrieval and search have power to improve services and systems in digital libraries, education, authoring multimedia, museums, art galleries, radio and TV broadcasting, e-commerce, surveillance, forensics, entertainment, so on [13]. There are many researches and developments of audio, video, and multimedia retrieval techniques and systems. Earlier researches used their own description metadata to describe media contents and to retrieve efficiently [14, 15, 16, 17]. As the MPEG-7 has been released as a multimedia metadata standard, researchers started to use it as the media content description tool [18, 19, 20, 21, 22, 23, 24]. However, currently, there are very few cases that a system has a complete framework based on MPEG-7 including media content metadata generation, metadata repository management, user query interface enabling content-based search, XQuery processing, and information retrieval technique.

3 System Architecture

3.1   MPEG-7 Metadata Creator

The MPEG-7 Metadata Creator is a graphic user interface. It receives an image and text annotation explaining the image as input and creates the MPEG-7 metadata instance for the image. The physical information of the image such a color histogram can be extracted from the image by using the feature extraction software [25]. Some information in the annotation data can be extracted by natural language processing, and automatically fill the corresponding fields of the MPEG-7 metadata. Other fields for semantic information should be filled manually. The MPEG-7 metadata and the image are passed to the Repository Engine so that it can store and manage them.

The MPEG-7 metadata instance is an XML document based on the XML schema. In order to create a metadata instance, users should know the structure of the MPEG-7 schema structure. However, the interface does not require the users to understand the schema in detail. The interface displays the metadata field entries and asks the users to fill the entries, and then it creates an MPEG-7 metadata from the information entered by the users. The interface displays the schema structure on the left hand side of the display for the MPEG-7 schema experts.

3.2   User Interface

The User Interface provides the users with an interactive, easy-to-use, and graphical interface. It translates a user query to its corresponding form in XQuery and passes it to the XQuery Engine. Moreover, it gets the retrieval result in XML passed from the XQuery Engine, converts it into the HTML format, and displays it to the users.

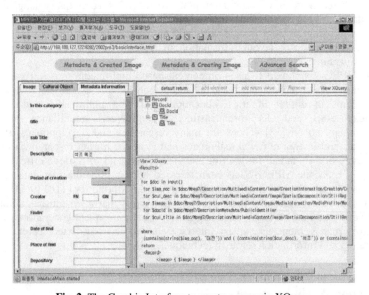

Fig. 2. The Graphic Interface to create a query in XQuery

XQuery consists of FLWR expressions that support iteration and binding of variables to intermediate results. Therefore, users must understand the XML schema and the FLWR expression to write user query in XQuery. It would be very difficult to write a query in this language XQuery correctly. The User Interface of the system allows the users to create a query in XQuery without knowing the XML schema and XQuery in detail.

The interface to create a query in XQuery is shown in Fig. 2. The window of the interface is divided into sub-windows, for for/let-clause, for where-clause (not shown in the figure), for return-clause, for XQuery-result. In the first three sub-windows, users fill in the retrieval conditions. The XQuery-result sub-window displays the result created so that users can confirm the query. While creating a query in XQuery, the Boolean expression for retrieval condition can be optimized. The result of optimization can be seen in another window. The query created is passed to the XQuery Engine for further processing of retrieval.

For example, let's consider the following query:

Retrieve titles of images created in Daejeon("대전") and containing

cultural objects of stone("석조") or wooden("목조") artifacts.

We type "대전", "석조", "목조" in the corresponding fields in the for/let-clause, build a Boolean expression in where-clause sub-windows, and build the format of the result in the return-clause sub-window. Then a query is created as shown in Fig. 3.

```
<Results>
{
    for $doc in input()
    for $img_poc in $doc/Mpeg7/.../Name
    for $cul_desc in $doc/Mpeg7/.../FreeTextAnnotation
    for $image in $doc/Mpeg7/.../MediaUri
    for $docId in $doc/Mpeg7/.../PublicIdentifier
    for $cul_title in $doc/Mpeg7/.../Title[@type="main"]
    where
        (contains(string($img_poc), "대전")) and
        ((contains(string($cul_desc), "석조")) or
        (contains(string($cul_desc), "목조"))))
    ranklimit(0)
    return
        <Record>
            <image> { $image } </image>
            <DocId> { $docId } </DocId>
            <Title> { $cul_title } </Title>
        </Record>
}
</Results>
```

Fig. 3. Example query in XQuery

Fig. 4. The Graphic Interface to display the result set

The query is passed to the XQuery Engine, and the User Interface gets the result set from XQuery Engine and displays the result set as shown in Fig. 4. In the result set, only thumbnail, title, and the object ID (not shown in the display) of the images are retrieved. Clicking a thumbnail image passes the object ID of the image to the Repository Engine. Then the Repository Engine searches the database for the metadata and the image with the object ID, and passes them to the User Interface. Now, users can get the detail information and the full image of the selected image. This method to display the final result set in two steps guarantees the fast service of the overall system.

For the user's convenience, the User Interface provides options to display the result set, in HTML format or in PDF format. Users can choose one of them as they want.

Moreover, it supports content-based retrieval query by example for images that uses features such as color histogram extracted from the query image by using the feature extraction software.

3.3   XQuery Engine

The basic function of the XQuery Engine consists of three sub-processes, (1) receiving a query in the form of XQuery from the User Interface, (2) getting an answer of the query from the IR Engine, and (3) returning it back to the User Interface.

Our XQuery Engine has the following useful aspects. First, any user interface that generates a query in XQuery is able to access any digital library system including our XQuery Engine. Second, we define a set of primitive operations for POTs so that they can become a standard interface between the XQuery Engine and an IR Engine. Third, some query optimizations over POTs can be done in the XQuery Engine so that better searching performance is expected.

PO Number	Primitive Operation
1	`list _MatchElement (path, string)`
2	`list _LessThanElement (path, value)`
3	`list _LessThanEqualElement (path, value)`
4	`list _GreaterThanElement (path, value)`
5	`list _GreaterThanEqualElement (path, value)`
6	`list _Contain (path, string)`
7	`list _SimilarTo (path, string)`
8	`list _MatchTitle (path, type, string)`
9	`list _ContainTitle (path, type, string)`
10	`list _MatchStructuredAnnotation (path, definition, string)`
11	`list _ContainStructuredAnnotaiton (path, definition, string)`
12	`list _Or (list, list)`
13	`list _And (list, list)`
14	`list _AndNot (list, list)`
15	`list _Return (int, string)`

Fig. 5. Primitive Operations

The portability is an important issue for the design of the XQuery Engine. Since we adopt a standard XML query, called XQuery, for user queries, any user interface that can generate XQuery can interface with the XQuery Engine. Another relationship between the XQuery Engine and the IR Engine also requires a standard information exchange method. For this purpose, we define 15 primitive operations as in Fig. 5. Each primitive operation is an atomic operation for IR Engine. Any query can be represented by a Primitive Operation Tree (POT) whose leaf nodes are primitive operations. POT is a more general data structure than any system-dependent storage representation. By using POT, our XQuery Engine can run on top of any IR Engine that can understand POT.

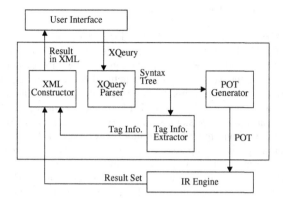

Fig. 6. XQuery Engine Architecture

Fig. 6 shows the architecture of the XQuery Engine. A user query is given to the XQuery Parser. The parser analyses the query and produces a syntax tree for the query. The syntax tree is used for two purposes. First, it is transformed into a POT by the POT Generator, which is passed to the IR Engine. Second, any answer to a query should be an XML instance, whose format is specified in the original XQuery and finally in the syntax tree. This tagging information is extracted from the syntax tree by the Tagging Information Extractor. Later after the XQuery Engine receives a result set from the IR Engine, the XML Constructor transforms the result set into an XML instance according to the tagging information. The result in XML is returned to the User Interface as an answer to the given user query.

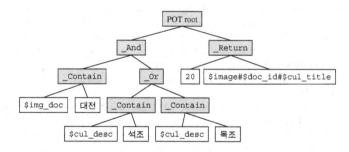

Fig. 7. The POT corresponding to the query in Fig. 3.

Fig. 7 is a POT for the query in Fig. 3. A POT is serialized as a string, which is actually passed to the IR Engine. Currently, XQuery is a working draft and does not fully support the functions for information retrieval. For our purpose, we slightly extend the XQuery syntax by adding the "ranklimit" phrase, which is used when a user wants to restrict the number of ranked results. An example of the ranklimit phrase is shown also in Fig. 3 (circled by an oval).

3.4   Information Retrieval(IR) Engine

In traditional information retrieval systems, a document as a whole is the target for a query. With increasing interests in structured documents like XML documents, there is a growing need to build an IR system that can retrieve parts of documents, which satisfy not only content-based but also structured-based requirements [10]. The retrieval engine we developed in this work supports the functionality with the goal of handling the semantics of the XQuery for MPEG-7 data (i.e. metadata of images).

Like conventional retrieval systems, our retrieval engine consists of two modules: the indexer and the retrieval modules. The indexer receives MPEG-7 data in the form of XML from the Repository Engine and parses them to create an index whose basic structure is in the form of an inverted file. The indexer takes the parsed elements and attributes of MPEG-7 data and creates the index structure as in Fig. 8 so that the traditional content-based and structure-based retrieval can be done together.

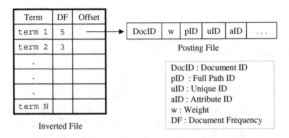

Fig. 8. Index structure for structure- and content-based retrieval

The retrieval module takes a POT from the XQuery Engine and searches the metadata (i.e. MPEG-7 metadata) using the preconfigured index. The IR Engine finally finds a list of documents represented by pairs of an object ID corresponding to an image and its path information to the element satisfying the term in a primitive operation, so that the structural requirement in the query can be examined. After the necessary operations combining the partial results (e.g. a Boolean operation), the results are given to the Repository Engine that fetches the actual image corresponding to the MPEG-7 data.

The dictionary part of the inverted file structure as depicted in Fig. 8 consists of terms, document frequencies (DF), and offset values. Terms are extracted from the elements of MPEG-7 metadata as if they are extracted from unstructured documents. DF is counted by considering the metadata for an image as a document. The offset part contains the starting location of the list of document information in the Posting File. Each segment of the list in the Posting File contains the document ID (DocID), weight, path ID (pID), unique ID (uID), and attribute ID (aID). DocID is the identifier of the document stored in the Repository Engine.

We use the well-known the *tf*idf* weight to calculate the weight of the term in a document. The next item, pID, is the identifier of the predefined absolute path from the root element to the leaf node containing the term in an XML document. Next to the pID is uID (unique ID) that uniquely identifies individual elements in the XML document. In order to locate a child or the parent of an element easily, we employ a *K*-ary tree by which the hierarchical structure of a tree (an XML document in this case) is well represented [26]. The relationship between a parent element and its child element can be directly obtained as follows:

$$Parent(i) = \left[(i-2)/K+1\right] \tag{1}$$

where i is an arbitrary node in K-ary tree and K is a degree that each internal node has.

The attribute ID, aID, serves as an identifier of an attribute value and is used for retrieval based on an attribute value assigned to an element.

Doc ID	Color
Doc N_i	35 26 34 4 20 27 8 14 16 25 17 11
Doc N_{i+1}	41 31 33 12 25 7 17 21 16 26 16 8
•••	•••
Doc N_n	28 26 34 4 20 28 14 16 17 35

Fig. 9. Index structure for a color-based retrieval

Fig. 9 shows an index structure that is used for high-speed retrieval and browsing by using the color information of images. This index structure consists of DocID (Document ID), and a vector of "color layout" values which specify a spatial distribution of colors. Each number in a color vector represents the degree of the particular color axis. The similarity of a query and an image in terms of a color vector is calculated based on the following formula:

$$Sim\,(Q,\,D_i) = \sum_{j=1}^{n} \left| q_j - d_{ij} \right| \tag{2}$$

where Q & D_i represent the color layout vector of a query & a vector for a document i. The retrieval module ranks a set of documents by using the p-norm model, and uses structural constrains as a filter [27]. For a query containing both term-based and color-based constraints, we perform a merge operation of the retrieval results: one set coming from term-based retrieval and another from color-based retrieval.

A query in XQuery can be divided into several primitive operations that are structure-based or content-based or even a combination of them. Table 1 shows an example of a retrieval query that is divided into three sub-queries.

For structure-based retrieval that takes into account the logical structure of a document, we first retrieve a set of documents that are relevant to a given keyword "대전" in the query, and filters out the documents that do not satisfy the structural constraints expressed with path information, "/MPEG7/Descripton/MultimediaContent/ Image/CreationInformation/Creation/CreationCoordinates/Location/Nam."

Table 1. An example of different types of queries

TYPE	QUERY
Structure-based	*Contain* (/MPEG7/Descripton/.../CreationCoordinates/Location/Name, "대전")
Content-based	*Similar_To* (/Mpeg7/Description/.../Image/VisualDescriptor, "29 22 36 14 8 7 15 3 16 13 15 19")
combination	*Contain* (/MPEG7/Descripton/.../CreationCoordinates/Location/Name, "대전") **AND** *Similar_To* (/Mpeg7/Description/.../VisualDescriptor, "29 22 36 14 8 7 15 3 16 13 15 19")

3.5   Repository Engine

The Repository Engine (RE) provides an effective storing and retrieval service of MPEG-7 metadata. The main functions of the RE are (1) extracting structural information, (2) storing XML documents and image (media) files, (3) retrieving XML data. The RE extracts the structural information of MPEG-7 metadata from metadata documents and stores the information in the database. Then RE stores metadata document instances sent by the MPEG-7 metadata creator according to MPEG-7 metadata structure. The RE stores media content files and provides them to the clients through HTTP. When the IR engine requests XML data specified with a document ID and an absolute path, the RE performs a retrieval task using the structure information and delivers the resulting XML metadata to the IR engine.

In the following subsections, we show the architecture of the RE and discuss how it carries out structure information extraction, XML document and image file management, and XML data retrieval.

Architecture of RE. The RE has three major components, the Structural Information Generator, the Storage Manager, and the Retrieval Manager as shown in Fig. 10.

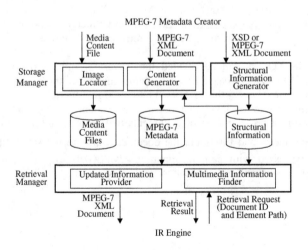

Fig. 10. Repository Engine Architecture

The Structural Information Generator extracts the structural information of MPEG-7 XML metadata and stores it into a database. It creates tables that store the metadata instances based on the structure. The Storage Manager stores the MPEG-7 metadata instances and media files into the database. It consists of Content Generator and Image Locator which manipulate XML document and media files, respectively. The Retrieval Manager interacts with the IR engine. In response to the requests from the IR engine, it transfers XML documents to the IR engine for indexing. It consists of Updated Information Provider and Multimedia Information Finder. The Updated Information Provider sends XML documents to the IR engine for index update and the Multimedia Information Finder carries out retrieval service.

Automatic Extraction of Metadata Structural Information. Registering the structural information of MPEG-7 description metadata, the RE stores and retrieves metadata according to the structure.

To extract and store the structural information, there are two often used methods: deductive and inductive methods. The former lets the system deal every form of document instances by using schema definition (XSD: XML Schema Definition)[28] defined in the standard MPEG-7 specifications. This method has advantages that can include the whole MPEG-7 definition and can accept many changes between document instances, but has problem of high developing cost and execution time. The latter extracts the structural information from a document instance. For the inductive method, the input document is required to satisfy only the minimum number of the MPEG-7 descriptors used by a specific application.

The RE adopts the inductive method because each MPEG-7 based system uses only several descriptors, and thus supporting all descriptors defined by the MPEG-7 standard specifications causes unnecessary overhead in the course of development and run-time performance degrade.

Storing XML Document and Media Contents. When a media content (i.e. image) file and its MPEG-7 description metadata document are transferred in a pair from MPEG-7 XML metadata creator, the Storage Manager stores them separately and maintains a mapping table of Uniform Resource Identifiers (URI) of media files and document IDs [29]. The Image Locator deals with storing media content files and the Content Generator maintains MPEG-7 description metadata documents.

When the Storage Manager receives a new XML document, the document is not stored in file format, but broken down into elements and attributes. Then it stores them in the database according to the pre-identified structure information. This database approach allows faster metadata access and media file retrieval. We used Microsoft SQL Server 2000 as the underlying database management tool in the prototype development.

After storing an XML document instance and a media content file, the Storage Manager generates a document ID for the XML document and a URI for the media content file. It keeps the pair in a database table, and transfers the ID with the document to the IR engine where the metadata document is indexed for retrieval service.

Metadata Retrieval. The Retrieval Manager receives two sets of arguments in a query from the IR engine: a set of MPEG-7 metadata document IDs and absolute paths of elements in the documents. From the absolute paths, the system finds the corresponding element IDs from the structural information table in the database. With the element IDs and other structural information in the database, such as sibling orders, a DOM tree of each element is constructed. The DOM trees are the result set of the query to be returned to the IR engine.

4 Discussion

Metadata has become an essential element for resource discovery and retrieval, especially with unstructured data such as text and multimedia. Among others, MPEG-7 is quite challenging and interesting to deal with because of the variety of features and the structural complexity that can be represented in its manifestation.

Our research is one of few efforts to handle MPEG-7 metadata using XQuery, a standard query language for XML, in a digital library setting. Our goal to this point has been to develop a system that consists of essential components that any digital library for MPEG-7 metadata should provide: a persistent storage and its manager for MPEG-7 metadata and the corresponding images, an indexing and retrieval engine that can handle various operations necessary for MPEG-7 metadata, an XQuery processing engine capable of handling queries targeted at MPEG-7 yet extensible for other purposes, and a query interface for users who are not an expert in XQuery nor in MPEG-7.

We have developed a system that can handle image data in Korean cultural heritage, with which the essential digital library functionality for MPEG-7 can be demonstrated. While we have addressed various technical issues in the course of designing and developing this system, we feel that this is still a test bed that can be used to enhance the technology from both theoretical and practical points of view and eventually build an operational digital library.

References

1. ISO,/IEC: Introduction to MPEG-7 (version 4.0). approved, N4675, March 2002
2. W3C: XML Query Language (XQL). Sep. 1998.
    (http://www.w3.org/TandS/QL/QL98/pp/xql)
3. W3C: A Query Language for XML. Note, Aug. 1998.
    (http://www.w3.org/TR/NOTE-xml-ql/)
4. IMB: An XML Query Language. May. 2000.
    (http://www.almaden.ibm.com/cs/people/chamberlin/quilt.html)
5. W3C: XML Path Language (XPath) 2.0. Working Draft, May. 2003.
    (http://www.w3.org/TR/xpath20/)
6. W3C: XQuery 1.0: An XQuery Language. Working Draft, May. 2003.
    (http://www.w3.org/TR/2003/WD-xquery-20030502)
7. Shanmugasundaram, J., Kiernan, J., Shekita, E., Fan, C., Funderburk, J.: Querying XML Views of Relatinal Data. Proc. of 27th VLDB, Rome, Italy, Sep. 2001

8. Fan, C., Funderburk, J., Lam, H., Kiernan, J., Shekita, E., Shanmugasundaram, J.: XTABLES: Bridging Relational Technology and XML. IBM System Journal, 2002
9. DSRG: Rainbow: Relational Database Auto-tuning for Efficient XML Query Processing. 2002. (http://davis.wpi.edu/dsrg/rainbow)
10. Myaeng, S.H., Jang, D., Kim, M., Zhoo, Z.: A Flexible Model for Retrieval of SGML Documents. In Proc. of the 21st SIGIR, 1998, 138–145
11. Navarro, G., Baeza-Yates, R.: Proximal Nodes, A Model to Query Document Databases by Content and Structure. ACM Trans. on Information Systems, 15 (4), 1997, 400–435
12. Bremer, J.M., Gertz, M.: XQuery/IR: Integrating XML Document and Data Retrieval. In Proc. of the 5th Int. Workshop on Web and Databases, Madison, Wisconsin, Jun. 6–7, 2002, 1–6
13. Manjunath, B.S., Salembier, P., Sikora, T.: Introduction to MPEG-7: Multimedia Content Description Interface. ISBN0471486787, John Wiley&Sons, 2002, 335–361
14. Hu, M.J., Jian, Y.: Multimedia Description Framework (MDF) for Content Description of Audio/Video Documents. Proc. of the 4th ACM Conf. on Digital Libraries, Aug. 1999
15. Chung, T.S., Ruan, L.Q.: A Video Retrieval and Sequencing System. ACM Transactions on Information Systems (TOIS), Vol. 13, Issue 4, Oct. 1995
16. Li, W., Gauch, S., Gauch, J., Pua, K.M.: VISION: A Digital Video Library. Proc. of the 1st ACM Int. Conf. on Digital Libraries, Apr. 1996
17. Chang, S.F., Chen, W., Meng, H.J., Sundaram, H., Zhong, D.: VideoQ: An Automated Content Based Video Search System Using Visual Cues. Proc. of the 5th Int. Conf. on Multimedia, Nov. 1997
18. Graves, A., Lalmas, M.: Video Retrieval using an MPEG-7 based Inference Network. Proc. of the 25th annual Int. ACM SIGIR Conf. on Research and Development in Information Retrieval, Aug. 2002
19. Rehm, E.: Representing Internet Streaming Media Metadata using MPEG-7 Multimedia Description Schemes. Proc. of the 2000 ACM workshops on Multimedia, Nov. 2000
20. Martínez, J.M., González, C., Fernández, O., García, C., de Ramón, J.: Towards Universal Access to Content using MPEG-7. Proc. of the 10th ACM Int. Conf. on Multimedia, Dec. 2002
21. Charlesworth, J.P.A., Garner, P.N.: Spoken Content Metadata and MPEG-7. Proc. of the 2000 ACM Workshops on Multimedia, Nov. 2000
22. Döller, M., Kosch, H., Dörflinger, B., Bachlechner, A., Blaschke, G.: Demonstration of an MPEG-7 Multimedia Data Cartridge. Proc. of the 10th ACM Int. Conf. on Multimedia, Dec. 2002
23. van Setten, M., Oltmans, E.: Demonstration of a Distributed MPEG-7 Video Search and Retrieval Application in the Educational Domain. Proc. of the 9th ACM Int. Conf. on Multimedia, Oct. 2001
24. Löffler, J., Biatov, K., Eckes, C., Köhler, J.: IFINDER: an MPEG-7-based Retrieval System for Distributed Multimedia Content. Proc. of the 10th ACM Int. Conf. on Multimedia, Dec. 2002
25. Lee, H.K., Yoon, J.H., Lim, J.H., Jung, K.S., Jung, Y.J., Kang, K.O., Ro, Y.M.: Image Indexing and Retrieval System Using MPEG-7. IWAIT 2001, Feb. 2001, 63–68
26. Bentley, J.L.: Multidimensional Binary Search Trees Used for Associative Searching. Comm. of the ACM, 18(9), Sep. 1975
27. Salton, G., Fox, E., Wu, H.: Extended Boolean Information Retrieval. Comm. of the ACM, 26 (12), 1983, 1022–1036
28. David C. Fallside: XML Schema Part 0: Primer, W3C Recommendation. May 2 2001, http://www.w3.org/TR/xmlschema-0/
29. Berners-Lee, T., Fielding, R., Masinter, L., Uniform Resource Identifiers (URI): Generic Syntax (RFC2396). Aug. 1998, http://www.ietf.org/rfc/rfc2396.txt

Multimedia Data Transmission Using Multicast Delivery in Digital Library

Iksoo Kim, Backhyun Kim, and Taejune Hwang

Department of Information and Telecommunication Engineering University of Incheon
177 Namku Tohwa-dong Incheon, Korea
{iskim,hidesky24,tjhwang}@incheon.ac.kr

Abstract. This paper presents the method for multimedia data transmission using multicast delivery in digital library. It is not conventional server-based multicast delivery but client-based on-demand one. The Multicast-Agent Scheduler for providing on-demand multimedia service using multicast in digital library generates immediately a multicast group address and port number when clients request an identical multimedia data, then it sends them to media server and clients. And then media server transmits requested multimedia streams to multicast group and the clients join the group automatically. This technique reduces media server load in digital library and maximizes the efficiency of network resources. And this paper implements multimedia transmission system in digital library with WMS (Window Media Services) and its API.

1 Introduction

In digital library, the problems for multimedia information service are excessive load of server and inefficient use of network resources. The services in digital library have to support the on-demand service that can be provided to the consumer whenever or wherever he or she wants it [1, 2]

To support the on-demand service for multimedia data must be developed high speed network, huge capacity of storage devices, compression technology and intelligent multimedia server which processes various data streams including audio, video, images, animations and text. One of the best ways to transmit multimedia data on Internet is multicast delivery technique.

Although the multicast has been shown to be very effective in reducing the server bandwidth and effective use network resources, the conventional multicast delivery systems are server-based multicast system that announces service time for a specific item in advance, and then clients access media server at that time [3,4,5,6]. Consequently, these systems do not support on-demand service and they never apply in digital library. The media servers in digital library have to implement client-based multicast system not server based one.

In this paper, multimedia data transmission using multicast delivery technique can support on-demand service. For providing on-demand service, Multicast Agent Scheduler (MAS) on client side generates multicast group address and port number the instant that clients request service, and it sends them to media server and clients.

T.M.T. Sembok et al. (Eds.): ICADL 2003, LNCS 2911, pp. 206–217, 2003.

When client A requests multimedia data including text, the service starts immediately. Let's assume other some clients request an identical item during he read a text. When one of the clients including client A requests video, audio or animation data within identical multimedia data, the scheduler generates one multicast address and port number. It sends them to media server and clients. Then media server sends multimedia data to multicast group and clients join that group automatically. The clients except the first client cache into their buffer the streams from media server. The first requester can be serviced directly from network and others are serviced through their buffer when they want to view it because the reason is that the instants of service request are different. Thus, this technique reduces the load of media server and uses efficiently network resources because many clients can be serviced through one multicast channel. Therefore, this technique supports multimedia on-demand service with multicast delivery in digital library.

This paper implements a multimedia data transmission system using multicast delivery with WMS (Window Media Service) and its API.

The rest of the paper is as follows: Section 2 describes the structure and operation of client-based multicast delivery for multimedia data in detail, and Section 3 addresses the implementation of media systems supporting multicast delivery for digital library with WMS (Window Media Service) and its API, Section 4 shows the result of improvement of proposed system through simulation, finally Section 5 concludes the paper.

2   The Structure and Operation of Media System Using Multicast

In this paper, the media system using multicast delivery for digital library consists of media server, scheduler on server side and a number of clients connected to their ADSL/Cable modem network as high-speed network, as shown in Fig. 1 [7,8].

The media server immediately performs streaming service through Internet as a source device that provides service of a requested multimedia data. It transmits multimedia streams requested to specific multicast groups that are transmitted from scheduler.

The Multicast Agent Scheduler (MAS) is a central control point that generates multicast group address and port number through scheduling process. Then it sends multicast group address and port number to media server and clients requesting service. The MA-Scheduler groups a same multicast group when some clients request an identical multimedia data in order to increase channel efficiency. Thus, if any client requests service for a multimedia item, the MA-Scheduler investigates whether the thread for scheduling to an identical item exists or not. The MA-Scheduler assigns the same multicast group address and port number to client when the thread for a multimedia item requested exists. Otherwise, it generates another multicast group address and port number to client. Therefore the MA-Scheduler creates different multicast address and port number to clients who request an identical item after the each grouping duration passed. Thus, this system is not server-based multicast delivery system but client-based one.

The media server transmits multimedia streams as soon as receiving multicast address and port number from scheduler and the clients join a specific multicast group automatically after receiving them.

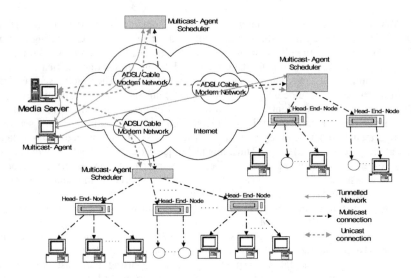

Fig. 1. The structure for VOD System using multicast

But the Internet does not fully support multicast delivery at present. So, this paper proposes Head-End-Network (HNET) that supports multicast, and HNET is similar to ADSL/Cable modem network. The HNET is composed of multicast-agent (MA)-Scheduler, some Head-End-Nodes (HEN) and a number of clients as shown in Fig. 1.

The MA-Scheduler is the heart of HNET. It establishes connection to media server in digital library with unicast, and then determines whether the requests from clients through some HENs are identical item or not. The MA-Scheduler is ready to support multicast when some clients request an identical item to media server. Media server transmits text page to each clients with unicast. And if one of clients requests multimedia data including audio, video or animation to media server, the MA-Scheduler generates a multicast group address and port number as explain before. The MA in media server and the MA-Scheduler on HNET generate multicast tunnel network between media server and HNET. Thus the requested multimedia streams from media server transmit to HENs through multicast tunnel.

The HEN manages clients' requests and multicast delivery. And it has a small buffer to store multimedia data for providing VCR operation in future study.

The clients access MA-Scheduler through HEN in order to request multimedia service and then they receive multicast group address and port number from the scheduler. Next, the clients join multicast group in order to receive the transmitted multimedia streams from server. The first request clients launches window media player with the aid of WMS (Window Media Service). The other clients who join same multicast group are cache those streams into their buffer, and then they drive window media player in order to view the requested multimedia streams from their buffer at the instant that they want to view them.

3   The Implementation of Media System Using Multicast Delivery

The implementation of Media system using multicast delivery in digital library uses WMS (Window Media Service) and its API, and it divides into three parts, client who requests service, MA-Scheduler as generation of multicast group address and port number according to clients' request, and Media Server as transmitting streams using received multicast address and port number.

The MA-Scheduler divides into two parts; main scheduler and socket thread. The main scheduler using server socket receives clients' request, generates multicast groups to each requested multimedia item and manages them. The socket thread maintains connection of client. The MA-Scheduler has three operating status; initialization, scheduling and termination. In initialization status, first, it generates *PubPoint( )* function to initiate COM library for WMS and creates *MovieInfoTable* which is the list of movies stored at Media Server that uses Hash function to reduce the seek time for finding the requested movie item. And then, MA-Scheduler generates *ServerSocket* to connect with client and maintains *Listen( )* until clients' request occurs.

When client requests service, MA-Scheduler generates scheduler thread object from socket object which is delivered by *accept( )* function of server socket object. The *accept( )* function is a member function that makes socket object accepting clients' request by *ServerSocket*. The *ServerSocket* of the MA-Scheduler receives clients' request and generates a thread per client who request service, and maintain each connection. It assigns multicast group address and port number and sends them to Media Server and clients that request service. For announcing available movie, scheduler transmits *MovieInfoTable* to client.

The Scheduler thread generates socket between scheduler and client in order to establish connection and gets ready for exchanging streams between them. Scheduling status has two conditions; new connection and join connection. When client requests service, Scheduler creates multicast information file (.nsc) for transmitting video items using *GenerateMServerNsc* which is a member function including client IP requesting service, the requested video item number and publishing point. *GenerateMServerNsc* defines a generation function for multicast group address and port number. Also, it defines arrays of multicast group addresses generated for scheduling video item and of flags indicating whether generated address is usable or not. If clients' request about an identical video item is in scheduling duration time, scheduler returns previously configured multicast information file to client. If not, scheduler creates new multicast information file and sends it to client. The scheduler thread disconnects socket connection when the scheduling is ended through socket object. Thus, the scheduler notifies Media Server to send requested video item to multicast group address as a destination and clients who request service to join a multicast group. Fig. 2 and 3 show overall service procedure of proposed system and MA-Scheduler procedure, respectively.

The MA-Scheduler is the heart of providing multimedia service in digital library. It receives clients' request for multimedia items, and generates immediately multicast group address and port number. Then it sends them to media server and clients who request service. But it generates another group address and port number when other clients request an identical multimedia item after media server terminates transmission. Fig. 3 shows the procedure of Multicast-Agent (MA)-Scheduler. The steps 5 to 7 in MA-Scheduler procedure of Fig. 3 perform these operations. If there is no request from other clients for an identical multimedia item, the MA-Scheduler does not generate multicast address and media server transmits multimedia streams with unicast the same as text-based page.

Step 1: Client accesses Multicast-Agent (MA)-Scheduler and media server for service request

Step 2: Media server starts text-based page service through unicast delivery

Step 3: The MA-Scheduler investigates whether the scheduling session for requested identical service exists or not.

If it exists go to step 5.

Step 4: The MA-Scheduler performs grouping and generates multicast group address and port number.

Step 5: The MA-Scheduler sends multicast group address and port number to media server and clients who request an identical multimedia item.

Step 6: Media server receives request to multimedia items within text-based page

Step 7: Digital library system establishes multicast tunnel network between MA on server side and MA-Scheduler

Step 8: Media server transmits requested item to a received multicast group.

Step 9: The clients join to their HEN with the received multicast group and port number.

Step 10: If the client who request first multimedia items, then launches Window Media Player for play-out them: Goto step 12

else the other clients cache them into their buffer.

Step 11: Each client launches Window Media Player for play-out them at appropriate time

Step 12: Media server terminates multimedia data transmission service.

Fig. 2. Overall multimedia service procedure using multicast delivery in digital library

Step 1: Initiate MA-Scheduler

Generates PubPoint ( ) to initiate Publishing Point and COM library

Creates MovieInfoTable

Generates ServerSocket

Step 2: The MA-Scheduler waits until the clients request multimedia service.

Step 3: The MA-Scheduler receives clients' request through HEN

Step 4: Scheduler thread wakes up

Step 5: The MA-Scheduler investigates whether the scheduling session for requested multimedia item exists or not.

If it exists, then go to step 7.

Step 6: The MA-Scheduler performs grouping and generates multicast group address and port number during grouping duration, generates Publishing Point and creates multicast information file (.nsc).

Step 7: The MA-Scheduler sends multicast group address and port number to media server and clients who request an identical multimedia item.

Step 8: The MA-Scheduler establishes multicast tunnel network with MA on media server side

Step 9: Completion Scheduling

Step 10: The MA-Scheduler receives multicast-delivered multimedia streams and transmits them to HENs

Fig. 3. MA-Scheduler procedure on HNET side

Fig. 4 and 5 show media server and client procedure, respectively. The media server generates **Datagram** socket and inserts the multicast group address and port number within the datagram packet, and transmits multimedia streams to clients. It divides into two parts; the one is **Datagram** socket as a maintaining indirect connection with clients and the other is data transmitting for sending requested multimedia streams.

Step 1: The MA-Scheduler accesses media server: Media server starts.

Step 2: Media server receives multicast group address and port number from the MA-Scheduler.

If it does not receive them, goto step 4; Requested multimedia streams are delivered by unicast

Step 3: Media server notifies MA on server side to establish multicast tunneling network to MA-Scheduler

Step 4: Media server investigates compression format and the rate of transmission.

If unicast transmission, media server transmits requested multimedia streams and goto step 6

Step 5: Media server transmits multimedia streams with received multicast address and port number through multicast tunnel.

Step 6: Media server completes transmission of multimedia streams; Completion server program

Fig. 4. Media server procedure

Step 1: Client starts Window Media Player and prepares connection to MA-Scheduler

Step 2: Client accesses to media server through MA-Scheduler

Step 3: Client requests multimedia items to MA-Scheduler after connection.

Step 4: If MA-Scheduler receives another request for an identical multimedia item, client receives multicast group address and port number from MA-Scheduler with multicast information file (.nsc), else goto step 8

Step 5: Client closes connection to MA-Scheduler

Step 6: Client joins multicast group address in order to receive transmitted video streams through multicast tunneled network from media server
If the client is the first requester for multimedia item, goto step 8

Step 7: All the clients who request and identical multimedia item cache the streams on their buffer

Step 8: Window Media Player plays out multimedia streams from their buffer or multicast tunneled network
Or Window Media Player plays out directly multimedia streams from unicast channel

Step 9: Window Media Player stops play-out.

Fig. 5. Client procedure

The media server investigates whether the server resources are consumed or not, and the requested multimedia streams store in the disk or not. It does not need to know clients' ID who requests service, their IP and how many clients request an identical multimedia item. The MA-Scheduler performs such operations. The media server performs only transmission of requested multimedia streams.

For requesting a specific multimedia item, client and MA-Scheduler generate sockets, and then client sends data to the main scheduler for service request. The client receives a multicast group address and a port number from the scheduler thread. Then, client generates multicast socket with received multicast group address and joins the group to receive transmitted multimedia streams through multicast tunnel network from the media server. Excepting the first request client, all clients who request an identical multimedia page cache the multimedia streams on their buffer and launch Window Media Player at the instant that they want to view and render the streams from their buffer. But the first request client play-outs directly multimedia streams through the multicast tunneled network.

Fig. 6 shows the GUI Console for monitoring MA-Scheduler. It has configured four information parts; current scheduling multicast movies, information about assigned publishing points, movie list in Media Server and the operating history in MA-Scheduler. Window Media Service uses publishing point and information file (.nsc) to delivery movie items.

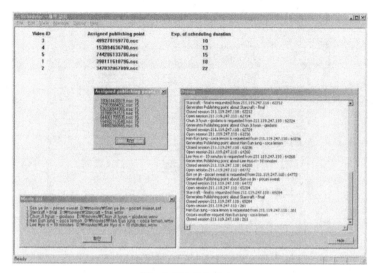

Fig. 6. MA-Scheduler

In Fig 6, MA-Scheduler is scheduling five movies assigned unique information file and shows time of remaining to service. Console of assigned publishing point shows publishing points assigned to movies that are served at present. Console of movie list has movie titles and their stored locations. Debug console indicates the clients' IP, port number and session status that is one of connect session such as client information, publishing point and close session. Each connection is maintained using TCP/IP for transmitting a movie information file. The MA-Scheduler indicates grouping requested video items list during a grouping duration time. The grouping item list is added requested multimedia item IDs when grouping item field within **GenerateMServerNsc** class becomes set. Also, the MA-Scheduler indicates generated multicast group addresses, port numbers, clients' IPs which request service and requested video items on window of User.

Fig 7 shows the publishing points in MA-Scheduler. Each publishing point is generated when a client requests a specific video item for the first time. If clients' request about an identical video item is in scheduling duration time in Fig 6, MA-scheduler returns previously configured multicast information file (.nsc) to the client. If not, scheduler creates new multicast information file and sends it to client. And when scheduling duration time expires, media server transmits the requested video items [9, 10].

Fig. 8 shows the result of GUI of client application. Client writes server IP or DNS name of scheduler on Client Console (Fig. 8.a), well-known port number and multimedia item number on corresponding window (Fig. 8.c). From the received multicast information file (.nsc), the transmitted multicast group address (226.21.44.65) and port number (24927) are written on Fig. 8.c. And then, the client automatically joins with 226.21.44.65 and 24927 (port number) using **ClientSocket** and **Window Media Player**.

Fig. 7. Publishing Point in Window Media Service

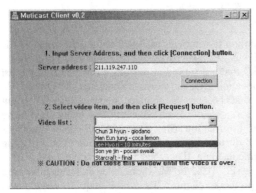

a. Console for Client   b. Media Player

c. Information of WMS

Fig. 8. Multicast Client

The **ClientSocket** generates socket to communicate with MA-Scheduler, receives the multicast information file (.nsc) and closes connection socket to MA-Scheduler. And then, it runs **Window Media Player** by executing **WinExec( )** as the member of information file (.nsc). Next, the **Window Media Player** attempts to join a multicast group assigned IP address and port number, and then receives multimedia streams transmitted from media server with a multicast group address. Window Media Player performs rendering of received multimedia streams. The result of execution of 8.a is shown in Fig 8.b.

4 Simulation and Results

This section performs simulation and analyzes on the results of performance of media server using multicast delivery. The request patterns depend on the popularity of the video serviced from media server. We use Zipf-like distribution for the probability of choosing i-th popular video among N multimedia items provided by media server. The probability that a specified multimedia is chosen with i_{th} frequency is Z/i, where $Z=1/(1+1/2+1/3+ \ldots +1/N)$. Using the Zipf distribution, if the overall clients' service request rate to the media server through scheduler is λ , the service requesting rate of the multimedia item for i_{th} frequency is $\lambda_i = \lambda \rho_i$ (where, $\rho_i = Z/i$)). Its rate based on popularity is used to determine the traffic for each multimedia item. The most popular multimedia item (i=1) must have higher weighted value than others because the request for popular multimedia item is more frequent than that for unpopular ones. We use ρ_i as a weighting parameter for selection of each multimedia item in simulation. Consequently, we perform simulation such that the more popular multimedia items, the higher probability of request for the multimedia item [11,12,13].

In the simulation, the number of multimedia item provided by the media server is N=100 and the length of each multimedia is 1 to 30 minutes, and the service request rate(λ) per head-end network(LAN) is 30 to 100 per minute. The service request rate λ follows Poisson distribution and the expression is as follows [14],

$$f_x(X = k) = \lim_{n \to \infty} \binom{n}{k} p^k (1 - p)^{n-k} = \lambda^k e^{-\lambda} / k! \tag{1}$$

Fig. 9 shows the number of required channel for service as the service request rate λ = 30 to 100 vary. The performance of proposed media system decreases the number of channel by 32.1%, 46.7% and 58.4% when the service request rate λ = 30, 50 and 100, respectively.

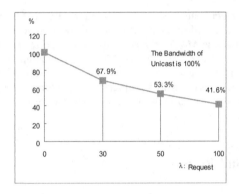

Fig. 9. The result of simulation for the load of server

5 Conclusion

The proposed system implements multimedia on-demand service in digital library using multicast which applies client-based system not server-based one. The Multicast-Agent-Scheduler performs efficient scheduling that immediately generates multicast group address and port number according to clients' multimedia request in digital library system. And it sends them to media server and clients who request service. Then the media server starts sending requested multimedia item to group, and the clients automatically join that group and play out receiving multimedia streams. Thus, we expect that the proposed system can perform on-demand service on Internet.

The proposed multimedia system in digital library shows that the number of channel for multimedia service decreases by 32.1%, 46.7% and 58.4% in comparison of that using unicast when service requesting rate • = 30, 50 and 100, respectively

This paper confirms that media server reduces the load of server and can efficiently use network resources through client-based scheduling for sharing multicast group address and port number. Thus, this system can use commercial multimedia service in digital library on ADSL/Cable modem network.

Acknowledgement. This work was supported (in part) by the Korea Science and Engineering Foundation (KOSEF) through the multimedia Research

References

1. M.A. Goncalves, E.A.Fox, L.T.Watson, and N.A.Kipp,"Streams, Structures, Spaces, Scenarios, Societies (5S): A Formal Model for Digital Libraries," Virginia Tech Dept. of Computer Science Tech. Report TR-01-12 July, 2001
2. D.Sitaram and A.Dan, "Multimedia Servers", Morgan Kaufmann Publishers 2000
3. T.D.C. Little and D. Venkatesh, "Prospects for Interactive Video-On-Demand" In MCL Technical Report 02-15-1994, 1994

4. K.C.Almeroth and M.H.Ammar,"The Use of Multicast Delivery to Provide a Scalable and Interactive Video-On-Demand Service," IEEE J. Selected Areas in Comm., Vol.14, No 6, Aug. 1996, pp. 1110–1122
5. Yen-Jen Lee, David H.C.Du and Wei-hsiu Ma, "SESAME: A Scalable and Extensible Architecture for Multimedia Entertainment", In IEEE, COMPSAC, 1996
6. K.Almeroth & M.Ammar, "An Alterative Paradigm for Scalable On-Demand Application: Evaluating and Deploying the Interactive Multimedia Jukebox", IEEE Trans. on Knowledge and Data Engineering Special Issue on Web Technology, April 1999
7. Iksoo Kim, Taejun Hwang, Youngjune Kim & Yoseop Woo, " New Distributive Web caching Technique for VOD Service," ITCOM2002 Conf. Boston U.S.A, 2002
8. Iksoo Kim, Backhyun Kim, Yoseop Woo, Taejun Hwang, Seokhoon Kang,"VOD Service using Web-Caching Technique on the Head-End-Network," ICCSA2003 Springer-Verlag LNCS 2668
9. Marc Melkonian, "Deploying Windows Media 9 Series over an Intranet,'' http://www. microsoft.com/windows/windowsmedia/howto/articles/Intranet.aspx, Nov. 2002
10. Tricia Gill, "Upgrading to Windows Media Services 9 Series," http://www.microsoft.com/windows/windowsmedia/howto/articles/UpgradeWMS9S.aspx, Sept. 2002
11. B.Kim, S.Moon, Iksoo Kim & Y.Woo, "A Buffering Algorithm for Providing Truly Interactive Video-on-Demand Service," PDPTA99, pp. 211–217, Las Vegas, 1999
12. P. Cao, L. Fan and G. Philips, "Web Caching and Zipf-like Distributions: Evidence and Implications," IEEE Infocom 1999
13. Carey Williamson, "On Filter Effects in Web Caching Hierarchies," ACM Transactions on Internet Technology, Vol. 2, No. 1, pp. 47–77, February 2002
14. H. M. Taylor and S. Karlin, "An Introduction to Stochastic Modeling," Academic Press 1994

Reducing Spatial Relationships for Efficient Image Retrieval[*]

SooCheol Lee, SiEun Lee, and EenJun Hwang

Graduate School of Information and Communication, Ajou University, Suwon, Korea
{juin,sfmovie,ehwang}@ajou.ac.kr

Abstract. Retrieval of images from image databases by spatial relationship can be effectively performed through visual interface systems. In these systems, the representation of image with 2D strings, which are derived from symbolic projections, provides an efficient and natural way to construct image index and is also an ideal representation for the visual query. With this approach, retrieval is reduced to matching two symbolic strings. However, using 2D-string representations, spatial relationships between the objects in the image might not be exactly specified. Ambiguities arise for the retrieval of images of 3D scenes. In order to remove ambiguous description of object spatial relationships, in this paper, images are referred by considering spatial relationships using the spatial location algebra for the 3D image scene. Also, we are removing the repetitive spatial relationships using the several reduction rules. A reduction mechanism using these rules can be used in query processing systems that retrieval images by content. This could give better precision and flexibility in image retrieval.

1 Introduction

The emergence of multimedia technologies and the possibility of sharing and distributing image data through large-bandwidth computer networks have emphasized the role of visual information. Image retrieval systems support either retrieval based on high-level semantics, which defines image content at the conceptual level, or retrieval based on visual content, which is based on image perceptual features like color, texture, structure, object shape, and spatial relationships.

Image retrieval based on spatial relationships among image object is generally known as spatial similarity based retrieval. This type of retrieval has been identified as an important class of similarity-based retrievals and is used in the applications such as geographic and medical information systems.

Spatial relationship is fuzzy concept and is thus often dependent of human interpretation. A spatial similarity function assesses the degree to which the spatial relationships in a database image conform to spatial relationships in the query image. A spatial similarity algorithm provides a ranked ordering of database images with respect to a query image by applying the spatial similarity function between the query image and the database image.

[*] This work was supported by grant No. R05-2002-000-01224-0(2003) from the Basic Research Program of the Korea Science & Engineering Foundation.

T.M.T. Sembok et al. (Eds.): ICADL 2003, LNCS 2911, pp. 218–229, 2003.

In this paper, we discuss the usage of 3D interfaces to provide query examples in retrieval by content of 2D images, based on reduced spatial relationship. A prototype system is presented which employs a 3D interface with navigation and editing facilities.

The rest of the paper is organized as follows. Section 2 describes some of the related works. Section 3 presents image indexing and symbolic coding of spatial relationship. Section 4 describes reduction rules to reason a spatial relationship between two objects. Section 5 explains measuring spatial similarity. Section 6 explains our implementation system and its user interface. Section 7 describes experimental results. Finally, Section 8 concludes the paper.

2 Related Works

So far, many CBIR systems and techniques have been reported. The QBIC system[18] at IBM allows an operator to specify various properties of a desired image including shape, color, texture and location. The system returns a selection of potential matches to those criteria, sorted by a score indicating the appropriateness of the match. Pentland et al.[2] presented another CBIR system that incorporates more sophisticated representation of texture and limited degree of automatic segmentation. Virage[3] and Chabot[12] also identify materials using low-level image properties. But, none of these systems considers spatial properties in a way that supports object queries.

Jagadish[9] has proposed shape similarity retrieval based on a two-dimensional rectilinear shape representation. Two shapes are similar if the error area is small when one shape is placed on the top of the other.

Lee et al.[15] propose a new domain-independent spatial similarity and annotation-based image retrieval system. Images are decomposed into multiple regions of interest containing objects, which are analyzed to annotate and extract their spatial relationships.

Chang et al.[14] developed the concept of iconic indexing by introducing the 2D string representation of an image. Since then, the 2D string approach has been studied further. 2D-H string is an extension of 2D string. 2D-PIR graph can consider both directional and topological relationships between all possible spatial object pairs in an image.

3 Indexing for Image Retrieval in Image Database

Image contents can be described in terms either of the image objects and their spatial relationships or of the objects in the original scene and their spatial relationships. In the first case, 2D objects are involved, and 2D spatial relationships are evaluated directly on the image plane. In the second, scenes associated with images involve objects that differ greatly in their structural properties from one application to the other. Specifically, scenes involve objects if objects have prevalently a 2D structure or involve 3D objects if they are common real-world scenes. Spatial relationships for the two cases are 2D and 3 D, respectively.

ROI(Region of Interest)[10, 15]for querying image databases are special images defined through a computer system by the user. They maintain a symbolic relationship with objects in the real world. According to the type of application, either a 2D or 3D structure can be associated with each icon to build virtual scenes with 2D or 3D objects, respectively.

3.1   Symbolic Coding of Spatial Relationships

Every image in the database contains a set of unique and characterizing image objects that scatter in any arbitrary locations. There could exist various spatial relationships among these image objects. The spatial location can be represented either by the relative coordinate or by the absolute coordinate.

In a 3-D space, the spatial location of an object O in an image is represented as a point P_o where $P_o = (X_o, Y_o, Z_o)$, and an image itself as a set of points $P=\{P_1, P_2,..., P_n\}$, where n is the number of objects of interest in the image. These points are tagged or annotated with labels to capture any necessary semantic information of the object. We call each of these individual points representing the spatial location of an image object a *spatial location point*[15]. For the sake of simplicity, we assume that the spatial location of an image object is represented by only single spatial location point, and hence, the entire image is represented by a set of spatial location points. In order to represent spatial relations among the spatial location points of an image, we decompose an image into four equal size quadrants. Figure 1 shows an image whose three spatial location points are located at the different quadrants.

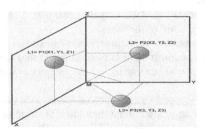

Fig. 1. Spatial location points.

This representation scheme is translation, orientation and scale independent. Based on this scheme, we can define image location algebra for image objects X, Y and Z as shown in Table 1

Suppose we are given an image with n objects of interest. We can describe its spatial information using unidirectional graph where each object corresponds to a vertex and any spatial relationship between two objects is indicated by a label along their edge. We refer to this graph as *spatial graph*. Figure 2 shows an original image and its spatial graph for the image objects.

Table 1. Image location algebra

Notation	Operator	Meaning
X < Y	*Lupper*	X is located in *Left upper* of Y
X ∧ Y	*Llower*	X is located in *Left lower* of Y
X > Y	*Rupper*	X is located in *Right upper* of Y
X ∨ Y	*Rlower*	X is located in *Right lower* of Y
X ∪ Y	*Upper*	X is located in *Upper* of Y
X ∩ Y	*Below*	X is located in *Below* of Y
X]Y	*Right*	X is located in *Right* of Y
X [Y	*Left*	X is located in *Left* of Y
X / Y	*Center*	X or Y is located in *Center* of M
X % Y	*Overlap*	X is *Overlapped* of Y
X ⊗ Y	*Inside*	X is *Inside* of Y
X ⊕ Y	*Outside*	X is *Outside* of Y
X • Y	*In front of*	X *is In front* of Y

***Definition* 1**. A spatial graph is a set of pair (V, E) where:

- $V = \{L1, L2, L3,..., Ln\}$ is a set of nodes, representing objects.
- $E = \{e1, e2, e3,..., en\}$ is as set of edges, where each edge is connecting two nodes L1 and L2, and labeled with a spatial relationship between them.

In the figure, some of the spatial relationships among the spatial location points are represented along their edges using image location algebra. Hear, M is a special spatial point called fiducial point.

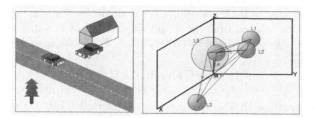

Fig. 2. Original image and its spatial graph

According to the definition 1, the spatial relationships for the figure are:

$V = \{L1, L2, L3, L4, L5\}$
$Rel = \{$L1 ∧ M}, {L1 % L2}, {L1 ∧ L3}, {L1 ∧ L4}, {L1 ∧ L5}, {L2 ∧ M}, {L2 % L1}, {L2 ∧ L3}, {L2 [L4}, {L2 [L5}, {L3 < M}, {L3 > L1}, {L3 > L2}, {L3 > L4}, {L3 > L5}, {L4 ∩ L1}, {L4] L1}, {L4 ∧ L2}, {L4 ∧ L3}, {L4 % L5}, {L5 ∪ L1}, {L5 [L2}, {L5 ∧ L3}, {L5 ⊗ L4}$

4 Reduction Rules for Spatial Relationships

To reduce spatial relationships between objects, we use some rules as reduction rules. Reduction rules are removing the redundant and inferable spatial relationships. As a result, we can represent more simple spatial relationships.

Let F be a finite set of relationships. We say that F is consistent if there exists an image that satisfies all the relationships in F. For example, the set {A left of B, B left of C} is consistent, while the set {A overlap B, A outside B} is inconsistent. We say that a relationship r is implied by F, if every image that satisfies all the relationships in F, also satisfies the relationship r. For example, the set of relationships {A left of B, B left of C} implies A left of C.

In this paper, we present various reduction rules for removing relationships for a set of relationships. Each rule will be written as $r : r_1, r_2, ..., r_k$, where r is called *head of the rule* and the list $r_1, ..., r_k$ is called *body of the rule*. We say that a relationship r is inferable by one step from a set of relationships F using a rule, if $r_1, ..., r_k$ are in F. Let R be a set of such rules. We say that a relationship r is inferable from F using a rule in R, if r is in F, or there exists a finite sequence of relationships $r_1, ..., r_k$ ending with r, i.e. $r_k=r$, such that r_1 is inferable in one step from F using one of the rules in R, and for each $i=2, ..., k$, r_i is inferable in one step from $F \cup \{r_{1}, ..., r_k\}$ using one of the rules in R.

Now we define six reduction rules for spatial relationships. A rule in R is said to be sound if, every image that satisfies all the relationships in the body of the rule also satisfies the relationship in the head of the rule. We say that a set of rules R is complete if for every consistent set F of relationships, every relationship implied by F is inferable from F using rules in R.

RR1 (Transitivity of left, right, upper and below): This rule indicates the transitivity of some of the relationships. For example, by this rule, the relationship A left of C can be inferred from the relationships A left of B and B left of C. Let × denote any relationship symbol in {"[", "]", "∪", "∩"}. We have the following rule for each such ×:

$$A \times C : A \times B, B \times C$$

RR2 (Interaction I): This rule captures the interaction between the relationships involving left, right, upper, below and the relationships involving overlap. For example, A left of D can be inferred from the relationships A left of B, B overlap C and C left of D. Let × denote any of the relationship symbols in {"[", "]", "∪", "∩", "%"}. We have the following rule for each such ×:

$$A \times D : A \times B, B \text{ overlaps } C, C \times D$$

RR3 (Interaction II): This rule captures the interaction between the relationships left, upper, outside (3D image only), and inside. For example, we can infer A left of C from the relationships A inside B and B left of C. The relationship A left of C can also be inferred from A left of B and C inside B. Let × denote any relationship symbol in {"[", "]", "⊗", "⊕"}. We have the following two types of rules for each such ×:

(**RR3-1**) A × C : A inside B, B × C

(**RR3-2**) A × C : A × B, C inside B

RR4 (Symmetry of overlaps and outside): This rule captures the symmetry of overlap and outside. Let × denote either overlap or outside. We have the following rule each such ×:

$$A \times B : B \times A$$

RR5 (Disjointness): This rule indicates that two objects are outside to each other if one of them is to the left or upper the other object. Let × denote any relationship symbol in {"[" , "]" , "∪", "∩"}. We have the following rule for each such ×:

$$A \text{ outside } B : A \times B$$

RR6(Overlap): This rule that if an object is inside another object, then the two objects overlap:

(**RR6-1**) A overlap B : A inside B

(**RR6-2**) A overlap B : C inside A, C overlap B

By taking into account the reduction rules, spatial relationship corresponds to the in figure 2 can be reduced into a more compact form:

$V = \{L1, L2, L3, L4, L5\}$

$Rel = \{L1 \wedge M\}, \{L1 \% L2\}, \{L1 \wedge L3\}, \{L1 \wedge L4\}, \{L1 \wedge L5\}, \{L2 \wedge L3\}, \{L2 [L4\}, \{L 2 [L5\}, \{L3 > L1\}, \{L3 > L4\}, \{L3 > L5\}, \{L4 \cap R\}, \{L4 \wedge L3\}, \{L4 \% L5\}, \{L5 \otimes L4\}$

Now, we prove the rules. We use the r : F to indicate that the relationship r is inferable from F using the set of rules in R.

Theorem 1: The set of rules in R is suitable for 2 and 3-dimensional images.

Proof: Clearly, **RR1** is theoretically correct. For example, assume that the relationships A left of B, B left of C are satisfied in a image p and let u, v and w be arbitrary points in image objects p_a, p_b and p_c of p respectively. Clearly, $u.x < v.x < w.x$. From transitivity of <, we see that $u.x < w.x$. Since u, v and w are arbitrary points, it follows that p satisfies the relationship A left of C. This shows the correctness of rule **RR4**. To see the theoretical correctness of **RR3-1**, assume that p is an image satisfying the relationships A inside B and B outside C. Clearly, $p_a \subseteq p_b$ and $p_b \cap p_c = \varnothing$. Hence $p_a \cap p_c = \varnothing$ and p satisfies the relationship A outside C. Similar claims can be used for other relationships such as left and upper and also for the difference case of **RR3-2**.

To prove the theoretical correctness of **RR2**, assume that p is an image that satisfies the relationships A left of B, B overlap C and C left of D. Let u and v be arbitrary points in p_a and p_d, respectively. Also, let w be a point in $p_a \cap p_c$. There exists such a point w since $p_a \cap p_c \neq \varnothing$. Clearly, the $u.x$ is < the $w.x$ which is < $v.x$ Using the transitivity of <, it follows that the $u.x$ is < $v.x$. Since u and v are arbitrary points in p_a and p_d respectively, it follows that the p satisfies the relationship A left of D.

It should be easy to see the theoretical correctness of **RR5**. Suppose the relationship A left of B is satisfied in a image p. Then, every point in p_a is strictly to the left of every point in p_b, and hence $p_a \cap p_c = \varnothing$. As a consequence, A outside B is satisfied in p. The theoretical correctness of **RR6** should be easy to see.

Table 2. Similarity between spatial operators

SIM	<	∧	>	∨	∪	∩	]	[	/	%	⊗	⊕	•
<	1	0.5	0.5	0.5	0.5	0.5	0.25	0.75	0.75	0.25	0.5	0.5	0.25
∧	0.5	1	0.5	0.5	0.5	0.75	0.25	0.75	0.75	0.25	0.5	0.5	0.25
>	0.5	0.5	1	0.5	0.75	0.5	0.75	0.25	0.75	0.25	0.5	0.5	0.25
∨	0.5	0.5	0.5	1	0.5	0.75	0.75	0.25	0.75	0.25	0.5	0.5	0.25
∪	0.5	0.5	0.75	0.5	1	0.5	0.5	0.5	0.75	0.25	0.5	0.5	0.25
∩	0.5	0.75	0.5	0.75	0.5	1	0.5	0.5	0.75	0.25	0.5	0.5	0.25
]	0.25	0.25	0.75	0.75	0.5	0.5	1	0	0.5	0	0.25	0.25	0
[	0.75	0.75	0.25	0.25	0.5	0.5	0	1	0.5	0	0.25	0.25	0
/	0.75	0.75	0.75	0.75	0.75	0.75	0.5	0.5	1	0.5	0.75	0.75	0.5
%	0.25	0.25	0.25	0.25	0.25	0.25	0	0	0.5	1	0.25	0.75	0
⊗	0.5	0.5	0.5	0.5	0.5	0.5	0.25	0.25	0.75	0.25	1	0.5	0.75
⊕	0.5	0.5	0.5	0.5	0.5	0.5	0.25	0.25	0.75	0.75	0.5	1	0.25
•	0.25	0.25	0.25	0.25	0.25	0.25	0	0	0.5	0	0.75	0.25	1

5 Metric for Measuring Spatial Similarity

The crucial point in similarity-based retrieval is to determine similarity metric that is efficient to calculate and capture the essential aspects of similarity that humans recognize. By quantifying the concept of "degree of similarity", we can measure the similarity degree between an image and a query image in terms of objects and their spatial relationships. In this paper, we denote the degree of similarity as a value in the range [0, 1]. For example, the degree of similarity between image P1 with object L1, L2, L3 and P2 with L4, L5, L6 is dependent on the degree of similarity between L1 and L4, L2 and L5, L3 and L6, respectively.

In this paper, we introduce the operator neighborhood graph[17, 19] which formally defines the distances among the spatial operators.

Definition 2. Spatial relationships between two objects are neighboring if they can be directly transformed to each other by a deforming operations (scaling, moving, and rotating).

Figure 3 shows an operator neighborhood graph for the spatial relationships corresponding to the spatial operators in Table 1.

The distance between two spatial operators δ_1 and δ_2 is defined by the shortest path from δ_1 to δ_2 on the neighborhood graph and is denoted by *distance* (δ_1, δ_2). The maximum distance on the neighborhood graph is 4 and the minimum is 0. We define the similarity degree using the following formula:

$$Sim\_Obj(\delta_1, \delta_2) = 1- (distance\ ((\delta_1, \delta_2)/D_{max}) \tag{1}$$

Table 2 shows the similarity degree that is derived from the operator neighborhood graph. Using the table, we can measure the similarity between two images. Query result is a set of images satisfying the condition expressed in it, i.e., the images than have a similarity degree greater that a specified threshold with respect to the query. We can define user query as follows:

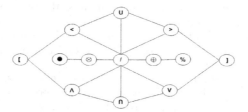

Fig. 3. Operator neighborhood graph

Definition 3. User query Q is a triple (ξ, S, t) where ξ is the set of objects in the query image. S is the set of spatial relationships among objects and t is the minimal required similarity between Q and database image (I_{DB}) and is between 0 and 1, inclusively.

As an example, let us consider the image in Figure 2. According to the definition 3, we can define the query image as follow:

$Q = \{\xi, S, t\}$

$\xi = \{L1, L2, L3, L4, L5\}$

$S = \{(L1 \wedge M), (L1 \% L2), (L1 \wedge L3), (L1 \wedge L4), (L1 \wedge L5), (L2 \wedge L3), (L2\ [L4],$
$\quad (L\ 2\ [L5), (L3 > L1), (L3 > L4), (L3 > L5), (L4 \cap M),(L4 \wedge L3), (L4 \% L5),$
$\quad (L5 \otimes L4)\}$

Given a query image Q of n objects, we can calculate its spatial similarity to a database image I_{DB} by the following function.

$$Sim\_Deg\ (Q, I_{DB}) = \sum_{i=1}^{n} \sum_{j=1}^{n-1} \left| O_i^q \vartheta O_j^{I_{DB}} \right| \tag{2}$$

In the formula, O_i^q and $O_i^{I_{DB}}$ are spatial relationships between the query and database images. Symbol ϑ compares two spatial operators by the value of similarity in Table 2. According to the formulation, the spatial similarity value between $O_i^q =$ L1 % L2 and $O_i^{I_{DB}}$ = L5 $\otimes$ L4 is 0.25.

The *Sim_Deg* function has been effectively used as a metric for measuring image similarity in our prototype content-based retrieval system.

6 Implementation

The system is designed according to three basic principles:
- To introduce a description of real world images in the database in terms of the 3D description of the scene that they represent;
- To perform querying through virtual scene that is defined with a direct manipulation of 3D symbol;
- To represent spatial relationships between objects both in the original and virtual scenes according to the representation language expounded previously.

Images and their descriptions are stored in an XML database. XML(Extensible Markup Language) is a simple, very flexible text format derived from SGML. Originally designed to meet the challenges of large-scale electronic publishing, XML is also playing an increasingly important role in the exchange of a wide variety of data on the Web and elsewhere.

XML permits document authors to create markup for virtually any type of information. This extensibility enables document authors to create entirely new markup languages for describing specific types of data, including mathematical formula, chemical molecular structures, music, recipes, etc.

We have represented spatial relationships and features of image objects using XML.

Figure 4 shows a snapshot of implemented image analysis process. For each image object marked by a rectangle, its edge is extracted and any necessary semantic information is coded into an XML document. The window on the left bottom shows the spatial graph for the marked image objects. Image objects in spatial graph can be modify its 3D location using forward and back button.

These represent object location and instance. The visual interface of the system is comprised of a ROI interface which supports the selection of images from the database and several operating facilities, as well as Query window, which is used for the definition and the visualization of the 3D query as shown in figure 5.

   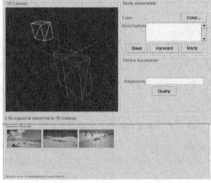

Fig. 4. Image analyzer interface   **Fig. 5.** Query window interface

7 Experimental Results

Using the image retrieval system, we have tested some of the typical queries under different combinations of stored annotation and spatial constraint of image objects. The image database contains 20,000 commercial Corel images that cover a wide range of nature scenes, buildings, construction sites, animals, etc Table 3 shows some of the results for the following query which finds images with a castle and trees beside it under different conditions, the following query is sent to the database:

Q1: "Find images that shows a castle with trees beside it"

Table 3. Simple query (Q1) results

Item	Spatial constraints	Keywords	Retrieved	Relevant	Precision
1	"-"	Castle	53	23	43.4
2	"-"	Tree	366	23	6.2
3	"-"	Castle and Tree	35	23	65.7
4	Left or Right	Castle and Tree	28	23	82.1
5	Overlap	Castle and Tree	14	9	64.2
6	Left or Overlap	"-"	2257	23	1.0
7	Right or Overlap	"-"	4323	23	0.5
8	Left or Right or Overlap	Castle and Tree	24	23	95.8

In the query Q1, the user has defined the spatial relationships between castle and trees as including images that have stored keyword "castle" associated with them. There are 23 images in the collection that satisfy the query.

In the table, item 1-3 used keyword search only, and item 4, 5, 8 used a combination of keyword and spatial constraints. Using the keyword "castle and tree" in conjunction with the spatial constraints "left or right and overlap" gives best precision.

As shown for item 6-7, images can be retrieved with 100% recall if the spatial constraints are broad enough, but the precision is too low: the 2257 and 4323 images retrieved from item 6-7 would require the user to browse whole thumbnails images to find the images of castle and tree.

As another example, a typical composite query including color, keywords and spatial relationship would be:

Q2: "Find the white car images inside the garage which is beside the lake"

The query Q2 returns all white car images in the database that were beside the lake and inside the garage. There were 24 images in the collection that satisfy the query.

Experiments have revealed that retrieving images based on keywords only gives marginal results. However, when incorporating spatial constraint in the query gives much better result.

Table 4. Composite query(Q2) results

Item	Spatial Constraint	Color	Keywords	etrieve	Relevant	Precision
1	"-"	"-"	Car	7865	24	0.3
2	"-"	White	Car	3589	24	0.6
3	"-"	White	Car and Garage	430	24	5.6
4	"-"	White	Car, Garage and Lake	142	24	17
5	Left or Right	White	Car, Garage and Lake	57	24	42.1
6	Overlap or Left or Right	White	Car, Garage and Lake	43	24	56
7	Overlap or Inside	White	Car, Garage and Lake	18	7	39
8	Inside or Left or Right	White	Car, Garage and Lake	24	24	100

8 Conclusion

In this paper, the subject of retrieval of contents of images depicting 3D scenes through 3D interface has been addressed. In this approach, images are referred to by considering spatial relationships between objects in the 3D image scene.

Also we have presented reduction rules for reducing spatial relationships from a given set of relationships. As it stands, this scheme is size, translation and orientation independent. A reduction mechanism using these rules can be used in query processing systems that retrieve images by content. This could give better precision and flexibility in image retrieval.

We have built a prototype system based on reduction rules and performed experiments to see how it works for typical image retrieval requests. The prototype system provides tools for analyzing, annotating, querying, and browsing images in a user friendly way.

References

1. A. Gupta and R. Jain, "Visual information retrieval," *Comm. Assoc. Comp. Mach.*, May 1997.
2. A. Pentland, R. Picard and S. Sclaroff, "Photobook: Content-based manipulation of image databases," *SPIE Proc. Storage of Retrieval for Image and Video Databases*, February 1994.
3. Bach JR, Fuller C, Gupta A, Hampapur A, Horiwitz B, Humphrey R, Jain RC, Shu C, "The virage image search enginee: An open framework for image management," *SPIE Proceedings of Storage and Retrieval for Still Images and Video Databases IV*, Feb 1996, San Jose, CA, pp. 76–86
4. C. Carson, S. Belongies, H. Greenspan and J. Malik, "Region-based image querying," *Proc. IEEE Workshop on Content-Based Access of Image and Video Libraries*, June 1997.

5. Eakins, J. P., " Automatic image content retrieval: Are we going anywhere?," *In proceedings of the 3rd Int. Conf. on Electronic Library and Visual information Research.*, May. 1996.

6. Egenhofer M. J. and Franzasa R. D, "Point set topological spatial relations., *Journal Geogr. Information System.*, vol 5-2, pp. 161–174, 1991.

7. J. R. Smith and S. –Fu Chang, "Visual SEEK: A Fully Automated Content Based Image Query System," *Proc. ACM Mult. Conf., Boston Ma., Nov. 1996.*

8. J. R. Smith and S. –Fu Chang, "Tools and techniques for color image retrieval," *Proc. IEEE Int. Conf. on Image Proc.*, pp. 52–531, 1995.

9. Jagadish HV, " A retrieval technique for similar shape." *Proc. ACM SIGMOD conf.*, May 1991, pp. 209–217.

10. L. H. Rodrigues, Building Imaging Applications with Java Technology, *Addison Wesley*, 2001.

11. Lee, S.Y. and F.J. Hsu, "Spatial reasoning and similarity retrieval of images using 2D-C String knowledge representation," *Pattern Recognition*, Vol 25-3, pp. 305–318, 1992.

12. M. Nabil, A.H.H. Ngu, and J. Shepherd, "Picture Similairty Retrieval Using the 2D Projection Interval Representation," *IEEE Trans. Knowledge and Data Eng.*, vol. 8, no. 4, pp. 533–539, Aug. 1996.

13. N. Chang and K. Fu, "Query by pictorial example," *IEEE Trans. Software Eng.*, Vol. SE-6, pp. 519–524, Nov. 1980.

14. S. Chang, Q. Shi and S. Yan, "Iconic indexing using 2-D strings," *IEEE Trans. on* Pattern *Analysis & Machine Intelligence*, Vol. 9, No. 3, pp. 413–428, 1987.

15. S. Lee and E. Hwang, "Spatial Similarity and Annotation-Based Image Retrieval System", *IEEE Fourth International Symposium on Multimedia Software Engineering*, Newport Beach, CA, December 2002.

16. S.L. Tanimoto, "An iconic/symbolic data structuring scheme," *in pattern Recognition and Artificial Intelligence. NY*: Academic, 1976, pp. 452–471

17. V. E. Ogle and M. Stonebraker, "Chabot: Retrieval from a Relational Database of Images," *IEEE Computer*, Vol. 28, No. 9, September 1995.

18. W. Niblack, et al. "The QBIC project: Query images by content using color, texture and shape," *SPIE V 1908*, 1993.

Effective Image Annotation for Search Using Multi-level Semantics

Pu-Jen Cheng and Lee-Feng Chien

Institute of Information Science, Academia Sinica
128 Academy Rd, Sec. 2, NanKang, Taipei 115, Taiwan, R.O.C.
{pjcheng,lfchien}@iis.sinica.edu.tw

Abstract. There is an increasing need of development of automatic tools to annotate images for effective image searching in digital libraries. In this paper, we present a novel probabilistic model for image annotation based on content-based image retrieval techniques and statistical analysis. One key obstacle in applying statistical methods to annotating images is the amount of manually-labeled images, which are used to train the methods, is normally insufficient. Numerous keywords cannot be correctly assigned to appropriate images due to lacking or missing in the labeled image database. We further propose an enhanced model to deal with the challenging problem. With the model, the annotated keywords of a new image are determined in terms of their similarity at different semantic levels including image level, keyword level and concept level. To avoid some relevant keywords missing, the model prefers labeling the keywords with the same concepts to the new image. Obtained experimental results have shown that the proposed models are effective for helping users annotate images in different training data qualities.

1 Introduction

With the explosive growth of images in digital libraries, there is an increasing need of development of automatic tools to help people annotate images. Given a set of images that have been labeled by keywords, the annotation problem of concern is how to aid one in assigning the keywords to new images. This task facilitates further image management such as text-based image retrieval, creation of metadata, organization and presentation of image content.

Most works in automatic image annotation focused mainly on inferring high-level semantic information from low-level image features. Some works [1,12,2] made use of image recognition techniques to classify images into semantically-meaningful categories and then labeled the images by the keywords that have been manually assigned to the categories. Image recognition methods are appropriate to constrained domains; however, they are not reliable in many complicated applications. There was other research applying relevant feedback methods to learn keywords from a set of labeled images. Generally, the feedback methods have the advantage of providing better accuracy than image recognition [7,8,13].

Differing from the previous works, the paper pursues the goal of integrating content-based image retrieval techniques and statistical analysis for image annotation.

T.M.T. Sembok et al. (Eds.): ICADL 2003, LNCS 2911, pp. 230–242, 2003.

We propose a novel probabilistic model for ranking a set of keywords according to the importance of them in representing the semantic of a given image. The model is based on the hypothesis that similar images may partially share the same keywords. Consider an example. Figure 1 shows 6 images pertaining to historical arts in the Palace Museum (referred to http://www.npm.gov.tw). Although it is very difficult to recognize the objects appearing in these images, content-based retrieval technologies provide a way to find out similar images based on low-level features such as colors, textures and shapes. In this case, the similar images include (a) and (b), (c) and (d), and (e) and (f). Suppose (a) has been labeled by keyword *china*. (b) will be probably labeled by keyword *china* because it is similar to (a).

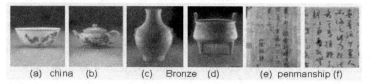

Fig. 1. Example of similar images

One key obstacle in learning keywords based on similar images is the amount of manually-labeled images is usually insufficient. In general, digital libraries contain numerous collections of images and keywords. Considerable keywords might be lacking and even missing in the labeled images. This problem is even more serious to the images whose similar images are few. Consequently, effective keywords are not easy to learn from a small set of similar images with insufficient labeled keywords.

To overcome the insufficiency (or sparseness) problem of manually-labeled images, in the proposed model the annotated keywords of a new image are determined in terms of their similarity at different semantic levels including image level, keyword level and concept level. The set of candidate keywords are mainly selected from the labeled keywords of the images that are visually similar to the new image. To avoid some relevant keywords missing in the candidate set, the concepts constituted by the candidate keywords are considered. Based on the concept level, the proposed model has capacity for suggesting the keywords with the same concepts. As a result, some keywords not appearing in the labeled images can be extracted, and some other keywords irrelevant to the overall concepts of the images can be eliminated. Consider the example again. Suppose most images similar to (e) and (f) contain keyword *penmanship* and the authors' names. The set of the authors' names constitute the concept of *calligrapher*. Though it is difficult to identify an image's author automatically, our model can recommend users a set of calligraphers as candidate keywords. In efforts to satisfy the needs for automatically annotating images, we also design an algorithm to generate the concept level in an automatically way. The method clusters relevant keywords based on the statistical analysis on term occurrences and co-occurrences in a corpus.

We have developed a prototype system based on the model for examining its performance. The system extracts both colors and textures for global and local features. It also supports relevant feedback strategies for automatically adjusting the meaning of similarity among different features. The experiments with the Corel image library show that the proposed method is effective and can achieve the performance of 55.0% recall and 55.4% precision.

The rest of the paper is organized as follows. Section 2 presents the related work. Section 3 describes the problem and its challenges. Sections 4 and 5 introduce the proposed methods and implementation issues, respectively. Section 6 describes performance evaluation. Finally, conclusion remarks are given in Section 7.

2 Related Work

There were different image classification or recognition techniques to classify images into categories and labeled them by the category keywords. Most of image recognition methods focused on certain semantic types whose features have high discriminability for particular user-defined classes. Chang et al. [3] presented semantic visual templates comprised of a set of example objects, which represent the semantic associated with the templates. The templates were generated semi-automatically. Paek et al. [9] combined visual and textual features. Visual objects were identified by clustering of segmented regions from images and represented with the *tf-idf* scheme [11]. Images were classified into two categories, indoor and outdoor, according to their visual objects.

Different from image recognition methods, Liu et al. [7] made use of users' feedback information to incorporate additional keywords for images. When users fed back a set of images being relevant to their queries, the system updated the annotation of feedback images by linking queries with these images. The relevance feedback technique provided better efficiency than manual annotation and better accuracy than image recognition.

3 Problem and Challenge

The image annotation problem can be formally defined as follows. Let $I = \{I_1, I_2,..., I_m\}$ be a set of images and $K = \{K_1, K_2,..., K_n\}$ be a set of keywords for labeling image $I_i \in I$. Let P be a probabilistic function mapping from $I \times K$ to real numbers varying from 0 to 1. $P(K_j|I_i) = v$ represents the conditional probability of keyword K_j given image I_i, which indicates the importance degree of keyword K_j in representing the semantic of image I_i. Suppose we have database images D and new images T such that $I = D \cup T$ and $D, T \neq \varnothing$, where D are the images that have been labeled already and T refer to the images to be annotated. For each new image $I_Q \in T$, the image annotation problem is to rank each keyword $K_j \in K$ according to the conditional probability $P(K_j|I_Q)$, which is estimated through $P(K_j| I_i)$ for all $I_i \in D$. Notice that once image I_Q is labeled ($D = D \cup \{I_Q\}$ and $T = T - \{I_Q\}$), subsequent new images in new T will be assessed based on new D.

The image annotation problem has two challenges in real-world applications. First, new image I_Q may have few similar images that have been labeled in database D. Secondly, the similar images may miss some satisfactory keywords to label them because manual labeling is usually incomplete. Thus, the labeled images in D probably contribute an incomplete set of keywords as candidates in the later annotation processing. This phenomenon explains why low-recall queries are easy to appear even in digital libraries with millions of images.

4 Image Annotation Processing

4.1 Probabilistic Model

In this section, we make use of *the semantic network* as a representation of the relationship between database images D and keywords K in the annotation problem. Based on the representation, we will propose a basic probabilistic model.

The basic semantic network consists of two levels of nodes, providing empirical associations between database images and keywords. More specially, the basic semantic network is defined as a tuple (D, K, M_{IK}) where

- D is a set of database images $\{I_i\}$ $(D \subset I)$ specifying *the image level*. Image I_i is a raw image, e.g. a JPEG image.
- K is a set of predefined keywords $\{K_j\}$ $(j=1..n)$ specifying *the keyword level*.
- M_{IK} is a set of weights $\{\beta_{ij}\}$ $(0 \leq \beta_{ij} \leq 1)$ on the links between database images D and keywords K. β_{ij} denotes the importance of keyword K_j to database image I_i.

Figure 2 illustrates an example of the basic semantic network, where $D=\{I_1, I_2, I_3\}$, $K=\{Dog, Grass, Lawn, Pet, Running\}$ and $M_{IK}=\{\beta_{11}=1.0, \beta_{12}=0.8, ...\}$. For simplicity, two nodes are connected if the weight on their link is non-zero.

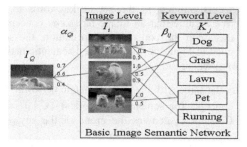

Fig. 2. Example of the basic image semantic network

For each new image I_Q, the candidate keywords can be simply selected based on the labeled keywords of its similar images. α_{Qi} varies from 0 to 1 and represents the similarity value between images I_Q and I_i. The higher the value is, the more similar the images are. Numerous works in content-based image retrieval [4,5] provide an automatic way to evaluate the similarity value and retrieve similar images. For example, in Figure 2 I_{1-3} are the similar images of I_Q, where $\alpha_{Q1} = 0.7$, $\alpha_{Q2} = 0.6$, and $\alpha_{Q3} = 0.4$. *Dog, Grass, Pet* and *Running* are candidate keywords, but *Lawn* is not considered as a candidate at this stage. We assume the annotation is incomplete here.

Given image I_Q and a candidate keyword K_j, the basic probabilistic model P_1 is defined as follows:

$$P_1(K_j \mid I_Q) = \frac{W_j^1}{\sum\limits_{j'=1..n} W_{j'}^1},$$

(1)

where W_j^1 is the weight of keyword K_j, which is computed as the weighted sum of β_{ij}:

$$W_j^1 = \sum_{\forall i} \alpha_{Qi} \times \beta_{ij}.$$

(2)

Taking Figure 2 as an example, the basic probabilistic model produces $P_1(Dog|I_Q)=0.466$, $P_1(Grass|I_Q)=0.236$, $P_1(Pet|I_Q)=0.15$, $P_1(Running|I_Q)=0.148$, and $P_1(Lawn|I_Q)=0$. The labeled keywords of the images similar to I_Q can be taken as a 'virtual document,' which yields a possible semantic interpretation of image I_Q. Each keyword in the document has a different weight W_j^1, which is calculated according to its importance to the similar images and the similarity between I_Q and the similar images. The basic probabilistic model P_1 provides a possible means to rank the keywords. However, some rankings are unsatisfactory. $P_1(Lawn|I_Q)=0$ because no similar images contain keyword *Lawn*. In addition, keyword *Running* is a noise and difficult to filter. It is expected *Pet* is better than *Running* for labeling image I_Q in this example. An enhanced model is, therefore, necessary.

4.2   Enhanced Model

To alleviate the inaccuracy mentioned previously, in this section we explore the use of the semantic concepts implicit in the set of keywords to build an enhanced probabilistic model. We assume that an image has some concepts constituted by its relevant keywords. Based on the conceptual information, the semantic network in Figure 2 can be extended to Figure 3. The extended semantic network is defined as a tuple $(D, K, C, M_{IK}, M_{KC})$ where

- D, K and M_{IK} are the same with the basic semantic network.
- C is a set of concepts (or semantic categories) $\{C_k\}$ $(k=1..q)$ specifying *the concept level*. Concept C_k denotes the group of the keywords pertaining to a certain concept.
- M_{KC} is a set of weights $\{\gamma_{jk}\}$ $(j=1..n,\ k=1..q,\ 0\le\gamma_{jk}\le1)$ on the links between keywords K and concepts C. γ_{jk} denotes the relevance of keyword K_j to concept C_k.

In the extended network, the concept level mirrors the other keyword level K' $(=K)$ on the right-hand side. Weight γ'_{kj} on the link between concept C_k and keyword K'_j is equivalent to weight γ_{jk}. This helps us explain how to compute the ranking for each keyword latter. Moreover, concept C and weights γ_{jk} and γ'_{kj} can be automatically generated with conventional term clustering and categorization methods, respectively, we will describe the details in Section 5.

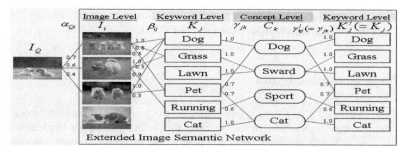

Fig. 3. Example of extended image semantic network

Like the basic probabilistic model, we assume the relevant keywords of image I_Q constitute another 'virtual document,' which provides a possible interpretation of image I_Q at the concept level. Again given image I_Q and a candidate keyword K_j, the enhanced probabilistic model P_2 is defined as follows:

$$P_2(K_j \mid I_Q) = \frac{W_j^2}{\sum\limits_{j'=1..n} W_{j'}^2},$$
(3)

where weight W_j^2 is computed as:

$$W_j^2 = \sum_{k=1..q} \gamma'_{kj} \times (\sum_{j'=1..n} W_{j'}^1 \times \gamma_{j'k}),$$
(4)

where W_j^2 is the weighted sum of the concept weights. γ'_{kj} denotes the weight and the formula in the parentheses denotes the concept weights.

Obviously model P_1 is a special case of model P_2 when each keyword corresponds to a concept with weight 1. However, this seldom happens in real applications. According to the example illustrated in Figure 3, the enhanced probabilistic model produces $P_2(Dog|I_Q)=0.44$, $P_2(Pet|I_Q)=0.22$, $P_2(Grass|I_Q)=0.155$, $P_2(Lawn|\ I_Q)=0.155$ and $P_2(Running|I_Q)=0.03$. In details the weight of concept *Dog* is 1.975, *Sward* is 0.774 and *Sport* is 0.27, respectively. The idea behind the enhanced model is that if keyword K_j's weight W_j^1 is low or even zero but K_j is highly relevant to the concept of its similar images, the ranking of K_j should be higher such as $P_2(Pet|I_Q)$ and $P_2(Lawn|I_Q)$. On the other hand, a keyword will be ignored if it is irrelevant to the concepts of the similar images, e.g. keyword *Running* and its concept *Sport*. Model P_2 prefers raising the rankings of the keywords with the same concepts to the image.

One possible drawback of the method is that it may carry other noisy information into the annotation process. The annotation accuracy relies on the performance of visual similarity estimation between images and of relevance estimation between keywords. As a result, linear combination of the two models will be helpful to support a more flexible and reliable method. The solution to the image annotation problem is, therefore, computed as:

$$P(K_j, I_Q) = \omega \times P_1(K_j, I_Q) + (1-\omega) \times P_2(K_j, I_Q).$$
(5)

where ω is a weighting parameter between 0 and 1. Given image I_Q, function $P(K_j, I_Q)$ serves as the ranking algorithm for each keyword $K_j \in K$.

5   Implementation Issues

We have developed a prototype system based on the proposed probabilistic model for facilitating image annotation. In this section, we present two major implementation issues: how to search similar images and how to automatically group keywords into concepts. Figure 4 shows our system architecture. The system consists of three main modules: *image similarity*, *keyword categorization*, and *keyword ranking*.

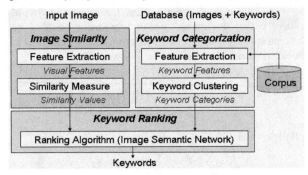

Fig. 4. System architecture of the prototype system

In the image similarity module, the *feature extraction* function produces a feature vector for each visual feature from the input image based on the image processing technologies. The features considered here include colors and textures for global and local features. The *similarity measure* function is responsible to calculate similarity α_{Qi} for each image $I_i \in I$ by estimating the weighted sum of the Euclidean distances among the extracted features. Details of visual feature extraction will be described in Section 5.1.

In the keyword categorization module, the *feature extraction* function generates a feature vector for each keyword by gathering the statistics of documents retrieved from a corpus. These feature vectors are then passed to the *keyword clustering* function, which is responsible to generate a set of keyword categories (or concepts) by clustering the keywords based on the similarity between corresponding feature vectors. The centroid feature vector of each concept is regarded as the feature vector of the concept. Weight γ_{jk} is determined by the similarity between the feature vectors of keyword K_j and concept C_K. Details of keyword-feature extraction and keyword clustering will be described in Sections 5.2 and 5.3, respectively.

The keyword ranking module accepts the weights necessary for the semantic network and estimates the relevance degree of each keyword K_j to image I_Q based on the probabilistic model P. If a keyword whose relevance degree is larger than a given threshold, it will be selected to annotate image I_Q.

5.1   Visual Feature Extraction

We employ both colors and textures for global and local image features. Local features representing the spatial layout of the colors and textures in an image are useful in providing object-level visual information. Given an image, we first rescale it to the 256×256 resolution and divide it into 16×16 square blocks. Then color and texture features are calculated for each block and the whole image.

Regarding the color features, we make use of a palette of 166 colors by uniformly quantizing the cylindrical HSV color space into 18 hues, 3 saturations and 3 values, which are augmented by 4 grey levels. For textures, we apply symmetric Gabor filters with 3 scales and 4 orientations defined in the spatial domain.

5.2   Keyword-Feature Extraction

Given a set of keywords K, keyword-feature extraction aims to create a N-dimensional feature space with term vocabulary $S = \{t_1, t_2, ..., t_N\}$ and then generate a feature vector $f = <a_1, a_2, ..., a_N>$ for each keyword $K_j \in K$. An extra training corpus is required to examine the statistics of term occurrence and co-occurrence. If a term frequently appears in the corpus with two keywords, the two keywords may be relevant to each other. Notice that the corpus should reflect users' knowledge in various applications. For instance, the labeled images in the Palace Museum provide information about historical arts. The Web provides abundant information about proper nouns such as persons' and companies' names. Herein, the Web is taken as an example. We adopt Google (referred to http://www.google.com) as our back-end search engine for providing such a corpus. To obtain term vocabulary S, each keyword $K_j \in K$ is submitted to Google and then top 200 most-relevant search results including titles and descriptions are returned. Search results of keyword K_j can be treated as a document corresponding to K_j. The training corpus will totally collect $|K|$ documents for all keywords. Then we use character/word bi- and tri-grams together to extract feature-terms from the corpus and top N most-frequent feature-terms are chosen to be our term vocabulary S.

Suppose there exists a vector $\vec{t_i}$ for each feature-term t_i. Keyword K_j can be represented as $\vec{K_j} = \sum_{i=1..N} a_i \times \vec{t_i}$. a_i is defined with *tf-idf* term weighting scheme [11] and is computed by:

$$a_i = (0.5 + 0.5 \frac{tf_i}{\max_{\forall j} tf_j}) \log \frac{n}{n_i}, \tag{6}$$

where tf_i is the number of occurrences of term t_i in the document corresponding to keyword K_j, n denotes the total number of documents in the corpus and n_i is the number of documents containing t_i in the corpus.

5.3   Keyword Clustering Algorithm

In order to cluster keywords K, we need to judge the similarity between two keywords K_1 and K_2 with feature vectors f_1 and f_2, respectively. The similarity between keywords K_1 and K_2 is defined as the cosine measure, that is, $cos(f_1, f_2)$.

We extend a hierarchical agglomerative clustering method to group keywords into concepts C. Algorithm *ConceptGeneration* starts with trivial clusters, each containing one keyword. Herein, a cluster in the clustering algorithm corresponds to a concept in C and vice versa. The algorithm cycles through a loop in which the two "closest clusters" are merged into one cluster. The distance between two clusters C_1 and C_2 is defined as the maximum of the distances between all possible pairs of keywords in the two clusters (the complete-linkage method) and is computed by:

$$FarthestNeighborDist\,(C_1, C_2) = \underset{\forall K1 \in C1, K2 \in C2}{Max}\, 1 - Sim(K_1, K_2). \tag{7}$$

The *FarthestNeighborDist* function typically identifies compact clusters in which keywords are very similar to each other and is less affected by the presence of noise or outliers in the data. Its major challenge is the problem of being biased in the direction of small compact clusters. Each loop will reduce number of clusters by 1 and is repeated until one global cluster is reached or the size of the minimum cluster C_k exceeds a given threshold δ. C_k's size is determined by *FarthestNeighborDist(C_k, C_k)*.

```
Algorithm ConceptGeneration (K: keywords, δ: threshold)
CS ← ∅
for each keyword Kⱼ∈ K do
        CS ← CS ∪ {{Kⱼ}}
while |CS|≥2 or FarthestNeighborDist(Cₖ, Cₖ) > δ ∀ Cₖ ∈ CS
do begin
        Select two clusters C₁ and C₂ from CS such that
        FarthestNeighborDist(C₁, C₂) is minimum
        CS ← CS-{C₁} -{C₂}
        CS ← CS ∪ {{C₁∪C₂}}
end
return CS.
```

6 Performance Evaluation

6.1   Experiment of Image Annotation

We tested our system over the Corel library with 5000 images to verify the efficiency of the proposed probabilistic model. The 5000 images have been manually partitioned into five collections (*animals, natural scenes, buildings, weathers* and *transportation*) and labeled with 20140 keywords, including 1432 distinct keywords, in advance. On average each image has 4.03 keywords to describe it. Table 1 shows the statistical information about the five collections.

Table 1. Statistical information about the data set

Collection Number of	Animal	Natural Scene	Building	Weather	Trans- portation
Images	1700	1300	500	500	1000
Keywords	6669	5221	1994	2008	4054
Distinct Keywords	556	406	267	160	386
Keywords Per Image	3.92	4.02	3.99	4.02	4.05

In this experiment, we directly used the Coral library as our corpus for clustering 1432 distinct keywords. For each collection, 100 images were randomly selected as new (or testing) images and the others were treated as labeled (or database) images. Initially, if image I_i is labeled by keyword K_j, their weight β_{ij} is set to be 1 by default. The goal of the experiment is to examine the performance of the proposed model in recall and precision and then explore its performance in insufficient labeled keywords.

Table 2 (a) shows the experimental result of applying the basic probabilistic model P_1 to labeling the images in the five collections. We represented the performance of annotation in the form of "recall/precision" for each top-K keywords, where K was varied from 1 to 8. Herein, we did not optimize the weights of the visual features for computing image similarity. The proposed probabilistic model can achieve the performance of 55.0% recall and 55.4% precision when the "top 4" set is selected for labeling. The result indicates that the proposed model P_1 is effective for helping users annotate images when there are sufficient images in the collection with good keywords assigned. We choose top 4 because in average each image is expected to be assigned four keywords in the database. When the "top 8" set is selected, its recall can achieve 69.2% with precision 34.2%.

To further assess the impact of insufficient labeled keywords to the basic probabilistic model, we restricted the number of the similar images to a new image to 10 (maximum) and 30% labeled keywords in the database were ignored for labeling the new images. We selected the *natural scene* collection as the data set in this case. Table 2 (b) shows that model P_2 outperforms P_1 in the situation that we have insufficient labeled keywords in the database. Although model P_2 could not fully recover the performance P_1 achieved with sufficient labeled data, as shown in Table 2 (a), P_2 does not depend strongly on the quality of the labeled data set.

Table 2. Performance of image annotation for five collecdtions (recall/precision)

(a) Use of model P_1

Category Top-K	Animal	Natural Scene	Building	Weather	Trans- portation
Top 1	.15 / .60	.20 / .86	.13 / .55	.23 / .81	.25 / 1.0
Top 2	.25 / .50	.32 / .64	.21 / .47	.35 / .63	.43 / .90
Top 4	.45 / .45	.54 / .54	.41 / .42	.58 / .56	.77 / .80
Top 8	.60 / .30	.68 / .34	.59 / .27	.72 / .35	.87 / .45

(b) Comparison between P_1 and P_2

Model Top-K	P_1	P_2
Top 1	.12 / .57	.18 / .71
Top 2	.22 / .51	.32 / .64
Top 4	.38 / .39	.50 / .50
Top 8	.57 / .21	.64 / .32

Manual annotation with keywords

forest, reflection, tree, water

Fig. 5. Example of a query image

The proposed probabilistic model can be integrated with relevance feedback strategies. Suppose a user plans to annotate the image in Figure 5. The system is able to adjust the weights of different visual features so that it can estimate the similarity weights based on users' information need. In other words, the system can be improved by better visual feature extraction for specific applications. Figures 6 and 7 shows the results of image retrieval and image annotation using relevant feedback, respectively.

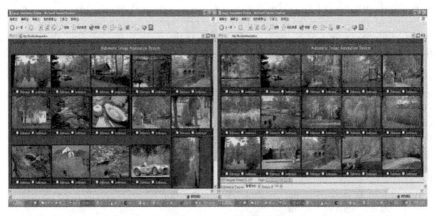

(a) Similar images before user's feedback   (b) Similar images after user's feedback

Fig. 6. Example of similar images using relevant feedback

1: water (P_2=0.111309)	1: leaves (P_1=0.137565)	1: water (P_2=0.126252)	1: forest (P_1=0.082275)
2: tree (P_2=0.099341)	2: forest (P_1=0.075725)	2: tree (P_2=0.082351)	2: water (P_1=0.073625)
3: sky (P_2=0.079239)	3: picnic (P_1=0.075725)	3: sky (P_2=0.075791)	3: sky (P_1=0.054357)
4: grass (P_2=0.049908)	4: sky (P_1=0.075725)	4: grass (P_2=0.042710)	4: leaves (P_1=0.054063)
5: mountain (P_2=0.024434)	5: rock (P_1=0.074199)	5: fish (P_2=0.025077)	5: grass (P_1=0.042807)
6: leaves (P_2=0.024272)	6: wall (P_1=0.074199)	6: leaves (P_2=0.021335)	6: field (P_1=0.035836)
7: rock (P_2=0.024108)	7: water (P_1=0.072779)	7: mountain (P_2=0.020786)	7: reflection (P_1=0.032362)
8: sand (P_2=0.018725)	8: grass (P_1=0.070913)	8: rock (P_2=0.020021)	8: barn (P_1=0.019956)
9: beach (P_2=0.017847)	9: tree (P_1=0.069099)	9: field (P_2=0.016695)	9: tree (P_1=0.019906)
10:ground (P_2=0.015914)	10:food (P_1=0.068772)	10:close-up (P_2=0.014543)	10: fish (P_1=0.018845)

(a) Annotation before user's feedback   (b) Annotation after user's feedback

Fig. 7. Example of image annotation with relevant feedback (P_1 & P_2)

6.2   Experiment of Keyword Clustering

In this experiment, we explored if the Web is appropriate to be treated as the corpus for clustering proper nouns. Our goal is to compare how closely the concepts generated by the *ConceptGeneration* algorithm matched those determined by human judges. The image taxonomy of the Chinese Web image search engine *want2* (referred to http://www.want2.com.tw) was served as our benchmark, in which 95313 images have been manually classified into 12 categories and 2712 sub-categories, including *entertainment, art, computer, nature, consumption*, etc. We randomly selected 90 sub-categories and 1000 terms as our keywords. The F-measure [6] was adopted as the performance metric.

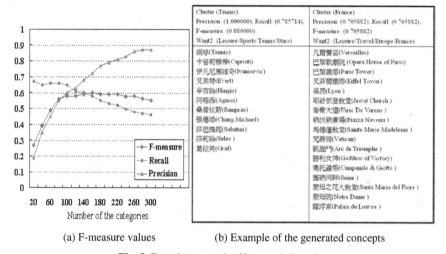

(a) F-measure values   (b) Example of the generated concepts

Fig. 8. Experiment result of keyword clustering

Figure 8 (a) shows the experimental result where the number of the generated clusters was varied from 20 to 300. The F-measure could achieve 0.61 when the number of clusters was around 160. This phenomenon explains that the complete-link method prefers to identify compact clusters in which keywords are very similar to each other in the same cluster. Increasing the number of clusters will produce smaller clusters with closely-related keywords which improve precision; however, in the meantime it might reduce the performance of recall. Figure 8 (b) illustrates the two generated clusters.

7   Conclusion

In this work, we have proposed two probabilistic models P_1 and P_2 to estimate the possibility of annotating keywords to given new images. With the models, the annotated keywords of new images are determined in terms of their similarity at different semantic levels. A prototype system based on the models has been implemented. Obtained experimental results have shown that model P_1 is effective for helping users annotate images when there are sufficient images in the collection with good keywords assigned. Model P_2 does not depend strongly on the quality of the labeled data.

References

[1]   Barnard, K. and Forsyth, D. Learning the Semantics of Words and Pictures. In Proceedings of the 8th International Conference on Computer Vision 2 (2001), 408–415.

[2]   Barnard, K. and Forsyth, D. Exploiting Image Semantics for Picture Libraries. In Proceedings of the 1st ACM/IEEE-CS Joint Conference on Digital Libraries (2001).

[3]   Chang, S.F., Chen, William and Sundaram, Hari. Semantic Visual Templates: Linking Visual Features to Semantics. In Proceedings of International Conference on Image Processing (ICIP), Workshop on Content Based Video Search and Retrieval (1998), 531–535.

[4]   Flickner, M, Sawhney, H.S., Ashley, J., Huang, Q., Dom, B., Gorkani, M., Hafner, J., Lee, D., Petkovic, D., Steele, D. and Yanker, P. Query by Image and Video Content: The QBIC System. IEEE Computer 28, 9 (1995), 23–32.

[5]   Gupta, A. and Jain, R. Visual Information Retrieval. Communications of the ACM 40, 5 (1997), 71–79.

[6]   Larsen, B., and Aone, C. Fast and Effective Text Mining Using Linear-Time Document Clustering. In Proceedings of the 5th ACM SIGKDD International Conference on Knowledge Discovery and Data Mining (1999), 16–22.

[7]   Lu, Y, Hu, C.H., Zhu, X.Q., Zhang, H.J and Yang, Q. A Unified Framework for Semantics and Feature Based Relevant Feedback in Image Retrieval Systems. In Proceedings of the 8th ACM International Conference on Multimedia (2000), 31–37.

[8]   Minka T.P. and Picard R.W. Interactive Learning Using a "Society of Models." In Proceedings of the IEEE Conference on Computer Vision and Pattern Recognition (1996), 447–452.

[9]   Paek, S. Sable, C.L., Hatzivassiloglou, V., Jaimes, A., Schiffman, B.H., Chang, S.F. and McKeown, K.R. Integration of Visual and Text-Based Approaches for the Content Labeling and Classification of Photographs. In Proceedings of ACM SIGIR Workshop on Multimedia Indexing and Retrieval (1999), Berkeley, CA.

[10] Rui, Y., Huang, T.S., Ortega, M. and Mehrotra, S. Relevance Feedback: A Power Tool for Interactive Content-Based Image Retrieval. IEEE Transactions on Circuits and Systems for Video Technology 8, 5 (1998), 644–655.

[11] Salton, G., and Buckley, C. Term Weighting Approaches in Automatic Text Retrieval. Information Processing and Management 24 (1988), 513–523.

[12] Vailaya, A., Jain, A. and Zhang, H.J. On Image Classification: City Images vs. Landscapes. Pattern Recognition 31, 12 (1998), 1921–1935.

[13] Zhao, R and Grosky, W.I. From Features to Semantics: Some Preliminary Results, In Proceedings of the IEEE International Conference on Multimedia & Expo (2000), 679–682.

Affective Contents Retrieval from Video with Relevance Feedback

Hang-Bong Kang

Dept. of Computer Engineering, The Catholic University of Korea
#43-1 Yokkok 2-dong Wonmi-Gu, PuchonCity, Kyonggi-Do, Korea
hbkang@catholic.ac.kr

Abstract. In this paper, we propose a new method to retrieve affective contents from video data using low level features such as color, motion and shot cut rate. First, we present a mechanism for computing a large number of low-level features that capture emotional characteristics. Then, we use AdaBoost method to select very highly meaningful features in detecting emotional events and to learn the boundary that separates data into two clusters. To learn the boundary adaptive to the query, we select positive examples and slightly negative examples which have short distances from the decision boundary. A user gives a relevance feedback to these examples. The learning process is repeated to these examples. Finally, a strong classifier is determined for emotional event detection. Experimental results are promising.

1 Introduction

Affective content or emotion analysis is necessary to represent a user's emotional preferences in various applications such as video data retrieval and video abstraction for digital libraries. For example, if affective content is analyzed effectively, users can retrieve the most interesting video clips or watch most exciting segments of video [1]. So, affective computing plays an important role in the intelligent human computer interaction [2].

To detect emotional video clips or events, it is necessary to analyze and abstract contents at affective level. It takes into account the subjectivity of the user and it also has an ability to recognize the emotions [1]. Relevance feedback is one of the most promising approach to reflect user's subjectivity in the retrieval process. The recognition of emotional events from low level features is not an easy task. One possible method is to use learning techniques. Therefore, it is desirable to develop a method with relevance feedback and learning to detect emotional events.

There have been several attempts to extract affective content from video. One method is to map low-level video characteristics into emotion space. Hanjalic and Xu [3] used motion and sound information to construct affect curves on the two dimensional emotion space consisting of arousal and valence. From the affect curve, the user's perception may be analyzed. Another method is to use sound energy dynamics to detect and classify affective sound events [4]. In this method, audio cues or sound patterns in horror films are detected automatically only for scene classification.

T.M.T. Sembok et al. (Eds.): ICADL 2003, LNCS 2911, pp. 243–252, 2003.

However, limitations still exist in the classification of emotional content because the extraction of emotion related features or the mapping of low-level features into high level emotions is very difficult. To deal with these problems, we detect a very large number of low level features from video data and then use AdaBoosting algorithm to select highly meaningful features to classify emotional events.

In this paper, we classify the most common emotional events such as fear, sadness, and joy, from video data using low-level features. The decision boundary that separates positive and negative examples is learned from AdaBoost scheme. The positive and negative examples used to learn the boundary are provided by the user with relevance feedback. Section 2 presents the computing method of affective features in video data. Section 3 discusses the classification of affective content using AdaBoost method. Section 4 presents affective content retrieval using Relevance Feedback. Section 5 shows experimental results.

2 Affective Feature Extraction

There are four basic common emotions such as fear, anger, sadness, and joy [4]. Since fear and anger have similar emotional characteristics with a view to arousal and valence [5], it is very difficult to discriminate fear and anger from low level features such as color, motion and shot cut rate. So, in this paper, we classify three emotional events such as fear, sadness and joy. To capture low level features which represent emotional characteristics, we have performed empirical study on the relationship between emotional events and simple low level features in video. The ground truth for three emotional events is manually determined on six 30-minute training video data such as "I Know What You Did Last Summer", "Home Alone", "Dying Young", "Ring", "Titanic" and "When Harry Met Sally", which are segmented into scenes. The scenes that belong to three emotional events are labeled by 10 students. If the video scene is labeled with the same emotional event by at least 7 of 10 students, we assign the scene as having one of three emotional events. From emotional events, we extract low level features. Table 1 shows the relationship between emotional events and low level features such as color, motion and shot cut rate. For example, at the fear events the colors are usually "dark and blue" or "dark and red" and "low saturated". The motion phase may be zoom, tilt or dolly and motion intensity is not related with fear events. The shot cut rate is usually fast. Based on the information like Table 1, we assume that color, motion and shot cut rate information is useful in classifying affective events from video data.

Since emotional events or scenes consist of consecutive shots, we compute low level features from each shot of video scene. We represent the video shot using three low level features as follows:

$$Video\ Shot := \{color,\ motion,\ shot\ cut\ rate\} \tag{1}$$

The color information is represented by contrast, accordance and dominant color.

$$Color := \{contrast,\ accordance,\ dominant\ color\}, \tag{2}$$

where   contrast:= {saturation contrast, light-dark contrast, warm-cold contrast},
accordance := {harmony color, complementary color}
dominant color :={single dominant color}.

To compute color features, we transform RGB color space into HSV color space and then quantize the pixels into 11 culture colors such as red, yellow, green, blue, brown, purple, pink, orange, gray, black and white [6]. We extract connected regions from the quantized image. Then, we choose five dominant regions and compute saturation contrast, light-dark contrast and warm-cold contrast. Accordance and dominant colors are also computed [7].

The motion information is represented as

$$Motion:=\{motion\ intensity,\ motion\ phase\}. \tag{3}$$

To detect motion information, we compute frame differences between two consecutive frames in the shot and if the frame difference is larger than the threshold value, we divide the frame into nine regions and compute motions using optical flow. The motion phase is quantized into 8 directions and classified into "pan", "tilt", "zoom", and "no camera motion" by template matching [8]. The motion intensity is also computed from dominant motion vectors. In the case of "no camera motion", object motion intensity or frame difference is computed as motion intensity.

The shot cut rate information is represented as

$$Shot\_cut\_rate:=\{Shot\ length\}. \tag{4}$$

We compute each shot's length and compared it with the median shot length because it shows a better estimate of the average shot length in the presence of outliers.

After experiments of the relationship between the feature vectors and emotional events using Fisher's LDA(linear discriminant analysis), we choose three color features such as *saturation contrast, light-dark contrast* and *single dominant color* as emotion-related color features. We also choose *pan, tilt, zoom, no camera motion* and *shot length* as emotion-related motion features. Figure 2 shows the LDA result using 9 features in classifying "Joy" and "Not-Joy" video shots. Two classes can be discriminated from low level features such as color, motion and shot cut rate.

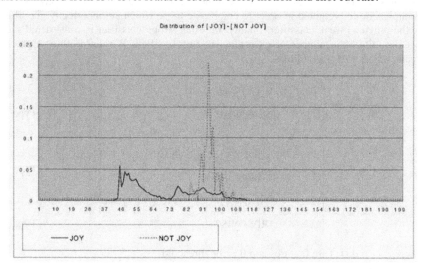

Fig. 1. The Feature Distribution using LDA

Table 1. Emotional event and low level features

	Color	Motion (Phase/intensity)	Shot cut rate
Fear	Dark and blue, sometimes dark and red Low saturated	Zoom, tilt, dolly /NA	Fast
Sadness	Dark Low Saturated	No camera motion / Small	Slow
Joy	Bright colors	NA / Large	NA

3 AdaBoost-Based Emotional Event Classification

To classify emotional events, we use a learning technique. From the empirical analysis shown in Table 1, we assume that a very small number of generated features can be combined to form an effective classifier. So, the most important thing is to find these features. To detect highly meaningful features for emotional event classification, we create a large number of low level features from video shot first. From color features, we can generate 17,898 features. Table 2 shows the rules for generating possible candidate features. Likewise, we also generate 13,000 features similarly from motion and shot cut rate.

In our system, we use a variant of AdaBoost algorithm to select the features and to train the classifier [9-11]. AdaBoost allows the user to continue adding weak learners until low training error has been achieved [9]. AdaBoost algorithm is shown in Figure 2. The weak learning algorithm is designed to select the weak classifier which separates the positive and negative examples best. For each round of learning, the examples are re-weighted in order to emphasize those which are incorrectly classified by the previous weak classifier. Finally, the final strong classifier is constructed such that the minimum number of examples are misclassified. We define three types of weak classifier $h_i(x)$ as follows,

$$h_i(x) = \begin{cases} 1 & \text{if } f_i(x) > \theta \\ 0 & \text{otherwise} \end{cases} \qquad \text{(Type 1)}$$

$$h_{ij}(x) = \begin{cases} 1 & \text{if } f_i(x) < \theta \text{ AND } f_j(x) > \theta \\ 0 & \text{otherwise} \end{cases} \qquad \text{(Type 2)}$$

$$h_{ij}(x) = \begin{cases} 1 & \text{if } f_i(x) < \theta \text{ OR } f_j(x) > \theta \\ 0 & \text{otherwise} \end{cases} \qquad \text{(Type 3)}$$

where $f_i(x)$ and $f_j(x)$ are features and θ is the threshold.

For color features, we make 570 classifiers like Type 1. The number of Type 2 and Type 3 classifiers is both 8,664 (see Table 2). For motion and shot cut rate, we make 13,000 classifiers. The total number of classifiers is 30,898. Based on these classifiers, we construct a strong classifier using AdaBoost algorithm shown in Fig. 2. The strong classifier is a weighted combination of weak classifiers. For each emotional event, a strong classifier is obtained.

Begin

    initialize

$$D = \{x^1, y_1,...,x^n, y_n\}, k_{max},$$
$$W_1(i) = 1/2m, 1/2l, i = 1,...,n$$

    where $y_1...y_n$ = 0 or 1, m and l are the number of negatives and positives, respectively.

       $K = 0$
       Do k = k+1

           Normalize the weights $W_k(i)$

           Train weak learner h_k using D sampled according to $W_k(i)$

       E_k = *training error of h_k measured on D using $W_k(i)$*

$$\alpha_k = \frac{1}{2}\ln[(1-E_k)/E_k]$$

$$W_{k+1}(i) =$$

$$\frac{W_k(i)}{Z_k} \times \begin{cases} e^{-\alpha_k} & \text{if } h_k(x^i) = y_i \text{ (correctly classified)} \\ e^{\alpha_k} & \text{if } h_k(x^i) \neq y_i \text{ (incorrectly classified)} \end{cases}$$

       until k = k_{max}

    return h_k and α_k for $k = 1$ to k_{max}

The final classifier is

$$h(x) = \begin{cases} 1 & \sum_{t=1}^{K\,max} \alpha_t h_t \geq \frac{1}{2}\sum_{t=1}^{K\,max} \alpha_t \\ 0 & otherwise \end{cases}$$

end

Fig. 2. AdaBoost algorithm [9]

Table 2. The Number of Color and Motion Features

CLASSIFIER	NUMBER OF COLOR FEATURE	NUMBER OF MOTION FEATURE
$F < \theta$	285	100
$F > \theta$	285	100
$F_1 < \theta_1$ AND $F_2 < \theta_2$	2166	1600
$F_1 < \theta_1$ AND $F_2 > \theta_2$	2166	1600
$F_1 > \theta_1$ AND $F_2 < \theta_2$	2166	1600
$F_1 > \theta_1$ AND $F_2 > \theta_2$	2166	1600
$F_1 < \theta_1$ OR $F_2 < \theta_2$	2166	1600
$F_1 < \theta_1$ OR $F_2 > \theta_2$	2166	1600
$F_1 > \theta_1$ OR $F_2 < \theta_2$	2166	1600
$F_1 > \theta_1$ OR $F_2 > \theta_2$	2166	1600
TOTAL	17898	13000

4   Affective Content Retrieval Using Relevance Feedback

In this Section, we propose a technique that learns a boundary adaptively that separates the positive and negative examples. To a given query, the test video shots in the database are filtered by the boundary which is learned from training data. Actually, some errors occur because some test images are not shown in the training stage. To learn a boundary adaptive to the query, we use relevance feedback on the retrieval results. We are only concerned with the examples located near the boundary in the feature space as shown in Figure 4(b). The distance $D(x,\lambda)$ represents the distance of x to the boundary characterized by λ. The distance from boundary is computed by

$$D(x,\lambda) = \sum_{t=1}^{K_{max}} (\alpha_t (h_t(x) - 0.5) \tag{5}$$

Some positive and negative examples whose distance-from-boundary is below the threshold value are filtered out like figure 4(b). The user gives relevance feedback to these examples. After that, new boundary is learned using AdaBoost. Using this boundary, we retrieve video shots for a given query. Some positive and negative examples around the boundary are used to learn the boundary again. We repeat this process until the number of filtered examples is smaller than the threshold value. Then, the final decision boundary is determined. Using this kind of strong classifiers, we retrieve affective content from video databases.

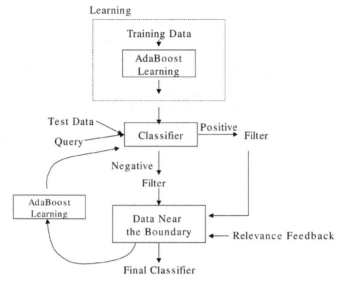

Fig. 3. Proposed Video Retrieval System

5   Experimental Results

Experiments have been done for affective content classification using AdaBoost learning algorithm. We made two data sets from ten video data such as "I Know What You Did Last Summer", "Scream", "Home alone", "Dying Young", "Autumn in New York", "Mask", "Titanic", "Jurassic Park" and "When Harry Met Sally". The video data was segmented into shots using color histograms and key frames were selected for each shot using color and motion information [12]. The ground truth for three emotional events such as "Fear", "Sadness", and "Joy" is determined by the user.

The training data set consists of 1,032 shots which consist of 294 fear shots, 132 sadness shots, 110 joy shots and 496 normal shots. We computed low level features at the shot level. For key frames of each shot, we transformed RGB color space into HSV space and finally computed 17,898 features from color information. The motion phase and intensity for each shot were computed. The relative shot length was also computed. For the motion and shot length features, 13,000 features were generated. The total number of features is 30,898. Three emotional classifiers are trained independently on the training data set. Only small number of features are selected by AdaBoost learning algorithm. For example, for fear classifier 20 features are selected from 20 rounds of learning.

To retrieve emotional events, we test each classifier using validation data set. The validation set consists of 1,522 shots which consist of 378 fear shots, 136 sadness shots and 120 joy shots and 888 normal shots. For a given shot, the classifier determines whether the shot is emotional is or not. Emotion-related shots are retrieved. We also browse the emotional and non-emotional shots whose distances from the boundary are short. To those shots, a user gives relevance feedback. A new boundary is formed. Recall and Precision are used to evaluate the retrieval performance. Figure 5 shows the precision and recall on the fear event. It should be noted that the recall curves go up with relevance feedback since more and more relevant video shots are retrieved when a user interacts with the system. However, the precision curves usually go down with respect to the times of relevance feedback since the number of relevant video shots returned to the user becomes small.

We also test the precision and recall based on color features only for each emotional event. They are shown in Table 3. We also tested our system with color and motion features. The results are a little improved and they are shown in Table 4. Even though we used simple low level features, the experimental results were encouraging.

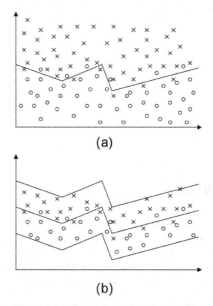

Fig. 4. (a) Original Data, (b) Filtered Data

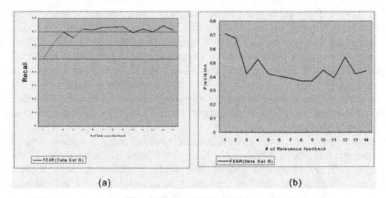

Fig. 5. (a) recall, (b) precision

Table 3. Emotional Shot Retrieval using Color Classifier only

	Number of Emotional Shots	Detected	False Alarms	Detection Rate	False Alarm Rate
Fear Classifier	378	313	129	82.8%	29.1%
Sadness Classifier	136	87	36	63.9%	26.4%
Joy Classifier	120	65	31	54.1%	47.6%

Table 4. Emotional shot retrieval using color and motion features

	Number of Emotional Shots	Detected	False Alarms	Detection Rate	False Alarm Rate
Fear Classifier	378	321	147	84.9%	31.4%
Sadness Classifier	136	98	32	72.0%	23.5%
Joy Classifier	120	75	46	62.5%	38%

6 Conclusion

In this paper, we propose a noble method to retrieve affective contents from video data using AdaBoost algorithm and relevance feedback. We use low level features such as color, motion and shot length information from video data. We generate a large number of simple features and select highly meaningful features using AdaBoost method. Video shot retrieval is realized by using AdaBoost classifier. To learn the boundary adaptive to the query, we select examples whose the distance-from-boundary is less than the threshold value. Then, the boundary is learned again. The recall is increased with respect to the times of relevance feedback.

To improve the detection results, it is desirable to add audio features to the classifier. Currently, we are experimenting with other learning schemes to improve the detection results.

Acknowledgements. This work was supported by the University Research Program of Ministry of Information & Communication in Republic of Korea.

References

1. Hanjalic, A.: Video and Image Retrieval beyond the Cognitive Level: The Needs and Possibilities. Proc. SPIE Storage and Retrieval for Media Databases 2001, San Jose, CA, pp. 130–140, (2001)
2. Picard, R.: Affective Computing. MIT Press, (1997)
3. Hanjalic A. and Xu, L.: User-oriented Affective Video Content Analysis, Proc. IEEE Workshop on CBAIBL'01, Kauai, HI, pp. 50–57, Dec. (2001)
4. Moncrieff, S.,Dorai, C. and Venkatesh, S.: Affect Computing in Film through Sound Energy Dynamics, Proc. ACM MM'01, pp. 525–527, (2001)
5. Lang, P.: The emotion probe: Studies of motivation and attention, American Psychologist, 50(5), pp. 372–385 (1995)
6. Goldstein, E. : Sensation and Perception, Brooks/Cole, (1999)
7. Bimbo A.: Visual Information Retrieval, Morgan Kaufman,(1999)
8. Lee, S., and Hayes, M.: Real-time camera motion classification for content-based indexing and retrieval using templates, Proc. ICASSP, pp. 3664–3667, (2002)
9. Duda, R., Hart, P. and Stork, D.: Pattern Classification, Wiley Inter-science, (2001)
10. Tiue, K. and Viola, P.: Boosting Image Retrieval, Proc. IEEE CVPR '00, (2000)
11. Viola, P. and Jones, M.: Rapid Object Detection using a Boosted Cascade of Simple Features," Proc. IEEE CVPR'01, (2001)
12. Zhang, H., Wu, J., Zhong, D., and Smoliar, S.: An integrated system for content-based video retrieval and browsing, Pattern Recognition, Vol. 30, No. 4, pp. 643–58, (1997)

IPSA: A Digital Archive of Herbals to Support Scientific Research

Maristella Agosti, Lucio Benfante, and Nicola Orio

Department of Information Engineering – University of Padua, Italy
{agosti,benfante,orio}@dei.unipd.it

Abstract. The work reported in this paper has been carried out in the context of a multidisciplinary project, named Ipsa, which has been launched at the University of Padua in 2002. Aim of the project is the design and the construction of a digital library of drawings and illustrations of historic documents, where the digital library is constructed for use of researchers of art and history of scientific illustration. This paper presents the first results of the ongoing project on the development of the digital archive of herbals, that are manuscripts containing hand drawings of real plants. The paper has a specific focus on the user requirements analysis, which has been conducted with a user-centred approach. According to user requirements, we designed tools to provide researchers with novel ways of accessing the digital manuscripts and sharing and transferring knowledge in a collaborative environment.

1 Introduction

The University of Padua has played a major role in the history of modern scientific illustration. Under the influence of Pietro d'Abano's rationalism, since the beginning of the 14th century, the Paduan School was characterised by the search for scientific objectivity [2]. Because of this approach the Paduan School produced, for the first time in Europe, a number of illuminated manuscripts including realistic botanical illustrations [4], detailed and realistic medical images, astronomic drawings inspired by scientific criticism, and astrological images that, although based on antique iconographic models, pointed to scientific and not merely magic astrology [3]. As a consequence, a highly innovative tradition of scientific illustrations was developed at the University of Padua, which had large renown in Europe and deep influence on European culture. The innovation and the appeal of this imagery have to be related not only to their scientific value, but also to the their high formal level and stylistic realisation quality.

The corpus of the historical and very innovative illustrations produced in the centuries under the influence of the Paduan School needed to be informatively documented and made digitally available to researchers of the University of Padua and of other worldwide distributed research institutions also for a secure remote access through an Internet connection. For this reason the University of Padua started a multidisciplinary project aimed at the creation of a digital archive of manuscripts, incunabula, printed books, drawings, prints of images related to this new approach to scientific illustration.

T.M.T. Sembok et al. (Eds.): ICADL 2003, LNCS 2911, pp. 253–264, 2003.
© Springer-Verlag Berlin Heidelberg 2003

The work reported in this paper regards the project and the development of the digital archive of a specific kind of illuminated manuscripts: herbals. Herbals are manuscripts containing hand-drawings of plants, either trees or bushes, or their parts, such as flowers or leaves. Herbals written and illustrated by the Paduan School, and successive herbals produced in Europe under its influence, have the rare characteristic of containing high quality and very realistic botanical illustrations directly drawn from nature. The digital archive of herbals has been named Ipsa, which stands for *Imaginum Patavinae Scientiae Archivum* (archive of images of the Paduan science). The user requirements analysis for the design and development of the digital archive has been conducted from Spring to Autumn 2002 also with the cooperation of a team of final year students of telecommunications engineering which have contributed to the analysis as part of the assignments of the database course. The requirements have been consolidated after an experimental usage of the initial working prototype made available to researchers after the Summer 2002. With the suggestions of the expert users on the utilization of that prototype, a first complete prototype has been made available to researchers at end of March 2003. From April to June 2003 the prototype is under evaluation of its final users, and a consolidated final version of the prototype, revised using the comments of the users, is going to be released in July 2003.

This paper addresses innovative aspects of the feasibility study of the project. The paper has a specific focus on the user requirements analysis and design, which have been conducted with a user-centred approach. According to user requirements, we designed tools to provide researchers with novel ways of accessing the digital archive and sharing knowledge in a collaborative environment. We believe that the results presented in this paper may be extended to other domains related to the exploitation and the preservation of cultural heritage, in particular the research on illuminated manuscripts.

2 Related Works

The preservation and dissemination of cultural heritage have contributed to the promotion and development of digital libraries and digital archives. The particular application to the cultural heritage domain poses interesting problems and challenges as reported in [5]. Some projects on digital libraries and digital archives regard illuminated manuscripts and, in particular, herbals. The description of a digital archive of illuminated manuscripts is reported in [8], while [7] describes the digital library of a herbal. Moreover, there is an increasing number of available commercial systems that give access to digital versions of manuscripts, incunabula, and old printed books.

In the particular field of the representation and the comparison of different images of plants, even if they are not taken from ancient herbals, [12] developed an agent-based tool aimed at helping the botanist inserting records of plants in a digital library and possibly finding similar records in the database. Another study regarding the graphical representation of the relationship among different plants, depending on their geographical distribution, is reported in [13].

We participated in a previous research project regarding the feasibility study of a digital archive for the preservation of the cultural heritage [1]. The feasibility study, named ADMV, which stands for *Archivio Digitale della Musica Veneta* (digital archive of the Venetian music), regarded the creation of a digital archive of images of manuscripts of musical scores, digitised versions in MIDI format, and recordings of performances of musical works by Venetian composers, as Marcello and Pellestrina. The ADMV system is now under development; information are available at the URL: http://www.marciana.venezia.sbn.it/admv.html.

The ADMV feasibility study was the motivation for a subsequent research project aimed at developing novel ways of indexing and retrieving musical documents in a digital library [10], both in symbolic and in audio forms [11].

3   User Requirements for Digital Herbals

The innovative characteristics of the creation of Ipsa digital archive of manuscripts, and in particular that the Ipsa application must be a supporting tool for research activities conducted by experts on drawings and illustrations of historic documents, give rise to a number of specific user requirements that was necessary to take into account and cosider in the development of the application.

3.1   Highly Dynamic Documents Records

Almost every digital archive dynamically changes over the years, mainly because of new acquisitions that increase the number of documents. This is also true for a digital archive of illuminated manuscripts, but there are other reasons that produce changes on the archive over time. The creation of records describing the documents and the images in a herbal, as for any collection of historical works, is part of the scientific research itself. Some examples of changes to records are, for instance, that new relationships with other works have been discovered, or that the attribution to a given author becomes less certain.

Those examples of possible changes make a collection of herbals more dynamic than, for instance, a collection of printed books. Moreover, unlike bibliographic records, there is no universal agreement on a fixed collection of metadata to use for a standardised description of the objects of the Ipsa archive, an example of which are hand-drawings of plants; apart from the name of the plant itself, a complete record should include the style, the way colours are used, the size of the original images and the correspondences among original and the different digital versions of images kept in the digital archive, to cite only a few relevant features that the experts need to have available for their work. Scientific research on herbals aims also at defining standards for the descriptions of documents like illuminated manuscripts.

Since creating a new record or modifying an existing one is part of the scientific work of researchers, the data management has to deal with intellectual rights. A researcher may prefer that some of the newly created records are not accessible by other users, at least until the results of his research have been published and his work have been acknowledged. This situation implies that users may decide which information can be shared with other users and which can not.

3.2   Research in a Collaborative Environment

The study of illuminated manuscripts, and in particular of herbals, involves a number of researchers from different fields. In fact, herbals are of interest for both the historian of art and the historian of science, but at the same time, they are also of interest for the botanist, because they represent plants and their possible variations through the years. Hence, the scientific research on herbals involves a number of persons with different expertise, which should be able to cooperate in order to share their different knowledge and background.

A digital archive of herbals has to provide a collaborative environment, where researchers should be able to interact and give different contributions on the definitions and redefinitions of objects in the herbals. For this reason, it is necessary to consider different levels of users of Ipsa. Apart from the administrators, it needs to be identified the group of research users that should be able to modify the records of the underlying database when new features of the stored objects are discovered.

3.3   Evolutions of Herbals

During the Middle Age the primary role of herbals as a tool for recognising plants was lost, because authors of drawings were more interested on aesthetics than on realism. For this reason, images were no more created looking directly at real plants, but they were copied from or inspired by images of existing herbals. The resulting drawings became increasingly different from the subjects they should represent, because each author added new modifications on parts of the plants depending on personal stylistic choices.

For researchers, it is of primary importance to state if drawings of a herbal are copied from existing herbals or if they are directly inspired by the nature. The disclosure of a link between two images belonging to two independent herbals, because one was the source for creating the other, allows to draw connections between the art of natural representations during the years and across the countries. On the other hand, the proof that two images have been independently created, notwithstanding their apparent resemblance, because for instance the authors could not have been in contact, allows to refine the map of existing connections among different herbals.

The use of realistic images in herbals come back to life since the XIVth century and further developed during Renaissance. Ipsa aims at helping researchers investigating the role played by the University of Padua in the creation of this modern realistic and exact iconography. The disclosure that the images of a herbal have been created as realistic copies of plants witnesses the emerging role of the scientific culture. The disclosure of a relationship between the style of images of different herbals, even if both are realistic representation of nature, helps tracking the spread of the new scientific culture over Europe. As a consequence, a major requirement of researchers is to create connections between objects in the digital archive. In particular, researchers should be able to create links for connecting an image to one or more images that are related, in some way, to it. It is important to keep in mind that images can belong to different herbals. We have investigated the requirements for the management of links among images and we have identified the features of links that it is necessary to manage:

- *Typed links*: Since two images can be related for a number of different reasons, they have to be connected by links that make explicit the type of relationship that correlate two or more images.
- *Link authors*: The creation of a link between two or more images depends on the scientific results of a researcher, who owns the intellectual rights on the disclosure of a new relationship between images; for this reason the author of each new link has to be memorized by the system.
- *Links one-to-one or Links one-to-many*: Links can connect an image to another one or an image to a set of images, because researchers needs both to compare two images for disclosing a possible relationship, and also to compare a set of images for disclosing common features in the representation.
- *Paths*: Links may form historical paths across images, because the images in a herbal can be copied by images of another one which, in turn, were copies themselves of previous drawings; hence two images can not be directly linked, because there is no direct relationship between them, but it could be possible to follow a path from one to the other exploiting existing links.

3.4   Presentation of Digital Images

A digital archive of herbals has the double role of preserving the cultural heritage and giving access to users in a networked environment. As it always happens in this situation, there is a trade-off between the high quality required for preservation and the small size needed for transfer over the network. Moreover, it has to be considered that research users should be able to perform comparisons among images belonging to different herbals that, in principle, may differ in their original size. According to research users, the number of images that should be presented on the computer screen varies from one to a maximum of six.

This last requirement implies that the image size, and hence its resolution, can dynamically vary depending on the context, because in principle a link can be created between any couple of images. The transfer load can be reduced through the use of thumbnails, at least for the first presentation of images. It can be noted that thumbnails can be also a viable solution when the comparison between images is not part of the scientific research but it can be used for dissemination to students or, if future releases of Ipsa will be available on the Web, to casual users without a controlled access.

Image acquisition is another important issue, because researchers need to analyse also small details of images. On the other hand, researches needs to see the image of the complete page of a manuscript, because it gives the context in which a particular plant is presented. Moreover, many herbals have more than a single image for each page, with images surrounding or overlapping with text. For these reasons, it is advisable to carry out multiple acquisitions of the same page, with different resolutions depending on the level of detail needed for the analysis by researchers. Image copyright management, which may be owned by libraries or institutions, is another important issue, even if it does not regard the collaborative environment of researchers.

4   Novel Ways of Using and Accessing the Digital Archive

Ipsa gives users the possibility of performing scientific research on herbals through tools for image annotation. The investigation of the use of annotations for easing the access to multimedia contents of digital libraries and archives is an emerging research field. A system that exploits annotations for creating a collaborative environment is reported in [9]. In our system, together with classical textual annotations, we provide users with linking annotations. Through textual annotation the user adds comments or descriptions to images, while through linking annotation the user creates a new link between different images.

4.1   Textual Annotations

Researchers study images of illuminated manuscripts in order to find new information on the iconography and on the representations. Users are then allowed to annotate each image; the text of the annotation can contains, for instance, considerations on the style or on the use of particular techniques. The same image can be annotated by different users of the same research group. Annotations may be for private use, for example when documenting an ongoing research work, but they can also be shared with colleagues of the same or other disciplines. Textual annotation of images is a step before the creation of new records of the database, and can be considered as a tool aimed at the enrichment of the database of the digital archive.

The user chooses when the textual content of annotations can be shared with the research group, with other users of Ipsa, or has to be private. The system for access controlling provides the necessary tools for hiding textual annotations to users without access to these information. Textual annotations are part of the multidisciplinary collaborative environment previously described, and so they are by default accessible to all the members of the research group.

Textual annotations, even when they do not become part of the records describing the manuscripts or their images, are a valuable contribution that increasingly enriches the digital archive. In fact, these annotations are added by authorised experts and they are the result of years of research work. For this reason, even if the access of the actual content of the annotations may be restricted to only a small number of users, we decide to use the annotated text for the indexing of documents and, in particular, of images. In this way the users contribution to Ipsa can be exploited to create more complete surrogates of the information contained in the digital archive. The user requirements study has shown that the search engine of Ipsa should index both normal records and annotations, allowing for the retrieval of images and documents that would not have been retrieved without the additional information carried by manual annotations.

4.2   Linking Annotations

As previously mentioned, one of the major goals of the research on illuminated manuscripts of herbals is the disclosure of relationships between images. These relationships may reflect the fact that images of a herbal have been copied from an existing one, as well as the common approach of realistic representation. Moreover, images can be related if they are considered similar by a researcher, where the concept of similarity takes into account historical, aesthetical, and technical considerations and goes beyond the simple concept or resemblance.

The researcher user can express a relationship between two or more images by adding a linking annotation to the image. Since there are a number of different reasons why two or more images are related, the system allows for a description of the link type. We propose the following taxonomy for linking annotations:

- `copy_of`: This link connects an image to the ones that have been used by the authors as the source for the pictorial representation; the link is one-to-many, because an image can be created by copying details from different sources; the presence of this kind of link expresses that the images was created with aesthetics rather than realistic aims.

- `copied_by`: The link represents a relationship symmetrical to `copy_of`.

- `influenced_by`: This link represents a weaker relationship than `copy_of` and, also in this case, it connects an image to the ones that have been a reference for its creation; the presence of this kind of link may be related to the aims of the author, for instance it can be a realistic representation of a plant but the style or the technique are inspired by other images.

- `influence_on`: The link represents a relationship symmetrical to `influenced_by`.

- `unrelated_to`: This type of link may seem useless, because images are more likely unrelated; nevertheless the analysis of user requirements highlighted that, for the domain of illuminated manuscripts, the disclosure of the independence of two different sources is part of the scientific research and it may need to be emphasised; the link is one-to-many, and it is created by the users only when the absence of a relationship is an important information; this type of link does not connects images that are simply different.

- `similar_to`: This type of link is created when a researcher wants to highlight that images can be considered similar according to some features, including style, technique, or subject; the link is one-to-many.

The proposed taxonomy regards only links created by the users. Because of the particular application domain, it does not include links created by the author of a hypertext or automatically created by the system. A taxonomy that includes also these different typologies can be found in [6]. From the description of link taxonomy it appears that some link types express a hierarchical relationship – e.g. influence or copy – while some others do not – e.g. similarity or no relationship. The presence of a hierarchical structure can be exploited by automatically building paths across the link structure, for instance to describe the creation over the years of copies of a renown herbal, and the subsequent creation of copies of the copies and so on. At the same time, paths can describe the dissemination of the scientific approach proposed by the Paduan School, its evolution over time and space. In Figure 1 an example of the structure given by different links is reported.

Thanks to linking annotations, Ipsa is dynamically enriched by a hypertext structure, which can integrate search through navigation inside the database. It is likely that both researchers and eventual other users, as students, would benefit from the presence of links: researchers may cooperate in their study on illuminated manuscripts by sharing the information on relationship between different sources; students, which may not be able to effectively search the digital archive, may take advantage of the navigation paradigm. It has to be noted that the disclosure of a relationship between images from different herbals is part of the scientific research, and then also in this case the system has to provide the possibility of restricting the access of linking information. For this reason, the same access rules applied for textual annotations are extended also to linking annotations.

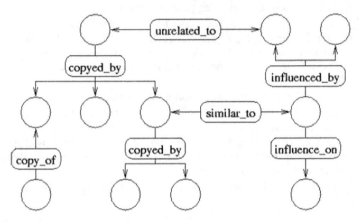

Fig. 1. An example of images connected by typed links

5   Issues on Image Management

As previously mentioned, a major requirement of research users is the possibility of studying and comparing complete images and their parts. In particular, users should be able to zoom images for analysing also small details. On the other hand, users gain access to the digital archive through the network and the transfer time of one or more high resolution images, of the size of a manuscript page, would be unreasonable. It has to be considered that research users may have different affiliations and, in general, may connect to Ipsa through the Internet. Moreover, the front end can be any commercially available Web browser, which may give additional problems when the file sizes become of several megabytes each.

We propose to overcome these problems by using variable resolutions for images. For each page of the different herbals, Ipsa stores both a low and a high resolution image. For complete pages, only the low resolution, which is in a lossy compressed format, is actually sent to the Web browser, because it has only to give a context to the researchers. The high resolution version of that same image is stored for preservation. Moreover, each separate drawing that belongs to the page is stored as a single image by itself. The process of acquiring both the complete page and all its images may seem costly, but we considered that in this way it would be possible to store different images from the same page with different resolutions, depending on their original size, the number of details, and the quality of the original drawing.

5.1 Variable Resolution Images

Research users need to compare up to six images that have to be contemporaneously displayed on the computer screen. The image size can be computed by the system, because it depends on the screen resolution and on the number of images. The preferred image resolution can be computed on-line for each image, considering that it is useless and time consuming to send an image with a resolution that cannot be displayed on the screen. For this reason Ipsa performs a downsampling of images, according to the needed resolution, before sending them to the user. The computational overload of this operation is compensated by the optimal transfer time from the system to the Web browsers. Moreover, the number of research users that are likely to gain access to Ipsa at the same time is reasonably low.

The same variable resolution approach is applied when users ask to zoom details of images. The system re-samples the images according to the new ratio between the original size of the image part and the size on the computer screen. The process can be summarised as follows:

- The user queries the system, using both the simple exact match search and the information retrieval engine – the system sends to the user the catalogue records and the image of the full page of the manuscripts in low resolution.
- If the retrieved information is of interest for the user, he can choose to visualise the images of the drawings – the system computes the size of the images on the screen, it re-samples the original images, and it sends them to the user.
- At this point the user can:
  - Add annotations to the images, by writing textual annotation or creating linking annotations to other images previously analysed – the system updates the hypertext structure of images.
  - Follow a linking annotation, if present, in order to navigate inside the hypertext or to compare different images – the system retrieves the linked images and performs the same operations as the second step.
- At any time the user may choose to zoom a given image – the system re-samples the image part with the new resolution and it sends the image to the user.

It can be noted that this approach overcomes the problem of variations in the original size of images contained in different herbals, because they are automatically resized depending on the available space on the computer screen.

6 The Architecture of IPSA

After having carried out the analysis of user requirements and the having developed the methodology for accessing the digital herbal, we started the project and the development of a prototype system, called Ipsa. We briefly describe the choices we made regarding the architecture of Ipsa. The system is based on software distributed under open source license; the application has been developed on Debian GNU/Linux platform.

Ipsa is a Web application that is based on a 3-tier architecture. Research users gain access to the functionalities of Ipsa through the Client Tier, which is a generic Web browser. The client tier communicates with the "Web Container", which is embedded in the Web/Application Tier, using the protocol HTTP. The Web Container is Tomcat developed by the Apache Software Foundation (http://www.apache.org/). It includes the Java Server Pages (JSP) and the Servlets that are the basis for the implementation of the presentation and application logic of Ipsa. These Java components exploit the functionalities of Java 2 Standard Edition. In particular, images are managed through the Java 2D and Java Advanced Imaging Apis, which are used for image processing and transfer. The implementation of the presentation login in the JSP has been carried out using the JSP Standard Tag Library developed by the Apache Software Foundation. The communication between the Web/Application Tier and the Information Tier is achieved through the library JDBC. The Information Tier contains the Database Management System PostgreSQL 7.2.4, copyright by The PostgreSQL Global Development Group (http://www.postgresql.org/), which is used both to store images and user annotations. A scheme of the architecture is reported in Figure 2.

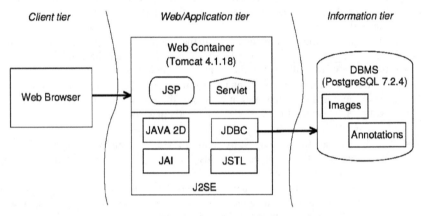

Fig. 2. The 3-tier architecture of Ipsa

7 Conclusions

In this paper we discuss the project and the development of a digital archive to be accessed by researchers on illuminated manuscripts of herbals. As it has been highlighted by our user requirement study, images and their possible relationships play a central role in this particular application domain.

We propose the use of textual and linking annotations as a tool for researchers working in a collaborative environment. In particular, linking annotations can be a valuable tool for representing the evolution of scientific representation over the years. The need of comparing different images, which may have different sizes and quality because they may belong to different herbals, has been addressed by representing images with variable resolution in order to find a good trade-off between image quality and problems related to the transfer over a network and to the display with common Web browsers. We believe that the proposed approach can be extended also to other application domains, in particular in the field of preservation and dissemination of cultural heritage.

Acknowledgments. The authors wish to thank the coordinator of the Ipsa project, professor Maria Giordana Canova together with professors Federica Toniolo and Elisabetta Saccomani, all from the Faculty of Humanities of the University of Padua, for the useful discussions on different aspects of the illuminated manuscripts. Sincere thanks to the members of the research group on Information Management Systems of the department for the useful discussions on aspects related to the fascinating area of annotating a digital library which take place during the meetings of the Operative Unit of the University of Padua in the ECD national project. ECD (*Enhanced Content Delivery*) is a research project launched by the Italian National Council of Research (CNR) in 2002 with the aim of developing methods and technologies for the enhanced delivery of contents to final users. Several academic, research, and industrial partners are participating nationwide on the project, further information can be obtained at the URL: http://www-ecd.cnuce.cnr.it/.

Thanks also to professors Franco Bombi and Concettina Guerra, of the department, for the useful discussions on aspects related to the representation of information on manuscripts, which have taken place in the context of the feasibility study conducted by a project team of the department for the National Committee of the Rectors of the Italian Universities.

References

1. Agosti M., Bombi F., Melucci M., Mian G., Towards a digital library for the Venetian music of the eighteenth century, in J. Anderson, M. Deegan, S. Ross, S. Harold (Eds), *DRH 98: Selected papers from Digital Resources for the Humanities.* Office for Humanities Communication, 2002, 1–16.
2. Canova M.G., La tradizione europea degli erbari miniati e la scuola veneta, Di Sana Pianta. *Erbari e Taccuini di Sanità.* Modena, 1988, 21–28.
3. Canova M.G., Per la storia della figura astrologica a Padova: il De imaginibus di Pietro d'Abano e le sue fonti, in T. Franco, G. Valenzano (Eds), *De lapidibus sententiae.* Padova, 2002, 213–224.
4. Cappelletti E.M., Le piante medicinali negli erbari veneti dei secoli XV e XVI, Di Sana Pianta. *Erbari e Taccuini di Sanità.* Modena, 1988, 61–66.
5. Crane G., Cultural Heritage Digital Libraries: Needs and Components, in M. Agosti and C. Thanos (Eds), *Research and Advanced Technology for Digital Libraries. Proc. of 6th ECDL.* Rome, 2002, 626–637.
6. DeRose S.J., Expanding the Notion of Links, in *Proc. of ACM Conf. on Hypertext and Hypermedia.* Pittsburgh, 1989, 249–57.
7. Don A., Teodosio L., Lambert J., Atchley D., From generation to generation: multimedia, community and personal stories, in *Proc. of ACM Int. Conf. on Multimedia.* San Francisco, 1994, 337–338.
8. Gladney H.M., Mintzer F., Schiattarella F., Bescòs J., Treu M., Digital access to antiquities. *Communications of the ACM*, Vol. 41(4), 1998, 49–57.
9. Lawton D.T., Smith I.E., The Knowledge Weasel Hypermedia Annotation System, in *Proc. of ACM Int. Conf. on Hypertext.* San Francisco, 1993, 106–117.
10. Melucci M., Orio N., Musical Information Retrieval Using Melodic Surface, in *Proc. of ACM Int. Conf. on Digital Libraries.* Berkeley, 1999, 152–160.
11. Orio N., Alignment of Performances with Scores Aimed at Content-Based Music Access and Retrieval, in M. Agosti and C. Thanos (Eds), *Research and Advanced Technology for Digital Libraries. Proc. of 6th ECDL.* Rome, 2002, 479–492.

12. Sànchez J.A., Lòpez C.A., Schnase J.L., An Agent-Based Approach to the Construction of Floristic Digital Libraries, in *Proc. of ACM Int. Conf. on Digital Libraries*. Pittsburgh, 1998, 210–216.
13. Schneider E.R., Leggett J.J., Furuta R.K., Wilson H.D., Hatch S.L., Herbarium Specimen Browser: A Tool for Accessing Botanical Specimen Collections, in *Proc. of ACM Int. Conf. on Digital Libraries*. Pittsburgh, 1998, 227–234.

HIT-DML: A Novel Digital Music Library

Chaokun Wang, Jianzhong Li, and Shengfei Shi

Department of Computer Science and Engineering
P.O.Box 318, Harbin Institute of Technology,
150001, Harbin, Heilongjiang, China
chaokun@hit.edu.cn
lijz@mail.banner.com.cn
shengfei@0451.com

Abstract. The design and implementation of Harbin Institute of Technology-Digital Music Library (HIT-DML) is presented in this paper. HIT-DML adopts a novel framework which is inherently based on database systems. In this framework, musical data is structurally stored in the database, some algorithms of musical computation are implemented as algebraic mirco-operations in the database management system, and thus database technologies and multimedia technologies are combined seamlessly. A musical feature-matching algorithm and the appropriate dynamic index are also applied in HIT-DML. HIT-DML can retrieve musical information based on content, especially against different kinds of musical instruments.

Keywords: Digital Music Library, Content-Based Music Information Retrieval

1 Introduction

Digital libraries have been a phenomenal success in terms of facilitating organization and processing of large volume of music data. Current music digital libraries, however, are either unscalable or unable to provide content-based retrieval and play based on musical instruments, e.g. just search "do-re-mi" on a certain musical instrument, or just play a combination of several musical instruments of a piece of music. Usually they are based on one of the following techniques: storing a piece of music as a file in a directory or as one binary large object in a database.

Besides the performance inefficiency, a common problem with most existing music digital libraries is that they usually ignore the transaction processing algorithms and other advanced features devised by the Database community through decades of refinement and evaluation, and thereby rely on ordinary file systems. For example, the replication mechanism in distributed database systems can be used to backup data between two remote libraries.

In this paper, a novel framework for digital music library and the prototype Harbin Institute of Technology-Digital Music Library (HIT-DML) are introduced. This framework is inherently based on database systems. HIT-DML is an instance of the framework. As a key part of Infinite Digital Library Project (IDLP) in Harbin Institute of Technology, HIT-DML is planned to realize the functions of acquisition, conversion, storage, management, computation, retrieval and consumption of musical data. It is also the platform for our music information research.

T.M.T. Sembok et al. (Eds.): ICADL 2003, LNCS 2911, pp. 265–274, 2003.

HIT-DML not only has the basic functions to navigate, query and play musical data, but also has the functions to acquire and load musical data, to extract features from them and compare musical features. Different from VARIATIONS [1], NZDL [2], and AVPROT [3], HIT-DML is inherently based on database systems. HIT-DML can retrieve musical information based on content, further it centers on database systems. It structurally stores musical data in a database, and implements some music operations, e.g. feature-extracting, in the database. It can utilize the advantages of database systems, and combine multimedia technologies and database technologies seamlessly. Besides that, HIT-DML can query musical data according to various musical instruments. As far as we know, this function is not implemented by other current digital music libraries.

The rest of this paper is organized as follows. Section 2 provides a review of related work. Section 3 introduces and describes the framework of digital music library proposed in this paper. This framework is the basis of HIT-DML. It is not only a blueprint for digital music library, but also a reference to digital libraries of other media. Section 4 reports the implementation of the current HIT-DML prototype, and presents some experimental results. Section 5 concludes the paper and highlights some future research directions.

2   Related Work

There is much work on digital music libraries. Almost all of this work has concentrated on music meta-data instead of raw data. In [4], Fingerhut describes the transition of the IRCAM Music Library from a traditional setup to one tightly integrating digital technologies. Self-describing objects and referencing object parts are introduced in this paper. The IRCAM concert recordings are transferred to self-describing hybrid compact discs, and URLs are used to reference multimedia objects and their parts.

NZDL is one of the successful digital music libraries. A comprehensive suite of tools built for NZDL are described in [5] [6]. These tools gather musical material, convert between many of these representations, allow searching based on combined musical and textual criteria, and help present the results of searching and browsing.

The VARIATIONS/VARIATIONS2 digital library project [7] [8] at Indiana University currently is one of the first practical applications of digital music libraries. It delivers online access to music in a variety of formats - sound recordings, scanned musical scores, computer score notation files, and video - and is designed to support research and learning in the field of music.

Blandford [9] et al. have evaluated four web-accessible music libraries, focusing particularly on features that are particular to music libraries, such as music retrieval mechanisms. The main challenges identified relate to the details of melody matching and to simplifying the choices of file format.

There is some work on MIR in peer-to-peer (P2P) networks. It can be used to establish digital music libraries based on P2P environments. Four models for content-based music information retrieval are proposed in [10]. A prototype and an accelerating algorithm are also given. One transaction mechanism for music files exchange in a P2P system is described in [11], but it can not protect copyrights.

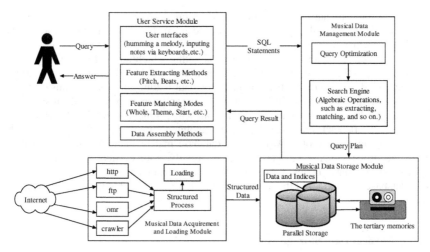

Fig. 1. The Framework of Digital Music Library

3 The Framework Design of Digital Music Library

The framework of digital music library is composed of four modules (Fig.1). This framework has two characteristics. One is that a novel data model [12] is adopted by it, and musical data instead of only musical features are structurally stored in databases. The other is that some music computing algorithms, such as feature-extracting and feature-matching, are realized as algebraic micro-operations of the database management system. In this framework, database technologies and multimedia technologies are combined organically. Not only meta-data based retrieval but also content based retrieval can be carried out. For example, search musical data similar to a piece of melody, especially to that in a certain musical instrument. Each module is described in detail as follows.

3.1 Musical Data Acquisition and Loading Module

There are a lot of musical data in a digital music library. It is the first step in the construction of a digital library to acquire these musical data. In order to more efficiently support applications of a digital library, musical data stored inside the library should be processed before loading.

There are various methods to acquire musical data. Using OMR (Optical Music Recognition) technique, music books can be scanned to pictures, from which digital musical information can be picked up. Through an AD converter, analog musical signals stored in tapes can be transformed into digital musical signals. Especially, with the increasing popularization of computer networks, there are very large musical data dispersed over the Internet. They can be gotten from FTP sites or Web sites, even by crawlers.

Musical data perhaps need be processed before loading of them into a database. For example, a musical file may be converted from its original format to a popular and better format, or be watermarked.

The loading of musical data is the process within which musical data is segmented and stored into the appropriate tables of a database based on the inherent structure of the data. In detail, there are two methods for data loading in a digital music library. The first method is to make a loading program, and use it to partition musical files outside the database, and then store the musical segments into the database. The second is to deposit musical files in a appointed directory, and then inside the database system use proper APIs of the database management system to read these files and process them, e.g. partition them, finally store musical segments into the appropriate database tables. Obviously the latter implements more operations inside the database system, and better combines multimedia technologies and database technologies.

3.2   Musical Data Storage Module

Musical Data Storage Module (MDSM) is an important component in a digital music library. This module is responsible for efficient storage and access of musical data to answer users' queries quickly. The digital library framework proposed in this paper supports not only meta-data-based query, e.g. titles of music, names of singers, but also content-based query, e.g. a piece of melody. These functions need the effective support from storage structures and access methods of musical data.

For storage structures, the structured storage schemas in a digital music library are designed in accordance with the data model proposed in [12]. In this model, musical data is stored in a database as certain structures instead of a BLOB (Binary Large OBject). This design supports more effective storage and retrieval of musical data. For instance, if a user only wants to listen the beginning of a piece of music, or the combination of several musical instruments of the piece of music, just the corresponding data is processed. It reduces the data transmitted, and increases the retrieval speed.

With the increase of musical data in the library, tertiary memories can be used to store the considerable volume of data. Parallel storage mechanism can also be used to accelerate the retrieval.

There are many kinds of meta-data and features for music. Features, e.g. frequency, hardness, loudness, pitch, harmony, energy spectrum, and Mel-Frequency Cepstral Coefficients (MFCC), are in common use with acoustic music. For access methods, many indices can be established based on various meta-data and features of music. These indices will improve the retrieval speed of the digital music library.

3.3   Musical Data Management Module

Musical Data Management Module (MDMM) is designed for query processing. After receiving the query extracted from a user's request, MDMM scans it and analyzes its grammar, and then carries out the optimization process based on certain rules to generate concrete query plan, finally executes the query codes of the plan to generate query result. With the introduction of new algebraic operations, some computing methods in music processing field, e.g. feature-extracting and feature-matching, are fused into database management systems. Thus musical data management module can directly manipulate musical data in databases instead of simply access them. It is a speciality that the proposed digital music library framework has. Of course, this needs the support from given storage structure discussed in the previous subsection.

Music feature-extracting means to extract features from musical data by a certain algorithm. As far as we know, music feature-extracting in other digital music libraries is finished outside databases, i.e. features are extracted before loading of musical data into databases. In the framework proposed in this paper, feature-extracting of musical data is implemented inside the database management system.

Likewise, in the proposed framework, feature-matching of musical data is also implemented inside the database management system. Besides that, music feature-matching is an approximate process because of the error between the ideal input and the melody hummed by a user, which is introduced by the imprecision of the user' memory and noise of the input devices.

The musical data management module has the ability of query processing, and the ability of music computing, e.g. feature-extracting and feature-matching of musical data, inside the database system. It can realize the musical computation, while exert the merit of database systems, e.g. separation of programs from data, integrity of information, universal functions, control of data redundancies, data share, various views of data, and so on. So it can be used to increase the efficiency of digital music libraries.

3.4   User Service Module

User Service Module (USM) of a library is the window for interaction with users. It usually provides navigation and retrieval services on musical data. Under the constraint of certain QoS (Quality of Service), USM takes in access requests posed by users, and returns the results.

The DML framework proposed in this paper offers services for users via Web pages. From the point view of user management, Web services can be divided into two kinds: anonymous user service and registered user service. For anonymous users, the library offers LFU (least frequently used) mechanism to cache most frequently used musical data. When a request is posed by a user, the library firstly searches in the cache. If the result is found, it will be returned to the user, otherwise the request will be sent to the database system for a new search. Besides that, the framework also offers active sending service for a registered user. For instance, a user can register the musical style he likes in the library, and then the library will send appropriate information to him when music of this style is added.

From the point view of library functions, Web services can be divided into two kinds: navigation service and query service. Navigation service means that a user can navigate musical data stored in the library according to some metrics, such as musical styles, years of creation, and so on. Query service can be classified as the following four levels:

A) A user poses a request based on meta-data, then the system returns the result, where meta-data means fields used in the conventional music information retrieval, e.g. titles of music, names of composers, and so on. Also, the request may be a combination of meta-data.

B) A user writes a piece of melody, USM extracts useful features from it as a query, and then the library processes this query.

C) A user uploads a piece of music, the library processes the query extracted from it.

D) A user hums and records a piece of melody by a microphone, then uploads it. The library begins a query on it.

The last three cases are queries based on content of musical data, i.e. content-based music information retrieval. The last one is most natural. After receiving the query result, the user has several choices. He can download some pieces of music, play a piece of music integrally, just listen to the theme of a piece of music, or enjoy the combination of several selected musical instruments in a piece of music, and so on. The user can play, pause, rapidly play, and rapidly back during his enjoyment.

4 The Implementation of HIT-DML

In this section, the implementation of HIT-DML is presented. The feature-extracting and feature-matching algorithms used in HIT-DML are described firstly.

According to the music theory and MIDI specification [13], the range of notes can be extended to C_3-G^6, which can be denoted by integers in $[0, 127]$. The set of notes $C_3...G^6$ is named the note set, that is $\{C_3, {}^\#C_3, D_3, ..., F^6, {}^\#F^6, G^6\}$. An interval is the difference in pitch between the current note and the previous note. The unit of interval used in this paper is semitone. Based on interval, an algorithm for musical feature-extracting is implemented in HIT-DML. This algorithm is applied widely, and the idea of it can be found in [15]. An example is as follows.

Example1. Let the feature character set be $C = \{R,U,W,D,B\}$. R means the latter note is same to the former note. U means the latter is higher than the former by at more 3 semi-tones. W means the latter is higher than the former by at least 4 semi-tones. D means the latter is lower than the former by at more 3 semi-tones. B means the latter is lower than the former by at least 4 semi-tones. Then a segment of melody $C^1 C^1 D^1 A E^1 {}^\# F^1 F^1$ is mapped to the feature string *RUBWUD*.

The music feature-matching used in current implementation of HIT-DML is based on an edit distance. The distance between two feature characters is as follows.

$$d = (d_{ij}) = \begin{bmatrix} d_{WW} & d_{WU} & d_{WR} & d_{WD} & d_{WB} \\ d_{UW} & d_{UU} & d_{UR} & d_{UD} & d_{UB} \\ d_{RW} & d_{RU} & d_{RR} & d_{RD} & d_{RB} \\ d_{DW} & d_{DU} & d_{DR} & d_{DD} & d_{DB} \\ d_{BW} & d_{BU} & d_{BR} & d_{BD} & d_{BB} \end{bmatrix} = \begin{bmatrix} 0 & 1 & 2 & 3 & 4 \\ 1 & 0 & 1 & 2 & 3 \\ 2 & 1 & 0 & 1 & 2 \\ 3 & 2 & 1 & 0 & 1 \\ 4 & 3 & 2 & 1 & 0 \end{bmatrix}$$

For example, the distance between W and U is 1.

The distance between two feature strings with the same length is the sum of the distances of corresponding feature characters. Given a positive integer n, called the standard feature string length, the distance between two feature strings, q and p, with different length can be computed as follows. Firstly, compute the distances between each substring of p and each substring of q with length n. Second, select the minimum of the distances of the substrings of p and q as the distance of p and q. Please note that the length of p and the length of q are all more than n.

Example2. Suppose the feature character set *C* is that used in Example 1, feature string *p* is *RUWUWWDRRRU*, *q* is *WRBRRWDBBU*. $|p| = 11 > |q| = 10$, the standard feature string length is selected as $n = min\{|p|, |q|\} = 10$. The substrings of *p* with the length *n* are $p_1 = RUWUWWDRRR$, $p_2 = UWUWWDRRRU$. The distance $Dis(p_1, q) = 15$, $Dis(p_2, q) = 14$, and then $Dis(p, q) = min\{\varphi(p_1, q), \varphi(p_2, q)\} = 14$.

Using the digital music library framework proposed in Section 3 and the previous feature-extracting and feature-matching algorithms, HIT-DML prototype has been developed. It stores music data structurally in databases, and implements feature-extracting and feature-matching algorithms in algebraic micro-operations in the database system to combine database technologies and multimedia technologies organically. HIT-DML shows that the correctness of the proposed DML framework and algorithms.

To simplify the implementation, the system can be developed upon any existing database system. The open source database system PostgreSQL is adopted in HIT-DML, which has the database server-Web server-Web client structure. The database server is constructed on Redhat Linux 6.22, and the Web server is IIS 5.0 on Windows 2000.

Currently, only music data in MIDI (Musical Instrument Digital Interface) format is processed in HIT-DML. There are 1069 midi music pieces stored in HIT-DML. The music data is acquired from some Web sites and ftp sites on the Internet. Some meta-data, e.g. nationalities of composers, cannot be gotten from MIDI music, so they have to be added by hand. This information can be collected into a text file, which will be loaded into the database by a tool developed by ourselves, or by tools of PostgreSQL. During the loading of music data, the second method discussed in Section 3.1 is used.

MIDI data is structurally stored in HIT-DML according to TRACKs. The database comprises 34 tables, which are used to store meta-data, raw data, and feature data of music. PL/pgSQL functions in PostgreSQL are used to simulate the algebraic micro-operations during the implementation of MDMM. In detail, 10 PL/pgSQL functions are developed to implement the feature-extracting and feature-matching operations on MIDI music. Web service is developed by ASP technique, and VB script is used. Anonymous user service is provided in current HIT-DML. The advanced query interface is shown in Fig. 2.

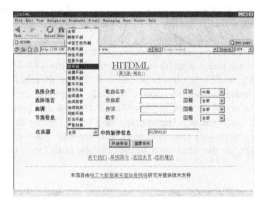

Fig. 2. The Advanced Query Interface of HIT-DML

In HIT-DML, a user can query music in two different methods. He can query music by meta-data of music, e.g. titles of music and styles of music. He can also query music based on content according to feature information, e.g. melody. Especially, HIT-DML can query music in accordance to different musical instruments, and play the combination of several musical instruments. In order to serve the ordinary users, a simplified user interface is provided. In this interface, letters a, b, ..., h, ..., u respectively denote bass do, bass re, . . . , medilant do, ..., alt si.

Experiments are made on the database server to test HIT-DML. A segment of feature string is randomly selected from the database, and then the returns are carefully checked. One SQL statement [12] used in this experiment is

Retrieve (id, title, rank) from midi_db query="DBWDB" top 10.

It retrieves the top 10 pieces of music whose melodies similar to "DBWDB" from the database "midi_db". The result is ordered by the degree of similarity.

Titles of Songs (chinese)	Queries	Positions in Results
忘情水	lmlkmmpommlllmlk	4
为情所困	onmmmnm	5
特别的爱给特别的你	hijloqp	1
太傻	ihfefdedd	5
天意	jjjiijh	6
零时十分	kihehjjihe	4
领悟	llmompqp	6
最浪漫的事	eefhhhhf	5
大哥你好吗	qqqpqsqqssqs	4
白天不懂夜的黑	ebcdcbab	5

Fig. 3. The Veracity Test Results in HIT-DML

In the experiments for veracity, the testing set is composed of 10 feature strings. The lengths of them are between 6 and 15, whose mean is 9. In the results illustrated in Fig 3, the correct music files are always listed in the top set of returns. 1 piece of music is located in the first position, and 3 in 4th, 4 in the 5th, 2 in the 6th. It shows that our system has higher usability, because the query submitted by a user is inherently fuzzy. It is reasonable that several pieces of music correspond to a same feature string. Besides that, the user can navigate the returns to select the music he liked.

There are some works of index structure on music data. For example, Lee and Chen [16] propose four index structures based on suffix trees for music data retrieval. In order to accelerate retrieval, a dynamic index based on inverted lists is designed in HIT-DML. This index structure can efficiently improve retrieval speed. The experimental results about feature strings whose lengths are between 4 and 12 are illustrated in Fig. 4. Each value is the average of 5 tests. During the testing, the return set is very large for the shorter testing strings, and the testing string will be partitioned for the longer strings, so the time used to process the both kinds of feature strings is more.

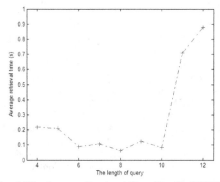

Fig. 4. The Average Retrieval Time Used in HIT-DML

5 Conclusion and Future Work

Our main contributions are: 1) A framework of digital music library is proposed which is constructed on a database system. Music data is structurally stored in a database. Many algorithms on music processing, e.g. feature-extracting and feature-matching, are implemented in the database management system. So multimedia technologies and multimedia technologies are combined seamlessly in the framework. 2) The implementation of HIT-DML, a digital music library prototype, is reported. A music feature-extracting and a music feature-matching algorithm are implemented in it. A dynamic index structure is also given. It shows the correctness of the proposed framework.

In the future, the fusion of database technologies and multimedia technologies will be further considered. Parallel distribution and query techniques on a large amount of music data will be studied.

References

1. VARIATIONS2: *Variations2* Digital Music Library Project Web Site. (http://dml.indiana. edu/)
2. NZDL: New Zealand Digital Library. (http://www.nzdl.org/)
3. AVPORT: Library of Congress. Digital Audio-Visual Preservation Prototyping Project Web Site. (http://www.loc.gov/rr/mopic/avprot/)
4. Fingerhut, M.: The IRCAM Multimedia Library: A Digital Music Library. In: Proceedings of the 6th IEEE Form on Research and Technology Advances in Digital libraries, Baltimore, MD, USA, IEEE Computer Society Press (1999) 129–140
5. Bainbridge, D., Nevill-Manning, C.G., Witten, I.H., Smith, L.A., McNab, R.J.: Towards a Digital Library of Popular Music. In: Proceedings of the 4th ACM International Conference on Digital libraries, Berkeley, California, USA, ACM Press (1999) 161–169
6. McNab, R.J., Smith, L.A., Witten, I.H., Henderson, C.L., Cunningham, S.J.: Towards the Digital Music Library: Tune Retrieval from Acoustic Input. In Fox, E.A., Marchionini, G., eds.: Proceedings of the 1st ACM International Conference on Digital libraries, Bethesda, Maryland, USA, ACM Press (1996) 11–18

7. Dunn, J.W., Mayer, C.A.: VARIATIONS: A Digital Music Library System at Indiana University. In: Proceedings of the 4th ACM International Conference on Digital libraries, Berkeley, California, USA, ACM Press (1999) 12–19
8. Minibayeva, N., Dunn, J.W.: A Digital Library Data Model for Music. In: Proceedings of the 2nd ACM/IEEE-CS Joint Conference on Digital libraries, Portland, Oregon, USA, ACM Press (2002) 154–155
9. Blandford, A., Stelmaszewska, H.: Usability of Musical Digital Libraries: A Multimodal Analysis. In: Proceedings of the 3rd International Symposium on Music Information Retrieval, Paris, France, IRCAM-Centre Pompidou (2002)
10. Wang, C., Li, J., Shi, S.: A Kind of Content-Based Music Information Retrieval Method in a Peer-to-Peer Environment. In: Proceedings of the 3rd International Symposium on Music Information Retrieval, Paris, France, IRCAM-Centre Pompidou (2002)
11. Grimm, R., Nutzel, J.: Peer-to-Peer Music-Sharing with Pro•t but Without Copy Protection. In: Proceedings of the 2nd International Conference on Web Delivering of Music, IEEE Computer Society Press (2002) 17–22
12. Wang, C., Li, J.: A Music Data Model and Its languages. Technique Report, CS, HIT (2003)
13. MIDINOTES: MIDI Notes. (http://www.argonet.co.uk/users/lenny/midi/notes.html)
14. Tang, M., Yip, C.L., Kao, B.: Selection of Melody Lines for Music Databases. In: Proceedings of the IEEE COMPSAC, Taipei (2000)
15. Dowling, W.J.: Scale and Contour: Two Components of a Theory of Memory for Melodies. Psychological Review 85(1978) 341–354
16. Lee W. and Chen. A. L. P.: Efficient Multi-Feature Index Structures for Music Data Retrieval. In Proceedings of SPIE Conference on Storage and Retrieval for Image and Video Databases (2000).

An XPath Reduction Algorithm for Fast Querying of Digital Libraries in XML

Hyoseop Shin[1] and Minsoo Lee[2]

[1] Software Center
Samsung Electronics, Co., LTD.
Seoul, Korea
hyoseop@samsung.com
[2] Department of Computer Science and Engineering
Ewha Womans University
Seoul, Korea
mlee@ewha.ac.kr

Abstract. Digital contents in XML are rapidly increasing on the Web. In our work, we assume that the XML data is stored in a relational database using the popular node numbering scheme and propose a technique to pre-process XPath queries in order to convert them into a much more efficient form that will run several times faster. Our algorithm uses a special data structure called XIP (XML Instance Path) tree of each XML document to reduce a given XPath query (i.e., path expression) into a more simpler form. The benefits of the approach is more significant for long length queries, making it useful for digital libraries storing large and complex structured XML documents for multimedia or business applications.

1 Introduction

With the rapid increase in the amount of XML data, various methods to store and retrieve the XML data are being researched. One of the most popular approaches to store XML data is to map them into a relational schema and then store them into relational databases. Others are to use native XML databases. Querying XML data is also in its early stage in terms of standards and research. XPath [2] and XQuery are currently the most commonly used languages to query XML, and much research is still needed to efficiently process queries on XML data. In our work, we assume that the XML data is stored in a relational database using the popular node numbering scheme [5,3] and propose a technique to pre-process XPath queries in order to convert them into a much more efficient form that will run in several times faster on the relational database that stores the XML data. More specifically, our approach uses a special data structure called XIP (XML Instance Path) tree of each XML document to reduce a given XPath query (i.e., path expression) with parent-child relationships into a simpler form that is specified with ancestor-descendant relationships.

T.M.T. Sembok et al. (Eds.): ICADL 2003, LNCS 2911, pp. 275–278, 2003.
© Springer-Verlag Berlin Heidelberg 2003

2 Motivating Example

We now give a simple motivating example to show how path reduction used by our proposed technique can improve the XPath processing time. Consider the following XML document that represents simplified information about a TV program.

```
<ProgramInformation>
    <programId>PROG-123<programId>
    <BasicDescription>
        <Title>Sunrise News</Title>
        <Synopsis>Morning News</Synopsis>
        <Keywords>
            <Keyword>politics</Keyword>
            <Keyword>economy</Keyword>
        </Keywords>
        <Genre>News</Genre>
        <CastList>
            <CastMember>
                <Role>Reporter</Role>
                <Agent>Richard Perry</Agent>
            </CastMember>
        </CastList>
    </BasicDescription>
</ProgramInformation>
```

A user can refer to the cast members of a program by using the following XPath expression:

/ProgramInformation/BasicDescription/CastList/CastMember/Agent   (1)

This long XPath, however, can also be represented as a shorter one without loss of meaning as follows:

/ProgramInformation//Agent   (2)

The length of the path expressions affects the performance of some XML storage schemes. It is especially critical for the popular node numbering scheme [6,4]. In this scheme, each element or attribute in the XML document is separately stored as a tuple within a relational table and thus a path expression that includes more than one parent-child or ancestor-descendant relationship requires multiple join operations. In general, for a path expression that has n nodes, $(n-1)$ joins are required to obtain the result[4,1].

In order to lesson the number of joins in processing path expressions, our path reduction method automatically finds a shorter XPath for a user-given XPath. For example, it would obtain expression (2) from expression (1) so that the XPath processor can execute the query more efficiently.

3 Equivalence Classes among Paths

A group of XPath expressions that are interchangeable among each other is defined to form an *equivalence class*.

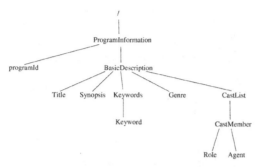

Fig. 1. An XML Instance Path Tree

To clarify the relationships between XPath expressions that belong to the same equivalence class, we introduce a structure called the *XML instance path (XIP) tree*. The XIP tree is dynamically extracted from the input XML documents, but it differs from the original XML documents in that the XIP tree does not repeatedly hold the child nodes of the same name under a parent node, but only hold once. Fig. 1 shows the XIP tree generated from the XML document in the previous section.

Two path expressions form an Equivalence class if and only if they are resolved into the same paths within an XIP tree.

4   Path Reduction

The basic idea of path reduction is that a chain of *parent-child* node pairs can be replaced by a single *ancestor-descendant* node pair, on condition that the resulting XPath belongs to the same equivalence class as the original XPath.

Given an XPath expression, however, it is difficult to list all the possible XPath expressions within the same equivalence class in order to find the shortest one. To simplify the path reduction process, we propose a greedy algorithm. The algorithm probes each node of the given XPath in order and determines whether it can be removed or not. When a node is removed, its preceding axis is replaced with '//' accordingly. A node can be removed only if the resulting XPath in which the node is removed still belongs to the original equivalence class. Fig. 2 represents the proposed path reduction algorithm.

5   Conclusion

This paper presented a path reduction method for optimizing XPath queries to efficiently retrieve XML data from a repository containing large and complex structured digital documents such as ebXML, MPEG-7, and so on. The assumed storage mechanism for XML is the popular node numbering scheme in a relational database. When using such a storage scheme, a long XPath query may have unacceptable query response time especially when users are using the repository as a digital library for multimedia applications or business applications.

```
PathReduction()
input: XPath P = A₁N₁A₂N₂ ... AₚNₚ
```

P_{set} ← Expand(P);
initialize $head\_expr_1$ ← NULL;

for each i from 1 to p-1 **do**
    cur_node ← A_iN_i;
    A_{i+1}' ← '//';
    $tail\_expr$ ← $A_{i+1}'N_{i+1} ... A_pN_p$;
    $candidate\_expr$ ← $head\_expr + tail\_expr$;
    P_{set}' ← Expand($candidate\_expr$);   /* '/' axis only path */
    if $P_{set} \equiv P_{set}'$ **then**   /* equivalence class */
        A_{i+1} ← '//';   /* remove node */

    end
    else   /* non-equivalence
class */
        $head\_expr$ ← $head\_expr + A_iN_i$; /* don't remove node*/
    end
end

$head\_expr$ ← $head\_expr + A_pN_p$;

return $head\_expr$;

Fig. 2. The Path Reduction Algorithm

The proposed method provides an XPath rewriting framework in which an XPath is rewritten into other shorter XPaths using the concept of *equivalence class* among XPaths. In our experiments, the proposed path reduction algorithm improved the query execution performance significantly and in some cases queries were executed up to five times faster than the original queries.

References

1. Shu-Yao Chien, Zografoula Vagena, Donghui Zhang, vassilis J. Tsotras, and Carlo Zaniolo. Efficient structural joins on indexed XML documents. In Proc. of the 27th VLDB conference, pages 263–274, Hong Kong, China, Aug. 2002.
2. James Clark and Steve DeRose. XML Path Language (XPath) Version 1.0, W3C Recommendation. WWW Consortium, Nov. 1999.
3. Quanzhong Li and Bongki Moon. Indexing and querying XML data for regular path expressions. In Proc. of the 26th VLDB conference, Rome, Italy, Sep. 2001.
4. Divesh Srivastava, Shurug Al-Khalifa, H. V. Jagadish, Nick Koudas, Jinesh M. Patel, and Yuqing Wu. Structural joins: A primitive for efficient XML query pattern matching. In Proc. of the 2002 IEEE conference on Data Engineering, San Jose, USA, Feb. 2002.
5. Chun Zhang, Jeffrey F. Naughton, Qiong Luo, and David J. DeWitt, and Guy M. Lohman. On supporting containment queries in relational database management systems. In Proc. of the 2001 ACM-SIGMOD conference, Santa Barbara, CA, USA, May 2001.

Continuous Naive Bayesian Classifications

Vinsensius Berlian Vega S. N. and Stéphane Bressan

Department of Computer Science, National University of Singapore,
3 Science Drive, Singapore 117543
VINSENSI@COMP.NUS.EDU.SG
STEPH@NUS.EDU.SG

Abstract. The most common model of machine learning algorithms involves two life-stages, namely the learning stage and the application stage. The cost of human expertise makes difficult the labeling of large sets of data for the training of machine learning algorithms. In this paper, we propose to challenge this strict dichotomy in the life cycle while addressing the issue of labeling of data. We discuss a learning paradigm called Continuous Learning. After an initial training based on human-labeled data, a Continuously Learning algorithm iteratively trains itself with the result of its own previous application stage and without the privilege of any external feedback. The intuitive motivation and idea of this paradigm are elucidated, followed by explanations on how it differs from other learning models. Finally, empirical evaluation of Continuous Learning applied to the Naive Bayesian Classifier for the classification of newsgroup articles of a well-known benchmark is presented.

1 Introduction

Many components and processes of modern Information Management Systems and Digital Libraries rely on machine learning algorithms and techniques. Classification, for example, is one of the key themes in Information Retrieval and Digital Libraries. Other areas include, to name a few, document analysis, document understanding [1], language identification, summarization [2], intelligent agents, text routing, document clustering, and relevance feedback [3], etc.

Our own research was motivated by the design and development of information tools for the Indonesian Language. Motivated by the lack of effective information retrieval tools for Indonesian Language speakers, we set ourselves the twofold goal of identifying and investigating research issue pertinent to Information Retrieval for the Indonesian Language [4] and of building a full-fledge effective Indonesian web search engine. In order to do so, one important step that must be accomplished is to build a web crawler that will find and index Indonesian web pages from the Internet. An implementation of a tool to sieve out non-Indonesian pages is therefore essential. In [5], we propose a learning algorithm to tackle the problem. The algorithm is a positive only learning algorithm based on weighted trigrams. With this method, we were able to attain an initial performance of over 94% recall and 88% precision.

The already high performance coupled with the requirement that the algorithm needs to be adaptive towards changes in language trends, had led us into asking whether the algorithm could create its own new experience (e.g. data for training) and

T.M.T. Sembok et al. (Eds.): ICADL 2003, LNCS 2911, pp. 279–289, 2003.

effectively learn from it. The idea of algorithm that creates its own experience is timely. With the explosion of machine-readable information, manually constructing experience (e.g. manually collecting and labeling data) could prove to be cumbersome and costly. Coupled with the high dynamism of information medium, content, and user requirements, algorithms that need minimum human intervention are desirable. We formulated the first notion of Continuous Learning according to which, new data labeled by the classifier (or by other kind of machine learning algorithm) is used to extend the training set indefinitely. The paradigm targets two important goals. First and foremost, it is aimed to reduce the amount of manual experience[1] needed. The desired effect of which is clear, that is to lessen the amount of human labor. Second, it is intended to make the underlying algorithm adaptive towards the change in environment. For example, in the past "Bill Clinton" would be a major keyword under the topic of U.S. politics. However as time passes, the major keyword has changed to "George Bush". Note that we use the term underlying algorithm here. The reason is because Continuous Learning is a learning paradigm, which needs to be applied to some learning algorithm, i.e. the underlying algorithm. In [5], we report the initial application of continuous learning idea to language identification and distinction. The result was encouraging. Continuous learning improved the initial 94% recall and 88% precision to 100% recall and about 90% precision.

This paper elaborates the generic idea of Continuous Learning. Section 3 explicates the intuition behind Continuous Learning. An application of continuous learning to a classification algorithm is presented to exemplify. Following that, some experimental results are described in section 4. In the next section, previous related researches are discussed and compared. Finally, in the conclusion we summarize our contribution and outline our plan for future work.

2 Continuous Learning and Its Application

The most common model of Machine Learning involves two life-stages. The first stage is the training stage. In this stage, a learning algorithm gains experience from some form of teacher or oracle.   The experience is commonly given in form of a set of training examples, be it perfectly labeled, a mixture of labeled and unlabeled [6,7], probabilistically labeled [8], or even erroneously labeled [9]. Given the training set, the learning algorithm then uses it to construct or update its internal parameters. This process could be a single-pass over the training data (e.g. Naive Bayesian Classifier and Candidate-Elimination in (Mitchell, 1997)) or it could be iterative/multi-pass method (e.g. ID3 and EM algorithm [11]). By iterative, we mean that the algorithm runs through or analyze a fixed set of training data multiple times until some condition is reached or satisfied.

In the next stage, which we call the application stage, the trained algorithm is then used as is to solve problems that it was originally intended for without any further significant modification towards the internal parameters of the algorithm. In other words, the learning process only occurs during the training stage.

---

[1] By manual experience we mean experience or data that are not automatically gathered by the algorithm itself and/or data that need to be manually labeled

2.1 Continuous Learning

Continuous Learning extrapolates this two life-stages model. Here the learning process is interwoven in the application stage. After the initial training, the algorithm is presented with some data that it needs to process. The most common task of a learning algorithm would be to perform some form of labeling (e.g. relevancy, categories, probability assignment, etc). Normally the information output by the algorithm is of the same kind as the information associated with the training data set. Let us say that the process transforms the given data from unlabeled data to self-labeled data. In the continuous learning algorithm, these self-labeled data are then used to retrain (or incrementally train) the algorithm. The interweaving of learning and labeling can continue ad lib. Here is the key of Continuous Learning, trusting one's own judgment to enlarge one's knowledge base. Although it may seem peculiar for an algorithm to do so, such a strategy is quite commonly used by humans, we believe. In some instances, it seems that the foundation of our knowledge is augmented with experience funded on this sole and self-knowledge without external feedback. Similarly, a Continuous Learning algorithm would indefinitely learn from its own judgment without any external feedback or guidance. External feedback includes predefined fitness function (such as those used in genetic algorithm), reward function (like in reinforcement learning), as well as human intervention. Simply put, a continuously learning algorithm is entirely on its own in the effort to improve its performance.

Given that the algorithm is going to determine its own fate, the arising question is to determine under which circumstances a performance increase actually occurs. One would expect that, if the performance of the algorithm after the initial training is relatively high, Continuous Learning have chances to improve its performance. However, should the initial performance be insufficient, the algorithm could worsen over time. This is not unlike the ability of better students to study on their own. The existence of such a threshold has been verified in the application of Continuous Learning to language distinction [5]. We now illustrate the algorithm and the existence of a threshold for the performance improvement on a Naïve Bayesian Classifier.

2.2 Continuous Naive Bayesian Classifier

As an illustrating example, we propose to apply Continuous Learning to a Naive Bayesian Classifier. The Naïve Bayesian Classifier is a simple and effective as well as commonly used Machine Learning algorithm.

The Continuous version of Naive Bayesian Classifier goes as follows. First, a generic Naive Bayesian Classifier is trained using a set of manually labeled initial training examples. Then, in the application stage, stream of documents is given to it to be classified. For each document, the classifier determines the most appropriate class of the document based on its current probability terms table. The assigned class is then assumed as the true class of the document. The classifier then incorporates the self-labeled documents as a new example of the assigned class, which is further used to update its internal probability terms table. The pseudo code for Continuous Naive Bayesian Classifier is given below. Note that in step 1, the document d is not obtained from any predefined set, rather it is obtained from the environment, e.g. the web, sensors' input, etc.

```
[Initial Training]
Let S_j = Set of sample documents of class j
For each class j
   Build the probability terms P(W|v_j)based on S_j
[Continuous Learning]
Loop forever
   1. obtain an arbitrary new document d to be
      classified
   [Data labeling]
   2a. k ← classify document d from based on
          current P(W|V)
   2b. output k as label of d
   [Training from Self-labeled Data]
   3a. Let S_k = S_k ∪ {d}
   3b. update the probability terms P(W|v_k) using
       the updated Sk
End Loop
```

3   Experimental Results

In this section, the results gathered from the experiments done with the Continuous Naive Bayesian Classifier are presented. The base Naive Bayesian Classifier is implemented according to the algorithm given in [10]. In each experiment, the Continuous Naïve Bayesian Classifier was trained with a set of manually labeled documents. Then, one by one, new documents from a predefined set were given to the Continuous Naïve Bayesian Classifier to be classified and learned from. At some interval, the current state of the classifier, i.e. the values of the probability terms P(W|V), is saved. Along with that, the performance of the Continuous Naïve Bayesian Classifier at the current state is measured against a test set.

From the results, we observed that in general, performance increase is attainable. However, the increase depends on the inherent difficulty of the problem and the initial performance. Initial performance here refers to the performance of the classifier after it has been trained with a set of manually (and correctly) labeled documents. While inherent difficulty of the problem refers to how hard the task in terms of how much experience is needed before a level of performance could be attained.

3.1 Experimental Setup

The data set used for the experiment is the 20 Usenet Newsgroups data set used in [7] (obtained from http://www.cs.cmu.edu/~textlearning). The data set contains 19997 postings that are spread among the 20 newsgroups, namely alt.atheism, comp.graphics, comp.os.ms-windows.misc, comp.sys.ibm.pc.hardware, comp.sys. mac.hardware, comp.windows.x, misc.forsale, rec.autos, rec.motorcycles, rec.sport.baseball, rec.sport.hockey, sci.crypt, sci.electronics, sci.med, sci.space, soc.religion.christian, talk.politics.guns, talk.politics.mideast, talk.politics.misc, and talk.religion.misc. Each of the 20 newsgroups, except soc.religion.christian, contains exactly 1000 postings. To balance up the numbers, we decided to create three postings into the group that contains only 997 documents by duplicating three different entries from the group. This duplication is justifiable, as a great portion of newsgroup postings are replies of previous postings that sometimes carry a significant portion of the previous postings' content. With the duplication, the total size of the data set is now 20000 and is distributed evenly to 20 newsgroups.

Before the experiment was carried out, the data set was preprocessed. First, the Usenet headers were removed. Then it was tokenized. Token is defined as contiguous alphabetic characters. No stemming was done, but we did stop-word removal. These settings are similar to that done in [7]. With one little difference, in that for the stop word list, we used the stop word list provided in the SMART Information Retrieval[2].

Definitions and Data Setup. As described in section 2.2, Continuous Naive Bayesian Classifier will learn indefinitely from documents given to it to be classified. In the experiments, the process is simulated by asking a trained classifier (i.e. classifier that has been trained with labeled data) to judge some sets of documents (which will be used by the Continuous Learning algorithm to retrain itself). At some interval (i.e. after a certain number of documents are presented to the continuous classifier) the classifier's performance is measured. The set of documents used between two consecutive intervals is called running set and the period between two consecutive intervals is termed as iteration, just for the lack of better word. Note that the term iteration here means differently with the term iterative used earlier. In the earlier usage, iterative means the algorithm

Given the above settings, the data set needs to be divided into three subsets: initial training set, set of running sets, and test set. In our experiment, the initial training set was comprised of the first n-documents from each newsgroup. The next 800-minus-n-documents from each newsgroup composed the set of running sets. Documents from the running sets were handed to the classifier in chronological order. The test set was chosen to be the last 20% of the postings from each newsgroup, similar to what was done in [7]. This simulate the situation where initial training set is collected from past documents, the current documents are used to continuously train the classifier, and the overall performance is measured in terms of its classification accuracy over future documents. Note also that none of the running sets overlapped.

Varying Initial Performance. The aim of the experiments is to discover whether the proposed framework could yield some increase of performance and under what condition could it do so. To obtain a good picture of what is happening, various parameters are introduced. The first parameter is the size of initial training set used. The reasoning is straightforward. Initial performance of the classifier vary with different number of documents used in initial training, by varying it we could observe how great the effect of Continuous Learning given different starting performance. In

---

[2] The SMART system (version 11.0) was developed at Cornell University and is available from ftp.cs.cornell.edu/pub/smart.

our experiments, we varied the initial training set to be 10, 20, 30, 40, or 50 documents per group.

Given that different initial training set sizes were used, the issue of how large the running set need to be resolved. A running set of 10 documents per group means differently for classifier X, trained initially with 10 documents per group, or classifier Y, trained initially with 50 documents per group. For classifier X, the self-labeled 10 documents per group have the equal weigh as the manually labeled 10 documents per group that it sees during the initial training. However for classifier Y, 10 per group self-labeled documents weigh much less than the 50 manually labeled documents per group that it was given in the initial training. Thus, suppose that the two classifiers wrongly label the entire running set, the effect would be greater for classifier X than to classifier Y. Therefore, to be fair, we should compare the performance of classifier X after seeing a running set of 10 documents with the performance of classifier Y after seeing a running set of 50 documents. In the light of this, we opted to set the saving and measurement interval to be equal to the size of the initial training set, e.g. for classifier X, the classifier state is saved and its performance is measured every 10 documents. While for classifier Y, it is done every 50 documents. In each of our experiments, the classifier was given 10 running sets, i.e. going through 10 iterations.

Varying Inherent Difficulty. Varying the size of initial training set show how the proposed idea performs under different starting position, i.e. different initial performance. However, altering the initial training set size may not be enough, as performance is also determined by how hard the problem is. Modifying the initial training set size challenges the idea to solve a same problem under different initial condition. Here is when the second parameter comes into play. Given a fixed size initial training set, we alter the difficulty of the problem by altering the number of groups that the classifier needs to classify. It may not be so obvious as why reducing the number of classes (or groups) means reducing the difficulty as well. As even for two groups, e.g. soc.religion.christian and talk.religion.misc, it might be very difficult to separate the two. However, as mentioned earlier, we would like to view difficulty as the amount of experience needed to achieve a certain level of performance. For example: assuming that the each document has an equal probability to be belong to a group, to achieve performance of 50% accuracy for the two-group problem, the classifier needs no experience, as it could be as easy as always assigning new documents into one of the classes. However, it is not the case for four-group problem. To exemplify the experiments, let's say for an initial training set of 10 documents per group, we change the problem from classifying new documents into one of 20 newsgroups to classifying into 7 newsgroups. Suppose also that the 7 newsgroups are selected to be the first 7 groups when the 20 groups are listed in alphabetical order. Thus, for this experiment, we take 7000 documents (1000 for each group). Out of this 7000, the last 20% or 1400 documents are set aside to be the test set. The initial training set and the running sets are formed as per normal. Hence, with this variation, we hope to discern the effectiveness of Continuous Learning for different inherent problem difficulty level. Here we use seven different numbers of classification problems: 7, 10, 12, 14, 16, 18, and 20 newsgroups.

Comparison with Upper Bound Performance. To further comprehend the effect of Continuous Learning, we compared the performance of each experiment setting of Continuous Learning with self-labeled data against the theoretical upper bound performance. The theoretical upper bound performance is achieved by feeding the algorithm with manually (and correctly) labeled data for it to learn from, instead of letting it learn from self-labeled data that may contain some error. Naturally, we expect the performance of the all-information setting to surpass that of the self-labeled. What we look into is whether there is some relation in performance between the two configurations.

3.2 Results

From our experiments we gathered a total of 12 pair of graphs, which depict the classification accuracy attained for 10 iterations. As stated earlier, in each iteration, the Continuous NBC is given a set of training set, whose size is equivalent to the size of the initial training set. Four pairs of graphs are shown in this section whereas the rest can be found in the Appendix[3]. In each pair, the performance graph of the continuous learning with self-labeled data is contrasted with the all-information performance.

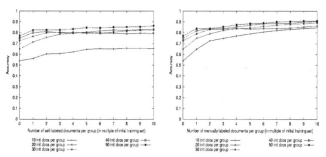

Fig. 1. Accuracy for classification on 7 newsgroups varying the initial training set

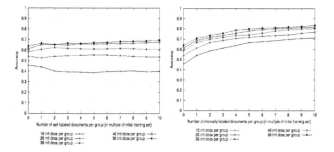

Fig. 2. Accuracy for classification on 16 newsgroups varying the initial training set

---

[3] The Appendix is available in the longer version of this paper, which can be downloaded from http://www.comp.nus.edu.sg/~vinsensi/publications.html

From Figure 1 and 2, we can see that Continuous Learning were able to improve performance given a good initial performance. Below some initial performance, however, Continuous Learning caused the performance to drop over time. Further, faced against a harder problem (i.e. more groups), not only that initial performance is generally lower, the improvement is attained at somewhat slower rate or even not at all. This claim is further validated with the two pairs of graphs below.

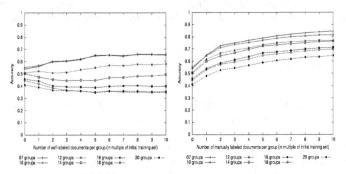

Fig. 3. Accuracy for initial training set of 10 documents per group and varying number of groups

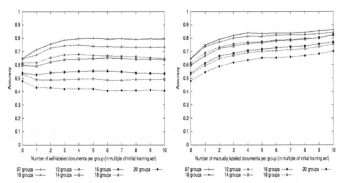

Fig. 4. Accuracy for initial training set of 20 documents per group and varying number of groups

The overall shape in the four pairs of graphs above clearly support the intuition behind the idea of Continuous Learning, in that an already good performing learning algorithm could improve itself by learning from self-labeled data. Vice-versa, not-so-good performing algorithm should be wary if it to use self-labeled data to improve itself, as it could end up with declining performance. It is also shown in the above that for a similar initial performance, the Continuous Learning concept works better for easier problem. Again, this is in line with the intuition that for easier subjects, less formal training is needed for a person to be able to self-study effectively. From this we can say that the minimum value for the initial performance needed to guarantee performance gains depends on the inherent difficulty of the problem.

In each pair of graph, we can observe that the performance of all-information (i.e. manually labeled) setting is almost always increasing. This is quite obvious, as in all-information, the data are all correctly labeled. The important point to note is that, for the self-labeled plots that are increasing (e.g. figure 1), their shape mimics the shape of the all-information plots. It seems to imply that for self-labeled settings that experience performance increase, the performance increase in self-labeled setting is a fraction of that in all-information setting.

4   Related Work

To the best of our knowledge, this idea of continuous learning has never been explicitly and formally formulated before, although the idea is somewhat straightforward or even obvious. The most relevant works are those on using unlabeled data to boost performance [6,7]. Although not directly equivalent, they have some common ground with the idea proposed in the paper. Both are aimed to reduce the need of large labeled sample data. Both tries to leverage the value of unlabeled data, using the information gathered from the small set of labeled data, to increase performance. Both avoid the need of external feedback.

The difference lies on how the unlabeled data are obtained and used. In [6,7], the training data set D consists some labeled data L and some unlabeled data U. The algorithms are first trained using L. After that, U is used to train the algorithms in the iterative fashion until some condition or state is satisfied. In the Continuous Learning paradigm, the training data set D consist only labeled data L, i.e. D = L. The algorithm is then trained with L. Whenever a document d is presented to the algorithm to be evaluated (or to be classified), it will give its judgement j (e.g. d belongs to class j) and retrain itself with d as if j is the actual label of d.

In fact, the concept of Continuous Learning can be applied to the algorithms for learning from unlabeled data, such that the algorithm will continue to collect unlabeled data, which upon reaching a certain size n will be used to retrain the algorithm. The resulting algorithm is shown below. Note that the initial training stage below is exactly the conventional learning from unlabeled data.

```
[Initial Training:
 Conventional Learning From Unlabeled Data]
Let D = L ∪ U
Let A be an algorithm capable of learning from
    unlabeled data
Train algorithm A using L
Train algorithm A using U
[Continuous Learning]
Let U = ∅
Loop forever
    1a. obtain a new document d to be classified
    1b. Let U = U ∪ {d}
```

```
[Data labeling]
2a. k ← classify document d using algorithm A
2b. output k as label of d
[Continuous Learning from Unlabeled Data]
3. If sizeOf(U)=n then
       Train algorithm A using U
       Let U = Ø
   End of if
End Loop
```

Compared with other online algorithm (e.g. reinforcement learning), the key difference is the non-existence of external feedback (e.g. predefined fitness function, reward function, and human interference) in Continuous Learning.

5   Conclusion

In this paper, we proposed the idea of continuous learning. The idea is inspired by the human natural ability to use experience to learn in the absence of a teacher. It is conceived with two objectives in mind, namely (1) reducing the need of human labor in creating, setting up, and labeling data for training a learning algorithm and (2) forging an adaptive algorithm. These goals are critical in the ever-growing and ever-changing realm of modern information systems. Continuous learning was contrasted to other learning models, such as the common two life-stages model (single pass or multi-pass/iterative) and other seemingly similar approach (e.g. reinforcement learning and EM), the most similar one being online algorithms. The key distinguishing point is that in continuous learning, the learning process is extended indefinitely relying only on self-labeled examples without any external feedback, a luxury that is available for online algorithms.

We have illustrated how the framework could be applied to Naive Bayesian Classifier. The empirical results obtained from a comprehensive set of experiments corroborate the intuition behind the proposed paradigm: under the right circumstances it can learn. It is shown that the effectiveness of Continuous Learning is not only determined by the initial performance, but also by the inherent difficulty of the problem. Harder problems would require higher initial performance for the Continuous Learning to be successful. In addition, the comparison with all-information accuracy suggests that learning from self-labeled data improves the performance proportionally to that of learning from manually labeled data.

In other words, a learning algorithm that has reached a certain level of performance can be expected to improve its own performance autonomously.

Yet an important task remains, namely the formalization of the Continuous Learning paradigm. We are currently attempting to define a theoretical framework that could help us to identify and quantify the conditions under which the Continuous Learning algorithm can actually learn.

References

1. Esposito, F., Malerba, D., Semeraro, G., Fanizzi, N., and Ferili, S.: Adding Machine Learning and Knowledge Intensive Techniques to a Digital Library Service. In International Journal on Digital Libraries (1998), 2(1), pp. 3–19, Springer-Verlag.
2. Kupiec, J., Pederson, J., and Chen, F.: A trainable document summarizer. In Proceedings of SIGIR 1995, pp. 68–73, ACM Press.
3. Bartell, B. T., Cottrell, G. W., and Belew, R. K.: Learning the optimal parameters in a ranked retrieval system using multi-query relevance feedback. In Proceedings Symposium on Document Analysis and Information Retrieval. (1994)
4. Vega, V. B. and Bressan, S.: Indexing the Indonesian Web: Language Identification and Miscellaneous Issues. In Poster Proceedings of 10th World Wide Web Conference. (2001)
5. Vega, V. B. and Bressan, S.: Continuous-Learning Weighted-Trigram Approach for Indonesian Language Distinction: A Preliminary Study. In Proceedings of 19th International Conference on Computer Processing of Oriental Languages. (2001)
6. Blum, A. and Tom Mitchell, T.: Combining Labeled and Unlabeled Data with Co-Training. In Proceedings of the 11th Annual Conference on Computational Learning Theory. (1998)
7. Nigam, K., McCallum, A., Thrun, S., and Mitchell, T.: Text Classification from Labeled and Unlabeled Documents using EM. In Machine Learning (2000), 39(2/3). pp. 103–134.
8. Smyth, P.: Learning with Probabilistic Supervision. In Petsche, T., Hanson, S., and Shavlik, J. (Eds.) Computational Learning Theory and Natural Learning Systems 3, (1995). Cambridge, MA: MIT Press, pp. 163–182.
9. Kearns, M. and Li, M.: Learning in the presence of malicious errors. SIAM Journal on Computing (1993), 22(4):807–837.
10. Mitchell, T. M.: Machine Learning. McGraw-Hill. (1997)
11. Dempster, A.P., Laird, N. M., and Rubin, D. B.: Maximum Likelihood from Incomplete Data via the EM Algorithm. Journal of the Royal Statistical Society, Series B (1997) 39:1–38.

Web Mining for Identifying Research Trends

Quan Thanh Tho, Siu Cheung Hui, and Alvis Fong

Nanyang Technological University, School of Computer Engineering, Singapore
{PA0218164B,asschui,acmfong}@ntu.edu.sg

Abstract. This paper proposes a web mining approach for identifying research trends. The proposed approach comprises a number of data mining techniques. To perform web mining, the Indexing Agents search and download scientific publications from web sites that typically include academic web pages, then they extract citations and store them in a Web Citation Database. The Temporal Document Clustering technique and Journal Co-Citation Clustering technique are applied to the Web Citation Database to generate temporal document clusters and journal clusters respectively. The Multi-Clustering technique is then proposed to mine the document and journal clusters for their inter-relationships. Finally, the knowledge that is mined from the inter-relationships is used for the detection of trends and emergent trends for a specified research area. In this paper, we will discuss the proposed web mining approach, and the performance of the proposed approach.

1 Introduction

The knowledge on research trends, especially emergent trends, is particularly important for researchers when they embark on a new research topic. It is also applicable for those existing researchers who would like to review their research works to make sure that their works are new and current. Although most scientific publications are made available now on the Web, the knowledge on current trends of research areas cannot be retrieved or extracted directly. Nevertheless, web publications provide an important source of information for automatic detection of research trends.

Trend detection applications are mainly divided into two categories [1]: semi-automatic and fully automatic. Semi-automatic systems [2,3] require human assistance in detecting trends. In this research, we focus on fully automatic systems [4,5] that can take in a corpus from users and generate the research trends, and in particular the emerging trends in research areas. In addition, citation database has also been considered as a source for finding trends [6]. Papers published in journals, conferences and workshops also provide important clues for trend detection [1,2,3], especially when we need to locate and label the research areas automatically. It is challenging to combine all this information in identifying research trends in scientific research areas.

In this paper, we propose a new web mining approach for identifying research trends and emergent trends. Our proposed approach is based on the mining of the Web Citation Database that was generated using the Indexing Agents [7,8,9]. To mine

T.M.T. Sembok et al. (Eds.): ICADL 2003, LNCS 2911, pp. 290–301, 2003.
© Springer-Verlag Berlin Heidelberg 2003

the database for trend detection, we first generate document clusters and journal clusters, and then we mine the inter-relationships from the generated clusters to identify trends. The aim of this research is to provide an additional function to our web citation-based retrieval system, PubSearch [8,9], to support users to find research trends in a specified area.

The rest of the paper is organized as follows. Section 2 discusses the system architecture for trend identification. Section 3 discusses the Temporal Document Clustering and the Journal Co-Citation Clustering techniques. In Section 4, the Multi-Clustering technique is discussed. Section 5 describes the process for trend detection. Section 6 presents the experimental results. Finally, Section 7 concludes the paper.

2   System Architecture

Figure 1 gives the system architecture for trend detection, which is a function provided by the PubSearch system [8,9]. Currently, PubSearch supports document clustering search [8] and author clustering search [9]. To support trend detection, we have developed the following components: Indexing Agents, Temporal Document Clustering, Journal Co-Citation Clustering, Multi-Clustering and Trend Detection Engine. Indexing Agents search for research web sites, especially those from academic institutions, download scientific publications from the web sites. Then, they identify the bibliographic section and parse the section to extract the citation information, which is then stored in the Web Citation Database. In addition, other document information such as authors, journals, date of publication, etc. is also stored in the Web Citation Database.

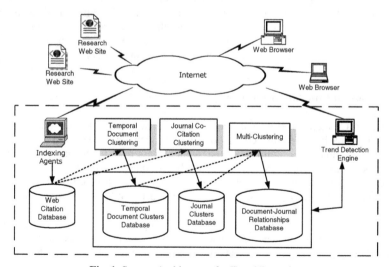

Fig. 1. System Architecture for Trend Detection

3 Clustering Methods

To identify research trends, we base on the premise that documents published in the current issues of the journals, conferences or workshops will indicate trends at that time. In addition, temporal (or date of publication) information on the documents published is also important for the retrieval of information on the trends. Hence, for trend detection purpose, we perform Temporal Document Clustering and Journal Co-Citation Clustering on the Web Citation Database. The Temporal Document Clustering clusters documents based on their keywords and temporal information. As each journal, conference or workshop contains documents, and each document contains references (or citation information), document co-citation analysis is applied in Journal Co-Citation Clustering to cluster journals, conferences and workshops.

3.1   Temporal Document Clustering

In PubSearch, we had performed document clustering [8] to mine the Web Citation Database. First, each document in the Web Citation Database was processed to extract a set of keywords based on their citation information. The extracted keywords were then converted into document vectors. Then, Kohonen's Self-Organizing Map (KSOM) was used to generate document clusters from document vectors.

For trend detection purpose, we perform Temporal Document Clustering based on the document clustering technique. In this approach, we first classify documents by their publication dates before clustering them. As a result, we have obtained many subsets of documents. Each subset contains a set of documents published in the same year. Then, we apply the document clustering technique to each subset. Eventually we get a set of clusters for each subset, called Temporal Document Clusters Subset, in which documents in each cluster will have the same publication year and similar as indicated by keywords. The information on the generated Temporal Document Clusters Subsets, the associated keywords of documents in subsets and their publication dates are stored into the Temporal Document Clusters Database.

3.2   Journal Co-citation Clustering

Journal Co-Citation Clustering is the technique that clusters journals, conferences, and workshops based on the co-citation analysis technique. The journal co-citation clustering technique is similar to the author clustering technique [9]. Journals, conferences and workshops are clustered based on co-citation analysis of their documents. We analyze the co-citation information of papers published in journals, conferences and workshops, which are available in the Web Citation Database. The correlation information is stored in the correlation matrix. The Agglomerative Hierarchical Clustering (AHC) algorithm [10] is applied to the correlation matrix to generate the journal clusters. As discussed earlier, topics discussed in journals, conferences and workshops indicate the current trends, therefore each generated journal cluster is considered as a potential trend.

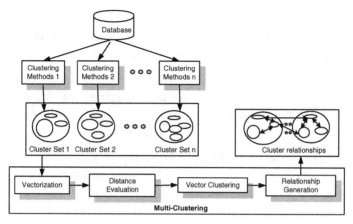

Fig. 2. Multi-Clustering Technique

4 Multi-clustering Technique

For Temporal Document Clustering, documents are clustered based on their dates and keywords. For Journal Co-Citation Clustering, journals, conferences and workshops are clustered based on co-citation analysis, which produces journal clusters; and each cluster implies a potential trend. To identify research trends, we propose to mine the temporal document clusters and journal clusters from the Temporal Document Clusters Database and Journal Clusters Database to discover the inter-relationships between the potential trends indicated by journal cluster, and documents with the associated keywords and date. To achieve this goal, we propose the Multi-Clustering technique to mine the inter-relationships from the multiple clusters. As shown in Fig. 2, the Multi-Clustering technique consists of the following steps: Vectorization, Distance Evaluation, Vector Clustering and Relationship Generation.

4.1 Vectorization

Vectorization extracts and represents multiple clustering data as vectors called *combined vectors* in a multi-dimensional space. Vectorization can be defined formally as follows.

Definition 1 (Cluster Set): Let $S = \{D_1, D_2, ..., D_m\}$ be a set of data items. A *clustering method CM* clusters the data items in S into a set of k *clusters* $CS = \{C_1, C_2, ..., C_k\}$ such that

- If $D_s \in C_p$ and $D_t \in C_p$, where $1 \leq s,t \leq m$ and $1 \leq p \leq k$, then D_s and D_t are similar.
- If $D_s \in C_p$ and $D_t \in C_q$, where $1 \leq s,t \leq m$, $1 \leq p,q \leq k$ and $k \neq l$, then D_s and D_t are dissimilar.

CS is called *cluster set*.

Definition 2 (Cluster Number): Let $CS = \{C_1, C_2,..., C_k\}$ be the cluster set obtained from applying a clustering method CM to a set of data items $S = \{D_1, D_2,..., D_m\}$. If $D_i \in C_j$, where $1 \le i \le m$ and $1 \le j \le k$, then j is the *cluster number* for D_i in CS.

Definition 3 (Combined Vector): Let $S = \{D_1, D_2,..., D_m\}$ be a set of data items. Let $CS_1, CS_2,..., CS_n$ be the cluster sets obtained from applying the clustering methods $CM_1, CM_2,..., CM_n$ to S. The *combined vector* for a data item D_i where $1 \le i \le m$ is the vector $v_i = (d_1, d_2,..., d_n)$ where d_j, with $1 \le j \le n$, is the cluster number for D_i in CS_j.

Definition 4 (Vectorization): Let $S = \{D_1, D_2,..., D_m\}$ be a set of data items. Let $CS_1, CS_2,..., CS_n$ be the cluster sets obtained from applying the clustering methods $CM_1, CM_2,..., CM_n$ to S. *Vectorization* generates a set of m vectors $V = \{v_1, v_2,..., v_m\}$ from the cluster sets $CS_1, CS_2,..., CS_n$ where v_i, $1 \le i \le m$, is the combined vector for a data item D_i in S.

4.2   Distance Evaluation

To discover relationships from the combined vectors, we can cluster the combined vectors into clusters of similar vectors. However, in order to perform clustering, we need to obtain the distances between the combined vectors. In this research, we adopt the Mahalanobis distance [11] to calculate the vectors' distances, since the Mahalanobis distance can incorporate the correlation of the dimensions of vectors. Mathematically, the correlation of dimensions can be inferred from their *covariance*. Let $V = \{v_1, v_2,..., v_m\}$ be a set of n-dimensional combined vectors. The *mean* of the ith dimension of V, where $1 \le i \le n$, is defined as

$$\overline{V}_i = \frac{\sum_{k=1}^{m} v_{ki}}{m} \qquad (1)$$

where v_{ki} is the value of v_k on the ith dimension.

Let $V = \{v_1, v_2,..., v_m\}$ be a set of n-dimensional combined vectors. The covariance $c(i,j)$ of the ith dimension and j^{th} dimension is defined as

$$c(i, j) = \frac{\sum_{k=1}^{m}(v_{ki} - \overline{V}_i)(v_{kj} - \overline{V}_j)}{m-1} \qquad (2)$$

The covariance $c(i,j)$ can be used to determine whether the ith and j^{th} dimensions have correlation or not. If $c(i,j) = 0$, then the ith and j^{th} dimensions have no correlation.

Let $V = \{v_1, v_2,..., v_m\}$ be a set of n-dimensional combined vectors. The covariance matrix C_V of dimensions in V is defined as

$$C_V = \begin{bmatrix} c(1,1) & c(1,2) & ... & c(1,n) \\ c(2,1) & c(2,2) & ... & c(2,n) \\ ... & ... & ... & ... \\ c(n,1) & c(n,2) & ... & c(n,n) \end{bmatrix}$$

Having the covariance matrix defined, we use the Mahalanobis distance to calculate the vectors' distances, which is defined as follows. Let $V = \{v_1, v_2, ..., v_m\}$ be a set of n-dimensional combined vectors. The Mahalanobis distance between v_i and v_j, where $1 \le p,q \le m$, is calculated as

$$d_M(i,j) = \sqrt{(v_i - v_j)^T C_V^{-1}(v_i - v_j)} \qquad (3)$$

4.3   Vector Clustering

To discover the hidden relationships from multiple clustering data, which are represented as combined vectors, we have adopted the Agglomerative Hierarchical Clustering (AHC), one of the most popular agglomerative clustering techniques, to perform a bottom-up clustering process. Using the set of combined vectors and the distance matrix as input, the AHC algorithm generates a set of *combined vector clusters*. Then, the combined vector clusters are further analyzed to discover the cluster relationships.

4.4   Relationship Generation

In Relationship Generation, we identify the knowledge on the relationships of the multiple clustering data from the results of the AHC clustering process on the combined vectors. Let S be a set of data items. The *entropy* [11] of S is defined as

$$e(S) = - \sum_{i \in value(S)} (p_i \log(p_i)) \qquad (4)$$

where p_i is the proportion of items in S that has the value i.

Definition 5 (Purity Set): Let S be a set of data items and T_p be a *Purity Threshold*. S is a *purity set* if and only if $e(S) \le T_p$.

According to experimental results given in [9,12], efficient clustering often results in clusters that have entropy with a value less than 0.4. Based on this result, we set T_p to 0.4.

Next, we define *common value*. Common values are the values that occur frequently in a set of data items S compared to the number of items. Generally, in the purity set, there are two kinds of values: common values and noisy values. We assume that if we eliminate noisy values from a purity set, then the set obtained is *similar* to the original set. The Jaccard measure is commonly used to evaluate set similarity [12]. Based on Jaccard measure, the similarity of two sets is defined as follows:

$$C_J(S_1, S_2) = \frac{|S_1 \cap S_2|}{|S_1 \cup S_2|} \tag{5}$$

Definition 6 (Common Value): Let S be a set of data items and T_C be a *Common Value Threshold*. A value I is the common value of S if and only if (i) S is a purity set, and (ii) $C_J(S, (S/\{I\})) < T_C$, where $\{I\}$ denotes the subset of items in S that has the value I.

T_C is set intuitively. Since the similarity between two sets ranges from 0 to 1, T_C should be greater than 0.5 to imply that the two sets are "similar". In this research, we set T_C as 0.75, which is the average value of 0.5 and 1.

Definition 7 (Common Value Set): Let S be a set of data items. We define *common value set* $S_{CM}(S)$ of S as the set of all of common values in S. A common value set can be an empty set.

Definition 8 (Dimension Set): Let $VC = \{v_1, v_2, ..., v_m\}$ be a combined vector cluster, where v_k is a n-dimensional combined vector, with $1 \le k \le m$. We define the ith *dimension set* $d_i(VC)$ of VC, with $1 \le i \le n$, as $d_i(VC) = \{v_{1i}, v_{2i}..., v_{mi}\}$, where v_{ki}, with $1 \le k \le m$, is the value of v_k on the ith dimension.

Definition 9 (Relationship Vector): Let $VC = \{v_1, v_2, ..., v_m\}$ be a combined vector cluster, where v_k is a n-dimensional combined vector, with $1 \le k \le m$. The *relationship vector* V_R of VC is defined as $V_R = (S_1, S_2, ..., S_n)$, where $S_i = S_{CM}(d_i(VC))$ with $1 \le i \le m$.

Each dimension of a relationship vector corresponds to a certain clustering method. The values stored in each dimension of a relationship vector are the cluster numbers of clusters generated by the corresponding clustering method. Each generated relationship vector represents an inter-relationship among these clusters. Example 4.1 gives an example of such cluster set relationship.

Example 1: Let $V_R = (\{1\}, \{2,3\})$ be the generated relationship vector. Let CM_1 and CM_2 be the two clustering methods corresponding to the first and second dimensions of V_R. Then, there exists an inter-relationship between cluster 1 from CM_1 and cluster 2 and cluster 3 from CM_2.

4.5   Keyword-Journal Relationship Subsets Generation

For trend identification purpose, we mine the citation information using the clustering techniques to generate temporal document clusters and journal clusters, which are stored in Temporal Document Clusters Database and Journal Clusters Database, respectively. Then, the Multi-Clustering technique is used to mine the temporal document clusters and journal clusters. Each set of temporal document clusters in each Temporal Document Cluster Subset and journal clusters are mined using the Multi-Clustering technique to generate a Document-Journal Relationships Subset, which contains the generated relationship vectors. Each relationship vector has two elements. The first element contains cluster numbers of temporal document clusters, and the second contains cluster numbers of journal clusters. Thus, each relationship vector represents an inter-relationship between temporal document clusters and journal clusters, which called *document-journal relationship*. As a result, the

Document-Journal Relationships Subsets are generated as shown in Fig. 3. Information on Document-Journal Relationships Subsets is stored in the Document-Journal Relationships Database.

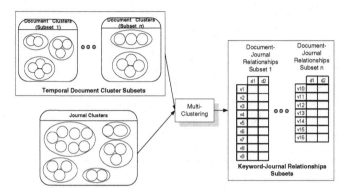

Fig. 3. Keyword-Journal Relationship Subsets Generation.

5 Trend Detection Engine

The architecture for the Trend Detection Engine is shown in Fig. 4, which comprises the followings: Trend Detection, Trend Information Retrieval and Emerging Trend Identification.

5.1 Trend Detection

In trend detection, users can specify the research area, which is needed to identify the trends, as query keywords. To detect trends in a research area, we use the relationship vectors in the Document-Journal Relationships Subset corresponding to the current year. As discussed earlier, each relationship vector represents a document-journal relationship between temporal document clusters and journal clusters. Each temporal document cluster corresponds to a set of keywords. Information of such keywords can be retrieved from the Temporal Document Clusters Database. Hence, each relationship vector can generate a set of keywords. By comparing the input keywords with keywords generated from the relationship vectors, we can retrieve relationship vectors corresponding to the input query. Each relationship vector retrieved is considered as a trend detected in the research area. The keywords generated can also be used to label the detected trends.

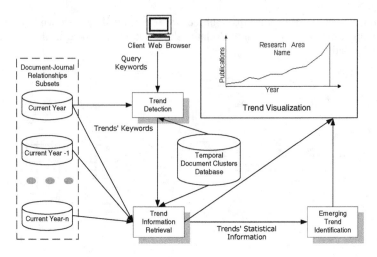

Fig. 4. Trend Detection

5.2   Trend Information Retrieval

Trend information is considered as statistical information of the documents relevant to the trend of the research area published in the last few years. This is retrieved as follows. From a certain year (beginning with the current year), the Document-Journal Relationship Subset corresponding to the preceding year is retrieved. Then, based on the information of the temporal document clusters in each document-journal relationship in the subset, the keyword clusters that are relevant to the input query's keywords are retrieved. Next, the number of publications is counted based on information stored in the Temporal Document Clusters Database. This step is repeated for a specified year (e.g. 10 years), and the number of publications is counted on a yearly basic as the statistical information for the detected trend. The statistical information of the detected trends can also be visualized as a graph as illustrated in Fig. 4.

5.3   Emerging Trend Identification

To identify emergent trends, we use the statistical information of documents published in the research areas of a certain detected trend. We assume that an emerging trend of a research area is the trend that the document publications in that research area have increased almost yearly. To identify this, we calculate the total number of publication increment as follows:

$$I_a = \sum_{i \in Y} (d_i - d_{i-1}) \tag{6}$$

where Y is a sequence of last N years (where N is experimentally set as 5) and d_i is the number of documents published in year i. If the value I_a in a certain trend is greater than a certain specified threshold T_e, which can be interpreted from the experimental results, it means that the publications in that trend have significantly been increased in recent years, then the trend should be considered as an emerging trend.

6 Experimental Results

The approach has been implemented and applied to a collection of over 1400 scientific publications on Information Retrieval domain from 1987-1997 [7,8]. For experimental purpose, we performed the trend identification process using the query input "Information Retrieval." Five trends were detected. The statistical information of the detected trends was retrieved. Based on the retrieved trends' information, we label the detected trends manually, as shown in Table 1.

Table 1. Manually Labeled Trends in Information Retrieval Field in 1998

Trend	1	2	3	4	5
Trend's Name	Hypertext Retrieval	Text Classification	Knowledge Representation	Web Search	Citation Analysis

For performance evaluation, we measured the recall, precision and F-measure [13] based on the retrieved documents corresponding to each trend. Four methods were used to calculate cluster similarities in Vector Clustering of the Multi-Clustering technique. They are the single link, complete link, average link and Ward's methods [11]. The performance results are given in Figure 5.

As shown in Figure 5, the single link method obtains very good precision, but its recall performance is poor. Generally, the precision performance is better than the recall measured in all methods. It is due to the use of citation keywords to retrieve documents belonging to the trends. Since a certain keyword can belong to more than one trend, trends can share some keywords. Hence, documents that are retrieved using keywords of a certain trend usually contain some noisy data, which reduces the recall values. The Ward's method has achieved the best recall performance and the complete link method has the best performance in terms of F-measure. The single link method obtains poor values in terms of recall and F-measure. However, the other methods have high recall, precision and F-measure values, which imply good performance.

The retrieved trend information can be visualized as graphs, as shown in Fig. 6. The three most frequent keywords generated from each trend are used for labeling them. The manual labeled names of the trends are also given in Fig. 6 for reference. There are three trends which have their number of publications increased consistently from 1992. They are Hypertext Information Retrieval, Web Search and Citation Analysis trends. Using the equation (6) with the threshold T_e set to 20, these trends are detected as emerging trends in 1998.

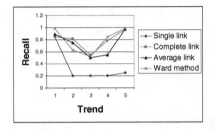

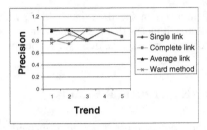

(a) Performance Evaluation Based of Recall   (b) Performance Evaluation Based of Precision

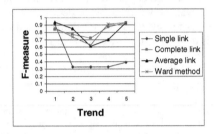

(c) Performance Evaluation Based of F-measure

Fig. 5. Performance Results

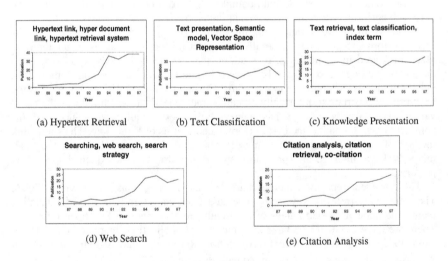

(a) Hypertext Retrieval   (b) Text Classification   (c) Knowledge Presentation

(d) Web Search   (e) Citation Analysis

Fig. 6. Trend Visualization

7 Conclusion

In this paper, we have proposed an approach to detect research trends and determine emerging trends using web mining techniques. The Temporal Document Clustering technique, Journal Co-Citation Clustering technique and Multi-Clustering technique have been proposed to mine the Web Citation Database to support trend detection from user specified areas. The approach had been applied to a collection of over 1400 scientific publications on the Information Retrieval domain. The performance results are good and high recall, precision and F-measure values have been obtained.

References

1. Kontostathis, A., Galitsky, L., Pottenger, W.M., Roy, S., Phelps, D.J.: A Survey of Emerging Trend Detection in Textual Data Mining. A Comprehensive Survey of Text Mining. Michael Berry. Springer-Verlag (2003)
2. Roy, S., Gevry, D., Pottenger, W.M.: Methodologies for Trend Detection in Textual Data Mining. Proceedings of the Textmine'02 Workshop. Second Society for Industrial and Applied Mathematics (SIAM) International Conference on Data Mining. Washington, DC (2002)
3. Blank, G.D., Pottenger, W.M., Kessler, G.D., Herr, M., Jaffe, H., Roy, S., Gevry, D., Wang Q.: CIMEL: Constructive, collaborative Inquiry-based Multimedia E-Learning. Proceedings of the 6th Annual Conference on Innovation and Technology in Computer Science Education (ITiCSE). United Kingdom (2001)
4. Pottenger, W.M., Yang, T.: Detecting Emerging Concepts in Textual Data Mining. Computational Information Retrieval. Michael Berry. SIAM, Philadelphia, PA (2001)
5. Swan, R., Jensen, D.: TimeMines: Constructing Timelines with Statistical Models of Word Usage. Proceeding of the 6th ACM SIGKDD International Conference on Knowledge Discovery and Data Mining. Boston, MA, USA. (2003)
6. Popescul, A., Flake, G.W., Lawrence S., Ungar L.H., Giles, C.L: Clustering and Identifying Temporal Trends in Document Databases. IEEE Advances in Digital Libraries. Washington, DC (2000) 173–182
7. Bolacker, K., Lawrence, S., Giles, C.: CiteSeer: an autonomous Web agent for automatic retrieval and identification of interesting publications. Proceedings of the 3rd ACM Conference on Digital Libraries. Pittsburgh, PA (1998) 116–123
8. He Y., Hui, S.C., Fong, A.C.M.: Mining a Web Citation Database for Document Clustering. Applied Artificial Intelligence, Vol. 16, No. 4 (2002) 283–302
9. He Y., Hui, S.C.: Mining a Web Citation Database for Author Co-citation Analysis. Information Processing & Management, Vol. 38, No. 4, (2002) 491–508
10. Everitt, B.:Cluster Analysis. Edward Arnold, 3rd Edition. London (1993)
11. Cios K.J., Pedrycz W., Swiniarski, R.W.: Data Mining: Methods for Knowledge Discovery. Kluwer Academic Publisher. Norwell, MA, USA (1998)
12. Boley, D.: Principal Direction Divisive Partitioning. Data Mining and Knowledge Discovery, Vol.2, No. 4, (1998) 325–344
13. Van Rijsbergen C.: Information Retrieval. Utterworths, London, England (1979)

Ontology Learning for Medical Digital Libraries

Chew-Hung Lee, Jin-Cheon Na, and Christopher Khoo

Division of Information Studies, School of Communication and Information,
Nanyang Technological University, Singapore
lchewhun@dso.org.sg
{tjcna,assgkhoo}@ntu.edu.sg

Abstract. Ontologies play an important role in the Semantic Web as well as in digital library and knowledge portal applications. This project seeks to develop an automatic method to enrich existing ontologies, especially in the identification of semantic relations between concepts in the ontology. The initial study investigates an approach of identifying pairs of related concepts in a medical domain using association rule induction and inferring the type of semantic relation using the UMLS (Unified Medical Language System) semantic net. This is evaluated by comparing the result with manually assigned semantic relations based on an analysis of medical abstracts containing each pair of concepts. Our initial finding shows that the automatic process is promising, achieving a 68% coverage compared to manually tagging. However, natural language processing of medical abstracts is likely to improve the identification of semantic relations.

1 Introduction

The Semantic Web [1] is a vision to extend the current Web into an environment where computers can cooperate with people to perform sophisticated tasks. This environment relies on information provided with well-defined meanings that computers can process and use. Ontologies as formal knowledge bases provide such machine-processable semantics. An issue facing the Semantic Web community is the lack of rich ontologies as the creation of ontologies is non-trivial requiring analysis of domain sources, background knowledge, and consensus among the users of the ontologies.

The conventional approach in constructing an ontology is to manually enumerate the concepts and relations found in a domain from domain sources. This labour intensive approach is unsuitable for developing a large ontology as it is likely to give rise to inconsistencies. An alternative is to use automatic or semi-automatic methods to extract the concepts and relations [4, 5]. We have embarked on a project to develop an automatic method to enrich existing ontologies, especially the identification of semantic relations between concepts in the ontology, by analyzing domain texts.

As an initial study, we carried out a small experiment using a sample of abstracts of medical articles to identify pairs of related concepts related to "Colon Cancer Treatment" and inferred the semantic relations between the terms in each pair using the UMLS (Unified Medical Language System) [6] semantic network. The purpose

T.M.T. Sembok et al. (Eds.): ICADL 2003, LNCS 2911, pp. 302–305, 2003.

was to find out how effective this simple method is in identifying ontological relationships, and to what extent natural language processing techniques need to be applied to the text to infer relationships between the concepts.

The rest of the paper is organized as follows. Section 2 highlights related works and our framework for ontology learning. Section 3 discusses the results of an initial experiment involving the colon cancer domain, and Section 4 concludes the paper.

2 Ontology Learning

Blake and Pratt [2] mined semantic relationships among medical concepts from medical texts. They focused on "Breast Cancer Treatment" using association rule mining to find associated concept pairs like magnesium-migraines. They were mainly interested in mining the existence of relationships between medical concepts and not in identifying specific semantic relations for the associated concept pairs. For example, the relationship between magnesium and migraines pair could be one of the following semantic relations: treat, prevents, disrupts, and cause. Because identifying specific semantic relations is very important for ontology learning, our work focuses more on finding specific semantic relations.

For the ontology learning, we use UMLS as a seed ontology. UMLS consists of three components: (i) the Metathesaurus containing information about biomedical concepts and terms from many controlled vocabularies and classification systems used in medical information systems, (ii) a semantic network providing a consistent categorization of all concepts represented in the UMLS Metathesaurus, and (iii) the Specialist lexicon providing lexical information on concepts.

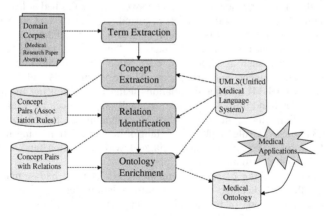

Fig. 1. Ontology Learning Processes

Our ontology learning process is shown in Figure 1. Abstracts of medical research papers are first collected from MedLine through the PubMed interface [6] using a specific medical query such as "Colon Cancer Treatment". Important terms are then extracted from the medical abstracts. Currently, we use the MeSH (Medical Subject Headings) terms used in indexing the abstracts as important terms (we also plan to extract important terms by processing the domain corpus using text mining techniques). Next we map each extracted term to a medical concept in the UMLS, and an association rule tool [3] is applied to the concepts to find associated concept pairs.

After finding associated concept pairs, we proceed to extract specific relations. The UMLS semantic network provides information about the set of basic semantic types that may be assigned to concepts in the Metathesaurus. It also defines the set of relationships that may hold between the semantic types. The 2003AA release of the semantic network contains 125 semantic types and 54 relationships. The relations are stated between high level semantic types in the semantic network whenever possible, and are generally inherited via the "is-a" link by all the children of those types. In some cases there will be a conflict between the placement of types in the semantic network and the link to be inherited.

In the initial experiment reported in this paper, the semantic relations between associated concepts are inferred from this semantic network. First each concept in a concept pair is mapped to one of the semantic types, and the direct or indirect semantic relations that are predefined between the two semantic types in the semantic network are taken as the semantic relation for the target concept pair. Finally, at the ontology enrichment stage, we merge the extracted concepts and their semantic relations with the seed ontology. The generated ontology can then be used as a domain knowledge base for medical digital library applications.

3 Results of Initial Experiment

In our experiment, we extracted the association rules from a sample of 387 medical abstracts following the framework outlined above. These rules had at least 2% support and 80% confidence -- i.e. both concepts occurred in at least 2% of the abstracts, and of the abstracts containing the first concept, 80% also contained the second concept.

We also filtered out rules involving "human", "mice" and "rats" as these concepts yielded trivial rules, such as "Mice, Inbred-> Mice", and we are interested in rules relating to colon cancer and treatment. The remaining 34 rules were tagged automatically with UMLS semantic relations using the inferencing method outlined earlier. The second and third authors also manually tagged each association rule with a semantic relation after examining 10 abstracts containing the pair of concepts.

Of the 34 rules, 11 rules had no matching semantic relation using the automatic method. Four rules were automatically tagged with a relation, and 19 rules were automatically tagged with multiple relations.

In the manual tagging of semantic relations, all 34 rules had semantic relations assigned to them, indicating that a semantic relation between the concepts was expressed in at least one of the abstracts examined. 19 of the rules were manually assigned 1 relation, and 15 rules had multiple relations assigned.

The automatically tagged relations were compared with the manually assigned relations. As mentioned earlier, 11 rules (or 32%) were not tagged with a semantic relation by the automatic method. Of the remainder, 4 rules (12%) were assigned the same semantic relation by both the automatic and manual tagging. 19 rules (56%) had partial matches – the automatic and manual tagging had at least 1 relation in common.

As an example of interesting relations found through this process, the relation "Leucovorin/administration & dosage *interact_with* Fluorouracil/administration &

dosage" with a support of 3% and a confidence of 100% was automatically tagged and concurs with the manual tagging of "*interact_with*". Another interesting rule is the relation between "Liver Neoplasms/secondary" and "Colonic Neoplasms/pathology" with a support of 7% and a confidence of 82% although the automatic method was not able to differentiate between the three semantic relations *affects, manifestation_of* and *result_of.*

In ontology learning, finding semantic relations between concepts is not an easy problem but the usage of a domain-related seed ontology (e.g. the UMLS semantic network) eases the difficulty of semantic relation identification somewhat. However, as our result shows, the seed ontology is not a panacea and analysis of medical texts such as medical abstracts is needed to identify both missing relations as well as to select an appropriate relation from a set of identified relationships.

4 Conclusion

The major benefit of this project will be the provision of a new tool for ontology engineers to create ontology automatically or semi-automatically. We are able to infer semantic relations between concepts automatically from a seed ontology 68% of the time (23/34), although the method cannot distinguish between a few possible relation types. Our next step is to investigate the use of natural language processing (NLP) of medical abstracts to identify the appropriate relation. As associated concept generally occurs within the same compound noun, or in two noun phrases linked by a verb, this suggests that NLP could be used to identify the relations between the concepts.

The generated ontology will be helpful for building the digital library applications like updating a medical treatment website with new treatments identified in the ontology and navigating medical digital encyclopedias using the generated ontology.

References

1. T. Bemers-Lee, J. Hendler and O. Lassila. The Semantic Web. *Scientific American,* May 2001, pp. 35–43.
2. C. Blake and W. Pratt. Better Rules, Fewer Features: A Semantic Approach to Selecting Features from Text. *In Proceedings of the IEEE Data Mining Conference*, San Jose, California, IEEE Press, 2001, pp. 59–66.
3. C. Borgelt, "Apriori Implementation", Available at http://fuzzy.cs.uni-magdeburg.de/~borgelt/doc/apriori/, visit on June 2003.
4. A. Maedche. Ontology Learning for the Semantic Web. Kluwer Academic Publishers, 2002.
5. B. Omelayenko. Learning of Ontologies for the Web: the Analysis of Existent Approaches. *In Proceedings of the International Workshop on Web Dynamics,* London, UK, January 2001.
6. Unified Medical Language System, National Library of Medicine, Available at http:www.nlm.nih.gov/research/umls, visit on June 2003.

LVS Digital Library Cluster with Fair Memory Utilization

MinHwan Ok, Kyeongmo Kang, and Myong-soon Park

Dept. of Computer Science and Engineering, Korea University
Seoul, 136-701, Korea
panflute@korea.ac.kr
{kinghor,myongsp}@ilab.korea.ac.kr

Abstract. A digital library system consists of LVS(Linux Virtual Server) operating with software clustering technology provides is designed on Linux environment. In the cluster of servers fair load distribution scheme that exploits memory utilization was proposed on the assumption that it reflects each server's load more effectively, and was simulated.

1 Digital Library Web Cluster

In digital library systems, most tasks are searching for information about archives including books and viewing the archive. It usually takes longer the time a person seek to find out wanted information from a result window than the time a server prepares the result window. Moreover each window opened reflects imminent search task or the past one for the server. Each window occupies a server memory. Viewing the archive by a person takes much longer time than processing the archive content by a server. More importantly, a large number of viewing the archive of complex content may exhaust a server memory.

From this respect, we learn that using memory utilization can be rather precise than using CPU utilization to distribute load of the requests fairly in digital library cluster. The model of digital library system, in this paper, is a cluster structure, constituted Linux cluster of replicated web servers. The cluster structures of replicated web servers provide scalability with ability to respond quickly to requests from clients. Each replicated web server presents an identical, entire web site. Replicated web servers need publish consistency among them[1], however, this paper makes a premise that the web servers are consistent in publishing the web pages.

The digital library cluster is based on Linux Virtual Server or LVS[2]. It has a centralized structure thus primary connection point to the system is the load balancer. Many web server clusters adopt centralized structure due to its performance.

2 Scheduling Methods of LVS

The scheduling method greatly affects the performance of the whole cluster system. It also affects the scalability and the reliability of the whole cluster system, and

T.M.T. Sembok et al. (Eds.): ICADL 2003, LNCS 2911, pp. 306–309, 2003.

decreases the response time for the client request by evenly distributing the requests over all work servers. The scheduling method can be divided into two methods. One is the method that considers the real load information of work servers. The other is the method that doesn't consider.

Round-robin scheduling is the method that doesn't consider the real load information. All the requests are treated as equals regardless of their loads. In the digital library cluster when the load balancer distributes client requests to the work servers, it uses information from the TCP layer or below. That is, the load balancer doesn't know the contents of the request from the client since it processes the requests with an IP address or a port number only. The least-connection scheduling method and the agent-based scheduling method are appropriate to this restriction.

The least-connection scheduling algorithm directs the network connections to the work server with the least number of established connections. The increment and decrement of live connections can be counted by detecting SYN(initializing a session) and FIN(terminating a session) flags in the TCP packets sent from the client side respectively. That is, the established connection is considered as the real load of a work server. All the requests are treated as equals regardless of their load.

The agent-based scheduling method is presented in 'Bit Project No.61'.[3] An agent is installed in the work servers and in the load balancer. Throughout the action of the agent, the load balancer gains the load information of the work servers each time and saves it in their own Load Information Table. When the request is received, the load balancer selects a work server that has the least load for offering the service, and so is able to achieve a sophisticated load balancing. However the load balancer has a lot of communication overhead since it sends to the work servers the packets that have requested the load information and also receives response packets from the work servers. As the work servers increase, the communication overhead of the load balancer is further increasing. It compounds the single-point-of-bottleneck problem of the load balancer. Our earlier works proposed the agent based sophisticated and scalable scheduling method that supplements this problem.

3 Agent-Based Sophisticated and Scalable Scheduling Method

Various model of the cluster system has been devised.[4] The dispatcher-based architecture showed the best performance in the article, and ABSS is proposed for dispatcher-based architecture. The architecture of digital library cluster is illustrated in Figure 1. The agent runs in the load balancer and work servers. The Load Information Packet itinerates between work servers and gains the load information of work servers. The load balancer distributes client requests to work servers using the real load information of work servers. The basic composition of the ABSS scheduling method is illustrated in Figure 2. The load balancer consists of a scheduler part and an agent part. The scheduler performs the role that decides which work server will process a client request referring to the Load Information Table. The Server Management module of the load balancer performs the role that decides the order among the work servers when the work server is added or removed.

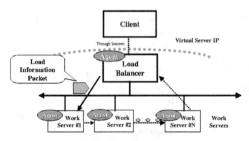

Fig. 1. Architecture

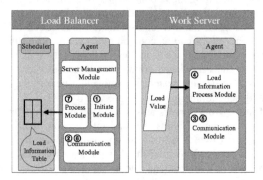

Fig. 2. Agentmodule

The Initiate module creates a new Load Information Packet(LIP) and calls the Communication module. The Communication module sends the LIP packet to the first work server. The Communication module of the work server gets a LIP and calls the Load Information Process module. The Load Information Process module has the load information of the work server and adds it to the LIP packet. Then the Load Information Process module calls the Communication module again. The Communication module sends the LIP to the next work server. The LIP packet gathers the load information of each work server while itinerating between the work servers. The Communication module in the load balancer gets the LIP packet from the last work server. The Process module copies the LIP to its own Load Information Table. And the load balancer distributes the client requests to the work servers referring the load information of work servers.

4 Scheduling Method of Fair Memory Utilization

The memory utilization doesn't show the throbbing of CPU utilization. Therefore we consider the correct load information of work servers than the CPU utilization that is not stable.

The BSD class' network code is assigned three types of memory, *socket, inpcb* and *tcpcb*.[5] The socket information is correlated with the communication link. The inpcb has the information correlated with an IP protocol control block, transport layer.

Table 1. Simulation environment

Packet transmission times between two nodes	3*ms*
request creation rate	60(*requests/sec*)
Average processing time per request	67*ms*
Total simulation time	10 *sec*
number of Load Balancer	1
number of Work Server	4

Table 2. Simulation environment

Scheduling method	Average standard deviation
Least Connection	21.87
ABSS	11.73
FairMem	9.88

The tcpcb has the information correlated with TCP control block, TCP. The assigned memories are kept until the connection is released. Also the memory utilization expresses the utilization of present memory unlike the CPU utilization.

Three scheduling methods was conducted. The first, least-connection scheduling, is the method that considers the number of connections as load information of the work server. The second, ABSS, is the method that considers the CPU utilization, and the third, FairMem, is the method that considers the memory utilization.

5   Simulation and Conclusion

In table 2, we can see that the standard deviation of FairMem is less than those of least-connection and ABSS, respectively. This implies that the FairMem scheduling method is the even fair load distribution scheme than the other two methods.

References

1. Rendal C. Burns, Darrell D.E. Long.: Efficient Data Distribution in Web Server Farm. IEEE Internet Computing (2001)
2. Bryhni, H. Klovning, E. Kure, O.: A comparison of Load Balancing Techniques for Scalable Web Servers. IEEE Network (2000)
3. High Available Cluster System, Bit Project No.61. (2001)
4. Valeria Cardellini, Michele Colajanni, and Philip S. Yu.: Dynamic load balancing on Web-server systems. IEEE Internet Computing (1999)
5. http://home.postech.ac.kr/~jysh/research/IDS/survey/synki ll/synkill.html

So Near and Yet So Far: The Digital Divide among the Information Professionals

Ahmad Bakeri Abu Bakar

Kulliyyah of Information and Communication Technology
International Islamic University Malaysia
Jalan Gombak, 53100 Kuala Lumpur, MALAYSIA

Abstract. Content development of indigenous collection for global access is spreading rapidly throughout the developed world. The tempo of development in the developing world, however, is not that encouraging. One of the reasons could be the gap of digital divide among the information professionals in terms of skills and knowledge in certain areas of the information and communication technology (ICT) is expanding due to the emergent technologies. As information professionals are responsible for the effective handling of digital libraries the level of ICT skills and knowledge possessed by these professionals are critical issues that need to be addressed by the digital libraries. This paper is aimed at identifying the current level of ICT skills and knowledge among the information professionals who are working in the academic and public libraries of Malaysia. Insight from the findings will indicate the extent of the gap of digital divide among the information professionals in Malaysia.

1 Introduction

Digital collection of indigenous materials can be accessed globally if there is a good information and communication infrastructure in place at the local, national, and international level. But having a well equipped infrastructure does not guarantee access to knowledge can take place smoothly as we are confronted with the knowledge explosion and technology revolution whereby only those who are affluent, educated and ICT literate can partake effectively in such a society. This implies that those who do not possess these characteristics have serious shortcomings and may be considered as the less unfortunate or the disadvantaged citizens. Let us for example look at the issue of access to global knowledge over the Internet. We know that in order for us to perform this task we need to have firstly electricity, telephone wires and other infrastructure, secondly we need a computer and appropriate softwares and thirdly, we need a community of users who are skillful and proficient in the use of ICT, particularly those who are providing the Internet services in the digital libraries, i.e. the information professionals. We might think that these requirements which are basic for any Internet connection are in place in most countries. It is not so.

Kennedy pointed out, "From UNESCO's standpoint, the Internet may have more influence than any single medium upon global educational and cultural developments in the coming century. Yet only 2.4 percent of the world's population is on the

T.M.T. Sembok et al. (Eds.): ICADL 2003, LNCS 2911, pp. 310–316, 2003.

Internet, or one out of 40. In Southeast Asia, only one person in 200 is linked to the Internet. In the Arab states, only one person in 500 has Internet access, while in Africa only one person in a 1,000 is an Internet user" [1].

The pertinent question then is how should we address this problem of the **digital divide** where various geographic, socioeconomic and cultural subpopulations have widely varying access to a range of information technologies. In other words there must be efforts to bridge the digital divide so that the chasm between the affluent and the poor communities, the urban and rural communities, racial and professional groups, gender, nations and regions is narrowed or closed. There are market adherents, however, who might say that there is no need for any form of intervention because market forces could eliminate the divide without any government or private sectors involvement. Market forces intervention might happen in developed countries as the number of people, including the information professionals, going online is increasing dramatically assisted by a reduction in net access costs. But this is highly unlikely in developing countries where the gap between the poor and the affluent has exacerbated and enlarged due to the digital technology. Poverty, poor ICT infrastructure and a lack of technical knowledge are insurmountable barriers existing in developing countries. Hill highlighted the case in which a PC costs the average Bangladeshi more than eight year's income while it costs just one month's wage for the average American [2].

2   Methodology

The digital divide remains an issue that needs to be addressed. Efforts made by the public and private sectors at national level will determine the extent of success in bridging the digital divide. Success on the other hand can only be effectively assessed if the gap in the technical competencies of the people are known. For lack of knowledge in these areas might frustrate our efforts to curb the situation. Therefore, the need to have a better picture of the current strengths and weaknesses in the technical competencies of those who are responsible for handling the digital libraries is highly important. For this purpose a sample of 30 respondents was taken as the basis for data collection. Their responses were part of a larger research project on ICT competencies of information professionals in Malaysia that are currently being undertaken by the researcher. The respondents in this study were limited to those who were working in the academic and public libraries only.

3   Results and Discussion

There were 27 categories of skills and knowledge that the respondents were tested in order to find out whether there is a need for them to further develop the skills and knowledge that they lack. Their responses and detail of the categories are as shown in the Table. Based on the ranking as shown in the table there were 15 categories of skills and knowledge that the respondents felt they really lack while doing their routines. Ten or more of the respondents in each case gave a 'very high' score indicating that there is a serious gap of proficiency in technical competencies among them. It is quite disturbing to note that they lack proficiency in skills such as ability to use the Internet for accessing online services, ability to use Internet to search for information using common search engines effectively, ability to use Internet for accessing electronic sources such as electronic journals and content pages, ability to employ effective search technique, search logic and syntax while using the Internet. Skills in Internet and Intranet are essential for information professionals to access globally. Without these skills it would be difficult for them to handle effectively the digital libraries.

The responses also indicate that they lack skills in web-based publishing which is important if content and portal development is to be implemented in the digital libraries. This is manifested by the 'very high' score attributed to ability to use *Microsoft Frontpage* for web pages development, ability to create applications using HTML programming and ability to set up a web site and implement it for own use, including type of communication link, communications bandwidth requirements, web server, hardware and software requirements. The dismal picture of the digital divide among the information professionals currently working in public and academic libraries would be exacerbated if the 'very high' and the 'somewhat high' scores are consolidated. It seems that all the 27 categories with the exception of two, will carry a proficiency gap at least 70 percent. The two exceptions are in the ability to use a business graphic programme and the knowledge of computer graphics.

4   Conclusions

The challenges of the digital divide among the information professionals are real and awesome. Evidently, steps taken by Government to cope with this problem are not bringing expected results. Efforts by the Government to balance the inequalities between those people in the urban and rural areas by bringing in e-libraries to both urban and rural communities are not enough. It is good for the Government to ensure that no sections of the society is without a digital opportunity by providing public and academic libraries with PCs with Internet and telecommunications access irrespective of their locations. The question now is will these strategies be enough to narrow the digital divide. Or how much is enough? Well, there is no definite answer to these questions. One thing which is certain is that the information professionals irrespective of their workplace are facing problems in trying to adjust to the digital environment. This study indicates that there is a profound proficiency gap among the information professionals in areas where we least expected such as accessing globally through the Internet and web–based publishing. Curbing these problems require further e-training and e-retraining of information professionals. Unless the Government provide enough funds for the training programmes in all libraries we will find the digital divide among the information professionals in Malaysia instead of narrowing will be expanded and perhaps it will never be closed forever.

Table 1. Academic and Public Librarian Response

COMPETENCY	DEVELOPMENTAL NEED My need to further develop my skills in this competency is				
	Very High	Sometime High	Neither High / Low	Very Low	Irrelevant
Ability to use anti-virus programme – scan a file/directory, set-up anti-virus shields, check on the DAT files for list of virus.	4	14	9	2	1
Ability to use computer software and understand the hardware and communication interfaces.	11	14	4	1	0
Ability to use Web browsers and knowing their functions.	8	14	7	1	0
Ability to analyze data such as determining the sources, types, form and format of the data, type of storage media on which data is located.	6	14	6	4	0
Ability to gather data from various sources and to store data using paper, electronic, etc.	12	13	4	1	0
Ability to use word processors to create documents using such features as printer control, page formatting, footnotes, cross referencing, mail merge, indices, tables and graphics.	10	10	8	2	0
Ability to use the Internet for e-mail, file transfer protocol (FTP) and telnet.	13	11	4	1	0

COMPETENCY	DEVELOPMENTAL NEED My need to further develop my skills in this competency is				
	Very High	Sometime High	Neither High / Low	Very Low	Irrelevant
Ability to use the Internet for accessing online services – foreign or local.	15	9	6	0	0
Ability to use the Internet to search for information using common search engines effectively.	16	7	6	1	0
Ability to employ effective search technique, search logic and syntax while using the Internet.	13	4	10	3	0
Ability to use the Internet for collection development activities.	8	7	11	4	0
Ability to use the Internet for cataloguing and classification.	8	8	9	5	0
Ability to use the Internet for reference queries.	10	9	11	0	0
Ability to use the Internet for interlibrary loan and document delivery.	7	9	10	2	2
Ability to use the Internet for accessing electronic sources such as electronic journals and content pages.	14	8	7	1	0
Ability to use a video conferencing software application such as Microsoft NetMeeting for teleconferencing via the Internet.	6	5	10	6	3
Understand what an Intranet is.	9	9	9	3	0

Ability to use a business graphic programme capable of producing flow charts, office space plans such as Visco.	3	5	9	5	8
Understand computer graphics – CRT displays, pixels, RGB/HSV colour spaces, clipping and transformation matrics, develop a simple application to display and rotate a cube.	4	5	6	6	9

COMPETENCY	DEVELOPMENTAL NEED My need to further develop my skills in this competency is				
	Very High	Sometime High	Neither High / Low	Very Low	Irrelevant
Ability to create presentations using Adobe Photoshop.	10	9	8	2	1
Ability to create presentations using Microsoft PowerPoint.	11	10	6	3	0
Ability to create multimedia products using Macromedia Director.	10	7	8	2	3
Ability to use Microsoft FrontPage for web pages development.	6	11	10	3	0
Ability to use Microsoft Excel to manipulate and create tabulated data.	11	8	8	3	0
Ability to create applications using HTML programming.	7	8	6	4	5
Understand Web Publishing – use of web-safe palette, FTP and telnet.	11	6	3	6	4

Ability to set up a Web site and implement it for own use – type of communication link, communications bandwidth requirements, Web server hardware and software requirements.	12	4	3	6	5

References

1. Kennedy, Paul, *Electronic gap,* UNESCO Courier 54 (12), 2001, pp. 48
2. Hill, Steve, *The Global View*, New Statesman, 129 (4494), 2000, pp. xxii.

Where Does Professional Education on Digital Libraries Lead Our New Librarians?

Yan Quan Liu

School of Communication, Library and Information Science
Southern Connecticut State University, USA
Liu@southernct.edu

Abstract. This study investigates the state of school education for digital libraries. For this study, a web survey was conducted of syllabi of courses on the subject of digital libraries. Similarities and differences on such subjects as teaching emphases, course outlines, textbooks and assignments were compared. The majority of classes now contain a "hands-on" element, a practical component of the course that requires that the students interact with digital libraries. Those students who have received practical experience with digital libraries, like those provided in the "hands-on" courses, are best served for future practice in the field of librarianship.

1   Introduction

In 1999, Spink and Cool examined how schools were teaching the subject of digital libraries. They examined twenty educational institutions that offered courses on the subject of digital libraries. From their investigation, they concluded that students taking courses on digital libraries ("DL") often had only vague notions of the nature of digital libraries and that a sound conceptual framework for DL education had yet to be developed. In Spring 2003, to follow-up on Spink and Cool's study, the course instructor for DL course at the School of Communication, Information and Library Science, Southern Connecticut State University ("SCSU"), in conjunction with his students, surveyed courses on the subject. The survey and the content of this paper was based on the review and analysis of the course syllabi and/or course descriptions of DL courses that was available on the Internet.

2   Universities Offering DL Courses

The survey revealed that thirty-six (36) educational institutions located in North America, Europe and East Asia, offered courses on digital libraries. (It is possible that more institutions offered courses but did not post any information about the courses on the Web.) Since Spink and Cool (1999) only located twenty (20) institutions offering courses on the subject, it appears that since 1999, the amount of courses on the subject of DL has approximately doubled, from 20 in 1999 to 36 in 2003. Institutions offering courses in DL include the following institutions:

T.M.T. Sembok et al. (Eds.): ICADL 2003, LNCS 2911, pp. 317–321, 2003.

Table 1. Educational Institutions Offering 'Digital Libraries' Courses: (If available, links are provided to the pertinent course page. In the alternative, links are provided to the school website or course listings.)

Catholic University of America, School of Library and Information Science	Cornell University, Computer Science	Drexel University, College of Information Science and Technologies
Indiana University, School of Information and Library Science	Old Dominion University, College of Sciences, Computer Science	State University of New York at Oswego, Department of Computer Science, Information Science Program
Queen's College/City University of New York	Rutger's University, School of Communication, Information & Library Studies	Simmons College, Graduate School of Library and Information Science
Southern Connecticut State University, Information and Library Science	Syracuse University, School of Information Studies	University of Alabama
University of Alberta, School of Library and Information Studies	University of British Columbia, School of Library, Archival and Information Studies	University of California, Berkeley, Computer Science Division
University of Iowa, School of Library and Information Science	University of Maryland, College of Information Studies	University of Michigan, School of Information
University of Missouri-Columbia, School of Information, Science & Learning Technologies	University of Pittsburgh, School of Information Sciences	University of South Florida, School of Library and Information Science
University of Wisconsin, School of Library and Information Studies	Virginia Tech, Computer Science	Dalhousie University, School of Library and Information Studies, Canada
University of Western Ontario, Canda, Information and Media Studies	Universidade Federal de Minas Gerais Escola de Biblioteconomia (Brasil)	Loughborough University (UK), Department of Information Science
University of Strathclyde in Glasgow (UK), Department of Computer and Information Science	Monash University (AU), School of Information and Management Systems	University of Technology, Sydney, (AU) Information & Knowledge Management
Peking University, Department of Information Management	Sung Kyun Kwan University (Korea), Department of Library and Information Science	Hebrew University of Jerusalem, School of Library, Archive and Information Studies
University of Malaya (Malaysia), Computer Science	Victoria University, School of Communications and Information Management	Nanyang Technological University (Singapore), Division of Information Studies, Applies Science

Some institutions offer more than one course on DL. For example, the University of Michigan offers "Special Topics: Digital Libraries", "Practical Engagement Workshop: Digital Librarianship", and "Practical Engagement Workshop: Advanced Digital Workshop". The University of Pittsburgh offers a specialization in DL.

3   Similarities between Digital Courses

Course Emphases

Most DL courses were offered as part of a graduate level program in library and/or information science, although some were part of doctoral programs and/or computer programs. (Examples of each can be found through the links offered in Table 1.) DL courses offered through library and/or information science departments tended to emphasize organizing, preserving, managing and providing access to information. *See, e.g.*, "Digital Library Foundations" course syllabus (Catholic University's School of Library and Information Science) and "Digital Libraries" course syllabus (School of Information Management, Victoria University). DL courses in computer science departments, like the one offered through Cornell University's Computer Science department, tended to concentrate on metadata, databases and information retrieval. DL courses in schools outside North America, like Sung Kyun Kwan University, also tended to emphasize technology.

Textbooks

The majority of universities, whether online or on-ground, relied on at least some traditional materials such as print textbooks. Only two U.S. universities (Drexel and Dalhousie) relied exclusively digital materials, including web sites, online articles to teach the course. SungKyunKwan University in South Korea also used only digital materials, justifying his decision in the course syllabus based on his opinion that that the technology of digital libraries was changing so rapidly that no proper textbook could be found. Among all the courses surveyed, Lesk's *Practical Digital Libraries: Books, Bytes and Bucks,* (1997) is the most popular and appeared in the syllabi of seven school courses. The second and third most popular texts were Borgman's *From Gutenberg to the Global Information Infrastructure: Access to Information in the Networked World* (2000) (5 classes) and Arm's (2000) *Digital Libraries* (3 courses).

Class Assignments

Several classes required that the students engage in a practical exercise involving digital libraries. The most commonly assigned project among the classes was the creation of a digital library. At the library schools, the project could count anywhere between 30% to 40% of the course grade. However, where the subject was offered as part of a computer studies course, the project tended to weigh more, as much as 70% of the course grade. The project, creation of a digital library, had different criteria at the various educational institutions. For example, some institutions, like Indiana University, require the creation of a digital library that is fairly formally structured. At SCSU, while there are specific requirements, they are not fit to a mold on a specific format on a website. Other projects included having the students "digitize" information and perform hands-on investigations. Creative assignments included an internet survey evaluating and comparing the syllabi and course descriptions of other programs offering DL courses (Southern CT State University), case studies (Old Dominion University), and comparing and contrasting the digital collections of the Library of Congress' American Memory Project with digital collections from two others types of libraries or museums (Indiana University).

3.1   Differences between Digital Libraries Courses

The major difference in courses did not emanate from online versus on-ground presentation. The major difference in courses arose from whether the school took a "hands-on" or a "hands-off" approach to DL education. These terms, "hands-on" and "hands-off", refer to the amount of interaction that the course requires that the students have with digital libraries. "Hands-off" classes require little or no interaction with digital libraries. The main course objectives are related to *examining* current digital library projects – as opposed to *creating* digital libraries. Those courses that do not include practical assignments appear to be avoiding the technological side of digital libraries. "Hands-on" classes include a practical element, a physical interaction with digital libraries, in addition to more traditional learning processes, like reading textbooks, etc. For example, as noted above, students might be required to digitize materials or create entire digital libraries.

3.2   Suggestions for Improvement and Conclusions

- The notion of sharing digital libraries and technology with the "have-nots' of the world did not seem to receive much attention. Courses on digital libraries would be enriched by the inclusion of at least one major assignment where students are required to articulate opinions on this issue. This assignment might also ask for suggestions about *how* to share resources.

- Courses should devote additional class time to the needs and information seeking behaviors of the end-users of digital libraries.

- Courses in digital libraries should provide students both a theoretical study of and practice in designing, constructing and evaluating digital libraries. An ideal course would cover the following topics: foundations and architectures of digital libraries, technologies of digital libraries, management and organization of digital resources, knowledge representations and discovery, metadata and standards, intellectual property rights, and case studies.

- A majority of courses require that students interact with DLs. These "hands-on" courses will serve their students well in future practice in the field of librarianship. Those courses that do not have practical elements are lacking and appear somewhat technophobic and overly dependent on outdated pedagogical methods.

References

1. Coleman, Anita. (2001, July/Aug.). Interdisciplinarity: the road ahead for   education in digital Libraries. *D-Lib Magazine*, 8(7/8).
2. Fox, E. A. & Marchionini, G. (1988). Toward a Worldwide Digital Library. *Communications of the ACM*, 41(4):28–32.
3. Roes, Hans. (2001, July/Aug.). Digital libraries and education: trends and opportunities. *D-Lib Magazine,* 7(7/8).
4. Spink, Amanda and Cool, Colleen. (1999, May). Education for Digital Libraries. *D-Lib Magazine,* 5(5). Retrieved January 28, 2003 from http://www.dlib.org/dlib/may99/05spink.html

Towards Building Sociable Library System through Negotiation Engine

S.M.F.D Syed Mustapha

Faculty of Computer Science and Information Technology,
University of Malaya, 50603 Kuala Lumpur, Malaysia
smfd@um.edu.my

Abstract. The emerging of digital technology has made the research field in digital library a multidisciplinary research area. Incorporating social factors such as interactiveness and negotiation are novel approach in making digital library more sociable and approachable. Our research represents embedding this capability using case-based reasoning approach. Searching of documents, articles and books will no longer be merely displaying its retrieval list which is considered as very unfriendly. We introduce negotiation engine which gives extended assistance in getting more specific material the user is looking for without the need to manually flip pages for every potential books. The system takes into account the social appearances of the references besides the physical appearances.

1 Introduction

Library system has made rapid progress from the manual cataloging to an OPAC system. In the last decade, many researches have been focused to the internal mechanism of a digital library especially in the areas of digital archives [11, 15], document representations [9, 10], document understanding [1, 4] and digital imaging [3]. It is equally important for us to consider the social factors of the library system in building the front-end for the users. Conventional approach of digital library system has only made advancement to the searching in electronic format. An extension of human assistance is still needed when the searching requires complex semantic understanding of the references that need to be searched. It would be everyone's fantasy to have a library system which can provide assistance in a negotiable manner using natural dialogue during the searching process. We illustrate the imaginings scenario in Fig. 1.

The negotiation dialogue as shown has brought in many technical issues in various disciplines if it needs to be fully implemented. The natural language is obviously necessary to understand user's response and generate natural text as feedback. Semantic hierarchical tree [6, 8] is necessary to understand the categories of terminologies in contextual manner rather than a pure syntactical matching. For example, the system needs to know that "embodied conversational agent" may be closer to "knowledge conversational" than "knowledge-based system" using some probabilistic reasoning. Among all of these essential technologies, the main technology that we are addressing in this paper is the negotiation technique.

T.M.T. Sembok et al. (Eds.): ICADL 2003, LNCS 2911, pp. 322–328, 2003.

System: Good day! How can I help you?

User: Good day to you too. I'm looking for something on organizational memory.

System: Well, we do not have any books with that title exactly. However, I have found fifty titles on different categories of knowledge management such as Advanced Knowledge Management, Organization in Action, Knowledge Worker....

User: I am writing a paper about how to build ontology for organizational memory and how to make the knowledge conversational.

System: We do not have any title on ontology, so can you be more specific about ontology.

User: It is advance theory to knowledge representation.

System: OK. I have topic on Recent Issues on Knowledge Sharing which has collection of articles on ontology. We do not have anything on knowledge conversational but we have something on embodied conversational agent.

User: Yah! That's what I am looking for. Also, please give me the detail on Organization in Action.

Fig. 1. Negotiation dialogue

Negotiation is apparent in the entire dialogue session given above. It negotiates the demand of the user as well as meaning of certain concept. Users are frequently unsure about the exact title of a book or what are the set of books or articles s/he must have in his/her study. Modern library system overcomes the problem by displaying the content of the book online so that the user does not need to make unnecessary physical visit. Despite this feature, we still regard the searching as time-consuming since the user has to browse the content of each book before deciding its relevancy. The above dialogue shows that the system not only negotiates the scope of the topic but also the possible substitution on the non-availability of the book. For example, the user has been more specific in the searching that is from "organization memory" into "how to build ontology for organizational memory and how to make the knowledge conversational". The system has also negotiated with the user to change to other title; "knowledge conversational" to "embodied conversational agent".

In Section 2, we show the architecture of the negotiation engine which may support the kind negotiation described above for a library system. In Section 3, we discuss the social issue in library system and finally we conclude our discussion with future work in Section 4.

2   Architecture of Negotiation Engine

Employing Case-based reasoning (CBR) in negotiation is a new direction in this field [14], We developed the negotiation engine which has been applied to match-making process [7]. Conceptually, this is also applicable to any type of negotiation with the following characteristics:

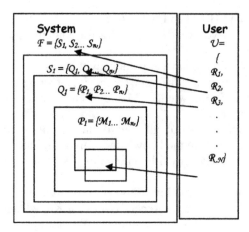

Fig. 2. Feature representation schema for $\mathcal{N} \times \mathcal{N}$ dimensions

1. There are two parties involved in the negotiation whereby the demand and supply do not have exact matches. The demand is referred to the user who makes request and demand is the negotiation engine who supplies information.
2. The demand party is willing to adjust the features of the original request while the supply party has static properties. In the context of a library, the user can change his/her searching terms while the list of books in the library should remain the same throughout the negotiation session.
3. The negotiation is performed in multi-dimensional manner. That is, the features are arranged in a hierarchical order from the most general at the top and most specific at the bottom. The negotiation begins from the top on general features and moves downward. It will backtrack from deepening in the tree in either two situations; whether the user does not have any specific interest on that feature to move on or "deadlock" has occurred. This is based on logical assumption that there are certain features which the demand party may not want to compromise at all. Backtracking helps to reduce the computational time if features at higher level have reached some agreement or deadlock.
4. If the negotiation ends but not fulfilling the demand party's requirements, it still guarantees the searching is exhaustive. Exhaustive means all possible combination of features have been negotiated or tested with the user as the alternative solutions.

We illustrate the feature representation schema of the negotiation engine as shown in Figure 2. The feature representation schema is composed of the system and user's components. The system component is made of several layers in which each layer is a collection of common features of a category. We use alphabets to name the set of features and also for the subsequent set of sub-features. The features in the inner layer have more detail information than any outer layer surrounds it. For example, Q_1 is more specific than S_1. The value $\mathcal{N}$ is not fixed for each layer as it depends on the number of features that are needed to describe the category. Since it is not possible to construct $\mathcal{N} \times \mathcal{N}$ dimensional layers, we show only the first element of each layer which is the expansion of S_1. We use $\rightarrow$ to indicate the flow expansion of the features and the linear flow expansion of S_1, S_2 and S_3 can be written as follows.

$$S_1 \rightarrow Q_1 \rightarrow P_2 \rightarrow M_3 \rightarrow \dots$$
$$S_2 \rightarrow Q'_1 \rightarrow P'_2 \rightarrow M'_3 \rightarrow \dots$$
$$S_3 \rightarrow Q''_3 \rightarrow P''_1 \rightarrow M''_4 \rightarrow \dots$$

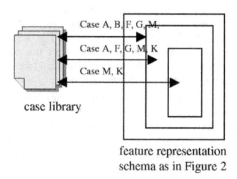

Case A, B, F, G, M,

Case A, F, G, M, K

Case M, K

case library

feature representation
schema as in Figure 2

Fig. 3. Architecture of the negotiation engine

Our system has been designed such that the negotiation is performed from vertical to horizontal order. That means the flow expansion of S_1 will be performed first before S_2 and S_3. This maintains the coherency of the series of questions prompted to the user. Each linear expansion will end either as the user has reached agreement or deadlock. The user's request is a set of linearly construct features. Each feature from a set R may correspond to a feature at different layers of the system.

In Figure 3, we show the architecture for the negotiation engine. In the conventional case-based reasoning approach, the best-match cases are only searched after the information on the key features has been collected from the user. In our approach, the nearest cases (based on nearest neighbor estimation) are searched from the entire case library for every session as shown in Figure 3. That means at every interaction, the system informs the user whether the requested feature is available in the case library or not. User is asked if s/he wants to modify any of the original features when they could not be found in the case library. For this reason, the entire case library has to be researched if the requested features anew. This could be a weakness in terms of computational time but it guarantees the exhaustiveness of the searching.

In Figure 3, we also show that a new case such as case K could pop up in the subsequent intersession. This is possible to happen when user makes major revision to his/her original requests and case K matches them. Despite this, the number of potential cases will always be reduced at every session as the key features are more specific.

3 Negotiation Engine in Sociable Library System

Our scope of library is mainly the conventional "brick and mortar" library where the collections of books, journals, encyclopedias, theses, magazines etc are organized and administratively maintained. Internet is sometimes can be considered as digital information resource but it is not structured, organized, scattered and owned by multitude of web masters. Nevertheless, we also consider online bookstore such as Amazon.com to be a potential user of our system.

Books, journals, magazines (thereon called references) are not merely typed pages but can be treated as sociable item depending on how we perceived them [2]. In match-making system, people are categorized in two ways, the physical appearance and "social appearance". Social appearance is referred as a person's race, religion, education background etc as these factors may affect the social relationship and preferences of another person. In similar manner, we need to categorize references so that they possess certain properties which are retrievable.

Physical appearance: Title, abstract/synopsis, number of pages, publisher, publication date, author, type, content of the book such as the main theory it discusses, popular diagrams or pictures etc. Physical appearances are properties which can physically be derived and obtained through objective interpretation. The values are more static and permanent than social appearance. For example, the content of the book does not decay throughout the years.

Social appearance: Type of frequent reader which consists of reader's education background (social science, linguistic, economics), potential use (for academic program, research, survey, advance topics), highly cited/referred or even the impact factors, reputation to public or certain relevant group etc. Social appearance is the properties based on social interpretation and the values can be dynamic. For example, a popular contemporary book may no longer be read by certain community and therefore its social value has changed.

The concept of social appearance of references is rather new and not well-established. However, we believe the values of social appearance are of great importance in relation to answering the questions such as

- why certain books must be read by many people compare to its counterpart.
- which book is commonly used by other universities in teaching knowledge management.
- what are the references I must have in order to study community in terms of social aspects.

Using the feature representation schema we introduce earlier, sociable library system can be built on similar schema as shown in Figure 4.

The sample of feature representation schema expands the first element of category S_1 and S_2. For example, for S_1 the *Discipline* is expanded into *Subject* and *Synopsis*; and the *Subject* is expanded into *Title* and *Social Science*. In this example, user is asked about the physical appearance and followed by the social appearance. All the features which are input by the users during the session on physical appearance will be kept together as part of key features with the key features input during session on social appearances. The integration of key features is important to ensure the searching results presented after taking into consideration of both physical and social issues.

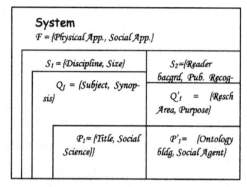

Fig. 4. Feature representation schema for sociable library system

4   Future Work and Conclusion

Inclusion of social factors in building intelligent communication system has been our major interest recently [12,13]. This paper emphasized on social factors of library system besides the physical information which is available in the current system. We demonstrate a futuristic dialogue session which will be addressed as a long term research. The feature representation scheme is the key element enabling the negotiation process as it is structured in multidimensional manner. The negotiation is done iteratively that allows the user to change minds or reconsider the change of values in which enables him/her to obtain some results after exhaustive negotiation. Our approach leads the way to a more flexible and realistic human way of negotiation.

An important aspect which needs to be considered using this approach is the preparation of feature representation. Feature representation in the context of library system is not actually new since it can look similar to a record presentation. However, the semantic information and the process of extracting can be costly and laborious. For example, to find out whether Book A is still popular among researcher in certain field may require some statistical process and comparison with other contemporary books. There are many more social appearance features which may not be easy for library administrator to get the information. However, we believe that these information could also be obtained from the borrow cooperation. Borrower can input comments about their feeling and opinion after reading the book. This approach is not new as it has been used mainly as testimonials for new books before they are launched in the market.

The work can be extended in many ways. In one aspect, the negotiation segregates the categories and deals with each category one after the other. The dialogue session we showed earlier looks more natural that the physical and social aspect of the reference is discussed together. Even though our method will not affect the accuracy of the searching results, natural presentation is vital issue in the respect of human computer interaction. Another aspect is that, the negotiation passes through all categories, subcategories and features of each category which can be a tedious negotiation process. A robust human computer interface program which understands the essence of the natural language and maps to only relevance key features within the category and subcategory will simplify the dialogue session.

References

1. Aiello, M., Monz, C., Todoran, L. and Worring, M. Document Understanding for a Broad Class of Documents. International Journal on Document Analysis and Recognition, 5:1–16, 2002.
2. Brown, J.S. and Duguid, P. (1996). The Social Life of Documents, First Monday, 1(1). http://www.firstmonday.dk/issues/issue1/documents/.
3. Chen-Y, Catthoor, F., Hugo J.D.M., "Efficient VLSI Architectures for a High-Performance Digital Image Communication System", IEEE Journal on Selected Areas in Communications, no. 8, October 1990 pp. 1481–1491
4. Clark, J., Slator, B. , Perrizo, W., Landrum, J., Frovarp, R., Bergstrom, A., Ramaswamy, S., Jockheck., W. Digital Archive Network for Anthropology, Journal of Digital Information, Vol 2, Issue 4, (May 2002). http://jodi.ecs.soton.ac.uk/
5. Dingli, A., Ciravegna, F., Guthrie,D., Wilks, Y. Mining Web Sites Using Unsupervised Adaptive Information Extraction. In Proceedings 10th Conference of the European Chapter of Asociation for Computational Linguistics, Budapest, Hungary, 2003.
6. Duygulu, P and Atalay, V. A hierarchical Representation of Form Documents for Identification and Retrieval. International journal on Document Analysis and Recognition, 5:17–27, 2002.
7. Esyin, C. Iterative Matching On Multi-Dimensional Case-Based Reasoning System For Negotiation. Master Thesis, University of Malaya (2003).
8. Kuo, Y-H and Wong, M-H. Web Document Classification based on Hyperlinks and Document Semantics. In A.-H. Tan and P. Yu (Eds): PRICAI 2000 Workshop on Text and Web Mining, Melbourne, pp. 44–51, August 2000.
9. Schimdt, A and Junker, M. Mining Documents for Complex Semantic Relations by the Use of Context Classification. In D. Lopresti, J. Hu and R. Kashi (Eds): DAS 2002, LNCS 2423, pp. 400–411, 2002.
10. Shepherd, M., Nunberg, G. Genre in Digital Documents, Thirty-Second Annual Hawaii International Conference on System Sciences-Volume 2, January 05–08, 1999, Maui, Hawaii. http:// computer. org/ proceedings/ hicss/ 0001/ 00012/ 00012002abs.htm
11. Smith, J.R., Digital video libraries and the internet, IEEE Communications Magazine, no. 1, January 1999 pp. 92–97.
12. Syed Mustapha, S.M.F.D, Nishida, T. and Kubota, H. Communicative Social Intelligence: An Application to Malaysian Industries. Conference of Scientific and Social Research, The Palace of Golden Horses, Seri Kembangan, Selangor, 2003.
13. Syed Mustapha, S.M.F.D, Nishida. Communicative Social Intelligence: An analysis of community of practice. Submitted to International Conference of Knowledge Management, 2003.
14. Wilke, W., Bergmann, R., Wess, S. Negotiation During Intelligent Sales Support with CBR, Negotiation During Intelligent Sales Support with Case-Based Reasoning", Proceedings of the 6th German Workshop on CaseBased Reasoning, GWCBR'98, Germany, 1998.
15. Wong, S.T.C and Tjandra, D.A. A digital library for biomedical imaging on the internet, IEEE Communications Magazine, no. 1, January 1999 pp. 84–91

Browsing a Digital Library: A New Approach for the New Zealand Digital Library

Dana McKay and Sally Jo Cunningham

Department of Computer Science,
University of Waikato
Private Bag 3105, Hamilton, New Zealand
{dana,sallyjo}@cs.waikato.ac.nz

Abstract. Browsing is part of the information seeking process, used when information needs are ill-defined or unspecific. Browsing and searching are often interleaved during information seeking to accommodate changing awareness of information needs. Digital Libraries often support full-text search, but are not so helpful in supporting browsing. Described here is a novel browsing system created for the Greenstone software used by the New Zealand Digital Library that supports users in a more natural approach to the information seeking process.

1 Introduction

Browsing is a vital part of the information seeking process, allowing information seekers to meet ill-defined information needs and find new information [16,19]. Despite the importance of browsing in information seeking, however, it is relatively unsupported in many information systems [13]. The Greenstone digital library software [1] created by the New Zealand Digital Library research group [2] is an example of software that does support browsing, though to a limited extent. Greenstone is used by numerous organizations worldwide to manage and present collections of documents.

The aim of the work presented here was to create a new browsing system within Greenstone that had the flexibility to allow users to follow a more natural information seeking process. The resulting system allows users to specify parameters such as the metadata by which they wish to browse and the maximum number of documents on a page. It also allows the user to combine searching and browsing activities.

Section 2 of this paper discusses the information seeking process: examining what browsing is, why it is important and how information systems can best support it. Section 3 describes Greenstone's current browsing capabilities and considers their weak points. Section 4 presents an overview of a new browsing system and Section 5 describes an evaluation of the new system. Section 6 draws some conclusions about this work.

T.M.T. Sembok et al. (Eds.): ICADL 2003, LNCS 2911, pp. 329–339, 2003.

2 Human Information Seeking

Human information seeking behaviour is more than full text search, or wandering among the shelves in a library. The information seeking process begins with the conception of a need for information, and (if successful) ends with the satisfaction of the information seeker that they have the information they require [16]. Section 2.1 will examine more closely the information seeking process and the role that browsing plays; Section 2.2 will examine the implications of this process for information systems and their users.

2.1   The Information Seeking Process

Traditional information retrieval models have tended to marginalise human behaviour and focus almost entirely on querying using structured languages. It is on these methods that the standard (recall and precision) measures of a system's success are based, and there is a large research literature about making searching more effective [17,27].

Searching may be most of information *retrieval*, but it is not all of information *seeking* [10]. Information seeking is a process that has been studied and broken down numerous ways (see [7,16,19] for examples of this work). These models have their differences, but there are also some striking similarities. All the models begin with the user perceiving their need for information (though they may not know how to express what it is they need [23]). The models, representative of an ideal world, all end with the satisfaction of this need (though in reality users often "satisfice" [3], or simply give up [23]). All the models also describe a stage ideally suited to browsing, where the information seeker knows they have a need for information but may not know how to fulfil that need. This stage is variously called source selection [18], exploration [16] and browsing [7].

While browsing is one part of the information seeking process, it is not all of it. Moreover, the process is not necessarily linear; users generally seek information in an iterative manner switching back and forth between stages [5,18,27], particularly searching and browsing.

2.2   Information Seeking Interfaces

To be as useful as possible, information seeking interfaces should support the activities of information seekers as naturally as possible. This means supporting all stages of the information seeking process, not just searching. Despite research having long emphasized that browsing is a fundamental information seeking activity (Bates described this is 1989 [6]), many systems still do not support it [13,25].

Browsing can be supported by many different facilities, including semantic browsing using such tools as self organising maps [9,26] or phrases [24], metadata based browsing like the Greenstone classifier system [4], and subject categorisation (for example the Library of Congress classification scheme). Browsing may be within a document (for example leafing through a book) or between documents (for example wandering the library shelves). Browsing may occur for a number of reasons, including evaluation of an information source, information discovery, and clarification of an information problem [8,18,25]. A common definition of browsing is an exploratory information seeking strategy relying heavily on serendipity and being used to meet an ill-defined information need [6,8,22]

One way that conventional libraries support browsing is through subject classification of documents. However, physical libraries cannot rearrange the shelves at whim to meet the needs of the user (say, if they wanted to browse by author and they changed suddenly to title). Electronic information systems (such as digital libraries) have the opportunity to "rearrange the shelves".

For a system to support browsing effectively, and add something to conventional physical libraries, it must be flexible, to allow the user to modify their information need and information seeking strategy at will. It should support browsing for any number of reasons, including those mentioned above. For optimum information seeking effectiveness interleaving of browsing and searching should ideally be simple [11,13].

Browsing is easily shown to be a vital part of the information seeking process, and very effective when combined with searching. Information systems need to recognise this importance and support browsing in ways that will allow users to become effective information seekers. The system described in this paper is a metadata-based system that allows users to configure their browsing structures and combine them with searching, thus giving the flexibility recommended in the literature.

3   Greenstone and Browsing

Greenstone is a complete digital library management system, handling everything from collection building to collection presentation via a web browser. It facilitates full-text and metadata searching, and various kinds of browsing [1,4]. Greenstone is designed to allow collections to be built fully automatically (that is, to not require the manual processing of source documents) and served by inexpensive machines over a slow internet connection [28]. Greenstone is largely stateless, not keeping information about what users do from one action to the next, so as to help reduce server load. Section 3.1 discusses the current browsing facilities available in Greenstone and Section 3.2 explains why these facilities inadequately meet information seekers' needs.

3.1   Greenstone's Current Browsing System

Greenstone's current browsing system is known as the "classifier" system. This is because documents are classified at collection build time according to their metadata, and browsing structures are pre-built ready for loading. Greenstone supports a number of different types of classifier, each suited to a specific kind of metadata. Each classifier displays information in its own way.

There are five main types of classifier currently implemented in Greenstone: the list, the alphabetic classifier, the hierarchic classifier, the date classifier [4] and a phrase-based classifier called "Phind"[24]

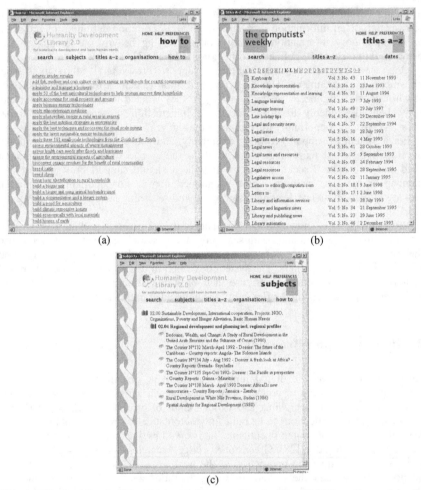

Fig. 1. The classifiers in Greenstone. (a) Shows a list classifier of "How to" metadata. (b) Shows an alphabetic classifier, viewed by title. The section being viewed is "K-L". (c) Shows a hierarchic classifier. The classification being viewed "02.04" is two levels deep

The list classifier is the simplest of the classifiers; it merely sorts metadata alphabetically, and presents documents in a single long list (see Figure 1a).

The alphabetic classifier also sorts documents alphabetically, but the document list is then divided up into preset classes according to initial letter, and the classes are displayed across the top of the page (see Figure 1b). If the classes are smaller than a pre-set size the classifier will merge them (for example, 'K-L' in Figure 1b). There is no limit on the number of documents in a class.

The hierarchic classifier deals with numerical hierarchies – documents are assigned a number indicating their position in the hierarchy (much like the Dewey decimal system), and the user views the hierarchies by progressive drill-down clicking (see Figure 1c).

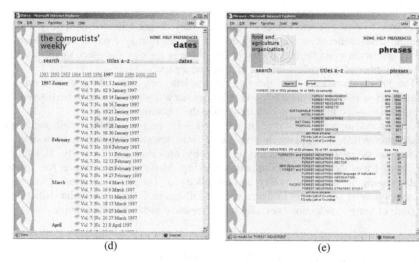

(d)   (e)

Fig. 1. (cont.) The classifiers in Greenstone. (d) A date classifier. Note the months down the side of the page. (e) The "Phind" classifier. The word "forest" is being browsed

The date classifier is very much like the alphabetic classifier, though it uses the year as a basic unit, (as opposed to initial letter) and it displays month information down the side of the hierarchy (see Figure 1d).

The Phind classifier is not based on traditional metadata. Instead, it creates an index of phrases when the collection is built, and allows the user to browse by entering a single word or phrase and drilling down through phrases to documents (see Figure 1e).

3.2   Problems with Browsing Using the Classifiers

The classifier system in Greenstone does not support users as well as it might. The failings are in two major areas – the fact that uses cannot combine searching and browsing, and in the rigidity of the system.

As discussed in Section 2, users locate information most effectively when they can switch easily between searching and browsing. Search results in Greenstone are currently always displayed in lists, and if a search is not ranked, these lists are unsorted. Classifiers present all the documents in a collection that have the classification metadata; there is no way to search a classifier. Thus the cognitive cost of switching between searching and browsing is high, reducing information seeking effectiveness.

The rigidity of the classifier system is built-in – each classifier uses static, pre-built browsing structures, thus allowing collections to be presented only in one pre-determined manner without input from the user. To illustrate how this can become a problem, imagine a collection with a number of distinct documents with the same title and different authors. The user cannot specify that they would also like to see the author metadata when browsing, much less insist upon the documents being sorted by author. Another example of how the rigidity of the classification system is detrimental to the information seeker's experience is the size of the groups displayed. Users are better able to navigate and evaluate options if they do not have to scroll [21]; yet in medium-sized collections (say 1,000 documents) users may have to scroll through three screens on a single classification, and there is no way for users to specify the largest number of documents they wish to see on a page.

The Phind classifier solves the rigidity problem, but allows browsing of only a single kind of metadata (phrases), and still does not allow collections to be filtered by search terms—and thus does not entirely solve the browsing problem.

Greenstone supports browsing in a limited way: non-searchable, static metadata classifiers. While this approach goes some way towards supporting browsing, it hinders users in their information seeking by not allowing them the flexibility necessary for truly effective information seeking. Moreover, Greenstone has strong goals relating to usability, utility and simplicity of collection creation. The work describes here is an attempt to overcome the failings in Greenstone while still taking its goals of simple collection provision on inexpensive hardware into account.

4 A New Browsing System for Greenstone

This project focussed on a between-documents metadata-based browsing system. This approach was chosen because Greenstone is about presenting collections of documents (rather than single documents) and Greenstone already has an effective semantic browsing system in Phind [24]. The user capabilities the new system was to support were defined with the failings of the current system and the research on human information seeking behaviour in mind. These capabilities are as follows: users must be able to combine searching and browsing, users must be able to choose the metadata by which they browse, users should be able to browse by more than one kind of metadata at a time, and users should be able to restrict the amount of information on any one screen. The guiding principle is to give the user the richest possible browsing experience.

The new browsing system is designed to provide a rich browsing experience without being too taxing on the user—allowing users flexibility in specifying how they wish to browse, while providing a simple interface with sensible defaults. This also involved creating the system to handle alphanumeric and date metadata.

One of the major advantages of this system over the existing classifier system is that searching and browsing can be easily combined. The search offered by this interface is functionally identical to the ordinary Greenstone search, but results are presented in a browsing structure defined by the user. To avoid the loss of the useful ranking information provided by Greenstone's underlying search technology MG [29], where the search is an "any words" search, rank information is displayed next to the document metadata, similar to search engine results (see Figure 2b). If the user does not enter any search terms, then the user can browse the whole collection (see Figure 2a).

The mechanism for specifying how documents are to be browsed must allow great flexibility, but it also must to be simple enough to use without training. To that end, the user is presented with familiar web-based controls and simple language to determine their browsing preferences. They may browse one or two kinds of metadata at a time (the lists of metadata available for browsing are requested from the collection, and inserted into the interface when the browse page is displayed), and they may specify how many documents they wish to see on a page.

Because Greenstone is stateless and combining all this information to form a browsing structure is computationally expensive, the browsing structures are created only once, and the classes that are not being currently viewed are hidden in the page using dynamic HTML and JavaScript. This means that the user will get an instantaneous response when switching between the classes in a browsing structure.

Browsing more than one kind of metadata at a time allows the user to view distinguishing metadata where the primary browsing metadata values occur more than once (for example many books with the same author but different titles, when browsing first by author). It also allows the user to sort the duplicates by the second piece of metadata, (so sorting the books by author, and then sorting the books with the same author by title). Both pieces of metadata are displayed for each document, even where documents may only have one of the two pieces (see Figure 2a). Documents without the first piece of classification metadata are slotted into the browsing structure under the label "no metadata available".

The system accommodates the "number-of-documents-per-page" option by creating a two-level hierarchy, with basic divisions (for example initial letter in the first level of the hierarchy), and the second level of the hierarchy divided up so as to provide the required number of documents in each class. The classes at this level are labelled such that they are distinct from neighbouring classes (for example, if the first document in one class is called "teak chests" and the first document in the next class is called "teas of the world", the classes will be labelled 'teak-' and 'teas-' respectively). See Figure 2b for an example of such a browsing situation.

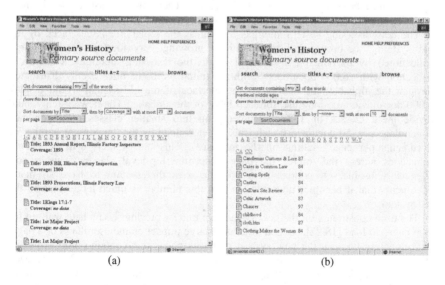

(a)   (b)

Fig. 2. The new browsing system. (a) Shows browsing of a whole collection by two pieces of metadata. (b) Shows browsing of ranked search results by title metadata. Note the ranking information on the right and the second level of the hierarchy

Users rarely change the defaults on information seeking interfaces; therefore while this interface offers a lot of flexibility it must also have sensible defaults [14]. By default, the entire collection is displayed for browsing by title metadata; this default is with a view to giving the user a good overview of the system. The default second piece of metadata by which to browse is determined by whatever metadata the collection has — it is hard to tell automatically what will be useful for any given collection, so the default second piece of metadata is the first detected piece of metadata that is not the title. The default number of documents per page is 20 – this is approximately one screen-full, so as to avoid wasted screen real-estate, but also to lessen the need for scrolling. Searching defaults to "any" words, as this is less likely to give a "no match" result and therefore less likely to frustrate the user [14].

The new browsing system has been designed to offer flexibility in a very simple manner. The major advantages it has over Greenstone's existing classifier system are the combination of searching and browsing, and the ability to interactively change browsing structures to meet changing information needs.

5   Evaluation

There were two main components to the evaluation of this system: a technical evaluation (in Section 5.1) and a user study (in Section 5.2).

5.1   Technical Evaluation

Systems must be technically sound to be useful. There are two aspects of the new browsing system that can be meaningfully evaluated: scalability and time constraints.

The new browsing system attempts to address the scalability issues faced by the old system (i.e. browsing lists potentially growing very long in medium large collections) by introducing a second level to the browsing hierarchy. Consider a collection with 26,000 documents, with the initial words of titles evenly distributed through the alphabet; the title browsing interface of the old system would display 1,000 documents in a long list, for each letter of the alphabet. The new system would divide these classes of 1,000 documents up into smaller classes of documents, containing, say, 50 documents each (this is determined by the "maximum number of documents per page" setting on the interface). This means there will be twenty subclasses across the top of the page under the top-level classes. This is still reasonably usable. Of course, it is possible with this system to have so many documents that it becomes unusable too, but this number is much larger than in the old system.

The time constraints on the new system are more worrying. Users hate waiting for web pages to load [18,22], so load time has a large impact on the usefulness of a page. Unfortunately because the new system produces pages that contain entire browsing structures, the pages are very large. The browsing interface itself is 6.78kB and each document is .04kB in the browsing structure. This means that over a 56kbps modem the interface will take 1 second to load, and each document in the browsing structure will add about 0.05 seconds – with a large collection this adds up very quickly. A collection of 1,073 documents (browsed by title and coverage) was shown to take 66 seconds to load over a 56kbps modem connection, precluding this interface from being used over a low speed connection. However, for a high speed connection or a local collection, this time drops to under 1 second, and once the page is loaded then the entire browsing hierarchy is available instantaneously. When we compare this to the classifier system, the total load time over a 56kbps would be 88 seconds for title metadata only. However, this time is in smaller chunks as the user loads each part of the hierarchy, and thus the wait time is more palatable to the user (each individual page would take about 3 second to load over a 56kbps connection).

A transaction log analysis of 42 collections in the New Zealand Digital Library [2] from June 21st to December 19th 2001 shows that approximately 9.5% of all actions are browsing with the classifier system, and that 37% of the time when a user looked at one part of a classifier (say the 'A' section of a title classifier) their next action was to look at another part of the same classifier (say the 'B' section). This has an associated time cost under the old system, but under the new system it is instantaneous.

5.2 User Study

There were two user studies performed on the concept embodied by this interface, one to determine how users actually want to browse, and one to determine the predictability of the system (i.e. to determine whether users could guess what the system would show them given the interface). Both these studies were paper based studies using index cards to represent documents. For more information on these studies see [20].

The first study asked user to arrange the paper documents into a browsing structure that they would find useful for locating information on a specific topic. Eight out of ten study participants created some metadata-based browsing scheme. Moreover, of the participants who created metadata-based browsing structures, five used more than one kind of metadata, something they couldn't do with the old system. When asked to comment on whether the organisation they had created was appropriate for an electronic information system, three users commented that they "would also like searching", and three users said that an information system should be able to present more than a single view of an information system. This indicates that users want the flexibility offered by the new system but not available in the old system.

The second study asked participants to arrange documents as they believed the interface would arrange them (being shown a picture of the interface where the documents were to be sorted first by title and second by coverage). A high level of comprehension was shown, with seven out of eight users sorting the documents properly, and the eighth user commenting that this was not how he believed the interface would sort the documents, but it was how he would like it to.

Evaluating the new browsing system both technically and with user studies shows that it has only on major flaw: the amount of time a browse page may take to load (and even that is ameliorated by the fact that it then provides better performance than the standard browsing interface 37% of the time). The new system handles large numbers of documents better than the old system, is readily comprehensible, and allows users the flexibility they want in a browsing system.

6 Conclusions

A novel browsing system was created within the Greenstone software. The system fits cleanly within the Greenstone software, and does not require any extra effort on the part of the user or the collection maintainer to use. This new system is a metadata-based between documents system, and was designed with human information seeking needs and the failures of the old system in mind.

The new system has some technical issues when it comes to page load time, but this problem can be solved by using local collections or a fast connection. Furthermore the total load time for a browsing structure is actually less in the new system than the old system.

The new system allows users to combine searching and browsing, in keeping with both the literature on information seeking behaviour and the user experiment carried out as a part of the work done for this investigation. The new system also allows the user more flexibility in determining the way in which they browse, also in keeping with experimental results and information seeking literature. In both these areas, the new browsing system is a vast improvement over the old classifier system making information seeking easier and more effective. The new browsing system can handle many more documents than the old system before the browsing structures become unusable.

In sum, a novel browsing system that allowed users dynamic interaction with information collections and fully supported the three main browsing activities of evaluating information sources, finding "new" information and clarifying information problems was implemented in Greenstone.

References

1. The Greenstone Software. http://www.greentsone.org, accessed March 6 2003.
2. The New Zealand Digital Library. http://www.nzdl.org, accessed March 6 2003.
3. Agosto, Denise. Bounded Rationality and Satisficing in Young People's Web-Based Decision Making. *Journal of the American Society for Information Science and Technology* 53:1 2002 16–27.
4. Bainbridge, David, Mckay, Dana and Witten, Ian. The Greenstone Developer's Guide. Dept. of Computer Science, University of Waikato 2001. Available at http://www.greenstone.org, accessed March 6 2003.
5. Baldonado, Michelle Q. Wang. A User-Centered Interface for Information Exploration in a Heterogeneous Digital Library. *Journal of the American Society for Information Science* 51:3, 2000 297–310.
6. Bates, Marcia J. The Design of Browsing and Berrypicking Techniques for the Online Search Interface. *Online Review* 13:5 1989 407–424.
7. Beaulieu, Micheline. Interaction in Information Searching and Retrieval. *Journal of Documentation* 56:4 2000 431–439.
8. Chang, Shan-Ju and Rice, Ronald E. Browsing: A Multidimensional Framework. *Annual Review of Information Science and Technology* 28 1993 231–276.
9. Chen, Hsinchun, Houston, Angela L., Sewell, Robin R., and Schatz, Bruce R. Internet Browsing and Searching: User Evaluations of Category Map and Concept Space Techniques. *Journal of the American Society for Information Science* 49:7 1998 582–603.

10. Crabtree, Andy, Twidale, Michael B., O'Brien, Jon and Nichols, David M. Talking in the Library: Implications for the Design of Digital Libraries. *Proc. 2ⁿᵈ ACM International Conference on Digital Libraries*, Philadelphia, Pennsylvania 1997 221–228.
11. Cunningham, Sally-Jo, Knowles, Chris, and Reeves, Nina. An Ethnographic Study of Technical Support Workers: Why We Didn't Build a Tech Support Digital Library. *Proc. 1ˢᵗ Joint ACM/IEEE-CS Conference on Digital Libraries*. Roanoke, Virginia 2001 189–198.
12. Henninger, Scott and Belkin, Nicholas. Interface Issues and Interaction Strategies for Information Retrieval Systems. *CHI Companion '95*. Denver, Colorado 1995 401–402.
13. Jacso, Peter. Savvy Searching Starts with Browsing. *Online and CD-ROM Review* 23:3 1999 169–172.
14. Jones, Steve, Cunningham, Sally Jo and McNab, Rodger. An Analysis of Usage of a Digital Library. *Proc. 2ⁿᵈ European Conference on Research and Advanced Technology for Digital Libraries*, Heraklion, Greece 1998 261–277.
15. Knepshield, Pamela A. Savage and Belkin, Nicholas. Interaction in Information Retrieval: Trends Over Time. *Journal of the American Society for Information Science* 50:12 1999 1067–1082.
16. Kuhlthau, Carol. Inside the Search Process: Information Seeking from the User's Perspective. *Journal of the American Society for Information Science* 42:5 1991 361–371.
17. Lawrence, Steve and Giles C. Lee. Context and Page Analysis for Improved Web Search, *IEEE Internet Computing* 2:4 1998 38–46.
18. Lazar, Jonathon, Bessiere, Katie, Ceaparu, Irina and Shneiderman, Ben. Help! I'm Lost: User Frustration in Web Navigation. *IT&Society* 3:1 2003 18–26.
19. Marchionini, Gary. Information Seeking in Electronic Environments. Cambridge University Press, New York. 1995
20. McKay, Dana. Browsing and Greenstone: a Study of Browsing in Digital Library Software. Available from the Dept. of Computer Science, University of Waikato. 2002.
21. Nielsen, Jakob. The Changes in Web Usability Since 1994", *Alertbox* December 1 1997, available at http://www.useit.com/alertbox/9712a.html, accessed March 6 2003
22. Nielsen, Jakob. The Top Ten New Mistakes of Webpage Design, *Alertbox* May 30, 1999, available at http://www.useit.com/alertbox/990350.html, accessed March 6 2003.
23. Nordlie, Ragnar "User Revealment" – a Comparison of Initial Queries and Ensuing Question Development in Online Searching and Human Reference Interactions.*Proc. 22ⁿᵈ Annual International ACM SIGIR Conference on Research and Development in Information Retrieval*, Berkley, California 1999 11–18.
24. Paynter, Gordon, Witten, Ian, Cunningham Sally Jo, and Buchanan, George. Scalable Browsing for Large Collections: a case study. *Proc. 5ᵗʰ ACM Conference on Digital Libraries*, San Antonio, Texas 2000 215–218.
25. Salampasis, Michail, Tait, John and Bloor, Chris. Evaluation of Information Seeking Performance in Hypermedia Digital Libraries. *Interacting with Computers* 10 1998 269–284.
26. Shukla, Preeti. *Cartography for Collections*. Masters Thesis. Available from the Dept. of Computer Science, University of Waikato. 2003.
27. Spink, Amanda, Bateman, Judy and Jansen, Bernarnd J. Searching the Web: a Survey of Excite Users. *Internet Research: Electronic Networking Applications and Policy* 9:2 (1999) 117–128.
28. Witten, Ian, and McNab, Rodger. The New Zealand Digital Library: Collections and Experience. *The Electronic Library* 15:6 (1994) 495–504.
29. Witten, Ian, Moffat, Alistair and Bell, Timothy. Managing Gigabytes: Compressing and Indexing Documents and Images. Van Norstrand Rheinhold, New York (1994).

The Inevitable Future of Electronic Theses and Dissertations within Malaysia Context

Eng Ngah Looi and Suit Wai Yeng

Mimos Berhad, Technology Park Malaysia,
57000 Kuala Lumpur, Malaysia
{looi,wysuit}@mimos.my

Abstract. The intellectual wealth of nations is becoming increasingly visible online. Therefore, providing scholarly materials available electronically has become part of the learning culture. Many universities are now in the process of digitizing their theses and dissertations in an effort to preserve it and to make it more widely available. As more and more electronic documents disseminate from various universities, there is a critical need to formally manage the distribution of resources across institutional boundaries. Hence, this paper examines the proposed framework of ETD initiatives within Malaysia context as well as various issues and concerns including accessibility/availability, scalability, security and searchability of the electronic theses and dissertations. Equally, this paper will also address other issues such as intellectual property rights, archiving and preservation of ETDs.

1 Introduction

Theses and dissertations are the fundamental pillar for the application and development of knowledge. It provides tangible evidence of the scholarly development of students and their ability to discover and communicate research findings. Generally, traditional ways of submitting theses and dissertations have a very limited reach. In Malaysia, theses and dissertations are submitted, disseminated and stored in paper. Students are required to submit multiple hard copies of theses or dissertations for preservation purpose. These printed publications are rarely viable in a massive way and are not easily accessed by potential scholars and interested researchers.

Moreover, handling and storing of paper theses in the library and the graduate office is time-consuming and expensive. The graduate office and library pays space and maintenance costs, and need to manually cataloging the submitted theses. The students pay high photocopy fees in procuring copies of their works. Many original research projects, to which authors have devoted long working hours, lie moldering in library basements, with no efficient way for students, researchers or publishers to locate the information that may be contained in them.

Electronic submission, distribution, and storage of theses will address these problems. Electronic publishing makes the theses and dissertations possible to reach every corner in the world and thus open new research and communication paths. A number of universities worldwide have now begun to accept electronic submission of

T.M.T. Sembok et al. (Eds.): ICADL 2003, LNCS 2911, pp. 340–350, 2003.
© Springer-Verlag Berlin Heidelberg 2003

theses and then post these documents on library web servers. Therefore, it is the intention of our research to explore the governance issues and technical feasibility of electronic theses submission, storage and distribution in Malaysia universities. The overall goal of our research is to investigate and propose optimum framework architecture for universities in digitizing theses and to lead universities to form a solid foundation of information infrastructure.

2 Electronic Theses and Dissertations (ETDs)

Electronic Theses and Dissertations (ETDs) are defined as those theses and dissertations submitted, archived, or accessed primarily in electronic formats. ETDs are a positive development in graduate education on several counts. Students can now be more expressive than black ink and white paper allow them to be. They are freed to include color diagrams and images, dynamic constructs like spreadsheets, interactive forms such as animations, and multimedia resources including audio and video. Besides, to ensure preservation of the raw data underlying their work, promote learning from their experience and facilitate confirmation of their findings, they may also enhance their ETDs by including the key datasets that they have assembled.

On the other hand, by requiring graduate students to publish theses and dissertations in digital format, universities are able to archive and store the theses more economically. This is a key responsibility of the university library, and it is easier and less costly to fulfill when the workflow involves electronic documents. ETDs reduce the need for library storage space and advance digital library technology, which improves library services. As a result, graduate student research achieves broader exposure and new opportunities for creative scholarship can be opened up.

However, there are some challenges that lie ahead if the academic communities intend to digitize theses submission, storing and dissemination process. As more and more electronic documents disseminate from various universities, there is a need of an optimum framework that can present heterogeneous resources in a coherent way. What's more, by unifying multiples resources into a single interface, we may face the legal concerns associated with access, copying and dissemination of digital theses. To solve the problems, we propose a framework architecture for ETDs system that can handle digitalized documents from various universities. The proposed framework will be discussed in the next section.

3 Proposed Framework

In this paper, we would like to propose an ETD framework, which can evolve the learning culture in Malaysia in the near future. This framework is embedded with grid technology, which supports the sharing and coordinated use of diverse resources in dynamic environment. With the adoption of this technology, it allows students or even researchers to access and share resources/information across distributed and wide area networks. Conventionally, the theses and dissertations are lying moldy in the bookshelves of the library and only limited access to particular university only.

Moreover, there is no collaboration among universities even though they are researching in the same research areas. The aim of this proposed framework to build an interoperable and accessible of ETD collections within the universities in Malaysia and thus establish a scientific research community within Malaysia society.

3.1   Grid Technology

Grid technology enables large-scale of sharing of resource within formal or informal consortia of individuals or institution. It necessitates increased collaboration between all universities. Basically, Grid technology can be divided into two large sub-domains: Computational Grid and Data Grid. Whereas a Computational Grid is a natural extension of the former cluster computer where large computing tasks have to be computed at distributed computing resources; a Data Grid deals with the efficient management, placement and replication of large amounts of distributed data. In this paper, we are only focused on Data Grid rather than Computational Grid. From the application's point of view, Data Grid is a collection of middleware services that provide applications with a uniform view of distributed resource components and the mechanisms for assembling them into system. The middleware services will allow secure access to massive amount of data in a universal namespace, to move and replica data at high speed from one geographical site to another, and manage synchronization of remote copies.

Our proposed architecture is built on the notion of grid-defined services. It attempts to abstract diverse elements of the data grid by providing a set of core services that can be used to construct a higher-level service for ETDs application. The details of our proposed architecture will be illustrated in the following section.

3.2   System Infrastructure

Figure 1 shows the ETD infrastructure with the adoption of grid technology. This implementation allows university to derive value from the promise of grid technology. Each and every university will collaborate through a common platform, which is grid platform. This approach is pragmatic and through this approach realization and capacity of grid technology will be illustrated.

Figure 2 shows the core services provided by grid technology that are necessary to provide the basic functionality: object naming and storage, object discovery and user access. In the next section, we present an overview of the services, sketching its elements and how they are supposed to function together.

Conceptually, the system works as follows:

As an undergraduate, postgraduate or doctorial student of the university, he/she is required to prepare his/her theses or dissertations in digital form or in other word it is represented as digital object. This digital object is a data structure which principal component is digital material, or data. This digital object is then post to the grid framework and then deposits to grid repository. Upon depositing the digital object in the repository, its key metadata and the repository name or IP address are registered with a naming server and an URN will be given to that particular digital object. Besides, the key-metadata will also be deposited into the index server via index service for querying or searching purpose.

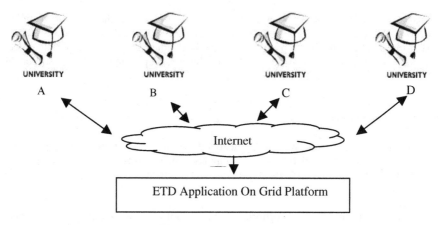

Fig. 1. ETD Infrastructure

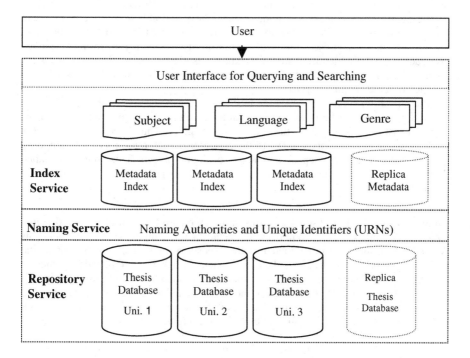

Fig. 2. Services provided by Grid

Accessing digital objects in repositories is accomplished using a repository access protocol (RAP) and the URN of that particular digital object. A URN is sent to a naming server to locate network addresses of repositories containing that digital object. The naming server maintained as part of the infrastructure map the URNs by hashing them. Naming servers may use any other techniques to do the mapping. No guarantee is made that the identified repository will provide the designated digital object. Rather, the user is assured only that the specified repository is where authorized maintainer of repository service has indicated particular digital object resides. The right to download the digital object is depending on the condition of access stated in the key-metadata of that digital object

3.3   Core Services

In the previous section, we have illustrated the overview flow of our proposed architecture. We now define our terminology more formally, and describe the operation of the various services of the system in more details.

Repository Service. ETD repositories should be able to store a variety of traditional types of contents –DF file, raw experimental data, and software – as well as complex multimedia entities that are mixtures of text, images, full-motion video and data. While each form of content has unique aspects, it is desirable to manage this content in a uniform manner. The repository service forms the first layer of functionality in the architecture. It addresses the need for uniformity by treating all forms of content as opaque, uniquely identified structures known as digital objects. Digital objects are identifiable only by their unique names. These unique names are URNs that are registered in the Naming Service.

The repository service provides the mechanism for the deposit, storage, and access to digital objects. A digital object is considered contained within a repository if the URN of that object resolves to the respective repository. Thus, access to the object is only available via a service request to the repository. Each repository must support a simple protocol to allow deposit and access of digital objects. This protocol is called Repository Access Protocol (RAP). RAP is meant to provide only the most basic capabilities and may evolve over time.

Index Service. Each repository contains an index record for each of its stored digital objects. The index record comprises all metadata for a digital object, including its key-metadata, and also other metadata the repository may maintain for that digital object. Notionally, the key-metadata component is a subset of metadata which is invariant for a digital object over repositories. No attempt is made in this paper to delineate how much of the metadata should be included in the key-metadata. The possible elements in the key-metadata are the description of the digital object, condition for access, the date and the time deposit. Figure 3 shows an example of key-metadata in an index server.

Index service provides the mechanism for discovery of digital objects via query. Index service indexes actual or surrogate information of digital object from the repository. Queries submitted to these index servers return result sets that contain URNs of digital objects that match the query. The index service also provides metadata about the content of its indexed information and the capabilities of its query mechanisms. This retrieved metadata is also used by other services, such as the collection service described below.

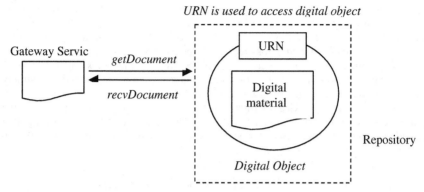

Fig. 3. Accessing to Digital Object in repository

```
<OBJECT>
  <TYPE> text/pdf </TYPE>
  <TITLE>Electronic Theses & Dissertations</TITLE>
  <SUBJECT>Digital Library</SUBJECT>
  <KEYWORDS>Electronic publishing</KEYWORDS>
  <AUTHOR>Eng Ngah Looi</AUTHOR>
  <DATE>20 June 2003</DATE>
  <TIME>1400</TIME>
  <ACCESS>public</ACCESS>
</OBJECT>
```

Fig. 4. Example of key metadata

Index Mining Service. The index mining service is an independent mechanism for introducing structure into a distributed information space. It works as an enhance service for our ETD framework. The index mining service provides the mechanisms for aggregation of access to resources into meaningful collection. It helps to define set of digital objects into different collection. These may be all the resources in the repositories or a subset of the total resources. A index mining service create collection by, for example, scanning a set of index services, reading their metadata and applying its collection definition criteria to define which objects indexed by index servers are elements of its defined collections.

Index mining service defines collection membership through criteria rather containment – resources become members of the collection because they conform a set of formal criteria. Such criteria allow dynamic selection of resources from a set of distributed repositories, based on either metadata about those resources or the content within the resources themselves. There is no fixed notion of collection definition criteria. One example of a collection definition criterion is subject, which may be determined by reading a controlled vocabulary metadata field derived some natural language analysis.

The life cycle of collections can be either stable or created in response to short-term, yet important needs. Physical location of resources, which is relatively static, is unrelated to their membership in a collection – the resources that are members of a collection maybe distributed across multiple repositories. A single digital object may exist in multiple collections, which are defined by multiple index mining services under separate administration. A static and degenerate example of collection is simply a list of resource identifiers, for instance, URNs.

The index mining service facilitates resource discovery that is tailored to the characteristics of the collection. It acts as a distributed metadata repository that provide efficient resource discovery according to the management and administration of digital objects in the collection.

Gateway Service. Entry services or gateways provide human-centered entry points to the functionality of the digital library. The main purpose of this service is to present distributed repositories to the user as a single entry. Each entry gateway uses the information provided by one or more index mining services to permit search for and access to digital objects within those collections. User interface service also use information provided by index mining service and index service to make query routing decisions based on factors such as content, cost, performance and the like. Thus, this entry service provides an easy mechanism for users (through the browser of their choice) to gain access to variety of repository services in a consistent manner.

Naming Service. The naming service maps URNs to network resources at which the corresponding digital objects are available. It is intended to be a means of universal basic access to registered objects. Digital objects are identified by globally unique names –URNs – that are registered with the naming server. The naming service is able to resolve a URN to one or more physical locations. Since a URN is just a string, it can be mapped to an actual repository by any of several mechanisms. Repository names are not actual network addresses; they must first map to network locations.

A URN is presumed to have two logical components, a local naming authority name and an identifier unique to that naming authority. For example, there may be a naming authority named "utm", which will authorizes other naming authorities within the "utm" domain. Thus, the name "utm.ee" might be assigned to the authority responsible for naming the electronic theses archive of Electrical Engineering faculty. Particular naming authorities may follow their own conventions for assigning semantic or non-semantic strings to their objects. For example, "utm.ee" may follow a proposed convention for its theses and dissertations, and give each of the corresponding objects a local URN, "ee-ae97093". The full unique URN for this digital object would be:

<URN:ASCII:ETHESES-v.3.0:utm.ee/ee-ae97093>
<URN:ASCII:ETHESES-v.3.0:utm.ee/ee-ae97093/theses.pdf>
<URN:ASCII:ETHESES-v.3.0:utm.ee/ee-ae97093/theses.ppt>

where the "/" separates the naming authority name from the string unique to that authority. Here "ETHESES-v.3.0" is supposed to suggest that this is an URN for electronic theses archive and also that some particular naming convention (v.3.0) is used by the naming authority. The string "ee-ae97093/theses.pdf" might be the unique local part of URN of the digital object corresponding to the Adobe Portable Document format of this work; "ee-ae97093" is the URN for PowerPoint representation.

Hence, any of the services would be able to determine the location(s) of an object through resolution via the naming service. Any of the services would be able to access any digital object in any repository in a standard manner through URN.

4   Discussion

The basic architectural that described in the previous section has stood up well, and provides a demonstrable model of how a collaborative ETD system should be designed. In this section, we will address and discuss the issues and challenges that occur while building this collaborative ETD system.

4.1   Issues & Challenges

Accessibility/Availability. The ETD system provides students/ universities with the option of distribution choices, including the option of restricting access to certain campus or denying access altogether. With our proposed framework, all the universities will gather together in a common platform thus provide maximum access to the students or even researchers to locate information from various universities in Malaysia. However, access control of the information is very important and this depends on the university whether they want to release their intellectual property or want to make it available for public.

Scalability. The most important scaling issue in this system is the storage of the ETDs. It is imperative that new members will start participating in this system thus increasing the storage requirements. However, the proposed framework is designed to be scalable. With the networked infrastructure and the use of technology that is modular and distributed within the universities, it is capable to handle the rising of the e-documents submitted by the students. Each university can store and archive their e-documents on their local machine and make it accessible through the grid platform later. This no only eases the management of database but also help to build up a collaborative community among the universities in Malaysia.

Searchability. Ability to search plays a central role in helping users find information in ETD system since the system that we proposed rely on distributed architecture: components and collections are located in separate places, coupled with a heterogeneous set of search engines. Consequently, students or even researchers are led to consult more than one search engine. While it would be helpful to automate this process, there are no widely accepted standards for submitting queries to multiple search engines simultaneously. Thus, there is a need for a simple, distributed retrieval system that can route searches to multiple search engines. Hence, federated search plays an important role to mediate the user queries to multiple heterogeneous search engines. This federated search determines how the query should be formulated and how to deliver it to each search engine specified by the users.

On the other hand, as in Malaysia, theses or dissertations are submitted either in Malay or in English. A powerful search engine, which is embedded with multilingual retrieval and query translation, is needed in order to retrieve the information from various universities with both languages. Multilingual retrieval and queries translation that embedded in the search engines makes resources in other languages more accessible and thus overcome the language barriers within the community.

Security. As the collaborative ETD framework is mainly for University or Higher Institutional Organization, policies typically have to be defined in order to control the access of information and resources. In our proposed grid infrastructure, any grid information service must hence incorporate security mechanisms so that it can comply with these policies. The aggregation of the information versus different repositories pose interesting security issues as these services make available to others information obtained from information provider(s). This distribution of information must be performed in a fashion consistent with the policy of the underlying provider(s).

Furthermore, security issues also arise with respect to the registration protocol. We need to ensure that registration messages are authentic and control which registration events are accepted and which are denied.

Archiving & Preservation. The most serious issue that prevents the students and universities to participate in the electronic theses and dissertations is their doubt on the archival stability and long-term sustainability. There is no assurance to ensure them that the electronic theses or dissertations will be accessible even ten years in the future. However, there are several strategies for addressing this problem. One of the solutions is to emphasize the importance in adopting the non-proprietary standards such as SGML, JPEG, VRML, and PDF as the document formats for the completed ETDs.

If the Adobe's Portable Document Format (PDF) is the final format representation for the completed ETDs, the ETD system need to have the ability to convert any format of the documents to PDF files. Though there are minor complexities related to fonts and special formatters like LaTeX, these can be worked out by investment in the Adobe software. If SGML is the final format representation for the completed ETDs, there are various solutions. One to use a standard editor that allows the students to insert tags like what is done by many HTML authors. The ETD system also can have conversion software running that enables the students to automatically make 100% accurate conversion to SGML.

Intellectual Property Rights. Intellectual property rights of electronic theses and dissertations remain with the author. However, students assign rights to the university to publish the electronic version online. For a university to participate in our ETD framework, it must agree to just three conditions. First, all document metadata is to be freely distributable. This allows index service to replicate indexing data without constraint. Second, each university agrees to state its policy on intellectual property rights (IPR), which is displayed by the gateway service when a reader accesses a thesis. Finally, the university certifies that the documents it deposits to repository service meet its (local) selection policy. Otherwise, we set no conditions. This flexibility allows participation by sites that charge for theses either individually or by subscription. These conditions are stated informally. We could have set stricter or more formal conditions with a contract, but this would have raised a barrier for participation far too high. For most, if not all our members, the expense of having a corporate attorney examine and execute the contract would have outweighed the benefits of joining.

5 Conclusion

Many theses and dissertations are now moldering, unread in the libraries. In order to make these scholarly collections more visible and more accessible to a broader community of students and researchers, these theses and dissertations have to be digitalized. Students, faculties or even universities have to start thinking of text on the digitalized documents rather than words on paper.

Thus, in our paper, we outline the infrastructure that can be applied to develop the ETD system in a heterogeneous compute environment. These preliminary exposures help us to continue the work on expanding the functionality of our ETD framework and apply its concepts in more advances research in digital archive architecture.

We plan to further expand the scope of our framework in the future, with the possibility of including technical materials from other disciplines. A major theme of this research will also be extensibility and interoperability of security mechanism for digital data and repositories. Finally, our goal is not only the mere publication of research work, but to build a rich and open communication channel for the global scientific community.

References

1. Hussein Suleman, Edward A.Fox, "*Towards Universal Accessibility of ETDs: Building the NDLTD Union Archive*"
2. Christian Weisser, John Baker, Janice R.Walker, "Electronic Theses and Dissertations: Problems and Possibilities"
3. Yong-Hyo, Lee, Yong-Soon, Kim, Dae-Joon, Hwang, "Developing Integrated Theses and Dissertations System and Improving University information Infrastructure: The Korean Experience"
4. ETD-ms: an Interoperability Metadata Standard for Electronic Theses and Dissertations – version1, [Online] Available: http://www.ndltd.org/standards/metadata/current.html
5. Carl Logoze, David Fielding, D-Lib Magazine, Nov 1998 "Defining Collections in Distributed Digital Libraries"
6. The Guide for Electronic Theses and Dissertations [online] Available: http://etdguide.org/content/
7. Edward A.Fox, Gail McMillan, John L. Eaton, 1999, "The Evolving Genre of Electronic Theses and Dissertations"
8. Edward A. Fox, John L. Eaton, Gail McMillan, Neill A. Kipp, Laura Weiss, Emilio Arce, Scott Guyer, 1996 "National Digital Library of Theses & Dissertations"
9. James Powell, Edward A. Fox, 1998, "Multilingual Federated Search Across Heterogeneous Collections"

10. Matthew G. Kirschenbaum, Edward A. Fox, "Electronic Theses & Dissertation in Humanities"
11. Heinz Stockinger, "Distributed Database Management Systems and the Data Grid"
12. Karl Czaikowski, Steven Fitzgerald, Ian Foster, Carl Kesselman, "Grid Information Services for Distributed Resource Sharing"
13. Wolfgang Hoschek, Javier Jaen-Martinez, Asad Samar, Heinz Stockinger, Kurt Stockinger, "Data Management in an International Data Grid Project"
14. Sandra Payette, Christophe Blanchi, Carl Lagoze, Edward A. Overly, 1995 "Interoperability for Digital Objects and Repositories"
15. Robert Kahn, Robert Wilensky, 1995, "A Framework for Distributed Digital Object Services"

MAG2DL: A Framework for Information Retrieval and Integration of Distributed Geographic Digital Libraries

Jihong Guan[1,2], Shuigeng Zhou[4], Junpeng Chen[1], Xiaolong Chen[1],
Yang An[1,2], Fuling Bian[2], and Zhiyong Peng[3]

[1]School of Computer,
[2]Spatial Information and Digital Engineering Research Center,
[3]State Key Lab of Software Engineering,
Wuhan University, Wuhan, 430079, China
jhguan@wtusm.edu.cn
flbian@yahoo.com
zypeng@public.wh.hb.cn
[4]Dept. of Computer Science & Engineering,
Fudan University, Shanghai, 200433, China
sgzhou@fudan.edu.cn

Abstract. Geographic Digital Libraries (GDLs) are Digital Libraries (DLs) that provide an infrastructure for organizing, structuring, creating, storing, distributing, retrieving, and processing geo-referenced information, which is inherently heterogeneous with many distinct formats and collecting procedures. The standardization of GDLs involves not only the organization of data, but also issues related to the retrieval and integration of these data. In this paper, we propose the MAG2DL framework for information retrieval and integration of distributed GDLs by using mobile agent and GML technologies. Mobile agents are used for distributed information retrieval to benefit distributed computing in (mobile) Internet context, and GML is used to solve the heterogeneities of various geographic information sources.

Keywords: Digital libraries, geographic data, mobile agent, GML, framework.

1 Introduction

Conventional libraries usually support three main functions [1]: collection, organization & representation, and access & retrieval. Digital Libraries (DLs) provide not only the above functions but also an infrastructure for organizing, structuring, creating, storing, distributing, retrieving, and processing multimedia digital information. Owing to the wide variety of users and the distribution and heterogeneity in nature of the stored information, DL technology is beginning to support major increases in both the availability and usefulness of geo-spatial information [2]. For example, the Alexandria DL [3] and Digital Earth [4] projects develop DL prototypes for geo-referenced information.

Geographic Digital Libraries (GDLs) are DL that can handle geo-referenced data, which describe geographic entities through three components [5]: geographic location (the position and shape of an entity on the Earth's surface); descriptive attributes

T.M.T. Sembok et al. (Eds.): ICADL 2003, LNCS 2911, pp. 351–364, 2003.

(conventional data defining the properties and features of the entity); and time (date or period related to the capture or to the validity of the data). Geo-referenced data is inherently heterogeneous with many distinct formats and collecting procedures. The standardization of GDLs involves not only the organization of data, but also issues related to the retrieval and integration of these data. These problems are inherent to DLs, but are aggravated in the case of geo-referenced data.

In the last decade, from the point of DL and GDL view, many efforts have been engaged in handling distributed and heterogeneous repositories to facilitate user's information retrieval and integration across diverse geographic data resources. ScholOnto [6] shows an ontology-based DL representational and technical infrastructure with a 'living' semantic network of concepts and discourse. [7] outlines a metadata architecture that addresses a broad class of the needs found in a distributed, heterogeneous, proxy-based architecture - Stanford InfoBus DL. [8] presents an operational, object-oriented, hierarchical metadata framework for searching, indexing, and retrieving distributed geographic information services. A dynamic mediation infrastructure [9] allows mediators to have a set of modules implementing a particular mediation function each. FEDORA [10] architecture supports the aggregation of mixed distributed data into complex objects and associated multiple content disseminations with these objects. [11] copes with interoperability among heterogeneous resources by using distributed object technology. Since XML is becoming the de facto standard of Web data exchange, a lot of research work has been conducted on modeling, querying and managing semi-structured and non-standard data to handle the heterogeneities in information integration [12-17]. Despite these fruitful achievements, to meet with various users' information needs, current GDL still needs further extending of their interoperability, flexibility for information sharing and exchange under (mobile) Internet environment.

In this paper, we propose a framework for information retrieval and integration of distributed GDLs by using mobile agent and GML (Geography Markup Language) technologies. We term this framework **MAG2DL**, that is, **M**obile **A**gent and **G**ML based **GDL**s. Here, mobile agents are used for distributed information retrieval to overcome the limitations of traditional distributed computing paradigms in (mobile) Internet context, and GML is used to solve the heterogeneities of various geographic information sources. The project is under the cooperation of Spatial Information and Digital Engineering Research Center, State Key Lab of Software Engineering, and School of Computer at Wuhan University, aimed to setup a platform for searching geographic information services, retrieving and integrating geographic data from distributed GDLs.

Mobile agent is a recently developed computing paradigm that offers a full-featured infrastructure for development and management of network-efficient applications [18-24]. Agent-based computing can benefit Internet (especially mobile Internet) applications by providing asynchronous task execution and more dynamics, supporting flexible and extensible cooperation, reducing communication bandwidth, enhancing real time abilities and higher degree of robustness, and enabling off-line processing and disconnected operations. As a new and promising distributed computing paradigm, mobile agents have been employed in many applications, including information retrieval [19], Web search [20], electronic commerce [21], network management [22], and personalization Web services [23], etc. Here we introduce mobile agents to access and share geographic information in GDLs.

GML is the instantiation of XML in geo-spatial domain [25]; it provides common grammar for encoding and exchanging geo-spatial content. Recently increasing research has been seen to employ GML in GIS applications. [26] reports a prototype that wraps and visualizes geographic data in distributed environment by using XML technology;   [27] introduces a XML-based mediator for heterogeneous GIS query; [28] gives a XML-based approach to integrating GIS and tourism information; [29] proposes a GML format to represent moving object in mobile environment; and [30-31] presents the specification of a spatial query language over GML and compares three query processing approaches. Representing map by using GML has some merits, such as better quality map, better query capability, editable map, customizable map styling, etc. [25]. So it is natural to utilize GML for integrating geo-referenced data in GDLs.

The rest of this paper is organized as follows. Section 2 presents the MAG2DL framework; Section 3 gives techniques of geographic information integration and heterogeneity handling in MAG2DL; Section 4 concludes the paper.

2 The MAG2DL Framework

2.1   Overview of the Framework

The proposed MAG2DL framework is composed of client sites, sever sites, (mobile) Internet or Intranet connecting these sites, and mobile agents roaming on the Internet/Intranet for retrieving information on behalf of the clients. A client site is referred to as a client machine, which can be a desktop or laptop PC, a PDA or a mobile phone, used for query submission and results presentation. A server site is also a MAG2DL server, which provides geographic information services for local or remote users. Figure 1 is an overview of the MAG2DL framework.

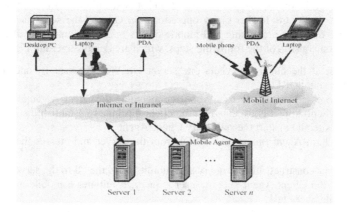

Fig. 1. MAG2DL overview

A user submits a query from a client machine to a server *via* web browser. The query is analyzed and optimized by the server, from which one or multiple mobile agents are created and dispatched to accomplish the query task cooperatively. Each mobile agent along with its sub-task travels from one remote server to another to gather the related information. Retrieved information is then taken back to the original site after the mobile agent finishes its mission. All returned information is further merged there and presented to the user. The servers also provide docking facility for mobile agents in case they cannot travel back to the destinations promptly due to network problems.

2.2   The Client Site

A user can access to MAG2DL system *via* a client machine or a local server as shown in Figure 1. First, a user should log in one server in the system. Then the server returns a Web (HTML) page to the client, in which there is a Java Applet termed as Client-Applet composed of one Mobile Agent Environment (MAE), one stationary agent and one mobile agent. The Client-Applet is executed at the client site to establish the Mobile Agent Environment (MAE) for the client and to start the stationary agent encoded in the Client-Applet. We call this stationary agent 'Client-Agent', which is responsible for the following two tasks:

- To obtain the Data Sources Description Information (DSDI) from the visited server. DSDI is something like the global data dictionary of MAG2DL, which includes all data sources' metadata (e.g., names, URLs and schema of each data source). Client-Agent gets DSDI from the stationary agent of the visited server. At each server, DSDI is maintained by the local stationary agent.
- To create the Query Interface (QI) in Web browser with which the user submits queries and gets retrieved data.

Thus when the query environment is set up at the client site, QI is only what a user can see, while Client-Agent, mobile agent and its execution environment are at the backend. A user starts his/her query operations *via* QI, and the server accessed will take charge of query processing and mobile agents manipulation. Typically, a whole query session consists of the following steps, which are demonstrated in Figure 2.

1)   A user at the client site visits one server *via* Web browser by specifying the server site's URL.
2)   The accessed server returns a Web page including the Client-Applet.
3)   The Client-Applet is executed on the client machine to establish the MAE at the client site and to start the stationary Client-Agent.
4)   The Client-Agent obtains the DSDI from the server and creates the QI for the user.
5)   The user constructs his/her query and submits it *via* the QI to the server.
6)   When the Client-Agent gets the user's query, it initiates a mobile agent to take over the query task.
7)   The mobile agent with user's query task leaves the client site and migrates to the server to which the client first visited for further query processing.
8)   After the query task is completed at the server site, the mobile agent migrates back to the client site and returns the results to the user *via* web browser.

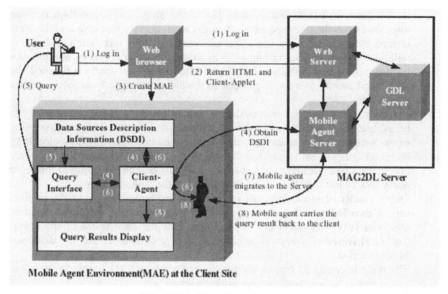

Fig. 2. The Client Site of MAG2DL

2.3   The Server Site

A server in MAG2DL at least consists of three main components: Web server (or simply WSever), GDL server (GSever), and Mobile Agent server (MAServer). WServer is the interface for a user to connect to MAG2DL server, and it is responsible for providing Client-Applet to the user. GServer is composed of GDL repositories, and spatial query processing engine that provides support for local query processing. MAServer is the key component of MAG2DL server, which provides the facilities to support mobile agents to carry out query processing. A MAServer contains four stationary agents: Local Services Agent (LSA), Query Optimization Agent (QOA), Querying and Wrapping Agent (QWA) and Mediation and Transformation Agent (MTA). Figure 3 illustrates the architecture of a typical MAG2DL server and the procedure of how a query task is completed by using mobile agent and GML technologies. The procedure includes the following steps:

1)   The query task is transferred to QOA for optimization. After optimization QOA creates a query plan, which includes a set of sub-queries, sites on which the sub-queries are executed respectively and the execution sequences of these sub-queries. QOA returns the result of query optimization to the main query agent. Main query agent then decides whether additional mobile agents are requested to carry out sub-queries processing.

2)   If the query involves only local data, the main query agent will go on to finish the query task itself without necessity of spawning other mobile agents. The main query agent assigns the query task to QWA, who is in charge of retrieving data and wrapping the results into a standard GML document.

3) If the query involves data of multiple server sites, and the sub-queries are requested to evaluate in sequence, then the main query agent or a mobile agent created by the main query agent will take over the query task. The mobile agent will be dispatched out according to its itinerary arranged previously, and the sub-queries will be accomplished one by one. After the last sub-query is finished, the dispatched mobile agent will go back to the client site directly or to its original server site.

4) Otherwise, if the query involves data of multiple sites, and the sub-queries can be evaluated in parallel, and the local site and other remote sites corresponding to the sub-queries are connected, then multiple mobile agents will be cloned by the main query agent to execute the sub-queries in parallel so as to gain better efficiency. The main query agent may join the mobile agents group to finish the query task or just take the role of coordinator of the multiple agents.

5) Query results obtained from all related sites are brought back to the original server, then MTA at the server site will do data integration and transformation, and one SVG [32] document is transformed as the final result of the query. Technical issues of wrapping and mediation of geographical data are discussed in next section.

6) The main query agent carries the final query result in SVG format to the client site, which is presented to the user via browser.

Another function of the MAG2DL server is to provide the docking mechanism for mobile agents when the connection between the current site and the destination site of agent migration is disrupted. LSA will take the role of deactivation and activation of mobile agent's when such a situation happens.

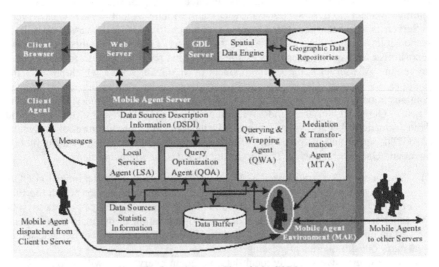

Fig. 3. The Server Site of MAG2DL

2.4   Mobile Agent Environment

Mobile Agent Environment (MAE) exists at both the client sites and the server sites. It provides an environment for mobile agents' creating, executing, dispatching and migrating. Besides the mobile agents, MAE is composed of the following functional modules: Mobile Agent Manager (MAM), Mobile Agent Transportation (MAT), Mobile Agent Naming (MAN), Mobile Agent Communication (MAC), and Mobile Agent Security (MAS).

- MAM, the heart of MAE, is responsible for all kinds of management of mobile agents, providing a full-fledged environment for agent creating and executing, basic functions to make mobile agent migrate precisely to its destination, functions for agent scheduling locally, support for agent's remote management.
- MAT controls the transferring of mobile agents, *i.e.*, sending and receiving mobile agents to and from remote sites.
- MAN manages mobile agents' naming service, which provides the mechanism of tracing mobile agents.
- MAC serves mobile agents communication, which serves as the protocol of communication, collaboration, and events transmission among agents.
- MAS provides a two-facet security mechanism. First, it is responsible for distinguishing users and authenticating their mobile agents to protect server' resources from being illegally accessed or even maliciously attacked. Second, it ensures mobile agents not be tampered by malicious hosts or other agents.

3 Geographic Information Integration Based on GML

3.1   The Integration Scheme

A popular integration method nowadays is mediator based approach, which usually adopts a three-layer architecture, *i.e.*, the bottom layer is data repositories with wrapper, the middle layer is mediator supporting query and result transformation between repositories and applications, and the top layer is the interface for users and applications. In MAG2DL, mobile agents are used to accomplish query tasks on behalf of users, which introduces a new approach for geographical information integration based on mobile agent and GML. Our integration scheme adopts a four-layer architecture as shown in Figure 4. The four layers are Client layer, Mobile Agent layer, Mediator layer and Wrapper layer respectively.

Here, GML is adopted as the common format of geographical information exchanging. Stationary agents at server sites take the roles of mediator and wrapper. That is to say, QWA takes the role of wrapper, and QOA and MTA together act as the mediator. Figure 5 illustrates the procedure of a user's query being processed at the server site with the mediator and wrapper.

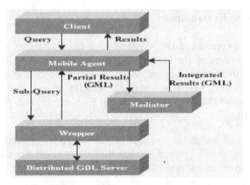

Fig. 4. A four-layer integration architecture

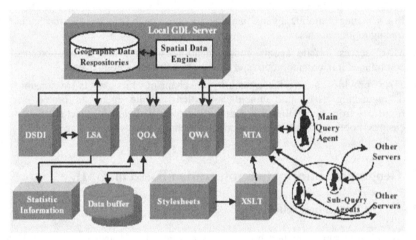

Fig. 5. Integration framework based on mobile agent and GML

3.2   From Geographic Data Files to GML Documents

Conventional spatial data of geographic information is usually stored in files (e.g. ArcInfo's shapefile), and aspatial data is stored in relational database or database files. To integrate distributed geographic information, we have to first transform spatial and aspatial data files into GML documents. Considering there are a lot of researches on transforming relational data into XML documents [33-36], we will not discuss the issue of transforming aspatial data into GML here.

GML is based on the abstract model of geography defined by OGC, which describes the world in geographic entities called features. A feature is a set of geometries and properties; while geometries include points, lines, curves, surfaces and polygons; and properties are the descriptions of name, type, and value. A feature collection is a collection of features. In what follows, to illustrate the transformation process from spatial data to GML document, suppose the spatial data is stored in

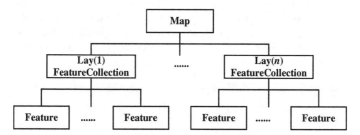

Fig. 6. GML document hierarchy

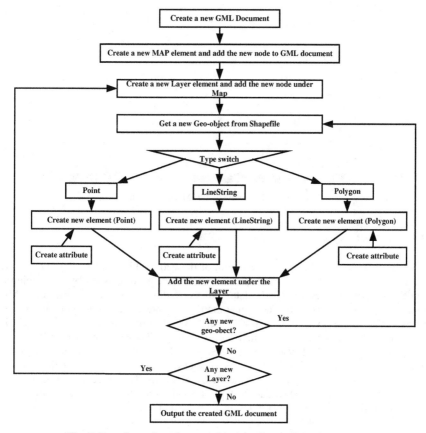

Fig. 7. Transformation of geographic data files to GML documents

Arcinfo's Shapefiles, we define the destination GML document schema according to the hierarchy as shown in Figure 6. Here, Map corresponds to the root of a GML document, which refer to any map of real world. Under map, there is one or multiple layers, each of which corresponds to a specific FeatureCollection. A

FeatureCollection indicates a set of similar features, such as rivers, roads *etc*, and each feature has its own elements and (or) attributes. Figure 7 illustrate the flowchart of transforming Shapefiles to GML document. We implement the transformation procedure in agents. Figure 8 gives a transformed GML document (parial) from the Shapefile of a USA state map.

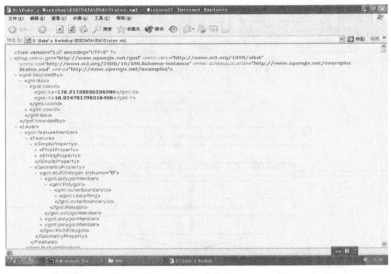

Fig. 8. A transformed GML document

3.3   GML to SVG

GML is concerned with the representation of the geographic data content. Of course we can also use GML to make maps. This might be accomplished by developing a rendering tool to interpret GML data, however, this would go against the GML thought of standardization and separation of content and presentation. In our framework, we use SVG to publish web map. SVG document is generated from GML document and sent to client terminal for displaying. Transformation from GML to SVG is accomplished by using XSLT (eXtensible Style-sheet Language Transformations) [37]. With XSLT, it is very easy to write a style-sheet that locates and transforms GML elements into other XML elements. The procedure of generating a spatial web map from GML data to SVG format with XSLT is shown in Figure 9. And a stylesheet sample is also given in Figure 10. To facilitate stylesheet defintion, we implemented a tool to edit stylesheet. At every server, different stylesheets are prepared for different requirements of devices and users. In our framework, mobile agent from the client brings information about the client devices, and appropriate stylesheet catering for such king of devices is selected, and later used to generate the SVG document.

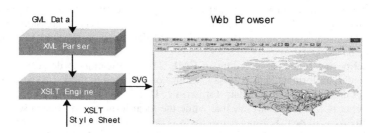

Fig. 9. The scheme of generating SVG map from GML with XSLT

Fig. 10. A style sheet sample

3.4   Heterogeneity Handling

In reality, information from any two geographic resources may adopt different models or/and are developed under different software environment or packages, and data may have different structures and semantics, these are the heterogeneous issues that amount to the major challenge to distributed GDLs accessing and sharing over Internet. To handle the heterogeneity for MAG2DL, common data schema, common data format and common query expression are used.

The common schema provides definitions of all the features and feature collections accessible to users. It is based on the OpenGIS specification. So it can be understandable to all data objects in the system. The common data format is based on the Spatial Archive and Interchange Format (SAIF), which uses an object-oriented approach and is possible to model most kinds of spatial data. In the common data format, geo-spatial data are structures as objects and are organized according to a class hierarchy described in OpenGIS [38].

When the common schema is adopted, the common query expression is practicable. Based on the common query expression, a query has three major parts: an input list, an output list and a search condition. Sub-query transferring between different server sites is based on the common query expression. The processing of a query implies two transformation procedures: transformation from common query expression to local query expression, and transformation from local data schema (format) to common data schema (format).

We define the schemas according to GML 2.0 specification to describe the data schema and data format. That is to say, we use one schema to represent the common data schema and the common data format, i.e. DSDI as we described in section 2. This schema is called Global-Schema, while the local information of each server can be described by a Local-Schema respectively. Data wrapping is in deed the procedure for data transformed from Local-Schema to Global-Schema. And the transformation from GML documents to SVG documents of query results can be seen as the transformation between different schemas. Global-Schema can be obtained by merging all Local-schemas at different server sites. The key issues while merging is to resolve semantic conflicts.

Data wrapping and integration, GML to GML and GML to SVG transformation all essentially amount to transformation between different schemas, i.e. transformation of elements and attributes from one schema to another according to mapping rules. The mapping rules are described by XSLT. Roughly, we can classify the mapping rules between the elements and attributes of two schemas into four types: *1:1* mapping, *1:n* mapping, *n:1* mapping and m:*n* mapping.

1:1 **mapping** is the simplest and mostly used mapping. It is used when elements and attributes in two schemas have different names but the same semantics.

1:n **mapping** rule is used when one element or attribute in a schema semantically corresponds to several elements or attributes in another schema and the transformation is from the former to the latter. XSLT provides the mechanism for mapping XML elements or attributes and analyzing the text content of an element or an attribute to separate it into several smaller elements or attributes with the support of XPath.

n:1 **mapping** is just the opposite of *1:n* mapping. *n:1* mapping rule is used when several elements or attributes in a schema semantically correspond to one element or attribute in another schema.

m:n **mapping** is much more complicated. It is used when transformation between schemas is related to the situation that certain complete semantic information is distributed over multiple elements or attributes in schemas.

4   Conclusion

Internet has greatly changed the ways of data accessing, sharing and disseminating. Digital Libraries (DLs) provide an infrastructure for organizing, structuring, creating, storing, distributing, retrieving, and processing multimedia digital information. Geographic Digital Libraries (GDLs) are DL that can handle geo-referenced data, which are inherently heterogeneous with many distinct formats and collecting procedures. The standardization of GDL involves not only the organization of data, but also issues related to the retrieval and integration of these data. In this paper, we propose the MAG2DL framework for information retrieval and integration in distributed GDLs by using mobile agent and GML technologies. MAG2DL brags off the advantages of these two different technologies. Mobile agents are used to overcome the limitations of traditional distributed computing paradigms in (mobile) Internet context for distributed information retrieval, and GML is used for integrating and heterogeneity-handling of various geographic information sources.

References

[1]   H.M. Gladney, E.A. Fox, Z. Ahmed, R. Ashany, N.J. Belkin, M. Zemankova. Digital library: gross structure and requirements: report from a March 1994 Workshop. In: J.L. Schnase, J.J. Leggett, R.K. Furuta, T. Metcalfe (eds.): Proc. Of Digital Libraries'94, 1st Annual Conf. On the Theory and Practice of Digital Libraries. College Station, TX: pp.101-107. 1994 Electronic proceedings at URL: http://atg1.wustl.edu/dl94.

[2]   R.R. Larson. Geographic information retrieval and spatial browsing. In L.C. Smith, M. Gluck (eds.): Geographic Information Systems and Libraries: Patrons, Maps, and Spatial Information. University of Illinois, Champaign, IL, 1996, pp. 81–124.

[3]   J. Frew, M. Freeston, N. Freitas, L. Hill, G. Janee, K. Lovette, R. Nideffer, T. Smith, Q. Zheng. The Alexandria Digital Library architecture. Int. J. on Digital Libraries, 2000(2), pp. 259–268.

[4]   The Alexandria Digital Earth Modeling System (ADEPT). http://www.Alexandria.ucsb.edu/adept/proposal.pdf.

[5]   J.L. Oliveira, M.A. Goncalves, C.B. Mederios. A framework for designing and implementing the user interface of a geographic digital library. Int. J. on Digital Libraries, 1999(2), pp. 190–206.

[6]   S.B. Shum, E. Motta, J. Domingue. ScholOnto: an ontology-based digital library server for research documents and discourse. Int. J. on Digital Libraries, 2000(3), pp. 237–248.

[7]   M. Baldonado, C.C.K. Chang, L. Gravano, A. Paepcke. The Stanford Digital Livrary metadata architecture. Int. J. on Digital Libraries, 1997(2).

[8]   M.H. Tsou. An operational metadata framework for searching, indexing, and retrieving distributed geographic information services on the Internet. In M. Egenhofer, D. Mark (eds.): Geographic Information Science (GIScience 2002). LNCS 2478, pp. 313–332.

[9]   S. Melnik, H. Garcia-Molina, A. Pacepcke. A mediation infrastructure for digital library services. Technical report, Stanford University, 2000.

[10] S. Payette, C. Lagoze. Flexible and extensible digital object and repository architecture (FEDORA). In Poec. Of the 2nd European Conf. On Research and Advanced Technology for Digital Libraries. 1999, pp. 41–59.

[11] A. Paepcke, S.B. Cousina, H. Garcia-Molina, S.W. Hassan, S.K. Ketchpel, M. Roscheisen, T. Winograd. Using distributed objects for digital library interoperability. Technical report, Stanford University, 1998.

[12] P. Buneman, A. Deutsch, W.C. Tan. A deterministic model for semi-structured data. In Proc. Of the 1999 Intl. Workshop on Query Processing for Semi-Structured Data and Non-Standard Data Formats, January 1999.

[13] C.E. Dyreson, M.H. Bohlen, C.S. Jensen. Capturing and querying multiple aspects of semistructured data. In Proc. Of the 1999 Intl. Conf. VLDB, pp. 290–301, 1999.

[14] J. Powel, E. Fox. Multilingual federated searching across heterogeneous collections. D-lib Magazine. Sep. 1998. http://www.dlib.org/

[15] G. Aloisio, G. Millilo, R.D. Williams. An XML architecture for high performance web-based analysis of remote-sensing archives. Future Generation Computer System. 1999, vol.16, pp. 91–100

[16] A. Rauber. A management of distributed information repositories. Department of Software Technology, Vienna University of Technology, 1999.

[17] I. Papadakis, V. Chrissikopoulos. A digital library framework based on XML. Department of Informatics, University of Piraeus, Greece. 2000.

[18] D. Kotz, R. Gray. Mobile agents and the future of the Internet. *ACM Operating Systems Review,* 1999, 33(3), pp. 7–13.

[19] B. Brewington. Mobile in distributed information retrieval. *Intelligent information agent,* Matthias Klusch (ed.), Springer-Verlag, Berlin, Germany.1999.

[20] K. Kato. An approach to mobile software robots for the WWW. *IEEE Transactions on Knowledge and Data Engineering,* 1999, 11(4), pp. 526–548.

[21] P. Dasgupta. MagNET: Mobile agents for networked electronic trading. *IEEE Transactions on Knowledge and Data Engineering,* 1999, 11(4), pp. 509–525.

[22] A. Sahai, et al. Intelligent agents for a mobile network manager (MNM). http://www.irisa.fr/solidor/doc/ps97/

[23] G. Samaras, C. Panayioyou. A flexible personalization architecture for wireless Internet based on mobile agents. Proceedings of ADBIS 2002, LNCS, vol. 2435, pp. 120–134. 2002.

[24] J. Guan, S. Zhou, A. Zhou. Mobile-agent based distributed Web GIS. Proceedings of 9th International Conference on Cooperative Information Systems (CoopIS'2001). LNCS, Springer-Verlag, 2001, Vol. 2172, 53–66

[25] Geography Markup Language (GML). http://www.opengis.org/techno/specs/00-029/gml.html

[26] J. Zhang, M. Javed, A. Shaheen, L. Gruenwald. Prototype for wrapping and visualizing geo-referenced data in a distributed environment using XML technology. ACM-GIS2000:27–32

[27] I. Zaslavsky, A. Gupta, B. Ludascher, S. Tambawala, Query evaluation and presentation planning within a spatial mediator: extending XML-based mediation to heterogeneous sources of GIS and imagery data. Proceedings of 12th International Workshop on Database and Expert Systems Applications, 2001, 853–855

[28] F. Pühretmair, W. Wöß. XML-based Integration of GIS and Heterogeneous Tourism Information. In Proceedings of CAiSE 2001, pp. 346–358.

[29] A. Garmash, A Geographic XML-based Format for the Mobile Environment. Proceedings of the 34th Hawaii International Conference on System Sciences (HICSS34), IEEE Computer Society, 2001

[30] J. E. Corcoles, P. Gonzales. A Specification of a Spatial Query Language over GML. ACM-GIS 2001, 2002, 112–117

[31] J. E. Corcoles, P. Gonzales. Analysis of different approach alternatives for a spatial query language over GML. ACM-GIS 2002, 2002.

[32] Scalable Vector Graphics (SVG) 1.0 Specification, W3C Work Draft, August 1999, at URL address http://www.w3.org/tr/svg

[33] M. Carey, D. Florescu, Z. Ives, Y. Lu, J. Shanmugasundaram, E. Shekita, S. Subramanian. XPERANTO: Publishing object-relational data as XML. Intl. Workshop on the Web and Databases (WebDB), Dallas, May, 2000.

[34] M. Fernandez, W.C. Tan, D. Suciu. SilkRoute: trading between relations and XML. 9th Intl. World Wide Web Conf. (WWW), Amsterdam, May, 2000.

[35] M. Klettke, H. Meyer. XML and object-relational database systems-enhancing structural mappings based on statistics. Intl. Workshop on the Web and Database (WebDB), Dallas, May, 2000.

[36] G. Kappel, E. Kapsammer, W. Retschitzegger. X-Ray-towards integrating XML and relational database systems. Technical report. Department of Information Systems, Institute of Applied Computer Science, Johannes Kepler University Linz. July, 2000.

[37] XSLT. http://www.w3.org/XSLT

[38] Open GIS Consortium (OGC). http://www.opengis.org/

Digital Libraries in Asian Languages – A TCL Initiative

Md Maruf Hasan, Kazuhiro Takeuchi, Hitoshi Isahara,
and Virach Sornlertlamvanich

Thai Computational Linguistics Laboratory, Communications Research Laboratory
112 Paholyothin Road, Klong 1, Klong Luang, Pathumthani 12120, Thailand
mmhasan@acm.org
{kazuh,isahara}@crl.go.jp
virach@crl-asia.org

Abstract. The Greenstone Digital Library (GSDL) system, developed by the
New Zealand Digital Library (NZDL) Consortium at the University of Waikato
is a suite of open-source software for building and distributing digital library
collections. At the Thai Computational Linguistic (TCL) Laboratory of CRL
Asia Research Center, we plan to implement and host digital libraries in several
major Asian languages. In this paper, we describe our experiences in
implementing Thai and Japanese digital libraries using Greenstone.

1 Introduction

In October 2002, CRL Asia Research Center - the Asia Pacific headquarters of
Japanese Communications Research Laboratory (CRL) is established in Thailand.
The Thai Computational Linguistics (TCL) Laboratory is one of the research
laboratories of CRL Asia Research Center across Asia. With the aim of becoming the
foothold of collaborative research on computational linguistics in Asia, TCL carries
out research in Human Language Technologies, Intelligent Information Infrastructure,
and Open Source Software related to language and knowledge processing. At TCL,
we initiated a project on hosting digital libraries in major Asian languages.

As defined by the Digital Library Federation [1], 'digital libraries are organizations
that provide the resources, including the specialized staff, to select, structure, offer
intellectual access to, interpret, distribute, preserve the integrity of, and ensure the
persistence over time of collections of digital works so that they are readily and
economically available for use by a defined community or set of communities'. We
need efficient digital library (DL) systems which can manage multilingual and
multimedia information to achieve the above goals. We choose Greenstone Digital
Library (GSDL) suite [2], developed by the New Zealand Digital Library (NZDL)
Consortium [3] at the University of Waikato.

GSDL is a suite of open-source software for building and distributing digital
library collections [4]. The main reasons behind choosing GSDL suite are (1) it uses
Unicode [5] and XML-compliant format internally, and (2) it supports indexing of
large collection of information including multimedia [6]. We developed interfaces in
Thai and Japanese for Greenstone. We also aim at developing Greenstone interfaces
for other Asian languages in the near future.

T.M.T. Sembok et al. (Eds.): ICADL 2003, LNCS 2911, pp. 365–372, 2003.

Unlike English, in written Japanese and Thai, words are not delimited with explicit boundaries. Japanese and Thai also have complex morphology and other unique linguistic properties. We are in the process of developing new tools for and integrating existing ones with the GSDL suite for effective processing of information in Asian languages.

We hope to build collections of electronic information in major Asian languages, which have cultural and historical values as well as collections of technical reports and thesis available in the universities and research centers written in the local languages. Our digital libraries will also host multilingual language resources such as parallel aligned corpora. Upon completion of the projects, such digital libraries will become an invaluable one-stop source of digital information ubiquitously available over the Internet for general public and researchers equally. We hope that this initiative will also circumvent digital divide in the Asian region [7].

2   The Greenstone Digital Library System

We choose Greenstone as the digital library suite for many reasons. Some of which are listed below:

- Greenstone runs on almost all popular computing platforms: Windows, Macintosh and popular Linux/Unix platforms. Greenstone can also be easily integrated with the two most popular Web servers: Apache and Microsoft IIS.
- The entire system is well-documented in terms of User's Guide, Installation Guide, Developer's Guide and two active mailing lists for users and developers.
- Greenstone is an open-source software suite which makes intensive use of many open source software behind the scene: for example Apache Web server, GNU database manager, *gdbm*, open-source indexing and retrieval system, *mg* [8], and several other plug-ins and utilities.
- Greenstone is capable of handling multilingual information using Unicode.
- Greenstone uses XML-compliant internal representation.
- Greenstone is capable of handling multilingual information and scalable [9].

The overview of a general greenstone system as described in the GSDL Developer's Guide [10] is summarized as follows:

Two components are central to the design of the GSDL system: "receptionists" and "collection servers." From a user's point of view, a receptionist is the point of contact with the digital library. It accepts user input, typically in the form of keyboard entry and mouse clicks; analyzes it; and then dispatches a request to the appropriate collection server (or servers). This locates the requested piece of information and returns it to the receptionist for presentation to the user. Collection servers act as an abstract mechanism that handle the content of the collection, while receptionists are responsible for the user interface.

As Figure 1 shows, receptionists communicate with collection servers using a defined protocol. The implementation of this protocol depends on the computer configuration on which the digital library system is running. The most common case, and the simplest one, is when there is one receptionist and one collection server, and both run on the same computer. However, CORBA based distributed configuration is also possible [11]. Another notable advantage of using Greenstone is its capability of empowering end-users with the power of building collection over the Internet [12]. Such a feature could be very useful in building linguistic resources collaboratively.

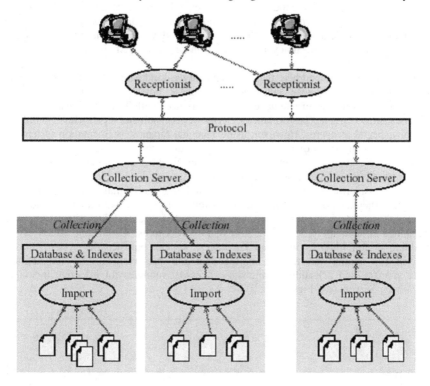

Fig. 1. Overview of a general Greenstone system *(Source: Greenstone Developer's Guide)*

It should also be mentioned here that Greenstone uses a series of open-source software within the above framework. Such software include pre-processing Plug-Ins (e.g., HTML, Image, PDF and MS-Word Plug-Ins) and a set of other programs and scripts (e.g., collection builder, *buildcol.pl* Perl script, *mg* Indexer, *gdbm* GNU database manger and *wget* Internet crawler, etc.

In the following section, we will describe our framework for using Greenstone effectively in processing Asian language information in the context of digital libraries

3   Digital Libraries in Asian Language – The TCL Initiative and Framework

The Greenstone framework is a flexible digital library framework that offers plenty of freedom and advantage to work with multilingual and multimedia information.

However, to use Greenstone for Asian language digital libraries we must at least address two major issues.

Firstly, we must develop the interfaces (c.f., Figure 1, *Receptionists*) for the respective languages. Secondly, we must identify the language specific issues which may interfere with effective indexing and retrieval. For some Asian languages such as Japanese and Thai, where there are no explicit word boundaries, and the morphological structures are complex, we need to develop (or integrate) respective modules to boost the accuracy of indexing and retrieval (c.f. Figure 1, *Collection Server/Indexing*).

It should be mentioned here that a straight forward indexing which may be suitable for English like European languages may cause potentially poor indexing and retrieval results for Asian languages. Our experiences with Thai and Japanese digital libraries show degraded performance in terms of precision and recall when we did not add any special measures. However, using Thai and Japanese segmentation systems in the preprocessing steps of the digital collection, did overcome some of the indexing problems. We assume that integration of proper NLP tools with GSDL core system may further improve the retrieval accuracies.

After considering the above issues, the Asian Language Digital Library Framework at TCL is therefore designed around Greenstone core system with auxiliary modules around the core (c.f., Figure 2). From the overview of a general Greenstone system as explained in Section 2.0, it is imperative that in order to use Greenstone effectively in building digital libraries in Asian languages, we can enhance the system in two stages: (1) adding the native interface for the presentations and interactions: *Receptionists*, and (2) adding linguistic processing modules for effective indexing: *Collection Servers* (c.f. Figure 1 & 2).

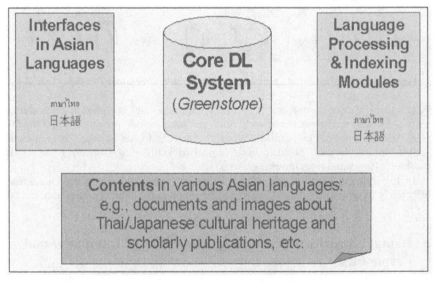

Fig. 2. Overview of TCL digital library framework for Asian languages

We invite the reader's attention to another non-trivial issue of automatic metadata extraction. In order to create rich digital library contents, metadata play crucial roles. At the moment, we have not yet initiated any work in this area. However, we foresee that automatic extraction of metadata in each language and collection is a crucial issue in building large digital libraries for that particular language or collection. It is almost impossible to employ manual labor to create and maintain a large scale digital library using manually annotated metadata. The above framework can essentially accommodate seamless integration of such metadata extraction tools.

4 Current Status and Future Work

At TCL, we developed Thai and Japanese interfaces for the Greenstone suite using the macro language explained in Greenstone Developer's Guide. Figure 3 shows the screenshot of Japanese Digital Library Interface.

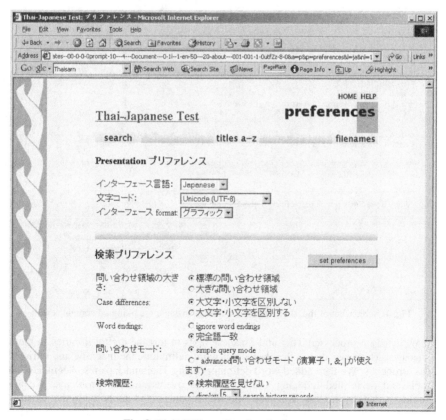

Fig. 3. Digital Library Interface for Japanese

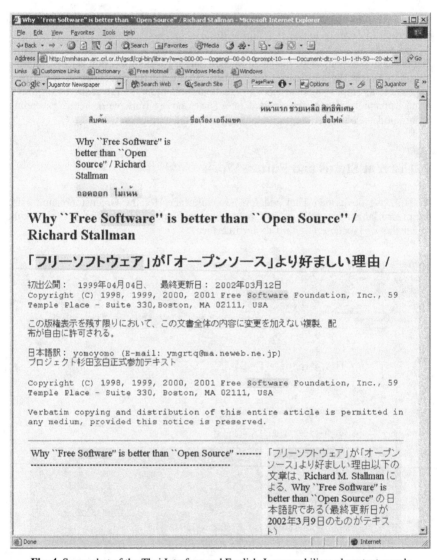

Fig. 4. Screenshot of the Thai Interface and English-Japanese bilingual content search

We used un-processed Thai and Japanese texts to test the digital libraries in these languages. However, due to the absence of word delimiters, the indexing and retrieval was erroneous. We then added word delimiters using Thai and Japanese Segmentation Tools and performed indexing and retrieval to overcome such problems. We are confident that by adding language specific modules and tools with the existing Greenstone suite we will make the GSDL system effectively useable with Asian languages. We are in the process of integrating *Chasen* [13], a Japanese morphological analyzer, and the Thai Segmenter, *Swath* [14] developed at NECTEC with the core GSDL suite.

We are also searching for digital contents (which can be used without violating copyrights) in Asian languages which can be placed under the DL systems at TCL, and can be made available to the general public and researchers. Once the above-mentioned integration task is complete and significant amount of digital contents are acquired, we will make the digital libraries in Asian languages available on the Internet for broader range of users.

The following figure (Figure 4) is a screenshot of the digital library where Thai digital library interface is used with bilingual (English/Japanese) query terms; keywords are highlighted in the retrieved documents.

As for the future work, we are focusing on developing tools which can automate the process of metadata extraction in the context of digital library.

5 Conclusions

We warmly invite the participants of ICADL-2003 and others to join hands with us by providing digital contents in Asian languages and by jointly developing tools for processing those contents under the Digital Library Framework initiated by TCL.

We are especially interested in acquiring digital contents which reflect Asian values, culture and heritage. We are also interested in networking with the universities and research institutes in Asia which can provide us with scholarly digital documents (thesis and technical reports, multilingual corpora and NLP tools, etc.) for making them available publicly through our digital libraries.

Acknowledgements. The first author likes to acknowledge the financial supports from Communications Research Laboratory (CRL), Japan in terms of a visiting fellowship to work at TCL, Thailand. Thanks to Kazuhiro Takeuchi, Thatsanee Charoenporn, Phanicha Phavananun, Woranuch Wasinanont and Nartdanu Suttinon for their helps in translation and proof-reading in Japanese and Thai.

We also thank and acknowledge the continuing help and support we are receiving from the GSDL development team. Among them, Michael Dewsnip deserves special thanks for his timely reply of our e-mail queries with the right answers.

References

[1]   Digital Library Federations: http://www.diglib.org/
[2]   Greenstone Digital Library Suite: http://www.greenstone.org/
[3]   New Zealand Digital Library Consortium: http://www.nzdl.org/
[4]   itten, I.H., David Bainbridge and Stefan J. Boddie (2001), Open Source Digital Library Software. http://www.dlib.org/dlib/october01/witten/10witten.html
[5]   Unicode Home Page: http://www.unicode.org/
[6]   New Zealand Digital Library music library
       http://nzdl2.cs.waikato.ac.nz/cgi-bin/gwmm?c=meldex&a=page&p=coltitle

[7]   itten, I.H., Loots, M., Trujillo, M.F. and Bainbridge, D. (2001) "The promise of digital libraries in developing countries." Comm. ACM, Vol. 44, No. 5, pp. 82–85.
http://www.acm.org/pubs/articles/journals/cacm/2001-44-5/p82-witten/p82-witten.pdf

[8]   Witten, I.H., Moffat, A. and Bell, T.C. (1999) Managing Gigabytes: Compressing and Indexing Documents and Images. Morgan Kaufmann, San Francisco, CA.
http://www.cs.mu.oz.au/mg/

[9]   aynter, G.W., Witten, I.H., Cunningham, S.J. and Buchanan, G. (2000) "Scalable browsing for large collections: a case study." Proceedings of the Fifth ACM Conference on Digital Libraries, San Antonio, TX, pp. 215–223.
http://www.acm.org/pubs/articles/proceedings/dl/336597/p215-paynter/p215-paynter.pdf

[10]   ainbridge, D., Dana McKay and Witten I.H., Greenstone Digital Library Developer's Guide, http://flow.dl.sourceforge.net/sourceforge/greenstone/Develop-2.39-en.pdf

[11]   ainbridge, D., Witten, I.H., Buchanan, G., McPherson, J., Jones, S. and Mahoui, A. (2001) "Greenstone: A platform for distributed digital library applications." Proc. European Digital Library Conference, Darmstadt, Germany.
http://www.cs.waikato.ac.nz/~davidb/ecdl01/platform.ps

[12]   Witten, I.H., Bainbridge, D. and Boddie, S.J. (2001) "Power to the people: end-user building of digital library collections." Proc Joint Conference on Digital Libraries, Roanoke, VA, pp. 94–103.
http://www.acm.org/pubs/articles/proceedings/dl/379437/p94-witten/p94-witten.pdf

[13]   Japanese Morphological Analyzer: *Chasen,* http://chasen.aist-nara.ac.jp/

[14]   NECTEC Thai Wordbreak Insertion Service: *Swath*
http://ntl.nectec.or.th/services/wordbreak/

A Knowledge Network Approach for Building Distributed Digital Libraries

Minsoo Lee

Dept of Computer Science and Engineering,
Ewha Womans University,
11-1 Daehyun-Dong, Seodaemoon-Ku, Seoul, Korea 120-750
mlee@ewha.ac.kr

Abstract. The Web is becoming increasingly popular as an infrastructure to efficiently share information. This infrastructure can be used to create a distributed digital library. A distributed digital library can be formed by allowing the digital content to be managed at several different Web sites while pointers to the content can be published on a delegate Web site. This simple scheme protects intellectual property as well as reduces privacy concerns. However, there are several problems that need to be considered when implementing the distributed digital library with current technology. First, the delegate Web site needs a mechanism to be notified from the participating Web sites regarding changes. Second, processing logic such as integration steps and security enforcement procedures should be easily specified and installed in the Web sites. Third, complex relationships among the Web sites in the digital library need to be specified and processed when integration occurs on the delegate Web site. We propose a Knowledge Network approach to implement a distributed digital library that solves such problems. The Knowledge Network is based on an event-trigger-rule model, where each participating Web site includes an extension to process these components. The automatic event notification, rule processing, and flexible trigger modeling of the Knowledge Network effectively supports the creation of the distributed digital library. An example implementation of the distributed digital library is also presented to verify the usefulness of the approach.

1 Introduction

Almost any digital content that you want or need can be found on the Web today. There exist specialized Web sites that deal with news articles, conference publications, art images, pop songs, etc. The amount of content available on the Web is increasing everyday, but we are still not able to make sufficient use of the Web. Although search engines may provide a nice starting point to find information, we often find that the information provided is not what we want or not credible information. Therefore, people mostly look for very popular Web sites that are related to their interest, such as going to amazon.com for books or going to mp3.com for music, and initially use the site to retrieve the desired information or travel to the linked sites.

T.M.T. Sembok et al. (Eds.): ICADL 2003, LNCS 2911, pp. 373–383, 2003.

This form of interaction shows that the Web can be conceived as a collection of digital libraries each with a specialized topic. Each digital library has a credible delegate Web site that provides links to other related Web sites with the same specialized topic. This provides a nice mechanism to cluster relevant Web sites together. It becomes much more easier for the delegate Web site to extract information from the Web sites in the digital library due to the smaller number of Web sites, and also much easier to check the credibility of the Web site content because of the expertise in the specialized topic. Even so, the content is owned and managed by each individual Web site for the purpose of protecting intellectual property rights as well as respecting the individual security restrictions. This kind of concept is what we will refer to in this paper as a distributed digital library.

In order to implement a distributed digital library, we find that a few problems need to be first addressed. First, the content on the Web sites are individually created and managed on each Web site in the digital library and therefore the delegate Web site may miss some important modifications. This would lead to poor information on the delegate Web site which could misguide users. Therefore, other Webs sites need to be able to notify the delegate Web site of such changes. Second, processing logic needs to be easily specified and embedded into the Web sites of the digital library. The delegate Web site needs to be easily populated with processing logic to integrate the changes from source Web sites. Source Web sites may contain processing logic to enforce security constraints before the notifications are sent to the delegate Web site. Third, complex relationships among different source Web sites need to be modeled and processed when integrating changes into the delegate Web site. An example of such a relationship is to only update the delegate Web site once all of the mirrored source Web sites are updated.

Our approach to build a distributed digital library that solves the discussed problems above is based on the concept of a Knowledge Network[1]. Knowledge Networks form an infrastructure among Web sites capable of event-trigger-rule processing. Events represent interesting things that happen on a Web site and can be notified to other Web sites. Rules are a granule of logic that are specified in a high level language and can be executed on the Web sites. Triggers tie events to rules and support modeling of complex relationships among events and rules. The Knowledge Network follows a publish-subscribe model among Web sites, and each Web site in the Knowledge Network includes extensions that can process events, triggers, and rules. The publishing and management utilities for the events, triggers and rules are provided as well. Using the concept of Knowledge Networks, the distributed digital library can be implemented by interconnecting the delegate Web site and other Web sites through events and enable processing logic to be specified and installed as rules, while the complex relationships among events can be modeled with triggers in the delegate Web site.

We have developed a simple example distributed digital library using the Knowledge Network concept to verify the usefulness of the Knowledge Network approach for distributed digital library implementation.

The organization of the paper is as follows. Section 2 provides a survey of related work regarding digital libraries and rule systems and event notification architectures. Section 3 discusses the requirements for a distributed digital library. Section 4 explains the knowledge network. Section 5 describes a distributed digital library application using the Knowledge Network. Section 6 explains some implementation details of the knowledge network and section 7 gives the summary and conclusion.

2 Related Research

There are a variety of different ways to define a digital library. Digital libraries consist of information retrieval systems and occasionally may include the tools to create and organize the digital contents. As digital libraries are the basis for several key applications such as e-learning, e-commerce, customer relationship management systems, and geographical mapping systems, it is being widely researched in a variety of fields by all kinds of researchers. There have been integration issues concerning digital content in various infrastructures. One of the research projects was InfoBus at Stanford. InfoBus is a testbed running the InfoBus protocol which provides a uniform way to access a variety of services and information sources through proxies using CORBA's distributed object technology[2]. Other interesting research issues were integrating metadata from different sources using distributed object technologies [3].

Digital libraries can greatly benefit from an infrastructure that combines event and rule technology to support easy integration among distributed digital contents. Our approach uses these technologies on the Web to form a distributed digital library.

There have been several approaches to provide an abstraction of the communication infrastructure over the Internet. One of the most popular approaches is modeling the communication as event notifications. Interesting things that happen are modeled as events and delivered to other systems on the Internet while hiding the details of the communication protocols from the users of the event notification mechanism. The issues that need to be dealt with are the scalability and selective subscription of information when using the event notification infrastructure. Several systems such as Keryx [4], NeoNet [5], and Gryphon [6] have been developed with focuses on these issues and have provided solutions in their own way. Keryx uses a publish-subscribe model for a language and platform independent event infrastructure. NeoNet provides a rule-based message routing, queueing and formatting system. Gryphon implements a message brokering middleware via an information flow graph, which specifies selective delivery, event transformation and new event generation. Standards bodies and communities have also proposed standards such as the CORBA Notification Service [7] and JMS [8]. The CORBA Notification Service uses an event channel concept and extends the Event Service by providing event filtering and quality of service. JMS supports reliable, asynchronous communication among distributed components.

Rule technology was initially researched in the fields of artificial intelligence and expert systems, and were soon introduced into active database systems[9,10]. Rules are expressed in a high-level language to specify executable logic. Many rule systems use Event-Condition-Action (ECA) rules that capture the semantics of "When an event occurs, check the condition. If the condition is true, then execute the action". An early application of rule technology to the Internet can be found in the WebRules [11] framework. The WebRules framework enables integration of Web servers by using rules, however it does not include concepts such as event and rule publishing or event filtering.

3   Requirements for a Distributed Digital Library

The concept of a distributed digital library is based on the idea that specialized topics on the Web should be maintained together as a group to provide information of better quality to the users of the Web. Distributed digital libraries consist of a delegate Web site that acts as a gateway to other relevant Web sites. The delegate Web site would typically contain summary information of Web sites as well as URL links to the Web sites. Current technologies to implement such a distributed digital library would create a huge burden on the delegate Web site because it would need to continuously monitor the related Web sites in the digital library for any changes. Also, most of this implementation would be done using a Web programming language such as Java or Perl, making it almost impossible for a less technical person to administer the platform and make any changes to the way content is extracted from other Web sites and integrated into the delegate Web site. Therefore, in order for such a distributed digital library to be realized the following requirements need to be satisfied.

(1) A notification mechanism is needed to automatically alert the delegate Web site when any new or changed information is available on other Web sites in the digital library. This reduces the burden of the delegate Web site and is the key to providing scalability in the distributed digital library.

(2) An efficient and powerful filtering mechanism to deliver only those notifications that are of interest to the delegate Web site should be supported. This will allow the delegate Web site to concentrate only on the information that is of interest and can greatly reduce network traffic.

(3) A simple way to add processing logic into Web sites without performing any programming is needed in order for administrators of delegate Web sites and source Web sites to easily participate in distributed digital libraries. Delegate Web sites need to provide mechanisms to easily specify and install the processing logic related to the integration of information. Participating Web sites of the digital library may want to enforce security constraints on the notifications as well.

(4) A mechanism to model and process the various relationships among the notifications to the processing logic in the Web sites should be supported. Complex relationships among Web sites almost always exist when integrating information from different Web sites.

These requirements can be satisfied if we use knowledge networks to implement the distributed digital library.

4   Concept and Architecture of Knowledge Network

The goal of the knowledge network is to enable users of the Web to easily share knowledge over the Web. By sharing knowledge, individual expertise can be integrated to form a much larger and valuable network of knowledge. This would make the Web into a more active and intelligent environment to develop advanced applications such as distributed digital libraries.

The knowledge network uses an ETR (Event-Trigger-Rule) model as a tool for users to represent knowledge. The ETR model is composed of the three knowledge elements - events, triggers, and rules - that carefully reflect the complexity and distributed characteristics of the Web environment. The events encapsulate timely information of what is happening on the Web and can be automatically notified to a large audience on the Web. The rules contain the decision-making procedures allowing the intelligence of humans to be embedded into the knowledge network. The triggers model complex relationships among events and rules, checking histories of events and enabling various reasoning or activation sequences of rules to reflect complex decision making processes. These knowledge elements altogether make the knowledge network an active infrastructure without the need of human intervention.

The knowledge network is realized by adding a component into the existing Web servers. Therefore, the knowledge network is composed of these symmetric nodes on the Web. Each node contains a component that is capable of processing the events, triggers, and rules. A Web server extended with such a component is referred to as a Knowledge Web Server (KWS).

The knowledge network takes a publish-subscribe approach for sharing knowledge on the Web. The publish-subscribe happens in a two stage process. The first stage consists of building and setting up the publish-subscribe information by both the knowledge publishers and the knowledge subscribers. The second stage is characterized as the run-time part of the knowledge network, where processing of the knowledge elements occur.

The architecture of the knowledge network is shown in Figure 1 as an example to explain the key features of the knowledge network: publishing events and rules, event filters, push-based event delivery, knowledge profile, and processing of triggers and rules. In Figure 1, several knowledge Web servers (KWS) are interconnected through the Internet. Only the modules related to the KWS extensions are shown in the figure for simplicity. The modules are the Event Server, ETR Server, and Knowledge Profile Manager. Assume that user A takes the role of a knowledge provider on the knowledge Web server A, while users B and C are knowledge consumers on knowledge Web servers B and C, respectively.

The publishing and subscribing activities form the build-time stage of the knowledge network.

Publishers (or providers) of knowledge may publish events and associated rules on their Web pages. The data that the events can carry are defined and rules that are useful to subscribers yet preferred to be executed on the publisher site are defined. This process is carried out through a GUI provided by the Knowledge Profile Manager. Figure 1 shows that the user A on knowledge Web server A has published two events E1 and E2, and two rules R1 and R2.

Subscribers (or consumers) of knowledge may visit the publisher's Web page and undergo a registration process to subscribe to the events and also specify filters on the events. Filters specify conditions on the events to enable selective subscription of the events. Additionally, subscribers may select published rules to be tied to the event. In figure 1, User B has subscribed to event E1 and linked it to rule R1, while user C has subscribed to event E2 and linked it to rule R2. Also, the event filter F1 is installed on event E1 by user B, while the event filter F2 is installed on event E2 by the user C.

After the registration, the consumers can configure their own site to automatically execute several rules when the subscribed event is notified. Complex relationships among the events and rules can be defined by complex triggers. Figure 1 shows that user B has linked the subscribed event E1 to its own rules R3 and R4 via a complex trigger T3. User C has linked the subscribed event E2 to its own rule R5 via a simple trigger T4.

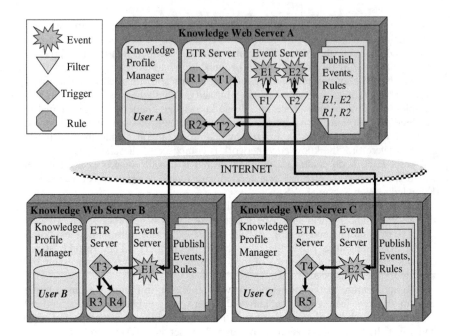

Fig. 1. Architecture of the knowledge network

The event, trigger, and rule definitions that are created during this stage are all stored into the Knowledge Profile Manager as a knowledge profile for each user. This enables a single point of management for all knowledge elements in a KWS. Figure 1 shows the knowledge profiles existing on different knowledge Web servers.

The execution of the knowledge elements form the run-time stage of the knowledge network.

The events that are generated on the publisher's site are filtered and notified to subscribers of the events. At the same time, the rules related to this event are executed on both the publisher's site and subscriber's site by the ETR Server. Figure 1 shows the ETR Server residing on each knowledge Web server. Event E1 will be filtered and activate rule R1 on KWS A, while event E2 will be filtered and activate rule R2 on KWS A. At the same time, the filtered events E1 and E2 will be delivered to KWS B and KWS C, respectively. KWS B will execute rule R3 upon receiving filtered event E1, and KWS C will execute rule R4 upon receiving the filtered event E2.

5   Distributed Digital Library Implementation

The distributed digital library is currently one of the most interesting components that is gaining focus for various applications on the Internet. The knowledge network concept can be used to implement such a distributed digital library by adding active capabilities and intelligence to the Internet.

We give a simple example of a Web site that draws information from several Web sites that publish satellite images for a country. Each Web site is managed by a country that has a weather satellite, and the site mostly contains satellite images of that country. The images are very frequently published because a country may have several satellites. A Web site named GlobalWeather extracts the images from these Web sites. It doesn't need all of the available images, so it just extracts the images that are generated every hour. By integrating these images on a single Web site, GlobalWeather can become a digital library of weather images of the whole world.

5.1   The Local Weather Web Sites

The local weather Web sites will publish images every minute on their Web sites. At the same time, they will post an event to notify that a new image is generated on the Web site. The event carries such information as the country name, the location of the image file, the time the image file was generated. The local Web sites also have provided filters on the time the image file was generated. The description of these events and the supported filters are as follows:

- NewImage (String CountryID, String FileURL, Timestamp GeneratedTime, String SourceServer): This event is posted when a new image is generated on a local weather Web site. Anybody interested in the images can subscribe to this event. A filter on this event is supported for the GeneratedTime attribute.

The local weather Web sites also have the following parameterized rule (provider-side rule) that the subscribers of the events can make use of while subscribing for the event.

- HighlightCountry(String CountryID, String FileURL) : This rule will process the image file to highlight the country in the image and provide it to the subscriber.

5.2   The GlobalWeather Web Site

The scenario for the GlobalWeather Web site works as follows. The GlobalWeather Web site maintains a list of accredited Web sites that produce satellite images. It first goes to those Web sites and subscribes for the event that will notify that a new image is available. When subscribing for the events, it selects a filter to only receive notifications of images produced hourly. Also it selects the HighlightCountry rule on the local weather sites to obtain a an image with the country highlighted. On the GlobalWeather Web site, it creates a rule to store the image into a database. Table 1 shows the subscription information related to the GlobalWeather Web site.

Table 1. Subscription information of the GlobalWeather site.

Local Weather Sites (Publisher)			GlobalWeather (Subscriber)	
Subscribed Event	Event Filter	Provider Rule	Trigger [Event](Rule)	Rule
NewImage	Generated Time.minute = 0	Highlight Country	[NewImange] (StoreRule)	StoreRule C: true; A: Store in DB;

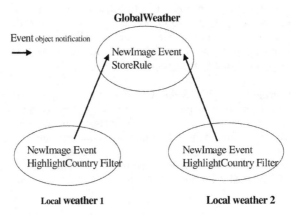

Fig. 2. A simple example scenario for GlobalWeather

5.3   The Big Picture

An overall diagram, which puts all of these knowledge elements together, is shown in Figure 2. The figure shows two local weather Web sites and the GlobalWeather Web site. NewImage events are posted on the local weather sites and the HighlightCountry filters are activated. The events that satisfy the filter condition are delivered to GlobalWeather, and for those events the StoreRule is executed.

As shown in the above scenario, the knowledge network provides an ideal infrastructure for collaboration and for adding knowledge into the web to make it more intelligent and applicable to the emerging areas of Internet applications such as distributed digital libraries as well as enterprise integration applications.

6 Knowledge Network Modules

The Event Server, ETR Server, Knowledge Profile Manager are the core modules that compose the knowledge Web Server. The modules were developed using Java (JDK 1.4) with a combination of applet, servlet and RMI technology. The popular Apache Web Server and Tomcat servlet engine were used in our prototype implementation.

6.1 ETR Server

The ETR Server has the following key features that are not supported by other rule systems.
- The ETR Server is developed in Java and is thus deployable on any platform.
- Processing of complex event relationships are done by an Event History Processor module and processing of complex rule sequences are done by a Rule Scheduler.
- The ETR Server has an extensible interface that enables it to receive events from various communication infrastructures.
- The ETR Server supports run-time modifications of rules.
- Rules are grouped and can be activated or deactivated as a group.
- Synchronous/Asynchronous events are supported.
- The ETR Server can process various built-in rule variable types that are useful for different applications.

6.2 Event Server

The Event Server consists of the following 4 key parts that cooperatively form the basis of the communication infrastructure of the knowledge network.
- An event registration part automatically generates event subscription forms that are shown to event subscribers during the event registration process. Events and their associated filters are stored in XML format and an XSL is applied to create the HTML forms. This part is implemented as a servlet.
- An event delivering part sends events over the Internet through HTTP or RMI. Once a generated event is filtered and the appropriate subscribers are identified, the delivering part will post the event to the destination.
- An event filtering part keeps the event subscription information along with the event filters that have been defined. The event filters are maintained and persistently stored in three kinds of data structures : inverted index, modified 2-3 tree, Range Table.
- An event receiving part is implemented as a servlet or RMI server to receive events through HTTP or RMI. It then forwards the event to the ETR server through RMI.

6.3 Knowledge Profile Manager

The Knowledge Profile Manager is implemented as an applet, servlet and RMI server combination. The front end of the Knowledge Profile Manager is developed as an applet. The applet enables users to access menus for defining and viewing events, triggers, and rules. Two different menus such as the Provider menu and the Subscriber menu are available. The backend is formed as a servlet and talks to an RMI server that is used to persistently store the knowledge information.

7 Conclusion

The concept and an implementation of a distributed digital library was presented in this paper. The distributed digital library can be realized by making use of the knowledge network infrastructure. The knowledge network extends the current Web infrastructure by adding processing capabilities for events, triggers, and rules as a part of the information infrastructure. Events, rules, and triggers can be used to capture human and enterprise knowledge in the Internet, making the Internet an active knowledge network instead of a passive data network. The event, event filter, event history, and rule processing capabilities of the knowledge network offer very powerful and useful services to enable the timely delivery of relevant data and the activation of operations that are necessary for the realization of a distributed digital library application. We have shown how such an application could be developed by providing an example scenario.

A few future research issues are identified as follows. First, security issues need to be further investigated due to the executable characteristics of rules on the provider (i.e., source Web sites in the digital library) site. Rules can have potentially damaging effects if the proper authorization and security issues are not clearly specified. Second, an event ontology is required to effectively make the infrastructure more scalable for a global marketplace. The event definitions may be controllable within a limited size group of nodes. However, when the target platform becomes the whole Internet, ontology issues need to be resolved. One way to practically solve this problem would be to provide an ontology server for specific topic domains. Third, interconnecting rules in this way could have a potential to contradict each other or have infinitely looping effects. Therefore, a validation mechanism for global rule chaining is needed.

References

1. M. Lee, S.Y.W. Su, and H. Lam. Event and Rule Services for Achieving a Web-based Knowledge Network. Technical Report, UF CISE TR00-002, University of Florida (2000).
2. M. Roscheisen, M. Baldonado, C.-C. K. Chang, L. Gravano, S. Ketchpel, and A. Paepcke.The Stanford InfoBus and Its Service Layers: Augmenting the Internet with Higher-Level Information Management Protocols. Digital Libraries in Computer Science: The MeDoc Approach, LNCS Series no. 1392, Springer, 1998.
3. C. Yang and F. Hsiao. Integrating Metadata with Distributed Object Technologies for Resource Discovery. In Proceedings of the 3rd International Conference of Asian Digital Library (ICADL 2000), Seoul, Korea, pp. 163-170, December 6-8, 2000.
4. S. Brandt and A. Kristensen. Web Push as an Internet Notification Service. W3C Workshop on Push Technology. http://keryxsoft.hpl.hp.com/doc/ins.html, Boston, MA, September (1997).

5. NEONet, http://www.neonsoft.com/products/NEONet.html
6. G. Banavar, M. Kaplan, K. Shaw, R.E. Strom, D.C. Sturman, and W. Tao. Information Flow Based Event Distribution Middleware. In Proc. of Electronic Commerce and Web-based Applications Workshop at the International Conference on Distributed Computing Systems (ICDCS99), Austin, TX, May 31–June 4 (1999).
7. Object Management Group (OMG), CORBA Notification Service, specification version 1.0. June 20 (2000).
8. Sun Microsystems. Java Message Service API, http://java.sun.com/products/jms/, January 22 (2001).
9. U. Dayal, B.T. Blaustein, A.P. Buchmann, et al. The HiPAC Project: Combining Active Databases and Timing Constraints. In ACM SIGMOD Record, Vol. 17(1), March (1988) 51–70.
10. J. Widom, (ed.). Active Database Systems: Triggers and Rules for Advanced Database Processing. Morgan Kaufmann, San Francisco, California (1996).
11. I. Ben-Shaul and S. Ifergan. WebRule: An Event-based Framework for Active Collaboration among Web Servers. In Computer Networks and ISDN Systems, Vol. 29(8–13), October (1997) 1029–1040.
12. H. Lam and S.Y.W. Su. Component Interoperability in a Virtual Enterprise Using Events/Triggers/Rules," in Proceedings of OOPSLA '98 Workshop on Objects, Components, and Virtual Enterprise, Vancouver, BC, Canada, Oct. 18-22 (1998) 47–53.
13. M. Lee, S.Y.W. Su, and H. Lam. Parallel Rule Processing in a Distributed Object Environment. In Proc. of the Int'l Conference on Parallel and Distributed Processing Techniques and Applications (PDPTA'99), Las Vegas, NV, June (1999) 410–416.

An Architecture of a Distributed Archive for Re-useable Learning Objects

Daniel Tan[1], Mohamed Ismail Fazilah[2], Tony Chan[2], and Ravi Sharma[2]

[1] Centre for Educational Development
[2] School of Computer Engineering
Nanyang Technological University
Republic of Singapore

Abstract. In this paper, we describe our efforts at developing and rolling out a content-centric e-learning service. In what we have defined as a distributed archive for re-useable learning objects, teachers and learners may draw from reputable content sources and concentrate on the value-added activities of devising learning paths, conducting assessments and carrying out collaboration. We believe that we have an architecture that will fulfill the above objective. The paper first articulates the rationale for such an approach, then reviews the relevant work of others, and finally presents our architecture for the e-learning trials being carried out at our institution. We conclude with some thoughts on the future directions.

Keywords: e-learning framework, models and experiments; digital learning library; courseware development and delivery; computer aided instruction.

1 Introduction

Education and training (especially at the post-secondary levels) have become the critical and necessary ingredient of the knowledge economy. However, the scarcity of expertise and the costs of providing such services have meant that demand continues to exceed the supply. Therefore, traditional models for the delivery of education and training are being radically transformed from the classroom, student-teacher mode to one that is IT-based and unsupervised, and includes peer-learning.

At its most basic level, education is about teaching and learning. This educational process is increasingly seen as beyond transmitting static knowledge from teacher to student. In recent years and in the light of recent dramatic developments in the use of IT in education, the complex, interactive effort of the learner engaging in ideas, applying principles and skills, and solving problems with guidance and facilitation by the teacher and in collaboration with other learners, is seeing a change in the traditional paradigm.

This approach to education depends on easy and direct access to information in all its forms and on good support for communication and collaboration between fellow students, their instructors, and others beyond the physical campus boundaries. The rapid development of the Internet has resulted in wired campuses that facilitates students and teachers to be in touch with each other, as well as to access digital resources like web pages, digital libraries and information assets.

T.M.T. Sembok et al. (Eds.): ICADL 2003, LNCS 2911, pp. 384–397, 2003.

The research direction of the Institute of Higher Learning (IHL) focuses on the development of new discoveries, knowledge, methods and technologies. They aim to produce new scholars and skilled professionals for the nation in the creation of wealth. Innovations are recognized as the seeds of new applications and the economies of the future.

IHLs also recognize their role and need to reach back to the communities and the society that supports them. Whilst students enroll in their campuses and graduate after a time in their environment and join the business and industrial communities, it recognizes the role it can play to reach these and others beyond the campus walls. Such a process is on-going and the flow of information and knowledge transfer is facilitated by an ever-growing network.

"E-learning" is becoming "e-earning" as manifested in life-long learning initiatives and practices in education, corporate training, product launches, and so on. The paradigm shift of local economies in job skill sets and the concept of "free agent" demands that learning does not stop formally after graduation at a formal university.

One such impetus for the offering of education and training is the conceptualization and implementation of entities known as *learning objects*. The University of Wisconsin's Global Passport Project [www.uwm.edu/Dept/CIE/AOP/LO_what.html] has a consensus of what researchers and practitioners define as a learning object:

- "modular digital resources, uniquely identified and metatagged, that can be used to support learning" National Learning Infrastructure Initiative
- "any entity, digital or non-digital, which can be used, re-used or referenced during technology supported learning" Learning Object Metadata Working Group of the IEEE Learning Technology Standards Committee (LTSC)
- "any digital resource that can be reused to support learning... the main idea of 'learning objects' is to break educational content down into small chunks that can be reused in various learning environments, in the spirit of object-oriented programming" David A. Wiley

There is considerable agreement therefore that the learning objects be multimedia in nature, with animation if necessary, indexed so as to promote efficient and effective searches, and be based on a sound learning paradigm. In order to promote application efficiency as well as computational economy, these objects ought to be distributed (i.e. shared), authoritative, comprehensive, modifiable and re-useable. We may also add to these notions, the design goals of all distributed systems – transparency, openness and scalability.

In this paper, we present our thoughts on an architecture for a digital archive for re-useable learning objects (DARLO). This remains an integral part of the e-learning initiative at the Nanyang Technological University which began about two and a half years ago and today covers some 200+ semester courses and 15000+ students. We believe that learning per se is an acquisition of knowledge and skills and therefore an e-learning platform must be DARLO-centered without ignoring learning models and community interaction. In Section2, we review some of the e-learning work that we have drawn inspiration from. Section 3 covers our framework and architecture. We conclude this paper with a discussion on future directions.

2 Background Review

2.1 Theories about Learning

Much of the theories of learning that have evolved over time have developed models to help us put theory into practice [Dorin et al., 1990]. There are four popular theories of learning: Behaviorism, Cognitivism, Constructivism and Contextualism. These theories of learning can be applied to online learning design and development.

Behaviorism. The behaviorist perspective is based upon the idea that an individual's behavior can be shaped through external stimuli from the environment. In behaviorism, learning is defined as a sequence of stimulus and response actions in observable cause and effect relationships. The pedagogical implication of such a perspective would be that the learning has to be very structured and achieved through specific objectives and learning outcomes. The drills and practice approach, with immediate corrective feedback provided at each step, is a common application of the behaviorist framework.

Cognitivism. The focus of the cognitivist perspective is the internal mental processes of the mind and how they could be utilized in promoting effective learning. Learning, for cognitive theorists, is viewed as "involving the acquisition or reorganization of the cognitive structures through which humans process and store information" (Good and Brophy, 1990, pp. 187). The pedagogical implication of such a perspective would be that the acquisition and application of knowledge and understanding is categorized into meaningful parts. The careful organization of instructional materials from simple to complex, building on prior knowledge is a natural next step. Objectives-based learning and task-oriented learning are common applications of the cognitivist framework.

Constructivism. The constructivist theory of learning focuses on learners' ability to mentally construct meaning of their own environment and to create their own learning. For the constructivists, learning, as argued by Merril (1991), is an active process of constructing meaning from experience where conceptual growth is through the negotiation of meaning, the sharing of multiple perspectives and the changing of our internal representations through collaborative learning. This should be situated in realistic settings where testing is integrated with the task and is not a separate activity. The pedagogical implication of the constructivist perspective would be that learners have a role in determining the direction of their learning by setting their own learning objectives. The assessment is much more subjective because it depends on the process and self-evaluation of the learner instead of specific quantitative criteria. Active learning, facilitated learning, simulated learning, and metacognitive learning are common applications of the constructivist framework.

Contextualism. Contextualism states that learning is most effective when learners process knowledge within specific contexts of the learners' lives and interests as the mind has a natural inclination to search for meaning that makes sense and is useful in his/her context. The pedagogical implication of such a perspective is similar to those of constructivism but the emphasis is on applying knowledge in context and reiterative cycles. Problem-based learning, cooperative learning and service learning are common applications of contextualism.

2.2   Platform Design Issues

The four theories of learning span the continuum from teacher-centred to learner-centred. These provide a pedagogical guide for e-learning which would have implications in the development of an architecture for a digital archive for re-usable learning objects. For example, the contextualist framework, which requires the acquisition of integrated and relevant knowledge via solving real world problems as one of its curriculum outcomes, would require the development of a repository of learning objects relevant to curriculum modules and the provision of access to online learning resources like digital libraries, journals, etc. to facilitate learning.

A blending of the application of these theories can occur in an e-learning platform where the re-usable learning objects that are offered, whether standalone or combined, support the important learning theories. Thus, it is important that standards are set for the re-usable learning objects so that learners are able to select the most appropriate platform according to their learning needs and mix and match the re-usable learning objects from a wide variety of producers to design an effective online course. The technical design parameters of an e-learning platform include: separation of services from implementation; backward compatibility; re-usable learning objects; and service delivery. It was instructive for us to examine the various standards in order to draw a conceptual architecture of our own.

The IEEE Learning Technology Standards Committee (LTSC) is chartered by the Computer Society Standards Activity Board to develop accredited technical standards, recommended practices and guides for learning technology. The current areas of interest are:

Architecture and Reference Model
Digital Rights Expression Language (DREL)
Computer Managed Instruction (CMI)
Learning Objects Metadata (LOM)
Platform and Media Profiles
Competency Definitions

Sharable Courseware Object Reference Model (SCORM) is an example of a Learning Management System (LMS) which has a set of services that launch re-usable learning objects, keep track of learner progress, sort out the order (sequence) in which learning objects are to be delivered, and report student mastery through a learning experience. It is a suite of technical standards that enables web-based learning systems to find, import, share, reuse, and export re-usable learning objects in a standardized way. It is thus important that such re-usable learning objects are grounded in learning theories so that the learning content can be effectively reused, moved, searched and re-contextualized. The SCORM suite also contains recommended best practices of how it may be used within a given community, user/developer guides, test implementations, sample content and a conformance test suite [Rehak 2002]. Re-usability of content, migration of objects to a different platform and creating searchable content are some of the issues that are addressed within the SCORM suite.

Koppi and his co-workers [Koppi and Lavitt 2003] have previously described "how learning objects can be part of an institutional learning environment by an integration of four components of online learning: an administration management system; an authoring system; a learning resource catalogue (LRC); and a delivery system." In their approach, RLOs were the means by which content authoring and the follow on learning resource catalog were developed. In a view that is consistent with the IEEE standard as well as other notable efforts, [cf. subsection below] learning objects interfacing with other learning objects build a learning environment. The LRC comprising metadata that describe learning objects in standard terms facilitates search and interoperability. Cataloging is a non-trivial task – learning objectives, contexts and behavioral descriptions are non-standard. Typically, the metadata reside in the catalog server whereas the learning objects themselves may be distributed across all participating repositories.

2.3   E-learning Exemplars

There are two distinct, emerging trends in the delivery of e-learning:

1. At a national level, adoption of e-learning and aligned standards, such as AICC, IMS, SCORM, OKI, with reusable learning objects are becoming common. The establishment of e-learning Competency Centres (eCC) in Singapore and its role of/in publishing and defining local e-learning standards provides a reference point for the educational industry and practitioners. There are also institutional activities to use e-learning standards in the definition of content.
2. At an international and organizational level – transnational alliances are being formed. These include U21, UK e-universities, OpenLearning Australia (OLA), Digital University, as well as trans-national initiatives in Europe, Canada, the United States, Japan and Malaysia.

The learning framework derived from learning theories tells an LMS what learning experience was intended by the instructional designer when he/she designed the learning object. An example of an LMS that uses re-usable learning objects is the Multimedia Educational Resource for Learning and Online Teaching [MERLOT 2002], a free and open resource, which has a collection of links to online learning materials that are annotated with peer reviews and assignments. Search and indexing are features built-in. Members, who can join MERLOT for free, may add materials, comments and assignments to MERLOT. **ARIADNE** (**A**lliance of **R**emote **I**nstructional **A**uthoring and **D**istribution **N**etworks for **E**urope) is among the better known international collaborative efforts.

Lydia is a learning object repository that assists in organizing and reusing learning objects by providing a platform for authors, developers and distributors to contribute. Lydia may be utilized as an add-on module or as an independent product [The Lydia Global Repository, 2003]. Another repository of learning objects is Alexandria, Canada's first national repository for educational objects that makes digital educational materials readily available to students, researchers and educators across

Canada and beyond [Alexandria: A Digital Content Repository Homepage, 2003]. The University of California – Berkeley's "Interactive University" and University of Wisconsin – Milwaukee's "Global Passport" projects are "public domain" instances of shared learning objects.

Australia is arguably the world's most pervasive user of "online units - subjects or course components, in which at least some of the content is delivered and/or some of the interaction is conducted via the Internet" in the delivery of higher education. In a recent study [DEST, 2001} it was reported that:

> The use of the Internet in university units ranges from a high of 99 or 100 per cent of units in seven universities to a low of 9 per cent in one university. All universities are employing the Web to some extent for teaching and learning purposes. Universities reported that 50 704 of their units (54 per cent) have content available on the Web. The most prevalent form of online delivery was Web-supplemented with 46 per cent of units. Fully online units represent a small percentage of units, i.e. 1.4 per cent, (0.8 per cent of undergraduate units, 2.7 per cent of postgraduate units). The discipline areas that have the highest percentage of fully online units are: Management and Commerce with 2.6 per cent fully online units, Education 2.5 per cent, Information Technology 2.3 per cent and Health 2.2 per cent. The discipline areas that make least use of the Web are Food, Hospitality and Personal Services (56.6 per cent make No Use of the Web), Creative Arts (55.7 per cent), and Society and Culture (52.1 per cent). Information and Technology (I.T.) units appear to make the highest use of the Web, compared with other discipline areas; 40.5 per cent of I.T. units are either fully online or Web-dependent.

Cisco [1999] and Microsoft [Lang, 2003] are notable, industry led efforts in the learning objects space. In what they call an architecture for *reuseable information objects* (RIO), Cisco has prescribed a collection of tools that support authoring, browsing, type-metadata definition, and repository management.

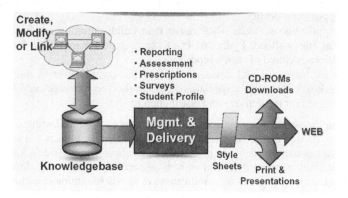

Fig. 1. Source: [Cisco 1999]

The Microsoft corporate learning specification, in addition, distinguishes between learning object (lesson), learning unit (module) and learning solution or path (course). This modularized approach to content is supported by the generic NET suite of services over standard and open platform.

In the next section, we apply some of the paradigms and concepts that we have drawn from the work of others, to our framework.

3   Framework and Architecture

We reiterate our belief that learning is an acquisition of knowledge and skills and therefore an e-learning platform must be DARLO-centered without ignoring learning models and community interaction. In this section, we present our architecture for a DARLO-centered platform and some of the thought process that went towards its conceptual design.

NTU started a pilot trial of e-learning in May 1999. We adopted a then leading e-learning platform. However, after a year, only 22 courses went on-line. This was not the result we expected of our ambitious investment. On hindsight, some reasons for unsuccessful trial were that the solution lacked a user-friendly graphical interface, used a proprietary database format, and was a cost-ineffective business (US$7.50 per named user). We re-engineered our solution beginning with the following design goals:

- Ease of Use, Installation and Maintenance
- Positive User Experience
- Scalable Performance
- Integration with Student Information System
- Compliance with Standards (IEEE, IMS, SCORM, etc.)

and the following architectural requirements:

- The platform –a back-end operating system that has robustness and scalability
- The relational database system – off-the-shelf package with track record of being put in production.
- The application software –buy rather than build; currently available solutions such as HarvestRoad, Lydia and POOL can perform many of the functions and operations required of such a repository.
- Network interfaces and devices – due to the complexities in the supporting network infrastructure, a specialized content delivery network (or CDN) would be required for the delivery and distribution model.

Based on the above, we conceived an architecture with the following components: authoring tool, distributed archive of re-useable learning objects, cataloging and searching functionalities, delivery platform (3 tier client-server model), collaborative tools (for student-teacher interaction as well as peer-to-peer learning), learning paths (for customization of courseware), and gateways to other learning communities. This architecture, which is still at the conceptual stage, is shown below. In the proposed architecture shown below, the cataloging and assessment components are not shown as they constitute future work.

However, we have proceeded to put in place a generic platform that will support the above architecture along with all other current e-learning initiatives at NTU. This is basically: Hardware: SUN Enterprise E1000016 processors, 18 GB RAM, 450 GB network storage, Gigabit Ethernet network connection; Software: Application-Blackboard 5.5.1 Level 3, Database- Oracle8i, Web Server- Apache (3 tier architecture). Sage snapshot (on 31-Oct-2002) is Course-sites 4,194, Page Hits 46,271,441, Students 26,385, Instructors 1,976.

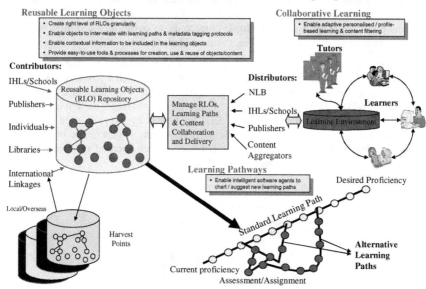

Fig. 2.

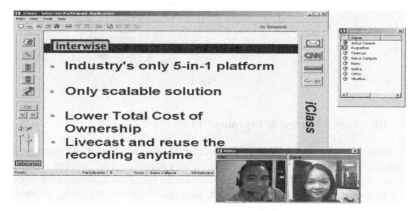

Fig. 3.

The look and feel of the e-learning platform we have developed is WIMP based and further supports multimedia communication and controlled sharing of resources.

The concept of Reusable Learning Objects is not new. In software engineering, the concepts of code re-use are manifested in basic programming "procedure" and "routine" structures. The use of code and algorithm libraries (notably mathematical libraries such as NAG) has been successfully integrated into standard practice. However, in the hardware design community, the scenario is somewhat different. The idea of electronic building blocks through the use of standard components such as resistors, capacitors as well as integrated circuits is now the prevalent industry practice. Engineers recognize the need and advantage of the use of standardized components for speeding up the design process. Manufacturers of such devices accept that the pie is large enough for multiple companies to compete for similar products. When put together, they become useful (value-added) appliances.

We have adopted the Integrated Circuit (IC) design metaphor for the organization of content as opposed to the Lego or atoms or grapes favored by others. We do not prescribe that our learning objects be in a given set of standard shapes and sizes, identical or differ only cosmetically. Instead, we envisage an environment of heterogeneous objects with hyperlinks defining how they may be used or re-used together. Such a metaphor is amenable to describe the organization of hierarchic Learning Objects drawing from the properties of object-oriented modeling such as inheritance, polymorphism and information hiding.

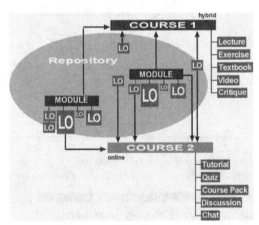

Fig. 4.

3.1   Repository of Reusable Learning Objects

For some time now, the e-learning community has become aware and more receptive to Internet technologies and its application to education. The concept of RLOs is gaining wide intellectual and practical acceptance, though it is recognised that there are still issues to be resolved. Standards and specifications are being defined, and adopted by the industry. These include IMS, AICC, IEEE LOM, Dublin Core (with derivatives like CanCore), OKI. Of these, SCORM appears to be the one that is gaining wider adoption. Many national initiatives tend to include SCORM as the basic specification for their collaboration among its partners.

The process of standardization of RLOs involves selecting a set of meta-data definitions and organizing these objects in a repository. Each RLO is tagged with fields that have data defined in a dictionary (that is, taxonomy) for consistency of terms, etc. Examples of meta-data fields include "date of creation", "author", "level", "keywords", etc. While some of these might be understood and completed by the teaching staff, it is envisaged that a majority of them would not be "bothered" by or "conscientious" with this tedious process. Being inconsistent in defining similar RLOs can create problems in their use later on. When searched, they might be "false positives" that makes search results inaccurate. A sound approach would be to use information scientists (or those trained in the Library Sciences) to do this task to ensure data quality and consistency.

Having a repository will allow the learning community to have a collection of its content organized in a database system separate from the Learning Management System (LMS) or Courseware Management System (CMS). This would allow content reuse and independence on specific platforms like IBM LearningSpace, WebCT, TopClass, Blackboard, and so on.

Decomposing the course into learning objects allows reuse at a lower granular level. Such RLOs might be manifested as an image, equation, video clip, essay, etc. The RLOs might be a hierarchy of learning objects (like a module). The aggregation of modules would then result in a course. That the RLO has a small granule size permits its greater reuse. Such reuse might be within a closed community, an institution, or among a larger community of institutions, or even globally.

A repository *per se* merely has RLOs and possibly, some relationship between these objects. By themselves, they have limited use, much like a numerical data of a stock exchange database. It is as the data is used and applied contextually (like data trends from a series of related data, industrial development which might impact a change in price movement, etc.) that it becomes useful. For this reason, a complimentary project of learning paths was proposed by NTU.

3.2   Learning Pathways

A learning path is defined as a series of sequential events, activities and RLOs that would result in the learner attaining some competence, knowledge or capabilities. In that regard, for any given topic, a learning path can be comprehensively defined.

Depending on the learner, that path can then be customized or personalized. Some modules or nodes might be omitted because he/she is already familiar with it. The path can be customized by the teacher according to an approved syllabus or publisher's road map or recommended pathway. The learning path must be customizable – the instructor should be able to add/remove/replace additional modules as he sees fit.

The original learning path might present alternative branches or pathways within the generic learning path to RLOs that permits the instructor or learner to opt for customization options. In this regard, the simple sequential path might be multi-dimensional, in that instead of a single simple path, it might have multiple paths, to describe two routes of specialization or alternatives, like different ways to prepare a surface for adhesion depending on the material type or process.

3.3 Deployment Plans

DARLO will be deployed in four phases. **Phase I** would be the creation of the digital archive utilizing currently available productized technology. The DARLO framework would be further refined to consider the database architecture, repository organisation, taxonomy and other related issues. This can be set up rather quickly within 9 to 12 months.

Phase II will look into the design of learning paths and associated issues in creating course modules, design tools, authoring and editing tools, schemes for path generation and learning object retrieval and learner's interface. Other potential applications such as payment gateways and assessment tools would also be developed.

At the end of Phase II, the project would enter operational **Phase III** status. By this time, the operations would be managed by an independent entity. This entity would likely operate as a business. Also, at this point, there will be industrial and business involvement in DARLO-centric businesses, like content creation and deposition, assessment pool, and such.

Phase IV would be a milestone when mirror DARLOs are created overseas to facilitate ease of access to content in other countries. Such local proxy, mirror and replicated sites can also act as harvest points in addition to providing convenient access points. As the former, it now becomes a collection point of RLO that will add to the diversity and richness of the learning objects, which in turn will enhance the position and value of DARLO to the Internet community.

4 Future Directions

We have described an architecture for the delivery of e-leaning services using the pilot efforts at NTU as a useful test-bed for ideas in content development and dissemination. While we are fairly content with the learning paradigm and technical platform that we have adopted, much work remains in seeing the field trials through to a stage where we can empirically show the efficacy of our architecture and its applicability beyond the NTU environment. This work is on-going and we envisage the following future research activities. For example:

- The automated process of decomposing content into RLOs (into maps);
- Classification and tagging of such RLOs (using some identifier system);
- Organisation of the repository structure;
- Pedagogy *of* and *in* learning paths – this is an area where our colleagues in the National Institute of Education can play an active and meaningful role;
- Design of learning path structures and supporting tools;
- Fine-tuning of content delivery networks for course delivery;

- Intelligent user-based profiling and impact on the learning path generation;
- Retrieval of RLOs to the Learning Path as the learner progresses in the learning; and
- Auto-generation and intelligent user adaptation to the learner.

On the subject of learning objects in particular, we wish to benchmark our pilot efforts with the best practices suggested in the literature – for example, the Advanced Distributed Learning (ADL)'s accessibility, interoperability, re-usability, durability and affordability criteria [Rehak 2002] or Rehak and Mason's [2003] key steps in forming a learning object economy – integration, interoperability, re-usability, heterogeneity. We intend to define some design parameters as well as success measures that would capture some of these relationships between architectural choices and success outcomes. Rehak and Mason [2003] also suggest that the holy grail of reuse would be to facilitate it on-the-fly and there is a need for success measures that capture the dynamic, just-in-time nature of packaging re-useable learning objects along with the currency of the contents.

There is no reason why this may not interoperate with like efforts throughout the world. This is the object of our participation as an affiliate in a trans-European project led by the ICPNM Academy – International Certificate Program for New Media – known as LOCUS – Localization of Digital Content and Services for E-Learning – which investigates a methodological framework for describing subjects, strategies, instruments and methods of localization of content and services for e-learning so that they may be shared and exchanged to the largest extent possible. In working towards a network of learning communities, we hope to demonstrate to ourselves and others that such a goal is not only desirable, but also achievable.

But perhaps the most challenging issue in the design of a DARLO-centric e-learning platform is the implication for the key participants – teachers/facilitators and students/learners. Along with the obvious lament about the "impersonalization of education", there is also a paradigm shift in terms of mass customization of curricula, anytime, anywhere, "at-your-own-pace" delivery, and significantly, the incentive/ reward structure. The resultant changing nature of learning as well as teaching evaluation; taking "best practices" in teaching beyond borders and the impact of globalization; peer review of content and curricula; and providing incentive as well as rewarding impactful participation – invoke controversial and sensitive issues that unfortunately cannot be brushed aside at the architectural phase.

We do not claim to have thought through all of the above issues at NTU, but we do take heart from analogies from the more general discipline of knowledge management and experiences on the Internet as reasons to be optimistic that these challenges are surmountable. Knowledge (even when implicit) can indeed be captured, improved upon, disseminated for review, shared, traded commercially and so on. Tools and techniques have already been developed for storage and distribution, cataloging and searching, bartering and micro-payments, and critically, the management of digital rights. Add to this, the precedence over the Internet of building communities which work toward a common good, the devolution/decentralization of control, and the adherence to an agreed upon code-of-conduct in transactions, and we have some striking similarities to the notion of a global archive for re-useable learning objects. And this would be the final goal of our DARLO-centric approach to e-learning.

Acknowledgements. Daniel Tan (ethtan@ntu.edu.sg) is the Director of the Centre for Educational Development at NTU. Fazilah Mohamed Ismail (asfazilah@ntu.edu.sg) is a Communication Skills Lecturer and Ravi Sharma (asrsharma@ntu.edu.sg) a Senior Fellow at the School of Computer Engineering. Tony Chan (askychan@ntu.edu.sg) is Associate Professor of Computer Engineering and Director of the Centre for Advanced Media Technology. The authors are grateful to the funding agencies and numerous discussion collaborators for the on-going e-learning initiative being undertaken at NTU. Many thanks are also due to Stuti Nautiyal for critiquing the manuscript.

References

1. Alexandria: A Digital Content Repository Homepage. 2003.
   http://alexandria.netera.ca/cgi-bin/WebObjects/Repository?theme=alexandria
2. Cisco Learning Forum Whitepaper, Reuseable Information Object Standards.
   http://www.elearningforum.com/meetings/1999/RIO-Nov99.pdf
3. DEST 2001 : Universities Online: A survey of online education and services in Australia. Commonwealth, Department of Education Science and Training, Government of Australia.
   http://www.dest.gov.au/highered/occpaper/02a/default.htm
4. Dorin, H., Demmin, P. E., Gabel, D., Chemistry: The study of matter. (3rd ed.), Prentice Hall, Englewood-Cliffs, 1990.
5. Good, T. L., Brophy, J. E., Educational psychology: A realistic approach. [4th ed], Longman, White Plains, New York, 1990.
6. IEEE Final Draft Standard for Learning Object Metadata (LOM): IEEE 14854.12.1-2002, http://ltsc.ieee.org
7. Tony Koppi and Neil Lavitt, "Institutional Use of Learning Objects Three Years on: Lessons Learned and Future Directions" Proceedings of the Association for the Advancement of Computing in Education Learning Objects Symposium, pp. 39–43, Honolulu, June 2003.
8. Gerry Lang, Creating a Common e-learning Infrastructure, Microsoft Learning Forum Whitepaper.
   http://www.elearningforum.com/meetings/2003/january/eLearningForum_MS2.pdf
10. *The Lydia Global Repository*, 2003. http://www.lydialearn.com/repository.cfm MERLOT : Multimedia Educational Resource for Learning and On-line Teaching, 2002,
   http://www.merlot.org/.
11. Daniel Rehak, "ADL/SCORM - What Does it Mean for Developers of ICT Projects?", Presentation at International Conference on *Reusale Learning Designs: Opportunities and Challenges*, 2002,
   http://www.lsal.cmu.edu/lsal/expertise/papers/presentations/rldoz05122002/rld05122002.pdf
12. Daniel Rehak and Robin Mason, "Keeping the Learning in Learning Objects", in *Reusing Online Resources: A Sustainable Approach to eLearning*, Allison Littlejohn [ed], Kogan Page, March 2003. is a good review of the issues and challenges confronting the design of learning objects and platforms.
   http://www.lsal.cmu.edu/lsal/expertise/papers/chapters/reusing/learninginlo.pdf
13. Merrill, M. D., "Constructivism and instructional design", Educational Technology, pp. 45–53, May 1991.
14. SCORM Version 1.3 Application Profile Working Draft Version 1.0, Advanced Distributed Learning, 2003,
   http://www.adlnet.org/adldocs/Other/SCORMV1.3_AppProfile.zip
   http://www.adlnet.org/index.cfm?fuseaction=scormabt gives an introduction to SCORM.

15. UC Berkeley Interactive University Project Digital Learning Materials, Index Building Connections To A World Of Ideas, http://iu.berkeley.edu/iu/
16. University of Wisconsin-Milwaukee Centre for International Education's Global Passport Project, http://www.uwm.edu/Dept/CIE/AOP/LO_bib.html is an excellent bibliography for learning objects http://www.lsal.cmu.edu/lsal/expertise/papers/index.html is a fairly current and comprehensive collection of articles about e-learning.

Creativity in Digital Libraries and Information Retrieval Environments

Shu-Shing Lee, Yin-Leng Theng, and Dion Hoe-Lian Goh

Division of Information Studies, School of Communication and Information
Nanyang Technological University, Singapore 637718
{ps7918592b,tyltheng,ashlgoh}@ntu.edu.sg

Abstract. Inspired by Weisberg's [20] argument that creativity exists in everyone and on the assumption that every information seeker is creative and undergoes a creative process in information seeking, this paper synthesizes a holistic "creativity" model and "information seeking" model to identify stages in a creative process for information seeking. A pilot study was conducted to verify these stages and also examine if present digital libraries and information retrieval environments provide "creative" features to support creative information seeking. We discussed these initial findings and made recommendations for further work to better support creative information seeking in digital libraries and information retrieval environments.

1 Introduction

Most information retrieval (IR) systems are designed to judge precision and recall of documents based on a match between index and query terms. However, precision and recall measures are limited, as they do not consider the contextual nature of human judgment. Measures of precision and recall should take into account that relevance is influenced by the knowledge state and intentions of the user [3], implying that relevance judgment is subjective. Moreover, since everyone has creative traits as argued by Weisberg [20], it can be inferred that the extent of creativity in a person influences his/her judgment of relevancy. If creativity is built on past experiences, then a creative person's judgment of relevancy will also be affected. In other words, if a person's past experience shows that some sources are not useful, he/she may judge documents from these sources as irrelevant and hence likely not use them in his/her creative process for information seeking.

Our study is inspired by Weisberg's [20] argument that creativity exists in everyone and results from ordinary thinking, which is a continuity of the past. Individuals deal with new situations based on previous experiences in similar situations. However, it must not be misunderstood that works based on past experiences have no novelty. Based on this theory, we make the assumption that *every information seeker is creative and undergoes a creative process in information seeking*.

This paper, therefore, attempts to establish a relationship between "creativity" and "information seeking". Establishing such a relationship is important as it provides a

T.M.T. Sembok et al. (Eds.): ICADL 2003, LNCS 2911, pp. 398–410, 2003.

different perspective of information seeking leading to new and perhaps improved ways of developing interfaces for supporting IR. Such a perspective sees a creative process as inherent in information seeking and may therefore improve query formulation and refinement, searching, browsing, and filtering, thereby, helping users better meet their information needs.

Sections 2.1 and 2.2 survey "creativity" models and "information seeking" models respectively to provide a basis for developing stages in creative information seeking in Section 3, resulting in a set of design features for supporting creativity in digital libraries (DLs) and information retrieval environments (IREs). A pilot study was then conducted to address two objectives: (1) to verify the stages in a creative process for information seeking and (2) to examine if ACM Digital Library and EI Engineering Village 2, examples of DLs and IREs respectively, have implemented "creative" features to support users' creative process for information seeking.

2 Creativity and Information Seeking

2.1 Survey of Creativity Models

Creativity means different things to different people. One definition associates it with the genius. Weisberg [20] highlights that attempts to understand creativity in our society is largely dominated by the "genius" view, which associates creative achievements as a result of great individuals using extraordinary processes. However, he argues that creativity is a trait that everyone has and that novelty results from the use of similar thinking processes when a particular person is put in a particular environment. Weisberg [20] emphasizes that his argument is not trying to claim that great individuals who produce original works are the same as ordinary individuals but that the thinking processes used are similar. Other definitions of creativity associate it with process-oriented or product-oriented views. Process-oriented definition highlights creativity as a process that results in innovative products [7, 12]. Product-oriented views associate creativity to the attributes of the outcome. Only when an outcome is both novel and valuable can creativity be said to have happened [1].

Synthesizing the different views for creativity, we define attributes of a holistic model of creativity focusing on the four fundamental aspects of a creative person, process, product, and environment [17, 18, 20]:

o   Attribute #1 - Creative Person. The creative person should have imagination, independence, and divergent thinking ability [5]. The ability to think 'holistically' is a key feature. It is vital to help a person break away from conventional ideas when one faces a dead end. King and Pope [13] also associate the creative person with psychological richness, complexity, and openness to experience.

o   Attribute #2 - Creative Process. The creative process can be broken down into four stages [11]:

1.   *Preparation.* The individual gets interested in the problem and collects all necessary data needed.

2.   *Incubation.* The individual unconsciously works on the problem.

3.   *Illumination.* Possible ideas start to surface to consciousness.

4.   *Verification.* The idea is worked into a communicable form.

o Attribute #3 - Creative Product. A creative product satisfies two properties: novelty and value [1, 10, 20]. Novelty is determined by a comparison of the new product with existing ones [1, 10]. Value is concerned with the relevance of the product to human purposes [1]. Amabile [2] explains that judgment of a creative product is dependant on a group of appropriate observers.

o Attribute #4 - Creative Environment. A creative environment's characteristics include boldness, courage, freedom, spontaneity, clarity, and self-acceptance [16]. The environment should support collaboration since idea generation and creativity do not occur in isolation [6, 15].

2.2   Survey of Information Seeking Models

To help us establish a mapping between "creativity" models and "information seeking" models, we briefly revisit some established information seeking models. Taylor's [19] model focuses on the importance of negotiation between the inquirer and librarian so that information needs can be addressed. On the other hand, the Sense Making Model focuses on how individuals use observations of others as their own to construct pictures of reality and use these pictures to guide their search behavior [4]. Wilson's [21] model focuses primarily on how information needs arise, context of the information as well as barriers that may prevent the actual search for information. Other models focus specifically on the activities and behaviors characteristic in information seeking. Kuhlthau's [14] model concerns the feelings, thoughts, and actions associated with different stages of the "information search process".

In this paper, we make use of the behavioral model of information seeking as postulated by Ellis [8] and Ellis, Cox and Hall [9] as it takes into account the subjective sequence of information seeking behavior/activities, which varies according to the context and circumstances of the seeker at that point of time. In addition, it also focuses specifically on the activities in information seeking. Using this model, the information seeker undergoes eight generic activities [8, 9]:

o Activity #1 - Starting: This refers to activities characteristic of the initial search for information on a new topic or area. The seeker may have some or no familiarity with the topic or area. Examples of these activities include asking colleagues, consulting literature reviews, catalogues, abstracts, and indexes.

o Activity #2 - Chaining: This refers to following chains of citation connections between materials, which can be forward chaining and backward chaining. Forward chaining involves the use of citation indexes or bibliographic tools to identify citations to relevant materials. Backward chaining refers to following up references cited in materials consulted.

o Activity #3 - Browsing: Semi-structured or semi-directed searching in an area of potential interest. Activities in this stage include browsing table of contents of journals, checking sources available in the library, browsing along shelves, and using the "browse" and "search" features of IR systems.

o Activity #4 - Differentiating: Using characteristics/differences in information sources to filter the amount of information obtained. Some characteristics for filtering include topic of study, creditability, author, type of source, and language.

o Activity #5 - Monitoring: Maintaining awareness of developments in a field through regular monitoring of particular sources. Methods that information seekers use to monitor sources include the use of informal contacts, monitoring services, research directories, and journals and publishers' catalogues.

o Activity #6 - Extracting: Systemically working through a particular source to locate materials of interest. This activity requires the seeker to set aside substantial amount of time to go through sources, like journals, books, computer databases, and indexes to locate information of interest. This activity is the most directed among all information seeking activities.

o Activity #7 - Verifying: This involves checking the accuracy of information.

o Activity #8 - Ending: Activities characteristic of information seeking found at the end of a topic or project, for example, during the preparation of papers for publication.

3 Stages and Design Features for Creative Information Seeking

In Section 3.1, we establish and present a proposed mapping between a holistic creativity model and an established information seeking model. Section 3.2 identifies potential design features to foster a creative process for information seeking. Section 3.3 develops stages in a creative process for information seeking and design features to support creative information seeking in DLs and IREs.

3.1 Establishing Mappings between 'Creativity''and 'Information Seeking''

A walkthrough of the "creative process" (as discussed in Attribute #2, Section 2.1) and the "information seeking activities" (as discussed in Activities #1-#8, Section 2.2) revealed four common links between the two models. We synthesized and organized these common links to reflect the *creative process* in *information seeking* and they are presented as follows:

o Link #1. Preparation in the "creative process" is concerned with collecting all necessary information to facilitate creativity. Thus, this stage can be linked to starting, chaining, and browsing in "information seeking" (see Activities #1-#3; Section 2.2) as these behaviors are also concerned with collecting information.

o Link #2. Incubation as described in the "creative process" involves unconsciously solving the problem. This means that the creative person is unconsciously trying to make linkages among information and some sort of filtering must occur to facilitate the linking process. Hence, incubation can be mapped to differentiating in "information seeking" (see Activity #4; Section 2.2).

o Link #3. Illumination happens when an idea strikes. The possible information seeking behaviors that facilitate this process include monitoring developments and extracting relevant information from information sources (see Activity #5, #6; Section 2.2), which also relates to illumination in the "creative process".

o Link #4. This stage involves working the idea into a communicable form. Checking accuracy of information takes place before the idea is worked into such a format. Thus, verification in creativity is linked to verification behavior in information seeking (see Activity #7; Section 2.2).

The common links identified between the "creative process" and the "information seeking activities" provide a basis for identifying stages in creative information seeking. Hence hereinafter, we would rename these links to describe "stages" in a creative process for information seeking.

3.2   Identifying Stages in Creative Information Seeking and Its Design Feature

Having established the common links/stages between the "creative process" and the "information seeking activities", we then brainstormed on a set of design features together with information specialists that might foster creativity in DLs and IREs. Design features that might foster each stage (as highlighted in Section 3.1) between "creativity" and "information seeking" are described as follows:

o   Stage #1. Features here should assist users to acquire information to begin the creative process. Such features are: search/browse, iterative searching, relevance feedback, customization and personalization, cross-referencing, subject classification, and query refinement. It is also important for DLs and IREs to clearly state sources available and its domain of focus. Other value-adding features include: collaboration, encouraging learning from mistakes, and providing rewards and praise.

o   Stage #2. Features that help users reduce information and make connections between materials are: collaboration with domain experts, providing sources from different domains, relevance feedback, and filtering criteria. Incubation can be long and frustrating. Features that help make the process more pleasant would be: encouraging learning from mistakes, providing rewards and praise, showing interest in helping users, providing system usability, offering learning opportunities, and allowing users to stop and begin searching.

o   Stage #3. Features that foster monitoring and extracting for idea discovery could be: collaboration, current awareness searching and profile, subject classification, and relevance feedback. Features should also motivate and encourage users towards illumination. They could be: encouraging learning from mistakes, providing rewards and praise, showing interest in helping users, providing system usability, offering learning opportunities, and guiding users from novices to experts.

o   Stage #4. Features that facilitate verification would include: iteration of search process; relevance feedback; providing collaboration and contacts among subject experts, and search/browse. Value-adding features to enhance usability include: encouraging learning from mistakes; guiding users to move from novices to experts; providing rewards and praise, and system evaluation/feedback.

3.3   Establishing Stages in a Creative Information Seeking Process

A further examination of the features described in Section 3.2 to foster stages in a creative process for information seeking showed that repetitions existed among features in the different stages. This was because too many information seeking behaviors were grouped to each creative stage. For example, in Stage #1, preparation in a creative process was linked with starting, chaining, and browsing activities in information seeking (see Stage #1; Section 3.1). Thus, the stages were refined. This time, a stage was established only when there was an obvious similarity between stages in a creative process (see Attribute #2; Section 2.1) and activities in information seeking (see Activities #1-#8; Section 2.2). Otherwise, concepts were kept separate. In other words, in Stage #1, preparation in a creative process (see Attribute #2; Section 2.1) could only be mapped to starting in information seeking activities (see Activity #1; Section 2.2) since both were concerned with commencing. Chaining and browsing in information seeking (see Activity #2 and #3; Section 2.2) should be kept separate, as they were not related to preparation in creative process.

This new set of mappings created the revised six stages in a creative process for information seeking. Terminology used for these stages were derived from creativity and information seeking models and hence grounded in these models. A final set of design features to foster each stage was iteratively refined and is presented as follows:

o Stage #1 - Preparation for starting information seeking. Features here focus on how the DLs and IREs prepare users for information seeking and how DLs and IREs prepare themselves for information seeking. The basis for this stage and features came from Stage #1 (Sections 3.1 and 3.2). These features could be: customization and personalization according to creative/information seeking ability, offering learning activities to enhance creativity, showing interest in helping users achieve need, and stating the domain focus of its sources.

o Stage #2 - Chaining information sources. Features included here are: cross-referencing within system, subject classification to help users obtain sources on a particular topic, and offering a variety of sources from various domains. These features help users find/track related materials. The rationale behind this stage and features were derived from Stage #1 (Sections 3.1 and 3.2).

o Stage #3 - Browsing and searching. This stage and its features are grounded in Stage #1 (Sections 3.1 and 3.2). Features here are concerned with facilitating browsing and searching so that sufficient information is acquired to support incubation and illumination. Such features would be: providing clear structured ways of searching, guiding users to move from novices to experts, mapping design features to information seeking, query formulation, browse/search features, relevance feedback, and search iteration.

o Stage #4 - Incubation for differentiating purposes. This stage is concerned with unconsciously filtering information and establishing linkages. Supportive features included are: encouraging learning from mistakes, providing reward and praise, filtering criteria, offering access to subject experts, and allowing users to stop and continue information seeking at any time. The formulation of this stage and its supportive features were derived from Stage #2 discussed in Sections 3.1 and 3.2.

o Stage #5 - Monitoring and extracting for illumination. The foundation for this stage and its features are provided by Stage #3 (Sections 3.1 and 3.2). Monitoring developments in a field and extracting relevant information are essential for illumination. Facilitating features could be: collaboration to enhance creativity, and providing current awareness search and profile.

o Stage #6 - Verification of information sources. After illumination, it is important that ideas are verified and worked into a communicable form. Features that support these processes are: providing contacts of subject experts/authors for verification as well as evaluation features to verify system uncertainties and for designers to improve the system. The rationale for this stage and features arose from Stage #4 in sections 3.1 and 3.2.

4   Pilot Study

A pilot study was conducted to fulfill 2 objectives:

(1) To verify the stages in a creative process for information seeking; and
(2) To examine whether ACM Digital Library and EI Engineering Village 2, examples of DLs and IREs respectively, have implemented design features (see Section 3.3) to support users' creative process for information seeking.

Subjects and Selected Digital Library / Information Retrieval Environment
The six subjects (denoted as S1-S6) selected were post-graduate research students: three 2nd-year PhD students and three 2nd-year Masters students. Three subjects were from the Communications Division and others were from the Information Studies Division in the School of Communication and Information (Nanyang Technological University). All subjects had experience using DLs and IREs. These subjects were divided into two groups. Group 1 (S1-S3) was asked to find an article using a digital library (DL), ACM Digital Library (ACMDL; see http://www.acmdl.org). Group 2 (S4-S6) was asked to find another article using an information retrieval environment (IRE), EI Engineering Village 2 (EV2; see http://www.engineeringvillage2.org). ACMDL and EV2 were chosen, as they were among the most commonly used DLs and IREs, after consultation with information specialists.

Protocol for Objective 1
Subjects were asked to solve an information need related to vocabulary problems in information retrieval using their respective DL and IRE. S1-S3 were first briefed on ACMDL and S4-S6 were briefed on EV2. Then they were provided a search query, which they used to find a specified article related to the information need. Subjects could use the query provided or develop their own. After they had found the article, they noted the steps taken in a form provided.

Protocol for Objective 2
We did a walkthrough of ACMDL and EV2 based on the proposed design features (as discussed in Section 3.3) that might foster creative information seeking. For each proposed design feature, implemented features in ACMDL and EV2 that satisfied the proposed one were noted.

5   Findings and Analyses

In Section 5.1, we present findings for objective 1 of the study and focus on whether the steps taken by the subjects matched the six stages proposed in Section 3.3 in a creative process for information seeking. Section 5.2 presents findings for objective 2 of the study and focuses on whether ACMDL and EV2 have incorporated design features to support users' creative process for information seeking.

5.1   Findings for Objective 1: Creative Information Seeking Behavior

Findings for objective 1 seemed to indicate that subjects went through similar stages in creative information seeking as those discussed in Section 3.3. The only differences among them were the query terms used and how they executed the query within the system. When these stages were compared with proposed stages in a creative process for information seeking, similar behaviors were evident. Discussion of findings following these proposed stages (see Section 3.3) are as follows:

o   <u>Preparation for starting information seeking.</u> Subjects began information seeking by first reading and understanding the task presented.

o   <u>Chaining information sources.</u> Subjects did not exhibit forward and backward chaining. However, subjects did some sort of chaining by picking up keywords based on the information need and specified article. They chained these keywords together to establish a query. S1 and S2 selected the title as a query term while S3 selected keywords from the title as query terms. S4-S6 used the query provided and added the article's author as a query term.

o   <u>Browsing and searching.</u> During browsing, subjects constructed the query that mapped the system's design using previously selected query terms and executed the query. S1 and S2 did a title search using the simple and advanced search interface respectively. S3 did a keyword search in the simple interface. S4-S6 combined keyword, title, and author search to look for the article.

o   <u>Incubation for differentiating purposes.</u> Based on information presented in the results list, subjects filtered out irrelevant records, and decided which record was most likely to be the correct one.

o   <u>Monitoring and extracting for illumination.</u> After deciding which was the most likely record from the results list, subjects went to the actual record to extract more information about the article.

o   <u>Verification of information sources.</u> Information extracted from the actual record was used to verify that it was indeed the correct article needed.

These findings seemed to indicate that subjects' steps taken matched the proposed stages of a creative process for information seeking except for stage #2. Findings showed that stage #2 should include aspects such as chaining of keywords to create a query other than forward and backward chaining. Certainly, more studies need to be carried out to verify these stages with different users DLs and IREs.

5.2   Findings for Objective 2: Examining ACMDL and EV2

This section discusses the findings and analyses collected for objective 2 of the study, examining ACMDL and EV2 for "features" that might support the six stages in a creative process in information seeking.

ACMDL
Stage #1 – Preparation for starting information seeking. ACMDL's features which assisted this stage were: personalized "bookshelves" for users to save relevant documents, allowing users to receive search updates based on saved queries, search guides, free access to some portions of the digital library, recommendations of relevant documents, and brief description of its domain focus. These features helped

ACMDL prepare users for information seeking and ensured that it was prepared to facilitate users' information seeking process.

Stage #2 – Chaining of information sources. ACMDL supported chaining of information sources by providing links to available documents used in references of other documents, enabling links to past journals/proceedings, offering a variety of sources by ACM, and presenting index terms and subject classification of documents. These features helped users find related documents.

Stage #3 – Browsing and Searching. In terms of facilitative features for searching and browsing, ACMDL provided tools that were mapped to information seeking activities and guided users to move from novices to experts. Features implemented were: basic/advanced search interface, search fields and guides, enabling users to search similar documents, searching within results set, browse feature for different journals/proceedings, sorting of results by relevance, title and publication date, and displaying a maximum of 200 records in results set.

Stage #4 – Incubation for differentiating purposes. Features in ACMDL that facilitated incubation for differentiating purposes involved helping users filter and establish linkages among documents. These features included: offering query suggestions when no results or spelling errors occurred; displaying a maximum of 200 records in results set; ranking of results by relevance; providing citation and abstract information in records, and automatic and personal updating of saved queries.

Stage #5 – Monitoring and extracting for illumination. Supportive features for stage #5 within ACMDL were: discussion forums for documents, sharing of documents among users, e-mail alerts of new issues of publications, and personal/automatic search updating of saved queries.

Stage #6 – Verification of information sources. Implemented features that fostered Stage #6 included: discussion forum for documents for verification purposes and feedback features for users to verify any system uncertainties with designers for further improvement.

Figure 1 highlights some features in ACMDL and the stages these features might support in the creative process for information seeking.

EV2
Stage #1 – Preparation for starting information seeking. Supportive features for stage #1 included: search updates via e-mail; search guides and tips; access to librarians and subject experts; auto-stemming feature to include all variations of a query term, and different views and output formats. These features helped EV2 prepare users for information seeking and ensured that it was prepared to facilitate users' information seeking process.

Stage #2 – Chaining information sources. In terms of fostering chaining of information sources, implemented features in EV2 included: providing different types of sources from applied science and engineering domains; displaying index terms of documents, and browsing of different indexes to help users find related documents. These features helped users find related documents and understand the sub-domains in a main domain.

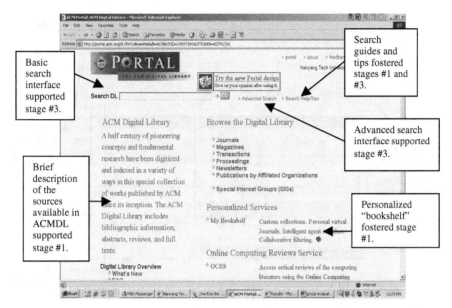

Fig. 1. Some Features in ACMDL and Its Supportive Stages

Stage #3 – Browsing and searching. Facilitative features for browsing and searching within EV2 were: search guides, access to librarians and subject experts, allowing browsing of index to find suitable query terms, basic/advanced search interface, search refinement, search history, reset search query, ranking of results by relevance, and viewing of records in citation, abstract and detail formats.

Stage #4 – Incubation for differentiating purposes. Features in EV2 that might foster incubation for differentiating purposes included: providing brief/detail citation and abstract information for each record; access to librarians and subject experts, and receiving e-mail search updates of saved queries.

Stage #5 –Monitoring and extracting for illumination. Facilitative features for stage #5 were: access to librarians and subject experts and allowing receipt of search updates via e-mail.

Stage #6 – Verification of information sources. Features for assisting verification of information sources in EV2 were: access to librarians and subject experts for verification and feedback features for verifying any system uncertainties with system designers for further enhancement.

Figure 2 highlights some features in EV2 and the stages these features might support in the creative process in information seeking.

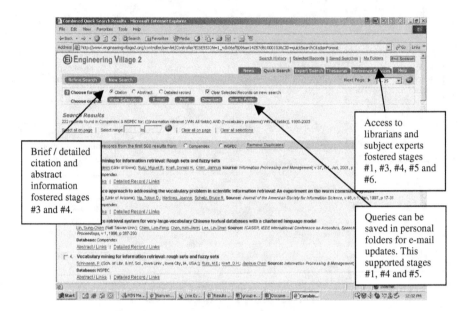

Fig. 2. Some Features in EV2 and Its Supportive Stages

6   Conclusions and On-Going Work

Through synthesizing a holistic model of creativity and an established information seeking model, six stages in a creative process for information seeking and design features were developed. These stages in creative information seeking differ from Ellis' [8, 9] information seeking model as they focus on cognitive processes in information seeking rather than behavioral activities in information seeking. Such a focus may have different implications on the design of DLs and IREs when compared with traditional information seeking models. DLs and IREs designed to support stages in a creative information seeking process might have features that focus on cognitive aspects of information seeking, such as ranking of results based on seekers' subjective relevance rather than a match between index and query terms and allowing users to create a mind map of related documents and their associations.

Findings gathered from a pilot study seemed to indicate that subjects' steps matched the six proposed stages in a creative process for information seeking except for stage #2, chaining for information sources. Findings showed that stage #2 should not include just forward and backward chaining but should also encompass chaining of terms to form a query. The study also inspected and found features in ACMDL and EV2 that might support creative information seeking.

This is an on-going research. Proposed stages in a creative process for information seeking and its supportive design features need to be further refined, tested, and used in real-world situations before they can emerge as stages and principles for the design of DLs and IREs to support users' creative information seeking behaviours.

More work needs to be done in objective 1 with different users, DLs, and IREs to refine the proposed stages in creative information seeking. Further work to objective 2 include studies on different DLs and IREs, and the usefulness and usability of the design features to support users' creative process in information seeking.

References

1. Akin, O., & Akin, C. (1998). On the process of creativity in puzzles, inventions and designs. *Automation in Construction, 7,* 123–138.
2. Amabile, T. M. (1990). Within you, without you: The social psychology of creativity, and beyond. In M. A. Runco & R. S. Albert (Eds.) *Theories of creativity* (pp. 61–91). California, U.S.A: Sage Publications.
3. Case, D. O. (2002). *Looking for information: A survey of research on information seeking, needs, and behaviour.* California, USA: Elsevier Science.
4. Dervin, B., & Dewdney, P. (1986). Neutral questioning: A new approach to the reference interview. *Reference Quarterly, 25*(4), 506–513.
5. Diakidoy I. N. & Kanari, E. (1999). Student teachers' beliefs about creativity. *British Educational Research Journal, 25*(2), 225–243.
6. Drazin, R., Glynn, M. A. & Kazanjian, R. K. (1999). Multilevel theorising about creativity in organisations: A sensemaking perspective. *Academic Management Review, 24*(2), 286–307.
7. Edmonds, E., & Candy L. (2002). Creativity, art practice, and knowledge. *Communications of the ACM, 45*(10), 91–95.
8. Ellis, D. (1989). A behavioral approach to information retrieval design. *Journal of Documentation, 45*(3), 171–212.
9. Ellis, D., Cox, D., & Hall, K. (1993). A comparison of information seeking patterns of researchers in the physical and social sciences. *Journal of Documentation, 49*(4), 356–369.
10. Fischer, G., & Nakakoji, K. (1997). Computational environments supporting creativity in the context of lifelong learning and design. *Knowledge-Based Systems, 10,* 21–28.
11. Gabora, L. (2002). Cognitive mechanisms underlying the creative process. *Proceedings of the Fourth Conference on Creativity and Cognition,* UK, 126–133.
12. Kazanjian, R. K., Drazin, R., & Glynn, M. A. (2000). Creativity and technological learning: The roles of organisation architecture and crisis in large-scale products. *Journal of Engineering and Technology Management, 17,* 273–298.
13. King, B. J., & Pope, B. (1999). Creativity as a factor in psychological assessment and healthy psychological functioning. *Journal of Personality Assessment, 72*(2), 200–207.
14. Kuhlthau, C. C. (1993). A principle of uncertainty for information seeking. *Journal of Documentation, 49*(4). 339–355.
15. MacCrimmon, K. R. & Wagner, C. (1994). Simulating ideas through creative software. *Management Science, 40*(11), 1514–1532.
16. Maslow, A. H. (1959). Creativity in self-actualising people. In H. H. Anderson (Ed.) *Creativity and its cultivation* (pp. 83–95). New York: Harper Collins.
17. Mooney, R. L. (1963). A conceptual model for integrating four approaches to the identification of creative talent. In C. W. Taylor & F. Barron (Eds.) *Scientific creativity: Its recognition and development* (pp. 331–340). New York: Wiley.
18. Rhodes, M. (1961). An analysis of creativity. *Phi Delta Kappan, 42*(7), 305–310.
19. Taylor, R. (1968). Question-negotiation and information seeking in libraries. *College and Research Libraries, 29*(3), 178–194.

20. Weisberg, R. W. (1993). *Creativity beyond the myth of genius.* New York: W.H. Freeman and Company.
21. Wilson, T.D. (1981). On user studies and information needs. *Journal of Documentation, 37*(1), 3–15.

Towards a Digital Document Archive for Historical Handwritten Music Scores

I. Bruder, A. Finger, A. Heuer, and T. Ignatova

Database Research Group, Computer Science Department,
University of Rostock, Germany
{ilr,af,ah,ti005}@informatik.uni-rostock.de

Abstract. Contemporary digital libraries and archives of music scores focus mainly on providing efficient storage and access methods for their data. However, digital archives of historical music scores can enable musicologists not only to easily store and access research material, but also to derive new knowledge from existing data. In this paper we present the first steps in building a digital archive of historical music scores from the 17th and 18th century. Along with the architectural and accessibility aspects of the system, we describe an integrated approach for classification and identification of the scribes of music scores.

1 Introduction

Handwritten music scores were a way to record, copy and disseminate music during the late 17th century until the beginning of the 19th century. There exist large collections of such music scores in libraries, archives etc. around the world. The information encoded in these music sheets, such as melody, title, time and place of origin, composer and scribe is of great interest to musicologists. Some of these data are often not found in alphanumeric form in manuscripts, but have to be derived analyzing other document features. Complex typographic and visual features such as handwriting characteristics, water marks etc. are used in practice for the analysis.

This paper represents the latest results from the ongoing project "eNoteHistory", realizing a digital archive for a collection of about 1000 historical music scores from the 17th and 18th century, property of the Library of the University of Rostock. Apart from the scanned score images we store a considerable number of corresponding metadata such as bibliographic and feature data, reflecting the diverse aspects on the content of the manuscripts. We employ full-text, structural and feature-based retrieval techniques to provide complex searching possibilities for different user scenarios. So far our system does not differ to a great extend from existing digital music archives, such as Meldex[1] or DIAMM[2] and many others. However we see the novel challenge of our work in the design of an effective approach for combining the various data in the digital archive to extract new information of interest to the musicologists and in

---

[1] http://www.nzdl.org/fast-cgi-bin/music/musiclibrary
[2] DIAMM – Digital image archive of medieval music, http://www.diamm.ac.uk/

T.M.T. Sembok et al. (Eds.): ICADL 2003, LNCS 2911, pp. 411–414, 2003.

particular to identify the scribes of the manuscripts. As classification base we use the handwriting characteristics of the scribes. We have defined a so called Feature Dictionary data structure, resembling a systematisation of the external knowledge used for the description of handwriting characteristics. Currently we develop algorithms for building classes for identifying music scribes based on these features.

2 Architecture and User Scenarios

The digital document archive is implemented using object-relational database system (ORDBMS) techniques, provided in the IBM DB2 UDB environment, offering extensions such as user-defined types, user-defined functions, XML-, text- and data mining-extensions. The advantages of ORDBMS are discussed in [5]. The document workflow considered by the system design is illustrated in Fig. 1.

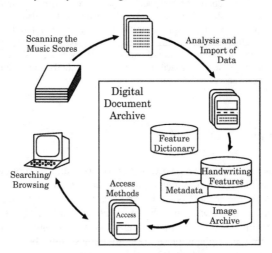

Fig. 1. Digital Document Archive Workflow

The first steps in designing the digital library as suggested in [6] were to define the sources of material and the required data models. We have identified the following groups of material: scanned music scores, corresponding metadata and feature data from the handwriting analysis. The scanned *music scores* build up the image archive. The image attributes and characteristics are also included in the image archive data model to provide enough information for later image processing, browsing or displaying. The *metadata* includes bibliographic data, descriptions of the documents and works, place and time of origin, composer's name etc. These data exist in LaTeX format and is the result of a scientific work published in [3]. In the produced material the RISM[3] database for historical music manuscripts has been referenced and links to it are provided in the metadata schema by shelf mark references. We have defined a relational data model to represent the semi-structured text data. Then we extracted the

---

[3] RISM - Répertoire International des Sources Musicales, http://rism.stub.uni-frankfurt.de/

content of the LaTeX sources by parsing and transforming the LaTeX document elements and items into XML structures. The XML structures were afterwards mapped to the relational database schema. Employing Text- and XML-based access structures and mechanisms in the ORDBMS provides enhanced possibilities to store, update, retrieve, browse and represent the metadata.

The third group of source material comprises the *handwriting features*, generated from the analysis of the music scores. The extraction and determination of handwriting characteristics from the manuscripts requires experts' knowledge, which is supported by a predefined Feature Dictionary, stored and maintained also in the database. The Feature Dictionary data structure comprises a set of classification trees, where each tree represents a single feature, such as a note stem form, clefs forms etc. A node in the tree corresponds to a certain expression of a feature, represented by a pictogram and a description. A musicologist will be able to browse these trees to find the best matching feature expressions for the analyzed document. Thus the handwriting specific features are stored in the database along with the corresponding images of the scanned manuscripts. These features can be defined on different levels: for a manuscript page, for a whole manuscript, or for a single scribe. The final aim is to be able to gather enough representative material to build classes for all scribes of the analyzed collection. To each class a unique handwriting signature will be appointed, represented by a set of handwriting feature vectors. Therefore we currently implement and evaluate clustering and classification functions using the DB2 Intelligent Miner for Data. A second approach for handwriting feature extraction and scribe identification will be implemented incorporating Optical Music Recognition (OMR) techniques, which are currently in an advanced phase of development and testing. Recent results from the OMR study have been published in [1]. The handwriting characteristics, which are the output from the OMR analysis, are also based on the Feature Dictionary representations used by the manual analysis. The OMR algorithms will become part of the ORDBMS by implementing them as a set of user-defined function for processing the score images supporting the manual analysis. The integration of image analysis functions into ORDBMS and content-based retrieval systems, is discussed in [2,4].

To provide comprehensive methods for data access and retrieval the implementation of different user scenarios illustrated in Fig. 2 is required. One of the most frequently used data access methods is searching. We provide the opportunity to search the archive for words and phrases in bibliographic metadata and source description data using the full-text extension. A second data access possibility is a convenient browsing through metadata, score images, or the Feature Dictionary. The last one and most complex search scenario is a very important access method for musicologists, where a scribe identification can be performed using the Feature Dictionary. Two approaches are implemented: a manual analysis and an automatic analysis and identification. The manual identification is based on browsing through the Feature Dictionary to find similar features to the unknown scribe. Known scribes with similar characteristics are retrieved from the database after comparing the handwriting characteristics of the unknown scribe with those of the scribes classes stored in the database. The scribe identification by automatic analysis is based on the OMR algorithms mentioned above. A scanned page of a score is processed to extract the corresponding handwriting characteristics automatically and then the scribes with the highest score of similarity on their handwriting characteristics from the database are presented as candidates for the identification. If the degree of similarity in both cases is not satisfactory a procedure for adding a new scribe class will be carried out.

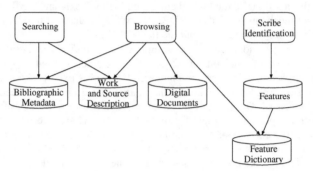

Fig. 2. User Scenarios

3 Conclusions

The presented digital archive of historical music scores enables data storage, analysis, retrieval, access and presentation of music material. Moreover the intelligent system extension for scribe identification, supporting the data analysis and mining is an essential part of the implementation, which sets new requirements to digital archives and libraries. Considering the need to integrate other regionally and historically varying music scores a reliability and validity evaluation and possibly adaptation of the results from the handwriting characteristics extraction and the methods for their analysis will be carried out.

References

1. R.Göcke. Building a System for Writer Identification on Handwritten Music Scores. In *Proceedings of the IASTED International Conference on Signal Processing, Pattern Recognition and Applications 2003*, Rhodes, Greece, 2003.
2. W. Kiessling, K. Erber-Urch, W.-T. Balke, T. Birke, and M. Wagner. The HERON Project - Multimedia Database Support for History and Human Sciences. In J. Dassow and R. Kruse, editors, *Informatik '98: Informatik zwischen Bild und Sprache*, pages 309–318. Springer Verlag, Heidelberg, 1998.
3. E. Krueger, The Handwritten Music Scores in the Collection of the Prince Friedrich Ludwig of Wuerttemberg and the Duchess Frederica Louise of Mecklenburg-Schwerin at the Library of the University of Rostock. Ph.D. thesis, University of Rostock, Germany, 2002.
4. M. Ortega-Binderberger, K. Chakrabarti, and S. Mehrotra. Database Support for Multimedia Applications. In V. Castelli and L. D. Bergman, editors, *Image Databases – Search and Retrieval of Digital Imagery*. 2002.
5. M. Stonebreaker, P. Brown. Object-Relational DBMS: Tracking the Next Great Wave. Morgan Kaufmann, 1999.
6. I. Witten, D. Bainbridge. How to Build a Digital Library. Morgan Kaufmann, 2003.

Knowledge Seeking Activities for Content Intelligence*

Key-Sun Choi[1] and Yeun-Bae Kim[2]

[1] Computer Science Division, Korterm, KAIST, 373-1 Guseong-dong Yuseong-gu
Daejeon 305-701 Korea
kschoi@cs.kaist.ac.kr
[2] Human Science Division, NHK STRL, 1-10-11 Kinuta Setagaya-ku
Tokyo 157-8510 Japan
kimu.y-go@nhk.or.jp

Abstract. This paper proposes a problem on the knowledge seeking activities compared with information seeking and knowledge discovery from text. A knowledge seeking activity is accomplished by a dynamic linkage of contents that is called "content intelligence." An algorithm called "crossover" of knowledge units is proposed.

1   Introduction

"Content" can be anything that is conveyed or contained by a medium with proper handling method(s) or algorithms. We assume that the content is a text-based entity, e.g. Web documents, semantic web, captions for video data, dialog text, speech-recognized audio data with metadata. By the term "content intelligence", "content" itself will be able to acquire and apply knowledge from other chunks of "content", and will be capable of self-reasoning and being autonomous.

For example, suppose that we have a series of lecture files (e.g., PowerPoint slides), whose file names are $f_1, f_2 ... f_n$. Each file has its own segmentations. That is, each file contains several subtopics: m subtopics for the file f_1 are $f_{1,1}, f_{1,2} ... f_{1,m}$. If a student asks a question $q(t)$ about a topic t, the answering against $q(t)$ can be found in several lecture files (say, f_1, f_3, f_5) and the right answers can be assembled from subtopics inside of each file, with the consideration of the student's prior-knowledge about the topic t. For example, a right answer is a sequence $f_{1,1}, f_{3,5} ... f_{5,2}$. Here we need to assume that there is an effective way to extract or be aware of the student's prior-knowledge on the topic t. A "causality" relation among answering segments (e.g., $f_{1,1}$, $f_{3,5} ... f_{5,2}$) is one of obligatory properties for justification of answers.

"Content intelligence" is enabled by metadata attached to the content, topic-specific ontology, resource ontology (to denote the real resource linked to nodes in

---

* This research was supported by Ministry of Science and Technology, Korea under Brain NeuroInfomatics Research Program for "Knowledge Base Prototype Construction and Its Application for Human Knowledge Processing Modeling" (2001~2004). The major work also had been supported by NHK Science & Technology Research Laboratories (STRL) during the period from March/2002~Feb/2003 while the first author stayed in NHK STRL.

T.M.T. Sembok et al. (Eds.): ICADL 2003, LNCS 2911, pp. 415–426, 2003.
© Springer-Verlag Berlin Heidelberg 2003

ontology), and the methods (or programs) to handle them. "Method" means the reasoning faculty as well as the knowledge acquisition/application capacity. A method constitutes the "explanation" capabilities through the "causality" tracking.

"Networked content intelligence" assumes that "content" features (1) format diversity as well as (2) the distributedness of their location. In this context, we will say: first, "intelligence" in a content (say, c_i) wants other relevant contents in the network probed and merged in order to answer the question $q(t)$ through the causal reasoning based on its own knowledge:(say, $\{c_j|$ relevancy(c_i,c_j) is important or causal-related}). Second, this process does not assume the physical integration of ontologies in different contents, but it assumes the integration of logical causal ontologies, depending on the question and its intention. This means that we can escape from any noise of totally physical integration between two different knowledge spaces.

First, some of the most precious things we get from content intelligence are: explanations about facts or incidents with multi-aspectual proofs based on solid contents (e.g., multimedia), and discovery of new facts and rules/patterns from networked contents by exploring causality residing inside of contents. *Second*, "causal justification" is important in knowledge-seeking activities. There are two different concepts: knowledge-seeking and knowledge-discovery. The act of seeking requires an explicit circumstance but discovery is an implicit, passive and natural act. Some discovery activities may require more than causal justification (maybe some factual or belief patterns). *Third*, causal justification has been studied in the knowledge-based logical inference as well as probabilistic causal reasoning, for example, based on Bayesian belief net [1]. But the "why"- or "how"-type question-and-answering has not been solved fully.

2   Relevant Works and Problem Definition

Two relevant problems about information seeking and knowledge discovery from text will be discussed in order to define our problem "knowledge seeking". Then an example is shown.

2.1   Comparison and Definition

"Information seeking problem" assumes "resource ontology" associating query components with the resources including the information that is searched for. "Resource ontology" lets the users (or the program) know the exact location of the relevant information for the specific type of query. For example, consider the question "How far is it from Mascat to Kandahar?" [2]. The resource ontology directs to the map information (longitude/latitude) resource for two locations ("Mascat and Kandahar") and the geographical formula resource for "How far." For a given query, the resource ontology guides the query's seeking goal to find the relevant set of information, which will be synthesized to an answer for the given question. The query type is not limited to any specific one but it covers resource-relevant questions (e.g., "how far", "yes/no") rather than "why" or "how"-type question.

On the other hand, "knowledge discovery from text" (hereafter "KDT") is to automatically identify linguistic patterns used to extract information relevant to a particular task (e.g., knowledge about "causal relation") from a collection of documents [3]. This problem is different from the information seeking such that KDT does not require any resource ontology but discovers the mapping between query terms and lexical patterns.

Our problem about "knowledge-seeking" assumes that a set of lexical knowledge bases[1] is available. While "information-seeking" focuses on the query decomposition to use resource ontology, "knowledge-seeking" focuses on how to link virtually lexical knowledge bases depending on the question type[2] for a given query. While the knowledge discovery problem focuses on the identification of linguistic patterns for a given semantic relation (e.g., causality), the problem of knowledge-seeking assumes that linguistic patterns have been absorbed in the lexical knowledge bases.

2.2   An Example [4]

Consider the question: "Tell me whether mad cow disease (BSE) causes human brain disease." In Fig. 1, how can you justify (or refute) its corresponding hypothesis (b4) about the "causal" relation between mad cow disease and human brain disease? The hypotheses (b) resides in knowledge space (a2), but the justifying (a3) facts are located in databases (a1) of contents such as TV programs, books or other digital media. The hypotheses (b) could be proved or disproved based on facts acquired from databases (e.g., D1, D2 in a1). The question is how to link the components (e.g., "cow disease", "human disease" in b1) of the hypothesis to their appropriate database units. In (c1) of disease hierarchy, BSE is a disease. Consider the hypothesis (b4) of "causal link between BSE and human brain disease." The justifying facts are acquired from two different supporting databases relevant to BSE and human brain disease (in a1). If a TV program in the database justifies the hypothesis that mad cow disease causes a human brain disease, the program is one "referent" (a4) of the fact. This hypothesis is an instance (d1) of a "causal" relation (d2) between disease (under c1) and food (under c2). Human brain disease can be caused by eating beef, a food (under c2), that is made edible (d4) from cow, infected (d3) by the disease, BSE (under c1), according to the ontologies. Ontology means all the relations linking concepts in the knowledge space.

Two different ontologies of living things (c3) and food (c2) are connected by the "edible" link (d4) between cow and beef. The "causal" link (d2) between food (c2) and disease (c1) represents the possible causality between the two ontologies. Because these links (e.g., d2, d3, d4) help connect differently classified databases, they will be called "contextual ontologies". Different databases (in a1) for human disease (D3, D4) and cow disease (D1, D2) are connected to different concepts, but a contextual ontology links them. Examples of contextual ontology are CAUSE in (d2) and INFECTED in (d3) of Fig. 1.

---

[1] For example, consider HowNet [5]. A typical representation of "lexical knowledge base" is a set of triplets (relation, node1, node2) that represents the "relation" between "node1" and "node2", where node1 or node2 may be a concept or a non-concept term. For example, if "human is an animal", then it is represented by (is-a, human, animal).

[2] For example, "why"-type question to ask about the causality.

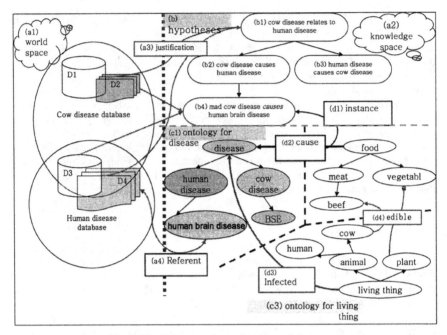

Fig. 1. World (resource) space and knowledge space

3   Hypothesis

Varieties of knowledge bases make physical ontology integration more challenging
[6]. The idea behind this paper is to virtually integrate various ontologies according to
question types and intention. Consider the question: "Why does the patient pay money
to the doctor?" The answer is not found in the lexical dictionary, but the component
of the query is in the dictionary. We found that the causality (for "why") answering is
possible to integrate the relevant components. See the paths in Fig. 2 where a symbol
* stands for AGENT, $ for OBJECT or PATIENT, and # for RELEVANT. Follow the path
from (2): "doctor cures patient", "doctor is relevant to occupation", "occupation is to
earn (the money)" in (4), and "(patient) giving money is equal to (doctor) taking
money" in (6). We will call this path-finding algorithm "crossover". In the following,
three hypotheses are shown:

Hypothesis 1: Dynamic virtual ontology integration is effective and transparent in the
local pragmatics for the question type and intention.

We have performed the construction of ontology integration as well as lexical
mapping between word senses and ontologies. As shown in [6], they eclipsed the non-
resolved higher hierarchies in case of direct plugging, whose physical integration is
not a complete hypothesis. It has much risk unless it serves ontological purposes. Our
hypothesis is to make a virtual integration of various ontologies by different linking
algorithms for ontological use (say, causality).

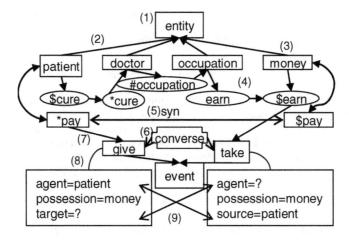

Fig. 2. Virtual linking of knowledge bases

Hypothesis 2 (Crossover Similarity): Causality relation between two nodes can be calculated whether they are causally related or not.

As shown in Fig. 2 for a query "Why does doctor cure patient?", two pairs of a partially shared unit between "doctor=*cure" and "patient=$cure" are used to form one unit of knowledge "cure(doctor, patient)". We will call this "concept crossover" for units of partially shared concepts under some principle. This thinking is just similar to "weighted abduction". Abduction is inference to the best explanation [7]. This achieves the goal on how to seek the ontologies for a hypothesis. Lexical chain [8] is a relevant theory, but limited to topical-relatedness in general.

Hypothesis 3 (Knowledge Uploading): Any pair of syntactically related words in a document is uploaded to knowledge space.

This is intended to solve problems with "prior knowledge" construction. The question is how to easily absorb the information in world space into the knowledge space.[3] Our hypothesis is to respect the syntactical binding. For example, if we find "patient pay money to hospital" in context, the new fact "patient paying to hospital, not to doctor" will be absorbed, e.g., $pay=hospital.

4   Virtual Integration of Underlined Knowledge Bases

Some issues on ontology integration have been discussed from various points of view. Pinto et al. [9] classified the notions of **ontology integration** into three types: **integration, merging** and **use/application**. The term **virtually integrated** means the view of ontology-based use/application. The followings are excerpted from [10].

---

[3] Truth-maintenance is necessary when absorbing (or acquiring) knowledge.

4.1   Example: A Snapshot of Virtually Integrated Knowledge Base

Each marked numbering in Fig. 2 has the following meaning:
(1)   Entity hierarchy: **entity** is the top node in the hierarchy of entities.
(2)   **entity** is the hypernym of **patient, doctor, occupation**, and **money** in the line (3).
(3)   Concepts or word entries are listed in this line. All concepts and word entries represent their definition by a list of concepts and marked pointers.
(4)   A concept (or word) in (3) features definitional relations to a list of concepts. For example, a **doctor** definition is composed of two concepts and their marking pointers: **#occupation** and ***cure**. Pointers in HowNet represent relations between two concepts or word entries, e.g., "#" means "relevant" and "*" does "agent".
(5)   **syn** refers to the syntactic relation in the question "Why do patients pay money to doctors?"
(6)   **converse** refers to the converse relation between events, e.g., **give** and **take**.
(7)   Event hierarchy: For example, the *hypernym* for **pay** is **give** and the *hypernym* of **give** is **event**.
(8)   Event role: Now, event roles are partially filled with entities, e.g., **patient** and **money**.
(9)   Event role shift: The *agent* of **give** is equalized to the *source* of **take**.

An overview of each component of the knowledge base is in Figure 2, where three word entries **why, patient**, and **money** are in the *dictionary*. The four *concept facets* of **entity, role, event**, and **converse** are described in this example, mainly as part of linguistic knowledge.

4.2   Interpretation of Lexical Knowledge

Consider the following three sentences:
1. Doctors cure patients.
2. Doctors earn money.
3. Patients pay money.

One major concern is to find *connectability* among words and concepts. As shown in Fig. 3, the following facts are derived:
4. Doctor is relevant (#) to occupation.
5. Occupation allows you to earn money.

Because a converse relation exists between **give** and **take**, their hyponyms **earn** and **pay** also fall under converse relation. It is something like the following social commonsense as shown in Fig. 3: "If someone X pays money to the other Y, Y earns money from X." We humans now understand the reason for "why patients pay money." The answer is that "doctors cure patients as their occupation allowing them to earn money." The following is a valid syllogism where Y is being instantiated to **doctor**:
6. If "X pays money to Y" is equivalent to "Y earns money from X" by converse relation, and "a doctor earns money from X", then "X pays money to the doctor".

Consider the next syllogism:

7. If "a doctor cures X" and "doctor is an occupation" and Axiom 1, then "the doctor earns money from X".

Axiom 1 is needed to make such a syllogism that *"If Y cures X and Y is an occupation, then Y earns money from X."* Then our challenge is to find out this **Axiom 1** from the lexical knowledge bases. It is a commonsense and thus there is a gap in the lexical knowledge base.

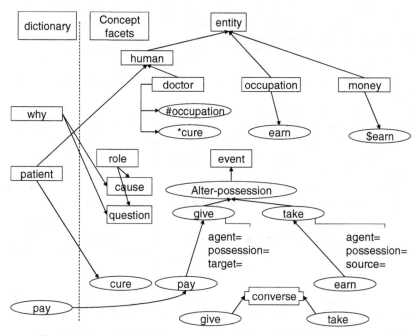

Fig. 3. An Example of Dictionary and Concept Facets in HowNet Architecture [5]

5   Connectability

Consider the query "Why do doctors cure patients?" Tracing Fig. 3 back through Fig. 2 leads to obtaining logical forms from (8) through (11). The best connectable path is planned from the first word (say, "why") of the question.

8. sufferFrom(patient,disease)
9. cure(doctor,disease)
10. cure(doctor,at-hospital)
11. occupation(doctor)
12. cure(doctor,patient)

For each pair of words, the function called "**similar**(*,*)" will be estimated to choose the next best tracing concepts (or words). **similar**'s missions are summarized as (1) checking the connectability between two nodes[4], (2) selecting the best sense of the node,[5] (3) selecting the best tracing candidate node in the next step. Finally, following the guidance by **similar** allows us to explain the question.

5.1   Observation and Evidence of Topical Relatedness

Let's try to follow the steps 8-12 given in the logical forms. In the question "Why do doctors cure patient?" that focuses on three words **doctor**, **cure**, and **patient**, we can trace some keywords given in example sentences as follows: **patient ~ disease ~ cure ~ doctor ~ occupation ~ earn ~ pay ~ patient**.

What kind of lexical relations are relevant to each pair of words or concepts? Their observation can be summarized as follows:

- The relation between **patient ~ disease** is a role relation of **sufferFrom(patient, disease)**.
- A sequence of **cure ~ doctor ~ occupation ~ earn** lets us infer the relation among **cure ~ earn**, which are closely linked by their *relevance* relation to **occupation**. Furthermore, **earn** and **cure** shares a common subject of these two events.
- The sequence of **earn ~ pay** is the result of a converse event relation between **earn** and **pay**.
- **pay ~ patient**: The agent of **pay** is a generic **human**. In other words, **pay** is a hyponym for the **act** of **human**, one of whose hyponym is **patient**.

Consider again the match between the tracing sequences of concepts and the knowledge base. Going into more details, notations with footnotes will be given to each example. At this point, we will give *names* and *formalization* based on the observed characteristics.

Feature comparison: To find the role relation among patient ~ disease, search the definition of entities (referring to patient and disease) in ways that two entities share the same event concept (referring to cure):[6]

```
patient ⊃ human ∧ $cure ∧ *sufferFrom.

disease ⊃  medical ∧ $cure ∧  undesired.
```

Interrelation: To find the event interrelation among cure ~ earn, two possible paths are presented as follows.

   – **Inverse interrelation**: Two event's role entities can be found by searching all of entities using ***earn ~ *cure** that share the same subject, and using ***earn ~ \$cure** where the subject of **earn** is the object of **cure**.
   – **Sister interrelation**: The following logical form can be derived from Fig. 3:

---

[4] A **node** means either concept or word.
[5] It is similar with word sense disambiguation.
[6] According to HowNet convention, "$" represents patient, target, possession, or content of an event, and "*" represents agent, experiencer, or instrument. "⊃" means **implies** or **has features**.

```
doctor ⊃ *cure ∧ #occupation.
occupation ⊃ earn.
```
Because **cure** and **occupation** is in the definition of **doctor**, a *probable* (~) logical implication can be derived as follows:
```
*cure ⊃ ~#occupation
```

Converse/antonymy: earn and **pay** have their respective hypernyms **take** and **give**. There exists a converse relation between these two hypernyms.

Inheritance: The relation among **pay ~ patient** is represented as follows: ("<" stands for "is a hyponym of")
```
pay < act
human ⊃ *act
patient < human
```

5.2   Rationale of Connectability

In the former section, we summarized four characteristics of causality (relatedness)-based path finding: feature comparison, interrelation, converse/antonymy in their hypernym's level, and inheritance. Among search spaces available, it is necessary to find out a measure of guiding the optimal path tracing.

We will call such a measure **similar** which will be defined according to the four characteristics just mentioned. Further details about the calculation formula will be presented again later.

Feature comparison:
The measure **feature similar(X,Y)** defines the notion of similarity between the features in **X** and **Y**.

Two interrelations:
- For "inverse interrelation", **inverse similar(X,Y)** calculates how much similarity exists between X'θ and Y'θ in a manner that X'θ = {Z | Z ⊂ θX}, where θX is an abstraction of role-marked concepts like *X, $X, #X, etc. Thus **inverse similar(X,Y) = similar(X'θ,Y'θ)**. In Fig. 4, "payer*" means that "payer" can be an agent role of "pay".
- For "sister interrelation", the measure **sister similar(X,Y)** means the following two situations: First, X and Y are features to define one concept (say, W). Second, one of them, say, Y's definitional feature concepts (referring to Z) are *similar* with X such that X and Z are similar if W ⊃ X ∧ Y and Y ⊃ Z.

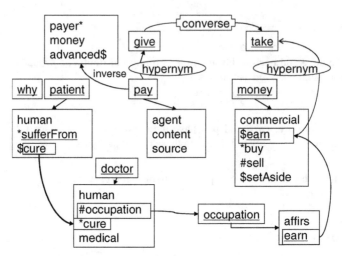

Fig. 4. Definition of Words and Virtual Linking by Crossover. "pay" is defined by two ways: one from case frame (agent, content, source), and the other from the objects in arguments of "pay". "payer" is an agent of "pay" such that payer*=pay or pay.agent=payer

Converse or antonymy:
The converse relation **converse(X,Y)** can be found by the measure **feature similar**. **converse(X,Y)** is formulated by $X \subset \theta Y$ and $Y \subset \theta X$ where $\theta = $ converse.

Inheritance:
Using inheritance property in the concept hierarchy, relations between hypernym of concepts X and Y are inherited to X and Y in a way that X and Y is similar if there exist X' and Z such that X<X', $Z \supset \theta X'$, and Y<Z where θ is a pointer or null. This inheritance tracing can be determined by how much similar X and Y are in terms of their path upward based on the relation of hypernym. We will define path similar. But tracing the path upward following hypernym links is to be described later according to the algorithm.

5.3   Algorithm CROSSOVER

The main idea of algorithm **Crossover** is obtained by switching over the role pointers θ whenever tracing is performed. [10] Consider again the question "Why do patients pay money to doctors?" As shown in Fig. 2, the best trace is **\$cure ~ *cure ~ *earn ~ \$pay**. It provides an explanation for the statement that "patients are cured by doctors ~ doctors earn money ~ patients pay money to doctors". This minimal path is obtained by crossing **\$cure** over to ***cure**. By crossover operation, **patient** and **doctor** are meaningfully and causally linked through **cure**. Note the following equations:
```
*cure = {doctor, medicine}
$cure = {patient, disease}
```

6   Conclusion

The proposed "justification probing" puts a new frontier line forward to the Turing test[7] about machine intelligence, as well as the current open problem in why/how-type question-answering area. But, although the linguistic knowledge bases have been developed enormously during the last several decades, we have few applications to use them for the knowledge-based reasoning. The reusability of knowledge resources is very important in the sense that we can merge and use the already available knowledge resources[8]. Such knowledge bases required too much cost and human labors. They have to be reused in ways that meet our needs.

The concepts "content intelligence" and "networked content intelligence" are proposed. Content itself is adapted to environment with its own methods. One of methods is investigated under the term "knowledge seeking". It is to use the already made knowledge bases and to link them virtually whenever they are necessary to keep the content intelligent. This approach has advantages over other approach in aspects of dynamic use of already made online ontologies and why-type question handling as shown in Table 1.

Table 1. Comparison of Three Approaches

	Goal direction	Prior knowledge	Prior knowledge use	Query types
Information seeking	from hypotheses[9] to world space	resource ontology	static, physical	what, where, when, who
Knowledge discovery	from world space to ontology	lexical ontology	static, physical	5W1H
Knowledge seeking	from hypotheses to ontology	networked ontologies, from world space to ontology	dynamic, virtual integration	5W1H (how, why)

References

1.   Pearl, J.: Causality: Models, Reasoning, and Inference, Cambridge University Press (2001).
2.   ACQUAINT: http://www.ai.sri.com/aquaint/.
3.   Girju, R., Moldovan, D.: Mining Answers for Causation Questions. Proc. of AAAI – Spring Symposium (2002).
4.   Choi, K.-S.: Knowledge and Standards – A Scenario toward Personalized Interactive Television Services -. Broadcast Technology. No. 12, Autumn. NHK STRL, Tokyo (2002).

---

[7] The Turing test is that the computer is interrogated by a human via a teletype, and passes the test if the interrogator cannot tell if there is a computer or a human at the other end. [11]

[8] For example, electronic dictionaries, online encyclopedias, electronic usage databases, Web, SemanticWeb resources, eJournal, etc, .

[9] "Hypotheses" stands for (b) in Fig. 1.

5. Dong, Z. and Dong, Q.: HowNet, http://www.keenage.com/. Beijing (1999~2003).
6. Magnini, B. and Speranza, M.: Merging Global and Specialized Linguistic Ontologies. Proceedings of Ontolex 2002 (Workshop held in conjunction with LREC-2002), Las Palmas (2002).
7. Hobbs, J.R., Stickel, M., Appelt, D., Martin, P.: Interpretation as Abduction. Proceedings of the Conference on 26th Annual Meeting of the Association for Computational Linguistics (1988).
8. Moldovan, D. and Novischi, A.: Lexical Chains for Question Answering. Proceedings of COLING 2002, Taipei (2002).
9. Pinto, H. S., Gómez-Pérez, A. and Martins, J.P.: Some Issues on Ontology Integration, Proceedings of the IJCAI-99 workshop on Ontologies and Problem-Solving Methods (KRR5), Stockholm (1999).
10. Choi, K.-S., Kim, J., Miyazaki, M., Goto, J., Kim, Y.-B.: Question-Answering Based on Virtually Integrated Knowledge Base. Proceedings of the Sixth International Workshop on Information Retrieval with Asian Languages (IRAL2003), Sapporo (2003).
11. Russel, S., Norvig, P.: Artificial Intelligence - A Modern Approach. Prentice-Hall (1995).

Knowledge Management in a Chinese Genealogy Information System

Jian-Hua Yeh[1] and Chao-Chen Chen[2]

[1] Department of Computer Science and Information Engineering, National Taiwan University.
System designer, Taiwan Genealogy Online Project, Taipei, Taiwan, R.O.C.
jhyeh@mars.csie.ntu.edu.tw
[2] Graduate Institute of Library and Information Studies, National Taiwan Normal University.
Project Leader, Taiwan Genealogy Online Project, Taipei, Taiwan, R.O.C.
cc4073@cc.ntnu.edu.tw

Abstract. The Chinese genealogies are the best resources for the family histories. They contain excellent information for people's root tracing and for academic researches. Our Taiwan Genealogy Online Project aims to digitalize genealogy material and to provide online services. This paper explains the design theory and implementation ideas of our system for Chinese genealogy.

Keywords: genealogy, metadata, pedigree, visualization, Taiwan Genealogy Online Project.

1 Introduction

It is estimated that there are about sixty thousand titles of Chinese genealogies around the world. These huge amounts of genealogies are excellent resources for people's root tracing, besides, for researchers, there are many valuable undiscovered phenomena in those genealogies to be revealed. And it is a good point to put those valuable resources to be widely used. But unfortunately they are traditionally book form or microfiche form. Those forms of materials are not convenient for full text information retrieval. For the sake of efficiencies, it needs a new transformation of those genealogies. At the present time, "digitalizing" is the good choice. But there is little related research on the digitalization of Chinese genealogies, so we present one comprehensive research project about that. In this paper, we will introduce how to using the XML technology to create the metadata of genealogy, maintaining relations among the individuals, and how to developing management and visualization utilities to representing pedigree information.

2 Genealogical Metadata Design Issues

In this project, we analyze attributes of Chinese genealogical information, then design three sets of metadata: (1) format for ancestors; (2) format for families; (3) format for surnames.

T.M.T. Sembok et al. (Eds.): ICADL 2003, LNCS 2911, pp. 427–431, 2003.
© Springer-Verlag Berlin Heidelberg 2003

The part (1) records the relations of an individual and his families. This is the basic materials for building pedigrees. The part (2) records the origin and the history of a family, including its organization rules and residence places. The part (3) gives general descriptions for each surname. The three formats altogether give a complete development history of patriarchal clan.

In addition, this project also implements a management system for Chinese genealogy. Our system can automatically link individuals to their ancestors or offspring and establish pedigree charts. The system is interfaced with Web. Users can create metadata of genealogy through Internet.

3   Object Structures for Representation of Genealogical Information

The researches of digital libraries have been inspired in recent years. Among these researches, a lot of them are based on an object-oriented model [6,7,8]. The object-oriented model is also applied in genealogy information system design. In this paper, we apply the object structures defined in NTUDLM [9] to manage genealogical information along with XML-based metadata. The rationale of this design is to facilitate both management and visualization of object relationships: the XML-based metadata is able to render Web output more directly, while the object relationships can be visualized more efficiently. The object structure in the genealogy information system is used to keep both metadata attributes and relations to other objects. While an attribute describe an object from one aspect, a relation associates one object with another object. As a result, the relationships among objects will form an object network. Figure 1 illustrates the structures among objects.

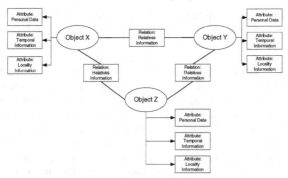

Fig. 1. The structures among objects

4   Genealogical Information Visualization

The visualization issues in genealogy information system are based on the object structures and object network discussed in the previous section. Because the objects in the system form object networks, the visualization of the network will become a graph presentation problem. However, the pedigree information contained in the Chinese genealogy is characterized as a paternal system, as far as the traditional genealogy material concerns, the pedigree is presented as a tree structure, as shown in Fig. 2. There are many related pedigree-drawing approaches found in historical material use tree-like structure as presentation format, as listed in Table. 1.

Fig. 2. A page of traditional genealogy material

Table 1. Several chart types of pedigree tree presentation

Chart Type	Sample	Chart Type	Sample	Chart Type	Sample
Tree chart		Ancestor chart		Descendant list	
Box chart		Collapsed chart		Group list	
Fan chart					

Since the Chinese genealogy material is based on the paternal system, the presentation of a Chinese pedigree is therefore a tree visualization problem. In the previous visualization researches [1], the visualization which concerns of a graph or tree structure is based on several factors: node placement, link management, scalability, and interactivity. These issues lead to the adoption of hyperbolic tree presentation [3,4,5] in our system, which is able to present a lot of tree nodes in a pedigree chart while keep good interaction with users. The presentation of a hyperbolic tree is shown in the sample figure in the next section.

5   Genealogy Information System Architecture

The design of object structures and the adoption of visualization techniques are two important bases of the genealogy information system. Fig. 3 depicts the system architecture of the system. Fig. 4 shows a sample screenshot of the system.

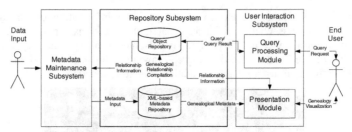

Fig. 3. System architecture

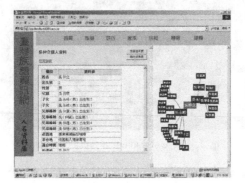

Fig. 4. A sample screenshot of pedigree presentation

The object repository is the module that stores and manages the metadata records in the system and is responsible for resolving the user's query. To the query process module, the object repository is an object-oriented data store and its objects structures have been elaborated in section 3. The XML-based metadata repository is the module that stores the contents of the genealogy metadata in a physical form.[2] On the other hand, the object repository stores the contents of the genealogy metadata in an abstract form.. When an update to the metadata contents is to be carried out, the update is first made to the structure of the XML-based metadata repository. Then the structure of the contents repository is compiled to create a new object structure for the object repository.

6   Conclusion

This paper discusses the design of a Chinese genealogy information system aimed at providing management and visualization utilities to extend the applications of digital libraries to a new dimension. The discussion particularly focuses on maintaining relations among the objects in the digital library from the genealogy metadata information stored in the digital library. The motivation is to develop management and visualization utilities that represent pedigree information. With such utilities, human beings are able to maintain and visualize genealogical information in a more efficient way.

References

1. Battista, G.D., Eades, P., Tamassia, R., and Tollis, I.G., Annotated Bibliography on Graph Drawing. Computational Geometry: Theory and Applications, 4(5), 235–282, 1994.
2. Chen, Chao-chen, Chen, Hsueh-hua. and Chen, Kuang-hua. "The Design of Metadata Interchange for Chinese Information and Implementation of Metadata Management System." Bulletin of the American Society for Information Science and Technology, 27:5(June/July 2001): 21–27.
3. Munzner, T., H3: Laying Out Large Directed Graphs in 3D Hyperbolic Space. Proceeding of Information Visualization '97, Phoenix Arizona, 1997.
4. Munzner, T. and Burchard, P., Visualizing the Structure of the World Wide Web in 3-D Hyperbolic Space. Proceedings of VRML'95, San Diego, CA, 33–38, 1995.
5. Teraoka, T. and Maruyama, M., Adaptive Information Visualization based on the User's Multiple Viewpoints – Interactive 3D Visualization of the WWW. Proceeding of Information Visualization '97, Phoenix Arizona, 1997.
6. William Y. Arms, Christophe Blanchi, and Edward A. Overly. An architecture for information in digital libraries. D-Lib Magazine, February 1997.
7. Schatz, Bruce R. and Chen, Hsinchun. Building large-scale digital libraries. Computer theme issue on the US Digital Library Initiative, May 1996.
8. Kahn, Robert and Wilensky, Robert. A framework for distributed digital object services. Technical report, CNRI, May 1995.
9. Yeh, Jian-Hua, Chang, Jia-Yang, and Oyang, Yen-Jen, "Content and Knowledge Management in a Digital Library and Museum", Journal of American Society for Information Science(JASIS), Special Topic Issue on Digital Libraries, 51(4), pp. 371–379, March 2000.

Approximating Fair Use in LicenseScript

Cheun Ngen Chong, Sandro Etalle, Pieter H. Hartel, and Yee Wei Law

Faculty of EEMCS, University of Twente,
PO Box 217, 7500 AE Enschede, The Netherlands
{chong,etalle,pieter,ywlaw}@cs.utwente.nl

Abstract. Current rights management systems are not able to enforce copyright laws because of both legal and technological reasons. The *contract rights* granted by a copyright owner are often overridden by the users' *statutory rights* that are granted by the laws. In particular, *Fair Use* allows for "unauthorized but not illegal" use of content. Two technological reasons why fair use cannot be upheld: (1) the current XML-based rights expression language (REL) cannot capture user's statutory rights; and (2) the underlying architectures cannot support copyright enforcement. This paper focuses on the first problem and we propose a way of solving it by a two-pronged approach: (1) rights assertion, to allow a user to assert new rights to the license, i.e. freely express her rights user fair use; and (2) audit logging, to record the asserted rights and keep track of the copies rendered and distributed under fair use. We apply this approach in LicenseScript (a logic-based REL) to demonstrate how LicenseScript can *approximate* fair use.

Keywords: Intellectual property rights, copyright, fair use, rights expression language, metadata security.

1 Introduction

Current rights management systems are not able to enforce properly copyright laws. The reason is both legal and technological and lies mainly in the fact that user's rights are a result of the reconciliation of two different and often-conflicting rulings. On one hand, there are the rights granted *by contract* by the copyright owner (e.g. author or digital library) to a user; these are called *contract rights* because they are granted when user agrees on the terms and conditions imposed by the copyright owner. On the other hand, there exist *statutory rights* granted by the law.

An example of statutory right is the right of *fair use* [10]. Contract rights and statutory rights often contradict each other: a contract may for instance forbid making copies of a given book, while the law grants the user to make copies for educational use. Statutory rights depend on a number of *circumstances*. For instance, according to the United States Codes (U.S.C) (http://uscode.house.gov/), Section 107 Title 17 Chapter 1 (Fair Use Doctrine), "fair use of copyrighted content, including reproduction for purposes such as criticism, comment, news reporting, teaching, scholarship, or research does not violate or infringe the copyrights".

T.M.T. Sembok et al. (Eds.): ICADL 2003, LNCS 2911, pp. 432–443, 2003.

In general, statutory rights are restricted by the contract rights in the rights management systems. In other words, from the legal perspective, the copyright owner holds far more control than the copyright laws endorse [11]. Questions of the legality of overriding the statutory rights by contract rights are yet to be answered [6], however the legal perspective is beyond the scope of the paper.

To fully understand why it is impossible to render this situation in current rights management systems we have to take a look at their structure; which consists of: (1) a rights expression language (REL), and (2) an underlying architecture. A REL provides a vocabulary, associated with a set of grammatical rules, to express a fine-grained usage control over a content. A *license* is written in a REL, governs the terms and conditions under which the content should be used. In practice, the most widely used RELs are XML-based, for instance XrML [7] and ODRL [8].

Mulligan and Burstein [9] have pointed out the inadequacies of the aforementioned XML-based RELs in expressing a user's statutory rights: (1) the RELs can only describe contract rights; (2) the RELs provide insufficient support for rights assertion by the user; and (3) the RELs cannot provide contextual information consistent with the copyright laws that accommodate the user's statutory rights. In short, the user's statutory rights become "unauthorized" under the contract rights because they cannot be captured in the license written in an XML-based REL. On the other hand, the user's statutory rights must be upheld under the copyright laws.

Fair use allows the users to exercise these "unauthorized but not illegal" rights.

In addition, it is neither a legal nor a practical requirement for users to declare these rights explicitly before enjoying these rights. Last but not least, the architecture cannot determine if some content is used for non-profit or commercial purposes [5]. Although it is impossible for a REL to capture the semantics of fair use completely we may *approximate* fair use [9].

In this paper, we propose a method for implementing a digital right management system that takes into account statutory right. For this we refer to the LicenseScript right expression model [2], and we use a two two-pronged approach based on (1) *rights assertion*; and (2) *audit logging* (see Fig. 1). To the best of our knowledge, this is the first attempt to approximate fair use by using a REL. We elaborate this approach in the later sections. In addition, we have pinpointed the distinction of LicenseScript with the XML-based RELs in our earlier work [3].

This paper is organized as follows. Section 2 introduces our approach to approximating fair use. Section 3 briefly explains the LicenseScript language with a simple scenario. Section 4 details our approach to approximating fair use in LicenseScript. Section 5 describes briefly some related work. Finally, section 6 concludes this paper and presents future work.

2 Our Approach

In this section, we explain how LicenseScript may be used to approximate fair use. As mentioned in section 1, we are using a two-pronged approach (Fig. 1): (1) *Rights assertion*: to allow the user to assert new fair use-compliant rights in addition to the rights dictated by the license; and (2) *Audit logging*: to keep a record of the rights asserted and exercised by the user and to keep track of the copies of the licenses created.

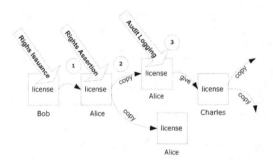

Fig. 1. Our approach to approximating fair use

Fig. 1 shows that Bob issues a license to Alice, allowing Alice to make copies of the license (and therefore she is able to make copy of the licensed content too). Alice performs rights assertion on the license before making copies of the license. Alice in turn gives a copy of the license to Charles. All the actions performed by the users (i.e. Alice and Charles) are logged in the appropriate license.

Using this approach, on one hand, the users can freely exercise their statutory rights; on the other hand, the copyright owner can track the source of possible copyright infringement. Note that our proposal is more advanced than *rights issuance*, which is performed by the copyright owner for issuing and granting rights to a user.

We use the following illustrative scenario of a *digital library* to aid in our explanation in the next two sections:

Example 1. Alice borrows an ebook, entitled "An Example Book" from Bob's Digital Library (herefrom we simply call it Bob). Bob sends the license to Alice, allowing her to view, copy and give the rendered copies of the ebook to other users.

2.1   Rights Assertion

Imagine a license for Alice, which states the following rights that are granted to Alice by Bob: *view*, *copy*, *give* and *assert*. Suppose Alice wants to print the ebook. The license does not state the *print* right. Therefore, Alice must assert a new *print* right by adding this right to the license. We believe that the users ability to assert new rights contributes to fair use because the user can express their rights according to their will, in addition to the rights granted by the copyright owner.

We make a few what we believe to be reasonable assumptions. Alice must have a content renderer, in this case an ebook viewer to use the ebook. A set of rules are embedded in the firmware of this ebook viewer. Bob may define these rules. Bob may not trust Alice, but he trusts the rules he defines. If Alice's asserted right in the license can be exercised by any corresponding rule Bob defines, Bob may logically trust this right (unless the asserted right causes conflicts in the license, which we will discuss later). This is because Alice's asserted rights must conform to the semantics of the rules. The implicit assumption is that the content renderer is secure.

Bob may specify some of the contextual information by using LicenseScript. This information may be, for instance, the usage purpose, the location of use etc. that the fair use doctrine refers to, as discussed in section 1. Then, Bob can write the rules such that oblige Alice to provide the contextual information. The rules then validate the provided information using the contextual information stated in the doctrine. In other words, Alice must declare her intention to perform fair use. The attestation of his declaration is performed by the underlying architecture (presumably by using some cryptographic means). We consider architectural support to enforce all this as our future work. Here we are concerned only with a higher level of abstraction that defines *what* may or may not happen, and not *how* actions may be performed.

2.2   Audit Logging

Alice should not be able to assert arbitrary rights nor must she be able to override existing rights (in the license) that may undermine the rights management system. While we might be able to avoid some problems by syntactic checks (e.g. to check for duplication of rights in the license caused by the rights assertion), many other potential ambiguities will remain (e.g. if the rights asserted can expire). Therefore, we record all the asserted rights (along with the user's identity, the date the right is asserted and the purpose of asserting the rights) in the license.

Bob may check the record and the license if the asserted rights have overridden or violated the contract rights. Therefrom, Bob may take further action, e.g. to allow/disallow the Alice's asserted right or to take Alice to court if the asserted rights violate the copyrights or the contract rights.

Additionally, Bob also tracks the copies of the licenses distributed by Alice. We can put a history record in the license to log this distribution pattern. Thus, Bob (i.e. the copyright owner) can trace the distribution of the licenses by inspecting the history record in these licenses. This helps the copyright owner track possible sources of copyrights infringement. Audit logging requires cryptographic support from the underlying architecture. We have already addressed the issue of secure audit logging in our previous work [4].

This concludes the introduction to our two-pronged approach towards approximating fair use. We will now present the details of the approach using License Script.

3 LicenseScript Language

LicenseScript [2] is a language that is based on (1) multiset rewriting, which captures the dynamic evolution of licenses; and (2) logic programming, which captures the static terms and conditions on a license. LicenseScript provides a judicious choice of the interfacing mechanism between the static and dynamic domains.

A license specifies when certain operations on the object are permitted or denied. The *license* is associated with the *content*, as can be seen in Fig. 2. A license carries *bindings*, which describe the attributes of the license; and *clauses*, which determine if a certain operation is allowed (or forbidden). The license clauses consult the license bindings for their decision making and may also alter the values of the license bindings.

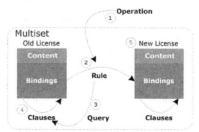

Fig. 2. Transformation of licenses

Licenses are represented as terms that reside in multisets. A multiset can be thought as part of the user's system. For the specification of a license, we use logic programming. The readers are thus assumed familiar with the terminology and the basic results of the semantics of logic programs.

Fig. 2 illustrates that (1) an *operation* (performed by a subject) (2) invokes a *rule* in the multiset. The rule then generates and executes a (3) *query* on the (4) license clauses and bindings. The (5) execution result of the rule is a newly generated license. Now we use a simple illustrative scenario to explain this process:

Example 2. Amanda gets an ebook, titled "A Book" from Ben Publisher. Ben issues a license with an expiry date fixed at "23/06/2004".

This license allows Amanda to print two copies of the ebook ($L01, \ldots, L14$ are line numbers included for reference purposes, they are not part of the code):

```
license(ebook:a_book,                               L01
    [ (canprint(B1,B2,User) :-                      L02
            get_value(B1,consumer,C),               L03
            C = User,                               L04
            get_value(B1,expires,Exp),              L05
            today(D), D>Exp,                        L06
            get_value(B1,printed,P),                L07
            get_value(B1,max_prints,Max),           L08
            P < Max,                                L09
            set_value(B1,printed,P+1,B2)],          L10
    [ (company=ben_publisher),                      L11
      (consumer=amanda),                            L12
      (expires=23/06/2004),                         L13
      (max_prints=2), (printed=0) ])                L14
```

A license is represented by a term of the form `license(content,C,B)`, where `content` is a unique identifier referring to the real content; `C` is a list of *license clauses* consisting of Prolog programs describing when operations are permitted or denied; and `B` is a list of *license bindings* capturing the attributes of the license. We define two multiset-rewrite *rules*, as shown below, to model the interface between the system and the licenses. The rules can be thought of as a firmware in the user's system. The user's content renderer would contain the rules as embedded firmware. Only the copyright owner (or a trusted third party on behalf of the copyright owner) can define a set of rules for the firmware of the content renderer.

The syntax of the rules is based on the Gamma notation [1] of multiset rewriting (again, $R01, \ldots, R04$ are line numbers):

```
print(Ebook,User) :                                 R01
    license(Ebook,C,B1) ->                          R02
    license(Ebook,C,B2)                             R03
    <= C |- canprint(B1,B2,User)                    R04
```

We will step through the example assuming Amanda would like to print the eBook with the available license on her system (as shown above):

1. Amanda's system wants to know whether she has the print *right* on the ebook. This is achieved by applying the print *rule* (line R01) with appropriate parameters: `print(ebook:a book,amanda)`.
2. The rule finds the `license(ebook:a book,[...],[...])` (line R02, line L01) in the system. The first list refers to the license clauses (lines L02–L14), while the second list refers to the set of license bindings (lines L15–L18).

3. The rule then executes a *query* in the form of `canprint(B1,B2,User)` (line `R04`), where `B2` designates the output generated by the query; This will form a few set of license bindings.

4. The license interpreter retrieves the value of the license binding `consumer` from the list of license bindings `B1` (line `L03`) and compares the retrieved value with the user identity `User` (line `L04`). `User` is passed in as an argument to the license clause (line `L02`).

5. Similarly, the interpreter retrieves the value of the binding `expires` (line `L05`).

6. The interpreter calls the primitive (which is discussed later) `today(D)` (line `L06`) to obtain the current time and date.

7. The expiry date of the license must be greater than current time and date (line `L07`).

8. Similarly, the value of `printed` is checked if it is smaller than the value of `max_prints` (lines `L07`–`L09`).

9. If all conditions are satisfied (the user is valid, the license has not expired and the number of printed copies does not exceed the allowable maximum copies), the query returns `yes` (line `R04`) to the interpreter, with the newly generated license bindings in `B2`.

10. The value of the license binding `printed` is incremented (line `L10`) every time the print operation succeeds.

11. The value `yes` indicates that the execution of `canprint(B1,B2,User)` yields *success* in the license clauses `C`.

12. The rule `print(Ebook,User)` generates a new license with the newly generated license bindings `license(Ebook,C,B2)` (line `R03`).

The function `get value(B,n,V)` is to report in `V` the value of n from `B`, whereas the function `set value(B1,n,V,B2)`, to give value `V` to n in `B2`.

We also use a number of primitives to model the interface of the system with the license (interpreter): (1) `today(D)`, to bind `D` to the current system date/time; and (2) `identify(L)`, to identify the current environment to `L`. For further details of the LicenseScript language, see Reference [2].

In the following section, we explain how LicenseScript can be used to approximate fair use.

4 Fair Use in LicenseScript

As we have seen, licenses are just objects in the multiset. Many other types of objects can be modelled, such as wallets and policies.

We use this LicenseScript-specific feature to define (1) the *license* issued by Bob to Alice, which allows her to *view*, *copy* and *give* the ebook, as well as *assert* new rights (section 4.1); (2) the *doctrine* that carries the contextual information consistent with fair use (section 4.3); (3) the *record* that logs Alice's asserted rights (section 4.2); and (4) the *rules* defined by Bob as the firmware of Alice's system, which include *view*, *copy*, *give*, *print* and *assert* (section 4.4).

4.1   The License

Following Example 1, this is the license that Bob issues to Alice:

```
license(ebook:an_example_book,
        [ (canloan(B1,B2,Loaner,User) :-
                get_value(B1,digital_library,L), L=Loaner,
                get_value(B1,loaned,Loaned), Loaned=false,
                set_value(B1,loaned,true,B2), set_value(B1,user,User),
                today(D), set_value(B1,expires,D+7,B2)),
          (canreturn(B1,B2) :-
                set_value(B1,loaned,false,B2)),
          (canview(B1,B2,User) :-
                get_value(B1,user,U), U=User,
                get_value(B1,expires,Exp), today(D), D>Exp),
          (cancopy(B1,B2,B3,User) :-
                get_value(B1,user,U), U=User, get_value(B1,expires,Exp),
                today(D), D>Exp, get_value(B1,copies,N),
                append([(User,D),N,NN), set_value(B1,copies,NN,B2),
                set_value(B1,copies,NN,B3)),
          (cangive(B1,B2,User1,User2) :-
                get_value(B1,user,U), U=User1,
                set_value(B1,user,User2,B2), get_value(B1,trace,T),
                today(D), append([(User1,D,User2)],T,T2),
                set_value(B1,trace,T2,B2)),
          (canassert(C1,C2,B1,B2,Clause,Binds,User,Purpose) :-
                get_value(B1,user,U), U=User,
                get_value(B1,expires,Exp), today(D), D>Exp,
                get_value(B1,asserted,As),
                append([(User,D,Purpose)],Clause,NC),
                append(NC,As,As2), set_value(B1,asserted,As2,B2),
                append(C1,Clause,C2), append(B1,Binds,B2)),
          (canperform(B1,B2,User) :-
                get_value(B1,expires,Exp), today(D), D>Exp,
                get_value(B1,user,U), U=User) ],
        [ (user=alice), (digital_library=bob), (loaned=true),
          (asserted=[]), (trace=[]), (copies=[]), (expires=15/8/03) ])
```

The function append(L1,L2,L3) is a built-in Prolog program that produces a new list (L3) by combining two lists (L1 and L2).

The license clause canloan determines if the ebook can be loaned to the user, and *only* by the digital library. The return date (represented by expires) is set at the seventh day from the date this ebook is loaned. The license clause canreturn is the counterpart of the license clause canloan, which resets the binding loaned to false.

The license clause canview determines that *only* Alice (the user) can view the ebook and the return date expires has not expired. The license clause canassert allows Alice to assert new rights (represented as the Clause with necessary bindings Binds). The license clause canperform determines if the user who performs fair use is the genuine user who owns the license.

The license binding asserted records all the rights asserted by the user. The license binding trace records the distribution of the license when it is given away. The license binding copies records the user who generates a new copy of this license.

4.2   The Record

The `record` that belongs to Bob and which logs the rights asserted by Alice to a license looks like this:

```
record(ebook:an_example_book,
        [ (canlog(B1,B2,User,Action) :-
                get_value(B1,history,H), today(Date),
                append([(User,Action,Date)],H,NH),
                set_value(B1,history,NH,B2)) ],
        [ (history=[]), (digital_library=bob) ])
```

The term `record` records (clause `canlog`) all the actions (the argument `Action`) performed by the user (the argument `User`) at the current time (the value `Date`) on the ebook.

4.3   The Doctrine

The `doctrine` (defined by Bob) that encodes the contextual information of fair use is:

```
doctrine(fairuse,
        [ (canallow(B1,B2,Purpose) :-
                get_value(B1,purposes,Ps), member(Purpose,Ps),
                identify(Loc), get_value(B1,location,L), L=Loc) ],
        [ (purposes=[criticism,comment,newsreport,
                eduction,scholarship,research]),
                (location=united_states_of_america) ])
```

The function `member(E,L)` checks if the element `E` belongs to the list `L`. The license clause `canallow` determines if the purpose attested by the user for using the content is under the fair use context and if the user is in the U.S. The license binding `purposes` state all the usage purposes allowed under the fair use doctrine. The license binding `location` indicates that this doctrine applies in United States. The copyright owner can define different types of `doctrine`, e.g. first sale `doctrine` to encapsulate the corresponding contextual information.

4.4   The Rules

The rules that Bob defines for Alice's firmware are:

```
loan(Ebook,User)  :
                    license(Ebook,C,B1) -> license(Ebook,C,B2)
        <= C |- canloan(B1,B2,User)
return(Ebook) :
        license(Ebook,C,B1) -> license(Ebook,C,B2)
        <= C |- canreturn(B1,B2)
view(Ebook,User,Purpose) :
        license(Ebook,C,B1) -> license(Ebook,C,B2)
        <= C |- canview(B1,B2,User)
view(Ebook,User,Purpose) :
        doctrine(fairuse,Cp,Bp1),license(Ebook,C,B1) ->
        doctrine(fairuse,Cp,Bp2),license(Ebook,C,B2)
        <= C |- canperform(B1,B2,User),Cp |- canallow(Bp1,Bp2,Purpose)
copy(Ebook,User)  :
        license(Ebook,C,B1) -> license(Ebook,C,B2),license(Ebook,C,B3)
```

```
                <= C |- cancopy(B1,B2,B3,User)
    copy(Ebook,User,Purpose) :
            doctrine(fairuse,Cp,Bp1),license(Ebook,C,B1) ->
            doctrine(fairuse,Cp,Bp2),license(Ebook,C,B1),license(Ebook,C,B2)
            <= C |- canperform(B1,B2,User), Cp |- canallow(Bp1,Bp2,Purpose)
    give(Ebook,User,Purpose) :
            license(Ebook,C,B1) -> license(Ebook,C,B2)
            <= C |- cangive(B1,B2,User1,User2)
    give(Ebook,User,Purpose) :
            doctrine(fairuse,Cp,Bp1),license(Ebook,C,B1) ->
            doctrine(fairuse,Cp,Bp2),license(Ebook,C,B2)
            <= C |- canperform(B1,B2,User), Cp |- canallow(Bp1,Bp2,Purpose)
    print(Ebook,User,Purpose) :
            license(Ebook,C,B1) -> license(Ebook,C,B2)
            <= C |- canprint(B1,B2,User)
    print(Ebook,User,Purpose) :
            doctrine(fairuse,Cp,Bp1),license(Ebook,C,B1) ->
            doctrine(fairuse,Cp,Bp2),license(Ebook,C,B2)
            <= C |- canperform(B1,B2,User), Cp |- canallow(Bp1,Bp2,Purpose)
            assert(Ebook,Clause,Binds,User,Purpose) :
            license(Ebook,C1,B1),record(Ebook,Cr,Br1) ->
            license(Ebook,C2,B2),record(Ebook,Cr,Br2)
            <= C1 |- canassert(C1,C2,B1,B2,Clause,Binds,User,Purpose)
               Cr |- canlog(Br1,Br2,User,Clause)
```

The assert rule says: to assert a new Clause with corresponding Binds, the user must show her identity User and states the Purpose of asserting this right; and the user's asserted clause is recorded by the term record (see section 4.2).

The first view rule says: to view the Ebook, the user must present her identity User and declare to the usage Purpose; the license must contain the license clause canview. If the first rule does not apply to Alice's execution, the second rule may be executed: the usage Purpose attested by the User must conform to the contextual information stated in the doctrine (see section 4.3).

The rules show how the various objects in the multiset are used, in a cooperative fashion to achieve fair use. For example, as shown in Figure 1, (1) Alice has asserted a print right to the license (as shown in section 4.1) on "1/8/2003" for the purpose of education (by executing the assert rule). The new license is as follows:

```
    license(ebook:an_example_book,
            [ ...,
              (canprint(B1,B2,User) :-
                    get_value(B1,onlyalice,U), U=User) ],
            [ ...,
              (asserted=[
              (alice,1/8/2003,education),
              (canprint(B1,B2,User):-get_value(B1,onlyalice,U),U=User)]),
              (onlyalice=alice) ])
```

(Herefrom, the symbol ". . ." represents the unchanged part of the object.)

The asserted clause canprint allows *only* Alice to print the ebook (she adds a new binding, namely onlyalice to the license). Alice can execute the print rule to print the ebook with the asserted *print* right. The asserted right is logged at the license binding asserted and Bob's record (from section 4.2) becomes:

```
    record(ebook:an_example_book,
            [ ..., ],
            [ ...,
              (history=[(alice,
                    (canprint(B1,B2,User):-get_value(B1,user,U),U=User),
                    1/8/03)]) ])
```

Now, (2) Alice makes an additional copy of the license by executing the `copy` rule. The third version of the license becomes:

```
license(ebook:an_example_book,
        [ ...,
          (canprint(B1,B2,User) :-
              get_value(B1,onlyalice,U), U=User) ],
        [ ...,
          (asserted=[(alice,1/8/2003,education),
          (canprint(B1,B2,User):-get_value(B1,onlyalice,U),U=User))]),
          (onlyalice=alice), (copies=[(alice,1/8/2003)]) ])
```

Alice's copy action is logged in the binding `copies`. (3) ←Alice gives a copy of the license to Charles on "2/8/03" (by executing the `give` rule). Charles' license (given by Alice) will look like this:

```
license(ebook:an_example_book,
        [ ...,
          (canprint(B1,B2,User) :-
              get_value(B1,onlyalice,U), U=User) ],
        [ ...,
          (asserted=[(alice,1/8/2003,education),
          (canprint(B1,B2,User):-get_value(B1,onlyalice,U),U=User))]),
          (onlyalice=alice), (copies=[(alice,1/8/2003)]),
          (trace=[(alice,2/8/03,charles)]), (user=charles) ])
```

The distribution is logged in the license binding `trace`. The value of the binding `user` is assigned to `charles` indicating the transfer of the ownership of this license.

We have demonstrated how rules can transform the objects in the multiset by using the example as illustrated in Figure 1. This concludes the detailed description of the approach to approximating fair use in LicenseScript.

5 Related Work

Mulligan and Burstein [9] suggest several extensions of the XML-based RELs to approximate fair use. We summarize their suggestions as follows: (1) to define a set of rights that might simulate some "default" rights the users have with physical copies of the content, e.g. for a music album, the default rights may be *play, rewind, seek, excerpt* and *copy*; (2) to provide some contextual information description in the REL to support the fair use modelling, e.g. the usage purpose etc.

Similar to Mulligan and Burstein first suggestion, our approach constrains the content user's fair use rights by the firmware rules. However, the copyright owners (or content providers) cannot make the predictions on how the users would use the con tent. Therefore, it is a cumbersome process for the copyright owners to define a set of default rights for all available content. Our approach, on the other hand, allows user to freely express their rights. At the same time, the copyright owner may control the user's fair use actions to the extent confined by the rules. The copyright owner may flexibly define some contextual information in LicenseScript that consistent with the fair use that the rules may comply with.

Secure Telecooperation SIT, Darmstadt and the Fraunhofer Institute for Integrated Circuits, Erlangen, Ilmenau have developed the Light Weight Digital Rights

Management System (LWDRM) (http://www.iis.fraunhofer.de/amm/
techinf/ipmp). They introduce two distinct file formats, namely local media
format (LMF) and signed media format (SMF). The LMF is bound to the machine
where the content is generated, whereas the SMF is intended for small-scale
distribution. The SMF is generated when the user mark the content with her personal
digital signature.

There are three levels of functionality defined in the LWDRM. The first level is the
LWDRM player, to play the SMF/LMF content. The second level allows the user to
generate LMF from the content. This level offers more extensive features to the user,
e.g. improved compression algorithms etc. The third level allows the user to sign the
LMF content, i.e. to generate the SMF content. Thereby, the user could distribute and
use this SMF content in other machines. LWDRM may track the leak the copyright
infringement by using the signature. However, the user must willingly sacrifice her
privacy to perform fair use. Our approach is complementary to the SIT approach, in
that we manipulate licenses while SIT manipulates content.

6 Conclusion and Related Work

Current rights management system can only enforce contract rights that are granted
by the copyright owners to the users. Other rights, such as the statutory rights granted
by copyright laws cannot be enforced in the rights management systems. Fair use is
an example of statutory rights, because fair use allows "unauthorized but not illegal"
actions.

In this paper, we focus on one aspect of the technological issues related to the
rights expression language (REL). We argue that current RELs (1) cannot capture
user's statutory rights, (2) do not support rights assertion performed by the users, and
(3) cannot provide useful contextual information that is consistent with the fair use.
We have introduced a two-pronged approach for approximating fair use in
LicenseScript: *rights assertion* and *audit logging*. Then, we have demonstrated the
use of LicenseScript to *approximate* fair use.

We would also like to investigate if LicenseScript is capable of expressing other
copyright laws, e.g. first-sale doctrine as well as privacy protection in the future. In
addition, we are implementing our architecture for LicenseScript, namely the
LicenseScript Engine.

Acknowledgement. We would like to thank (in alphabetical order) Aaron Burstein,
Séverine Dusollier, Lucie Guilbault, Pamela Samuelson and Mark Stefik for their
invaluable help with this paper.

References

1. J-P. Banâtre, P. Fradet, and D. L. Métayer. Gamma and the chemical reaction model: Fifteen years after. In C. Calude, G. Paun, G. Rozenberg, and A. Salomaa, editors, *Workshop on Multiset Processing (WMP)*, volume 2235 of *Lecture Notes in Computer Science*, pages 17–44. Springer-Verlag, Berlin, August 2001.
2. C. N. Chong, R. Corin, S. Etalle, P. H. Hartel, W. Jonker, and Y. W. Law. LicenseScript: A novel digital rights language and its semantics. In *3rd International Conference on WebDelivering of Music (WEDELMUSIC)*, page 122–129, Los Alamitos, California, United States, September 2003. IEEE Computer Society Press.
3. C. N. Chong, S. Etalle, and P. H. Hartel. Comparing Logic-based and XML-based Rights Expression Languages. In *Workshop on Metadata for Security, On the Move Int. Federated Conference (OTM)*, page To appear, Berlin, Germany, November 2003. Springer-Verlag.
4. C. N. Chong, Z. Peng, and P. H. Hartel. Secure audit logging with tamper-resistant hardware. In *18th IFIP International Information Security Conference (IFIPSEC)*, pages 73–84. Kluwer Academic Publishers, May 2003.
5. E.W. Felten. A skeptical view of DRM and fair use. *Communications of ACM*, 46(4):57–59, April 2003.
6. L. Guibault. Copyright limitations and contracts: Are restrictive click-warp license valid? *Journal of Digital Property Law*, 2(1):144–183, November 2002.
7. H. Guo. Digital rights management (DRM) using XrML. In *T-110.501 Seminar on Network Security 2001*, page Poster paper 4, 2001. ISBN 951-22-5807-2.
8. R. Iannella. Open digital rights management. In *World Wide Web Consortium (W3C) DRM Workshop*, page Position paper 23, January 2001.
9. D. Mulligan and A. Burstein. Implementing copyright limitations in rights expression languages. In J. Feigenbaum, editor, *Proceedings of 2002 ACM CCS-9 Workshop on Security and Privacy in Digital Rights Management*, volume 2696 of *Lecture Notes in Computer Science*, page To appear. Springer-Verlag, November 2002. ISBN 3-540-40410-4.
10. D.K. Mulligan. Digital rights management and fair use by design. *Communications of ACM*, 46(4):31–33, April 2003.
11. P. Samuelson. Digital rights management {and,or,vs.} the law. *Communications of ACM*, 46(4):41–45, April 2003.

A Study on the Digital Right Management of MPEG-4 Streams for Digital Video Library

Dongkyoo Shin, Junil Kim, and Dongil Shin

Department of Computer Science and Engineering, Sejong University
98, Kunja-Dong, Kwangjin-Ku, Seoul 143-747, Korea
{shindk,junil,dshin}@gce.sejong.ac.kr

Abstract. This paper presents encryption techniques for digital right management solutions of MPEG-4 streams, suitable for digital video library. MPEG-4 is a format for multimedia streaming and stored in the MPEG-4 file format. We designed three kinds of encryption methods, which encrypt macro blocks (MBs) or motion vectors (MVs) of I-, P-VOPs (Video Object Planes), extracted from the MPEG-4 file format. We used DES to encrypt MPEG-4 data. Based on theses three methods, we designed and implemented a DRM solution for video on demand services, which enabled a MPEG-4 data streaming, and then compared the results to get an optimal encryption method.

1 Introduction

Digital libraries need to provide secure environments for development, management, preservation and archiving of proprietary and copyrighted material [1]. While current systems employ sophisticated techniques for distributed access and search [2, 3], more attention needs to be paid to access controls and copyright information for archived data. Especially for digital video library such as the Informedia system at Carnegie Mellon University [4], which enables full content search and retrieval of the multimedia materials, copyright protection for offered materials is necessary.

Multimedia materials offer a rich source of information, with aspect of content available both visually and acoustically. The multimedia materials can be copied without loss in quality and distributed easily over the communication channels. The great opportunity is that these data can be described digitally as well, so that producers' identities and rights can be tracked and consumers' information needs can be effectively addressed [5]. Numerous strategies exist to reduce the number of bits required for digital video in lossy compression, in which some information is sacrificed to reduce significantly the number of bits used to encode the video. MPEG-4 is such a lossy compression format developed as an ISO/IEC standard by MPEG (Moving Picture Experts Group), the committee that also specified the widely adopted multimedia standards such as MPEG-1 and MPEG-2. This standard made interactive video on CD-ROM, DVD, digital television and Internet broadcasting possible [6].

Right management for MPEG-4 is important for multimedia streaming services using it, such as video on demand system in digital video library, since it is desirable that only those who have paid for services can view their digital contents [16]. In

T.M.T. Sembok et al. (Eds.): ICADL 2003, LNCS 2911, pp. 444–455, 2003.

general, digital rights management (DRM) systems restrict the use of digital contents to protect the interests of copyright holders. DRM technologies can control number of views, length of views, altering, sharing, copying, printing, and saving for digital contents. These technologies may be contained within program software such as viewer or plug-in, or in the actual hardware of a device. DRM systems take two approaches to securing content. The first is to encrypt digital content in a shell so that authorized users can only access it. The second is to place a watermark, flag, or a XrML (eXtensible Right Markup Language) tag on digital content as a signal to a device to protect copying of media [7].

In this paper, we adopt the first approach to secure multimedia services using MPEG-4 and encrypted MPEG-4 data using DES (Data Encryption Standard) [8, 9]. We designed three kinds of encryption methods which encrypt macro blocks (MBs) or motion vectors (MVs) of I-, P-VOPs (Video Object Planes) extracted from the MPEG-4 file format. Based on theses three methods, we designed and implemented a DRM solution for video on demand services, which enables MPEG-4 data streaming.

2 Background

The MPEG-4 visual standard provides standardized core technologies allowing efficient storage, transmission and manipulation of textures, images and video data for multimedia environments. The MPEG-4 video coding algorithms will eventually support all functionalities already provided by MPEG-1 and MPEG-2, including the provision to efficiently compress standard rectangular sized image sequences at varying levels of input formats, frame rates and bit rates. In addition the content-based functionalities will be assisted [6, 10].

The input to be coded can be a VOP (Video Object Plane) image region of arbitrary shape and the shape and location of the region can vary from frame to frame. Successive VOP's, belonging to the same physical object in a scene, is referred to as Video Objects (VO's) - a sequence of VOP's of possibly arbitrary shape and position. The shape, motion and texture information of the VOP's belonging to the same VO is encoded and transmitted or coded. Similar to MPEG-1 and MPEG-2, I-VOP, P-VOP and B-VOP are basic types of VOPs, and each VOP is decomposed into Macro Blocks which is again decomposed into 6 Blocks in which DCT (Discrete Cosine Transformation) is applied [10, 14].

2.1 Traditional MPEG Video Encryption Method

Traditionally MPEG-1 and MPEG-2 uses video encryption algorithms to prevent unauthorized users from decoding the video programs by scrambling them [17,18]. The general scheme is to apply an invertible transformation, E_{kl}, to video stream, S, called plaintext, that produces a bitstream C, called ciphertext, $C = E_{kl}(S)$. An authorized user, who has a secret key, $k2$, can decrypt the encrypted video stream by the transformation $D_{k2} = E_{kl}^{-1}$. The decryption operation is as follows:

$$D_{k2}(C) = E_{kl}^{-1}(C) = E_{kl}^{-1}(E_{kl}(S)) = S \tag{1}$$

Parameter *k1* is called an encryption key, and *k2* is called a decryption key. Some video encoding algorithms use a selective encryption algorithm, which only operates on the sign bits of DCT coefficients of a MPEG compressed video [11, 18]. In VEA, the encryption key and the decryption key are the same. The block encryption algorithms developed to secure text data is used since they usually use short keys and complex computations, such as DES. We should use long keys to prevent adversary attacks and use simple computation algorithms to pursue real time performance for multimedia applications such as streaming service.

2.2   MPEG-4 File Format

While MPEG-2 is the standard for entertainment quality video and audio and is the format of choice for DVD (Digital Versatile Disc) and DVB (Digital Video Broadcasting), MPEG-4 is an emerging digital media standard currently being defined by ISO's Moving Picture Experts Group (MPEG) that will enable users to select, view and manipulate audio, video and other forms of digital content. By the adoption of the MPEG-4 file format standard, users are assured that all digital media content can be authored in a common file format that also supports real-time video and audio streaming [6]. This digital stream can then be delivered over the Internet, corporate networks or broadcast directly into the home.

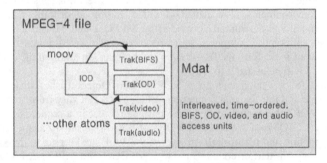

Fig. 1. Example of a MPEG-4 file format

The MPEG-4 file format is designed to contain the media information of an MPEG-4 presentation in a flexible, extensible format, which facilitates interchange, management, editing, and presentation of the media. The design is based on the QuickTime format from Apple [12]. The MPEG-4 file format is composed of object-oriented structures that are called atoms. A unique tag and length identify each atom. Most atoms describe a hierarchy of metadata giving information such as index points, durations, and pointers to the media data. This collection of atoms is contained in an atom called the movie (MOOV) atom. The media data is located elsewhere; it may be in the MPEG-4 file or located outside the MPEG-4 file and referenced via URLs. Figure 1 gives an example of a simple interchange file, containing three streams [6].

The file format is a streamable format, as opposed to a streaming format. That is, the file format is never actually streamed over a transmission medium. Instead, metadata in the file known as hint tracks provide instructions, telling a server application how to deliver the media data over a particular delivery protocol. There can be multiple hint tracks for one presentation, describing how to deliver over various delivery protocols. In this way, the file format facilitates streaming without ever being streamed directly [15, 17].

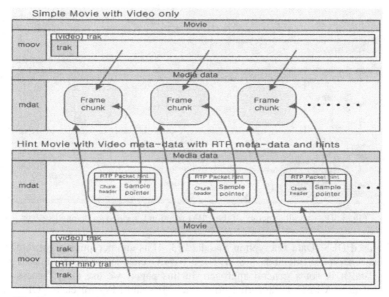

Fig. 2. Relationship with RTP protocol hint tracks to stream a simple video movie

Figure 2 shows the container relationship with RTP protocol hint tracks to stream a simple video movie. The metadata in the file, combined with the flexible storage of media data, allows the MPEG-4 format to support streaming, editing, local playback, and interchange of content [6, 13].

3 Design and Implementation of a Video on Demand System by Applying DRM

In this paper, we designed and implemented a DRM solution for video on demand system suitable for digital video library, which enables MPEG-4 data streaming and download. The overall structure of the solution is shown in Figure 3. The user accesses the digital library containing DRM server which can interpret metadata and copyright information. Streaming server offers encrypted data to the user with the DRM information.

The video data is extracted from MPEG-4 file and three kinds of encryption methods are applied to the video data.

1) Encryption of macro blocks (MBs) within I-VOP (We call it method-1.)
2) Encryption of MBs and motion vectors (MVs) in P-VOP (mehod-2)
3) Encryption of both MBs in I-VOP and MBs and MVs in P-VOP (method-3)

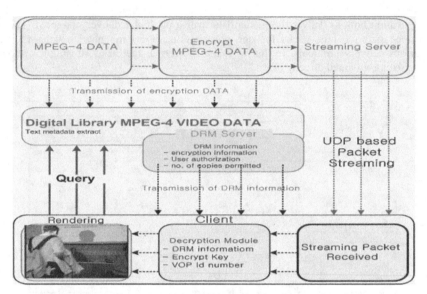

Fig. 3. The overall structure of the DRM solution for video on demand system

We used DES (Data Encryption Standard)[3, 4] as an encryption algorithm. Since previous encryption methods [18, 19] use MPEG encoder program sources to get video data, it is not a general approach. In this paper, we use direct access to the MPEG data in MPEG-4 file format to extract MBs and MVs for each VOP, and we can access the already-encoded data. In addition, we can insert the DRM information into the MPEG data file so that we can efficiently manage already encrypted MPEG-4 files. The structure of the DRM metadata information is shown in Figure 4.

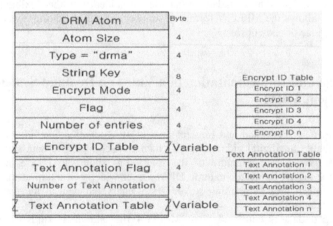

Fig. 4. The structure of DRM metadata

The DRM metadata information is inserted to MPEG-4 data and follows MPEG-4 file format. This metadata is used for efficient encryption of the data and indexing of digital library. The first 4 bytes, that is Atom Size, defines the size of the atom itself, and the next 4 bytes (Type) defines the type of this atom as "drma". The client and server interpret and separate this information from the actual data. The metadata information does not affect the streaming of video data. The details of the metadata items are explained as follows.

- Key String: string for the key generation is stored. The DES algorithm used the same key for both encryption and decryption.
- Encryption Mode: encryption method (that is method-1, method-2 or method-3) is defined
- Flag: flag for selective encryption is defined.
- Number of Entries: the number of encrypted VOP is defined. That is, this metadata defines the size of Encryption ID Table.
- Encrytpion ID Table: The IDs of encrypted VOP are listed. Each entry has a size of 4 byte.
- Text Annotation Flag: flag for text annotation is defined. Explanation of a video stream is defined as a text annotation which can be used as an indexing key.
- Number of Text Annotation Entries: the number of text annotation in Text Annotation Table is defined.
- Text Annotation Table: The text annotations are listed.

The encrypted MPEG-4 data is transmitted to the client with DRM metadata information offered by DRM server. The client decrypts the transmitted media data in real time using the decryption module and renders the decrypted media data. Figure 5 shows the transmission of DRM information by the DRM server between clients and streaming server. In this architecture, we need not to modify the video or audio codec to decrypt the data because the decryption module deals each VOP as a preprocessing fashion in the buffer.

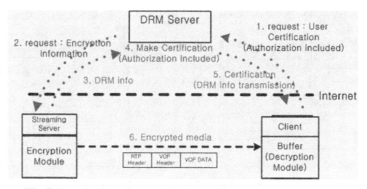

Fig. 5. Transmission of DRM information between client and server

3.1   Video Frame Extraction Algorithm

As mentioned in section 2.2, the MPEG-4 file format is composed of atoms. A MPEG-4 file is divided into two parts: metadata and data. Metadata is contained in a Movie (MOOV) atom and actual media data is contained in a mdat atom [6, 12].

To encrypt video data from the MPEG-4 file format, we have to parse the metadata of MPEG-4 file and extract video frames such as I-, P-, B-VOPs. Figure 6 shows how to interpret metadata of MPEG-4 file format to extract video data.

The procedure to extract a video sample is as follows:

1) Identify the video track by checking the existence of a video media information header atom.

2) Obtain sample table (stbl) atoms within the video track. Sample table atoms include location of actual media data and description information etc.

3) Obtain table information from sample to chunk (stco), sample per chunck (stsc) and sample size (stsz) atoms.

From the procedure described above, we obtain the sample table within the video track and location information of each sample. Figure 7 shows how to get actual data from mdat atom by calculating an offset using the location information of each sample [6, 12].

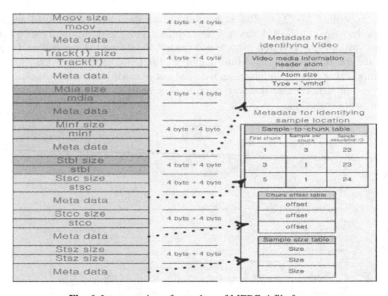

Fig. 6. Interpretation of metadata of MEPG-4 file format

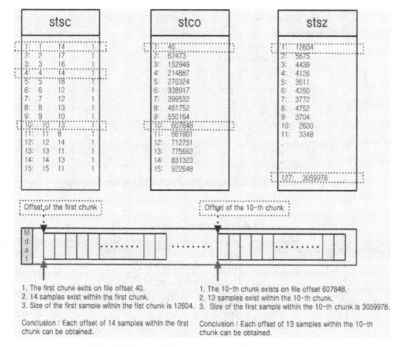

Fig. 7. Obtain video data by calculating an offset.

3.2   Macro Block Extraction from I-VOP and Its Encryption (Method-1)

I-VOP is extracted from the video data, and DES is applied to the I-VOP. Since DES is a block encryption algorithm, which takes 64-bit data as an input and output 64-bit encrypted data, it does not affect the size of the data. If we choose an encryption algorithm, which has different input and output size, it will cause padding bits and offsets in the MPEG-4 file and should be changed. We choose DES due to this reason. We apply only multiples of 64 as an input not to change the file size and prohibit the padding of DES from occurring.

To extract an I-VOP from the video data, we follow an MPEG-4 visual standard [10]. As shown in Figure 8, each video object plane (VOP) has a video_start_code. The value of a video_start_code is x00 00 01 B6 (in hexadecimal) and vop_coding_type identifies the VOP type for I-, P-, and B-VOPs. Table 1 shows the vop-coing_type.

Figure 9 shows the results of the encryption of macro blocks (MBs) within I-VOP. The figure on the left hand side is the original data and the one on the right hand side is the play back of an encrypted data without decryption. Because the intra coded macro blocks of P-VOP preserve considerable information, we can see some shapes in the figure on the right hand side.

```
VideoObjectPlane() {              No, of bits
Mnemonic
            vop_start_code        32        bslbf
            vop_coding_type       2         uimsbf
            do {
                  modulo_time_base 1                 bslbf
            } while (modulo_time_base != '0')

            marker_bit 1          bslbf
            vop_time_increment 1-16          uimsbf
            marker_bit 1          bslbf
............
}
```

Fig. 8. Structure of video object plane in MPEG-4 visual standard

Table 1. VOP coding type

vop_coding_type	coding method
00	Intra-coded (I-VOP)
01	Predictive-coded (P-VOP)
10	Bidirectionally-Predictive-coded (B-VOP)
11	Sprite

Fig. 9. Encryption of macro blocks within I-VOP

3.3 Encryption of Macro Blocks and Motion Vectors in P-VOP (Method-2)

In P-VOP, intra coded macro blocks (MBs) and motion vectors (MVs) are encrypted. Figure 10 shows the results of the encryption. Because the intra coded macro blocks of I-VOP preserve a lot of information, we can see some perfect still images periodically during the streaming. If the ratio of I-VOP is small in the video sequence, encryption of P-VOP can be an efficient encryption method.

Fig. 10. Encryption of macro blocks and motion vectors in P-VOP

3.4   Encryption of Both Macro Blocks in I-VOP and Motion Vectors in P-VOP (Method-3)

Both method-1 and method-2 do not offer satisfiable results because the intra coded macro blocks preserve a lot of coding information. We encrypt both Macro Blocks in I-VOP and Motion Vectors in P-VOP to solve this problem. Figure 11 shows the results. It is the strongest encryption method among the three methods, but the amount of data for encryption is increased which decreases the performance of the client which playback the streaming sequence.

Fig. 11. Encryption of both macro blocks in I-VOP and motion vectors in P-VOP

4 Simulation on Encryption Speed

In this paper, we propose three encryption methods for MPEG_4 data. While method-3 offers the strongest encryption results, it requires large amounts of data for encryption. Even though we can control the amount of data for encryption by adjusting I-VOP ratio, to encrypt only macro blocks of I-VOP, it requires small amounts of data for encryption in general. The time for encrypting VOP is represented as follows:

$$E(t) = DES(t) + M(t) \tag{2}$$

$E(t)$ is processing for encryption of VOP, DES(t) is processing time for DES encryption and $M(t)$ is processing time for pre-processing.

Table 2 shows the results from "very_huge.mp4" (which was used in the encryption results of Figures 9, 10 and 11) based on $E(t)$ in the above formula. The time unit is a second.

Table 2. Measures of encryption speed for the three methods

Encryption Method	Number of VOPs used in the encryption	Average encryption time per VOP (second)	Total encryption time (second)
Method-1	361	0.0000030736	0.0011094883
Method-2	540	0.0000048096	0.0025975620
Method-3	901	0.0000139419	0.0125523652

The results show that the encryption speed for the media stream depends on the amount of data for encryption. Even though method-3 spends 10 times more than method-1 for encryption and decryption, it may not affect the playback because the client has a buffer for decryption and can delay the playback.

5 Conclusion

In this paper, we designed and implemented a DRM solution suitable for digital video library, which extracts video data from MPEG-4 file formats and encrypts VOPs using DES. We use three different encryption methods to encrypt the macro blocks (MBs) or motion vectors(MVs) in VOPs. While method-3 offers the strongest encryption results among the methods, it requires large amounts of data for encryption and takes time to process. Each encryption method may be optimal for a certain constraint.

In addition, DRM information combined with the encrypted data is pursued for multimedia streaming services. That is, DRM information is inserted into MPEG-4 file format to efficiently support the services without affecting the streaming of video data. The methods proposed in this paper also can apply to interactive video on CD-ROM, DVD, digital television and Internet broadcasting services.

References

1. Vemulapalli, S., Halappanavar, M., Mukkamala, R.: Security in distributed digital libraries: issues and challenges, Proceedings of International Conference on Parallel Processing (Aug. 2002)
2. Barrett, B.H.: A digital library architecture for interactive television, IEEE International Conference on Systems, Vol. 3, 12–15, Man and Cybernetics (Oct. 1997)

3. Adams, W.J., Jansen, B.J. and Howard, R.: Distributed digital library architecture: the key to success for distance learning, Proceedings of Eighth International Workshop on Continuous-Media Databases and Applications (Feb. 1998)
4. Michael, G. Christel, Andreas, M. Olligschlaeger and Chang Huang.: Interactive Maps for a Digital Video Library, pp. 60–67, IEEE Multimedia 7(1) (2000)
5. Wactlar, H.D. and Michael, G. Christel.: Digital Video Archives.: Managing Through Metadata, Issues in Digital Media Archiving, Commissioned for and sponsored by the National Digital Information Infrastructure and Preservation Program, pp. 80–95, Library of Congress (April, 2002)
6. Information technology - Coding of audio-visual objects - Part 1: Systems ISO/IEC 14496-1:2001, ISO/IEC/SC29/WG11 (2001)
7. EPIC(Electronic Provacy Information Center) Digital Right Management and Privacy Page, http://www.epic.org/privacy/drm/
8. Data Encryption Standard (DES), FIPS PUB 46-3 (Oct. 25. 1999)
9. William Stallings.: Principles and Practice (3rd Edition), Cryptography and Network Security, Prentice Hall (2002)
10. Information Technology – Coding of Audio-Visual Objects – Part 2:Visual, ISO/IEC 14496-2, ISO/IEC/SC29/WG11 (Nov. 1998)
11. Shi, C. and Bhargava, B.: A Fast MPEG Video Encryption Alogrithm, proceedings of the ACM Multimedia (Sep. 1998)
12. QuickTime File Format, Apple Computer (June. 2000)
13. RTP Payload Format for MPEG-4 Audio/Visual Streams, RFC 3016 (Nov. 2000)
14. Thomas Sikora.: The MPEG-4 video standard verification model, pages 19–31, IEEE Transactions on Circuits and Systems for Video Technology (Feb. 1997)
15. QuickTime Streaming Server Modules, Apple Computer (2002)
16. Frank Hartung and Friedhelm Ramme.: Digital Rights Management and Watermarking of Multimedia Content for M-Commerce Applications, pages 78–84, IEEE Communications Magazine (Nov. 2000)
17. Sieven Gringeri, Sami Iren.: Transmission of MPEG-4 video over the Internet, pages1767 -1770, IEEE International Conference on Multimedia and Expo (July 30–Aug. 2, 2000)
18. Shi, C. and Bhargava, B.: An Efficient MPEG Video Encryption Algorithm, pages 381–386, Proceedings of Seventeenth IEEE Symposium on Reliable Distributed Systems (Oct. 1998)
19. Adnan M, Alattar and Al-Semari.: Improved Selective Encryption Techniques for Secure Transmission of MPEG Video Bit-Streams, pages 256–260, Proceedings of 1999 International Conference on Image Processing (Oct. 1999)

Gradient-Based Edge Detection of Songket Motifs

Nursuriati Jamil[1] and Tengku Mohd Tengku Sembok[2]

[1] Faculty of Information Technology & Quantitative Sciences,
Universiti Teknologi
MARA, Shah Alam 40450, Selangor, Malaysia
liza@tmsk.itm.edu.my
[2] Faculty of Technology and Information Sciences,
Universiti Kebangsaan Malaysia,
Bangi, Selangor, Malaysia
tmts@pkrisc.cc.ukm.my

Abstract. This paper discussed the effectiveness of several popular gradient-based edge detection techniques when applied on binary images of songket motifs. Five edge detector algorithms that is Roberts, Sobel, Prewitt, Laplacian of Gaussian and Canny are applied to twenty-five Malaysian traditional songket motifs. These scanned motif images are initially preprocessed to remove noise using several morphological operations. Other than noise removal, binarization of color images are also done to produce binary images. To determine the performance of the edge detectors, the results are evaluated by five human subjects based on several pre-conceived criteria.

1   Introduction

Edges can be defined as where gradient of image intensity function reaches its local maximum. In other words, edge points are points in the image where pixel brightness changes drastically. Typically, edge points are associated with the boundaries of objects in the image and edge detection can also be used for region segmentation and feature extraction.

2   Gradient-Based Edge Detectors

Edge detection methods can be classified into directional and non-directional or gradient-based operators [5]. Directional operators uses two masks and two convolutions. While non-directional use single mask and convolution but they are sensitive to noise due to gradient nature of the operators. In this paper, five popular gradient-based edge detection algorithms were experimented on the binary images. The algorithms are Roberts, Sobel, Prewitt, Laplacian of Gaussian and Canny.

T.M.T. Sembok et al. (Eds.): ICADL 2003, LNCS 2911, pp. 456–467, 2003.

2.1   Roberts Edge Detector

Roberts cross operator is the simplest edge detection operators and will work best with binary images [6]. It provides a simple approximation to the gradient magnitude: Using convolution masks, this becomes G[f[i, j]] = | f[[i, j] − f[i + 1, j + 1]| + f[i + 1, j] − f[i, j + 1]|, where Gx and Gy are calculated using the following masks:

$G_x =$

1	0
0	-1

$G_y =$

0	1
1	0

Roberts operator is very easy to compute and there are no parameters to set. Its main disadvantages are that since it uses such a small kernel, it is very sensitive to noise. It also produces very weak responses to edges unless they are very sharp.

2.2   Sobel Edge Detector

Consider the arrangement of pixels and pixel [i, j] shown in Figure 1 below.

p_0	p_1	p_2
p_7	[i+j]	p_3
p_6	p_5	p_4

Fig. 1. Neighborhood pixels used in Sobel and Prewitt operators

The Sobel operator is the magnitude of the gradient computed by:

$$M\sqrt{s_x^2 + s_y^2} \qquad (1)$$

where the partial derivatives are computed by:

$$s_x = (p_2 + cp_3 + p_4) - (p_0 + cp_7 + p_6) \qquad (2)$$

$$s_y = (p_0 + cp_1 + p_2) - (p_6 + cp_5 + p_4) \qquad (3)$$

with the constant c = 2. Like the other gradient operators, s_x and s_y can be implemented using convolution masks:

$S_x =$

-1	0	1
-2	0	2
-1	0	1

$S_y =$

1	2	1
0	0	0
-1	-2	-1

Note that this operator places an emphasis on pixels that are closer to the center of the mask or on-axis pixels.

2.3   Prewitt Edge Detector

The Prewitt operator uses the same equations as the Sobel operator, except that the constant c = 1. Thus, the convolution masks are:

$S_x =$

-1	0	1
-1	0	1
-1	0	1

$S_y =$

1	1	1
0	0	0
-1	-1	-1

Unlike the Sobel operator, this operator does not place any emphasis on pixels that are closer to the center of the masks.

2.4   Laplacian of Gaussian Edge Detector

The Laplacian is seldom used on its own in edge detection because it is sensitive to noise. It is more useful to enhance edge of an image after the image has been blurred using a Gaussian filter. Edge localization is then done by finding the zero crossings of the second derivative of the image intensity. The idea is illustrated for a 1D signal in Figure 2. The first graph represents an edge in 1D. Gaussian filter is used for smoothing and the second derivative of which is used for the enhancement step. The detection criterion is the presence of a zero crossing in the second derivative with the corresponding large peak in the first derivative.

In this approach, noise is first reduced by convoluting the image with a Gaussian filter. Isolated noise points and small structures are filtered out. With smoothing, however, edges are spread. Pixels that have locally maximum gradient are considered as edges by the edge detector in which zero crossings of the second derivative are used. To avoid detection of insignificant edges, only the zero crossings whose corresponding first derivative is above some threshold are selected as edge point. The edge direction is obtained using the direction in which zero crossing occurs. The output of the Laplacian of Gaussian (LoG) operator, h(x,y), is obtained by the convolution operation:

$$h(x, y) = \Delta^2[g(x, y)* f(x, y)] = [\Delta^2 g(x, y)] * f(x, y) \tag{4}$$

where

$$\Delta^2 g(x, y) = \left(\frac{x^2 + y^3 - 2\sigma^2}{\sigma^4} \right)^{-(x^2+y^2)/2\sigma^2} \tag{5}$$

The value of σ determines the filter width and controls the amount of smoothing so that edges at different scale can be detected using different value of σ.

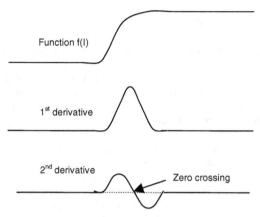

Fig. 2. First and second derivative of an edge illustrated in one dimension

2.5 Canny Edge Detector

Canny edge detector provides the most possible compromise between noise reduction and edge localization and is observed to give good results with real images [2]. Its edge detection algorithm has the following steps:

1. Smooth the image with a Gaussian filter. Let I[i, j] denote the image; G[i, j, σ] be a Gaussian smoothing filter where σ is the filter width. The result of convolution of I[i, j] with G[i, j, σ] gives an array of smoothed data as:

$$S[i, j] = G[i, j, \sigma] * I[i, j] \tag{6}$$

2. Compute the gradient magnitude and orientation using finite-difference approximations for the partial derivatives. Firstly, the gradient of the smoothed array S[i, j] is used to produce the x and y partial derivatives P[i, j] and Q[i, j] respectively as:

$$P[i, j] \approx \frac{S[i, j+1] - S[i, j] + S[i+1, j+1] - S[i+1, j]}{2} \tag{7}$$

$$Q[i, j] \approx \frac{S[i, j] - S[i+1, j] + S[i, j+1] - S[i+1, j+1]}{2} \tag{8}$$

The x and y partial derivatives are computed with averaging the finite differences over the 2x2 square. From the standard formulas for rectangular-to-polar conversion, the magnitude and orientation of the gradient can be computed as:

$$M[i, j] = \sqrt{P[i, j]^2 + Q[i, j]^2} \tag{9}$$

$$\theta[i, j] = \arctan(q[i, j], p[i, j]) \tag{10}$$

Here the arctan(x,y) function takes two arguments and generates an angle.

3. Apply nonmaxima suppression to the gradient magnitude. Nonmaxima suppression thins the wide ridges around local maxima in gradient magnitude down to edges that are only one pixel wide. After nonmaxima suppression, an image N[i, j] which is zero everywhere except the local maxima points is produced.

4. Use the double (hysteresis) thresholding algorithm to detect and link edges. To remove noise in the nonmaxima suppressed magnitude image N[i, j], two threshold values are applied to it. With these threshold values, two thresholded edge images $T_1[i, j]$ and $T_2[i, j]$ are produced. The image T_2 has gaps in the contours but contains fewer false edges. With the double thresholding algorithm, the edges in T_2 are linked into contours. When it reaches the end of a contour, the algorithm looks in T_1 at the locations of the 8-neighbours for edges that can be linked to the contour. This algorithm continues until the gap has been bridged to an edge in T_2. The algorithm performs edge linking as a by-product of thresholding and resolves some of the problems with choosing a single threshold value.

3   Edge Detection Performance Evaluation

An edge detector's performance can be evaluated either subjectively or objectively in an experimental framework. Ziou and Tabbone [8] in their report used experimental evaluation to show edge detectors failures and characterize their performances. Failure of an edge detector is established by doing subjective evaluation where a human subject rates the detector by looking at the detected edges. Meanwhile, the performance of an edge detector is measured by doing an objective evaluation where criteria that describe the characteristics of the edge to be detected are done beforehand. Some of the measurements used by several authors in objective evaluation are:

1. Non-detection of true edges, detection of false edges, and edge delocalization error [1].
2. Combines errors that arise due to edge's thickness and lack of continuity [4].

Heath et al. [3] combine subjective evaluation and statistical techniques to compare edge detectors in the context of object recognition. Results of the evaluation make statements whether the outputs of one edge detector are rated statistically higher than the outputs of another. The human judge rates the edge detectors based on how well they capture the salient features of real objects. The results are interpreted using the analysis of variance technique to establish the statistical significance of observed differences.

4   The Experiments

The binary images used in this experiment are traditional songket motifs of Malaysia which originated from Kelantan and Terengganu. The overall process of detecting edges of the motifs consists of two main steps, which are image preprocessing and boundary detection.

4.1 Preprocessing

Songket motifs are designed on graph paper and thus the shapes are geometrically inclined and only two values (0 and 1) are necessary to store the shape information in digital form. Even though several songket motifs nowadays are weaved using colored threads, neither color nor texture play an important role in determining the type of songket motifs. Thus, this paper will focus only on the shape of the songket motifs, which is the utmost important criterion in categorizing the motifs.

The operations involved in preprocessing of the motifs images are noise removal and binarization. The motifs collected and used for the experiment are scanned from books, manuscripts and color photographs. Noises produced from scanning operation have to be removed so that true representations of the songket motifs are correctly archived. This is done by manually editing the images using a paint program or performing filtering and morphological operations such as dilation or erosion. Figure 3 shows an example of noise removal operation done using a mean filter. The *Anggur* motif scanned is filtered using a 7x7 kernel containing equal weights. The value of the output pixel is computed as the average of the pixels in the local neighborhood.

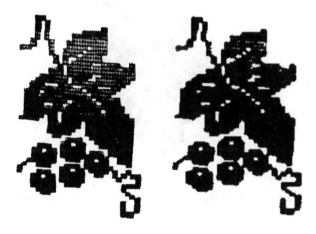

Fig. 3. Originally scanned *Anggur* motif (left) and filtered *Anggur* motif (right)

Another method used to remove noise is by using morphological operation such as dilation. In Figure 4, a dilation operation was performed on the *Bunga Raya* motif to fill in the holes in the image. A structuring element of size 3x3 is applied over the image and an OFF pixel is set to ON if any of the structuring element overlaps ON pixels of the image. The problem with using dilation is that the operation might completely closes up or narrows down holes (shown in circles) in the image. A way to solve this problem is to combine several different operations such as dilation, mean filter and *k*fill filter to remove as much noise as possible as shown in Figure 5. However, no same operation can be applied to all motifs to effectively reduce or remove the noise. Depending on the amount of noise and shape of the motif, different operations have to be experimentally applied to the motif for the best result.

Fig. 4. Originally scanned *Bunga Raya* motif(left) and dilated *Bunga Raya* motif(right)

Fig. 5. Mean filter, dilation and *k*fill filter applied to *Bunga Raya* motif

Dilation can also be used to add pixels at region boundaries or to connect disjoint pixels. For example, the motif *Sulur Kacang* in Figure 6 (left) has disconnected pixels and will cause problem during boundary detection. Thus, dilation was applied to expand the image as shown in Figure 6 (right).

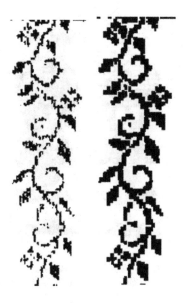

Fig. 6. Originally scanned *Sulur Kacang* motif(left) and dilated *Sulur Kacang* motif(right)

For colored motifs, binarization of the images is done by converting the color image to grayscale image by eliminating the hue and saturation information while retaining the luminance. The grayscale image is then thresholded to binary image based on whether a pixel in the greyscale image has intensity greater than or less than or equal to a given constant value (the threshold). The output binary image has values of 0(black) for all pixels in the input image with luminance less than the threshold value and 1(white) for all other pixels.

In performing binarization, choosing the appropriate threshold level is very important. Threshold value is a normalized intensity value that lies in the range [0, 1]. Figure 7 demonstrates the results of thresholding *Sarung Celak* motif with different threshold values. The second image chooses a threshold value too low, resulting in breaks in what is supposed to be complete regions. While the third image shows too high a threshold value, resulting in larger blobs than necessary. The final image however uses a threshold value that is most acceptable for *Sarung Celak* motif. Similar to noise removal operation, there is not a single optimally suited method for binarization for all images. It is often best to make the decision by experimentation.

4.2 Boundary Detection

After the preprocessing stage, process of boundary detection begins. To facilitate discussion of boundary detection, the following terms used in this paper are defined [7]:

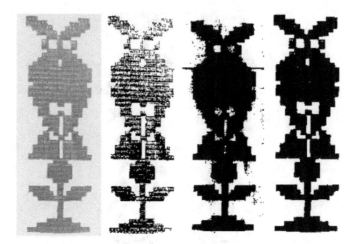

Fig. 7. The originally scanned *Sarung Celak* motif is shown as the leftmost image, while the following images are thresholded at value 0.5, 0.9 and 0.77, respectively.

1. True edge point – a pixel that corresponds to an actual edge point of the image motif.
2. Edge connectedness – measures how edges are connected with each other to form closed boundaries of the image motif.

In this experiment, twenty-five traditional songket motifs, ranging from simple to complex shapes of four different categories (Flora, Fauna, Food, Others) are used. Five methods of edge detection which are Canny, Prewitt, Sobel, Laplacian of Gaussian and Roberts were applied to all these motifs. As subjective measures tend to be more useful in many computer imaging applications [6], these results are given to five human subjects to be evaluated based on some objective measurements. The measurements used to determine unsuccessful edge detectors are by detecting errors such as missing true edge points, classifying noise pulses as true edge points and lack of connectivity between edge segments. If these errors do not occur, the edge detector can be classified as successful. However, the final judgment relies on the criteria that the most suitable edge detector for songket motif should produce horizontal and/or vertical edges only because these characteristics conform to the weaving process of songket motifs.

5   Results and Discussion

In the first stage of evaluation, the human subjects were asked to eliminate all edge detectors that can be deemed as unsuccessful based on the errors produced by them. For example, Figure 8 show sample of errors detected as a result of boundary detection of the motifs. The first image shows one-third of the scanned Air Muleh motif, the second image shows the motif applied using Canny method resulting in noise pulses (shown in circle) classified as edge points, while the third image is the same motif applied with Prewitt method resulting in disconnected edges (shown in circle).

Fig. 8. A portion of *Air Muleh* motif shown as the leftmost image while the others show samples of errors produced during edge detection.

Another type of error is demonstrated in Figure 9, where a smaller section of *Air Muleh* motif is applied with Laplacian of Gaussian method resulting in missing true edge points.

Fig. 9. A section of *Air Muleh* motif and its corresponding missing true edges error produced during edge detection process.

The overall result of the human evaluation on all twenty-five motifs is summarized in Table 1. As can be seen from the table, Canny edge detector is highly subjected to detection of false edges due to the noise signals. Noises are produced in varying clusters in all twenty-five motifs especially within or near holes. This is probably due to the high threshold value used to detect weak edges in the Canny detector. The most common error that occurred in four detectors (Canny, Prewitt, Sobel and LoG) tested are missing true edges. This is especially obvious in Laplacian of Gaussian detector probably due to the smoothing operation prior to edge detection. The last type of error is edge connectedness, which existed in all twenty-five motifs applied with Prewitt detector. Laplacian of Gaussian detector also produces a small degree of disconnected edges especially in complex shapes such as Bunga Berdiri and Awan Larat.

Table 1. Summary of Human Evaluation Based on Errors

Edge Detector	Canny	Prewitt	Sobel	LoG	Roberts
Detection of False Edges	√				
Missing True Edges	√	√	√	√	
Lack of Connectivity		√		√	

As the only detector that can be considered as successful, Roberts operator is finally evaluated based on the most important criteria, that is it should resulted in only horizontal and vertical edges. Figures 10, 11 and 12 demonstrate few examples of motifs applied with Roberts detector in comparison with LoG and Sobel detector. As shown in these Figure 11, Roberts detector produce exact replicas of the original motifs. Thus, it is very important that noise is non-existent in the original motif to get an accurate edge representation. While Figure 12 show existence of diagonal edges (in circles) as a result of LoG operator and Sobel operator applications on the motifs.

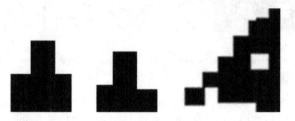

Fig. 10. Original scanned motifs of *Wajik* (left) and *Ayam Jantan* (right)

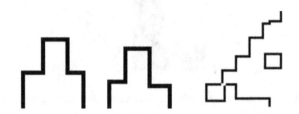

Fig. 11. *Wajik* (left) and *Ayam Jantan* (right) motifs produced using Roberts edge detector

Fig. 12. *Wajik* (left) motif produced using LoG and *Ayam Jantan* (right) motifs produced using Sobel edge detector

6   Conclusion

The process involved in edge detection discussed in this paper consists of preprocessing and boundary detection. Preprocessing of the songket motifs is very crucial because the existence of noise in the scanned motifs produced very inconsistent and unreliable results of boundary detection. It is also very important that the image represents the actual songket motif because this is a first attempt of archiving songket motif in digital form in Malaysia. After experimenting on twenty-five motifs using five popular edge detector algorithms, the results clearly shows that Roberts operator is most suitable for detecting edge of binary images. Even though Laplacian of Gaussian operator's results can be improve by experimenting on different filter width , σ, Roberts operator has the advantage of using very simple and easily computable kernel. However, Roberts operator is very sensitive to noise, thus a small amount of noise in the image will produce very undesirable and useless results.

References

1. Abdou, I. E.: *Quantitative Methods of Edge Detection.* Technical report, No. 830. Image Processing Institute, University of Southern California (1978)
2. Efford, S.: *Digital Image Processing.* Pearson Education Limited (2000)
3. Heath M., Sarkar S., Sanocki T., and Bowyer K.: Comparison of Edge Detectors: A Methodology and Initial Study. *Computer Vision and Image Understanding*, 69(**1**): 38–54 (1998)
4. Kitchen L. and Rosenfeld A: Edge Evaluation Using Local Edge Coherence. *IEEE Transactions Systems, Man and Cybernetics*, 11(**9**): 597–605 (1981)
5. Muhammad Bilal Ahmad and Tae-Sun Choi: Local Threshold and Boolean Function Based Edge Detection. *IEEE Transactions on Consumer Electronics*, 45(**3**): 674–9 (1999)
6. Umbaugh, S.: *Computer Vision and Image Processing.* Prentice Hall Inc (1998)
7. Zhu Q.: Improving Edge Detection by an Objective Edge Evaluation. In: *The 1992 ACM/SIGAPP* Symposium *on Applied Computing*, Kansas City, MO: 459–68 (1992)
8. Ziou D. and Tabbone S.: *Edge Detection Techniques- An Overview*, Technical report, No. 195, Dept Math & Informatique. Universit de Sherbrooke (1997)

Assessing the Usability of Political Web Sites in Malaysia: A Benchmarking Approach

Hassan Shahizan[1] and Shiratuddin Norshuhada[2]

[1] Department of Information Management, Faculty of Information Technology,
Universiti Utara Malaysia, 06010 UUM Sintok, Kedah, Malaysia
shahizan@uum.edu.my
[2] Department of Multimedia, Faculty of Information Technology,
Universiti Utara Malaysia, 06010 UUM Sintok, Kedah, Malaysia
shuhada@uum.edu.my

Abstract. This paper presents the findings on a study that evaluates the usability of political Web sites in Malaysia by using the benchmarking approach. The outcome of the study indicates that the step-by-step processes proposed by the approach, despite some weaknesses, were very useful, easily followed, and executed. The result of the benchmarking shows that the overall level of usability for the selected Web sites was low and thus need some immediate attention. Although these Web sites performed well in the areas of screen appearance, consistency, accessibility, and navigation, they suffered some usability problems in other aspects including media use, interactivity, and most importantly content.

1 Introduction

One of the major areas of concern facing many Web sites is Web usability. Web sites with low usability could result in low page hits and failure of Web sites. Thus, determining how usable a Web site is indeed imminent. Until now there has been lack of reliable methods for assessing the usability of Web sites particularly the methods that utilise benchmarking approach. With this in mind, this paper will present a study that attempt to utilise the benchmarking approach in assessing the usability of political Web sites. The paper begins with the definition of the concept of Web benchmarking, followed by statement of research objective. Then, the methodology used in this research is explained. Finally, findings and discussion on research contribution will be presented.

2 The Concept of Benchmarking?

Benchmarking is about comparing ones' current performances and practices with others in the same area of interest or business [1,2]. The main objective is to determine ones' position compares to others. American Productivity and Quality Centre (APQC) defines benchmarking as "...the practice of being humble enough to

T.M.T. Sembok et al. (Eds.): ICADL 2003, LNCS 2911, pp. 468–479, 2003.

admit that someone else is better at something, and being wise enough to learn how to match and even surpass them at it."[3]. The result of benchmarking is normally used for bridging the gap with the competitors and move from where ones are now to where ones want to be [4]. There are many advantages that an organisation could gain from benchmarking, which include creating awareness of changing consumer needs, generating a sense of urgency for change, and enabling improvements through learning from others who are better.

Benchmarking can also be performed on Web sites and can be divided into two types [4,6]: Internal benchmarking and external benchmarking. Internal Web benchmarking is comparisons of Web sites within the organisations' units, departments, or branches. External Web benchmarking is direct comparisons of one's Web sites against those of competitors outside an organisation

3   Objective and Methodology

A benchmarking framework for assessing the usability of Web sites was developed by Shahizan [7]. This framework offers complete step-by-step processes for benchmarking Web usability. The main objectives of this study were twofold: to test the applicability of the framework in political Web site domain and to identify the level of usability of major political Web sites in Malaysia. In order to achieve these two objectives, the methodology proposed in Shahizan's framework was adopted, which will be discussed in the next section.

3.1   Eight Steps to Web Benchmarking

Web benchmarking is a continuos process of measuring and comparing one's Web sites with others, which involves at least, eight steps as shown in figure 1.

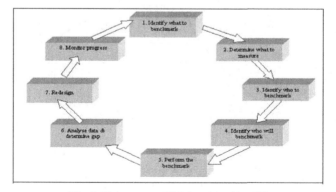

Fig. 1. Eight steps to Web benchmarking [7]

Step 1: Identify What to Benchmark. Although there are many aspects of Web sites, which can be evaluated in order to improve their effectiveness and usefulness, the focus of this study was on usability. Web usability is a concept that relates to how convenient, practicable, and useful a Web site is for a user [8,9]. It is a broad concept covering at least seven major factors namely Screen Appearance, Consistency, Accessibility, Navigation, Media Use, Interactivity, and Content . Screen Appearance refers to visual layout and structure of a Web site. It relates to how a Web site is designed and how the information is presented on the screen. Consistency refers to design consistency, which is vital in determining users' familiarity with a Web site in terms of for example, navigation icons, colouring scheme, and page structure. Apart from appearance and consistency, one also needs to take into consideration the issue of Web accessibility of the target users who use different technology to access the Internet.

Navigation relates to how easy users can move around a Web site. Good navigation will help users find information easily and quickly . Another factor, media use refers to proper use of multimedia elements, both of static media (text and graphics) and continuos media (audio, animation, and video) to present information within Web sites. Interactivity, on the other hand, refers to the interactivity elements of Web sites such as facilities for users to contact Web masters, communicate with other users, and perform online enquiries. Finally, content relates to the services & information provided by Web sites.

Each of the SCANMIC factors has sub-categories as summarised in figure 2.

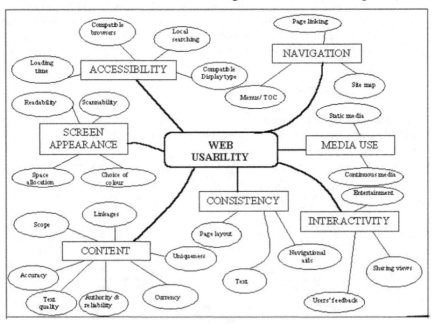

Fig. 2. Factors affecting Web usability

Step 2: Determine What To Measure. All factors listed in table 1 as proposed by the framework were measured. Figure 3, 4, and 5 outline all criteria used to measure each factor.

Table 1. The number of Web usability criteria arranged by SCANMIC factors

SCANMIC Factors	No of Criteria
Screen Appearance	8
Consistency	3
Accessibility	3
Navigation	8
Media use	5
Interactivity	3
Content	55
Total	85

Web Usability Benchmarking

URL: _____

Date: _____ Time: _____

Evaluator's Name: _____

1. Screen Appearance

Subcategory	Criteria	YES	NO
Choice of colour	1. Non excessive use of colour for text (e.g. brown for titles and all black for main content)	( )	( )
	2. Sharp colour contrast between text and its background (e.g. black fonts on white background)	( )	( )
	3. Use of colour to differentiate functional area (e.g. tool bar, menu bar and list of contents) with content display area	( )	( )
Readability	4. Different text sizes to differentiate between titles, headings and texts	( )	( )
	5. Avoidance of background images in the content display area	( )	( )
Scannability	6. Clear titles for each pages	( )	( )
	7. Clear headings, sub headings for text/ document	( )	( )
	8. Use of typography and skimming layout (e.g. bold fonts and highlighted words)	( )	( )
Total		(/8)	(/8)

2. Consistency

Criteria	YES	NO
1. Consistent page layout through out Web site excepts main page (e.g. placement and size for content display, banners, and menu bar).	( )	( )
2. Consistent use of text in terms of its type, font size and colour.	( )	( )
3. Consistent use of navigational aids (e.g. menu bar, buttons and links in terms of graphics metaphor, size and colour).	( )	( )
Total	(/3)	(/3)

3. Accessibility

Subcategory	Criteria	YES	NO
Display compatibility	1. Compatible contents for all main browsers (e.g. Netscape and Microsoft Explorer)	( )	( )
	2. Compatible contents between different versions of the same browser	( )	( )
Fast content retrieval	3. The use of local search facility	( )	( )
Total		(/3)	(/3)

Fig. 3. Benchmarking form for Screen Appearance, Consistency, and Accessibility

4. Navigation

Criteria		YES	NO
1.	Menu/ list of key categories of contents in the main page*	( )	( )
2.	Menu/ list of key categories of contents in all sub-pages*	( )	( )
3.	Links to the main page in all sub pages*	( )	( )
4.	Accurate/ unbroken links	( )	( )
5.	Use of sitemap	( )	( )
6.	Menus are fit on screen (i.e. users do not have to scroll to see menus)	( )	( )
7.	Use of text within text link(where applicable) so that users can explore more if they wanted to	( )	( )
8.	No/ short page scrolling	( )	( )
Total		(/8)	(/8)

Note : '*' these criteria are not applicable to Web sites that use frames or separate windows for sub-pages because the menu are displayed on the screen all the time. In this case, tick 'YES' for assessment purposes.

5. Media Use

NA (i.e. Not Applicable) option is provided in the form for this category since not all Web sites utilise all media elements.

Subcategory	Criteria	YES	NO	NA
Continuos/ time-based media (audio, animation and video)	1. Control features for continuous media where appropriate (e.g. replay, control volume and turn off)	( )	( )	( )
	2. Alternative access (e.g. text version) to any information presented through continuous media	( )	( )	( )
	3. Avoidance of looping animation to prevent users' distraction	( )	( )	( )
Static media (graphics, images, pictures)	4. Labelling of all static media especially those used for menus and icons	( )	( )	( )
	5. Use of thumbnails to display photos (i.e. small icon-sized pictures with options for larger images)	( )	( )	( )
Total		(/5)	(/5)	(/5)

6. Interactivity

Criteria		YES	NO
1.	Availability of features for users' feedback about the site (e.g. Web master's email address and on-line form)	( )	( )
2.	Availability of features for sharing views and discussions (e.g. e-forum, net conference and net chatting)	( )	( )
3.	Availability of entertainment features (e.g. online games and puzzles)	( )	( )
Total		(/3)	(/3)

Fig. 4. Benchmarking form for Navigation, Media Use, and Interactivity

7. Content (specific to political Web sites)

Subcategory	Criteria		YES	NO
Scope ATTRACT	1.	Guest book	( )	( )
	2.	Readers' corner (comments/ opinion)	( )	( )
	3.	Q&A with politicians/ public figures	( )	( )
	4.	Recorded political events (video & audio clips)	( )	( )
	5.	Give-aways (e.g. free email, e-post cards)	( )	( )
	6.	Photo gallery	( )	( )
	7.	Registration for email news	( )	( )
	8.	Job advertisement	( )	( )
	9.	Enquiries on membership	( )	( )
	10.	Speakers corner	( )	( )

	11. Online membership	( )	( )
	12. Campaign banners	( )	( )
	13. Online shopping	( )	( )
	14. Suitable language for audience	( )	( )
	15. News coverage of various issues	( )	( )
	16. Civic/ religious corner	( )	( )
INFORM	17. Profile/ about us	( )	( )
	18. Press release	( )	( )
	19. Archive of previous press release	( )	( )
	20. Organisational chart	( )	( )
	21. History	( )	( )
	22. Mission and vision	( )	( )
	23. Policies (e.g. on education, crime, health etc)	( )	( )
	24. Campaign	( )	( )
	25. Logo with description	( )	( )
	26. Announcements of activities/ events	( )	( )
	27. Fund raising/ donation appeal	( )	( )
	28. Reports/ publications	( )	( )
	29. Statistics (e.g. election results analysis)	( )	( )
POSITION	30. Up-to-date contents especially news	( )	( )
	31. Choices of languages for multi-ethnic audience	( )	( )
	32. Contact of politicians & public leaders	( )	( )
	33. Parliamentary debates/ reports	( )	( )
	34. Technical help	( )	( )
	35. Track record/ report card	( )	( )
DELIVER	36. On-line forms (e.g. for feedback & registration)	( )	( )
	37. On-line polls/ readers polls	( )	( )
	38. Database search (e.g. registered voters, media release)	( )	( )
	39. Web TV	( )	( )
	40. Web radio	( )	( )
	41. Chatting room	( )	( )
Accuracy	42. Clear distinction between informational and opinion content	( )	( )
Authority and Reliability	43. Information on authors and other documents (e.g. names and affiliation)	( )	( )
	44. References or sources of text and other documents	( )	( )
	45. Background information of institution/ organisation/ owner of the site (i.e. logo, name, address, phone number and email address)	( )	( )
Uniqueness	46. Options for output/ print format when appropriate (e.g. long pages)	( )	( )
	47. Choices of media type for a particular information (e.g. text only, audio or video)	( )	( )
	48. Information or warnings before executing users' requests (e.g. file type and size for downloading)	( )	( )
Linkages	49. Clear distinctions between internal and external links	( )	( )
	50. Links to other relevant sites (e.g. local branches, sponsors)	( )	( )
	51. Links to online news (local and international)	( )	( )
	52. Links to politicians' homepages	( )	( )
Text Quality	53. News/articles/documents/stories with pictures	( )	( )
	54. Summary of news/articles/documents/stories with links to full versions	( )	( )
	55. Divide news/articles/documents/stories according to scope (e.g. local & international)	( )	( )
Total		(/55)	(/55)

Fig. 5. Benchmarking form for Content that are applicable only for political Web sites

Step Three: Identify Who To Benchmark Against. This benchmark could be considered as an external benchmarking because it involved comparisons between different political Web sites in Malaysia. Four major political Web sites were selected with justifications as shown in the following table.

Table 2. A list of Web Sites used in the benchmarking

	Web Site Owner	URL	Reasons for Selection
1.	National Front Party (BN)	http://www.bn.org.my	Very strong ruling party
2.	Pan-Islamic Party (PAS)	http://www.parti-pas.org	Very strong opposition party dominated by Malays.
3.	Democratic Action Party (DAP)	http://dapmalaysia.org	Very strong opposition party dominated by Chinese.
4.	ABIM	http://www.abim.org.my	One of the largest NGOs

Step Four: Identify Who Will Benchmark. Two evaluators were invited to participate in the benchmarking. They were both expert Internet users who have been using the Internet for more than 5 years.

Step Five: Perform the benchmark. The participants were grouped in a room occupied with two computers with the different specifications as described in table 3.

Table 3. Computer specifications for Web benchmarking

	Processor	Random Access Memory (RAM)	Internet access	Internet browser	Screen resolution
Computer 1	Pentium 1	32 Megabytes	33 Kbps Modem	Netscape 4.5 & Int. Explorer 5.0	640 X 480 pixels
Computer 2	Pentium 2	128 Megabytes	56 Kbps Modem	Netscape 6.2 & Int. Explorer 6.0	800 X 600 pixels

The evaluators were briefed on the purpose of the benchmarking and what they were supposed to do. Four benchmarking forms were supplied to the evaluators before they started the benchmarking (refer to figure 3, 4, and 5). Using the forms, the evaluators then, performed the benchmarking for about 3 hours on the selected Web sites (see figure 6).

Step Six: Analyse data and determine gap. After the benchmarking, all forms were collected from the evaluators. The number of criteria existence and non-existence were calculated and summarised as presented in figure 7.

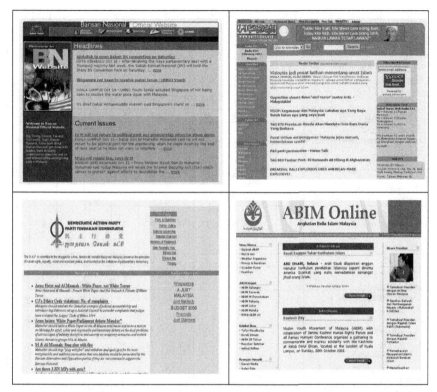

Fig. 6. Four selected political Web sites in the benchmarking: The National Front Party (http://www.bn.org.my), The Malaysian Pan Islamic Party (http://www.parti-pas.org), The Democratic Action Party (http://www.malaysia.net/dap) and The Islamic Youth Movement (http://www.abim.org.my)

Detailed analysis of the results will be discussed in section 4.

Step 7 (Redesign) and 8 (monitor progress). The results derived from steps 5 and 6 will help identify weaknesses and strengths of the Web sites being evaluated. This would then, to a certain extend, allows the designers to redesign their Web sites for better usability. Once the Web sites were redesigned, they should be monitored and re-evaluated to identify the progress made. Our study, however, finished at step six because its' main objective was only to identify the level of usability of the selected Web sites.

4   Discussion on Findings

All four political Web sites have very good design in terms of screen appearance. In general, designers of these sites utilised proper colour, text, titles, headings, and

	BN			PAS			DAP			ABIM		
	YES	NO	NA	YES	NO	NA	YES	NO	NA	YES	NO	NA
Screen Appearance (F1)												
Choice of colour (/3)	2	1		3	0	-	2	1		2	1	-
Readability (/2)	2	0		1	1	-	2	0		2	0	-
Scannability (/3)	3	0		2	1	-	3	0		3	0	-
Total (/8)	7	1		6	2	-	7	1		7	1	-
Consistency (F2)(/3)	1	2		3	0	-	3	0		2	1	-
Accessibility (F3) DisplayCompatibility (/2)	2	0		2	0	-	2	0		2	0	-
Search facility (/1)	1	0		1	0	-	1	0		0	1	-
Total (/3)	3	0		3	0	-	3	0		2	1	-
Navigation (F4) (/8)	6	2		5	3	-	7	1		3	5	-
Media use (F5) Static Media (/3)	1	1	0	0	1	1	0	2	0	1	1	0
Continuous Media (/2)	0	0	3	2	1	0	0	0	3	0	0	3
Total (/5)	1	1	3	2	2	1	0	2	3	1	1	3
Interactivity (F6) (/3)	0	3		2	1	-	2	1		2	1	-
Content (for political Web sites - F7) Scope												
Attract (/16)	2	14	-	4	12	-	5	11	-	7	9	-
Inform (/13)	5	8	-	7	6	-	7	6	-	11	2	-
Position (/6)	2	4	-	3	3	-	1	5	-	0	6	-
Deliver (/6)	0	6	-	3	3	-	2	4	-	1	5	-
Accuracy (/1)	1	0	-	0	1	-	1	0	-	1	0	-
Authority & Reliability (/3)	3	0	-	1	2	-	1	2	-	1	2	-
Uniqueness (/3)	0	3	-	1	2	-	0	3	-	0	3	-
Linkages (/4)	3	1	-	4	0	-	1	3	-	2	2	-
Text Quality (/3)	2	1	-	2	1	-	0	3	-	2	1	-
Total (/55)	18	37	-	25	30	-	18	37	-	25	30	-
Grand Total (/85)	36	46	3	46	38	1	40	42	3	42	40	3

Fig. 7. Summary of the number of existence and non-existence of Web usability criteria for each sub sections of the SCANMIC categories

skimming layout. Evaluators identified at least six criteria existence in all Web sites from a total of eight generic criteria. The selected Web sites were also benchmarked against three criteria for consistency. Web sites belonging to PAS and DAP were very consistent in all three aspects of page layout, use of text, and navigational aids. The other two Web sites (i.e. BN and ABIM), however, suffered from page layout inconsistency such as placement of content display and banners. Apart from page layout, BN's Web site also has inconsistent use of text in terms of its types, font size, and colour.

Accessibility is the third category of usability used in the evaluation. Three Web sites - BN, PAS, and DAP were highly accessible in both aspects of display compatibility and searching facility. ABIM's Web site, however, did not provide any searching function for better accessibility. DAP's Web site has the highest level of usability in navigation category. It met seven out of eight criteria used in the benchmarking. The only problem faced by this site was the non-existence of a site map. BN and PAS also scored fairly well with six and five criteria existence respectively. However, ABIM's Web site had major navigation problems including a few broken links, long page scrolling, and unavailability of site map. Consequently, this Web site only scored three out of eight.

When benchmarking the criteria for media use, it was found that most of the selected Web sites did not utilise continuous media in presenting information except PAS. All sites also failed to properly use static media where graphics, logos, and pictures were not labelled. The selected Web sites were also good in some aspects of interactivity. Although features for entertainment were not available, Web sites belonging to PAS, DAP, and ABIM provided all features for users' feedback and discussions. BN's Web site, on the other hand, had very severe interactivity problems where all three criteria were not utilised.

When benchmarking content criteria, PAS and ABIM performed better than BN and DAP by scoring 25 out of 55 criteria. Both PAS and ABIM had a wider scope of contents especially those that would attract and inform visitors. Despite performing slightly worse than the others in most aspects, BN's Web site scored perfectly for content aspect of authority and reliability. Other Web sites scored only one out of three criteria in this category. When measuring linkages, PAS Web site had all four criteria compared to DAP, which had only one. DAP also suffered severe text quality problems where all three criteria were not met. The scores in other areas were not much different between the four Web sites.

The score for the benchmarking together with the percentage usability index for all four Web sites were summarised in figure 8(a) and 8(b).

Nonetheless, the results of the benchmarking revealed some usability problems faced by all parties as described in step six. In general, the usability level of Web site belonging to PAS has the highest level of usability with 54.76 percent, followed by ABIM, DAP, and BN with 51.23 percent, 48.78 percent, 43.90 percent respectively (refer to figure 8(a)). The results also provide ideas to designers of all Web sites particularly BN and DAP on areas that need to be concentrated on in the redesign of their sites.

5   Conclusion and Recommendation

The benchmarking was conducted successfully with satisfactory results. The benchmarking processes or steps were easily followed and executed by all parties who were involved. Good feedback was obtained from the evaluators. The criteria used were easily understood and evaluated. The number of criteria for all categories was also considered adequate. Nonetheless, after the testing, several issues were noted which could improve the applicability of the framework:

- The whole process of performing the benchmarking in Step 5 was very time consuming. Two solutions are recommended to minimise this problem as follows:
    1) During Step 4 (i.e. identify who will benchmark), select more evaluators (e.g. one evaluator for each SCANMIC category);

SCANMIC Factors	BN			PAS			DAP			ABIM		
	YES	NO	NA	YES	NO	NA	YES	NO	NA	YES	NO	NA
F1 (/8)	7	1	-	6	2	-	7	1	-	7	1	-
F2 (/3)	1	2	-	3	0	-	3	0	-	2	1	-
F3 (/3)	3	0	-	3	0	-	3	0	-	2	1	-
F4 (/8)	6	2	-	5	3	-	7	1	-	3	5	-
F5 (/5)	1	1	3	2	2	1	0	2	3	1	1	3
F6 (/3)	0	3	-	2	1	-	2	1	-	2	1	-
F7 (/55)	18	37	-	25	30	-	18	37	-	25	30	-
Total (/85)	36	46	3	46	38	1	40	42	3	42	40	3

% Usability Index for BN = 36/(85- 3) X 100 = **43.90%**, % Usability Index for PAS = 46/(85-1) X 100 = **54.76%**
% Usability Index for DAP = 40/ (85-3) X 100 = **48.78%**, % Usability Index for ABIM = 42/ (85 - 3) X 100 = **51.23%**

Fig. 8(a). The benchmarking score and percentage Web usability index for the selected Web sites.

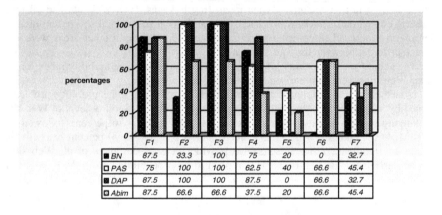

Fig. 8(b). Bar Chart of the benchmarking score (in percentages) for the selected Web sites

2) During Step 5 (i.e. perform the benchmark), instead of evaluating all Web pages, allow evaluators to test parts of the Web site using a proper sampling technique.
•   The outcome of the testing also revealed that the benchmarking evaluation method needs to be expanded. In particular, Step 7 (i.e. redesign) required enhancement. In addition to relying on the results of Step 6 (i.e. analyse data and determine gap) to redesign the Web site for better usability, other evaluation methods (e.g. expert reviews) could also be used particularly those that deal with the assessment of the subjective criteria.
•   The evaluators suggested that the assessment should be based on both the existence of a particular criterion and its functionality (i.e. whether it works or not). For example, if a Web site provides a menu for searching, it does not mean

that it can help users find information easily. The search function might not work properly or return an error page. Based on this suggestion, Step 5 of the framework should be expanded to include instructions to evaluators not only to look for criteria existence but also identify whether they are indeed working.

Results of the benchmarking indicated that the overall level of usability for the selected Web sites was low which ranged between 40 to 55 percent. Although these Web sites performed well in areas of screen appearance, consistency, accessibility, and navigation, they suffered some usability problems in some aspects of media use, interactivity, and most importantly content.

References

1. Codling, S.: Best Practice Benchmarking, The Management Guide to Successful Implementation. Industrial Newsletters Ltd., Great Britain (1992).
2. Bramham, J.: Benchmarking for People Managers. Cromwell Press, Great Britain (1997).
3. APQC: The Benchmarking Guide. Productivity Press, Portland, OR (1993).
4. Chang, R.Y., Kelly, P.K.: Improving Through Benchmarking. Kogan Page Ltd, London (1995).
5. Anderson, B., Pettersen, P.G.: The Benchmarking Book, Step-by-step Instruction. Chapman and Hall, Great Britain (1996).
6. Bendell, T., Boulter, L., Kelly, J.: Benchmarking for Competitive Advantage. Pitman Publishing, Great Britain (1993).
7. Shahizan Hassan: A Framework For Evaluating The Usability of Political Web Sites: Towards Improving Cyberdemocracy, PhD Thesis. University of Newcastle Upon Tyne, United Kingdom (2002).
8. Institute of Electrical Engineers: IEEE Standard Computer Dictionary. New York (1990).
9. Marcus, A.: Improving the User Interface (1999). Available: http://www.Webward.com/interviews/marcus.html [access: 2000, Dec. 16].

The Implementation of the Electronic Game Terminology Dictionary

Tae Soo Yun, Won Dal Jang, Jae Sang Lee, and Choong Jae Im

Division of Internet Engineering, Dongseo University, San69-1,
Churye-Dong, Sasang-Gu, Busan, South Korea
{tsyun,xdmz2000,jslee,dooly}@dongseo.ac.kr

Abstract. This paper presents the methodology to make the electronic dictionary and the design and implementation of the electronic game terminology dictionary prototype system. Before constructing database on game industry, the electronic game terminology dictionary is necessary. To construct the corpus, we collect the game-related documents such as game marketing reports, game technology reports, game introduction documents, etc. To make the effective electronic dictionary, the standardization of the corpus data is needed. Thus, we construct the corpus using the TEI (Text Encoding Initiative) of the SGML (Standard Generalized Markup Language). We extract the terminology from the corpus based on the frequency of term. And then we find the semantic relationships of the game terminology by the analysis and classification of the game terminology, which is called thesaurus. Based on the thesaurus, we can implement the semantic-based game terminology electronic dictionary.

1   Introduction

Recently, the world has been changed to knowledge-based society, which is dominated by the creation of knowledge information and the practical use. In this situation, the construction of digital library for a specialized field such as game industry is essential[1,2].

In the last several years, game industry has had a distinguishable growth in Korea. However, the field of systematic digital library such as technology based on game, trend on game industry, and planning of game contents, etc. still lags behind America and Japan[3]. Therefore, it is important that domestic petty game business secure high quality of information to cope with the advanced country.

To accelerate the growth of the game industry, government and some private companies have interest in constructing the game industry database. Prior to constructing database on game industry, the game terminology electronic dictionary is needed.

The general definition of electronic dictionary is online database of related language information on words. Through the electronic dictionary, we can find language information about words more fast, conveniently and cheaply. In recent years, language information processing technology becomes more and more important technology and the necessity of terminology dictionary is increasing. Many

T.M.T. Sembok et al. (Eds.): ICADL 2003, LNCS 2911, pp. 480–488, 2003.

countries invest so many manpower and capital in developing database of language information and electronic dictionary.

The major projects related to electronic dictionary in foreign countries are as follows. The *WordNet* is an online lexical reference system whose design is inspired by current psycholinguistic theories of human lexical memory. English nouns, verbs, adjectives and adverbs are organized into synonym sets, each representing one underlying lexical concept[4].

The *EDR Electronic Dictionary* is the result of a nine-year project (from fiscal 1986 to fiscal 1994) aimed at establishing an infrastructure for knowledge information processing. The project was funded by the Japan Key Technology Center and eight computer manufacturers[5].

EuroWordNet is a multilingual database with wordnets for several European languages (Dutch, Italian, Spanish, German, French, Czech and Estonian). The wordnets are structured in the same way as the American wordnet for English (*Princeton WordNet*) in terms of synsets (sets of synonymous words) with basic semantic relations between them[6].

On the other side, within the country, Yonsei editorial association has published the research papers for the theory on dictionary press and practical use, electronic dictionary, etc. And 21th century Sejong Electronic Dictionary Project which construct the electronic dictionary essential to korean information processing is going on[7].

In fact, however, there has been no case constructing the information in relation to game industry until now. So, in this paper, we present the methodology to make the electronic dictionary and the design and implementation of the electronic game terminology dictionary prototype system.

2   Introduction of the Electronic Terminology Dictionary

The research and development in reference to lexical information computerization focus on reusability and generality. Therefore, this research trends have two aspects, reuse and general utilization. Reuse of existing data means that we can integrate and reuse various information including existing printed dictionary to apply the natural language processing.

Generally, the information provided by electronic dictionary can be observed in the aspects of lexical item and user support system. The information provided by lexical item of dictionary is headword (lexical item), morpheme, grammar information, and example, etc. Also co-occurrence information and postposition, conjunctive relation of suffix, synonym and antonym, bilingual information for machine translation, corpus for extracting statistical information, etc. are provided to support natural language processing application system as standard dictionary.

One of the important points to implement standard electronic dictionary is that it must provide the user support system that the user can access easily. The user support system does not mean just user interface. It includes powerful supporting system. The user support system designed effectively will increase the usefulness of the electronic dictionary by providing more convenience. By reducing the time and efforts of the natural language processing application program development, we can get the economical gain.

3   Design of the Electronic Game Terminology Dictionary

The development process of the electronic game terminology dictionary is like Fig. 1. We implement the prototype system of the electronic game terminology dictionary using this methodology.

To construct the corpus, we collect the game-related documents such as game marketing reports, game technology reports, game introduction documents, etc. To make the useful electronic dictionary, the standardization of the corpus data is needed. Thus, we construct the corpus using the TEI (Text Encoding Initiative) of the SGML (Standard Generalized Markup Language).

We extract the terminology from the corpus based on the frequency of a term. And then we find the semantic relationships of the game terminology by the analysis and classification of the game terminology. Usually, the semantic relationship is represented by semantic network. We call that thesaurus. Using the thesaurus, we can implement the semantic-based electronic game terminology dictionary.

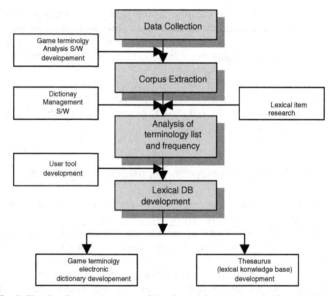

Fig. 1. The development process of the electronic game terminology dictionary

3.1   Corpus Extraction

The corpus translates into a bundle of words or a collection of words. The definition depends on each person, however, it is used as the following meaning : large-scale language database or storing voice language of human in large-scale computer and using it in the research of language when needed. The corpus to be used a special field should be the representative of corresponding special fields. The extraction method and sizing can be the most important basic works because most language information can be acquired by analyzing the corpus[2].

The corpus extraction process consists of two phases. In the first phase, we make the raw corpus based on game-related database and related-data collection. And then collected data are processed and standardized in the second phases.

We construct 50,000 corpuses from the 5 game-related documents and the data searched through the internet using the SGML. We extract the vocabulary using the terminology extractor from the 50,000 corpuses. Table 1 shows the number of words of the corpus based on previously described guideline.

In the second phase, we research and develop the specification of standardization for the corpus. The corpus collected in the first phase is suffered from the duplication and low quality because it is not formalized. To overcome this problem, we must make the specification of standardization for the corpus. We use the TEI (Text Encoding Initiative) guideline of the SGML (Standard Generalized Markup Language). Table 2 shows the words count of the corpus based on previously described guideline.

Table 1. The number of words of the extracted corpus

1999 Korea Game Industry Trends Research, KESIA, 1999 (10,000 words)
2001 Korea Game White Paper, KGPSC, 2001 (10,000 words)
From Internet information retrieval (12,5000 words)
From PC communication information retrieval (5,000 words)
From Newspaper and magazine related with game (75,000 words)

Table 2. The TEI representation of the game terminology (Example)

\<info\>
\<title\>game – A study on Promoting Online computer game industry **\</title\>**
\<author\>Kim Hyunbin, Kim Kiho, etc**\</author\>**
\<edition\>First edition**\</edition\>**
\<publish\>ETRI**\</publish\>**
\<year\>2000**\</year\>**
\</info\>
\<item\>Chap 2. Online Game Market**\</item\>**
\<item\>Section 1. Wired Online Game**\</item\>**
\<item\>1 Oversee Online Game Market**\</item\>**
\<p\>\<s\>Online game will be core .....**\</s\>**
\<s\>Overall game S/W market size is ....**\</s\>**

3.2 Thesaurus

The thesaurus is the database representing the relationship among the terminology in the natural language processing fields[8,9]. The relationship among terms used in the thesaurus can be classified by two category. The first case is macro level. It deals with equivalence relationship, hierarchical relationship, and associative relationship that are semantic relation among terms. The second case is micro level. It deals with a term having hierarchical relationship with a set of terms included in equivalence relationship, and inter-relationship of the term category included in associative relationship and relationship with everything. Thesaurus can be used to select the index word and search word used as keyword during the search using this relationship.

As a result of going over thousands of game terms listed to headword candidate for this research, the case occurred antonymous relation among words was rare or trivial. However, it seems that the whole-part relation is useful and hierarchical relation is essential. In terms of this point, we constructed the thesaurus for game terminology with priority given to hierarchical relation and whole-part relation.

We constructed the thesaurus based on the semantic network. Figure 2. shows the example of the semantic network. Each term is connected to other terms and relationship thorough the graph. Based on the semantic network, we can find the relationship among terminology easily.

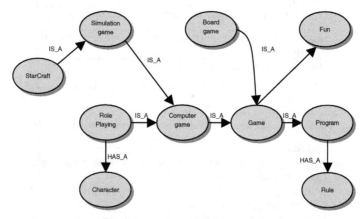

Fig. 2. Semantic network (Example)

Thesaurus consists of descriptor i.e. the priority word which is used to represent specific concept and non-descriptor which is non-priority word. It is represented by the equivalence relation and reciprocal relation between the descriptor and non-descriptor. For example, the term 'USE' and 'UF' are used to describe the synonym of descriptor and non-descriptor[6]. The reciprocal relationship is represented by hierarchical relation and association. The 'BT(Broad Term)' which is upper conceptual word represents more extended meaning, and the 'NT(Narrow Term)' that is, lower conceptual word represents detailed meaning. The 'RT(Related Term)' is used to represent the association of terms. Fig. 3. shows the example of thesaurus represented by using this relation of terms.

```
Arcade game
        USE Arcade
Arcade
        BT  Game
            Computer game
        NT  Action game
            Adventure game
            Shooting game
            Board game
        RT  Program
```

Fig. 3. Thesaurus (Example)

3.3 The Electronic Game Terminology Dictionary

After thesaurus construction of some special fields, what we have to do first is to select headword to make electronic terminology dictionary based on the semantic hierarchy. The headword is the entry of dictionary and keyword. Generally, we extract headword from corpus based on the frequency of the word.

The terminology database extracted from the corpus was integrated with database management system such as MS-SQL or Oracle to provide the information retrieval and management. It is better to manage with web-based structured document style.

SGML (Standard General Markup Language) is used as means to present and manage the language information. SGML is meta-language, which can define the syntax of markup language. SGML includes complex markup description rules to present various document. HTML (Hyper Text Markup Language) is good example utilizing the simple function of SGML.

Because the structure representation of each document and markup tag is different, TEI (Text Encoding Initiative) is announced to standardize this. Exactly, TEI has many description needed to encode existing printed dictionary or corpus.

SDML (Standard Dictionary Markup Language) is designed to represent various electronic dictionary using the some parts of the SGML. By markup dictionary and corpus using the SDML, we can accumulate various lexical information, extract, modify and edit information using this.

We design the electronic dictionary prototype system having about 1,000 game terminology extracted from 50,000 corpus. Our electronic game terminology dictionary satisfies the TDMS (Text and Dictionary Management System) specification and constructed based on TEI guideline of the SGML. Table 3 shows the example of game terminology information based on TEI guideline.

Table 3. Terminology information based on TEI guideline (Example)

```
<termEntry id = MS1>
<descrip type = 'subjectLevel1'>Genre</descrip>

<ntig lang = 'kor'>
<termGrp><term> Role Playing Game </term>
<termNote    type    =    'partOfSpeech'>    </termNote>
</termGrp>
<descripGrp><descrip type = 'definition'>
A genre of computer game and a kinds of game that player
playes the role of some characters......
</descrip>
<ptr type = 'sourceIdentifier' target = '...'></descripGrp>
<adminGrp><admin type = 'responsibility'></admin>
</adminGrp>
</ntig>
<ntig lang = 'en'>
<termGrp><term> role playing game </term>
<termNote    type    =    'partOfSpeech'></termNote>
</termGrp>
<descripGrp><descrip type = 'definition'>
</descrip>
<ptr type = 'sourceIdentifier' target = '...'></descripGrp>
......
```

4   The Implementation of the Electronic Game Terminology Dictionary

Using the thesaurus, we implement the prototype system of the electronic game terminology dictionary that is possible to retrieve the game information using semantic relationship. Fig. 4. shows the user interface of our electronic dictionary.

This electronic game terminology dictionary is implemented to provide semantic-based search. The user can easily find the meaning of game terminology and related terminology. We used ASP 3.0 and JavaScript as language, and MS-SQL 2000 as database to implement the electronic game terminology dictionary.

This electronic game terminology dictionary provides following functions:
- **Keyword search function:** If the user inputs the keyword, he can get the meaning of corresponding keyword.
- **Category search function:** To provide category-based search function, we classify the terminology as three aspects. Thus the user can search game terminology using category.
- **Indexing:** This dictionary also provides traditional dictionary function. The terminology is ordered by ascending in Korean and English.
- **Most frequently used terminology:** The user can see the most frequently used terminology.
- **Recently added terminology:** The user can see the recently added terminology.

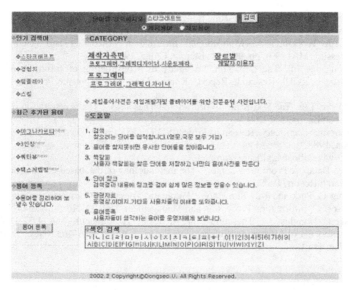

Fig. 4. The user interface of the electronic game terminology dictionary

- **Related terminology:** The user can find easily related terminology of the inputting terminology.
- **History list function:** History list stores the list of previously searched terminology.

5   Conclusion

In this paper, we present the methodology to make electronic dictionary and the design and implementation of the electronic game terminology dictionary.

We construct 50,000 corpora from the 5 game-related documents and the thesaurus based on the semantic network. We design the electronic dictionary prototype system having about 1,000 game terminology extracted from 50,000 corpora. This electronic game terminology dictionary provides keyword search function, category search function, indexing, most frequently used terminology, recently added terminology, related terminology and history list function.

Using the results of this research, we can develop the game information database containing the data of the game industry.

References

[1]   Juntae Yoon, Key-Sun Choi, Mansuk Song, "Corpus-Based Approach for Nominal Compound Analysis for Korean Based on Linguistic and Statistical Information", Natural Language Engineering vol. 7, No. 3, 251–270, 2001.

[2]   Young-Soog Chae, Young-Bin Song, Yong-Suk Choi, Key-Sun Choi, "Building Knowledge Base from KIBS Corpus and MRD:A Case Study of Verbs", Proceedings of the 1th Workshop on Multi-lingual Information Processing and Asian Language Processing(MAL`99), pp. 96–101, Beijing, China, 1999,11.

[3]   Choong Jae Im, Tae Soo Yun, "A Study on Constructing of Information on Game Industry", KGDI Research Report, Korea Game Development&Promotion Institute, 2002.

[4]   Jae Yoon Lee, Tae Soo Kim, "WordNet and Thesaurus", The investigation of Language information, pp. 232–269.

[5]   Electronic Dictionary Research Project(EDR), Electronic Dictionary Research Inst., Japan, 1988.

[6]   http://www.illc.uva.nl/EuroWordNet/

[7]   Korea Database Promotion Center, "The methodology of databased construction", KDPC Research Report, 1998.

[8]   Young C. Park and Key-Sun Choi, "Automatic Thesaurus Construction Using Bayesian Networks", Information Processing and Management, Vol. 32, No. 5, pp. 543–553, 1996.

[9]   Foskett, Douglas J, "Thesaurus" in A. Kent, H. Lancour, and J.E. Daily (eds.) Encyclopedia of Library and Information Science, 30: pp. 416–463. (New York: Marcel Dekker, Inc.)

Inculcating ICT Skills through a Collaborative Digital Library Initiative for Educational Use

A.N. Zainab, Abdullah Abrizah, and Nor Badrul Anuar

Faculty of Computer Science & Information Technology, University of Malaya
{zainab,abrizah,badrul}@um.edu.my

1 The Context

Digital libraries revolutionise the traditional pedagogy of providing learning resources and the way resources can be accessed. It helps students to practice self-accessed and self-directed reference learning at their own pace. It changes the conventional process of seeking information and the speed and spread of information obtained. Masullo and Mack (1996) succinctly summarize the three roles digital libraries can play in education; (a) as a resource for teaching; (b) as an environment for learning; and (c) as an authoring space. The educational value of digital libraries is in the authentic activities that they can allow students to engage in. The supportive interfaces, resource selection, organisation of documents are designed to provide learners with enough context and knowledge to enable them to use digital libraries as learning resources. Hedman (1999) pointed out that in the electronic world situation, anyone could be both an author and a publisher. This situation perpetuates the creation of communal resources in cooperation. The existing entities allow for the dynamic generation of content. This enables the creation of digital libraries from grass root levels. In the educational context, this type of collaborative venture brings about the achievement of the following objectives: a) creation of content collaboratively; b) enhance IT literacy through the very act of collaboration; and c) creative presentation of contents using multimedia elements (Stahl, 2000). These objectives are embedded the proposed digital library portal for historical resources that can be collaboratively used by educational and public institutions to develop digital resources. A proto-type system was developed and a biographical portal of selected Malaysian personalities and historical buildings is chosen as the domain for the test bed.

In Malaysia, the ICT infrastructure and supportive governance are already in place and Malaysians are appreciative of utilizing ICT. Schools connectivity and ICT penetration is growing. Surveys of various population pockets have indicated high computer ownership (Narisma and Zamree, 2002) but low Internet use. However, among the younger population, Internet use is higher. Although schools are provided with computers and ICT facilities, the opportunity for students to access the Internet is limited. To expedite ICT literacy among students and teachers, Internet use should be embedded in the current curriculum and the collaborative digital library initiative proposed this through the online publication and management of historical projects for lower secondary school students. The students are required to research on historical buildings, local administrator or historical figures. The aim of the digital library initiative is to expand access across high quality Malaysia's local history

T.M.T. Sembok et al. (Eds.): ICADL 2003, LNCS 2911, pp. 489–492, 2003.

resources for the public and the K-12 communities; and to strengthen collaboration on creating and sharing of local historical resources between partner members.

2 The Proposed Framework

The digital library project conceptualizes the following objectives: a) to develop a repository platform to preserve local history resources, and in this context, the test-bed is in the domain of Malaysian biographical information; b) to make the resources accessible through the Internet; c) to develop an effective and efficient search system that retrieve information from multi-format resources; d) to develop template-based systems that makes indexing multimedia contents easy for resource managers and student contributors; e) to develop a relevancy ranking algorithm that could be utilized in query searches; f) to create a user friendly and consistent interface; g) to ensure authorized access to the management functions of the system; and h) to assess participants basic IT literacy. In the implementation of this project, the use of the digital libraries would be an integral part of classroom activities. Students should be enabled to publish their own documents in the digital library and share them with others. In this case, students should be allowed to create and submit their project report in the electronic format. Reports that are submitted in the form of scrapbooks could be digitized and published in the "space" allocated for participating schools. Teachers would be given the opportunity to utilize their ICT knowledge by validating the quality of submissions to maintain content quality of the digital library, grading projects online, adding links to other useful resources found in the Internet. This would "push" teachers and students to be active players in building the digital library and indirectly inculcates ICT literacy among the education community.

In order to ascertain the basic features needed for the system, a pilot survey was carried out as the preliminary fact finding process. Interviewing stakeholders of the system is considered the most effective method of ascertaining the system's requirements. In the pilot phase, interviews are conducted with history teachers to gain information about the history project undertaken by all secondary three students, the need, requirements, functions, rules as well as expectations for the digital library. Questionnaire were distributed to 74 secondary three students. The schools chosen provide Internet connections and are situated near cyber cafes, putting the stakeholders in an ICT rich environment. The teachers interviewed saw the potential of a digital library in providing information to students for their project and are willing to participate in the development of the prototype. The pilot survey involves knowing the user community, understanding how they interact with systems, their changing needs, and students' information seeking behaviour when researching for their historical projects. Students in the sample are versatile in their downloading skills of resources from the web. Students also indicate the types of problems they face when searching for information. Over 90% of students feel that there is a need for digital libraries of local history information and this would definitely benefit them. The students also volunteer suggestions as to the functions they would like to see in a digital library. This feedback helps to ascertain the main features required for the proposed historical portal.

3 The System Functions

The Faculty of Computer Science and Information Technology's role is in studying the behaviour of players in the initiative and the development of the prototype. The ownership of the digital library would eventually be transferred to the main stakeholder that is, the Ministry of Education. The schools, teachers, students, the public, universities, and depositories are the expected stakeholders (users and content providers), with the helm of the system being hosted by the Ministry of Education. The portal has tried to incorporate features expressed by the "keystone principles" proposed by the US College and Research Libraries Group (An action plan...2001). The prototype portal incorporates the five main basic features proposed by IBM DB2 Digital Library (1998). The uploading, indexing, search and retrieval modules provides for creation, capturing and sharing data from distributed sites among various user groups. This is the strength of the system as it encourages active participation, which would in the long run produce the desired outcome in terms of ICT literate teachers and students. The system supports multi-format digital resources and therefore exposes the learning community to the unique features of digital libraries. It also provides search facilities by simple keyword searches, contextual searches and using Boolean operators. An extended feature is the provision of bilingual search and retrieval screens. Users could also determine the number of records to be displayed in search result page and browse the contents of the library by specific category of objects. Thumbnail images are displayed for browsing before users can zoom for specific detail of any objects. The Indexing module has incorporated a basic thesaurus of synonymous terms to facilitate indexing the resources. This list is not currently exhaustive and requires updating from time to time. In terms of access rights management, the portal allows uploads from any members but each uploads require validation from assigned resource managers before it is searchable through the Internet. Besides these basic features, the biographical portal provides additional facilities such as general information, help and edutainment modules as well as the reporting module.

During this preliminary stage, the prototype is pilot tested at a secondary school. The teachers interviewed give their opinion about the functionality of the system, its contents, its usefulness as a resource for student's project and its effectiveness in motivating students to learn history. One drawback from the evaluation exercise is the lack of skills shown by the teachers in handling the computer and it is foreseen that human factors could be the main problems in the successful implementation of the collaborative digital library. In general, the students are more adept in handling the system and rate the design features as either excellent or good. They also generally agree that such a system would be useful resource for the completion of their history project.

4 Conclusion

The biographical portal is the domain used as the test-bed towards the implementation of a fully integrated collaborative digital library of historical resources. The interviews and the pilot surveys provide invaluable information about information gathering behaviour and the community's perception of digital libraries. To successfully implement the collaboration between partners, a number of problems need to be ironed out. The teachers involved need to be given training in publishing digital resources and the skill of indexing and validating the resources to ensure that the contents of the library can be efficiently retrieved. Users must accept the reality that the richness in content of the digital library is dependent upon their willingness and active participation as partners. The outcome of this involvement is imparting ICT awareness and skills to the educational community. Another important skill needed is the ability to reference or cite resources used correctly. Subsequent phase of this digital library project will further investigate the requirements of users by applying the survey instruments to a wider sample groups; expanding contents; incorporating a digital library history lessons, teaching tools, and examination questions bank on history for lower secondary schools. Future study is also needed to gauge students and teachers level of ICT literacy as a result of their involvement in the development of the digital library.

References

1. An action plan for value-based librarianship: the Keystone Principles. College & Research Libraries News. (2001). Available at: http:/www.ala.org/acrl/keystone.html.
2. Hedman, Anders. 1999. Creating digital libraries together – collaboration, multimodality and plurality. Fourth *SIGCSE/SIDCUE on Innovation and Technology in Computer Science Education,* Cracow, Poland: 147–150.
3. IBM DB2 Digital Library Archtecture. (1998). Available at:
   http://www~4.ibm.com/software/is/dig-lib/v2factsheet/page3.htm
4. Masullo, Miriam J. and Robert Mack. 1996. Roles for digital libraries in K-12 education. *D-Lib Magazine*, September.
5. Narima Ismail and Zanree Yaacob. 2002. Masyarakat Melayu dan TMK: Persediaan untuk K-Masyarakat. [Malay society and the ICT: Readiness for the K-society], Seminar Kebangsaan Bahasa dan Pemikiran Melayu: Kecemerlangan Melayu dalam Era Teknologi Maklumat dan Komunikasi, 18–19 Jun 2002, APM, Universiti Malaya
6. Stahl, Gerry. 2000. A model of collaborative knowledge building. Proceedings of the Computer-Supported Collaborative Learning (CSCL). Also available at:
   http://orgwis.gmd. de/~gerry/publications/conferences/2000/icls/index.html

PAPER for an Educational Digital Library

Dion Hoe-Lian Goh[1], Yin-Leng Theng[1], Ming Yin[2], and Ee-Peng Lim[2]

[1] Division of Information Studies, School of Communication & Information
Nanyang Technological University, Singapore 637718
[2] Center for Advanced Information Systems, School of Computer Engineering
Nanyang Technological University, Singapore 639798
{ashlgoh,tyltheng,asmyin,aseplim}@ntu.edu.sg

Abstract. GeogDL is a digital library of geography examination resources designed to assist students in revising for a national geography examination in Singapore. As part of an iterative design process, we carried out participatory design and brainstorming with student and teacher design partners. The first study involved prospective student design partners. In response to the first study, we describe in this paper an implementation of **PAPER** – **P**ersonalised **A**daptive **P**athways for **E**xam **R**esources – a new bundle of personalized, interactive services containing a mock exam and a personal coach. The "mock exam" provides a simulation of the actual geography examination while the "personal coach" provides recommendations of exam questions tailored to suit individual ability levels. This paper concludes with findings from a second study involving teacher design partners to further refine GeogDL.

1 Introduction

GeogDL [2] is a digital library of geography examination resources designed to help students prepare for a national secondary-level geography examination in Singapore. GeogDL's collection consists of past-year examination questions, solutions, related supplementary content and user annotations.

With the initial phase of development completed, a first study was conducted to engage a group of intergenerational partners involving designers, secondary school students and usability-trained evaluators for the purposes of reinforcing and refining the initial design of GeogDL [11]. The study revealed that, among other issues, student participants' expectations for GeogDL went beyond the initial design goals for the system, which were to provide an environment for users to access past-year examination questions, view their solutions, explore related content and discuss with other users.

In response to the first study, we describe in this paper an implementation of **PAPER** – **P**ersonalized **A**daptive **P**athways for **E**xamination **R**esources – an assessment and coaching module, consisting of two major components:

- **Mock Exam.** Provides a timed and scored test that reflects the structure and content of the actual geography examination.
- **Personal Coach.** Provides recommendations of examination questions to attempt based on performance in previous mock exam sessions.

T.M.T. Sembok et al. (Eds.): ICADL 2003, LNCS 2911, pp. 493–504, 2003.

PAPER is built using the generic services of GeogDL and draws content from GeogDL's repository of examination questions and solutions.

The remainder of this paper discusses the design and implementation of PAPER. Section 2 describes PAPER's underlying educational design rationale and contrasts PAPER with related work in general computer adaptive testing systems and geography-oriented educational digital libraries. Section 3 provides an in-depth treatment of PAPER including its architecture and usage. A second study of PAPER involving teacher design partners is described in Section 4.

2 Related Work

In contrast to traditional computer adaptive testing systems attempting to replicate the expertise of a human teacher who can diagnose and respond to the needs of individual students [10], PAPER is designed based on analyses of students' individual and group performances. The underlying educational design rationale in PAPER is inspired by "successful learning experiences" theory postulated by Ellington, Percival and Race [6] in the provision of instant feedback and guidance to students' learning paths.

PAPER's main objective is, therefore, to supplement classroom teaching with a wider and appropriate range of assessment techniques to support individualised student learning and to record achievement, hence achieving one of the main goals of teaching in that performance of students undergoing a given educational system should improve in some desired way [8].

GeogDL's PAPER is also different from more recently developed geography-oriented educational digital libraries (e.g. ADEPT [3] and DLESE [4]) in that students can freely explore geography concepts but also utilize services that offer a more structured yet personalized approach to studying geography. In addition, while the mock exam shares similarities with existing online testing tools such as QUIZIT [12] and PILOT [1] in that all provide a Web-based environment for testing and grading, our approach differs in that the mock exam is integrated with GeogDL's other tools thus offering various interrelated avenues for learning and exam preparation. For example, because the mock exam operates in conjunction with the personal coach, students are not only able to ascertain their areas of weaknesses through their scores but also receive recommendations of topic areas and hence, exam questions, that should be explored further.

3 PAPER's Usage and Architecture

PAPER consists of two major components, the mock exam and personal coach. This section describes these components and their implementation, focusing on the adaptive aspects of the system to create a personalized learning experience for users.

3.1 Mock Exam

Figure 1 shows PAPER's mock exam interface for multiple-choice questions. It has a deliberate minimalist design to focus users on the content. Upon reading a question, users select an answer and proceed to the next question. Users may also revisit previous questions to modify their answers. PAPER monitors the time taken for each question to give an indication of how difficult a particular question is to a student.

Upon completion of the mock exam, PAPER grades it and displays a performance report (Figure 2). The report contains a summary of the results and includes the total score and total time taken. Performance data for individual questions are also provided. This includes the correct answer, time taken, question topic and difficulty level. Students and teachers may use the performance report to gauge mastery of geography concepts as well as areas for further improvement. Users may also review the solutions and explore supplementary resources from the report interface.

Navigation controls

Exam question

User selects answer here

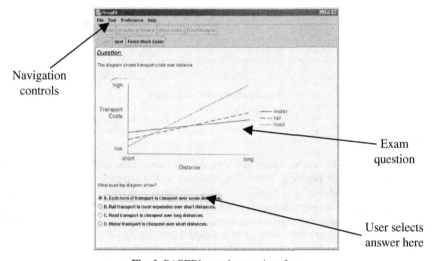

Fig. 1. PAPER's mock exam interface

The structure and content of a mock exam is defined by a **mock exam paper** – a virtual collection of examination questions. The paper is virtual because questions are not predefined. Instead, an author (e.g. a teacher) indicates the characteristics of questions that should appear. These include question type (e.g. multiple choice, essay), topic area (e.g. "natural vegetation"), number of questions and level of difficulty (as indicated by the questions' metadata). When a mock exam session is initiated, PAPER selects questions using the characteristics set in the paper. Students are thus presented with a unique exam each time a session is run, allowing them to attempt a wider variety of questions. Authors may also create static mock exam papers so that each session results in the same set of questions. This feature would be useful in situations when a teacher wants to measure the performance of his/her class, when a teacher wants students to attempt certain questions that are deemed important in the geography examination, or to emphasize a certain topic learnt in class.

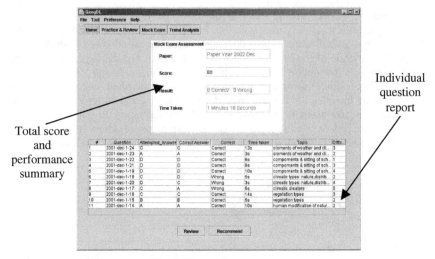

Total score
and
performance
summary

Individual
question
report

Fig. 2. The mock exam report

3.2   Personal Coach

Upon completion of one or more mock exams, students may wish to attempt more
questions for further practice. With print, teachers would typically help their students
identify such questions – a time-consuming, manual task. PAPER assists in this
process through the personal coach which analyzes a student's performance in
previous mock exams and then recommends questions pitched at appropriate levels of
difficulty. Questions are thus tailored to individual abilities.

The personal coach may be invoked from the mock exam report (Figure 2). The
interface consists of two major sections as shown in Figure 3. The panel on the left
provides a list of recommended questions organized into topics as described in the
geography syllabus [7]. The panel on the right presents a question selected by the user
and also allows users to attempt it. The solution may also be viewed and users may
explore any related supplementary resources found there. Currently, these resources
are Web sites identified by experienced geography teachers.

Questions are recommended based on a user's past performance in the mock
exams. Specifically, each question in a mock exam is associated with one or more
topics in the geography syllabus. The personal coach calculates a competency level
for each topic based on a user's performance for that topic in previous mock exam
sessions. This is a weighted score involving the most recent mock exam and a
cumulative score from previous sessions (see Section 4.2 for details of calculation).

Using this approach, the personal coach adapts to the student as he or she interacts
with PAPER. For example, if a student consistently answers questions correctly in a
topic such as "Agricultural systems", the personal coach will recommend questions
with a higher level of difficulty. Conversely, if a student performs poorly in a topic
such as "Elements of weather and climate", easier questions will be recommended.
Recommendations may change each time a mock exam is completed, and is
dependent on the student's topic scores. Difficulty levels range from 1 (easiest) to 5

(most difficult) and are stored in each question's metadata. These are once again assigned by experienced geography teachers to ensure validity.

Recommended
questions classified
by topics

Question selected from
the recommended list

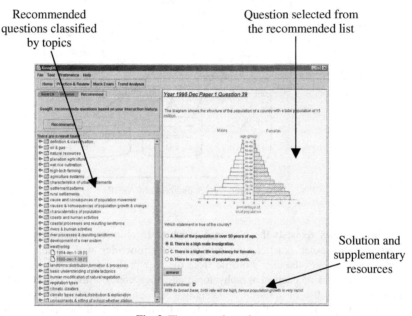

Solution and
supplementary
resources

Fig. 3. The personal coach

We term this approach **personalized adaptive pathways**, to refer to the ability of the personal coach to adapt to the changing needs of students by recommending learning paths in the form of examination questions, solutions and supplementary resources. It is hoped that this approach will better cater to the learning needs of individuals by providing challenging questions for familiar areas in geography while asking easier, confidence boosting questions for more problematic areas.

4   Implementation

4.1   Architecture

The major components of PAPER are shown in Figure 4. The collection of the digital library is maintained in the **question database** and contains examination resources (questions, solutions, supplementary content and mock exam papers) as well as their associated metadata.

The **mock exam module** extracts questions from the question database given a mock exam paper, and displays them to the user. Upon completion of a paper, the module grades it, generates the performance report and updates the user's profile through the **profile manager**. All profiles are maintained in the **user profile database** which keeps track of users' competencies in the various geography topics.

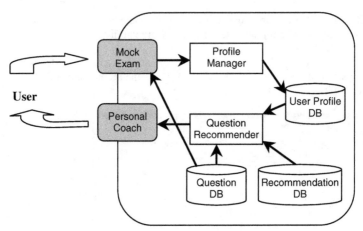

Fig. 4. Architecture diagram of PAPER.

When the user requests the **personal coach** to recommend suitable examinations questions for further practice, the **question recommender** will be invoked. This component retrieves the user's profile from the user profile database, determines the competency level of each geography topic and then consults the **recommendation database** for a list of questions matching each competency level. The question recommender then extracts the questions from the question database and delivers it to the personal coach for formatting and presentation to the user.

4.2   Profile Manager

PAPER's profile manager is responsible for updating a user's profile or topic competency scores. Each profile is a vector of values, with each value representing the competency score of a user in a particular geography topic. The profile is updated each time a user completes a mock exam.

The formula used for computing each new topic competency score ($\mathbf{h}_{new}$) is shown below. Each new topic competency score in the profile is a weighted sum of the existing topic competency score ($\mathbf{h}$, based on past mock exams) and the topic performance score ($\mathbf{p}$) in the current mock exam. Topic competency scores range from 0 (lowest competency score) to 1 (highest competency score). The rationale behind the formula is that the topic performance score in the current mock exam ($\mathbf{p}$) reflects the user's mastery of geography concepts more accurately than his/her previous performance ($\mathbf{h}$). Consequently, a higher weight ($\mathbf{W}$) should be assigned to the current mock exam topic performance score.

$$
h_{new} = \begin{cases} p \times \dfrac{n_m \times W}{n_m \times W + n_t} + h \times \dfrac{n_t}{n_m \times W + n_t} & \text{if} \quad \dfrac{n_m \times W}{n_t} >= T \\[2em] p \times T + h \times (1 - T) & \text{otherwise} \end{cases} \tag{1}
$$

where

h_{new}: the new topic competency score
h: the existing topic competency score prior to the current mock exam
p: the topic performance score for the current mock exam
n_m: the number of questions in the current mock exam on a particular topic
n_t: the number of questions previously attempted on a particular topic
W: the weight assigned to the current mock exam
T: the minimum weight assigned to the current mock exam

The value **p** is the percentage of the number of questions answered correctly over the total number of questions attempted on a particular topic in the current mock exam. **W** is a weight that determines the contribution of the current topic performance score in the calculation of a new competency score. To favor current topic performance over past performance, **W** is assigned a number greater than 1. **T** is the threshold of the minimum contribution of the current mock exam topic performance score **p**. In cases where n_t is very large, the contribution of the current performance is very small and cannot affect the calculation of a new competency score that adequately reflects the user's mastery of the topic. Therefore, there is a need to maintain a minimum contribution factor and this is denoted by **T**. Note that the parameters **W** and **T** are user defined.

4.3   Question Recommender

The personal coach's question recommender is responsible for recommending suitable questions based on the user's competency profile vector calculated by the profile manager. For example, if a student does not perform poorly in the topic "Elements of weather and climate" (e.g. h=0.4), the system will recommend questions with a lower level of difficulty. In contrast, if another student performs very well in that topic (e.g. h=0.85), the system will suggest more advanced questions.

In the current implementation, we make use of the recommendation database to maintain the set of questions that matches each level of difficulty. Conceptually, the database is a table of values whose columns represent levels of difficulty and rows represent topics. A cell found at the intersection of a row and column contains questions belonging to a particular topic and having a certain difficulty level. To locate a cell, the question recommender first maps a user's topic competency score to a difficulty level. This is done by approximating the competency score to a letter grade as defined by the requirements of the national examination, and using that grade as a proxy to the level of question difficulty. For example, exam scores of 75 or more are graded as "A" in the national examination, and competency scores within this range are thus assigned the most difficult questions (difficulty level 5). Conversely, competency scores of less than 50 ("F") are assigned the easiest questions (level 1).

5 Participatory Design

PAPER was developed using the participatory design (PD) methodology [5, 9]. In participatory design, a team of people representing the major stakeholders of a product work together to create that product that would reflect the way actual users would use it. In contrast with the first study employing student design partners, this section describes a second study using teacher design partners to carry out participatory design to further refine PAPER.

5.1   Participants

Two design partners (P1 and P2) in the education field were recruited. P1 is a secondary school geography teacher and head of the school's humanities department with over 30 years of experience teaching the subject. P2 is a school psychologist involved in teacher training at a university in Singapore. Both are well-versed in pedagogical theories and methods, and familiar with the intricacies of Singapore's education system.

5.2   Protocol

A facilitator involved in the first study and currently on the development team worked with each design partner in separate sessions to elicit opinions on PAPER. Each session lasted approximately 1.5 hours.

The session was divided into four parts. Part 1 was a familiarization segment that introduced the design partner to the project. The goals of the project were reviewed and the design partners were given an overview of PAPER's features. In Part 2 of the session, the facilitator provided a guided tour of the mock exam and elicited opinions on four areas: (1) positive aspects of the mock exam; (2) areas of improvement; (3) usefulness of the mock exam in helping students learn and prepare for the geography exam; and (4) usefulness of the mock exam as a tool for helping teacher meet their educational objectives. Part 3 was a repeat of Part 2 except that the focus was on the personal coach. Finally, Part 4 was an open-ended interview whose purpose was to identify, refine and brainstorm further ideas for improving PAPER.

5.3   Feedback on Mock Exam

Design partners were introduced to the three major tasks afforded by the mock exam: selection of static and dynamic papers; attempting questions in the mock exam; and viewing of the mock exam report.

Positive Comments. The design partners' responses to the mock exam were generally positive. P1 liked the dynamic paper concept since it lessened the work required for creating new exam papers. Teachers simply needed to select the desired topics and PAPER would then automatically generate an exam paper for students. P2 also liked the fact that students could review answers after the mock exam and explore supplementary resources as the latter would help reinforce concepts learnt, or elucidate areas of weakness. Both P1 and P2 also felt that the mock exam report was comprehensive and useful for diagnostic purposes. For example, the length of time taken for each question and the topic area would be helpful to identify strengths as well as areas for further revision.

In terms of usefulness to students, P1 thought that it would be a good alternative to print versions of past-year exam questions. For example, after completion of a lesson, teachers could ask students to attempt related questions to assess mastery of the topic. Further, being Web-based, students need not have to bring additional books to school and could access the system both at school and at home.

P2 felt that the mock exam would also be a useful tool for teachers in that "differentiated teaching" can occur, catering to individual differences and abilities. Through the dynamic paper, a teacher could create exams with varying levels of difficulty, and then instruct students to attempt a particular exam given his/her ability level. P1 commented that the mock exam would also help in easing a teacher's workload. In a typical classroom setting, students would attempt print versions of mock exams and upon completion, the teacher would painstakingly go through each solution, answering any questions that might arise during the process. With PAPER's mock exam, students could independently attempt the questions and then peruse the solutions and supplementary resources. The teacher now becomes a facilitator that assists students in interacting with PAPER, and provides additional instruction when students require more information than what PAPER can provide.

Negative Comments. P2 felt that there should be greater use of color and multimedia to take advantage of the digital medium, and differentiate the system from print. The use of such elements would not only help the learning process (e.g. animation depicting ox-bow lake formation) but also maintain the interest level of students. However, these should only be made available during the review phase of the mock exam, and not while students are attempting the questions. It was interesting to note that both P1 and P2 did not like the default grey "theme" of the system – a more colorful user interface would be more appropriate for PAPER's target group of users. P1 also pointed out that content was an integral part of the system and its acceptance by students and teachers would depend very much on the quality of the solutions and supplementary resources. Consequently, while P1 agreed with P2 that the introduction of multimedia would be an improvement to the existing system, content should never be sacrificed.

5.4   Feedback on Personal Coach

While PAPER's mock exam was relatively straightforward to describe since it had a print counterpart, the personal coach required more explanation as there was no physical parallel. Here, the design partners were shown how students could receive recommendations from the personal coach after the mock exam was completed, and how they could attempt the recommended questions. A non-technical overview of the recommendation algorithms used by the personal coach was also provided to assure the design partners that the questions were not haphazardly selected.

Positive Comments. Since adaptivity is difficult to achieve in print versions of exam questions except perhaps through manual analysis, both design partners felt that the personal coach had good potential as a tool to facilitate exam preparation. Further, they liked the fact the recommendations were fine grained (at the topic level), and that students would be provided with questions that met their ability levels. Both P1 and P2 agreed that this would be something that teachers would not have time to do in a classroom setting with large numbers of students, each requiring individual attention.

P1 felt that students would benefit from the personal coach because they will be able to determine for themselves whether they have grasped the presented concepts. That is, the better students perform in the mock exam, the more likely they will be able to attempt harder questions. Conversely for weaker students, the personal coach will recommend questions that are easier. In all cases, students will be able to find a level of question difficulty they are comfortable with. P2 added that this would be motivating factor since weaker students will not be discouraged and better performing students will be challenged by the more difficult questions. Further, P2 also noted that the personal coach would be useful for students who have just begun their exam preparation and are unsure what questions to attempt first. The system would also be useful for those who do not have the initiative to explore the repository of questions themselves. In both cases, the personal coach would serve as a good starting point.

Both design partners agreed that the personal coach would be useful from the teacher's point of view as well. Specifically, P1 felt that since students can be left on their own with PAPER, teachers would have more time to devote to individual students who are academically weaker or simply have trouble with certain topics or questions. P2 concurred and noted that since the personal coach (and the mock exam) runs without the need for intervention by teachers, there will be less resistance to adopting PAPER in the classroom. Teachers will also spend less time identifying suitable questions for students to attempt.

Negative Comments. P2 argued that one weakness of the personal coach is that it lacks comprehensiveness in terms of question coverage. In the long run, students simply cannot focus only on recommended questions. Instead, they need to attempt as many questions as possible since the actual examination contains both easy and difficult questions. Consequently, students cannot depend only on the personal coach but use features such as search/browse to retrieve and attempt questions that have not been recommended. P2 also felt that the personal coach could be extended to become a recommender system for teachers who are planning lesson materials and authoring exams. Specifically, the system could provide a teacher with the average difficulty level for each topic using the individual topic difficulty levels for each student in his/her class. These average values would serve as an overall performance indicator for the class, allowing the teacher to pitch the lesson or exam at an appropriate level.

5.5   Discussion

Given the feedback from both studies involving student and teacher design partners, several lessons were learnt that will be used to guide future development of PAPER. These are summarized in this section:

1. **The importance of differentiation.** PAPER should take advantage of the digital medium and differentiate itself from print versions of exam questions. The personal coach, which recommends questions tailored to individual ability levels, is one such example. An area that requires improvement is the use of color, sound, animation and other multimedia elements to maintain the interest level of users. This is especially so for PAPER's target group of users who are exposed to a variety of Web sites, computer games and other software.
2. **The importance of content.** An attractively designed system will still fail if users do not find the content useful or of sufficient quality. This is especially so in PAPER where students depend on it for exam preparation. Thus, future development of PAPER should occur in two tracks, one focusing on features and usability, while the other on geography content. The latter will require the services of experts such as geography teachers.
3. **Ease of use.** Teachers and students have only a fixed number of hours at school and a variety of activities to perform. To facilitate adoption, a new system such as PAPER should be intuitive, reliable and easy to use. It should not waste valuable time or users will focus on other tasks such as learning how to use a competing and better designed software.
4. **Consultation with actual users.** An educational tool such as PAPER should not be treated as an end in itself. In other words, teachers will not rush to adopt a system simply because it is available. Instead, the system must demonstrate that it is able to help meet the learning objectives set by teachers, and be easily integrated into the existing curriculum. Consequently, system developers need to work with target users to determine how best to design and deploy GeogDL.

6 Conclusion

With the development of PAPER, GeogDL now offers a suite of digital library services ranging from traditional search and browse to dynamic ones that integrate and adapt content. Using existing services in GeogDL, students are able to interact with individual resources such as attempting an examination question and viewing the associated solution. The new mock exam feature in PAPER assembles questions to create a timed, simulated version of the geography examination. The personal coach adapts to students' ability levels and utilizes past mock exams to recommend further questions for practice that are tailored to individual needs.

The PD sessions revealed that our design partners generally concurred with the goals and features of PAPER. From the students' point of view, they felt that PAPER offers an environment that helps students prepare for the geography exam in ways beyond what books can provide. Further, since students can independently interact with PAPER, teachers have more time to spend catering to individual students' learning needs. However, more work needs to be done. We plan to further refine

PAPER by incorporating the suggestions elicited from our design partners and running trials of the system in schools. Nevertheless, we anticipate that this richer, personalized, interactive experience offered by PAPER will better fulfill our goal of developing a digital library that meets the educational needs of students.

Acknowledgements. This work is funded by SingAREN Project M48020004.

References

1. Bridgeman, S., Goodrich, M.T., Kobourov, S.G., and Tamassia, R.: PILOT: an interactive tool for learning and grading. ACM SIGCSE Bulletin, Vol. 32, No. 1 (2000) 139–143.
2. Chua, L.H., Goh, D.H., Lim, E.P., Liu, Z., Ang, R.: A digital library for geography examination resources. Proceedings of the 2nd ACM/IEEE Joint Conference on Digital Libraries (2002) 115–116.
3. Coleman, A., Smith, T., Buchel, O., and Mayer, R.: Learning spaces in digital libraries. Proceedings of the Fifth European Conference on Research and Advanced Technology for Digital Libraries, Lecture Notes in Computer Science, Vol. 2163. Springer-Verlag, Berlin (2001) 251–262.
4. Digital Library for Earth System Education. http://www.dlese.org/
5. Druin, A., Bederson, B., Boltman, A., Miura, A., Knotts-Callahan, D., and Platt, M.: Children as our technology design partners. In Allison Druin (Ed.), The Design of Children's Technology (51–72). Morgan Kaufmann Publishers, San Francisco (1999).
6. Ellington, H., Percival, F. and Race, P.: Handbook of Educational Technology. 3rd Edition. Kogan Page, London (1995).
7. Geography: GCE Ordinary Level. http://www.moe.edu.sg/exams/syllabus/2232.pdf.
8. Gibbs, G.: Improving student learning through course design. Oxford Centre for Staff Development, Oxford (1997).
9. Muller, M.J.: PICTIVE – an exploration in participatory design. Proceedings of the SIGCHI Conference on Human Factors in Computing Systems (CHI'91) (1991) 225–231.
10. Nwana, H.S.: Intelligent tutoring systems: An overview. Artificial Intelligence Review, Vol. 4 (1990) 251–277.
11. Theng, Y.L., Goh, D.H., Lim, E.P., Liu, Z., Pang, N., Wong, P., Chua, L.H.: Intergenerational partnerships in the design of a digital library of geography examination resources. Proceedings of the 5th International Conference on Asian Digital Libraries, Lecture Notes in Computer Science, Vol. 2555. Springer-Verlag, Berlin (2002) 427–439.
12. Tinoco, L., Fox, E., and Barnette, D.: Online evaluation in WWW-based courseware. Proceedings of the 28th SIGCSE Technical Symposium (1997) 194–198.

Metadata for Online Resources and Learning Object

Norhaizan Mat Talha, Ismail Rohani, and Zaleha Abd. Rahim

MIMOS Bhd., Technology Park Malaysia, Kuala Lumpur
{zan,rohani,zara}@mimos.my

Abstract. If used effectively, metadata allows information to be accessible by labeling its contents consistently. It will also lead users to find information they need, all in one place. With that in mind, we have implemented the 'labeling'/'cataloging' of online resources and learning objects. This paper reports on our commitment in achieving this which includes, the development of Metadata Management System, a tool for creating, harvesting and maintaining metadata records, the development of our own application profile which draws elements from both IEEE Learning Object Metadata (LOM) and Dublin Core and the development of our own search engine to query and retrieve the metadata sets. In bringing the audience direct to the relevant resources, the metadata has been implemented at a pilot project that specifically aims to bridge the digital divide. This is achieved through the structured and systematic information classification and indexing.

1 Introduction

The Malaysia Grid for Learning (MyGfL) is a national initiatives aims to promote life long learning through the use of ICT and will be a one-stop center for quality assured online learning content, tools and services. The fundamental elements in MyGfL are the metadata repository and the learning services. Recognising the importance of standard in implementation of MyGfL, the Content and Technical standards was then developed for content providers who are developing content or wish to have their content published on MyGfL

The Content and Technical standards covers the general issues on content as well as the systems standards that serves as the platform to execute e-learning. This standards is developed to address Reusability, Accessibility, Interoperability and Durability of both content and systems.

In accessing the content of MyGfL which ranges from online training and accreditation programs, reading materials and references to information on various fields and subjects the users need to have a consistent way of discovering information. The information, even for resources where access is restricted (paid resources etc.), should be in standard format so that it may indicate to a prospective user the suitability of a resource to their interest.

T.M.T. Sembok et al. (Eds.): ICADL 2003, LNCS 2911, pp. 505–509, 2003.
© Springer-Verlag Berlin Heidelberg 2003

2 Metadata Implementation

Implementing metadata would result in the availability of consistent, accurate and well-structured descriptions of web resources. This would enable much greater search precision and more relevance ranking of the large result sets which a typical search engine would provide. Metadata can also be utilized in the management and administration of digital networked resources. It will have information about the date of creation and modification and responsibility for maintenance and is essential for ensuring that web resources are kept up to date.

We have decided to pilot the implementation of metadata tagging for one of our project called Titian Digital, which already have ready web content as a proof of concept. Titian Digital is a content exchange platform, targeted for rural communities with the objective to improve the socio-economic level of rural community by adopting ICT in their day-to-day activities, thus addressing the ultimate goal of bridging the digital divide. Titian Digital focuses on three specific domains, namely: Rural Economy, Health and Education. Our aim is to direct the targeted audience right to the relevant resources through application of metadata. Metadata maximised the opportunities for users to find the most relevant and comprehensive set of resources specifically for their purposes.

The resources in Titian Digital platform are already categorized according the domain mentioned above and the metadata creation process classify the resources according to the said categories and sub-categories. A search interface to allow for resource discovery within the Titian Digital environment will then direct user right to the information they are looking for. Furthermore, metadata records are presented bilingually, i.e. English and Malay for the benefits of rural communities.

2.1   Metadata Management Systems, MMS

In order to facilitate and automate the management of metadata tagging process the Metadata Management System, MMS, has been designed and developed, both as a tool and system specifically for creating, maintaining, storing and harvesting metadata records. Metadata will be generated and encoded in XML for interoperability purposes. MMS comprises of three main modules: Metadata Editor, Metadata Harvester and Metadata Administrator.

Fig.1. depicts a snapshot of the Metadata Editor. In designing the Editor we have a taken into account the user requirement so that metadata creation by generic users will be very simple, short, intuitive and easy to use. Users are be assisted in filling in the metadata information by providing them with metadata guidelines. These guidelines provide them the definition and explanation of each element in Dublin Core as to ensure consistency. It also provides the Graphical User Interface (GUI) to allow users to create and view metadata records for one resource at a time, and to generate metadata tags for embedding in the resource. They can save their records prior to submitting to metadata quality assurance, an authorized person who will go through the metadata record created and filled in the rest of the optional field wherever applicable.

The search interface will support simple search, guided search and advanced search. The category of the search result is also hyperlinked as one of the features that assist the users to bring them closer to the information they are looking for.

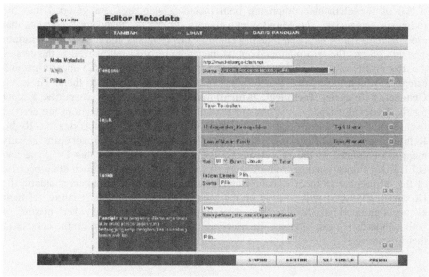

Fig. 1. Metadata editor

3   Achievement

The creation of metadata record for Titian Digital resources was done by the author herself and the content aggregators of Titian Digital. While the author has deeper understanding about metadata, the content aggregators have undertaken their task with their knowledge and experience of the content of Titian Digital resources. We are also aware of our immediate and potential audiences and the way which they will search for information. We have also discovered that a good resource, e.g. Web page design (information on date created/modified, authors, copyright statement, etc on the first page) will make metadata creation an easier task. Our biggest obstacle lies in the process of describing the resources. Here our knowledge of the resources as well as our writing skills proved to be our advantage. As the time this paper is written, we have created approximately to 500 metadata records describing the content on the Titian Digital.

4   Mixing and Matching Metadata

The content of our resources, which consists of collections of services and information across many disciplines requires a common, cross-domain metadata schema for their description. The metadata created to describe them is based on qualified Dublin Core with an extension that include educational metadata such as the IEEE Learning Object Metadata, LOM, which is used to facilitate search, evaluation, acquisition and use of learning objects.

All of the elements comprising both metadata standards are grouped into the following categories. The **Mandatory** category groups the mandatory elements that users have to fill in which are mainly Dublin Core elements and the **Meta Metadata** category groups the information about the metadata record itself as well as the data of the user profile of the metadata creator. The rest of the categories are under **Optional** category, which means that user only fill in the fields applicable to them. These are **General, Life-cycle, Technical, Educational, and Annotation** categories. Except for the **General** category, it is obvious that all of the **Optional** categories are derived from IEEE LOM. However we have omitted three IEEE LOM categories, the **Right**, **Relation**, and **Classification** because the elements in those category are already mapped or existed in the DC elements. It should also be noted that DC.Type and IEEE LOM Educational.LearningResourceType are not mapped to each other because of the differences in the vocabulary and schema value. Both metadata standard, the DC and IEEE LOM will co-exist on the Metadata editor with the "mixture" of their elements grouped into the above category. In the **General** category, where mixture of both standards is most obvious, the user will create metadata based on the content of their resources.

5   Conclusion

From our experience, we can conclude that the creation of metadata to describe resources assists in resource discovery and resource management. Consistent cataloguing of online resources maximised the opportunities for searchers to search and retrieve the most relevant and comprehensive set of resources for their purposes. Localization of our Metadata Management system has realized priority to bridge the digital divide in the country as well to tap indigenous knowledge of the community. This localization will benefit both the metadata creation process as well as the end users. Ultimately, Metadata can also be used to organize, store and retrieve items for information management purposes.

6   Future Work

To ensure general acceptance and the effectiveness of our Metadata Editor, a usability test with real end users need to be conducted to find out how successful the standard is in improving accessibility to information and to identify the need for improvements. We are also hoping that other government or private sectors with web resources would take similar initiatives and start to implement metadata for their web resources. To avoid being 'isolated' we planned to develop the Metadata Harvester as part of the MMS. We are currently in the process of implementing the Z39.50 and Open Archive Initiative (OAI) metadata-harvesting interface.

References

1. Pithamber R.Polsani: "Use and Abuse of Reusable Learning Objects", *Journal of Digital Information, volume 3 issue 4, 2003.* http://jodi.ecs.soton.ac.uk/Articles/v03/i04/Polsani/
2. Apps, A, MacIntyre, R and Morris, L: "Exposing Cross-Domain Resources for Researchers and Learners", *Proc. Int. Conf. On Dublin Core and Metadata for e-communities 2002: 71–80*
3. Heery, R, and Patel, M: "Application profiles: mixing and matching metadata chemas", *Adriadne, 25, 2000.* http:/www.adriadne.ac.uk/issue25/app-profiles
4. Milstead, J and Feldman, S: "Metadata: Cataloging by Any Other Name...", *ONLINE, January 1999.* http://www.onlinemag.net/OL1999/milstead1.html
5. Curie, M, Moss, N, Ip, A, and Morrison, I: "The Edna Metadata Toolsets: A Case Study". http://ausweb.scu.edu.au/aw2k/papers/currie/paper.html
6. Greeenberg, J, Pattuelli, M, Parsia, B and Robertson, W: "Author-generated Dublin Core Metadata for Web Resources: A Baseline Study in an Organization", *Journal of Digital Information, volume 2 issue 2, 2003.*http://jodi.ecs.soton.ac.uk/Articles/vo2/i02/Greenberg/
7. Friesen, N, Mason, J, Ward, N: "Building Educational Metadata Application Profiles", *Proc. Int. Conf.On Dublin Core and Metadata for e-Communities 2002: 63-69*
8. Miller, P: "Metadata for the masses", *Ariadne* http://www.ariadne.ac.uk/issue5/metadata-masses/
9. Gill, T: "Introduction to Metadata on the web", *Getty Research Institute.* http://www.getty.edu/research/institute/standards/intrometadata/2_articles/gill/index.html
10. Abdul Rahman, R and Mat Talha, N: "Metadata Management System, Business Requirement Specification", *MIMOS Bhd. 2003*
11. IEEE LOM, 2002. "Learning Object Metadata draft version 6.4" http://ltsc.ieee.org/w12/index.html
12. DCQ 2000, "Dublin Core Qualifiers" http://www.dublincore.org/documents/dcmes-qualifiers

Segmenting Chinese Unknown Words by Heuristic Method

Christopher C. Yang and K.W. Li

Department of Systems Engineering and Engineering Management
The Chinese University of Hong Kong

Abstract. Chinese text segmentation is important in Chinese text indexing. Due to the lack of word delimiters in Chinese text, Chinese text segmentation is more difficult than English text segmentation. Besides, the segmentation ambiguities and the occurrences of out-of-vocabulary words (i.e. unknown words) are the major challenges in Chinese segmentation. Many research works dealing with the problem of word segmentation have focused on the resolution of segmentation ambiguities. The problem of unknown word identification has not drawn much attention. In this paper, we propose a heuristic method for Chinese test segmentation based on the statistical approach. The experimental result shows that our proposed heuristic method is promising to segment the unknown words as well as the known words. We have further investigated the distribution of the errors of commission and the errors of omission caused by the proposed heuristic method and benchmarked the proposed heuristic method with our previous proposed technique, boundary detection.

1   Introduction

Text segmentation is defined as the segmentation of texts into linguistic units, normally words [8]. The problem can be formally defined as [6]

$$\arg\max_{W_i} P(W_i \mid C) = \arg\max_{W_i} P(W_i)P(C \mid W_i) / P(C) \qquad (1)$$

where $C = c_1c_2...c_m$ is an input character string, and $W_i = w_1w_2...w_n$ is a possible word segmentation.

Since $P(C|W_i)$ equals to 1 and $P(C)$ is a constant, the above formulation can be simplified to

$$\arg\max_{W_i} P(W_i \mid C) = \arg\max_{W_i} P(W_i) \qquad (2)$$

Unlike English, many Asian languages (e.g. Chinese, Japanese and Thai) do not have delimiters of words as spaces or punctuation marks. As a result, segmenting Chinese text is a more difficult task than segmenting English text. The techniques to segment Chinese character sequences into words can be divided into three categories: (a) statistical approach [2][7][6], (b) lexical rule-based approach [9], and (c) hybrid approach based on statistical and lexical information.

T.M.T. Sembok et al. (Eds.): ICADL 2003, LNCS 2911, pp. 510–520, 2003.

The segmentation ambiguities and the occurrences of out-of-vocabulary words (i.e. unknown words) are the most challenging problems in Chinese text segmentation. Many research works dealing with the problem of word segmentation have focused on the resolution of segmentation ambiguities. The problem of unknown word identification has not drawn much attention.   The unknown words are diverse, including personal names, organization names and their abbreviations. The unknown words are defined as the words which are not found in the lexicon [1], but they provide more precise and comprehensive meaningful terms for information retrieval. Lai and Wu [4] referred the unknown words or phrases as phrase-like units (PLU) that can be combinations of words in the lexicon or some meaningless characters. Due to the ever-changing nature of language, no general lexicon can be comprehensive. New words or phrases are created everyday. In this paper, we propose a heuristic method based on the statistical approach to segment Chinese text. In particular, the capability of the proposed technique to segment unknown words is investigated.

The followings are some types of unknown words that frequently occur:

1. *Abbreviation* (acronym): Abbreviations are difficult to be identified since their morphological structures are very irregular. Their affixes reflect the conventions of the selection meaningful components [1]. However, the affixed of abbreviations are common words which are least informative for indicating the existence of unknown words. For example, 中大 (CU) is the abbreviation of 香港中文大學 (The Chinese University of Hong Kong).

2. *Proper nouns*: Proper nouns can be classified into 4 subcategories: 1) name of people; 2) name of place; 3) name of organization; 4) specific terms, e.g. 大腸桿菌, 脫氧核糖核酸, 可卡因, 目眩神迷. Certain key words are indicators for each different subcategory. For instance, there are about 100 common surnames which are prefix characters of Chinese personal names. The characters, such as 道, 區, 路, frequently occur as suffixes of the names of places. However, names such as 香港仔, 黃竹坑, 粉嶺 are hard to identify.

3. *Derived words*: The derived words have affix morphemes which are strong indicators of unknown words, e.g. 電腦化.

4. *Compounds*: The compounds are very productive type of unknown word. Nominal and verbal compounds are easily formed by combining two or more words, e.g. 邊境禁區, 胡琴演奏會, 爆竊集團.

2 Statistical Approach

In the statistical approach of Chinese text segmentation, a text corpus is analyzed and the context specific information about syntactic structures and usage of words are obtained. Association formulae are utilized to measure the association among adjacent characters in Chinese text. The most popular association formulae are mutual information (MI) and significance estimation (SE).

Mutual information (MI):

Mutual information is first adopted by Sproat and Shih [7] to measure the association between two adjacent characters

$$MI(a,b) = \log_2 \frac{N\, freq(ab)}{freq(a)\, freq(b)} \tag{3}$$

where a and b are Chinese characters, N is the size of corpus, $freq(ab)$ is the frequency of occurrence of the character string ab, and $freq(a)$ and $frea(b)$ are the frequencies of occurrence of a and b, respectively.

Significant Estimation (SE):

Significant estimation is adopted by Chien [2] to measure the association of n characters where n can be any values greater than two.

$$SE(c) = \frac{freq(c)}{freq(a) + freq(b) - freq(c)} \tag{4}$$

where c is a string with n characters, a and b are two overlapping substrings of c with n-1 characters.

If $c = c_j c_{j+1} c_{j+2}$,

$$SE(c_j c_{j+1} c_{j+2}) = \frac{freq(c_j c_{j+1} c_{j+2})}{freq(c_j c_{j+1}) + freq(c_{j+1} c_{j+2}) - freq(c_j c_{j+1} c_{j+2})} \tag{5}$$

3 Heuristic Method

We propose a heuristic method with five rules to segment Chinese text using mutual information and significance estimation of all bi-grams and tri-grams, respectively, in the corpus. Given a Chinese strings with n characters, $c_1\, c_2 \ldots c_j \ldots c_n$, every character is initialized as a unigram. The heuristic method begins from the second character, c_2, and determines the matching rules. When a rule is matched, c_j is combined with the previous n-gram(s) to form a longer n-gram or remain as a unigram. If there is no other rule can be matched, the next character, c_{j+1}, will be considered. This process is repeated until the last character, c_n, is reached.

Rule 1:

If c_{j-1} is a unigram and $MI(c_{j-1}, c_j) > th_3$, c_{j-1} and c_j are combined as a bi-gram.

$$MI(C_{j-1}, C_j) > th_3$$

If c_{j-1} is a unigram and $MI(c_{j-1}, c_j) \le th_3$, c_{j-1} and c_j remain as unigrams.

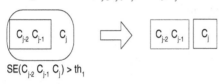

$MI(C_{j-1}, C_j) <= th_3$

Rule 2:

If $c_{j-2}\,c_{j-1}$ is a bi-gram and $SE(c_{j-2}c_{j-1}\,c_j) > th_1$, $c_{j-2}c_{j-1}$ and c_j are combined as a tri-gram.

$SE(C_{j-2}\,C_{j-1}\,C_j) > th_1$

If $c_{j-2}\,c_{j-1}$ is a bi-gram and $SE(c_{j-2}c_{j-1}\,c_j) \le th_1$, c_j is remained as a unigram.

$SE(C_{j-2}\,C_{j-1}\,C_j) > th_1$

Rule 3:

If c_{j-2} and c_{j-1} are unigrams, $SE(c_{j-2}\,c_{j-1}\,c_j) > th_1$, and $MI(c_{j-2}\,c_{j-1}) > th_2$, c_{j-2}, c_{j-1} and c_j are combined as a tri-gram.

$SE(C_{j-2}\,C_{j-1}\,C_j) > th_1$

$MI(C_{j-2}\,C_{j-1}) > th_2$

If c_{j-2} and c_{j-1} are unigrams, and $SE(c_{j-2}c_{j-1}\,c_j) \le th_1$ or $MI(c_{j-2}c_{j-1}) \le th_2$, c_j is remained as a unigram.

$SE(C_{j-2}\,C_{j-1}\,C_j) > th_1$

$MI(C_{j-2}\,C_{j-1}) > th_2$

Rule 4:

If $...c_{j-2}\,c_{j-1}$ is a n-1 gram and $SE(c_{j-2}\,c_{j-1}\,c_j) > th_1$, $...c_{j-2}c_{j-1}\,c_j$ are combined as a n-gram.

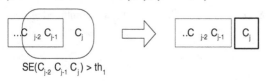

$SE(C_{j-2} C_{j-1} C_j) > th_1$

If $...c_{j-2} c_{j-1}$ is a n-1 gram and $SE(c_{j-2} c_{j-1} c_j) \leq th_1$, c_j is remained as a unigram.

$SE(C_{j-2} C_{j-1} C_j) > th_1$

Rule 5:

If $...c_{j-2}$ is a n-2 gram, c_{j-1} is a unigram, $SE(c_{j-2} c_{j-1} c_j) > th_1$, and $MI(c_{j-2} c_{j-1}) > th_2$, $...c_{j-2} c_{j-1} c_j$ are combined as a n-gram.

$SE(C_{j-2} C_{j-1} C_j) > th_1$

$MI(C_{j-2} C_{j-1}) > th_2$

If $...c_{j-2}$ is a n-2 gram, c_{j-1} is a unigram, and $SE(c_{j-2} c_{j-1} c_j) \leq th_1$, or $MI(c_{j-2} c_{j-1}) \leq th_2$, c_j is remained as a unigram.

$SE(C_{j-2} C_{j-1} C_j) > th_1$

$MI(C_{j-2} C_{j-1}) > th_2$

th_1, th_2, and th_3 are thresholds determined experimentally.

3.1   Example

Given a Chinese sentence, 財政司司長發表財政預算案的日子, the mutual information for all bi-grams and the significant estimation for all tri-grams are as follows:

Bi-gram	財政	政司	司司	司長	長發	發表	表財	財政
MI	6.83	4.27	4.49	4.69	0.51	3.80	-1.42	6.83
Bi-gram	政預	預算	算案	案的	的日	日子		
MI	3.43	7.65	5.79	0.73	0.82	6.43		

Tri-gram	財政司	政司司	司司長	司長發	長發表
SE	0.253	0.540	0.806	0.005	0.006
Tri-gram	財政預	政預算	預算案	算案的	案的日
SE	0.128	0.340	0.463	0.103	0.007

th_1, th_2, and th_3 are 0.3, 3.0, and 1.0.

Using Rule 1, MI(財政$)$ > th_3, [財] and [政] are combined as a bi-gram, [財政].

> Result: [財政]

Using Rule 2, SE(財政司$) \leq th_1$, [司] is remained as a unigram.

> Result: [財政][司]

Using Rule 5, SE(政司司$)$ > th_1 and MI(政司$)$ > th_2, [財政] , [司] and [司] are combined to form[財政司司].

> Result: [財政司司]

Using Rule 4, SE(司司長$)$ > th_1, [財政司司] and [長] are combined as [財政司司長].

> Result: [財政司司長]

Using Rule 4, SE(司長發$) \leq th_1$, [發] is remained as a unigram.

> Result: [財政司司長][發]

Using Rule 5, SE(長發表$) \leq th_1$, [表] is remained as a unigram.

> Result: [財政司司長][發][表]

Using Rule 1, MI(發表$)$ > th_3, [發] and[表] are combined as a bi-gram, [發表].

> Result: [財政司司長][發表]

Using Rule 2, SE(發表財$) \leq th_1$, [財] is remained as a unigram.

> Result: [財政司司長][發表][財]

Using Rule 5, SE(表財政$) \leq th_1$, [政] is remained as a unigram.

> Result: [財政司司長][發表][財][政]

Using Rule 1, MI(財政$)$ > th_3, [財] and [政] are combined as a bi-gram, [財政].

> Result: [財政司司長][發表][財政]

Using Rule 2, SE(財政預$) \leq th_1$, [預] is remained as a unigram.

> Result: [財政司司長][發表][財政][預]

Using Rule 5, SE(政預算$)$ > th_1 and MI(政預$)$ > th_2, [財政], [預] and [算] are combined as [財政預算].

Result: [財政司司長][發表][財政預算]

Using Rule 4, *SE(*預算案*)* > *th,*, [財政預算] and [案] are combined as[財政預算案].

Result: [財政司司長][發表][財政預算案]

Using Rule 4, *SE(*算案的*)* ≤ *th,*, [的] is remained as a unigram.

Result: [財政司司長][發表][財政預算案][的]

Using Rule 5, *SE(*案的日*)* ≤ *th,*, [日] is remained as a unigram.

Result: [財政司司長][發表][財政預算案][的][日]

Using Rule 1, *MI(*的日*)* ≤ *th₃*, [日] is remained as a unigram.

Result: [財政司司長][發表][財政預算案][的][日]

Using Rule 3, *SE(*的日子*)* ≤ *th,*, [子] is remained as a unigram.

Result: [財政司司長][發表][財政預算案][的][日][子]

Using Rule 1, *MI(*日子*)* > *th₃*, [日] and [子] are combined as a bi-gram, [日子].

Result: [財政司司長][發表][財政預算案][的][日子]

In this example, 財政司司長 and 財政預算案 are unknown words that are compound words formed by the combination of known words, 財政司 and 司長, and 財政 and 預算案, respectively. 發表 and 日子 are known words. It shows that the proposed heuristic method can successfully segment both the unknown words which is impossible to be identified by dictionary.

4 Experiments

Experiments are conducted to measure the precision, recall and error rate of the segmentation results using the Hong Kong local Chinese news articles and HKSAR government press releases as corpus. The formulations of precision, recall, and error rate are given as below:

$$Precision = \frac{c}{n} \qquad Recall = \frac{c}{N} \qquad Error\ rate = \frac{e}{N}$$

where   *c* is the number of words that are correctly segmented,
         e is the number of words that are incorrectly segmented,
         n is the number of words segmented, and
         N is the number of words in the corpus.

In the corpus of our experiment, there are totally 2000 documents. The number of known words and the number of unique known words are 317,386 and 44,189, respectively. The number of unknown words and the number of unique unknown words are 108,296 and 30,792, respectively. Many of the unknown words are names of persons, events, organizations, and technical terms. The average frequency of the known words and unknown words are 7.18 and 3.52, respectively. The average frequency of the known words is double of the average frequency of the unknown words.

4.1   Performance and Benchmarking

In this section, we present the performance of the proposed heuristic methods and benchmark its performance with that of our previous proposed technique, boundary detection [9]. The boundary detection is developed to detect the segmentation points in a Chinese sentence based on the abrupt changes on the mutual information between the adjacent bi-grams [9]. It is shown by experiment results that the boundary detection technique is efficient and effective. It only requires the mutual information but not the significance estimation.

Table 1 and Table 2 present the experimental result of the boundary detection and heuristic method for unknown words and known words, respectively.

Table 3 presents the overall experimental result of boundary detection and heuristic method for both known words and unknown words and their efficiency.

Table 1. Performance of Boundary Detection and Heuristic Method for segmenting unknown words

Algorithms	Precision	Recall	Error rate
Boundary Detection	0.801	0.752	0.187
Heuristic Method	0.918	0.903	0.081

Table 2. Performance of Boundary Detection and Heuristic Method for segmenting known words

Algorithms	Precision	Recall	Error rate
Boundary Detection	0.812	0.841	0.195
Heuristic Method	0.897	0.919	0.105

Table 3. Overall Performance of Boundary Detection and Boundary Heuristic Method

Algorithms	Precision	Recall	Error rate	Processing Time used in seconds
Boundary Detection	0.809	0.818	0.193	89.6
Heuristic Method	0.902	0.915	0.099	254.5

The result shows that the heuristic method is promising to segment the unknown words as well as the know words. Besides, the heuristic method is significantly better than the boundary detection in terms of precision and recall. It can be explained by the fact that the heuristic method utilizes both mutual information of bi-grams and significant estimation of tri-grams to form n-grams, but the boundary detection only utilize the mutual information on bi-grams to determine the segmentation points. Given more statistical information, the heuristic method is able to achieve higher performance. On the other hand, the heuristic method is significantly more time consuming than the boundary detection because it involves the computation of both mutual information and significant estimation. The rules matching in heuristic matching is also more computational expensive than identifying segmentation point in boundary detection.

4.2   Analysis of Error

The errors arose from using the boundary detection and heuristic method were analyzed based on the methods suggested by Dai et al. [3][4]. The errors in Chinese text segmentation can be divided into two types: a) errors of commission and b) errors of omission. The errors of commission refer to the segments that are identified by the automatic text segmentation techniques as words but in fact they are not. The errors of omission are words that are not identified by the automatic text segmentation techniques to be words but in fact they are. Table 4 presents the distribution of the errors of commission and the errors of omission caused by the boundary detection and the heuristic method.

Table 4. The Distribution of the Errors of Commission and the Errors of Omission

	Errors of Commission	Errors of Omission
Boundary Detection	93.5 %	6.5 %
Heuristic Method	84.9%	15.1 %

The result shows that both of the boundary detection and the heuristic method have significantly more percentage of the errors of commissions. Comparing between the boundary detection and the heuristic method, the heuristic method has relatively less percentage of the errors of commission and relatively more percentage of the errors of omission. It is due to the fact that the boundary detection determines the segmentation points purely by the abrupt changes of mutual information of adjacent Chinese characters. However, the abrupt changes may not always correspond to segmentation points especially when the statistical information provided by the corpus is not sufficient. Therefore, the boundary detection may identify segmentation points that indeed do not exist.

The error of commission can be further categorized into two types:

E1. A word is incorrectly segmented into segments that are simple words

For example, 中文大學 can be incorrectly segmented to [中文] and [大學].

[中文] and [大學] are both simple words

E2. A word is incorrectly segmented into segments such that one or both of the segments is not a word.

For example, 財政司司長 can be incorrectly segmented to [財政] and [司司長].

[財政] is a word but [司司長] is not a word.

Table 5 presents the distribution of E1 and E2 errors in the errors of commission caused by the boundary detection and the heuristic method.

Table 5. The Distribution of E1 and E2 Errors in the Errors of Commission

	Errors of Commission	
	E1	E2
Boundary Detection	57.0%	43.0%
Heuristic Method	55.5%	44.5%

The result shows that the percentage of E1 errors is higher that that of E2 errors in the errors of commission caused by both of the boundary detection and the heuristic method. The E1 errors are hard to be avoided especially when the frequencies of both of the simple words, which are incorrectly segmented, are relatively higher than the frequency of the word formed by these simple words. Using the statistical approach, both of the boundary detection and the heuristic method take the simple words as more probable than the compound words formed by these simple words. Unless the compound words appear more frequently in the corpus, it is impossible to be avoided. It is also found that the distributions of E1 and E2 errors in the errors of commission caused by the boundary detection and the heuristic method are approximately the same. None of these two techniques have advantages in resolving either type of errors.

5 Conclusion

In this paper, we propose a heuristic method for Chinese text segmentation using statistical approach. Such method employs mutual information and significance estimation to measure the association among adjacent characters and utilizes five rules to determine the segmentation points. Experiment results show that the heuristic method is promising to segment unknown words as well as known words. The heuristic method is significantly better than our previous proposed boundary detection. Error of analysis has also been presented. It is found that the percentage of errors of commission is significantly more than the percentage of the errors of omission. In terms of the errors of commission, there are more errors caused by segmenting compound words into simple words.

References

1. Chen, K. and Bai, M., "Unknown Word Detection for Chinese by a Corpus-base Learning Method," *Computational Linguistics and Chinese Language Processing*, vol.3, no.1, February, 1998, pp.27–44.
2. Chien, L.F., "Fast and quasi-natural language search for gigabits of Chinese texts," *Research and Development in Information Retrieval, ACM-SIGIR*, Seattle, 1995, pp.112–120.
3. Dai, Y., Khoo, C. S. G. and Loh, T. E., "A New Statistical Formula for Chinese Text Segmentation Incorporating Contextual Information," *ACM SIGIR*, 1999.
4. Khoo, C. S. G., Dai, Y., and Loh, T. E., "Using Statistical and Contextual Information to Identify Two-and Three-Character Words in Chinese Text," *Journal of the American Society for Information Science and Technology*, 53(3), pp.365–377, 2002.

5. Lai, Yu-sheng and Wu, Chung-hsien, "Unknown Word and Phrase Extraction Using a Phrase-Like-Unit-Based Likelihood Ratio", *International Journal of Computer Processing of Oriental Languages*, Vol. 13, No. 1, 2000, pp.83–95.
6. Meknavin, S., Charoenpornsawat, P., Kijsirikul, B., "Feature-based Thai Word Segmentation," *Natural Language Processing Pacific Rim Symposium* (NLPRS'97),1997
7. Sproat, R. and Shih, C., "A Statistical Method for Finding Word Boundaries in Chinese Text," *Computer Processing of Chinese and Oriental Languages*, 4, 1990, pp.336–351.
8. Wu, Zimin and Tseng, Gwyneth, "ACTS: An Automatic Chinese Text Segmentation System for Full Text Retrieval," *Journal of The American Society for Information Science*, 46(2):83–96, 1995.
9. C. C. Yang, J. Luk, S. Yung, and J. Yen, "Combination and Boundary Detection Approach for Chinese Indexing," *Journal of the American Society for Information Science, Special Topic Issue on Digital Libraries*, vol.51, no.4, March, 2000, pp.340–351.
10. Yeh, C.L. and Lee, H. J., "Rule-based Word Identification for Mandarin Chinese Sentences –A Unification Approach," *Computer Processing of Chinese and Oriental Languages*, vol.5, no.2, pp.97–118, 1991.

Using a Light-Weighted Cache Pool to Leverage the Performance of Web Picture Databases

Chao Li, Chun-xiao Xing, and Li-zhu Zhou

Department of Computer Science and Technology
Tsinghua University, Beijing, 100084, China
li_chao00@mails.tsinghua.edu.cn,
{xingcx,dcszlz}@mail.tsinghua.edu.cn

Abstract. In most web digital libraries, picture databases play an important role in making the contents more completed, illustrative and attractive. However, in some special purpose (e.g. for education or for news publication) digital libraries, in which picture databases are absolutely necessary at the back end, the phenomenon of "hotspot" often pulls down the response speed of queries on picture databases and makes the whole performance decline seriously. This paper brings forward the idea of caching "hot" data in a pool to alleviate the above problem. And by utilizing the characteristics of "hotspot", we implement a light-weighted cache pool which is very effective in improving picture access performance.

1 Introduction

Today most digital libraries provide a convenient access of their contents to users through Web. Generally speaking, pictures play an important role in making the contents more completed, illustrative or even attractive. And in some digital libraries for special purposes, such as for education or for news publication, there are so many pictures that maintaining a picture database to manage the pictures at the back end is absolutely necessary.

There are several system implementations [1] [2] [3] [4] and research papers [5] [6] on picture databases. And many of them contribute to the key problems such as picture classification, annotation or description, as well as searching methods based on certain ways of classification and annotation. These contributions offer various methods to mange or schedule the picture databases. However, in some digital libraries for special purposes (e.g. our THADL [7] for ancient Chinese architecture course learning), the phenomenon of "hotspot" occurs frequently, i.e. in a given time interval, more than half of the users focus on accessing (or, repeat to access) less than 0.5% contents. This phenomenon may become even severe when a teacher assigns a survey or discussion project on certain topics. And the phenomenon of "hotspot" often pulls down the response speed of queries on picture databases and makes the whole performance decline seriously. Similar situation may occur in other special purpose digital libraries, such as sports news digital libraries during the period of a famous game. The performance degrading may bring boring experience to users and bury all your construct effort with complains.

T.M.T. Sembok et al. (Eds.): ICADL 2003, LNCS 2911, pp. 521–532, 2003.

This paper brings forward an idea of caching "hot" pictures in a pool at the web application level to alleviate the "hotspot" performance decline problem of picture databases. As compared with equipment upgrading, this software-style method is more cost-effective and scalable. Actually, the idea of "caching" has a long history in Computer Science and the cache can be placed anywhere as long as you think it is suitable to pay some space cost to gain some time benefit. Initially, cache technology is used to smooth the speed difference between CUP and main memory in the field of computer architecture. Later on, the idea of "caching" is applied in other fields, such as: Web cache [8] in the field of Internet to reduce the network traffic, increase the response speed, and help load balance; connection pool [9] in the field of database-backed web application to save the database connection cost; etc. No matter in which context a cache is applied, no matter it is implemented by hardware or software, and no matter it is placed in system level, data management level, or application level, cache technology has some common problems to answer, such as: how to guarantee the freshness and validity of data in a cache? How to schedule or replace data in the cache when a cache is full? And how to keep a certain hit rate so that a cache is worthy of the cost? Although there are several classical methods or discussions to answer the above problems [10] [11] [12], the cache problem is always an open problem [13]. As the user access patterns, the data distribution characteristics and cache performance metrics are varied, there is no "golden solution" for cache problems.

For the above reasons, we try to put the application characteristics into full consideration to achieve an efficient solution. First, once picture data are deposited into the database, few of them will be revised, i.e. they will be there or be dropped off completely, and common users only view them through Web. So, our cache doesn't have to deal with the routine write-back matters, which makes the cache replacement algorithms light-weighted and much more efficient. The light-weighted property is very important as a heavy-weighted cache may make the workload of the system even heavier. Second, as mentioned before, the "hotspot" phenomenon here is time-related. To fully utilize this property, we arrange our cache under the combining principle of FIFO and LRU. Besides, a multi-map structure is specially maintained for history access records to accelerate the decision-making for cache replacement, and the pool size of the cache is adjustable so that this method is more scalable and adaptive.

With all these considerations, a picture cache pool is implemented on the picture database of THADL. The experiment results really show that this method can efficiently alleviate the performance degradation problem of picture database when "hotspot" occurs. And the same way can be applied to similar problems of web applications, as long as "hotspot" phenomenon of picture database pulls down the performance of the web application.

This paper is arranged as follows. In the preparation section, a brief comparison of several web picture database construct techniques is present. After that, our picture cache pool algorithm is analyzed and described in a detail. Then, the experiment and the results are given. And lastly, we discuss the future work and draw the conclusion.

2   Picture Database Construct Techniques

Although the method of our picture cache pool is adaptive, and the idea can be applied to different picture database implementations, it is still necessary to have a brief review on several construct techniques of picture databases. This is also for the belief that choosing a suitable technique can help to make our method more effective and more efficient.

Basically, there are three technical solutions to construct a picture database (as Fig. 1 shows), i.e., (1) purely on a file system, (2) purely on a relational DBMS, and (3) on a mixture of a file system and a relational DBMS.

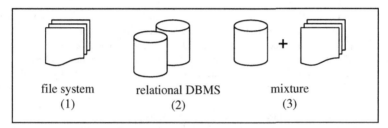

file system	relational DBMS	mixture
(1)	(2)	(3)

Fig. 1. Three solutions for web picture databases

But for the high cost of maintaining the integrity of file catalogs and the doubted query performance, the first solution is always abandoned. And the third solution is often deployed in the following way: hand all of the description information (or say, metadata) of the pictures to a relational database, often in a well-scheduled schema; store the pictures as files in a file system, often arranged in a directory tree according to the classification of the pictures; and maintain a file path reference from the metadata to the picture files, often as a text-type column in the relational schema. The advantage of this solution is that it is easy and convenient to implement for those development staff who are used to developing traditional database-backed web MIS applications without multimedia contents in the databases, while the disadvantages of it are the difficulties of maintaining the integrity (between metadata and picture data) of databases, and the performance restrictions when the quantity of users and pictures are increased beyond certain level.

For the considerations listed above, we prefer the second solution for the following reasons. First, storing both metadata and picture data in a relational database (picture data appear as a column) can make the whole database schema clean and simple. Second, by utilizing the power of DBMS, integrity maintenance becomes an easy and efficient job. And the last attractive reason is that the service performance is much more promising than the other two solutions, for some performance optimizations by DBMS.

So, the second solution is adopted in our picture database construction, and the following implementations and experiments are all based on it. For the briefness of the following description, we abstract the relational schema for pictures as (ID, description, picture_data).

3 Method Descriptions and Analysis

For the clarity of the analysis of our picture cache pool method, we present two traditional picture database retrieval methods before our method (to be compared with). And for the ease and unification of the description of the three methods, we abstract web picture database access pattern into three steps as a representative. At the end of this section, we list the detailed algorithm description in the form of pseudo code.

3.1 Web Picture Database Access Pattern

For the ease and unification of the description of the three methods, we abstract web picture database access pattern into three steps as a representative. In the implementations, these three steps correspond to three web pages (as Fig. 2 shows).

Step one: user browses the catalog or raises a query to find his/her interests.

Step two: the interested content's descriptions together with its hyperlink to the picture are shown, user reads the descriptions and decides to enter into the hyperlink to see the picture or not.

Step three: show the picture linked by the previous page.

So, in short, request is submitted in Page I, metadata are shown in Page II, and the real picture appears in Page III.

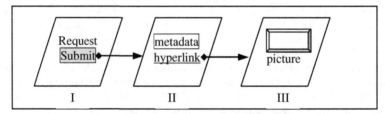

Fig. 2. Three-step web picture database access pattern

3.2 Picture Database Retrieval Methods

For the clarity of the analysis of our picture cache pool method, we present two traditional picture database retrieval ways before our method.

Method I: Simple retrieval without any optimizations. Query the database for corresponding metadata to generate Page II after Page I is submitted. And query the database for the picture data to generate Page III after the hyperlink of Page II is entered.

Method II: Prefetch picture to reduce the response time of the third page. After Page I is submitted, query the database for corresponding metadata (to generate Page II) and the picture data (to prefetch them into memory for later use). While after the hyperlink of Page II is entered, get the picture data from memory to generate Page III. Of course, this kind of method is impossible in practice for its bad scalability. We list it here just for performance comparison, as its response time of Page III is expected to be the shortest (can act as a performance upper limit) before the memory is filled up.

Our method: Using the picture cache pool to reduce the response time of the third page. Query the database for corresponding metadata to generate Page II after Page I is submitted. After the hyperlink of Page II is entered, check the picture pool to see if the requested picture is in it. If it is in the pool, get the picture data from the pool to generate Page III and update the history access records accordingly. Otherwise, query the database for the requested picture data and update the pool. The details of how to update/build the pool as well as the replacement algorithm is in section 3.4.

The reason why we only cache pictures in the pool but not the corresponding metadata is based on the following considerations. First, as the size of pictures is much bigger than that of metadata, the time cost of retrieval and load pictures is much higher than that of metadata. Second, users may not enter into the hyperlinks to see the pictures after they see the metadata in Page II, in fact, few percents of the pictures will be requested, which are the real "hotspots". So, caching pictures in the pool is aimed to solve the bottleneck of requesting pictures on "hotspot".

3.3 Analysis and Comparison

For Method I, the good side is that the implementation is simple and direct, but the bad side is that the performance will degrade severely in the occurrence of "hotspot".

For Method II, although through the way of prefetch, the response time of Page III is shortened much than that in method I, but this kind of prefetch consumes so much memory that the memory will soon be used up as the requests mount up. So the bad scalability restricts this method when the number of users increases. Yes, one variation of this method is the selective prefetch, which can control the memory using, but this is another way of cache and we don't put it in the discussion scope of this paper.

Compared with the two above methods, our method is expected to have the following advantages. First, compared with Method I, the database query and connection times are decreased because of the picture cache pool, which helps to reduce the workload of the database server and thus guarantees the performance to some degree under the rigorous situation of "hotspot". Although the DBMS may maintain a cache for itself, this cannot save the cost of database connections. Second, when the picture cache pool hits, the response time of Page III is almost as short as that in Method II; and the usage of memory can be controlled within a suitable scope by setting the size of the pool, which also shows the superiority in controllability and scalability than Method II and ensures the performance of application server to some extent. Third, when a picture is missing from cache pool, the cache pool system really has to pay some cost for the cache pool update/replacement (if the hit rate is 0%, this method is even poor than Method I), but it is worthy of the cost as long as the cache hit rate is kept to a certain percentage (the property of "hotspot" help to insure the percent); and by careful design of the data structure together with the algorithm in implementation, this kind of cost can be compensated.

3.4 Algorithm Description

In this section, we first introduce several important data structures we use to maintain the cache pool, and then give the algorithm.

Major Data Structures. The picture pool is implemented as an object list, in which a picture is an object item in the list. The length of the list (i.e. the size of the pool) can be set to a suitable value according to the number of "hotspot" pictures we predict.

For the quick look-up of the picture pool, a picture pool index is maintained in the form of a hash table (named *poolIndex*). In this hash table, the key is the ID of the picture, and the corresponding value is a 2-tuple: (Freq, Entry). Here, "Freq" records the access frequency of the picture (for the decision on which item to be dropped from the cache pool on update/replacement), and the "Entry" is the entry value of the corresponding picture in the picture pool (serve as a pointer from the index to the pool).

For the quick decision at the time of pool replacement (to find the picture whose access frequency is the lowest, and in all the pictures of the same "Freq" value whose enter time is the earliest), we adopt a hash tree (a map/hash table that further guarantees that it will be in ascending key order, sorted according to the *natural ordering* of its keys). The key of this hash tree (named *accessFreq*) is "Freq", and the corresponding value is a list of picture IDs with the same "Freq" value, i.e. each "Freq" value can be mapped to multiple ID values, which forms an ordered multimap [14].

Fig. 3 tries to give an example to illustrate the data structures.

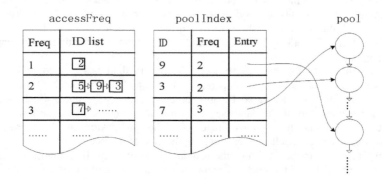

Fig. 3. Major data structures

Algorithm. The algorithm is implemented in an object-oriented style, but for the plainness of the description, we list it here in a mixture of object-oriented and procedure style.

```
Input: ID  //the ID of the requested picture
Output: picture_data
{ the followings have already been declared/existed
  List pool[size];
  HashTable poolIndex;
  HashTree accessFreq;}

Program Begin
  if (ID in the keys of poolIndex) //cache hit
  then begin
        curFreq:=poolIndex[ID].freq;
        poolIndex[ID].freq++;
        accessFreq[curFreq].IDs.remove(ID);
        accessFreq[curFreq+1].IDs.appendAtEnd(ID);
        return pool[poolIndex[ID].Entry];
      end
  else begin  //cache miss
        query database for picture_data(PD) by ID;
        if (ID not exits in database)
        then return //return a code: "not exits"
        else begin
              if (pool is full)
              then begin
                minFreq:=accessFreq.minKey;
                victimID:=
                   accessFreq[minFreq].IDs.remove(0);
                //get and remove the first ID from
                //the list of the min frequency
                pool[poolIndex[victimID].Entry]:=PD;
                tmpInd:=poolIndex.remove(victimID);
                tmpInd.Freq:=1;
                poolIndex.add(ID,tmpInd);
                accessFreq[1].IDs.appendAtEnd(ID);
              end
              else begin //pool is not full
                pool[pool.length]:=PD;
                tmpInd.Freq:=1;
                tmpInd.Entry:= pool.length;
                poolIndex.add(ID,tmpInd);
                accessFreq[1].IDs.appendAtEnd(ID);
              end
              return PD;
           end
        end
  end
Program End.
```

In the listed algorithm description, there are two things that can be parameterized. The first one is the size of the pool, which can be set to the approximate number of "hotspot" pictures. If this number is not certain, it can be adjusted according to the hit rate during the serving course of the pool. And the second one is the way to deal with *accessFreq* in the whole process of the pool, which reveals the pool management strategy. In our implementation, we arrange it following the principle of both LRU and FIFO, which is proved very efficient under the work mode in our application. Of course, this can be adjusted according to the characteristics of the application to achieve a satisfied improvement.

4   Experiment Results

4.1   Experiment Environment

This experiment environment is implemented as the picture database prototype of THADL. We use JSP to implement most of the web presentation work, and JAVA Beans to implement most of the processing logics.

Test Environment. As shown in Fig. 4, the test environment consists of two severs. Sever I acts as a back-end database server, and Sever II acts as an application server and web server (where the JSP Engine resides). The two servers are connected through the connection of LAN, and the users issue HTTP requests to Sever II to access our system through the campus network.

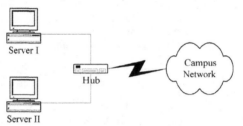

Fig. 4. System topology

System Configuration. The configuration (hardware, OS, and software) of Server I and Server II are listed in the columns of Table.1 respectively.

Data Set of the Picture Database. Now, all the THADL contents in the form of pictures are loaded in our picture database. The total picture number is 6,641, and the formats are bmp and jpeg. The size of the picture is varied, from 10KB to 100KB. Actually, the picture database has no restrictions on the picture formats, as the system

Table 1. System configuration

	Sever I	Sever II
CPU	AMD alhlon(tm)XP 2000+	AMD alhlon(tm)XP 2000+
Memory	512M DDR	256M DDR
OS	Windows2000 Professional	Windows2000 Advanced Server
DBMS	Oracle9i	
JVM	jdk1.4.0_03	jdk1.4.0
JSP Engine		Resin 2.1.6
JDBC		oracle.jdbc.driver.OracleDriver

treat all of them as binary streams. And at the time of display, the system will check out the format from the corresponding metadata and present the picture in a proper way. The picture database has no restrictions on the number of the pictures and the size of the pictures too, as long as the storage system can hold them all. For lager scale applications, we can utilize some massive storage solutions such as SAN [15][16][17].

4.2 Experiment Method

In the first section, the definition of "hotspot" has been given as follows: in a given time interval, more than 50% users focus on accessing (or, repeat to access) less than 0.5% contents. Of course, the shorter the time interval and the more the number of users, the more rigorous is the workload that the system has to afford. In our experiment, to make the result clear, we fix the time interval to 1 second, and change the number of users from 10 to 200 (increased by 10). That is, the toughest workload in the experiment is 200 simultaneous users/sec.

To simulate the simultaneous users and record the response time of each user request, JMeter 1.8 [18] is used. To drive JMeter to work as we expect above, a JMeter test script should be prepared for each time of the test. We generate the test scripts as follows: first randomly select 33 (6,641 * 0.5%) picture IDs, second randomly select 0.5n (n is from 10 to 200) users, and last randomly assign the selected IDs to the selected users and assign the left users with a random number between 1 and 6,641. This three-time-random procedure not only accords with our criterion of "hotspot", but also guarantees the evenness and impersonality of our experiment. You may define you own criterion of "hotspot", i.e. change the percent of selected picture IDs and users in step one and two accordingly.

4.3 Result

Although less database connection times and memory consumption rate are all potential benefits of our method as analyzed in section 3.3, we put the request response time here as our main metrics of performance as the request response time is the most concerned aspect, no matter from the side of the users or from the side of our initial motivation.

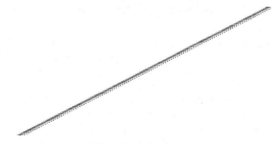

Fig. 5. Average response time of the three methods

Fig. 5 shows the average response time of the three methods (section 3.2). We can see that as the number of simultaneous users/sec increases, the same trend of the three methods is that the response time increases. But it is obvious that our new method, the picture cache pool method, always remains the lowest.

Fig. 6 and Fig. 7 show the minimum and maximum response time of the simultaneous user requests respectively. From these figures, we can see that, in most of the cases, the minimum response time of our method is under the value of 500ms, and the maximum response time of our method is under the value of 10,000ms. Compared with Method I and II, the upper bound and lower bound of the response time of our method have the obvious advantages, and thus guarantees the outstanding performance of our method.

Fig. 6. Minimum response time of the three methods

Fig. 7. Maximum response time of the three methods

5   Discussions and Future Work

Putting the characteristics of the web picture database of our digital library into full consideration, we work out this light-weighted and cost-effective solution, a picture cache pool, which is proved to be efficient in the aspect of improving the response time.

Although adopting a general-purpose reverse Web cache can also improve the performance of such kind of web application, it is not as economic as our method (more hardware consumptions and more sophisticated controls), at least. Furthermore, using a heavy-weighted cache may make the workload of the system even heavier. And this just is one of the reasons why we choose our light-weighted solution.

And although the database connection pool technology can do some help for saving the database connecting time, it cannot lighten the query process and response work of database servers. Besides, under the tough workload, e.g. more than 20 simultaneous user requests/sec, the performance is very poor. So, it is not very suitable for alleviating the "hotspot" problem as we describe above.

However, this method is not restricted to the application scenario of THADL. In fact, it can be applied to other similar scenarios. First, this idea can be used in the environment of other kinds of web picture database construct techniques (section 2). Second, this idea can not only be applied to web picture database applications, but also can be applied to other web database applications, e.g. web Patent databases, as long as the object in the database shares the similar physical properties and performance demands with the pictures in picture databases. Third, the implementation details can be varied according to the different application scenario, such as the size of the cache pool and the management strategy of *accessFreq* (section 4.3). Last, the same idea can do help to other larger scale applications, if only the storage system can hold all the data objects. And we can utilize some massive storage solutions such as SAN to make the storage system more scalable. But in this situation, there are still other issues to consider, e.g. as there are several separate storage devices work together, how to schedule the data placement to achieve a better performance? etc. This could be a promising research in the near future for THADL project.

6   Conclusion

In some special purpose (e.g. for education or for news publication) digital libraries, in which picture databases are absolutely necessary at the back end, the phenomenon of "hotspot" often pulls down the response speed of queries on picture databases and makes the whole performance decline seriously.

This paper brings forward an idea of caching "hot" pictures in a pool to alleviate the above problem. In the preparation section, a brief comparison of several web picture database construct technologies is present. After that, our picture cache pool algorithm is analyzed and described in a detail. Then, in the experiment, by utilizing the characteristics of "hotspot", we implement a light-weighted cache pool on the picture database prototype of THADL, which is proved very efficient in improving the performance. And lastly, we discuss the application scenarios and the future work.

Acknowledgment. Our work has been supported by the National Natural Science Foundation of China under Grant No. 60221120146, and the National Grand Fundamental Research 973 Program of China under Grant No.G1999032704.

We are grateful to HUANG Yao-qi for his hard work in preparing the test scripts and cleaning up the numerous and jumbled test results.

References

1. http://vasc.ri.cmu.edu/idb/
2. http://www.atlantaopera.org/photodb/index.cfm
3. http://collage.nhil.com/
4. http://www.quanjing.com/
5. Schreiber, A.T., Dubbeldam, B., Wielemaker, J., Wielinga, B.: Ontology-based photo annotation. Intelligent Systems, IEEE [see also IEEE Expert], Volume. 16, Issue. 3, May–June (2001) 66–74
6. Shneiderman, B., Kang, H.: Direct annotation: a drag-and-drop strategy for labeling photos. Information Visualization, 2000. Proceedings. IEEE International Conference on , 19-21 July (2000) 88–95
7. Xing Chun-xiao, Zhou Li-zhu, et al.: Developing Tsinghua University architecture digital library for Chinese Architecture study and university education. Proceedings of 5th International Conference on Asian Digital Libraries (ICADL2002), December (2002) 206–217
8. Greg Barish, et al.: World Wide Web Caching: Trends and Techniques. IEEE Communications Magazine Internet Technology Series, May (2000) 178–185
9. http://www.caucho.com/resin/ref/db-config.xtp#Pooling-Configuration
10. Scheuermann Peter, Shim Junho, Vingralek Radek: A case for delay-conscious caching of Web documents. Computer Networks and ISDN Systems, Volume: 29, Issue: 8–13, September, (1997) 997–1005
11. Miller Douglas W, Harper III D T: Performance analysis of disk cache write policies. Microprocessors and Microsystems, Volume: 19, Issue: 3, April, (1995) 121–130
12. Dolgikh Dmitry G., Sukhov Andrei M.: Parameters of cache systems based on a Zipf-like distribution. Computer Networks Volume: 37, Issue: 6, Dec, (2001) 711–716
13. Gupta Devidas, Malloy Brian, McRae Alice: The Complexity of Scheduling for Data Cache Optimization. Information Sciences, Volume: 100, Issue: 1-4, August, (1997) 27–48
14. http://java.sun.com/docs/books/tutorial/collections/interfaces/map.html
15. Clark Tom: Design Storage area network. Addison Wesley Longman, Inc (1999)
16. Marc Farley: Building Storage Networks. Chinese edition by China Machine Press (2000)
17. Li Chao, Xing Chun-xiao, Zhou Li-zhu: Study on Data Placement and Access Path Selection in FC-SAN Virtual Storage Environment. Proceedings of 5th International Conference on Asian Digital Libraries (ICADL2002), December (2002) 423–424
18. http://jakarta.apache.org/jmeter/index.html

An Object-Oriented Approach for Transformation of Spatial Data from Relational Database to Object-Oriented Database

Siew Teck Kiong and Wang Yin Chai

Faculty of Information Technology, Universiti Malaysia Sarawak, 94300
Kota Samarahan, Sarawak, Malaysia
siew_tk@yahoo.com
ycwang@fi.unimas.my

Abstract. Classical data models like the relational data models have proven to have limitations in modeling spatial data in many aspects. In the latest computer technology, object-oriented database technology extends support for the complex data types to deal with the today's complex applications. There are various attempts in integrating the two models to exploit the strengths of these two models to develop a flexible environment for the complex applications. However, these new data models such as extended and extensible relational database technology still suffer from various problems. In view of this, the perusal in this study is to develop an approach which constitutes the transformation system to transform spatial data fully from the relational database to the object-oriented database. The approach pursued is an object-oriented approach whereby the development of the transformation system is achieved through the applications of object-oriented features such as data abstraction, inheritance, polymorphism and behavior modeling. This involves the structural and the behavioral design of the transformation system around the objects.

1 Introduction

This study is in a period of intensive change and innovation regarding database technology. A different trend can be seen in the history of the last 20 years of software development. Relational database systems (RDBMS) revolutionized database management systems in the 1980s, and object oriented programming languages are revolutionizing software development in the 1990s. This results from the increasing needs to store and manipulate complex data in the databases as the complex data is getting imminent across a wide range of applications such as multimedia applications for the Wed, specialized application domains including medical care, geographical, space, and exploration systems and even financial systems. In addition, the classical databases based on the hierarchical, the network, and the relational data model have proven to be insufficient for these complex applications in many ways (Herring 1992). Due to these limitations, there is an urgent call for the advancement to the classical data models. This acts as an impetus to the development of the object-oriented database. Object-oriented model becomes the

T.M.T. Sembok et al. (Eds.): ICADL 2003, LNCS 2911, pp. 533–543, 2003.

trend of today database technology. The trend is towards the extended support for these additional data types, being called complex data which are spatially related. However, the dominant database in the real world applications is still the relational database due to the proliferation of the relational systems, and their dominance will remain in the near future. In view of the today database market and the needs to store and manipulate the complex data in the databases, there are various efforts in integrating relational and object-oriented systems. However, there are significant problems existing in these approaches in modeling the complex data. In view of this, this paper discusses a full transformation modeling for spatial data from relational databases to object-oriented databases, instead of the integration.

The rest of this paper is organized as follows: Section 2 gives a brief overview of the status and problems of today database market. Section 3 explains the research methodology adopted for the transformation. Section 4 describes the overall architecture of the full transformation system. Section 5 shows the performance of the transformation system, and finally, conclusion is given in Section 5.

2 Status and Problems of the Current Database Market

In spite of advances in the object technology, the dominant database in the market is still the relational database over the last decade. Many companies have made a significant investment in relational databases. They have actually converted many applications using CODASYL, and other data organizations to use relational databases. These companies are rightfully leery of converting once again to object technology. As the applications grow, huge amount of data is stored in the databases. Thus, all these factors hinder the adoption of object technology in these companies. In view of these situations, there are various efforts in continuing research in integrating the relational and object-oriented databases in order to enhance the database management in handling the complex applications using the rich features of the object-oriented systems while continue keeping the data in the relational databases. The followings are some of the approaches and problems encountered in bringing together the strength of both relational and object-oriented data models in order to produce a flexible database management environment that can be adapted to various applications' requirements.

The major area is extending the RDBMS with object-oriented capabilities to intelligently manage spatial data, which is a key development underway in database technology. Many organizations now want the RDBMS platform extended in an evolutionary way to leverage existing investments and applications while enabling the DBMS to support new applications. An implementation of a spatial data model in the context of object-relational databases consists of a set of spatial data types and the operations on those types. Much work has been done over the last decade on the design of spatial Abstract Data Types (ADTs) and their embedding in a query language. ORDBMS also support object-modeling techniques in the database. These techniques include encapsulation, inheritance, polymorphism, and others that push the benefits of OO application development into the database server itself. In any discussion of ORDBMS, the primary goal of object-relational vendors such as Informix is to build extensions on the relational platform to handle complex and spatial data. While ORDBMS are beginning to deliver some object capabilities, they do not offer the same level of support as the object DBMSs for features such as encapsulation, inheritance, pointer navigation and tight integration with object-oriented programming languages to provide persistent storage of native objects created in an application. Object features will be implemented differently in OR given its underlying data structure of tables and columns [12]. Adding flexible support for arbitrarily complex user-defined application objects and logic within the database server is not an easy task. Besides, the impedance mismatch becomes significant for application programming and querying.

In addition to the above integration approaches, there are attempts to study the data transformation in this technology age. This is converting relational database to object-oriented database system to benefit from the object-oriented technology in improving productivity and flexibility. At the same time these attempts try to avoid the problems encountered in the integration approaches by converting the data to the object-oriented databases and building the application on top of the object-oriented databases. In this way, the applications have no problem in benefiting from the object-oriented features such as inheritance, polymorphism, and data abstraction. The whole applications can be developed in the object-oriented programming environment, and this solves the problem of the "impedance mismatch". There are attempts in designing environment for migrating relational to object-oriented database systems. However, there are problems encountered in these attempts. Due to the semantic gap between the two data models, the schema transformation cannot be done fully-automatically. It involves SQL to extract information as attempted by Jens Jahnke 1996. This may give rise to the problem of "impedance mismatch".

3 Methodology

The study proposes the following steps in developing an algorithm for the transformation of the spatial data from the relational database to the object-oriented database. Besides, the methodology provides a systematic approach to solve different problems encountered during the transformation and is theoretically sound in preserving the semantics of the spatial data transformed.

Initially, the standard relational and object-oriented databases are identified in the development of the new model. As the relational and object-oriented databases are incompatible (Egenhofer etal 1992, Herring 1992, Worboys 1994), it is a prerequisite to study the structures of the source and target databases in detail for any semantic ambiguities. This is performed by querying both databases' schemas for the schema information. In order to resolve these semantic ambiguities, the semantic reconstruction is required based on the schema information obtained. Since the spatial data is transformed from relational to object-oriented databases, the study proposes an semantic reconstruction to enrich the object-oriented schema rather than relational schema. This aims to have the equivalent databases by preserving the semantic of the two databases equivalently in order to ensure the minimum loss of information. However, the constraint that the object-oriented database is not modified must apply during the semantic reconstruction so as not to modify the existing applications and functions of the database. To satisfy the constraint, the study employs object-oriented features such as data abstraction, and behavior together with inheritance and polymorphism properties to enrich the object-oriented schema. Based on the enriched schema, the mapping rules are derived that map the schema of the relational database to the schema of the object-oriented database, such that all the constraints or properties in the relational database are preserved in the object-oriented database. These are the steps required in the schema transformation, and hence constituted the schema transformation process.

With the completion of the schema transformation, the next step is to migrate the spatial data from relational database to object-oriented database by using the mapping rules derived. In this process, the data needs to be extracted from relational databases before depositing to the object-oriented databases. For the data extraction, it is necessary to know the data format and syntax that is stored as in the table header in the meta data of the relational databases. This requires the exploration of the table header for the meta data. The behavior modeling that is supported by the object-oriented system then performs the data deposition into the object-oriented database. This step forms the data transformation process.

It is also important to support the automatic transformation of the data manipulation operations. This is termed as the application transformation process in this study. It emphasizes on the retrieval of the deposited data and information, especially topology of the spatial data from the object-oriented database. Hence, the application consists of the retrieval and topology operations. This involves the dynamic modeling of the object-oriented database that can be achieved through the inheritance, and polymorphism concepts. The study describes a methods-based framework and event detection mechanism through the trigger activities of the operations to provide a reactive capability for handling spatial data topology in object-oriented database. This also makes the database active in manipulating the spatial data.

The above three processes make up the transformation system. The study proceeds to design the transformation system by applying the object-oriented analysis and design techniques that enable the implementation of the transformation system in the object-oriented environment. This is essential to solve the problem of the impedance mismatch that prevails in the relational database management systems. The design consists of the static and dynamic modeling of the transformation system. The Unified Modeling Language (UML) is applied to aid and simplify the design of the system, especially in the dynamic modeling. To have the system independent design, two standard databases are used in the design so that the transformation system designed is widely applicable to the databases as long as they are based on the standard requirements. A geo-relational database is utilized as the source data in the transformation, while a standard object-oriented GIS database as the target database.

With the completion of the design, there is sufficient detail to general code for the transformation system. This step is to perform the prototype implementation of the system in the object-oriented programming language. This is quite a trivial task as there is a tight coupling between the object-oriented designs and programming languages.

Finally, the transformation system is tested in order to ensure the full transformation of the spatial data. A sample of the spatial data from the source database is transformed to the target database. Then an analytical testing is performed on the sample data to evaluate the efficiency of the transformation system in terms of data accuracy and loss of information.

4 The Proposed Architecture of the Transformation Algorithm

A framework of an algorithm of the full transformation for spatial data from source database (VPF) to target database (OODGM) is proposed. In order to provide a generic transformation algorithm, two standard data models are selected for this study, namely Vector Product Format (VPF) and Object-Oriented Geo-Data Model (OOGDM). The Vector Product Format (VPF) is a standard format, structure, and organization for large geographic databases that are based on a georelational data model and are intended for direct use. VPF is developed by the U.S. Defence Mapping Agency and has become part of the DIGEST international standard formats for representing geographical data. OOGDM is a new object-oriented model for GIS, and is based on the concepts introduced by the Object Database Management Group (ODMG). Based on object-oriented design principles, OOGDM provides support for data types most commonly found in GIS-applications (Andreas 1997).

The algorithm is able to provide a systematic approach to solve different problems in schema and data transformation and must be theoretically sound in preserving the semantics of the source data being transformed without loss of information. It also enables the application transformation at the level of the transformed data. The following sections describe the algorithm which constitutes the new model of the transformation for the full transformation of spatial data from relational to object-oriented databases. The transformation algorithm has a three-layer architecture as shown in Figure 1 consisting of:

- Schema transformation process
- Data transformation process
- Application transformation process

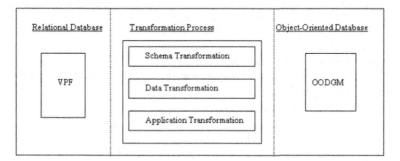

Fig. 1. The Architecture of the Transformation Algorithm

4.1 Schema Transformation

The schema transformation process is the most crucial step in the database transformation in order to produce an equivalent database especially in preserving the semantics of the relational data when transformed to the object-oriented data structures without the loss of information. Furthermore, this task of schema transformation must be as generic as possible so that it becomes possible to do schema transformations in a system-independent way.

Firstly, doing a good job at the schema transformation requires a solid understanding of both databases. This will entail the semantic differences between two databases. VPF employs the topological data structure representation. The nodes are stored as pairs of xy coordinates, and edges are ordered collections of two or more tuples and referenced by their endpoints. Polygons are modeled by referencing the first edge. Topology data are stored together with the geometry in the primitives' tables. For the topology data, only the connectivity information between nodes, edges and faces are provided. These structures represent directed or undirected graphs that do not consider the exact geometry of their vertices.

OODGM uses a boundary representation to describe the geometry. The geometry of individual elementary feature is represented directly using xy coordinates. Points are indicated by their xy coordinates. Polylines, and polygons or holes in the regions are modeled directly using a set of xy coordinates. Thus, the geometry of the elementary features can be retrieved directly without computation. This kind of representation is termed object-centered. There is no support for the topology data.

Next, the study performs semantic reconstruction to resolve any ambiguities between the schemas of VPF and OODGM spatial databases In terms of the geometry, there are equivalent representations for the nodes and edges primitives in both databases. However, for the face primitive, based on the information obtained from face and region schemas defined in VPF and OODGM respectively, face is represented indirectly in terms of the edges in VPF, and region is represented directly in terms of the boundary vertices in OODGM. In preserving the equivalent semantics in both databases, this indicates that semantically there is a need to reconstruct and redefine the schema of OODGM based on the semantic differences. The database structure of OODGM cannot be modified. Thus, in this semantic reconstruction step, this study will construct the virtual data structure which contains the geometry of the edges in term of a collection of vertices. Accordingly, the boundary vertices forming the region in OODGM are defined by the vertices of the edges. Then there is an equivalent structure between the virtual data structure and the OODGM structure. This study proposes to have this semantic reconstruction on the fly in order not to modify the existing schemas of both databases as shown in Figure 2. The following computations are performed:

a. Firstly, from the first edge information given for face geometry in VPF, all the edges forming the face are computed using the algorithms.

b. Secondly, the geometry of the edges, which are stored as a collection of points, is retrieved from the edge primitive database.

c. Finally, a virtual data structure is used to store the geometry of edges on the fly before being transformed to target database.

In terms of topology, the topology connectivity information is stored as the primary keys of the primitives in VPF. However, there is no support for the topology data in OODGM. The study defines a virtual data structure equivalent to the data structure of topology connectivity information in VPF to store the topology connectivity information for the OODGM. Object-oriented system supports data abstraction. A collection of data together with a set of operations on that data is called an abstract data type or ADT. So the study defines the data structure of ADT to be the virtual data structure for the topology connectivity information as indicated in Fig. 3.

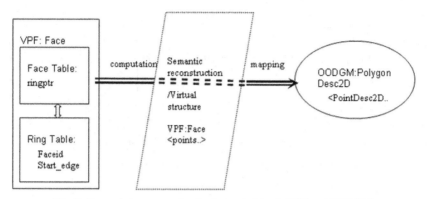

Fig. 2. Semantic reconstruction for face primitive in VPF and OODGM

Finally, the study derives the mapping algorithm based on the semantic reconstruction for the geometry and topology of the primitives. It adopts the ADT concept in OODGM. Based on ADT's definition, it consists of a data structure to store data and operations on the data. For the mapping purposes, the study examines the data structure first. A data structure is a construct that can be defined within a programming language to store a collection of data. For example, arrays and structures, which are built into C++, are data structures. ADT is not another name for a data structure. The study defines the data members of the data structure of ADT to be constituted of the geometry data member and topology data member. Then, based on the VPF tables, the following mapping algorithm as indicated in Figure 4 and Figure 5 are derived.

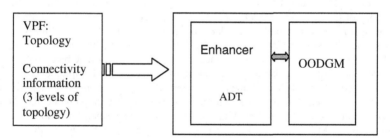

Fig. 3. Topology semantic reconstruction added to OODGM

Primary keys of the primitives in VPF map to the indexes of the respective data structure of ADT.
Geometry of the primitives in VPF maps to geometry data member of the data structure of ADT which is made up of the child classes of the elementary features in OODGM.
Topology connectivity information maps to the topology data member of the data structure of ADT.

Fig. 4. Mapping algorithm for the transformation

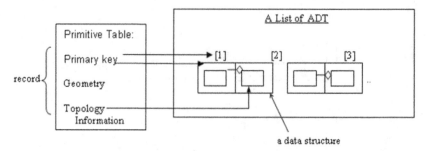

Fig. 5. Mapping rules from VPF to OODGM

4.2   Data Transformation Process

This process involves two steps in transforming the spatial data from VPF to OODGM. It involves the extraction of spatial data from the VPF and then deposition of the data into the OODGM. The data extraction is the extraction of spatial data from the source database. To achieve this, it is appropriate to create a generalized table interpreter which can be the user-defined data type defined to contain the metadata of the tables in the object-oriented programming environment based on the schema specification. The table interpreter can accommodate and facilitate the dynamic interpretation of the table, and enables the extraction of the records from the tables based on the metadata.

The data deposition is concerned with the deposition of the extracted data to the target's database. This is very much related to the mapping algorithms discussed in Section 4.1. There can be direct deposition whereby the topology information and geometry of the primitives in VPF are deposited directly to the topology data member and geometry data member of the data structure of ADT which is composed of the ADTs and the spatial database of OODGM. To achieve the data deposition in OODGM, the study employs the concept of data abstraction. Object data models provide data abstraction by a separation of the interface and implementation of an object. Abstract data typing "hides" the internal representation of objects from the outside world and protects the internal algorithms that implement the objects' behavior from external meddling. Changes in attribute implementation do not result in changes to the ADT interface. Further more, this information hiding capability allows the development of reusable and extensible software components. This is an advantage of having ADT. Based on this concept, the study defines the 'insert' operation to be included in the operations of ADT to deposit the data in the database. Then, a request is sent to the insert operation to deposit the data in the database, as Figure 6 illustrates. If we are on the program's side of the wall, we will see an interface that enables us to deposit the data in the database. In addition, object-oriented system supports the behavior modeling.

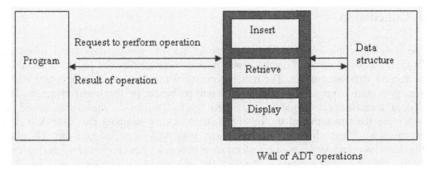

Fig. 6. ADT operations provide access to a data structure

4.3   Application Transformation Process

The application transformation process focuses only on the retrieval of the geometry and topological data structures of the elementary features in OODGM. This is performed by creating the interface which is defined by the wall of ADT operations enabling us to send the 'retrieve' operation to the database as shown in Figure 6. Then a system of messages is sent between the classes to trigger the operation to retrieve the data. The geometry and topology data are stored in the respective structures in the database. They need not be computed from the different structures using the table join. Instead, they can be retrieved directly from the data structures through the accessors methods of the operations of the primitives' classes. We can create a chain of events that will trigger the operations to extract the geometry of the topological structures using the accessors. For one data structure to send a message to another data structure to activate the operations to extract the geometry of the later data structure, the accessibility to one another data structure can be done through the inheritance concept. This type of dynamic modeling abstracts the topology behavior of the elementary features in the OODGM.

5 System Performance

System evaluation is concerned with any data inaccuracy and loss of information. This study has adopted an efficient approach named the 'check digit' approach to evaluate the system. The use of the 'check digit' approach will significantly check for the transcription errors including the incorrect or transposed data. This has great implications in evaluating the system in terms of data accuracy and any loss of information. From the check digit values, the amount of errors which is a measure of the unreliability of the system in the transformation can be detected. The less error, the more reliable the system. The study computes the values of reliability as a measurement of the efficiency of the transformation system in terms of the errors incurred from the check digit values. From the reliability values computed for each primitive in the sample data, the analysis has justified that the transformation system is perfect in the transformation of the spatial data from the relational database to the object-oriented database.

6 Conclusion

The development of a transformation model for the spatial data from relational database to object-oriented database was in part motivated by the problems faced by the current database market. The model consists of the three-layer architecture which is a systematic approach to solve different problems in the transformation. The schema transformation process supported by the model is theoretical sound in preserving the semantics of the relational databases by mapping the equivalent data structures after the semantic reconstruction, without loss of information. The data transformation and application transformation processes are supported by the features of the object-oriented models. Neither the schema transformation nor the data transformation process require any change to the data and both relational and object-oriented systems. This is important since it will greatly enhance the practical applicability of our model for most areas where standard relational and object-oriented systems are used today.

The primary contribution of this paper lie in the use of object-oriented features in enabling the transformation of the spatial data without modifying the target database. First, the data portion of ADT is designed to deal with the schema transformation involving the semantic differences between the two databases, as well as the topology connectivity information which is not supported by the target database. This necessitates the ability to derive the mapping algorithm between two databases. Second, the operations of ADT which act as an interface models the dynamic behavior of the transformation process. The ADT operations will trigger the operations of the database, which are implemented by the methods in the object-oriented database. Together with the inheritance and polymorphism features, the operations will model the geometry and topology in the object-oriented database.

References

1. Andreas Voigtmann.: An Object-Oriented Database Kernel for Spatio-Temporal Geo-Applications. University Munster (1997)
2. Arctur D.K., J.F. Alexander, K. Shaw, M. Chung, M. Cobb.: OVPF Report:Object-Oriented Database Design Issues. Internal research report for the Naval Research Laboratory, Stennis Space Center, MS.(1995a)
3. Arctur D.K., J.F. Alexander, K. Shaw, M. Chung, M. Cobb.: OVPF Report:Issues and Approaches for Spatial Topology in GIS. Internal research report for the Naval Research Laboratory, Stennis Space Center, MS. (1995b)
4   Cristiano Sacchi, Licia Sbattella.: An Object-Oriented Approach to Spatial Databases. Dipartimento di Elettronica e Informazione, Milano, Italy. (1994)
5   Daniel A. Keim, Hans-Peter Kriegel, Andreas Miethsam.: Integration of Relational Databases in a Multidatabase System based on Schema Enrichment. Institute of Computer Science, University of Munich. (1993)
6. David K. Arctur.: Design of an Extensible, Object-Oriented GIS Framework with Reactive Capability. University of Florida (1996)
7. Egenhofer, M. J., and A. U. Frank.: Object-Oriented Modeling for GIS. *URISA Journal*. 4:2, pp. 3–19 (1992)
8. Herring, J.R..: TIGRIS: A Data Model for an Object-Oriented Geographic Information System. *Computers and Geosciences* 18:4, pp. 443–452 (1992)

9. Frank, A.U.: Requirements for a database management system for a GIS. Photogrammetric Engineering and Remote Sensing, 54, 1557 (1988)
10. Jean-Luc Haivant.: Introduction to Database Reverse Engineering. Laboratory of Database Application Engineering, University of Namer (2002)
11. Jens Jahnke, Wilhelm Schafer, Abert Zundorf.: A Design Environment for Migrating Relational to Object-Oriented Database Systems. Proceeding of the International Conference on Software Maintenance (1996)
12. Judith R. Davis.: Informix-Universal Server Extending the Relational DBMS To Manage Complex Data. DataBase Associates International November, (1996)
13. Joseph Fong.: Converting Relational to Object-Oriented Databases. Computer Science Department, City University of Hong Kong, Kowloon, Hong Kong (1997)
14. Joseph Fong & Bloor, C.: Data Conversion Rules from Network to Relational Databases. Information and Software Technology, vol 36, (1994), no 3, 141–153
15. Nidia Posada, David Sol.: Object Oriented Database for a GIS. Universidad de las Americas, Puebla.(2000)
16. Sasa M. Dekleva.: Advances in Database Technology. DePaul University, School of Accountancy, 1E. Jackson Blvd, Chicago (1996)
17. Scott W. Ambler.: Mapping Objects To Relational Databases. SIGS Books/Cambridge University Press, (1998)
18. Shailesh Agarwal, Christopher Keene, & Arthur M. Keller.: Architecting Object Applications for High Performance with Relational Databases. OOPSLA Workshop on Object Database Behavior Benchmarks and Performance Austin (1995)
19. Worboys, M.F.: Object-Oriented Approaches to Geo-Referenced Information. International Journal of Geographical Information Systems. Pp. 385–399 (1994)
20. Worboys, Michael F. & Hearnshaw, Hilary M. & Maguire David J.: Object-oriented Data Modelling for Spatial Databases, International Journal of Geographical Information(1990)

Improved Variable Ordering for ROBDDs

P.W. Chandana Prasad, M. Maria Dominic, and Ashutosh Kumar Singh

Faculty of Information Science and Technology
Multimedia University, Jalan Ayer Keroh Lama, 75450 , Melaka, Malaysia.
{Penatiyan.prasad,murugeson.dominic,ashutosh.kumar}@mmu.edu.my

Abstract. Present here is a novel algorithm for minimization of the Reduced Ordered Binary Decision Diagram (ROBDD) by finding the best variable ordering for any Boolean function. Selection of ordering relation is achieved by considering each sub functions.

1 Introduction

Variable ordering relation plays a significant role for sizes of Reduced Ordered Binary Decision Diagrams (ROBDDs), which have found various range of applications such as circuit checking, logic synthesis and test generation [3], [4]. Therefore selection of appropriate ordering is challenging task, which is already handled by many researches [5]. Some heuristics have been also published to solve this problem [6].

We describe a new variable ordering algorithm, which exploits the notion of sampling in the context of variable ordering. Our sampling technique involve analyzing each sub Boolean function using ordering and repeating technique followed by eliminating each variable from the Boolean function to obtain a new Boolean function in order to find the rest of the variable order.

2 Background

We review some of the basic definitions [1] here for reference.

A binary decision diagram (BDD) is a directed acyclic graph (DAG). The graph has two sink nodes labeled 0 and 1 representing the Boolean functions 0 and 1. Each non-sink node is labeled with a Boolean variables v and has two out-edges labeled 1 (or *then*) and 0 (or *else*). The If–then–Else or ITE operation is a recursive form of the Shannon decomposition theorem given as below:

$$ite(f, g, h) = f \cdot g + \overline{f} \cdot h \tag{1}$$

Shannon's decomposition theorem can be shortly written as:

$$f = ite(x_i, \ f = ite(x_i, f\big|_{x_i=1}, f\big|_{x_i=0}) \tag{2}$$

T.M.T. Sembok et al. (Eds.): ICADL 2003, LNCS 2911, pp. 544–547, 2003.

An *ordered binary decision diagram (OBDD)* is a BDD with the constraint that the input variables are ordered an every source to sink path in the OBDD visits the input variables in ascending order.

A *reduced ordered binary decision diagram (ROBDD)* is an OBDD where each node represents a distinct logic functions.

Bryant [2] proved that the ROBDD is a canonical form for a logic function; that is, two functions are equivalent if, and only if, the BOBDD's for each function are isomorphic. It is well known that the size of the ROBDD for a given function depends on the variable order chosen for the function.

3 Proposed Method

Definition

Assume that the Boolean function *f* is a combination of sub sets of $f = \sum_{i=1}^{n} f_i$ with the variable order set of $S = \{x_1, x_2, ..., x_n\}$. Consider *J* as the variable sequence for the particular set *S*.

Following algorithm explains the procedure of finding the best variable order for different type of Boolean functions.

Algorithm

1. Input Boolean function *f* and variable order *S*
2. Sort the pattern of *f* according to the sub function f_i (length is depend on the number of variables it consist with)
3. If all the sub functions are with same number of variables as in *S* and each variable repeats in all sub functions,
4. {
5. for *j* =1 to *n* do
6.   {
7.   find the variable with less number of complement form in whole function
8.   pick that variable and move it to position *j* on *S*
9.   delete the variable from entire function
10.   take rest of the variable as new function
11.   }
12. }
13. else
14. {
15.   if sub expression does not contain repeated variables, then
16.   {
17.   for *j* = 1 to *n* do
18.   {

19. $S_j = f_i(x_k)$, where $i,k= 1$ to n

20.   }

21.   }

22.   else

23.   {

24.   find the sub function f_i with the minimum number of variables

25.   get the variable in that sub function that repeats more times in entire function

26.   for $j = 1$ to n do

27.   {

28.   pick the variable and move it to j on S

29.   }

30.   }

31.   }

32.   }

Following examples describes different type of Boolean expression for selection of variable orders with the use of above-mentioned algorithm.

Example 1

$$f = \overline{x_1} \cdot \overline{x_2} \cdot \overline{x_3} + x_1 \cdot \overline{x_2} \cdot x_3 + \overline{x_1} \cdot x_2 \cdot x_3 + x_1 \cdot x_2 \cdot \overline{x_3}$$

Since this Boolean expression consist with same number of variables and each variable repeats in all the sub functions, we check for the variable that has less number of complement form in the entire function. x_3 and x_2 have the lesser number of complement forms i.e. 2 each. So we can select either one as the 1ˢᵗ variable in S. If we select x_3 as the 1ˢᵗ variable, then it will be place in S, and eliminate that variable (both the normal variable and the complement form) from entire Boolean function.

$$f = \overline{x_1} \cdot \overline{x_2} + x_1 \cdot \overline{x_2} + \overline{x_1} \cdot x_2 + x_1 \cdot x_2$$

The Boolean function with the rest of the variables, consider as a new Boolean function and follow the same steps until we found all variables. According to the same rule what we used earlier, we can find x_2 as the variable with lesser number of complement form. Since we select x_2 as the 2ⁿᵈ variable in S, x_1 will be the last variable.

So the final variable order that gives lesser number of nodes will be: $x_3\, x_2\, x_1$ or $x_2\, x_3\, x_1$. Figure 1 shows the comparison for the above variable order.

Example 2

$$x_1 \cdot x_2 \cdot x_3 + x_4 \cdot x_5 + x_6$$

Since each variable repeats same number of times than the best possible variable order will be the variable sequence in the Boolean expression. So we can select the best variable order as $x_1\, x_2\, x_3\, x_4\, x_5\, x_6$. According to the basic Boolean rules if we change the variable order inside the sub functions and change the sub function location, it cannot effect the Boolean expression. This means for the above type of Boolean expression we can take the best variable orders as: $x_1\, x_2\, x_3\, x_5\, x_4\, x_6$ or $x_1\, x_2\, x_3\, x_6\, x_4\, x_5$.

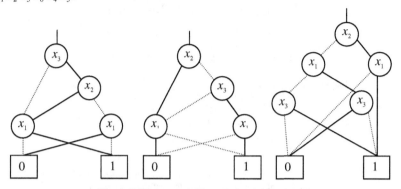

Fig. 1. Different variable ordering for ROBDDs

4 Conclusion

A more efficient and easy method was described in which produce the best possible variable order for any ROBDDs. Example comparisons were shown using the BDD software package. Even though this system gives the best variable order it is not the unique one. Instead of the variable ordering produced by this system, there could be more other ordering that can give the same number of nodes, but not less what this system had given The present results show that time and space complexity depend heavily on variable ordering.

References

1. Akers, S. B.: Binary Decision Diagram. IEEE Trans. On Comp., Vol. 27. (1978) 509–516
2. Bryant, R. E.: Graph–Based Algorithm for Boolean Function Manipulation. IEEE Trans. On Comp., Vol. 35. (1986) 677–691
3. Friedman, S. and Supowit, K.: Finding the Optimal Variable Ordering for Binary Decision Diagram. Design Automation Conf., (1987) 348–356
4. Steven, J. F. and Kenneth J. S.: Finding the Optimal Variable Ordering for Binary Decision Diagrams. IEEE Trans. On Comp., Vol. 39. (1990) 710–713
5. Yang, C. and Ciesielski, M.: BDS: A BDD–Based Logic Optimization System. IEEE Trans. On CAD of IC and Sys., Vol. 21. (2002) 866–876
6. Bollig, B. and Wegener, I.: Improving the Variable Ordering of OBDDs is NP–Complete. IEEE Trans. On Comp., Vol. 45. (1996) 993–1002

Applying UML to a New Model for Transformation of Spatial Data from Relational Database to Object-Oriented Database

Siew Teck Kiong and Wang Yin Chai

Faculty of Information Technology, Universiti Malaysia Sarawak,
94300 Kota Samarahan, Sarawak, Malaysia
siew_tk@yahoo.com
ycwang@fi.unimas.my

Abstract. The design of the new model for the full transformation of the spatial data from relational database to object-oriented database is performed in object-oriented environment using the object-oriented analysis and design tools. It consists of the static modeling of the software components of the new model. It involves the creation of the design class diagram, which indicates all the classes and the relationships identified in the new model. In addition, it couples the dynamic modeling of the software components which produces an active database in completing the data transformation and application transformation processes. This has contributed significantly in eliminating the prevailing problem of "impedance mismatch" in the database technology. The dynamic modeling involves the trigger mechanism that interacts among the software objects to accomplish the transformation. The application of UML enhances the design of the new model especially in the dynamic modeling of the active database. The artifacts created in this design phase by applying UML provide a significant degree of the information necessary to implement the transformation system. Besides, UML creates an easily reusable, extensible and maintainable design of the new model especially in the distributed computing environment.

1 Introduction

The study presents a practical look at the issues involved with the full transformation of the spatial data from relational to object-oriented databases by applying the UML to the design of the new model. Two standard databases, namely VPF and OODGM, are employed in the design of the new model for transformation system. The transformation system provides tools for the extraction of the data from the relational database, deposition of the extracted data to the object-oriented database, as well as the retrieval of the deposited data. The study is not performing any of these processes in the relational environment. The whole process is carried out in an object-oriented environment by using an object-oriented programming language to alleviate the common issue of "impedance mismatch" prevailing between the applications and databases as in the relational environment. In accordance with this proposal, the study uses the object-oriented analysis and design techniques to create a new model design for the transformation system. This study focuses on the design of the transformation system using UML. The study is making use of the object technology whereby there

T.M.T. Sembok et al. (Eds.): ICADL 2003, LNCS 2911, pp. 548–551, 2003.

is an emphasis on defining logical software objects that will ultimately be implemented in an object-oriented programming language. These software objects have attributes and methods.

The rest of this paper is organized as follows: Section 2 portrays the architecture of the transformation system. Section 3 gives an analyze phase of the static modeling of the new model. Section 4 describes the design of an active database of the new model. Section 5 applies the activity diagrams of UML in enhancing the dynamic modeling of active database. Finally, conclusion is given in Section 6.

2 Transformation System Architecture

Initially, the study considers the architecture of the new model for the transformation system. It is essential to have an architecture that produces the reusable components of the transformation system. The study adopts the three-tier architecture which has three distinct and separate layers namely presentation layer, application logic layer, and storage layer. The first tier, the presentation layer, is relatively free of application processing, and its main concern is to forward task requests to the middle tier. The middle tier is the application logic layer in performing the required tasks of applications. It is the core of the applications, which consists of the software components. The third tier, the storage layer, is storage for the databases.

According to this architecture, the study focuses on the middle tier in the design of the transformation system. The application logic layer consists of the domain objects and services objects, which accommodate the three processes of the transformation system namely, scheme, data and application transformation processes. The domain objects define the concepts required in the schema transformation process, while the services objects define the interfaces to perform the data and application transformation processes. Hence, the design of the transformation system involves solely the application logic layer, which is the middle tier. That means, the study needs to design the domain and services objects to develop the transformation system.

3 Analyze Phase in Static Modeling of New Model

Analyze phase of the object-oriented design technique focuses on identifying all the entities and their relationships of all the objects defined in the transformation system. The object-oriented step in this phase is the decomposition of the problem into individual concepts or objects. A conceptual model is a representation of concepts in a problem domain [6]. The primary task of the analysis phase is to identify different concepts in the problem domain and document the results in a conceptual model. Thus, the objective of this phase is to build a conceptual model, which identifies all the concepts existing in the problem domain and illustrates meaningfully these concepts in terms of the relationships among them and their attributes. These concepts are the representation of real-world things in the conceptual model but constitute the software classes in the construct phase. It emphasizes on identifying all the concepts required in the transformation processes, which involve scheme, data and application transformations. Here, the study is building the conceptual model through the following steps:

a.   Identifying the candidate concepts;
b.   Establishing the associations necessary to record relationships between the concepts;
c.   Adding the spatial data to the concepts necessary to fulfill the information requirements.

The UML contains notation in the form of static structure diagrams in which no operations are defined to illustrate conceptual models. In the UML, the term 'class' is used, but not 'concept'. Based on this term, the analysis phase is a process to identify the classes, attributes of the classes, as well as the relationships between the classes in the system.

4 Design Phase for an Active Database of the New Model

The study has completed the analyze phase in identifying all the classes involved in the transformation system. Now it proceeds to the design phase that focuses on the identification of methods required in the full transformation of the spatial data from the source database to the target database. In object-oriented environment, the classes are coupled with the methods to dynamically model their behavior in the object-oriented database. Hence, the new model of the transformation system is able to have the database in the object-oriented environment actively involved in the events. The software objects with both the attributes and methods constitute the active database. The events are implemented by the operations of the respective classes as well as the interactions among the classes. These operations are given by the methods of these classes. Hence, during this step a logical solution based upon the object-oriented paradigm is developed. The heart of this solution is the creation of interaction diagrams, which illustrate how objects will communicate with other objects by sending messages to complete operations. Following the generation of interaction diagrams, design class diagrams can be developed which summarize the definition of the classes (and interfaces) that are to be implemented in software.

5 Activity Diagrams in Enhancing Dynamic Modeling of Active Database

The collaboration diagrams show the interactions between objects of different classes via messages passing to trigger a chain of operations upon stimulating a system event. Now, the study is examining the behavior of these operations by using the activity diagrams of the UML. An activity diagram is designed to be a simplified look at what happens during an operation or a process. The entire activity is attached to the implementation of an operation. The purpose of this diagram is to focus on flows driven by the internal processing (as exposed to external events). It is different from a flowchart such that a flowchart is normally limited to sequential processes whereas an activity diagram can handle parallel processes. Activity diagram prevents unnecessary sequences in the behavior and to spot opportunities to do things in parallel. This can improve the efficiency and responsiveness of a behavior especially in the active database of the new model of the transformation system.

In this paper, the swimlanes are included to produce activity diagrams that have the ability to expand and show who has the responsibility for each activity in a process. An activity diagram may be visually divided into "swimlanes ", each separated from the neighboring swimlanes by the vertical solid lines on both sides. Each swimlane represents responsibility for part of the overall activity, and may eventually be implemented by one or more objects. Swimlanes are good in that they combine the activity diagram's depiction of logic with the interaction diagram's depiction of responsibility. This enhances the dynamic modeling of the active database that involves the trigger mechanism among the software objects. In illustrating this, the study presents some of the activity diagrams to represent and understand the behaviors for the situations that are dominated by workflow across many classes.

6 Conclusion

This study has coupled the new way of modeling, the UML (Unified Modeling Language), in explicitly designing the new model in the full transformation of the spatial data from the relational database to object-oriented database. UML contributes expressively in developing an easily extensible, easy-to-understand, and ready-to-use system. It is a modeling language, and has a tight mapping to a family of object-oriented programming languages, so facilitating the construct phase of the system. It plays a very important role in dynamic modeling. Due to the complication arising from the intercommunication via the messages in the chain-operations of the trigger mechanism, UML has simplified the tasks in a systematic way. The study has adopted two types of diagrams to achieve this: (i) an collaboration diagram which illustrates how objects interact via messages to fulfill the tasks, (ii) an activity diagram which is designed to be a simplified look at what happens during an operation or a process. The entire activity is attached to the implementation of an operation. The study has significantly verified that UML aids in improving the efficiency and responsiveness of the system especially in dynamic modeling of an active database in object, and thus results in the effective creation of the software systems of the new model in object-oriented environment.

References

1. Ali Bahrami.: Object-Oriented Systems Development Using the Unified Modeling Language. McGraw-Hill Book Co-Singapore (1999)
2. Craig Laman.: Applying UML and Patterns. An Introduction to Object-Oriented Analysis and Design. Library of Congress Cataloging-in-Publication Data (1998)
3. Cristiano Sacchi, Licia Sbattella.: An Object-Oriented Approach to Spatial Databases. Dipartimento di Elettronica e Informazione, Milano, Italy (1994)
4. David K. Arctur.: Design of an Extensible, Object-Oriented GIS Framework with Reactive Capability. University of Florida, Gainesville, FL 32611, USA.(1996)
5. Fatima Pires, Claudia Bauzer Medeiros, Ardemiris Barros Silva.: Modelling Geographic Information Systems using an Object Oriented Framework. Relatorio Tecjico DCC – 13/93.(1993)
6. Fowler, M.: Analysis Patterns: Reusable Object Models. Reading, MA.: Addison-Wesley (1996)

Proxy Searching of Non-searchable and Poorly Searchable Open Access Archives of Digital Scholarly Journals

Péter Jacsó

University of Hawaii, Department of Information and Computer Sciences,
2550 The Mall, Honolulu, HI 96882
jacso@hawaii.edu

Abstract. Many high quality, open access scholarly journals have been published on the Web. However, many of them do not offer a search program to find articles in their article archive. They provide access only via browsing through/digging down the volumes, issues, and table of content pages. Archives of many other open access scholarly journals do offer search options, but these have often very limited capabilities, lacking even such essential full-text search features as exact phrase searching. Both types of archives, however, can be searched using as a proxy the advanced options of some of the Web-wide search engines, such as Google, AllTheWeb and WiseNut, which spider the open access sites hosting the archives of full-text articles in HTML, Word and/or PDF format. The paper demonstrates the efficiency and – in case of directly searchable archives – the much higher precision and relevance of searching the archives by proxy.

1 Introduction

Traditional publishers of scholarly print journals, such as Elsevier, Springer Verlag, and MCB University Press have expensive and capable information storage and retrieval, or database management systems to offer sophisticated access to the full text of the large digitized collections of articles for their subscribers. All of them allow the use of Boolean operators, truncation of search terms, searching for exact phrase, limiting the search to specific fields, such as title, abstract, author or keywords (descriptors). Some of the programs allow restricting the search to journals, volumes or issues which the libraries subscribe(d) to. Elsevier's Science Direct even allows searching for cited works.

In contrast with the traditional large publishers, most of the publishers of open access single publications which were born on the Web to be distributed on the Web without any revenue or compensation, focus on providing current articles. Understandably, not much thought could be given to efficient searching of the growing archives in lack of funds and experienced systems staff for software installation, maintenance and customization. Many other single-title publishers chose to install one of the open source (free) but limited capability web site search engines.

T.M.T. Sembok et al. (Eds.): ICADL 2003, LNCS 2911, pp. 552–555, 2003.

2 The Problem

The problem is that for many of the valuable scholarly digital journals there is no appropriate access for efficiently discovering their content. The lack of search capabilities force the users to dig down in each issue and each article or other documents, such as editorials and letters to the editor, and judge from the table of contents entries and –if available- from the abstract whether the document may discuss a specific topic, product or service in which they are interested. The full text of articles, of course, can be scanned by using the browser's Find command, but it is a slow, awkward and less than perfect process, requiring too many unrewarding mouse clicks .

This happens, for example, with the archive of the *Journal of Medical Internet Research* (*JMIR*). Even though it has a relatively small archive of 120+ articles and other documents, finding all articles which discuss, for example, the MEDCERTAIN information quality assessment project and "trustmark" of health related Web sites is an arduous process.

The term appears on the table of content pages only in one article's title, and in another's subtitle. A few other titles and abstracts allude to the possible coverage of the project. A time consuming thorough check through the 15 issues of the 5 volumes of *JMIR* would discover a good dozen items which discuss MEDCERTAIN to various extent. To put this into perspective, the entire MEDLINE database has only four hits about MEDCERTAIN, and it is the one which has the richest coverage of this topic among the nearly 500 databases on the DIALOG information system.

The lack of appropriate access and efficient discovery is less obvious in case of those open access scholarly journal archives which do offer a web-site search engine. The problem, however, becomes apparent when you go beyond the single word query. The case of the WebSTAR Search software used with one of the best Web-born information science and technology journals, *First Monday* (*FM*), illustrates the problem well. It cannot do exact phrase searching, and its relevance ranking algorithm is overly simplistic. Searching for articles which include an exact term, such as "information organization" is not possible.

The software truncates the component words to `inform` and `organ`, and finds 262 articles even when relevance is set at minimum 90%. There are 7 articles in the entire archive (as of June 20th, 2003) in which the term "information organization" appears. The rest of the "hits" retrieved include articles with one of these word variants: `inform`, `informed`, `information`, `informatics` AND one of these variants: `organ`, `organs`, `organize`, `organizer`, `organizers`, `organized`, `organization`, `organizations`. Pluralizing the word organization adds insult to injury caused by degrading the adjacent, unidirectional word order relationship of the query to a simple Boolean AND operation between the two excessively truncated original words.

The more often those word variants occur anywhere in an article, the higher its relevance rank will be. Aggregate frequency of the truncated component words of the query and their density in the article are weighted higher for relevance ranking than adjacency, proximity, position and exact phrase matching.

This explains (but does not justify that the seven articles which have exact match for the original query "information organization" were ranked by WebSTAR Search as 6th, 13th, 27th, 84th, 103rd, 181st, and 210th. Irrelevant articles which include one of the modified query words on the first page and the other on the last page or in the next paragraph, push down the relevant ones in the result list. Users get tired of the deluge of irrelevant results before they would get to the relevant articles.

There are similar problems in searching the archives of open access scholarly journals which use the ht://dig software which cannot handle exact phrases in a search query. In addition, it offers only Boolean AND, and OR operators between the words in the query, and also engages in senseless, unsolicited pluralizing, such as `informations, knowledges, shelfs`, when encountering the singular form of these words in a query. Its relevance ranking also leaves much to be desired.

3   The Solution

The Web-wide search engines used as proxy agents can provide a) much needed access to many of those open access digital archives of scholarly journals which do not have site search engines and b) far more relevant search results from those archives which use site search engines of very limited capabilities.

Using the Web-wide search engines as proxy agents merely requires the appropriate domain specification of the archive to be searched along with the query. To make the search for articles about "information organization" on the primary host site of the archive of *First Monday* the user simply invokes the advanced search template, enters the query in the exact phrase cell, and specifies the domain to which the search must be limited.

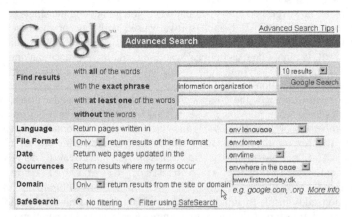

Fig. 1. Using Google as a proxy agent to search the First Monday archive

Query specification in the major Web-wide search engines is more powerful and flexible than those offered by most of the open source site-search engines. For example, Boolean NOT operator and exact phrase searching are available. Until recently, Google was my top choice for proxy searching, by virtue of its superiority in terms of the size of its database, the scope, depth and frequency of spidering relevant sites, its ability of harvesting HTML, Word and PDF documents, its speed and options for presenting results. Current test searches, however, proved that AllTheWeb, and WiseNut yielded as good results for most test queries as Google. AltaVista, and Inktomi were on par with them except for one test query shown below. The newest competitor, GigaBlast had the least results across all the archives tested, but it is worth trying. As the search engines command syntaxes are getting more and more similar, it is easy to switch from one to the other using such query syntax as `"information organization" site: www.firstmonday.dk.`

Title/Search Engine	First Monday	AllThe Web	Alta Vista	Giga Blast	Google	Ink tomi	TEO MA	Wise Nut
The Day the World Changed	6	4			7			2
After the Dot-Bomb	13	1		4	1			1
INFOMINE	27	3	1	1	4	2		6
Digital Image Managers	84	7		2	3		3	5
Media Lullabies	103	2		3	2	3	1	7
Searching for Authority	181	6	2		5	1	2	4
TOOL: The Open Opinion Layer	210	5			6			3

Fig. 2. Rank number of the exact matches in the native and proxy agents' result list

Apart from the number of hits, the biggest difference among the Web-wide search engines as proxy agents are in the relevance ranking. Relevance ranking of the results is better or much better using the proxy agents (except for GigaBlast) than using the open source web-site search engines, simply because the former are constantly being tuned and improved, while the open source search programs, understandably, get much less attention and improvement by the developers.

Special features, such as the cached versions of the articles with multi-color highlighting of the matching terms, the conversion of PDF files to HTML, or the sneak-preview of results will also determine which search engine is the best proxy agent for a user. Certain syntax limitations, such as the inability of specifying a secondary domain level in Google may also play a role in the decisions if the archive is not at the top domain of a host. For example, use of ATW as proxy is recommended when searching the *Bulletin of ASIS&T* because it allows the use of the specific secondary level domain www.asis.org/Bulletin. In Google, one can't go beyond www.asis.org and the query picks up many matching records from ASIS&T publicity announcements, not just articles from the *Bulletin*. Comparing results and their ranking from the users' preferred archives using different Web-wide search engines on a regular basis will help determine which are the best proxy agents for them.

Object-to-Multidimensional Database Mapping Algorithms

Tong Ming Lim[1] and Sai Peck Lee[2]

[1] Monash University Malaysia, School of Information Technology
2, Jln Kolej, Bandar Sunway, Selangor. Malaysia
lim.tong.ming@infotech.monash.edu.my
[2] University of Malaya, Faculty of Computer Science and Information Technology,
Kuala Lumpur, Malaysia
saipeck@um.edu.my

Abstract. An object wrapper [3,4] is a piece of middleware that provides an object view on top of a legacy database management system. But legacy database management systems such as relational database systems (RDS) and multidimensional database systems (MDS) [5,6,7] are different in many aspects from an Object-oriented Data Model. Among these aspects are semantic management, data structures and data types supported in these models. As a result, it is crucial to understand these data models in order to design and implement an efficient piece of middleware. In this paper, a short discussion on the real-world data modelling requirements is presented. Then, this is followed by a discussion on an Object View's requirements. The third section of the paper presents the architecture of the Object-to-Multidimensional Mapping Engine (O-MME) [10,11,12,13,14,15,16,17,18,19]. A detail discussion on major interfaces and classes in the Object-to-Multidimensional mapping algorithm are presented next. Issues such as data type conversion and database language statements generation are discussed in this paper also. Finally, some performance issues are presented and future possible researches are outlined.

1 Introduction

As requirements from users become semantically complex, legacy databases such as relational database systems and multidimensional database systems are not sufficient to handle requirements of these applications. Due to these demands, object-oriented database systems emerge as the next generation of database system that satisfies these new requirements. In order to satisfy these new requirements, features that an Object-oriented data model [1,2,8,9] must possess are inheritance, complex or user-defined types, object identity, association and aggregation, collection and computational completeness. With these features, applications such as CAD/CAM for engineering and multimedia information management systems could be constructed with ease. Nevertheless, the acceptance of object-oriented database systems is slow in the business sectors partly due to lack of a formal foundations. Hence, many of these applications are limited in certain software categories only. The non-procedural structured query language (SQL), simple two-dimensional table data structure and

T.M.T. Sembok et al. (Eds.): ICADL 2003, LNCS 2911, pp. 556–562, 2003.
© Springer-Verlag Berlin Heidelberg 2003

sound mathematical foundation are some of the strengths that make relational database systems (RDS) popular and widely accepted among business corporations for the last dozen years. The vast amount of investment on Information Technology (IT) systems utilising relational database technology have helped these business corporations in organising and managing data efficiently and effectively. To give up these working systems and adopt a new database technology means reinvesting human, time and monetary resources. As a result, many business corporations switch to other database technologies such as object/relational database systems or hybrid database technologies while waiting for object-oriented database technology to get mature. Multidimensional database system [6,7] (or post-relational or multi-valued database management system) is an enhanced relational database technology that emerged in the early 1970s. A Multidimensional Data Model (MDM) does not have to comply with the first normal form. MDM answered one of the problems faced by developers and users; that is to allow a table to hold another table in its field. This is one of the major enhancements besides flexible record size in the model. However, Multidimensional Database System (MDS) still don't solve all the problems faced by developers when building complex systems such as CAD/CAM and office document information (ODI) management systems.

2 Object View Requirements for Legacy Databases

The ODMG Object Data Model provides Type definition to define virtually any user-defined type, which provides an external specification and an internal implementation that is totally hidden from users. The implementation of a Type is languages dependent. ODM provides constructs such as Interface that can inherit from one or multiple parents. In addition, ODM uses EXTENDS so that a Class can inherit behaviour and state from a parent class, KEY construct permits a class to define index in order to speed up objects access and creation of an OID automatically as objects are instantiated. Simple atomic literal, collection literal such as LIST, BAG, SET, ARRAY and DICTIONARY and a set of predefined structured objects such as Date, Interval, Time and Timestamp are proposed as part of the ODMG standard. ODMG Object Data Model proposes many other features such as concurrency, transaction management, constant, exception and metadata. This part of the research will focus on essential characteristics of an Object Data Model and optional features will not be discussed and implemented in the Object-to-Multidimensional Mapping Engine.

3 Architecture of Object-to-Multidimensional Database Systems

The entire framework consists of twelve major groups of classes. They are Object-to-Legacy Mapper, ODL Parser, Datatype Converter, Persistent Storage Connection Handler, Meta Class Manager, Cache Manager, OSQL-SQL Translator, SQL Transaction Command Centre, Persistent Broker, Object Concurrency Sub System, Object Transaction Sub System, OSQL Parser, Persistent Object Manager, Persistent Object State, Virtual Proxy, and Business Classes Caster. Each component is explained in the following paragraphs.

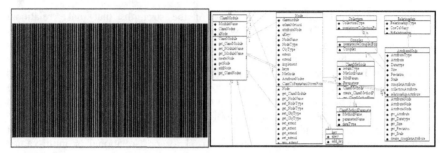

Fig. 1. Persistent Storage Connection Handler   **Fig. 2.** Meta Class Manager

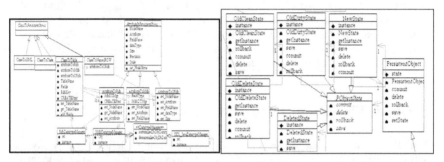

Fig. 3. Object-to-Legacy Mapper   **Fig. 4.** Persistent Object Manager

Persistent Storage Connection Handler (Fig. 1) is a set of classes that provide connection information for databases connected. It uses Singleton design pattern in the implementation of the classes in the handler. ODL Parser reads Object Definition Language input from users and this input is parsed for its syntax and semantic correctness based on the ODL grammar. ODL Parser also binds these business classes to specific object-oriented language by generating these language-specific classes. As input is parsed grammatically and semantically correct, classes of the problem domain will be saved as instances Meta Class Manager (Fig. 2) classes. Meta Class Manager maintains these classes' information active in the memory so that mapping and processing of instances of business classes are possible.

ODL Parser then instantiate classes of Object-to-Legacy Mapper (Fig. 3), which consists of type mapping, class-level, mapping, attribute-level mapping and key-level mapping mechanisms. Type mapping maps Interfaces, Structure and Class to appropriate data structure depending on the type of persistent stores. Class-level mapping involves mapping of inheritance, object persistency and extents of classes. Attribute-level mapping maps all types of attribute, which include simple type, complex or user-define type, relationship and collection.

All business classes generated by ODL Parser inherits from Persistent Object Manager (Fig. 4) if such business class is of persistent object type. Persistent Object Manager contains basic operation such as save, delete, select and update. Hence, based on the current object's state contained in Persistent Object State (Fig. 4) Controller, appropriate object operations are carried out.

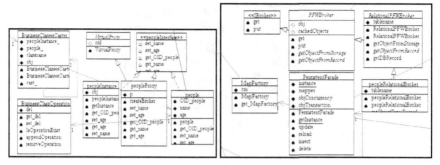

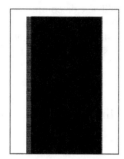

Fig. 5. Virtual Proxy   **Fig. 6.** Persistent Broker

Fig. 7. Cache Manager   **Fig. 8.** Object Concurrency Sub System

Persistent Object Manager uses lazy materialisation by implementing Virtual Proxy (Fig. 5) design pattern; where an object is materialised when users request such object. Business Classes Caster (Fig. 5) is used in conjunction with Persistent Object Manager and Virtual Proxy to materialise and de-materialise objects. Methods in Persistent Object Manager triggers methods in Persistent Object State Controller and this in turn call methods in the Persistent Broker (Fig. 6) that determines whether such object is currently in the Cache Manager or it has to be materialised by reading from persistent stores.

All instances of the business classes are maintained in the Cache Manager (Fig. 7) as soon as they are read from persistent stores or newly instantiated. It contains two-level cache management; In-Memory Cache and Persistent Cache. In-Memory Cache maintains a list of active transient objects so that traversing and navigating of these objects are quick. Second-level cache or Persistent Cache uses XML document structure to hold such objects when the main memory runs low. As an object is saved, Object Concurrency Sub System (Fig. 8) allows a user to request for a read or write lock. In this project, the locking system is kept in the most simplify manner. It implements dynamic priority locking system at the core of the sub system. Such locking system allows a user to request a higher priority in the case if it needs to grab this object and a read or write lock will grant to this object. In this project, a XML File System is created and Object Concurrency Sub System maintains a lock log in this file system. As an object request a lock, such lock is maintained in this file system. Until this user perform a rollback or commit, then, such lock is released.

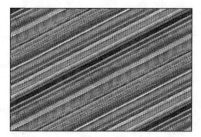

Fig. 9. Object Transaction Sub System

Object Transaction Sub System (Fig. 9), on the other hand, is designed to ensure ACID property of the persistent objects. It captures images of each object before any database operation is performed on it and upon a rollback or commit is called, then such object is removed from the transaction log. All logs are saved in the XML File System. Methods are provided to the users to validate the system's integrity in the case there is a system crash. Any incomplete transaction will be restored to its previous state. Hence, database regains its integrity.

4 Implementation of an Object-to-Multidimensional Mapping Engine

The mapping engine is implemented in Java by utilising robust and extensible software design patterns for ease of maintenance, lower coupling among classes with higher cohesion within classes. The complexity of the mapping engine gives rise to several issues. We found that the richness of the object-oriented data model needs intricate and sophisticated mapping algorithm in the mapping of class structure to legacy data structure. Due to the simplicity of the legacy data structures such as table, the mapping engine is designed to capture and manage most of the mapping detail. Hence, the legacy data structure is merely used to provide storage management. Caching facility is built as part of the research project. A cache manager implements in the project uses multi-tiers cache swapping with consistent monitoring on the availability of the working memory. This is aim to provide large object management and smooth object navigational characteristics. A transaction management system is implemented to provide concurrency and recovery features. The classical Two Phase Locking Protocol (2PLP) cannot provide the locking needs in this project. As a result, the enhanced multi-granularity locking [20,21,22] protocol imposes a fair amount of resources to maintain a rather large compatibility and commutative table active in the memory for such a protocol to work is attempted.

5 Enhancements and Conclusion

Mapping of classes to a multidimensional database system is a rather complicated piece of work due to their differences in the data models and their data structures. But, the new advanced applications and existing legacy applications have asked for a better development paradigm with a reliable and robust persistent mechanism. As a result, it is important to provide a smooth migration path in view of the slow maturity process and acceptance level among developers and database vendors. A number of enhancements are planned such as redesign using more robust framework for the mapping of class to legacy data structures, and re-examine caching and transaction techniques at the core of the middleware.

References

1. R.G.G. Cattell and Douglas K. Barry, The Object Database Standard ODMG 2.0, Morgan Kaufmann Publishers Inc. San Francisco, California
2. Alfons Kemper and Guido Moerkotte, Object Oriented Database Management, Application in Engineering And Computer Science, Prentice Hall International publication
3. Stephen Kurtzman and Kayshav Dattatri. Object-oriented wrappers for the Mach Microkernel, ROAD magazine, May-June 1996
4. Joshua Duhl. Integrating objects with relational data : architectural approaches, OBJECT magazine, May 1996
5. Douglas Barry. ODBMSs and complex data, OBJECT magazine, May 1996
6. Advanced PICK reference manual, Version 2.0, PICK SYSTEM , 1995
7. Roger J. Bourdon. Advanced Pick. Open database and Operating system, Addison Wesley, 1996
8. F. Bancilhon G. Ferran. ODMG-93: the object database standard, O^2 technology, Technical report No. 11, 1994
9. Loomis. Object Databases. The Essential. Addison Wesley, 1995.
10. Tong Ming, Lim and Sai Peck, Lee, 1997, Classes and Objects Management Multidimensional DBMS Data Model, IASTED International Conference Software Engineering (SE '97) San Francisco, 2-6 Nov. 1997, California, pp. 17–22
11. Tong-Ming, Lim and Sai-Peck, Lee, Classes And Objects Management In Multidimensional DBMS Data Model, Faculty of Computer Science and Information Technology, University Of Malaya, ISORC98 + ICSE98, Kyoto International Conference Hall, Kyoto Japan, April 20–22, 1998
12. Tong Ming, Lim and Sai Peck, Lee, 1999, Objects to Multidimensional Database Wrapping Mechanism, Annual AoM/IaoM International Conference on Computer Science, August 6-8, 1999, Westgate Hotel, San Diego, California
13. Tong Ming, Lim and Sai Peck, Lee, 2001, An Object to R/MDBMS Persistence Framework, REDECS2001 conferences, Kuala Lumpur, Oct. 22–25, 2001 UniTen-UPM.
14. Tong Ming, Lim and Sai Peck, Lee, 2002a, Object Schema Management Facilities in an Object Wrapper, The 2002 International MultiConferences in Computer Science, Las Vegas (14 Joint Int. Conferences).
15. Tong Ming, Lim and Sai Peck, Lee, 2002b, Object Schema Management Tool, Malaysia Journal Of Computer Science.
16. Tong Ming, Lim and Sai Peck, Lee, 2002c, Object Caching Using XML Document Structure, CITRA2002
17. Tong Ming, Lim and Sai Peck, Lee, 2003, Eol database language for object wrapper, International Conference on Software Engineering Research and Practice (SERP'03: June 23–26, 2003, Las Vegas, Nevada, USA)
18. Tong Ming, Lim and Sai Peck, Lee, 2003, Object-Relational Mapping Service Architecture, 3rd International Conference on Information Technology in Asia (CITA'03), Kuching Sarawak, Malaysia, July 17–18 2003

19. Tong Ming, Lim and Sai Peck, Lee, 2003, Object mapping algorithms for multidimensional database systems, The 3rd International Conference on Advances in Strategic Technologies, Kuala Lumpur, Malaysia, 12–14, August 2003
20. Hong-Tai Chou and Won Kim, 1988, Versions and Change Notification in an Object-Oriented Database System, Annual ACM IEEE Design Automation Conferences, Proceeding of the 25th ACM/IEEE Conference on Design Automation June 12–15, 1988, Anaheim, CA USA pp. 275–281
21. Wojciech Cellary and Waldemar Wieczerzycki, 1993, Locking Objects and Classes in Multiversion Object-Oriented Databases, Conference on Information and Knowledge Management, Proceedings of the second international conference on information and knowledge management, Nov 1-5 1993, Washington USA, pp. 586–595
22. Suh-Yin Lee and Ruey-Long Liou, 1996, A Multi-Granularity Locking Model for Concurrency Control in Object-Oriented Database Systems, IEEE Transactions On Knowledge and Data Engineering, Vol. 8, No. 1, Feb. 1996

An Architecture for Multischeming in Digital Libraries

Aaron Krowne and Edward A. Fox

Digital Library Research Laboratory Virginia Tech Blacksburg, VA 24061, USA
{akrowne,fox}@vt.edu

Abstract. In this paper we discuss the problem of handling many classification schemes within the context of a single digital library, which we term multischeming. This includes the tasks of representing which category describes an object in the digital library as well as understanding the browsing process which is performed by the user in this setting. We motivate this problem as related to digital library interoperability, and propose an architecture for representation of classification schemes in the digital library which solves it. We also discuss its implementation in the CITIDEL project.

1 Introduction

The use of classification schemes to organize information for retrieval and storage has a long history. Especially in the last century, classification began to receive more methodical treatment within the library science community [1–3, 14, 15]. Chiefly because of economic pressures, Dewey created his Decimal Classification system in the late 19th century [4]. Its subsequent adoption and standardization sparked a wave of theoretical and practical advances in classification. Many new classification systems appeared, including the Library of Congress Classification (LC), Ranganathan's Colon Classification (CC) [14], the Bliss Bibliographic Classification (BBC), and many others. These and similarlyinspired schemes have provided a standard, consistent, and expansible means for library patrons to efficiently find what they want (or simply browse).

These classification systems, meant for general collections, have inspired smaller-scale efforts within more specific domains. This is in spite of the fact that the general schemes are "universal" and aim to have full coverage of all human knowledge. The causes of this are chiefly social: the community most interested in making the narrow subject domain more detailed is relatively small, and further, the community which administers the general schemes is not the same as the community which is continually pushing the frontiers of knowledge within the subject domain, necessitating revisions.

This research work was funded in part by the NSF through grants DUE0136690, DUE0121679 and IIS0086227.

Examples of domainspecific classification schemes are the Medical Subject Headings (MeSH), the ACM Computing Classification System (ACM CCS), and the American Mathematics Society Mathematical Subject Classification (AMS MSC).

Classification schemes are now a nearly ubiquitous element of digital libraries. Since these digital libraries usually serve narrower communities than the general

T.M.T. Sembok et al. (Eds.): ICADL 2003, LNCS 2911, pp. 563–577, 2003.
© Springer-Verlag Berlin Heidelberg 2003

public, they typically contain materials from specialized subject domains. Therefore, they tend to utilize domainspecific classification schemes, like the ones listed previously. Further, the small scale of these communities (which may be fragmented globally and organizationally) and their focus on domainspecific work rather than standardization of the knowledge they produce has meant that multiple alternative schemes will often be in use. Lastly, ontologies not even intended for use as classification schemes may be profitably used as such, thus adding to the confusion. It is from this setting that our work emerges.

This paper is organized as follows. In the first section, we describe more specifics of the problem in the interoperable digital library setting, as well as some possible basic solutions and some requirements of a better solution. In the second section we describe how schemeinvariance is represented. In section three we present the scheme index, a structure necessary to make this representation work. In section four we discuss how the system was implemented in CITIDEL. In section five we introduce the distinction between schemelevel and categorylevel mappings. In section six we discuss interscheme mapping quality. In section seven we present data and results from the CITIDEL implementation of the system. In section eight we discuss our system and a related system. In section nine we discuss limitations and future work, followed by concluding remarks.

2   DL Classification in an Interconnected World

Digital libraries (DLs) rarely exist in isolation. The Internet has naturally become the entry point to the modern digital library. However, the Internet also facilitates interconnectedness between digital libraries. This interconnectedness can and will be used for a variety of purposes, including distribution of digital library services (federation) and direct sharing of content (harvesting). Facilitating this interconnectivity is the motivation and goal of the Open Archives Initiative [12]. The need for federated services between digital libraries was the driving force behind the development of Dienst and the Networked Computer Science Technical Reference Library (NCSTRL) [10, 11].

The Computing and Information Technology Interactive Digital Educational Library (CITIDEL) is a digital library which makes heavy use of harvesting from other digital libraries to build its catalog of content. Thus we deal chiefly with the scenario of harvesting of content in this paper. The issues and solutions we discuss should, however, be applicable to all tasks that are distributed across digital libraries, as we discuss what is fundamentally a knowledge management issue.

We already have discussed how nearly every digital library will likely have some sort of classification scheme to organize its content. However, we also pointed out that there is no standard classification scheme. Thus, the individual digital library often will have to select arbitrarily from a field of alternative classification schemes. This implies that differing classification schemes will be used by different digital libraries, even though their content domains overlap significantly. With interconnectivity, this poses a problem: categorizations supplied by one digital library may be meaningless to another. This shuts out those resources from utilization through services which build upon classification.

An illustration: if a harvested object is marked as a "nut", but "legume" describes the set of things that we call "nut" in our DL, we have a classification collision[1]. Now the user doesn't know whether to look in category "nut" or "legume" to find this object. Further, if they are simply browsing and not looking for a specific object, their task has been complicated by the need to scan over the contents of two categories. In this case, it is clear that we have no provision for interpreting and acting upon the fact that "nut" really is "legume"[2].

Indeed, in many cases, different classification schemes are really describing the same "universe" of objects. This overlap of the universes of content of digital library collections is, in fact, why harvesting is done in the first place.

One method of coping with this is to simply enforce standardization. Besides the fact that this is more easily said than done (and implies a significant wait), it is a misguided solution: domains of content (and classification schemes) often overlap only partially. We want to keep open the option of digital libraries sharing some subset of content which is the intersection of their domains, even if this intersection is not the same as the union. This mirrors the overlap in fields of knowledge. Those working with these fields have unique ontologies to describe and organize overlapping ideas or objects; these ontologies must accommodate their overall system of knowledge which others do not possess. Inasmuch as classification schemes are ontologies, we would lose something by their standardization.

On the other hand, we could fix the problem by supporting many classification schemes in parallel. Resources would simply appear under the schemes they were originally classified under (and no others). The result of this, however, would be a continual scavenger hunt through all of the schemes to find any resource, its original classification scheme being arbitrary. Furthermore, it is not really reasonable to expect users to memorize more than a few classification schemes which describe the same universe of content, nor is it likely this is practical. We are faced now with the problem of the user only being acquainted with the scheme which contains "legume": what happens if the object they want was harvested as a "bean"?

Another possibility is to add category remapping (classification conversion) to the harvesting pipeline, where metadata transforms are often already present. This has a whole host of drawbacks. Firstly, it presupposes that interoperability is only harvesting, when in fact it could also be other forms of federated services (such as searching or browsing). Secondly, it adds transforms even when implementers have relied on not needing them (such as when building services upon pure Dublin Core). Third, category transformations are very complicated, and certainly are not implemented easily in XSLT [18], the standard system for transforming XML. Fourth, it is a bad idea to make lossy transformations permanent. And finally, if one is ready to go about producing category mappings, one might consider reading on and seeing what else can be done with them.

---

[1] Note that in this terminology, it is the "description space" of the categories that is colliding, not the resources themselves. The result of this as the resources are concerned is that they become "far apart" in browsing space, rather than nearby, as would be preferred.

[2] To further compound the problem, note that it will grow in proportion to the number of schemes used by the digital libraries we harvest from. Now the user is in the position of having to guess whether the object they are looking for is classified as a "nut", "legume", "bean", or "seed", ad nauseum.

None of these possible solutions leads to a salient outcome: we are going to need a more elegant one. We need to accommodate both arbitrary schemes used during classification, as well as user familiarity with, and preference for, one or a small number of schemes at access time. Thus, we need our system to "know" about the semantic equivalence of categories between schemes, and for it to act accordingly. Digital libraries can, and must, smooth over these organizational incompatibilities. We propose a system that affords a schemeagnostic digital library; one where neither classification nor retrieval forces the selection of a particular classification scheme.

3 Representation

What does it mean to "act accordingly" in the context of semantic equivalence of categories? We know that when we ask to see objects in category X, we really want to see all objects in X, all objects in categories that X is the same as, and all objects in categories that are subsets of these. Essentially, we want the user's browse request to be translated into a wider request – what their request really would be if they knew all the classification schemes in our DL and how the content areas they describe are related to each other. We call this a multischeming system[3].

To do this, the system needs information about the semantic relationship between schemes – it needs connections between categories. This information takes the natural form of mappings.

The mappings would be defined by the maintainers of the digital library, and are of the logical form "X is a Y ", where X and Y are categories. Note that this takes care of the notion of subset; if X is a Y , but Y is not an X, then the category X is a subset of the category Y . This is our basic mapping primitive, and it is the only foundational element we need: to define equality, we simply tell the system "X is a Y " and "Y is an X".

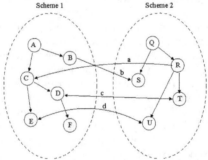

Fig. 1. A graphical representation of mappings between two schemes and their categories. A single arrow indicates that the destination category is a subset of the source. Arrows going both ways ("c" and "d") indicate that the source and destination categories are equivalent (they have equivalent content domains). Lettered arrows are interscheme mappings created by the DL maintainer; the other arrows are implicit in the hierarchy of the scheme

---

[3] This is not to be confused with multiclassification, which is the assigning of more than one category to a particular object. Our multischeming system does, however, subsume multiclassification.

We can represent these associations with a directed graph (Figure 1.) "X is a Y " corresponds to a node, labeled X, and a node labeled Y , with an arrow from Y to X. This may seem a little backwards from the natural language statement, but it makes sense for information retrieval: when we are "at" node Y and want to know which nodes we can "get to" (or "see"), logically the question is answered by following the arrows out of Y .

One of the things we will store in our system, then, is links between category "nodes" of classification schemes which represent classifications we can "see" from each node. To represent the fact that an object has a particular classification (or classifications), we must separately store pointers between objects and these category nodes (this part is just standard classification). An object may have pointers to more than one node. This is necessary because it is often difficult or impossible to classify an object as belonging entirely in one or another category.

The operation of browsing then works like this: the user selects a node (category) from a classification hierarchy with the intent of retrieving all objects which are classified as belonging in that category. This category is represented as a node, as discussed above, which we will call the "root node" of the browsing query. The system then does a lookup of this root node in the database and finds all nodes that the root node points to. This set is then merged with the set containing just the initial root node, and the search for objects is done on the resulting set. That is, the digital library translates the query "give me all objects in this category" to "give me all objects in this category or categories that are subsets of it"[4]. The above representation contains enough information for this question to be answered quite mechanically and succinctly in a standard relational DBMS.

4 Achieving the Representation: The Scheme Index

To make the above work, we need a structure which gives us that critical piece of information of all categories that should be considered along with a root query category. We call this structure the scheme index.

This index allows us to make the assumption that all the category nodes are linked together as fully as could possibly be determined by the set of "X is a Y " statements encoded by the system maintainers. What we mean by this is that, if "X is a Y ", and "Y is a Z", the system should immediately have access to the transitive fact that "X is a Z" via the scheme index. This notion should be extended to relationships not only once removed, but ntimes removed; the "distance" between nodes in the classification graph is purely accidental. We are concerned with semantics the graph represents, which is invariant regarding the number of arrows between connected nodes.

However, the distance between nodes is a practical matter, as it translates to work for the system maintainers and/or for the database system[5]. It should be enough to declare that a category, X, which contains categories A, B, and C, "is a" new category Z. The maintainer should not have to explicitly state that "A is a Z", "B is a Z", etc.

With categories of classification schemes as nodes in a large graph, and edges the semantic mappings between them as described above, it is clear that the solution to

---

[4] Note that here we do not mean proper subset.

[5] Standard relational database systems do not perform transitive closures, unfortunately.

our problem is to automate the transitive closure of this graph, at which point it becomes a complete scheme index. In other words, if it is possible to travel through this graph from category node A to category node B, then the transitive closure algorithm will create an arrow directly from A to B. The algorithm does this for all pairs of nodes, which will complete the semantics of our interscheme mapping layer.

This mapping layer effectively becomes a semantic "index" over our many schemes, which can be used as described in the previous section to expand a root category node query into a set of nodes it is semantically equivalent to (as far as browsing is concerned). This set, then, is processed conventionally for the union list of objects which are in these categories.

5 Implemented System

In this section we describe the CITIDEL implementation of the architecture outlined above. A synopsis of the whole process is given in Figure 2.

Multischeming System Initiation Process

1. Extract schemes from foreign and local sources; normalize.
2. Import normalized schemes to database, populate scheme index with parentchild links.
3. Create interscheme mappings.
4. Augment scheme index with category links from mappings file.
5. Dump scheme index from database to file.
6. Read schemes into memory as matrix; perform transitive closure.
7. Output new set of category links in SQL insert statement format.
8. Replace scheme index in database by executing SQL from last step.
9. Use index for category browsing tasks in digital library.

Fig. 2. The steps to setting up our multischeme browsing system

First, the scheme data was crawled from web sites, transformed by a script into a normalized syntax, and then imported into our database. At this stage, each category was given a unique identifier, and thus all categories become part of the same logical space (though they still kept a pointer to their originating scheme, for organizational purposes). The schemes we imported and support within CITIDEL are ACM CCS, ACM/IEEE Computing Curricula (CC, both 1991 and 2001 versions), the CoRR Subject Areas, and the Mathematical Subject Classification (MSC, which has a large computing subbranch)[6,7].

---

[6] To browse these, see <http://www.citidel.org/?op=cbrowse>.

[7] A wonderful consequence of using our system is that when schemes are revised, one can smoothly transition to the new scheme by simply loading in both schemes and creating mappings between them. The mappings are easier to create the less that has changed; one could even automate the generation of mappings to samenamed categories, then fill in the rest by hand. Optionally, one could drop the support of the old scheme from the user interface, as all resources classified under it will appear under the new scheme automatically.

Also automatically generated at scheme import time are some of the contents of the mapping "index": namely the portion that maps parent to child category within the same scheme. This parentchild information is all we need to leverage the transitive closure of our browsing engine such that we will get resource lists (and counts) at a parent node which take into account resources in all of its descendent nodes. For example, a category "Science" might have subcategory "Physics", which in turn has subcategory "Condensedmatter physics". With our system, the two implicit "has-child" relationships "Science haschild Physics" and "Physics haschild Condensed-matter physics" are all that are needed to infer that "Science" contains all resources from "Condensedmatter physics". Hence, our system solves for "free" the normally messy transitivecontainment problem in browsing by hierarchical classification schemes.

The scheme mappings in our system are made up of category mapping statements of the form contains C1, C2, for categories C1 and C2 (which are of course typically in separate schemes). A simple ASCII text file, mappings.conf, is made up of lines of this form, and serves as input to the transitive closure portion of our system. A portion of this file, mapping ACM CCS to CC, is given in Figure 3.

```
# computer vision > image processing and
computer vision contains CC2001.GV11,
CCS1998.I.4

# intelligent systems > artificial intelligence
contains CC2001.IS, CCS1998.I.2

# intelligent systems > pattern recognition
contains CC2001.IS, CCS1998.I.5

# fundamental issues in intelligent systems > artificial
intelligence contains CC2001.IS1, CCS1998.I.2

# information management > information
systems contains CC2001.IM, CCS1998.H

# information models and systems > models and
principles contains CC2001.IM1, CCS1998.H.1

# information models and systems > information systems
applications contains CC2001.IM1, CCS1998.H.4
```

Fig. 3. A portion of CITIDEL's interscheme mapping file. This is from the section mapping ACM CCS into CC 2001. That is, it supplies the data necessary to determine which categories from CCS can be "seen" from each category within CC

In our system, we map ACM CCS into all other schemes, and this is sufficient for ensuring that all resources classified under ACM CCS will appear when browsing by all other schemes, in addition to resources natively classified under those schemes. However, because we are not yet mapping the other schemes into ACM CCS as well, there are limitations in our instance of the system which have practical consequences we will discuss in the next section.

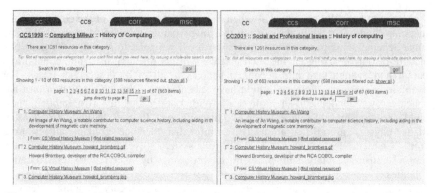

Fig. 4. A sidebyside comparison of browsing the history categories of the Computing Classification System and Computing Curricula schemes on CITIDEL. Note that the list of resources (the top of which you can see here) is the same in both cases. However, these resources are only classified under CCS

The next step after importing the schemes and writing the mappings file is to augment the contents of the current mapping index in the database with the contents of the mappings file. This is simple enough. It is handled by a script that reads and parses the mappings file and writes out links of the form (category_a, category_b) (where b is mapped into a) to the index table in the database.

After this step, the index is exported to disk, then read by a Clanguage transitive closure program. This program builds a large inmemory matrix from the data, interpreting category node identifiers as matrix indices. In our system this results in a greater than 6000×5000 matrix. Transitive closure is run on this matrix, producing a new matrix with the necessary transitive links. The program then outputs the results as insert statements of pairs (category_a, category_b), which are used to repopulate the scheme index table in the database. At this point, the index is complete.

Within CITIDEL, the "browse by subject" area leads to a simple tabbed "scheme navigator" interface, where each tab is a scheme. ACM CCS is selected by default (but can be reconfigured by the user). Below the selected tab is displayed the list of categories at the current level, along with the count of resources in that category (and all categories within it) as well as all categories in other schemes visible from it. Other than at the top level in a scheme, a synopsisstyle list of resources is displayed below the scheme navigator, once again, containing even resources classified in other schemes, as long as they were mapped into the current category.

When the user clicks on a category, the display reconfigures as is typical for standard category browsing interfaces, showing categories within the newlyselected category, and the resource list is updated to display synopses for resources at the current node or any category node mapped to it via our system.

Users also can initiate text searches from any classification category node. This dispatches a search to the search engine, then narrows the returned list of results, using the union of the current category and all categories mapped into it as a filter on the results set.

In this manner, CITIDEL allows users to browse by their favorite classification schemes without worry of "missing out" on resources categorized under the other four currentlysupported schemes. In addition, they have the option of utilizing more than one scheme if they choose, so they can exploit the strengths of one or the other depending on the information finding task. All of this is entirely without worry of whether the resource desired was classified under this or that scheme. In Figure 4, we give a demonstration of classification invariance on CITIDEL by way of sidebyside comparison.

6 Mappings and Schemes

There are really two logical levels to mappings, though there is no distinction at the implementation level. The category (or "low") level, already discussed, consists of mappings between the categories which are the "atoms" of the multischeming system and the primitive elements of all classification schemes. This is the level the system actually works with. However, we can think of the scheme (or "high") level (Figure 5) as mappings between entire classification schemes; which was really the goal of this entire enterprise.

We can view each scheme as a node in a graph, along with directed edges to other scheme nodes. We draw an arrow from scheme A to B when every category of A is mapped to a category of B. We would expect that normally schemes are mapped both ways (that is, their categories are comapped to each other). Optimally, then, we can drop the arrows and replace them with undirected edges.

However, we might not be able to do this if, for example, one scheme's content domain is just a small part of that of another scheme.

Using our multischeming system, the digital library maintainer need only make sure this highlevel graph is connected for the system to be able to guarantee that an object classified under one scheme will show up under all schemes. This implies that a new scheme can be added to the system by making mappings to a single scheme in an alreadyconnected graph. For convenience, all new schemes could be mapped to some canonical scheme C. In this case, the DL maintainer can leverage high familiarity with C to produce mappings rapidly and of a high quality. Alternatively, the DL maintainer can be opportunistic, and map a novel scheme to whatever is perceived to be the most similar scheme in the graph.

7 Mapping Quality

The previous section presented a rosy view of the schemelevel mapping situation. However, even in our CITIDEL implementation, we have not attained this ideal, which raises the issue of mapping quality. We introduce some definitions to aid in discussing and understanding this.

- A mapping M from scheme A to scheme B (or of scheme A into B) is a set of ordered pairs of the form (a,b), each of which defines a link from category a in A to a category b in B.
- We say that M is complete when there exists no $ca \in A$ such that M lacks a pair of the form (ca,b). In other words, every category of A is mapped to some category in B.

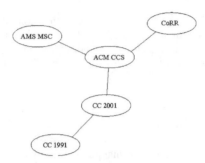

Fig. 5. A schemelevel view of optimal mappings between classification schemes (based on CITIDEL). Here we have formed a connected graph by mapping most schemes to "ACM CCS" and vice versa, except for "CC1991" and "CC2001", which are very close to each other. Note that the undirected edges mean that the mappings go both ways; an object classified with an "AMS MSC" category is viewable from ACM CCS, and vice versa. Since the graph is connected, this is true for all pairs of schemes.

> – Let MAB and MBA be complete mappings from A to B and B to A, respectively. We say that M = {MAB, MBA} is a symmetric mapping between A and B, or that A and B are symmetrically mapped

Thus, a more precise way of saying what was said in the previous section is that if the undirected graph formed by symmetrically mapped schemes in a digital library is connected, then every resource classified anywhere will be visible somewhere in every scheme.

This makes intuitive sense: a complete mapping means a resource classified in a source scheme must appear somewhere in the destination scheme; symmetric mappings mean that the same fact applies symmetrically, and a connected graph of such mappings (along with the use of transitive closure in our system) extends this symmetric relationship across all levels of graph indirection. This is what we mean by "completely schemeinvariant classification".

Due to limitations discussed later, in CITIDEL we only have complete mappings (mapping every other scheme to ACM CCS), and have no symmetric mappings at the present time. However, at the moment we mostly have resources classified under either CCS exclusively or CCS and X (where X is one of the other schemes). This means we can get "effective" classification invariance with our current set of resources simply by mapping ACM CCS into all schemes. Since objects classified natively in other schemes also happen to have CCS classifications, we luck out and do not yet need to map other schemes into CCS. This situation is illustrated in Figure 6.

The notion of quality discussed above can be extended. Completeness is a very rough metric; it does not take into account mapped categories which are mapped to the wrong places or mapped to the same place, for instance. Indeed, the notion of "wrong" may not be amenable to consensus at all. Thus, scheme mappings are ultimately as subjective as the schemes themselves. One could say that scheme mappings inherit the subjective nature of classification itself.

However, there does seem to be room for guiding metrics about the quality of interscheme mappings, based on notions of loss of information, precision, or accuracy. We leave development of such metrics for future work.

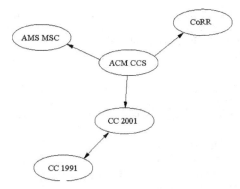

Fig. 6. A schemelevel view of a mapping situation closer to the current one on CITIDEL. "ACM CCS" is mapped into most other schemes, which means resources classified under CCS will appear when browsing via the other schemes. For resources natively classified under another scheme to appear under CCS, they must be multiclassified under both schemes (as some of our resources are). Here we have shown the two versions of CC as symmetrically mapped; an economical task due to their similarity. Note that, using this graph, one can intuit where resources classified under one scheme can appear by following the arrows.

8 Results

In Table 1, we give of statistics for our application of multischeming in CITIDEL. Transitive interscheme links are the most important links which are added by the transitive closure portion of our system, as they extend the category mappings to the set of mappings that is truly needed for schemeinvariant object visibility to work properly. The "virtual classifications" statistics show the number of true classifications that would be needed to match the effect of multischeming in our implementation. Note that we have attained the effect of a nearly tenfold classification verbosity without storing such a massive quantity of categorizations.

In Table 2, we give object interscheme visibility data. This consists of counts of objects visible natively in a scheme (those which are classified under categories in that scheme within their metadata), and those which are visible from categories in that scheme through our multischeming system. Clearly the data indicate that most resources, visible only through ACM CCS natively, become visible in all of the other schemes with multischeming. This serves as a rudimentary proof that a multischeming system can, even without complete and symmetric mappings, make objects exportable to other schemes.

Note that the counts are not all maximal (89,150) due to imperfections in the mappings. Still, the vast majority of resources become "portable", despite the small amount of work we put into the mappings, which we think is a testament to its utility.

These results do not close the book on evaluation: still useful would be studies comparing the enduser retrievability of mapped and unmapped resources (a more precise metric of mapping quality than we have given here), as well as studies of the usability of an interface which presents alternative schemes. Still, we think the figures here and the running system they are derived from are encouraging.

Table 1. Multischeming statistics for CITIDEL. In this table, "intrascheme links" refers to links between categories in the same classification scheme (implicit), and "interscheme links" refers to links between categories in different classification schemes (multischeming mappings). "Virtual classifications" are the effective classifications emulated via multischeming.

Schemes	4
Total categories	6,166
Total category mappings	244
Scheme index total links	12,419
Parentchild links	5,922
Transitive links	6,253
Intrascheme links	10,745
Transitive ancestor links	4,823
Interscheme links	1,674
Transitive interscheme links	1,430
Classified resources	89,150
Classifications	241,723
Average classifications/object	2.7
Virtual classifications	1,968,488
Average virtual classifications/object	22.1

Table 2. Counts of CITIDEL objects natively classified in each scheme, and visible under that scheme through the multischeming system

14   Krowne and Fox

Scheme Native Resources		Multischemed Resources
		89,150
		81,947
	89,150 0	81,222
CCS CC CoRR MSC	0 0	80,138

9 Discussion and Related Work

The architecture we have described above seems to have few drawbacks. The computational complexity does not increase as the digital library grows in size; instead it depends only on the number of categories within all classification schemes understood by the system. This complexity, however, only surfaces at the time of initializing or adding schemes. Processing for transitive closure need only be done offine at these times in order to update the scheme index, and is tractable on current machines for even a large number of categories (for 6000+ categories we found the transitive closure took less than a minute to run on a Pentium III 800MHz machine).

Nor does the addition of more schemes pose an increasing amount of work for the system maintainer; a new scheme need only be mapped to one other scheme for the complete invariance of our system to work.

Multiple classifications for a single object are handled naturally by representing classification as a pointer, which could be one among many, from one object into the set of classification category nodes. Adding more categories to an object poses no computational or architectural challenge to the system.

All of this has been demonstrated to be tractable, workable, and usable within CITIDEL, which is a largescale setting[8].

There exists a system called "Renardus"[9] [13], which is similar in many respects to the multischeming system we have proposed here. Renardus considers itself a gateway or brokering service; that is, its goal is to be a gobetween for users among many disparate digital library collections. In this spirit, Renardus will direct users to resources from many source collections through its text search and classification browsing systems.

Differing from most of our discussion here, Renardus has a universal subject scope. To provide its classification browsing, all schemes are mapped into the Dewey Decimal Classification (DDC). However, the user is not entirely limited to DDC, as the mapping relationships are exposed at browse time via lists of categories which are related to the current DDC category. These relations are of the type "Narrower Equivalent", "Fully Equivalent", "Minor Overlap With", and "Major Overlap With", and appear in separate lists.

However, upon clicking any of these related category hyperlinks, the user is whisked out of Renardus and to the remote digital library, suddenly browsing in a completely different format. This change in interface could be jarring to users. In addition, it is questionable whether exposing category mapping relations within a category hierarchy is not too confusing in the first place.

While not a multischeming system (it is lacking the retrieval half of scheme-invariance), the Renardus architecture has much in common with ours. Its support for many mapping relationships goes beyond our containment/equivalence model[10], and is certainly worth considering.

10 Limitations and Future Possibilities

There was a conspicuous omission from the above presentation: how to create the scheme mappings which are the semantic basis of the entire system. Indeed, this is one of the greatest limitations of the current system; we have no elegant method to create the mappings. This is a major reason why we have not created full mappings for CITIDEL, settling instead for "sufficient" mappings, given the characteristics of our collection.

Hence, one of the most attractive possibilities for the future would be to develop a program which would read in a classification scheme in a standard format, then provide a convenient graphical interface for drilling down into the schemes and

---

[8] CITIDEL carries about 450,000 resources in its current catalog, with near 1,000,000 expected by 2004.

[9] See <http://renardusbroker.sub.unigoettingen.de/>.

[10] Note that in our model, "overlap" relationships cannot be expressed elegantly: to avoid damaging resource recall, the mapper must map a category to multiple destinations if its content belongs to each of them in part.

drawing connections between certain parts. It also would be useful to maintain progress metrics regarding how much of the mapping is complete, and what the fidelity of the mapping is. At the end, the program could write out the mappings in the proper format.

This process could even be bootstrapped by automated inference, utilizing resources classified across schemes to suggest initial mapping links. For our purposes, however, this was not a useful approach to develop, as we did not have many resources which were crossclassified.

This tool could accelerate the development of standard mappings between schemes in certain domains, which could then be disseminated widely, essentially eliminating the need for most digital library builders to think about making interscheme mappings.

There have been related efforts which could possibly apply here. As we mentioned earlier, classification schemes are really just a type of ontology. Also qualifying as ontologies are thesauri, which can be seen as a generalization of dictionaries [17]. Work in thesauri has lead to many knowledgebased systems to do crosslanguage information retrieval, due to their ability to make connections between concepts [6–8, 16]. In fact, the types of relationships exposed by Renardus are precisely the kind one would see in a thesaurus, suggesting that thesauri subsume classification schemes [5] and indicating that methods and tools used to work with thesauri may be applicable to our system. This possible bridging between fields deserves further attention.

11 Conclusion

In this paper, we have introduced classification schemes and discussed their importance in digital libraries. We then discussed how the nature of specialized communities of study and interoperability among digital libraries introduces the problem of "colliding" classification schemes. We proposed a model that accommodates multiple classification schemes in a single digital library such that browsing is classificationagnostic. We discussed the details of the scheme index which is central to implementing this model, and the process of creating the mappings which it relies on. We discussed the implementation of this system in CITIDEL, and its scalability. We discussed a related system (Renardus) and compared it with our multischeming system. We also exposed limitations and discussed future possibilities, where connections might be made to work in thesauri.

We hope that this paper has focused attention on the looming problem of classification collision in the interoperable digital libraries environment, as well as our proposed and implemented system which can be used to solve this problem. We think our system turns this crisis into an opportunity: one for more powerful and flexible digital library features for end users and an improved overall digital library experience.

Acknowledgements. We would like to thank the ACM for sharing their content and classification schemes with us. We also thank colleagues in the Digital Library Research Lab at Virginia Tech for their useful suggestions.

References

1. Bakewell, K. G. B.: Classification and Indexing Practice. Linnet Books, Hamden, Conn. (1978)
2. Bengtson, Betty G., Janet S. Hill (eds.): Classification of Library Materials. NealSchuman Publishers, Inc., New York, New York (1990)
3. Bliss, Henry E.: The Organization of Knowledge in Libraries. The H. W. Wilson Company, New York (1939)
4. Chan, Lois M., John P. Camaromi, Joan S. Mitchell, Mohinder P. Satija: Dewey Decimal Classification: A practical guide. Forest Press, Albany, New York (1996)
5. Dykstra, M.: LC subject headings disguised as a thesaurus. Library Journal 113(4), 42–46. (1998)
6. Eichmann D., M. Ruiz, and P. Srinivasan. CrossLanguage Information Retrieval with the UMLS Metathesaurus. In: Proc. of the 21st Annual International ACM SIGIR Conference on Research and Development in Information Retrieval, Melbourne, Australia (1998)
7. Gonzalo J., F. Verdejo, and I. Chugur: Using EuroWordNet in a Conceptbased Approach to CrossLanguage Text Retrieval. In: Applied Artificial Intelligence, Vol. 13 (1999)
8. Hull D. A., and G. Grefenstette. Querying Across Languages: A Dictionary based Approach to Multilingual Information Retrieval. In: Proc. of the 19th Annual International ACM SIGIR Conference on Research and Development in Information Retrieval, ACM SIGIR (1996)
9. Kamps, Thomas, Christoph Hüser, Wiebke Möhr, Ingrid Schmid: Knowledge-based Information Access for Hypermedia Reference Works: Exploring the Spread of the Bauhaus Movement. In: Maristella Agosti and Alan Smeaton (eds.): Information Retrieval and Hypertext. Kluwer Academic Publishers, Norwell, Massachusetts (1996)
10. Lagoze C.: Dienst An Architecture for Distributed Document Libraries. Communications of the ACM, Vol. 38 No. 4 page 47 (April 1995)
11. Lagoze, C.: The Networked Computer Science Technical Reports Library. In: Cornell Computer Science Technical Reports (July 1996) <http://techreports.library.cornell.edu:8081/DPubS/UI/1.0/Browse>
12. Lynch, Clifford: Metadata Harvesting and the Open Archives Initiative. ARL Monthly Report No. 127 (August 2001) <http://www.arl.org/newsltr/217/mhp.html>
13. Neuroth, Heike, Traugott Koch: Metadata Mapping and Application Profiles. Approaches to providing the Crosssearching of Heterogeneous Resources in the EU Project Renardus. In: Proceedings of the International Conference on Dublin Core and Metadata Applications (2001) <http://www.nii.ac.jp/dc2001/proceedings/abst21.html>
14. Ranganathan, S. R.: The Colon Classification. In: Systems for the Intellectual Organization of Information, Vol. IV. Rutgers University Press, New Brunswick, New Jersey (1965)
15. Tauber, Maurice F., Edith Wise: Classification Systems. In: Ralph R. Shaw, (ed.): The State of the Library Art, Vol. 1(3). The Rutgers University Press, New Brunswick, New Jersey (1961)
16. Verdejo, Felisa, Julio Gonzalo, Anselmo Peñas, David Fernández, Fernando López: Evaluating wordnets in CrossLanguage Information Retrieval: the ITEM search engine. In: Proceedings of the International Conference on Language Resources & Evaluation (2000)
17. Fellbaum, Christine (ed.): WordNet: An Electronic Lexical Database. MIT Press, Boston, Mass. (1998)
18. XSL and XSLT. <http://www.w3.org/Style/XSL/>

Improving Automatic Labelling through RDF Management

Floriana Esposito, Stefano Ferilli, Nicola Di Mauro, Teresa M.A. Basile,
Luigi Iannone, Ignazio Palmisano, and Giovanni Semeraro

Dipartimento di Informatica, Università di Bari
via E. Orabona, 4 - 70125 Bari – Italia
{esposito,ferilli,nicodimauro,basile,iannone,semeraro}
@di.uniba.it
ignazio_io@yahoo.it

Abstract. Building a shared and widely accessible repository, in order for
scientists and end users to exploit it easily, results in tackling a variety of issues.
Among others, the need for automatic labelling of available resources arises.
We present an architecture in which machine learning techniques are exploited
for resources classification and understanding. Furthermore, we show how
learning tasks can be carried out more effectively if training sets and learned
theories are expressed by means of Resource Description Framework (RDF)
formalism and the storage/retrieval/query operations are managed by an ad hoc
component.

1 Introduction

Serious problems to full access, knowledge and exploitation of historic and cultural
sources are caused both by the fragility of the medium on which they are stored and
by their being distributed in various archives throughout the world. Moreover,
professional communities working in the cultural heritage field today still lack
effective and efficient technological support for cooperative and collaborative
knowledge working, thus often rely on informal and non-institutional contacts. A
solution to the former problem may come from a process of digitization, that
transposes the document in electronic form. Conversely, the latter problem can be
overcome by exploiting the Internet as an infrastructure to retrieve/access such a
material and bridge the distance among researchers.

The COLLATE project[1] aims at developing a WWW-based *collaboratory* [7] for
archives, researchers and end-users working with digitized historic/cultural material.
Specifically, it aims at providing suitable task-based interfaces and knowledge
management tools to support experts in their individual work and collaboration to
analyze, index, annotate and interlink all material. New user knowledge can be
continuously integrated into the COLLATE digital data and metadata repositories, so
that the system can offer improved content-based retrieval functionality and enable

---

[1] IST-1999-20882 project COLLATE - *Collaboratory for Annotation, Indexing and Retrieval
of Digitized Historical Archive Material* (URL: http://www.collate.de).

T.M.T. Sembok et al. (Eds.): ICADL 2003, LNCS 2911, pp. 578–589, 2003.

users to create and share valuable knowledge about the cultural and social contexts, allowing in turn other end-users to better retrieve and interpret the historic material.

The need of automatically labelling the huge amount of documents in the COLLATE repository suggested the use of Machine Learning techniques to automatically identify document classes and label significant components, to be used for indexing/retrieval purposes and to be submitted to the COLLATE users for annotation. Combining results from the manual and automatic indexing procedures, elaborate content-based retrieval mechanisms can be applied [2]. The challenge comes from the low layout quality and standard of such a material, which introduces a considerable amount of noise in its description. As regards the layout quality, it is often affected by manual annotations, stamps that overlap to sensible components, ink specks, etc. As to the layout standard, many documents are typewritten sheets, that consist of all equally spaced lines in Gothic type.

This paper is organized as follows. Next section describes the COLLATE system architecture. The documents in the collection that are to be automatically labelled by the embedded learning component are described in Section 3 along with its performance on such a dataset. Then, Section 4 describes the metadata management component in charge of handling all the information flowing in the system, and its interaction with the learning component. Conclusions are drawn in Section 5.

2 The COLLATE Environment

The overall architecture of the COLLATE system (Fig. 1) is structured into several functional layers: *Operational Layer*, *Domain Metadata Layer*, *Task Layer*, *Interface Layer*. The Operational Layer can be described as a digital data repository that comprises a variety of data, ranging from scanned-in text documents to multimedia data and the accumulated annotations related to one or more of these original data. The Domain Metadata Layer provides suitable tools for metadata management in order to organize the stored data in a way that supports the complex knowledge-intensive tasks users will want to perform on the repository contents. The knowledge structures, which are represented by specific XML schemata, constitute the Domain Model. The Task Layer concerns the possibility for the wide variety of the COLLATE types of users to access, work with and evaluate the digitized archive material. In order to support the users in accomplishing their tasks, COLLATE provides appropriate interfaces for convenient work with the digital documents, the Interface Layer. All the information handled by the system is encoded in XML and RDF[2] format, which allows the various modules to communicate by a single representation language; thus, communication between the layers is realized through XML-based communication protocols, as well.

Now, let us briefly summarize the workflow within the system, focusing our attention on the Document Pre-Processing and XML Content Manager modules. After the historical documents are scanned in, they pass through a pre-processing module which extracts from them relevant information using labelling rules automatically generated by a learning component. The meta-information discovered in this phase is stored together with the Web version of the corresponding documents by the *XML*

---

[2] Resource Description Framework http://www.w3.org/RDF

Content Manager, which serves as mediating management layer between the COLLATE system and its underlying databases. It will be used for document retrieval, also managed by the *XML Content Manager*.

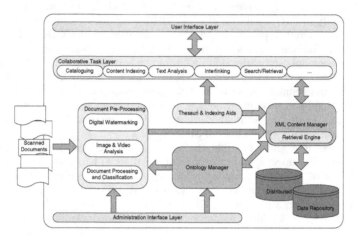

Fig. 1. Overall architecture of the COLLATE system

Though the developed tools and interfaces are generic, the COLLATE experimental domain concerns historic film documentation. Multi-format documents on European films dating from early 20th century are provided by three major European national film archives: DIF (Deutsches Filminstitut, Frankfurt am Main), FAA (Film Archive Austria, Vienna) and NFA (Národní Filmový Archiv, Prague). Such a collection includes a large corpus of rare historic film censorship documents from the 20ies and 30ies, but also newspaper articles, photos, stills, posters and film fragments. An in-depth analysis and comparison of such documents can give evidence about different film versions and cuts, and allow to restore lost/damaged films or identify actors and film fragments of unknown origin.

Specifically, the COLLATE repository (Fig. 2 shows examples of documents) includes several thousands comprehensive documents concerning film culture, and focuses on documents related to censorship processes. The importance of censorship for film production distribution lies mainly in the fact that it is often impossible to identify a unique film. Often, there are lots of different film versions with cuts, changed endings and new inter-titles, depending on the place and date of release. Exactly these differences are documented in censorship documents and allow statements about the original film. They define and identify the object of interest. Often they provide the only source available today for the reconstruction of the large number of films that have been lost or destroyed. Censorship documents support this restoration process by identifying and structuring the film fragments. They allow to put together film fragments from various copies in order to obtain a correct reconstruction. Each country developed its own censorship history embedded in the political history. The collection is complemented by further documents like press articles, correspondence, photos, etc.

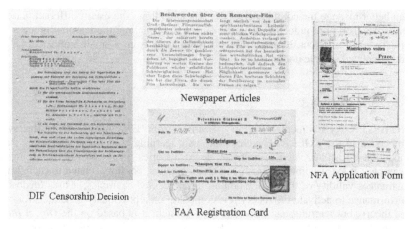

Fig. 2. Sample COLLATE documents

Typical documents analyzed are: Application Forms, Censorship Decisions, Registration Cards. The first kind of documents, Application Form, was required for applying to get the permission to show a film from a production or distribution company. The consequence of this application was the examination by the censorship office. It was usually accompanied by a list of intertitles or dialogue list that served to check whether a film shown in the cinema was the same as the one examined by the censorship office. As regards the Censorship Decision documents, they are about the permission of distributing or showing a film (with relative version) throughout a country. The Registration Card is a certification that the film had been approved for exhibition in the present version by the censoring authority. The registration cards were given to the distribution company which had to pay for this, and had to enclose the cards to the film copies. When the police checked the cinemas from time to time, the owner or projectionist had to show the registration card. Such cards constitute a large portion of the COLLATE collection and are an important source for film reconstruction. All these documents could be a source for information like: *Name of applicant* (production or distribution company), *title of the film*, *year of production*, *length* (before censorship), *brief content*, *information about earlier examinations*, *participants in the examination*, *juridical legitimization for the decision*, *conditions for permission* (for example cuts, change of title, etc.), *reference to previous decisions*, *costs for the procedure*, *production company*, *date and number of examination*, *number of acts*, *forbidden parts*. There are also a lot of documents from the contemporary film press, newspapers or magazines: They are necessary to reconstruct the context of a film, since they enlighten the reception background.

3 The Embedded Learning Component

Supported by previous successful experience in the application of symbolic learning techniques to classification and understanding of paper documents [3,5,9], we focused our attention on first-order logic learning techniques, whose high level representation can better manage the complexity of the task and allows the use of different reasoning strategies than pure induction with the objective of making the learning process more effective and efficient, to learn rules for such tasks from a small number of selected and annotated sample documents.

3.1   INTHELEX

INTHELEX[3] (INcremental THEory Learner from EXamples) [4] is the system embedded in the COLLATE architecture as a learning component. It carries out the induction of *hierarchical* first-order logic theories from positive and negative examples: it learns simultaneously *multiple concepts*, possibly related to each other; it guarantees validity of the theories on all the processed examples; it uses feedback on performance to activate the theory revision phase on a previously generated version of the theory, but learning can also start from scratch; it is based on the *Object Identity assumption* (different names in a description must refer to different objects). It exploits a previous version of the theory (if any), a graph describing the dependence relationships among concepts, and an historical memory of all the past examples that led to the current theory.

The learning cycle performed by INTHELEX can be described as follows. A set of examples of the concepts to be learned, possibly selected by an expert, is provided. Some initial examples, previously classified by the expert, are exploited to obtain a theory that is able to explain them. Such an initial theory can also be provided by the expert, or even be empty. Subsequently, the validity of the theory against new available examples is checked. In the case of incorrectness on an example, the cause of the wrong decision can be located and the proper kind of correction chosen, firing the theory revision process. In this way, examples are exploited incrementally to modify incorrect hypotheses according to a data-driven strategy. Test examples are exploited just to check the predictive capabilities of the theory, intended as the behavior of the theory on new observations, without causing a refinement of the theory in the case of incorrectness on them.

Another peculiarity of INTHELEX is the integration of multistrategy operators that may help solve the theory revision problem by pre-processing the incoming information [5]. The purpose of induction is to infer regularities and laws (from a certain number of significant observations) that may be valid for the whole population. INTHELEX incorporates two inductive refinement operators, one for generalizing hypotheses that reject positive examples, and the other for specializing hypotheses that explain negative examples. Deduction is exploited to fill observations with information that is not explicitly stated, but is implicit in their description, and hence refers to the possibility of better representing the examples and, consequently, the inferred theories. Indeed, since the system is able to handle a hierarchy of concepts, some combinations of predicates might identify higher level concepts that are worth adding to the descriptions in order to raise their semantic level. For this reason, INTHELEX exploits deduction to recognize such concepts and explicitly add them to the example description. The system can be provided with a Background Knowledge, supposed to be correct and hence not modifiable, containing complete or

---

[3] INTHELEX is currently available in binary format for i586 DOS-based platforms (http://lacam.di.uniba.it:8000/systems/inthelex/).

partial definitions in the same format as the theory rules. Abduction aims at completing possibly partial information in the examples, adding more details. Its role in INTHELEX is helping to manage situations where not only the set of all observations is partially known, but each observation could also be incomplete. Indeed, it can be exploited both during theory generation and during theory checking to hypothesize facts that are not explicitly present in the observations. Lastly, abstraction removes superfluous details from the description of both the examples and the theory. The exploitation of abstraction in INTHELEX concerns the shift from the language in which the theory is described to a higher level one. An abstraction theory contains information on the operators according to which the shift is to be performed. INTHELEX, automatically applies it to the learning problem at hand before processing the examples. The implemented abstraction operators allow the system to replace a number of components with a compound object, to decrease the granularity of a set of values, to ignore whole objects or just part of their features, and to neglect the number of occurrences of a certain kind of object.

3.2   Experimental Results on the COLLATE Dataset

INTHELEX was considered a suitable learning component for the COLLATE architecture based on its previous successful application to different kinds of documents, indicating a good generality of the approach. Moreover, many of its features met the requirements imposed by the complexity of the documents to be handled. In addition to being a symbolic (first-order logic) incremental system, its multistrategy capabilities seemed very useful [8]. For instance, abduction could make the system more flexible in the absence of particular layout components due to the typist's style, while abstraction could help in focusing on layout patterns that are meaningful to the identification of the interesting details, neglecting less interesting ones. Experimental results, reported in the following, confirm the above expectations.

The COLLATE dataset for INTHELEX consisted of 29 documents for the class Registration Card (FAA), 36 ones for the class Censorship Decision (DIF), 37 for the class Application form (NFA). Other 17 reject documents were obtained from newspaper articles. The complexity of the domain is confirmed by the description length of the documents, that ranges between 40 and 379 literals (144 on average) for class Registration Card, between 54 and 263 (215 on average) for class Censorship Decision; between 105 and 585 (269 on average) for class Application Form.

The examples needed to run INTHELEX describe the layout blocks that make up a paper document in terms of their size (height and width, in pixels), position (horizontal and vertical, in pixels from the top-left corner), type (text, line, picture, mixed) and relative position (horizontal/vertical alignment between blocks).

Each document was considered as a positive example for the class it belongs, and as a negative example for the other classes to be learned; reject documents were considered as negative examples for all classes. Definitions for each class were learned, starting from the empty theory, and their predictive accuracy was tested according to a 10-fold cross validation methodology, ensuring that each fold contained the same proportion of positive and negative examples. Table 1 reports the experimental results, averaged on the 10 folds, of the classification and interpretation process in this environment as regards Accuracy on the test set (expressed in percentage) and Runtime (in seconds).

As expected, the classification task turned out to be easier than the interpretation problem concerning the semantics of the layout blocks inside documents, but it should be considered that the high predictive accuracy should ensure that few theory revisions can be expected when processing further documents. Indeed, INTHELEX was able to learn significant definitions for the annotation of the given documents, as evident from the very high predictive accuracy in both cases, reaching even 99.17% for the classification task (in which never falls below 95.74%) and 98.95% in the interpretation problem (in which only 2 cases out of 28 fall below 90%).

Table 1. INTHELEX performance on COLLATE dataset

DIF	Accuracy	Runtime	FAA	Accuracy	Runtime
Classification	*99.17*	*17.13*	*Classification*	*94.17*	*334.05*
cens_signature	98.32	1459.88	registration_au	91.43	3739.36
cert_signature	98.31	176.59	date_place	86.69	7239.62
object_title	94.66	3960.83	department	98.95	118.62
cens_authority	97.64	2519.45	applicant	97.89	93.99
chairman	93.10	9332.845	reg_number	91.95	4578.20
assessors	94.48	12170.93	film_genre	93.02	2344.89
session_data	97.68	1037.96	film_length	90.87	3855.39
representative	92.98	13761.96	film_producer	94.05	4717.17
			film_title	89.85	4863.08

NFA	Accuracy	Runtime	NFA	Accuracy	Runtime
Classification	*95.74*	*89.88*	applicant	93.66	15588.15
dispatch_office	94.28	13149.31	film_genre	98.53	684.35
applic_notes	98.81	231.05	registration_au	94.64	5159.74
No_censor_card	95.47	8136.79	cens_process	98.51	4027.90
film_producer	93.98	5303.78	cens_card	94.62	3363.86
No_prec_doc	93.97	5561.14	delivery_date	95.52	3827.34

It is worth noting that the rules learned by the system have a high degree of understandability for human experts, which was one of the COLLATE requirements. For instance, Figure 3 shows a definition for the classification of documents belonging to Censorship Decision of DIF class to be read as "*a document belongs to this class if it has long length and short width, it contains three components in the upper-left part, all of type text and having very short height, two of which are medium large and one of these two is on top of the third*". An interesting remark is that, starting with descriptions whose average length was 215, the average number of literals in the learned rules is just 22.

Figure 4 shows the definition learned by INTHELEX to label the component *film_title* in Registration Cards from *FAA* and the mapping of the components of the learned description in a sample document. Again, such a rule contains 23 literals only.

```
class_dif_cen_decision(A) :-
    image_lenght_long(A), image_width_short(A),
    part_of(A, B), type_of_text(B),
    width_medium_large(B), height_very_very_small(B),
    pos_left(B), pos_upper(B),
    part_of(A, C), type_of_text(C),
    height_very_very_small(C),
    pos_left(C), pos_upper(C),
    on_top(C, D), type_of_text(D),
    width_medium_large(D), height_very_very_small(D),
    pos_left(D), pos_upper(D).
```

Fig. 3. Learned Rule for Classification

```
logic_type_film_title(A) :-
page_first(B),part_of(B,A),part_of(B,C),part_of(B,D),
    type_of_text(A),pos_upper(A),
    type_of_text(D),pos_upper(D),
    height_very_small(C),type_of_text(C),
    pos_center(C),pos_upper(C),
width_very_large(E),height_smallest(E),
type_of_hor_line(E),pos_center(E),pos_upper(E),
height_very_very_small(F),pos_left(F),pos_upper(F),
on_top(E,D),on_top(E,F),alignment_left_col(F,A).
```

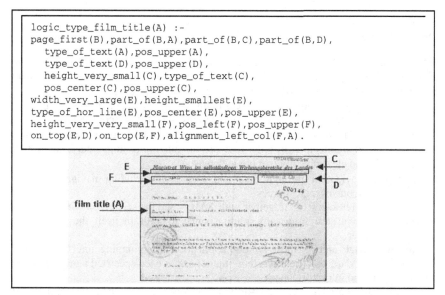

Fig. 4. Learned rules for the semantic components *film title* and the mapping on document

4 RDF Sub Architecture

Semantic Web stands for the next evolution of World Wide Web [1]. It will provide more intelligent services such as clever search engines, user tailored applications and data exchange based on semantics

World Wide Web Consortium (W3C) has been working through the most recent years in the development of technologies that could support the evolution towards the Semantic Web. While some of these technologies are still in early phases, others can already find an exploitation in real world applications. This is the case of Resource Description Framework (RDF). It represents the basic support to write metadata on

Web resources and to grant interoperability among heterogeneous applications when exchanging these metadata.

RDF describes resources in terms of primitives (classes, properties, resources, etc.) without taking into account the description structure itself. In fact, the description can be encoded in XML[4]. This ensures its portability across the Web.

Moreover, RDF represents a suitable solution to implement the Semantic Web vision also because it presents three key features:

- **Extensibility:** Each user can add its own description extending pre-existing ones without any limit.
- **Interoperability:** RDF descriptions can rely on XML serialization every time they need to be exchanged among heterogeneous platforms
- **Scalability:** RDF descriptions can be viewed as sets of three fields records (triples) (Subject, Predicate and Object). This makes them easy to fetch and manage even if a single description holds many triples in it.

4.1   RDF Management in COLLATE

COLLATE system could be easily assimilated to the wider scenario foreseen by Semantic Web: a huge quantity of resources (documents, assets) with many relationships among them. COLLATE requirements are:

- A uniform way of identifying resources (films, film related documents, cataloguing and indexing information, scientists' annotations, scientific discourses)
- Distribution of information: in fact archives still keep their resources in a decentralized architecture, in order to avoid the moving of huge data amount, both physically and electronically (for obvious reasons)
- Intelligent navigation through data and metadata: including navigation across scientific discourses on resources

For all these reasons RDF (together with XML – see the section on the COLLATE Environment) is a straightforward solution since it holds in itself the features we underlined earlier.

However, RDF and its most famous application programming interfaces (APIs) lack both in standard specifications (e.g.: there has not been specified a uniform query language yet) and in performances.

That is why the COLLATE consortium developed a component that aims to fill these gaps and embedded it into the aforementioned XML Content Manager.

We go on examining which added value our framework provides to COLLATE. It is quite obvious that a huge collection of documents and metadata such as COLLATE heritage needs a careful devising of a scalable component in order to manage storage and retrieval of both resources and relationships among them. While the solution for the former problem is delegated to efficient RDBMS, as far as the latter we developed a suitable RDF Persistence for granting scalability. This module relies on Jena Toolkit storage model for RDF. It consists on exploiting a relational representation of the RDF Triples (subject, predicate, object) stored in a database. This approach takes advantage of the outstanding performance rates of the most famous RDBMS (such as Oracle, MySQL and PostgreSQL). One of the most immediate benefits is the fact that

---

[4] But also in other different formats e.g.: http://mail.ilrt.bris.ac.uk/~cmdjb/2001/06/ntriples/.

applications need not to load in-memory RDF *Models* (Descriptions) in order to deal with small portions of them (typically small sets of *Statements*), saving lots of memory and time for each operation.

Moreover, Jena Toolkit offers RDF Description Query Language (RDQL[5]) as language for querying RDF Descriptions. This support has been extended for querying multiple *Models*, that together with multi-user environment and scalability, proved to be a suitable solution for COLLATE requirement.

The query language, however, remains a weakness point of all RDF APIs available, including Jena. At the time of writing, still no standard query language specifications are available. This hampers the interoperability between components and, therefore, between different systems; in other words, two systems using different APIs to manage RDF can exchange data, but cannot easily exchange queries on these data.

To address this issue, the subcomponent, named Enhanced Query Engine, is able to deal with different query languages. The design of this component exploits the Strategy pattern [6], enabling the use of a dynamic set of query languages. In order to add the support for a new query language, only the classes implementing the interfaces to wrap the parser of the language and the query engine are needed, allowing for easy update. This update, obviously, can be the standard query language the W3C (together with other organizations) is working on, as soon as it is available.

4.2   Experiments

In order to prove the efficiency of our framework we hereby provide a small empirical evaluation of its performances. We tested its efficiency and effectiveness as it deals with RDF Resources that are necessary for the integration with INTHELEX. More specifically, one point of integration with INTHELEX consists in storing training examples and subsequently in retrieving them by INTHELEX for theory building and tuning. As we stated earlier, there are many reasons because documents metadata had to be encoded in RDF within COLLATE and INTHELEX learns documents classifiers starting from document layout description (metadata).

In our test cases, we considered sets of examples whose size increased dramatically, as you can see in column "Triples" in table 2. We started from an example test bed that results in 334 Triples in its RDF translation, ranging till the biggest that reaches ~78000 Triples. We measured the times required for the following operations:

- Adding a whole training set
- Querying a training set

Furthermore we present also the average timings weighted on the number of triples (columns "Add time/triples" and "Query time/triples").

As we can see in Figure 5 (where the Y scale is logarithmic for the sake of readability), the complexity of the insertion of a new description is linear with the size of the description itself. This is outlined by "Add time/triples" ratio, that is almost constant. The time elapsed to execute queries on a particular description, on the other side, does increase with the size of the description but in a non-linear way. As clearly

---

[5] http://www.hpl.hp.com/semweb/rdql-grammar.html

shown by "Query time/triples" ratio, a query costs around 0,1 milliseconds per statement when the number of statements is limited, but costs less than 0,01 milliseconds per statement when the number of statements is over 78000. From the data in the table 2 and figure 5, it appears that the increase of size of a 230 factor (from 334 to over 78000) produces an absolute increase in time of about a 5 factor. On the basis of these data, we can assert that the size of the descriptions being queried is of very little relevance when evaluating application performances.

Table 2. Test Results

Name	Triples	Add time	Query time	Add time/triples	Query time/triples
first_rdf	334	2594	34	7,77	0,1
second_rdf	637	5458	43	8,57	0,07
third_rdf	1295	10104	85	7,8	0,07
fourth_rdf	2750	22282	42	8,1	0,02
fifth_rdf	6341	52927	167	8,35	0,03
sixth_rdf	17534	161573	235	9,21	0,01
seventh_rdf	78445	683813	182	8,72	<0,01

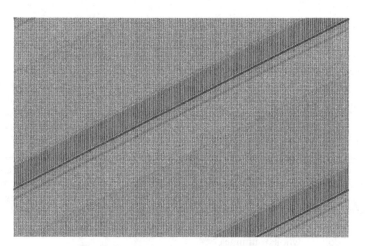

Fig. 5. Graphical representation of test results

Acknowledgments. This work has been partially funded by the European Commission under the IST Project COLLATE (IST-1999-20882) "Collaboratory for Annotation, Indexing and Retrieval of Digitized Historical Archive Material".

References

[1] T. Berners-Lee, J. Hendlers and O. Lassilla, The Semantic Web Scientific American, May 2001

[2] H. Brocks, U. Thiel, A. Stein, and A. Dirsch-Weigand. Customizable retrieval functions based on user tasks in the cultural heritage domain. In P. Constantopoulos and I.T. Sølvberg, editors, *Research and Advanced Technology for Digital Libraries*, number 2163 in LNCS, pages 37–48. Springer, 2001.

[3] F. Esposito, D. Malerba, G. Semeraro, N. Fanizzi, and S. Ferilli. Adding machine learning and knowledge intensive techniques to a digital library service. *International Journal on Digital Libraries*, 2(1):3–19, 1998.

[4] F. Esposito, G. Semeraro, N. Fanizzi, and S. Ferilli. Multistrategy Theory Revision: Induction and abduction in INTHELEX. *Machine Learning Journal*, 38(1/2):133–156, 2000.

[5] S. Ferilli. *A Framework for Incremental Synthesis of Logic Theories: An Application to Document Processing* Ph.D. thesis, Dipartimento di Informatica, Università di Bari, Bari, Italy, November 2000.

[6] E.Gamma, R.Helm, R.Johnson, J.Vlissides, *Design Patterns* Addison-Wesley Pub Co (1995)

[7] R.T. Kouzes, J.D. Myers, and W.A. Wulf. Collaboratories: Doing science on the internet. *IEEE Computer*, 29(8):40–46, 1996.

[8] G. Semeraro, F. Esposito, S. Ferilli, N. Fanizzi, T.M.A. Basile, and N. Di Mauro. Multistrategy learning of rules for automated classification of cultural heritage material. In E.P. Lim, C. Khoo, E. Fox, T. Costantino, S. Foo, H. Chen, and S. Urs, editors, *In Proc of the 5th International Conference on Asian Digital Libraries (ICADL)*, number 2555 in Lecture Notes in Computer Science, pages 182–193. Springer-Verlag, 2002.

[9] G. Semeraro, S. Ferilli, N. Fanizzi, and F. Esposito. Document classification and interpretation through the inference of logic-based models. In P.Constantopoulos and I.T. Sølvberg, editors, *Research and Advanced Technology for Digital Libraries*, number 2163 in LNCS, pages 59–70. Springer, 2001.

An OAI-Based Filtering Service for CITIDEL from NDLTD

Baoping Zhang, Marcos André Gonçalves, and Edward A. Fox

Digital Library Research Laboratory, Virginia Tech
Blacksburg, VA 24061 USA
{bzhang,mgoncalv,fox}@vt.edu

Abstract. One goal of the Computing and Information Technology Interactive Digital Educational Library (CITIDEL) is to maximize the number of computing-related resources available to computer science scholars and practitioners through it. In this paper, we describe a set of experiments designed to help this goal by adding to CITIDEL a sub-collection of computing related electronic theses and dissertations (ETDs) automatically extracted from the Networked Digital Library of Theses and Dissertations (NDLTD) OAI Union Catalog. We analyze the metadata quality of the NDLTD OAI Union Catalog and describe three different experiments that combine different sources of evidence to improve the accuracy in filtering out the computing related entries.

1 Introduction

CITIDEL [1] is part of the Collections Track activities in the National STEM (Science, Technology, Engineering, and Mathematics education) Digital Library (NSDL). In particular, CITIDEL operates and maintains the "computing" content of the digital library that includes information systems, computer science, information science, information technology, software engineering, computer engineering, and other computing-related fields. This work focuses on enhancing the current coverage of the CITIDEL collection by automatically extracting computing-related records from the NDLTD [2-4] collection and adding them into CITIDEL.

1.1 Background and Motivation

The Open Archives Initiative Protocol for Metadata Harvesting provides an application-independent interoperability framework based on metadata harvesting. There are two classes of participants in the OAI-PMH framework:

1. Data Providers administer systems that support the OAI-PMH as a means of exposing metadata;
2. Service Providers use metadata harvested via the OAI-PMH as a basis for building value-added services.

T.M.T. Sembok et al. (Eds.): ICADL 2003, LNCS 2911, pp. 590–601, 2003.

A repository is a network accessible server that can process the six OAI-PMH requests. A repository is managed by a data provider to expose metadata to harvesters. The NDLTD OAI Union Catalog [5] is an example of a service built by harvesting metadata via the Open Archives Initiative Protocol from Open Archives [6] of electronic theses and dissertations worldwide. At present there are 7507 records in the Union Catalog, but we expect that, through partnering with OCLC and because of its support by providing data from WordCat, there eventually will be millions of records.

In order to achieve the CITIDEL goal of maximum coverage of computing related information, we have designed and conducted a set of experiments that harvest metadata in Dublin Core [7] format from the OAI Union Catalog and then filter out the computing related entries.

One way to filter out computing entries from the whole NDLTD collection would be to look at the contributor fields of each record (in the case of ETDs where this entry corresponds to mentors and/or committee members). For example, if most of the contributors are computer scientists, one could expect that this record is computing related. Another way is to look at the subject fields.

Figure 1 shows the number of entries which have subject field(s) and contributor field(s) for the whole NDLTD collection. Figure 2 shows this for each university (site) in the collection, in a series of groups, organized according to size of collection. Figure 1 shows that only about 65% of the entries have contributor fields while about 92% have subject fields. Figure 2 also shows the inconsistency of using contributor and subject fields across universities. For example, all entries from USF have both contributor and subject fields while all entries from MIT are missing both fields. All entries from LSU have subject field but no contributor field. And some but not all entries from WUW have subject fields and some but not all entries from Duisburg have contributor fields. This analysis shows that the filtering task using only contributor is impossible. To address those entries with missing contributor fields, we need to look at other sources of evidence.

Though the subject fields are most useful overall in filtering, their sole use is prevented by a number of factors. The first factor, according to Figure 2, is that many records at several sites are missing subject fields. If we simply filter using subject information, we would exclude those records. The second factor is the inconsistency in use of subjects at several universities as an indicator of topical field. For example, at Virginia Tech, subject represents department name, so for a computing related

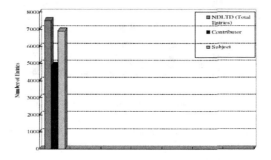

Fig. 1. Entry counts with *contributor* field(s) and *subject* fields

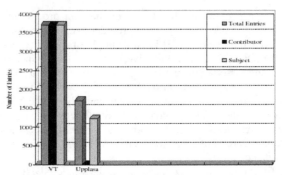

Fig. 2(a). Entry counts with *contributor* field(s) and *subject* field(s) for different sites

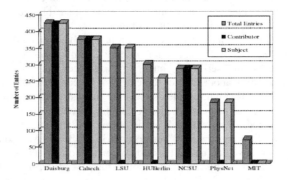

Fig. 2(b). Entry counts with *contributor* field(s) and *subject* field(s) for different sites

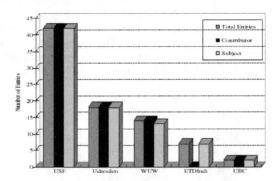

Fig. 2(c). Entry counts with *contributor* field(s) and *subject* field(s) for different sites

record, the subject would be "computer science". This subject entry clearly indicates the broad topic of the record. But this practice is not universal among universities. For example, in a record from Uppsala University, the subjects are "data assimilation", "multiblock", and "object oriented". These words are actually the keywords for the record. So we see that different universities use subject fields in different ways. Thus, in such an open-ended research collection, it's not possible to enumerate a list of words that will include all possible computing related entries for different universities. Another factor is the language problem. Some records from a particular institution (i.e., University Library of Gerhard-Mercator University Duisburg) may list the subject(s) in languages other than English but at the same time they do have the title and abstract in English. The fourth factor is that even considering two records with the same subject, one of them might be computing related and the other may not. For example, there are a number of records harvested from Virginia Tech with the subject "Electrical and Computer Engineering". One of these records is about "high-power three-phase PWM inverters" which is definitely not computing related. Another one is about "Multicast Networks", which is computing related. In this case, we cannot get rid of all the records with such a subject. We have to look at the contents of the record to determine if it's computing related or not.

So to get better filtering results, we need to combine several sources of evidence. If an instance lacks both the contributor field and subject field, we can only rely on the content based classification as evidence of the record being computing related (i.e., text from title and/or abstract). Accordingly our filtering experiment was composed of a combination of three major steps:

- Content-based classification – classify the data set into two sets: computing related and non-computing related using title plus subject plus abstract,
- Filtering based on contributor field(s) in the metadata – enhance the results achieved through content-based classification,
- Filtering based on subject field(s) in the metadata – enhance results when records of the second step are missing contributor fields or to correct possible records mistakenly filtered out.

The experiment aimed to test: 1) the relation between quality of metadata and quality of services; 2) the effectiveness of content-based filtering in the absence of explicit subject and/or contributor information; and 3) the effect of combining several sources of evidence.

2 Experimental Setting for Filtering Mechanism

2.1 Content-Based Classification – Weka

We have used the Weka data mining package [8] as our classification tool. Weka is a collection of machine learning algorithms for solving real-world data mining problems. It contains tools for data pre-processing, classification, regression, clustering, association rules, and visualization.

Classification aims to assign instances to predefined classes. Classification requires supervised learning; a training data set is used to specify the classes we are trying to learn. The performance of the classification model learned from a training set is tested on a test data set to see how well the model predicts the correct class for unseen data.

Since the collection was harvested using OAI, both the training and the test metadata were in XML files. The XML file is composed of fields like subject, title, abstract, and category for each record. The terms from title, subject, and abstract fields were used to produce the document vector for each record. Each element of the vector is a term along with its weight. Each term's weight was generated based on the *tf-idf* scheme. Term frequency *tf* provides one measure of how well a term describes the document contents. Inverse document frequency (*idf*) measures the inverse of the frequency of a term among the documents in the collection. The motivation for usage of an *idf* factor is that terms which appear in many documents are not very useful for distinguishing a relevant document from a non-relevant one.

Weka expects ARFF files [9] as input. An ARFF (Attribute-Relation File Format) file is an ASCII text file that describes a list of instances sharing a set of attributes. ARFF files have two distinct sections. The first section is the Header information, which is followed by the Data information. The Header of the ARFF file contains the name of the relation, a list of the attributes (the columns in the data), and their types.

The ARFF files for our experiment were generated by parsing the XML files. All the words are listed as attributes in the ARFF file, and the document vector along with the category of each document constitute the DATA part of the ARFF file.

Part of an example header on our training data set is:

```
@RELATION acmabstracts
@ATTRIBUTE word_1 REAL
% abandon 2.90252685546875

.................
@ATTRIBUTE word_9251 REAL
% computer 11664.530334472656
@ATTRIBUTE word_9252 REAL
% computer-based 39.0728759765625
@ATTRIBUTE word_9253 REAL
 % computerize 45.552978515625
@ATTRIBUTE word_9254 REAL
% computing 711.42822265625

.................
@ATTRIBUTE word_30000 REAL
% yeast 2.46429443359375
@ATTRIBUTE category_code {C, D}
```

The list of the attributes is composed of the words (stop words removed) and an enumeration of the category for each record. Each word attribute's type is a real number which is that word's total frequency in the collection. Each line that begins with a "%" is a comment line explaining what the word is and its total frequency in the collection. The category "C" represents a computing related record, and the category "D" represents a non-computing related record.

Part of the Data of the ARFF file is the following:

```
@DATA
{2545 0.04974365234375, 2867 0.14984130859375, 5890 0.19989013671875,
 30000 "C"}
{222 0.0372314453125, 1951 0.0372314453125, 2545 0.0372314453125, 30000
 "D"}
```

The Data part contains several rows. Each row represents a document and is surrounded by curly braces. The format for each entry is: <index> <space> <value>.

Here index is the attribute index (starting from 0). For example, in the first row of the above example, "2545" is the attribute index 2545 (word 2546) and its value is a real number which is that word's weight computed through using *tf-idf*. The last entry of each row is the attribute "category_code", which is the category of this document.

We chose to use the WEKA SMO [10] classifier. The SMO classifier implements the sequential minimal optimization algorithm. It is a fast method to train Support Vector Machines (SVMs) which has reportedly been the best classifier so far for text classification experiments [11-15]. The main idea of Support Vector Machines is that given a set of data points which belong to either of two classes, an SVM finds the hyperplane that leaves the largest possible fraction of points of the same class on the same side and maximizes the distance of either class from the hyperplane. The optimal separating hyperplane will minimize the risk of mis-classifying the training samples and unseen test samples. Figure 3 illustrates this idea.

Figure 4 shows the composition of the training and test sets for the experiments. Normal arrows represent how we selected the training collection and the test collection. Dotted arrows represent the input to the training and classification process. Dashed lines represent the output of the training process.

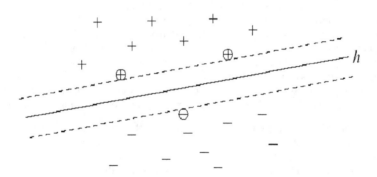

Fig. 3. Support Vector Machines (SVMs) find the *hyperplane h*, which separates the *positive* and *negative* training examples with maximum distance. The examples closest to the hyperplane are called Support Vectors (marked with *circles*)

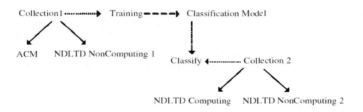

Fig. 4. *Training set* and *Test set* composition

For the experiments, the metadata harvested from the Union Catalog were manually divided into two categories for test purposes: computing related and others. We used records extracted from the ACM Digital Library (included in CITIDEL) to provide positive training examples to our classifier instead of some other computing related records because the previously identified computing sub-collection in NDLTD only has 138 entries. We felt this sub-collection was too small to serve as the computing category of the training set. Since we need to separate the computing related entries from the remaining records, all the ACM metadata was marked as one category - computing related. Half of the non-computing related entries from the Union Catalog served as the non-computing category of the training set. All the computing related entries and another half of the non-computing entries served as the test collection.

2.2 Contributor Filtering

To remove false computing entries from the classification result set, we decided to look further at the contributor fields for those classified as computing entries. For an ETD, the contributors are normally members of the committee. A simple heuristic was defined wherein if more than half of the contributors are computer scientists, this thesis or dissertation is assumed to be computing related.

We used a set of author names extracted from records of the ACM DL as our computer scientists list. When we match a name, different formats need to be considered. For example, we may have 'Edward A. Fox', but the contributor name might be in the format of 'Edward Fox', or 'E. A. Fox'. Even if the name in the computer scientists list doesn't exactly correspond to the contributor name, we should count this case as a match. If an exact name match fails, the mechanism we used was:

- If their middle initials are the same, we compare the initials of their first names and the whole last names. For example, if the contributor is in the format "E. A. Fox" and the computer scientist is in the format "Edward A. Fox", both the initials of the first name is "E" and both have the same last name, so this is counted as a match.

- If and only if one of the two compared names' middle is empty, we compare their first names and last names. For example, if the contributor is in the format "Edward Fox" and the computer scientist is in the format "Edward A. Fox", they have the same first name and last name, so this is counted as a match according to this rule.

In our experiment, we tried to match 495 contributor names with the names in the computer scientists list (extracted from the ACM DL). 277 of the 495 were matches. Among these 277, 156 had exact name matches. In addition, 35 are matched based on the first scheme above, and 86 are matched based on the second scheme above.

2.3 Subject Filtering

From the analysis of NDLTD records, it was noted that contributors were not used uniformly and consistently across institutions (see Sect. 1.1). Therefore many entries may not be filtered using only the contributor filter. For example, we noticed that 88 of 129 non-computing related entries were missing contributor fields in their metadata. So to deal with this situation, we applied a second filter on those entries missing contributor fields. We analyzed the metadata of those entries and found that 71 of 88 entries have subject fields. We noted that some non-computing words are subjects. For example, words like 'physics', 'animal science', 'Landscape Architecture', etc. appear. So we could use them to remove entries whose subject field had such kinds of words.

We also noticed that when the contributor filter was applied on the classified computing collection, a few positive entries were filtered out. So we also applied the subject filter in another way on these entries. That is, we check if these entries' subject field contains words like 'Computer Science' and if they do, we move them back into the computing collection.

We choose to pick contributors before subject(s) because we feel that contributor information is more reliable. Due to the inconsistency in use of subjects by several universities as indicators of field, it's hard to choose several words and say that records with such words in the subject field are computing related but otherwise are not computing related. So it's a better choice to use subject filtering as a supplement to the content based filtering and contributor filtering, to improve filtering accuracy.

3   Experimental Results

3.1   The Content-Based Classification Result Was as Follows

We have two classes in our classification. One is "C" which represents the computing related (positive) instances and another is "D" which represents the non-computing related (negative) instances. The total number of instances classified by the classification system in the test set was 3792, whereas 138 were positive instances and 3654 were negative instances. 96.3% (3652) of the total instances were correctly classified while 3.7% (140) were incorrectly classified.

Table 1 gives the detailed accuracy for these two classes. Table 2 shows information about actual and predicted classifications of the system.

Table 1. Detailed accuracy by class

Class	Precision	Recall	F-Measure
C	0.496	0.92	0.645
D	0.997	0.965	0.981

Table 2. Content-based classification result

Actual Class	Classified as C	Classified as D
C	127	11
D	129	3525

3.2 Contributor Filter Results

To remove those 129 entries which are classified as computing related entries but actually are non-computing entries, we run the contributor filter on the classified computing collection through the content-based classification system. Among those 129 entries, we were able to filter out 39 entries. This is mainly because 88 entries of those 129 don't have contributor fields. 2 non-computing entries failed to be filtered out because more than half of their contributors were in the computer scientists list that we extracted from the ACM DL. One of these two is a dissertation with the title "Numerical Differentiation Using Statistical Design" in the field of Statistics from North Carolina State University (NCSU), and the other is a dissertation with the title "Autonomous Solution Methods for Large-Scale MARKOV Chains" in the field of Operations Research from NCSU. We also filtered out 17 actual computing entries. We want to move back those 17 entries. To deal with the errors in filtering and missing contributor entries, we applied the subject filter on those entries.

3.3 Subject Filter Results

Among those 88 missing contributor entries, we were able to filter out 65 through the subject filter. 17 entries don't have subject fields. 6 of them failed to be filtered out by the subject filter because their subject contains words where it is hard to say if they are computing related, for example, phrases like "library and information sciences", "Electrical and Computer Engineering", etc.

We applied a subject filter on the 17 computing entries filtered out by the contributor filter. We successfully moved 16 of them back to the computing collection.

4   Evaluation

Table 3 shows the experimental results in terms of the changes of the number of positive and negative instances after each step of the experiment, and the number of positive and negative instances in the final computing collection.

Table 3. Experimental Results

	Computing	Non-Computing
Content-based classification	127	129
Contributor filter	-17	-39
Subject filter	+16	-65
Final computing collection	126	25

For completeness, we also tested the result of applying only a subject filter to the results achieved through the content-based classification. All the experimental results are summarized in the recall and precision measures in Figure 5. Precision is defined as the proportion of correctly classified records in the set of all records assigned to the target class. Recall is defined as the proportion of correctly classified records out of all the records having the target class.

Content based classification yields good recall but low precision. After applying a subject filter to the content based classification, we improved the precision without loosing recall. When we applied a contributor filter to the content based classification result, we also improved precision but at the same time filtered out some computing entries, so recall was reduced. On the other hand, after applying the subject filter, we could remove more false computing entries and at the same time bring back some real computing ones. So considering both recall and precision, we achieved the best results by combining these three types of evidence.

We also calculated the F-Measure for each step of the experiment. F-measure is defined as 2*Precision*Recall / (Precision + Recall). Table 4 shows the values of F-measure for each step.

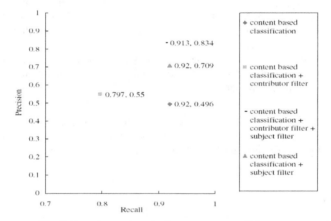

Fig. 5. Experimental results in *Precision Recall* format

Table 4. F-Measure values for each experiment step

Experiment	F-Measure
Content-based classification	0.645
Content-based classification + contributor filter	0.651
Content-based classification + subject filter	0.801
Content-based classification + contributor filter + subject filter	0.872

5 Conclusion

We have presented a set of experiments to extract computing related theses and dissertations from the NDLTD Union collection to include in the CITIDEL collection. Our experiments show that the quality of the filtering service was affected by the quality of the metadata. If the metadata contains more fields and if the fields were consistently used across all NDLTD data providers, we can utilize those fields to improve filtering. Several sources of evidence were combined to overcome the problem of inconsistency of the instances' metadata and to yield better results. To address the problems of absence, inconsistency, and ambiguity of contributor and subject information in NDLTD, content-based classification was studied. This procedure gives good recall but low precision. The contributor filter tried to look at the contributor field(s) and to filter out non-computing related instances. And to address the problem of lacking contributor field(s) for some instances, the subject filter tried to look at the subject information to filter out non-computing related instances. The final combination of the filtering mechanisms provided satisfactory precision and recall.

One area of future work is to enhance the content-based classification result by trying to apply different weights to the words in the title, subject, and abstract fields to reflect their relative importance. Another area of future work is to combine other sources of evidence like the department field in other formats of metadata like ETDMS (the recommended metadata standard for ETDs), when it is available, or the full-text of the ETD for the content-based approach. We also will formalize and extend our filtering methods by using probabilistic tools like belief networks to combine multiple sources of evidence. Finally we plan to apply similar strategies and methods to filter electronic theses and dissertations in many other fields covered by NDLTD (e.g., Physics, Mathematics, etc.).

Acknowledgements. This research work was funded in part by the NSF through grants DUE0136690, DUE0121679 and IIS0086227. The second author is also supported by CAPES, process 1702-98 and a fellowship by American Online (AOL).

References

1. Fox, E.A.: Computing and Information Technology Interactive Digital Educational Library (CITIDEL). Homepage (2002). http://www.citidel.org/
2. Fox, E.A.: Networked Digital Library of Theses and Dissertations. Nature Web Matters (1999) http://helix.nature.com/webmatters/library/library.html
3. Fox, E.A.: Networked Digital Library of Theses and Dissertations (NDLTD). Homepage (1999) http://www.ndltd.org
4. Suleman, H., Atkins A., Gonçalves, M.A., France, R.K., Fox, E.A., Virginia Tech; Chachra V., Crowder M., VTLS, Inc.; and Young, J., OCLC: Networked Digital Library of Theses and Dissertations: Bridging the Gaps for Global Access - Part 1: Mission and Progress. D-Lib Magazine, 7(9) (2001)
5. Suleman, H., Luo, M.: Electronic Thesis/Dissertation OAI Union Catalog. Homepage (2002) http://rocky.dlib.vt.edu/~etdunion/cgi-bin/index.pl
6. Van de Sompel, H.: Open Archives Initiative. WWW site. Ithaca, NY: Cornell University (2000) http://www.openarchives.org
7. DCMI: Dublin Core Metadata Element Set, Version 1.1: Reference Description. Available from http://www.dublincore.org/documents/dces/
8. Witten, I.H., Frank, E.: Data Mining: Practical Machine Learning Tools and Techniques with Java Implementations. Morgan Kaufmann, San Francisco, CA (2000)
9. Paynter, G.: Attribute-Relation File Format (ARFF). WWW site. http://www.cs.waikato.ac.nz/~ml/weka/arff.html

10. Platt, J.: Fast Training of Support Vector Machines using Sequential Minimal Optimization. Advances in Kernel Methods - Support Vector Learning, B. Schölkopf, C. Burges, and A. Smola, eds., MIT Press (1998)

11. Joachims, T.: Text categorization with support vector machines: learning with many relevant features. In Proceedings of ECML-98, 10th European Conference on Machine Learning (Chemnitz, Germany, 1998), 137–142

12. Dumais, S. T., Platt, J., Heckerman, D., and Sahami, M: Inductive learning algorithms and representations for text categorization. In Proceedings of CIKM-98, 7th ACM International Conference on Information and Knowledge Management (Bethesda, MD, 1998), 148–155

13. Joachims, T.: A statistical learning model of text classification for support vector machines. In Proceedings of the 24th annual international ACM SIGIR conference on Research and development in information retrieval (New Orleans, Louisiana, 2001), 128–136

14. Dumais, S., Chen, H.: Hierarchical classification of Web content. In Proceedings of the 23rd annual international ACM SIGIR conference on Research and development in information retrieval (Athens, Greece, 2000), 256–263

15. Sebastiani, F.: Machine learning in automated text categorization. ACM Computing Surveys (CSUR), Vol. 34, Issue 1 (2002), 1–47

Challenges in Building Federation Services over Harvested Metadata

Hesham Anan, Jianfeng Tang, Kurt Maly, Michael Nelson,
Mohammad Zubair, and Zhao Yang

Old Dominion University, Norfolk, VA 23529
{anan,tang_j,maly,mln,zubair,yzhao}@cs.odu.edu

Abstract. The Open Archives Initiative Protocol for Metadata Harvesting (OAI-PMH) is a de facto standard for federation of digital repositories. OAI-PMH defines how repositories (data providers) expose their metadata as well as how harvesters (service providers) extract the metadata. In this paper we will concentrate on our experience as service providers. Although OAI-PMH makes it easy to harvest data from data providers, adding specialized services requires significant work beyond the OAI-PMH capabilities. Harvesting provides only the basic services to get metadata from repositories. However, processing these data or retrieving related metadata is not part of the OAI-PMH. In this paper, we will present the impact of value-added services like citation and reference processing, equation searching, and data normalization on the process of dynamic harvesting in Archon. Dynamic harvesting introduces challenges of keeping specialized-services consistent with ingestion of new metadata records. Archon is a NSDL NSF funded digital library that federates physics collections. We present performance data for the overhead of using these services over the regular harvesting. We also present the implementation of Simple Object Access Protocol (SOAP) web services (and corresponding client) that enhances the usability of our collections by allowing third parties to provide their own clients to search our databases directly.

1 Introduction

Using the Open Archives Initiative Protocol for Metadata Harvesting (OAI-PMH) standardizes and facilitates the process of federating multiple digital libraries (DLs). However, by design this protocol does not provide support for services beyond basic harvesting of metadata records. For example, a service that provides reference information related to a document as well as links from references to their corresponding documents needs the original metadata along with the metadata of the references. Furthermore, the full text corresponding to the original metadata might be retrieved and scanned for references. Such correlated or full text harvesting is not directly supported by OAI-PMH. Additional processing is required to store reference linking information and to update references to and from exiting documents. Another service example is normalization, such as populating missing metadata fields (e.g. subject). We have implemented services to deduce the subject if missing from the harvested Dublin Core metadata. Other examples of value-added services include displaying and searching equations that are embedded in metadata fields such as title

T.M.T. Sembok et al. (Eds.): ICADL 2003, LNCS 2911, pp. 602–614, 2003.
© Springer-Verlag Berlin Heidelberg 2003

or abstract in formats such as LaTeX [4] or MathML [8]. Equations in these formats are not easy for users to browse or view, so we have added a service to render these equations. However, this requires metadata post-processing to identify and extract equations and to convert them to easily displayable images. Processes like the one mentioned above introduce some challenges in the process of harvesting and some processes might consume a long time that provides constraints on how and when these processes must be scheduled. In this paper we review our experiences with these issues in the implementation of Archon (a DL that federates physics collections) that is part of NSF's National Science Digital Library (NSDL) project [9]. We also discuss how the addition of these specialized services affects the harvesting time.

After harvesting, Archon can work as an OAI aggregator that enables other DLs to harvest from it using the OAI-PMH. However, while the OAI-PMH provides harvesting capabilities, it does not provide distributed searching capabilities. To that end we developed web services to support searching of our collection by third parties. To implement this, we used Simple Object Access Protocol (SOAP) based Web services. As an illustration, we developed the Personal Digital Library Assistant (PDLA), a reference implementation of a client that uses these services while adding its own services of book-shelving and reference creation.

2   Process Automation

In Archon, we harvest records using OAI-PMH. This protocol provides the capability to harvest records incrementally from OAI-enabled repositories using simple commands. However, at the core of Archon we have high level services that require post-processing of harvested metadata. To keep these specialized-services consistent with ingestion of new metadata records; we implement Archon's post-harvesting processes as tasks that can be run incrementally and automatically.

The Archon post-processing conceptually consists of tasks for citation and equation processing, normalization, and a subject resolver. Some of the metadata fields (e.g. dates) have to be normalized to compensate for many conventions used at the various repositories. Normalization is not time-consuming and integration with the harvester is straightforward. However, citation processing, equation processing and subject resolution have to be implemented as tasks either because they are difficult to integrate into other processes or because of performance issues. In the following subsections, we will describe these tasks in detail.

2.1   Citation Processing

The Archon reference-linking service provides the user a list of the references for specific metadata records. Where possible the service provides links to the documents at external source archives and within Archon. Figure 1 shows a screenshot of the bottom of a metadata record that includes a list of references with some references not being resolved and several resolved to both external sources and internal Archon links. The external links are generated by using the script from CERN [6].

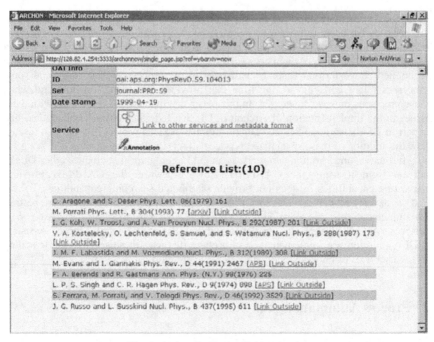

Fig. 1. Archon Reference-linking service

Figure 2 shows a screenshot of Archon's citation service. This service allows the user to search the records by citation relationship. When a user clicks the "Citations" link along each record (visible at the right of Figure 1), a window will appear that allows the user to specify a search either for all records citing this record (citation to) or all records cited by this record (citation from) in either the full Archon collection or the current result set.

Citation Processing is the background process to prepare and organize data for Archon's reference-linking service automatically after a harvest of metadata records. As shown in Figure 3, its main parts are the reference collector, bibliographic collector and reference process.

The reference collector is responsible for getting the references and uses separate approaches for different sources. One approach is to harvest reference information using OAI-PMH. For arXiv and APS records, the reference information is available as parallel metadata records. The second approach is to download the full-text document and use reference extraction software. For the CERN records we use a reference extraction script from CERN [2]. It can extract references from PDF files.

The bibliographic collector is responsible for getting bibliographic information. This is necessary because currently most DC records do not provide enough information establishing relations between metadata records with references. Where available we harvest parallel metadata records and obtain bibliographic information from them. Bibliographic information from different sources may be different for the same item. For example, some may use "Phys. Rev. D" while others use "Physics Review D". To address this problem, we normalize the bibliographic information.

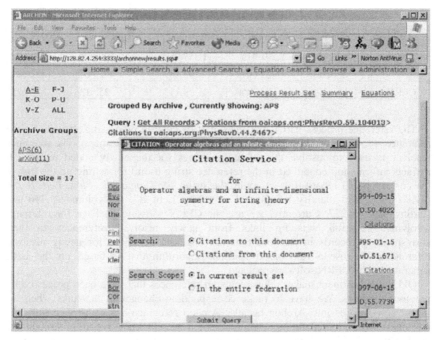

Fig. 2. Archon's Interface for Citation Service

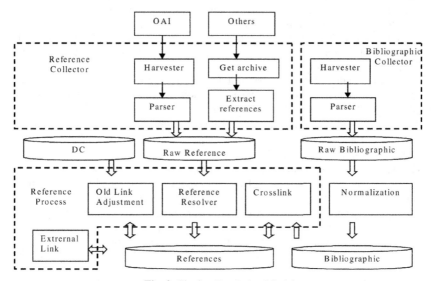

Fig. 3. Citation Processing Modules

Table 1. Archon Reference Status

Archives	Total	External	Internal	Linked	Resolved
arXiv	4,838,158	2,191,419	1,257,367	2,790,904	2,900,347
APS	686,521	427,601	195,187	432,604	520,843
CERN	58,105	24,345	9,115	25,513	27,753

The reference process part is the main part of citation processing. It includes the reference resolver, crosslink and external link and old link adjustment. The reference resolver is used to resolve the reference strings for the newly added records. It extracts information contained in the reference string useful for setting up the link to the corresponding record. For example, the string "*A. Donnachie, Phys. Lett. B 296 (1992) 227*", will identify the journal as "Phys. Lett. B", the volume is 296 and starting page is 227. Currently, we use the CERN software package for reference resolving. Crosslink sets up links from newly resolved references to their corresponding records in Archon. External link sets up URLs for newly resolved references. We use a rule based heuristic algorithm that is based on the URL generator of the CERN software package.

Old link adjustment makes adjustments on references that have been processed by previous modules. We have to make corresponding changes in the links when we ingest new records into Archon because Archon reference-linking service links the references within its federation. Therefore, when we add a new record in Archon, we need to check whether there are some old references that can be linked to this record.

The current status of references in Archon is shown in Table 1. It gives the total numbers of references for each archives as well as how many references have been resolved successfully, how many resolved references have external links (to an outside source), how many have internal links (within Archon), and how many have links (either external or internal or both). "Resolved" is higher than "Linked" because we may be able to resolve all components to a valid internal representation but the URL generator is unable to construct a link. In summary, we have a success rate ranging from 50% to 80%.

To test the validity of our rule based link generator we randomly select 20 records from Archon and analyzed the reference resolution. Table 2 shows the test result. We divide the result of links into three categories.

- Success: succeeds to point to an appropriate document.
- Success: but not to individual document, rather the link goes to a page which has a document list.
- Failure: fails to point to either the corresponding document or a document list.

In our test, the failure rate is less than 10%, which we have found fairly constant in larger random samples. The main reasons for failure links are:

- The link is to another resolver which fails to resolve it. For example, we generate the URL for the reference "I. G. Koh, W. Troost, and A. Van Proeyen Nucl. Phys., B 292(1987) 201" (a reference of oai:aps.org:PhysRevD.59.104013) as http://doi.crossref.org/resolve?sid=xxx:xxx&issn=05503213&volume=292&spage =201.
- However, the destination resolver, CrossRef, cannot resolve it.

Table 2. External Link Success/failure Ratio

Records	Total external links	Success	Success(but not to individual)	Failure
oai:aps.org:PhysRevD.59.104013	8	6	0	2
oai:aps.org:PhysRevD.16.3242	15	15	0	0
oai:arXiv.org:cond-mat/9906406	25	25	0	0
oai:aps.org:PhysRevD.64.017701	8	8	0	0
oai:arXiv.org:cond-mat/9906415	8	8	0	0
oai:arXiv.org:astro-ph/9902112	50	44	0	6
oai:arXiv.org:chao-dyn/9607003	19	17	1	1
oai:arXiv.org:hep-lat/9312002	9	9	0	0
oai:arXiv.org:nucl-th/9312002	19	16	1	2
oai:arXiv.org:hep-th/9311181	12	10	0	2
oai:arXiv.org:hep-ph/9312204	24	23	1	0
oai:arXiv.org:gr-qc/9312026	14	12	1	1
oai:arXiv.org:patt-sol/9402001	13	5	7	1
oai:arXiv.org:hep-th/9403119	25	20	4	1
oai:arXiv.org:nucl-th/9404010	13	12	0	1
oai:arXiv.org:cond-mat/9404026	17	14	1	2
oai:cds.cern.ch:CERN-PS-2002-011-AE	1	1	0	0
oai:cds.cern.ch:CERN-PPE-96-008	11	9	0	2
oai:aps.org:PhysRevD.10.357	4	4	0	0
oai:aps.org:PhysRevD.20.211	9	9	0	0
oai:aps.org:PhysRevD.30.2674	6	6	0	0
Total	310	273	16	21

- The requested object does not exist. For example, we succeed to generate the right URL for "Phys. Rev. A 26, 1179 (1982)" (a reference of oai:arXiv.org:chao-dyn/9607003) to APS. However, the cited object does not exist in APS.
- The request page does not exist. This may indicate that the URL we generated may not be right.

2.2 Equation Processing

In our federation we might find equations in some parts of the metadata that are represented in formats such as LaTeX or MathML. Viewing such representations is not as intuitive as viewing the equations themselves, so it is very useful to provide a visual tool to view the equations. We represent the equations as images and display these images when the metadata records are displayed. This requires tasks to be performed after harvesting new metadata records. Figure 4 shows the tasks involved in equation processing. These tasks include:

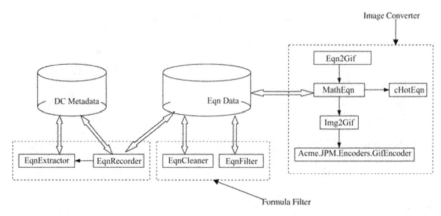

Fig. 4. Equation Processing

- **Identifying equations:** Depending on the format of the equations the boundaries of the equation within the text of the metadata are identified. For example LaTeX equations have special characters like $.
- **Filtering equations:** This task is applied to remove incomplete or incorrectly identified equations from the list of equations.
- **Equation storage:** For fast browsing images for the equations are generated and stored in a database.

Details on using equations in search can be found in [7]. None of these tasks done for the historic harvest of a collection differ from the equivalent tasks done after a dynamic harvest. In contrast to the citation services, we do not have to rely on other metadata and/or full text documents since all the information is in the regular metadata records. Thus, the task of automating this service was simply one of invoking the appropriate module after harvesting.

2.3 Subject Resolvers

Some of the metadata in the archives might not be available through OAI-PMH. For example in arXiv and APS we encountered many missing subjects and had to either guess some of them or use different resources and metadata archives to obtain them. In this section, we describe our subject resolver, which will try to fill the subject field for APS and arXiv DC records (CERN and NASA records already have appropriate subject fields). For each arXiv record without a subject field, the subject resolver will try to guess a subject based on its OAI identifier.

Figure 5 shows the process for resolving subject for an APS record. Some APS parallel metadata records contain PACS (Physics and Astronomy Classification Scheme) codes, which is a subject classification schema for physics and astronomy. Therefore, for an APS DC record without a subject field, we use the PACS codes from its corresponding parallel metadata record (which has been already obtained for citation service) and map the PACS codes into a string from the PACS schema. If its parallel metadata record does not contain PACS codes at all, we will try to guess its subject from its OAI identifier.

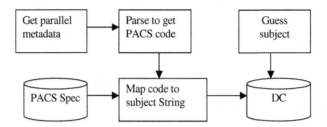

Fig. 5. Subject Resolving for APS Records

3 Web Services and Applications

Web Services are self-contained self-describing, modular applications that can be described, published, located, and remotely invoked. They can perform anything from simple requests to complicated business processes. Once a Web service is deployed, other applications (and other Web services) can discover and invoke the deployed service [14]. Web services usage promotes interoperability by minimizing the requirements for shared understanding as well as enabling just in time integration.

We implemented some web services to expose and extend the use of our collections. Two of these web services are:

- **Search service:** This service provides access to all search functionality without the need to use the Archon interface.
- **Book shelf service:** This service allows each user to have a personalized collection which is a subset of the overall archives. It can be used for different purposes. For example, teachers can use it to collect course materials and package it in a personalized collection.

Using the above web services, clients can be developed to provide special features according to requirements of different user communities. We developed a client, Personal Digital Library Assistant (PDLA), using the search web service. This is a Windows client that provides a customized interface to search the Archon collections. It can be used to select and store special sub collection of the search results locally. It can also be used to export selected documents' metadata in different formats such as XML, Text or Microsoft Word using selected templates like the ACM style or IEEE style. This allows an author to create her own bibliography of frequently used references and have them presented in formats appropriate for the intended journal. Figure 6 shows the results of using the PDLA client to search Archon for papers written by 'Maly'. In Figure 7 we specify that references to a select group of papers on the bookshelf be exported in Word format appropriate for an ACM publication with the result shown in Figure 8.

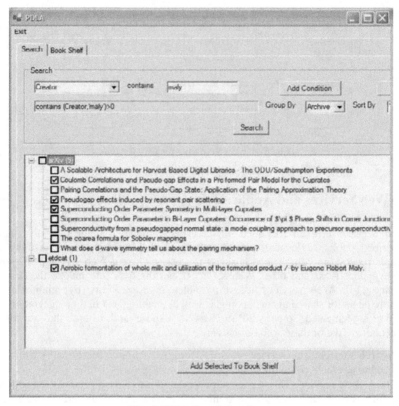

Fig. 6. PDLA Search Interface

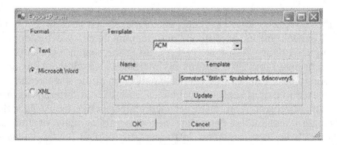

Fig. 7. PDLA Export Interface

4 Performance

Performance was an important consideration when we implemented the Archon background processing since it has to complete before the next dynamic harvesting

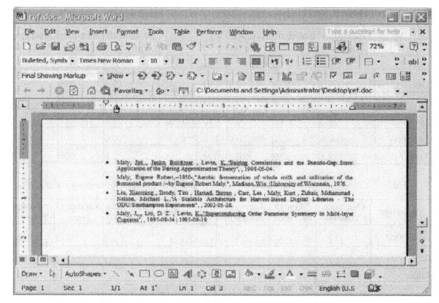

Fig. 8. References generated by PDLA

starts. We have done performance tests on the OAI harvester, Citation Processing and Subject Revolver for APS records. The objective was to identify any bottlenecks. The results for harvesting DC records for NCSTRL-NCSU (Table 3), arXiv from Arc (Table 4), APS (Table 5) and for harvesting parallel metadata records from APS respectively (Table 6) are shown below.

These tables show how many times each operation has been executed and how much time has been spent on each operation, where Identify, Resumption, ListRecords, ListSets stand for sending corresponding request and getting the result, and DB stands for database operation.

From these tables, we can see that the most time-consuming operation is ListRecords. And the performance of the OAI harvester greatly depends on the

<table>
<tr><td colspan="4">**Table 3.** NCSTRL-NCSU[1]</td></tr>
<tr><th>Operation</th><th>Operation Time (s)</th><th>Number of Times</th><th>Average Time (s)</th></tr>
<tr><td>Identify</td><td>0.6</td><td>1</td><td>0.6</td></tr>
<tr><td>DB</td><td>7.0</td><td>143</td><td>0.1</td></tr>
<tr><td>Resumption</td><td>0.1</td><td>2</td><td>0.1</td></tr>
<tr><td>ListRecords</td><td>46.2</td><td>2</td><td>23.1</td></tr>
<tr><td>ListSets</td><td>24.8</td><td>1</td><td>24.8</td></tr>
<tr><td>Total</td><td>80.5</td><td>143</td><td>0.6</td></tr>
</table>

<table>
<tr><td colspan="4">**Table 4.** arXiv (from ARC)</td></tr>
<tr><th>Operation</th><th>Operation Time (s)</th><th>Number of Times</th><th>Average Time (s)</th></tr>
<tr><td>Identify</td><td>0.17</td><td>1</td><td>0.2</td></tr>
<tr><td>DB</td><td>46</td><td>1,000</td><td>0.1</td></tr>
<tr><td>Resumption</td><td>0.50</td><td>10</td><td>0.1</td></tr>
<tr><td>ListRecords</td><td>3,805.8</td><td>10</td><td>380.6</td></tr>
<tr><td>ListSets</td><td>5.7</td><td>1</td><td>5.7</td></tr>
<tr><td>Total</td><td>3,858.3</td><td>1,000</td><td>3.9</td></tr>
</table>

---

[1] An entry '0.1' means a time less than 0.1s.

Table 5. APS (DC)

Operation	Operation Time (s)	Number of Times	Average Time (s)
Identify	0.2	1	0.2
DB	9.7	220	0.1
Resumption	0.1	4	0.1
ListRecords	10.3	11	0.9
ListSets	0.6	1	0.6
Total	22.5	220	0.1

Table 6. APS (Parallel)

Operation	Operation Time (s)	Number of Times	Average Time (s)
Identify	0.2	1	0.2
DB	45.1	906	0.1
Resumption	0.4	10	0.1
ListRecords	72.1	11	6.6
ListSets	0.6	1	0.6
Total	125.6	906	0.1

Table 7. Citation Processing for APS

Operation	Operation Time (s)	Number of Times	Average Time (s)
Adjustment	13.2	895	0.1
Biblio Parsing	21.8	906	0.1
Biblio Normalization	N/A	N/A	N/A
Ref Parsing	106.4	902	0.1
Ref resolving	624.6	13,129	0.1
Cross-linking	103	13,129	0.1
Total	868.9	906	1.0

Table 8. Citation Processing for arXiv

Operation	Operation Time (s)	Number of Times	Average Time (s)
Adjustment	8.2	614	0.1
Biblio Parsing	10.1	614	0.1
Biblio Normalization	21.9	453	0.1
Ref Parsing	134.2	614	0.2
Ref Resolving	923.7	18,797	0.1
Cross-linking	123.1	18,563	0.1
Total	1,221.3	614	2

performance of data providers. For harvesting one DC record, it took 0.1 seconds for APS, 0.6 seconds for NCSTRL and 3.9 seconds for ARC on the average. In addition, the size of the record has some effects on the performance of the OAI harvester. Harvesting one APS parallel metadata record, which is much larger than its corresponding DC record in average, takes more time than harvesting one APS DC record. Table 7 and Table 8 show the performance results for Citation Processing for APS and arXiv records.

These tables show how many times each operation has been executed and how much time has been spent on each operation, where Identify, Resumption, ListRecords, ListSets stand for sending corresponding request and getting the result, and DB stands for database operation.

From these tables, we can see that the most time-consuming operation is ListRecords. And the performance of the OAI harvester greatly depends on the performance of data providers. For harvesting one DC record, it took 0.1 seconds for APS, 0.6 seconds for NCSTRL and 3.9 seconds for ARC on the average. In addition, the size of the record has some effects on the performance of the OAI harvester. Harvesting one APS parallel metadata record, which is much larger than its corresponding DC record in average, takes more time than harvesting one APS DC record. Table 7 and Table 8 show the performance results for Citation Processing for APS and arXiv records.

Table 9. Citation Processing for CERN

Operation	Operation Time (s)	Number of Times	Average Time (s)
Adjustment	13.6	972	0.1
Download HTML	327.9	256	1.3
Download PDF	468.8	181	2.6
Ref Extraction	117.7	179	0.7
Ref resolving	75	1,397	0.1
Cross-linking	9.8	1,397	0.1
DB	16.8	2,369	0.1
Total	1,029.6	972	1.1

Table 10. APS Subject Revolving

Operation	Operation Time (s)	Number of Times	Average Time (s)
Initial operation	0.1	1	0.1
Get parallel metadata	14.3	1,000	0.1
Parse metadata	7.1	996	0.1
Map	2.1	514	0.1
Update	19.5	996	0.1
Flag	7.1	996	0.1
Index	18.5	1	18.5
Total	68.5	1,000	0.1

From these two tables, we can see that the most time-consuming operation is reference resolving. It took about 1 second for processing one APS record and about 2 seconds for processing one arXiv record. This difference is because for these test records one APS record has 14 references on average while one arXiv record on average has 30 references.

Table 9 shows the result of Citation Processing for CERN records. Citation Processing for CERN records is different from processing APS or arXiv records. CERN citation processing extracts references from the full-text downloaded documents instead of getting references from parallel metadata records. The identifier field of a CERN record contains a URL for an HTML page, which contains a URL for the PDF file. Hence, to download the full-text document involves two steps: downloading the HTML page and downloading the PDF page. However, not all CERN records contain extractable PDF files. To improve the performance, our program will not try to download the full-text documents for those without extractable PDF files.

From the tables, we see that bottlenecks are in downloading HTML pages, downloading PDFs and reference extraction. It took about 1 second to process one CERN record. Table 10 shows the result of subject resolving for APS records. In the table, Update stands for updating the subject field for the DC records, Flag stands for updating some flags in database, Map stands for mapping the PACS code to subject string and Index stands for re-index the database. From the table, we can see that it took about 68 milliseconds to process one record.

5 Conclusions

This paper reports on our experience with implementing higher level services for a collection that federates a number of other collections using OAI-PMH. Since there are few, if any, such services beside Archon, this paper is more of a study in itself than a comparative analysis. Our performance analysis shows that we can comfortably set the scheduler of the OAI harvester to about 1 day and have a safety factor for human intervention should the automatic process break down. Whether the search Web service is indeed a useful tool depends on the usefulness of the basic federation collection. We are in the process of adding to the current production service of federating CERN, arXiv, and APS, also NASA and plan to collaborate with AIP(American Institute of Physics) to have their collections included as well. Once all these are federated and working at the high service level at a dynamic basis, the Web services should prove to be attractive particularly to authors of papers who can thus maintain their own bibliographies.

Acknowledgement. We are extremely grateful for the cooperation and collaboration of Corrado Pettenati and Jean-Yves Le Meur from CERN who have graciously provided us their code for reference processing. They have worked with us to adapt their process to Archon; their code is one of the reasons for the high success rate of reference resolution.

References

1. CERN Document Server. Available at: http://cdsweb.cern.ch.
2. Claivaz J., Le Meur,J. , Robinson, N. , "From Fulltext Documents to Structured Citations: CERN's Automated Solution", High Energy Phys. Libr. Webzine : 5 (2001). Available at http://doc.cern.ch/heplw/5/papers/2/.
3. Lagoze, C., Van De Sompel, H., Nelson, M. & Warner, S. (2002), "The Open Archives Initiative Protocol for Metadata Harvesting (Version 2.0)". Available at: http://www.openarchives.org/OAI/openarchivesprotocol.html.
4. LaTeX project home page, http://www.latex-project.org/.
5. Liu, X., Maly, K., Zubair, M. & Nelson, M. L. (2001), "Arc - An OAI service provider for digital library federation.", D-Lib Magazine, 7(4). Available at http: //www.dlib.org/dlib/april01/liu/04liu.html.
6. Lodi, E., Vesely, M., Vigen, J., "Link managers for grey literature", CERN-AS-99-006, 4th International Conference on Grey Literature : New Frontiers in Grey Literature, Washington, DC, USA, 4–5 Oct 1999 /Ed. by Farace, D J and Frantzen, J - GreyNet, Amsterdam, 2000, pp. 116–134.
7. Maly K., Zubair, M., Nelson, M., Liu, X., Anan, H., Gao, J., Tang, J., & Zhao, Y., "Archon—a digital library that federates physics collections.", In *DC-2002: Metadata for e-Communities: Supporting Diversity and Convergence*, Florence, Italy, October 13–17 2002, pp. 25–37.
8. Mathematical Markup Language (MathML) Version 2.0, W3C Recommendation 21 February 2001, http://www.w3.org/TR/MathML2/.
9. NSDL project 2002. Available at: http://www.nsdl.org.
10. PACS 2003. Available at: http://www.aip.org/pacs/.
11. SOAP Version 1.2, W3C Working Draft 9 July 2001, Martin Gudgin, Marc Hadley, Jean-Jacques Moreau, Henrik Frystyk Nielsen, http://www.w3.org/TR/soap12/ .
12. Van De Sompel, H and Lagoze, C., "The Santa Fe Convention of the Open Archives Initiative", D-Lib Magazine, 6(2), February 2000. http://www.dlib.org/delb/february00/vandesompel-oai/02vandesompel-oai.html.
13. UDDI Specifications http://www.uddi.org/specification.html.
14. Web Services Description Language (WSDL) 1.1, W3C Note 15 March 2001, Erik Christensen, Francisco Curbera, Greg Meredith, Sanjiva Weerawarana http://www.w3.org/TR/wsdl

Effective Design Multimedia Content Materials: Child-Centered Design

Norhayati Abd. Mukti and Siew Pei Hwa

Information Science Department, Faculty of Technology and Information Science,
Universiti Kebangsaan Malaysia, 43600 Bangi, Selangor, Malaysia
nam@ftsm.ukm.my

Abstract. While interest is growing in the integration of ICT in learning and teaching, the use of multimedia technology has offered an alternative way of delivering instruction. Multimedia technology plays an important role in the education because of its ability to provide a virtual environment for learners to effectively acquire knowledge. This paper argues that if we are to design effective learning application for children then a child-centered approach to the design should be taken. This approach should be based on general human-computer interaction principles as well as educational theories.

1 Introduction

The rapidly growing amount of educational multimedia software is accompanied by increasing research in new forms of multimedia presentation and interactivity. Today, of course, multimedia is the use of text, graphics, audio, animation, and video to present information. This digital information environment is dynamic. Delivery of multimedia applications include such format as CD-ROMs, the Internet, CD or DVD/Web hybrids, videodiscs, laserdiscs, distance learning, video conferencing, and the ever-evolving handheld PDAs and e-books. These applications run the gamut from computer-based tutoring systems for adults to the new category of "edutainment" products for children. These very diverse applications seem to share a common perspective – multimedia information helps people learn.

According to Najjar (1996), people enjoy multimedia, prefer multimedia learning materials, and believe that multimedia helps them learn. These beliefs are exploited by the marketers of multimedia hardware, software and services to hype their products. Based on several research (e.g., "Eloquent Idea" 1992; Hofstetter 1994"; and Staff 1990;), Najjar noted that "People generally remember 10 percent of what they read, 20 percent of what they hear, 30 percent of what they see, and 50 percent of what they hear and see..." [1]. So, many people argue that multimedia has the potential to create high quality learning environments which actively engage the learner, thereby promoting deep learning. However there is growing evidence that the potential of multimedia is not being fulfilled. Hence, to ensure that educational multimedia applications realize their potential it is necessary to stand back and re-examine the key features of multimedia and how they can be used to enhance learning. In this paper, aspects that concern with child-centered educational multimedia materials design will be presented and discussed. The example for

T.M.T. Sembok et al. (Eds.): ICADL 2003, LNCS 2911, pp. 615–626, 2003.

discussion herein is referred to a multimedia-based instructional package called CITRA.

2 Description of CITRA

CITRA (Courseware development to project positive Images of TRAditional Malay oral narratives) is intended as an innovative and interactive multimedia application, which is designed and developed based on a well-researched conceptual model. The principle objective of developing CITRA is to create an application that combine multiple media in an enticing environment that allows the positive images and moral values to be projected via the multimedia capabilities and technologies in order to foster good moral sense in children. In addition, CITRA is designed and developed not only incorporates various media but also various instructional strategies based on sound pedagogical approaches and learning theories deemed suitable for children ages between 8-9 years old. CITRA merges the idea of stories with multimedia functionality to produce dynamic and flexible software to exercise thinking while acting, playing, exploring, navigating, and having fun. CITRA explore new horizons in the use of Malay traditional oral narratives as a mean for helping young learners construct and reconstruct their thinking structures and practice positive moral sentiments more effectively and expeditiously.

CITRA, which uses the CD-ROMs and computer as the means of dissemination, is a didactic tool made up of four key learning modules: Storytelling World module, Enjoyable Reading World module, Word Enrichment Corner module, and Mind Test Land module. Four activities that adopt the problem solving, interactivity and perpetual navigation approaches are built into this module. The activities are fun, mind stimulating and motivating, and are related to the previous three learning modules. The four activities are Knowledge Test, two educational electronic games, and Creating Story activity. Besides, there are four different tests or quizzes built into the Knowledge Test activity namely Comprehension Test, Vocabulary Quiz, Good Moral Values Appreciation Test and Application Test. CITRA comprises of eleven pieces of multimedia courseware which were developed using traditional Malay oral narratives as core content. There are many different types of traditional Malay oral narratives but had been categorized into three major types namely myth, legend and folktales. The focus of CITRA is on folktales, which comprise of humorous tales, edifying tales and animal tales. CITRA development is done using a Macromedia Director authoring environment. Macromedia Director is chosen to integrate and synchronize all the media elements that have been created or modified and stored digitally in the computer into one final application for the purpose of conveying a specific message to the audience or learners. Many multimedia technologies are available for authors to create CITRA. CITRA then is packaged into a distributed format for the end-user.

3 Principle Components of Educational Materials

Educational materials prepared in any medium consist of three discrete elements: content, organization and interface. These elements define the essential characteristics of the instructional package when they are combined to create the instructional sequence. The different media in which educational materials can be developed have unique and distinct attributes. Through these attributes, the content, organization and interface can all be varied to provide the unique forms which are instilled in instructional packages across the different media forms [2]. Before proceeding to further discussion on child-centered educational materials design, it is useful to consider each of content, organization and interface to distinguish between them and to establish the role of each in educational materials design.

3.1 Content

The content of a production is the specific story that we want to film, the specific topic that we want to address, and the events that will be the subject of our documentary [3]. In brief, this attribute describes the information that is contained within the product. Typically, this includes such elements as text, diagrams, graphics and photographs. Video materials are able to support temporal media forms such as audio, animations and moving images as well as static graphics. Multimedia materials support many different media forms combined in instructional settings [2].

According to Hartman, educators want the multimedia products to contain the high quality content that will enrich, complement, and supplement their existing curricular. They expect motivating multimedia to increase student interest, attention and retention. Hartman added that educators look for content without gender, ethnic or racial biases. Many want multimedia built around common thematic units or programs that provide opportunities for collaboration among students, or that provide different perspectives on an issue so that students learn to approach subject matter in ways that are rarely found in textbooks. Thus, content is much more than just factual and descriptive information. In order to be successful in the classroom, content must be based on a real understanding of schools' curricular emphases, how children learn, and how classrooms really work [4]. This means that designing educational multimedia materials needs greater effort in the presentation of the contents since this will partly determine the success of learning process.

Effective learning content and instructional design should be the fundamental of every learning system whether offline or online. Effective learning content is not just interactive or media-rich; it reflects the learner's work environment and reality. To be both interactive and job ready, learning materials must have at their core workplace competencies and industry standards representing the behaviour expectations placed on the learner. Content should support learner in their acquisition of knowledge and skills, and the transfer of their skills and knowledge into work performance [5]. Norshuhada and Landoni assert that it is important to carefully design the way content is structured, organized, and presented. The types of activity in which learners will be involved play significant roles in the success of pedagogic design. Thus, studies on what kind of activities cater for most learners' needs are indeed helpful in promoting better child-centered educational materials design [6].

Referred to Shiksha India's approach towards content development, the content in the child-centered environment will be taught in an interesting and interactive manner to ensure that the child learns to use computer as a tool to enhance his/her knowledge base. The approach addresses a number of key prepositions for content development as: (1) accredited quality syllabus-based courseware which makes learning enjoyable and interesting, (2) non-syllabus based international courseware which enables better understanding of concepts and broadens horizons, (3) ability to exploit the attractiveness of multimedia for creative pursuits, and (4) links with a wider community for collaborative learning [7]. Furthermore, content development should take into account the many source of curriculum: (1) the curriculum has an articulated description of its theoretical base that is consistent with prevailing professional opinion and research how children learn; (2) curriculum content is designed to achieve long range goals for children in all domains -- social, emotional, cognitive and physical -- and to prepare children to function as fully contributing members of a democratic society, (3) curriculum addresses the development of knowledge and understanding, processes and skills, dispositions and attitudes, (4) curriculum addresses a broad range of content that is relevant, engaging, and meaningful to children, (5) curriculum goals are realistic and attainable for most children in the designated age range for which they were designed, (6) curriculum content reflects and is generated by the needs and interests of individual children within the group. Curriculum incorporates a wide variety of learning experiences, materials and equipment, and instructional strategies, to accommodate a broad range of children's individual differences in prior experience, maturation rates, styles of learning, needs, and interests, (7) curriculum respects and supports individual, cultural and linguistic diversity. Curriculum supports and encourages positive relationships with children's families, (8) curriculum builds upon what children already know and are able to do (activating prior knowledge) to consolidate their learning and to foster their acquisition of new concepts and skills, (9) the curriculum provides conceptual frameworks for children so that their mental constructions based on prior knowledge and experience become more complex ever time, (10) curriculum allows for focus on a particular topic or content, while allowing for integration across traditional subject-matter divisions by planning around themes and/or learning experiences that provide opportunities for rich conceptual development, (11) the curriculum content has intellectual integrity; content meets the recognized standards of the relevant subject matter disciplines, (12) the content of the curriculum respects children's intelligence and does not waste their time, (13) curriculum engages children actively, not passively, in the learning process. Children have opportunity to make meaningful choices, (14) curriculum values children's constructive errors and does not prematurely limit exploration and experimentation for the sake of ensuring "right" answers, (15) curriculum emphasizes the development of children's thinking, reasoning, decision-making, and problem-solving abilities, (16) curriculum emphasizes the value of social interaction to learning in all domains and provides opportunities to learn from peers, (17) curriculum protects children's psychological safety, that is, children feel happy, relaxed, and comfortable rather than disengaged, frightened, worried, or stressed, (18) the curriculum strengthens children's sense of competence and enjoyment of learning by providing experiences for children to succeed from their point of view, and (19) the curriculum is flexible so teachers can adapt to individual children or groups [8].

In the context of designing CITRA, using local content and vernacular language is an important issue because the teaching and learning become more effective when the content suits local culture and way of life. CITRA adopted thematic literature-based approach. Literature here means local literature based on traditional Malay oral narratives. Literature or stories are chosen since the story response approach brings another dimension into moral development, that of story development. Many researchers in moral education have adopted this narrative approach influencing curriculum through a story response approach. Through interacting with story, children are given the opportunity to reason about such things as cause, effect and consequences, and to consider moral choices, but also use the word of story as a mirror for their own life experience [9]. The design of content and activities in CITRA was also made using the experience from other system and from education, Malay literature and ICT (information and communications technologies) specialist. It then adopted the holistic child development approach that takes account into the literacy experience of child, which assists in the cognitive, psychomotor and affective development of a child. It also incorporated a variety of pedagogical approaches and learning theories to meet diverse learning style of children. In addition, the activities concern with moral values learning and evaluation are designed based on the syllabus or curriculum of primary school (KBSR) moral education. The moral values infused into the curriculum are of affective and emotional domains. It has been emphasized that some moral values need to be instilled into all children, so that they can achieve overall and balanced development. There are sixteen good moral values infused into the curriculum of moral education. They are: (1) compassion, (2) self-reliance, (3) respect, (4) love, (5) freedom, (6) courage, (7) physical and mental cleanliness, (8) co-operation, (9) diligence, (10) moderation, (11) gratitude, (12) rationality, (13) public spiritedness, (14) humility, (15) honesty, and (16) justice. Each moral value entails a number of sub-values respectively.

3.2   Organization

The content within instructional materials is delivered according to the manner in which it has been stored and represented. With paper-based printed materials such as books, organization tends to be sequential where one chapter leads to the next. Video materials also embrace sequential organization and most materials designed with this medium are designed to flow from one point to the next in the order. Multimedia materials can support multiple organization modes when compared to conventional materials. The media elements and instructional materials can be organized and stored in many different ways ranging from linear to the more flexible referential forms [5]. Fig. 1 shows an example of the organization mode of multimedia materials in CITRA.

3.3   Interface

The interface of instructional materials describes the environment in which the information is presented [5]. Richer environments include a library with doors, help desk, rooms, collections, and shelves, and the City of Knowledge with gates, streets, buildings and landmarks. The information superhighway is often presented as a

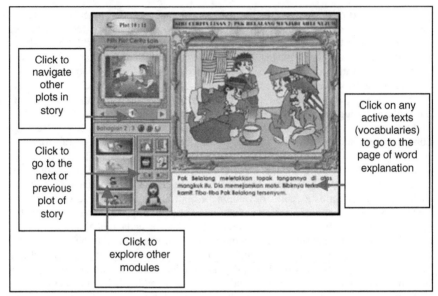

Fig. 1. A sample screen from Enjoyable Reading World module in CITRA. It adopts multiple organization modes

metaphor. The metaphor need to be useful in presenting high-level concepts, appropriate for expressing middle-level objects, and effective in suggesting pixel-level details. Designing of computer-based metaphor extends to support tools for the information seeker. Some system provide maps of information spaces as an overview to allow learners to grasp the relative size of components and to discover what is not in the database. History stacks, bookmarks, help desks, and guides offering tours are common support tools in information environments [10]. The representation of actions is often conveyed by action handlers: The labels, icons, buttons, or image regions that indicate where learners should click to invoke an action. Navigation action handlers can be turned page corner to indicate next page operation, a highlighted term for a link, a magnifying glass to zoom in or open an outline, a pencil to indicate annotation and so forth. Sometimes, the action handle is merely a pull-down menu item or a dialog box offering rich possibilities. The ensemble of handles should allow learners to decompose their action plan conveniently into a series of clicks and keystrokes [10].The aspect of user interface will be discussed in more depth in Section 5.

4   Interactions in Educational Multimedia Materials

Interactions and interactivity have become key elements characterizing much of the teaching and learning associated with new technologies. In essence, the terms describe the means by which the user communicates with the technology and brings about a change or response as a consequence [2]. In other words, interactivity means

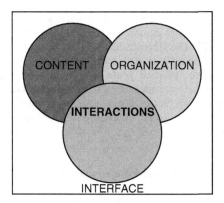

Fig. 2. The principle components of educational multimedia materials

the ability to interact with the media in such a way that improves the accessibility, usability and presentation of the information. Educational multimedia materials shall not just "deliver" information to the learners, but also enable interactive learning. Educators and learners should be capable of getting immediate responses of their actions during the process of knowledge seeking and exploration. The interactive nature allows the user to move independently and non-sequentially through the available material [11].

The forms of interactions that are supported by instructional materials are many and varied and serve many different purposes. Some of the interactions are designed as part of the instructional materials and as such are best seen as elements of content. Other interactions are present to enable the user to control and manage the materials and are elements of the interface. Yet another form of interaction is used to locate and access the content. This form of interaction is tied directly to the organizational structure of the materials. When interactions are considered in this broad context, it is evident that rather than being discrete elements within instructional materials, they become characteristic of the complete package [2]. Interactions and interactivity are evident in the content, the organization and the interface (see Fig. 2).

5 HCI for Children

What is HCI? The term human-computer interaction (HCI) was adopted in the mid-1980s to describe the emerging field of study that focuses on all aspect of interaction between users and computers. This includes, but is certainly not limited to, the design of the computer interface. HCI is concerned with understanding, designing, evaluating and implementing interactive computing system for human use [12]. It is highly interdisciplinary area of research; the main contributing disciplines are Computer Science, Cognitive Psychology, Social and Organizational Psychology, Ergonomics and Human Factors. Other areas of interest include: artificial intelligence, linguistics, philosophy, sociology, anthropology, engineering and design [13]. Emerging from HCI research, the emphasis is placed on the need to involve the users in activity when promoting deep learning. Users should not need to adapt to a system but rather than the system should be built to suit the needs of the users and therefore be usable by the users. The concept of usability is central to HCI and refers to making system easy to learn and easy to use [12]. The International Organization for Standardization (ISO) defines usability as "...the effectiveness, efficiency and satisfaction with which specified users can achieve specified goals in particular environments..." In some ways, usability builds on the older idea of user friendliness. This was a term that was popularly used to describe whether or not a system was easy for the user to operate [14]. Another important concept in HCI literature is affordance. This term means that the design of something should suggest (i.e., afford) its functionality [12].

5.1   Applying HCI for Children to Educational Materials Design

Children are certainly humans with needs that are different from those of adults. Establishing an understanding of HCI issues that are specific to children is a neglected area of HCI research. There is without doubt far more research into designing for adults. Children's issues are occasionally documented in the HCI literature. One area that covers learners in general is the area that looks at the needs of novice users versus the experienced user. The authors will cover the areas of novice versus experienced users as well as some issues in child-centered HCI in this section.

Novice versus Experienced Users. Although not all children are novices, it is probably safe to assume that some children are novices. When users are new to an application, they are generally two types of learning that takes place. This observation applies equally to children using educational software. The two hurdles are: (1) learning the educational content, and (2) learning the interface of the software. In 1987, Carroll pointed out the most of the user-interface research concentrated on expert users despite the fact that the more difficult issues, namely ease of learning and skill acquisition arose with novice users. Topic found in the literature that deal with novice users are the encouragement of exploratory learning, the use of animated demonstrations to facilitate exploratory learning, matching the user-interface to user-skill level, and the tailoring of colour, help explanations, and default values to novice users. Exploratory learning with respect to application software refers to learning how to perform a task through exploration of the software using trial and error. Carroll has shown that exploratory learning may have a positive impact on computer skill acquisition and he notes that there are a variety of minimalist training materials that support exploratory. Another method to facilitate exploratory learning has been suggested by Payne *et al.* They suggest the use of short animated demonstrations to help novice users in their initial exploration of a system. The animated demonstrations recommended are not task-by-task animations, but rather single animations that serve as an orientation to a system. Matching the user-interface to user-skill level has also been suggested as another way to accommodate novice users. Trumbly *et. al* found that task performance increases and error rates decrease when user interface characteristics are mated to user computer knowledge, for example novice interface to novice user. Examples of interface characteristics include the use of colour, the types of error messages, the degree of help provided, and the use of default values. Research findings revealed that colour can be beneficially employed to highlight or draw attention to special features (Wlliges and Williges 1984). The use of colour for experienced users however is considered to be less important because highlighting is not needed as much. With regard to help facilities, lengthy explanations have been shown to be useful for novice users while more concise error messages are recommended for experienced users (Shneiderman 1986). Lastly, default values are useful for reducing keystrokes are especially helpful to novice users because suggested inputs are supplied. Another interface characteristic that deserves discussion is audio. Earcons are sounds that inform the user about the state of the system. The majority of earcons have been symbolic but interface designers are beginning to explore the use of iconic earcons. A symbolic earcon is one in which the mapping between sound and action is entirely arbitrary, for instance, a beep for a wrong keystroke (Gaver 1986). Because of the arbitrariness of symbolic earcons, their affordances are not obvious. On the other hand, since the affordances of iconic earcons are more obvious, they will be helpful to novice users [12].

Child-Centered Design. One difference between adults and children is the mental models that they form. Mental models are formed by users in order to help guide them through attempts to perform tasks and correct errors while using computer software. One particular design strategy is to encourage the correct mental model of the user. This can be accomplished by having the application use of a metaphor for something that the user already knows (Flatten *et al.* 1989). A popular metaphor is that of the desktop, but Jones states that the desktop metaphor is not suitable for children. Typically, interfaces based on the desktop metaphor include icon for such things as file folder and in-out trays. However Jones argues that for a child to understand what these items represent, the child will need some knowledge of the office environment, which most children do not have. Jones suggestion of having children design the icons should be considered when designing educational materials [12]. The icons should be meaningful to children, for example, to indicate "Exit", the designer can use an animated "open-close door". Children prefer direct manipulation to dialogue and so, whenever possible, the educational materials should opt for direct manipulation.

Educators want multimedia that is intuitive and easy for children, as well as adults, to learn and navigate through right out of the box or upon first landing on a system. They want computer environments that are easy to handle by novice users and experienced users alike. Hartman suggests a number of characteristics of child-centered design as below [4]:

GUI Design. A product's graphical user interface (GUI) must contain the following types of elements to be deemed user-friendly for children: (1) simple, uncluttered screens, (2) age-appropriate graphics that enhance the content, rather than interfering with it, (3) fonts, styles, sizes and colours that are easy to read, (4) concise text that pays attention to grammar and punctuation and that avoids slang, (5) dialog boxes that have titles so the user knows what the box is meant for and that always offer a way out (fro example, a Cancel button), (6) background and foreground colors that aren't too bright or too dark, (7) menus (e.g., drop-down, cascading) that are group logically and structured so they make sense, even to novice users, (8) click-and-drag features with visual cues (e.g., a cursor that changes shape, icons that change appearance). While this is most crucial for early learning programs, it is a design plus for all education users, (9) icons that clearly represent what they are meant to represent, and

(10) on-line help (hypertext) systems that actually help users to get answers to their questions easily.

Navigation. Navigation should be seamless. On CDs, for instance, there should be more than one way to move around (e.g. via icons and menus).The program should be easy to navigate from any page. All links within a page should work smoothly, all the time, or enable users to easily jump back to the page they left.

Audio. Audio must sound crisp and clear and must serve to enhance learning. Narrated text should be spoken clearly and slowly enough so that the user can understand what is being said. Often, developers of early learning programs hire children as their audio talent. While this can significantly enhance the product, giving it a fun "kid" feel, it can also hurt the product if the children's speech is slurred or spoken too quickly. Volume control (as well as the ability to turn off audio completely) is a crucial feature that some multimedia developers overlook. The result is that in some schools, excellent products remain untouched because the schools' computers have no headphone and are located in a central area, like the library. Without volume controls, users can't use the product without disturbing others.

Video. Video clips can make an instructional material come alive, but they must play smoothly, each and every time. Users should be able to pause or stop the video in mid-play without causing the program to crash.

Feedback and Reinforcement. When users make an incorrect choice, how does the computer respond? Many teachers balk at feedback that seems punitive (e.g., "Wrong answer!") and look for multimedia that provides only useful, positive feedback (e.g., "Good try... try again.") so users will feel safe in making repeated attempts. Teachers also look for positive reinforcement that subtly guides students to the correct solutions by having them re-think facts or solutions. For example, if an incorrect path is taken, the program's response might be a pop-up dialog box or audio clip with a question to spur thinking and help guide students back to the correct path without directly pointing them to the answer.

Given that the user needs are paramount, one important aspect of HCI work is to understand the context and the environment in which systems will be used. Designing CITRA fits into the broad domain of HCI. The users are children and the goal is to produce usable materials that have educational content. The materials must be usable in that they must allow for diverse users and they must be enjoyable to use. Besides the careful choice of colourful graphics, a whole range of sound can be played including music, friendly narration and special sound effects to elaborate the situation and environment of a scene. Sounds are crucial in multimedia applications as they are often used to attract attention, elicit emotion or dramatize a point [15]. In addition to that, the presentation also entails animations like "birds fly", "butterflies fly", "running stream", and so forth. Animations play a significant role in providing action, realism, visualization and demonstration [16]. Children's titles, in particular rely heavily on animations to attract children's attention and increase their interests in exploring more content [15].

6 Conclusion

Educational multimedia materials that are played on stand-alone computers, as well as materials that can be played over computer networks such as Internet involve large amounts of learner initiated activity and action. While many consider that the interactions in programs make significant contribution to achieving learning outcomes. Interactions are present in all components of instructional materials, the content, its organization and the interface through which it is presented. Interactions play a communicative role in the human-computer dialogue. In considering the value of interactions from learning perspective, the key attribute is not the function or form of the interaction but rather the nature of the thinking it encourages in the learner. Effective educational multimedia materials require interactions that do far more than manage and control the program and provide choices for the user. Some research on educational multimedia materials has been conducted and the results are mixed. The success of the educational multimedia materials seems depend on the nature of the educational content and how the multimedia material compares to traditional classroom education. It has been argued that the goal should be to integrated multimedia materials into the classroom curriculum. The authors hope is that the discussion in this paper will encourage other researchers not only to do further studies on the learning of children in the context of computer-based environments but also to study the HCI issues arising in the design of educational multimedia materials for children, and investigate how to create a learning environments in which the above elements are cohesively and dynamically integrated.

References

1. Najjar, L.J.: Multimedia Information and Learning. Journal of Educational Multimedia and Hypermedia 5 (1996) 129–150
2. Oliver, R.: Interactions in Multimedia Learning Materials: The Things that Matter. British Journal of Educational Technology, [Online] Available:
   Elrond.scam.ecu.edu.au/oliver/docs/96/IMMS.pdf [2003, May 9]
3. The Content, [Online] Available: [2003, May 9]
   http://www.sign-lang.uni-hamburg/signingbooks/SBRC/Grid/d71/guide05.htm
4. Hartman, G.: Multimedia Product development: What Educators Really Want, [Online] Available: http://www.hartmanedtech.com/html/Hartman.pdf [2003, May 25]
5. Technologies for Learning Group. Content Development Solutions, [Online] Available: http://www.tlg.ca/contentdev.html [2003, May 9]
6. Norshuhada Shiratuddin & Landoni, M.: Multiple intelligence based e-Books, [Online] Available: http://www.ics.Itsn.ac.uk/pub/conf2001/papers/Shiratuddin.htm [2002, Aug 25]
7. Confederation of Indian Industry. Shiksha India, [Online] Available:
   http://www. 216.122.48.63/Shiksha/Content.html [2003, April 25].
8. National Association for the Education of Young Children: Guidelines for Appropriate Curriculum Content and Assessment in Programs Serving Children Ages 3 Through 8 (1990): A Position Statement of the National Association for the Education of Young Children and the National Association of Early Childhood Specialists in State Departments of Education, [Online] Available:
   http://www.naeyc.org/resources/position_statements/pscag98.pdf [2003, April 25]
9. Menz, O. & Dodd, J.M.: Stewardship: A Concept in Moral Education, [Online] Available: http://www.nexus.edu.au/teachstud/gat/dod_men1.htm [2003, May 23]

10. Shneiderman, B.: Designing the User Interface: Strategies for Effective Human-Computer Interaction. 3rd edn. Addison Wesley Longman, Inc Reading, Massachusetts (1998)
11. Siew Pei Hwa & Norhayati Abd. Mukti: Designing Interactive Multimedia Learning Environment for Moral and Values Education. Proceedings of ICEFA (International Conference on Education for All), Vol. 1 (2002) 376–391
12. McGrenere, J.L. (1996): Design: Educational Electronic Multi-Player Games A Literature, (Online) Available: http://www. cs.ubc.ca/labs/imager/tr/mcgrenere.1996b.html [2003, May 25]
13. Preece, J.: Human-computer Interaction. Addison-Wesley Publishing Company Wokingham, England (1994)
14. Faulkner, X.: Usability Engineering. Palgrave Houndmills (2000)
15. Neo Mai & Kent Neo: The Multimedia Mosaic. Federal Publications Singapore (1997)
16. Shuman, J.E: Multimedia in Action. Wadsworth Pub., ITP New York (1998)

Indigenous Digital Multimedia Content Development for E-learning: Instructional and Cognitive Design Model Approach

Badioze Zaman Halimah, Nazlena Mohamad Ali, and Yahya Aidanismah

Department of Information Technology, Faculty of Information Science and Technology,
Universiti Kebangsaan Malaysia, 43600 Bangi, Malaysia
{hbz,nma,aida}@ftsm.ukm.my

Abstract. The world do not need reminders that its population are living in a knowledge driven era. One is constantly aware of the amount of information/knowledge that is put at one's fingertips by the new communications and computing technologies. One of the central and most compelling applications for the 21st century is highly information based societies. E-learning is still being debated and researched and there is still much uncertainty about it in terms of what it means for culture, learning democracy, jobs, roles and society in general. Nevertheless, the growth of online or e-learning educational institutions has been phenomenal and it will continue to improve. Perhaps one of the most dramatic changes due to this phenomenon is the rapid convergence of computing, communications and indigenous content development initiatives. There is therefore a need to look at indigenous digital multimedia educational content development approaches that would meet the needs of indigenous community. This paper hopes to highlight the design of multimedia digital content based on the instructional and cognitive models thought suitable to create future knowledge workers (k-insan) in Malaysia. The paper shall also draw out in detail the characteristics of the k-insan and entities of the proposed indigenous content development initiatives based on the instructional and cognitive model approach with reference made to indigenous multimedia packages such as the ME, ME2 and MEL.

1 Introduction

Institutions and industries involved in information management, storage and retrieval globally are going to change dramatically in the next century. Due to the integrated technological and social forces, so as the globalization, the extension of time and place, the disembedment of social relations and the reflecting structuring of knowledge, the structural premises for information management practices and the product these institutions hope to hire as their future human resource will also have to change. On one level, these changes may lead to the disembedment of the process of services to be provided to their clients and an increasing competition between information service based institutions. Perhaps the scare scenario is that information storage, searching and retrieval becomes an abstract relation to the Internet or just-in-time service and content packages for different types and levels of users. Small,

T.M.T. Sembok et al. (Eds.): ICADL 2003, LNCS 2911, pp. 627–638, 2003.
© Springer-Verlag Berlin Heidelberg 2003

locally situated physical 'educational' institutions may disappear and be replaced by a few very big and prestigious world educational institutions through online digital institutions (virtual universities or virtual libraries). Yet on an exciting note, the technological changes also hold many possibilities. In today's information or knowledge-economy era, indigenous content developers need to be knowledgeable and skilled than ever before, they need to equip themselves with knowledge and skills in order to create or innovate content that would benefit the indigenous community as well as the global communities that have interest in the respective indigenous knowledge.

2   Entities of E-learning

During the industrial economy or i-economy era, the capital resources were from land, energy and money. Today with the k-economy, knowledge has become the most important and demanded capital. This has happened due to the rapid development of Information and Communication Technology (ICT), which enables information to be accessed, processed and used in problem solving, and the creation of new knowledge[20];[21][22]. ICT has also enabled organizations to receive, collect, store, process, create and disseminate information to relevant individuals for specific purposes.

The education sector is directly involved with knowledge. Thus, the use of ICT in the education sector is a practice that can no longer be ignored. This has led to the emergent of the new concept e-learning or mobile learning as the technology now advances, which uses ICT to support the education system (the management of teaching and learning process of formal, non formal and informal education; and lifelong learning). E-learning not only democratizes education, it also frees learning and teaching activities from being restricted to specific time and place; enhace the use of a variety of educational resources; enhance the quality of teaching and learning strategies; as well as hasten learning process based on the learning pace of the learners. E-Learning can help a nation develop a system of education with an effecient mechanism to create a society based on knowledge or knowledge based society through a lifelong learning concept.

The operational definition of e-learning for the development of ICT for education policy in Malaysia was defined as: The use of ICT in supporting teaching and learning process, and the management of lifelong learning education in the k-economy era [1].

3   Defining Knowledge

Due to the fact that for most times words like data, information and knowledge are often used loosely to describe the same phenomenon, it is important to begin a clear picture of what knowledge means for this purpose[23];[24]. For the purpose of this paper, data is defined as any signals which can be sent from the originator to a recipient-human or otherwise. Information is defined as data which are intelligible to the recipient. Finally, knowledge is defined as the cumulative stock of information and skills derived from use of information by the recipient. Where the recipient is a human being, knowledge thus reflects the processing (thinking or cognition) by the brain of the raw material supplied in the form of information.

From the description, knowledge thus subsumes information, which represents both the input to knowledge development and the form in which knowledge is transferred –its 'circulatory system'. The traditional economic view of information and knowledge is that they are the same thing. In practice, they are different but strongly complementary [2];[25];[26].

Perhaps a useful distinction can be made between knowledge about something and knowledge about how to do something ('know-how'). Knowledge about something generally relates to concepts and theories, and know-how to the acquisition of skills through practical implementation of such concepts and theories. Learning on the job in a work situation is a classic example of acquiring knowledge or skills through practice or what is sometimes termed as 'learning by doing'.

4   Creation of the Future Knowledge Worker (*k-insan*)

In order to ensure that the new educational system with its new approach and strategy shall produce the knowledge worker as deemed by the nation, the characteristics of the knowlege worker known as the *k-Insan* [3]was created as follows:

- **Knowledge and Skills**

  Possess a sound formal education; skills on how to learn,to use tools and technology; and lifelong learning.

- **Professionalism**

  Possess management and implementation skills in order to produce quality work in terms of cost and time;decision making based on knowledge and values; and possess Emotional Intelligence (EQ) in order to manage people.

- **Entrepreneurship**

  Possess entreprenial skills in commercializing products (innovation, discovery,and development) in order to create wealth.

- **Socialization**

  Ability to work in collaboration and cooperatively in groups.

- **Values and Internalization**

  Ability to understand and internalize moral values, ethics, culture, and religion within the organization and society; and possess a sound philosophy and principles of life.

Figure 1 shows the conceptual model of the *k-Insan* or Insan-i based on the characteristics discussed.

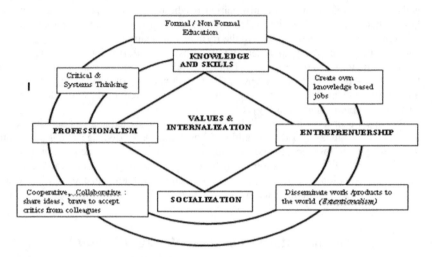

Fig. 1. Conceptual Model of k-Insan

5 Indigenous Multimedia Digital Content Initiatives Based on Instructional and Cognitive Design Models

Indigenous multimedia digital content initiatives in Malaysia began with the use of electronic technology in the educational environment (though not all educational institutions are electronically linked). There was a need to develop indigenous multimedia digital content that would meet the needs of indigenous learners (k-Insan) in the smart school pilot project which was conducted in 85 secondary schools and 5 primary schools based on indigenous content materials in Mathematics, Science, English and Bahasa Melayu. The smart school project will eventually include all primary and secondary schools in the country. The next roll out will include 2,000 primary and 2,000 secondary schools. Efforts on the development of indigenous content will have to improved based on sound educational and pedagogical approaches.

5.1 Instructional Design (ID) Model

Instructional Design (ID) models generally would mean the systematic process of translating principles of learning into plans for instructional materials and activities [4]; [5]. The instructional design models for indigenous multimedia digital content used for the ME, ME2 and MEL Packages took into consideration various entities such as depicted in the Holistic Instructional design model in Figure 2.

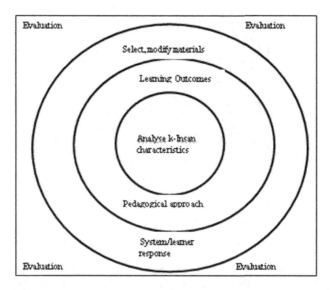

Fig. 2. The Holistic ID model for Indigenous Multimedia Digital Content

The Holistic ID models adopted by the indigenous multimedia packages involves six entities namely: Beginning from the center and spreading outwards are k-Insan characteristics, learning outcomes, selecting and modifying materials, pedagogical strategies, system/learner response and evaluation approach.

K-insan characteristics is as described in detail earlier; learning outcomes involve the outcome that is expected of the learning prepared in the content created; selecting and modifying materials involve the activities as well as media to be selected and modified for the content to meet the needs of the potential learner (k-Insan); pedagogical strategies involve approaches such as self-exploratory, simulation, randomization; system/learner response involve interactivity and navigational approach such as perpetual navigation; and evaluation approach such as formative or topical.

5.2   Cognitive Design Architecture

The structuring of indigenous content for e-learning involves the creation of a curriculum. Many software developers have deliberately underplayed this element. The careful structuring of content becomes increasingly important as learning becomes more complex [6]; [7].Various models have been used in multimedia courseware design in order to ensure that learning takes place. Due the fact that learning is a cognitive process, it makes sense that the architecture developed for multimedia courseware design must take into consideration various cognitive learning theories in order to ensure that multimedia coursewares developed are not merely teaching and learning machines or tools but they actually create dynamic learning environments. Piaget [8], Bruner [9], and Inhelder [10]were the early cognitive

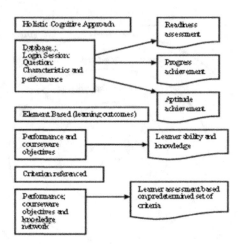

Fig. 3. Cognitive Architecture of the Indigenous Multimedia Coursewares

propagators of cognitive theories like the preferred modality theory and the cognitive flexibility theory. Then there were the information processing theories [11]; [12]; [27]and pattern recognition theories [13]which eventually lead to the idea of constructivism and contextual or CORE approach [6]; [29] in cognitive learning process. Cunningham [15]distilled seven main principles which forms the constructive architecture. The central tenet of constructivism is that knowledge of the world is constructed by the individual. The learner through interacting with the world constructs, tests and refines cognitive representations to seek truth and make sense of the world.

The ME [30], ME2[31] and MEL[32] packages were designed on a cognitive architecture (as depicted in Figure 3) taking into consideration the various cognitive theories not just in how the indigenous knowledge is presented to the learner in order that the learning process in not didactic, but the architecture also takes into account the use of cognitive theories in the design of the user interface and also the navigational approach as can be observed from examples of the print screens (Figures 4 – 8).

Due to the fact that learners have different learning styles, just as teachers have different teaching styles, the materials should help teachers set up a range of teaching and learning environments ranging from a teacher centred process to one of learner centred cognitive models as depicted in the diagrams below.

6   Elements in Cognitive Architecture

6.1   Different Learning Environments

Our approach to the development of the materials is designed to ensure that the differences in learning styles and pace of learning of individual learners will be accommodated. The assessment modules of the materials are designed with the aim of

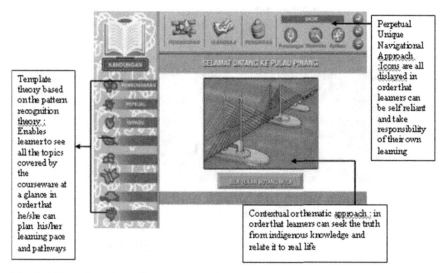

Template theory based on the pattern recognition theory : Enables learner to see all the topics covered by the courseware at a glance in order that he/she can plan his/her learning pace and pathways

Perpetual Unique Navigational Approach :Icons are all dislayed in order that learners can be self reliant and take responsibility of their own learning

Contextual or thematic approach : in order that learners can seek the truth from indigenous knowledge and relate it to real life

Fig. 4. ME package-Example of the use of the contextual approach in the presentation of knowledge and the design of User Interface and Navigational Approach

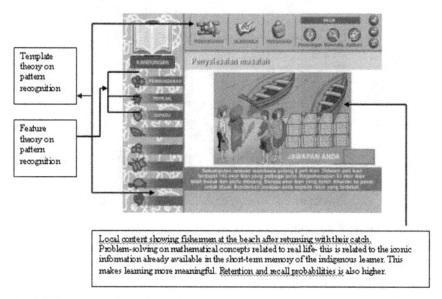

Template theory on pattern recognition

Feature theory on pattern recognition

Local content showing fishermen at the beach after returning with their catch. Problem-solving on mathematical concepts related to real life- this is related to the iconic information already available in the short-term memory of the indigenous learner. This makes learning more meaningful. Retention and recall probabilities is also higher.

Fig. 5. ME package - Example on the use of the Template and Feature theories of Pattern recognition in the design of user Interface and presentation of knowledge

making the courseware flexible and individualized enough to ensure that every learner is provided with the appropriate learning materials and opportunity.

Montage and Morphing using the Template theory which Gives the overall idea of the indigenous content of the Multimedia courseware

The traditional *tudung saji* or the food cover that symbolizes the malay culture and way of life –this helps the learner to make meaning or cognitive perception based on knowledge that is already familiar to his/her life

Fig. 6. Example of MEL package showing the indigenous content based on the cognitive architecture

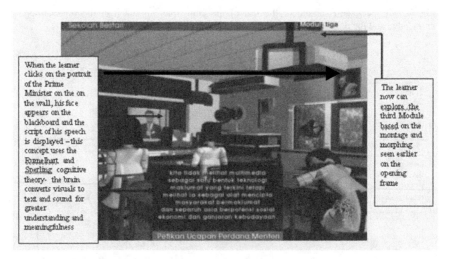

When the learner clicks on the portrait of the Prime Minister on the on the wall, his face appears on the blackboard and the script of his speech is displayed –this concept uses the Rumelhart and Sperling cognitive theory- the brain converts visuals to text and sound for greater understanding and meaningfulness

The learner now can explore the third Module based on the montage and morphing seen earlier on the opening frame

Fig. 7. Example of the MEL package of the indigenous content based on the Cognitive architecture

6.2   Self-Directed Learning

The indigenous teaching and learning coursewares designed using the cognitive architecture model was to provide flexibility in the classroom and to be able to adapt to self-paced and self-directed learning. The approach will enable learners to progress at a faster pace than the average learner and less able learners to receive more time and attention from the teacher. At the same time teachers will be provided with high quality materials to help them conduct group discussion of key concepts.

The learner begin the module by clearing the cans in the theme park. The cans are thrown in the rubbish bin by dragging the cans into the bin. This is in accordance with the values and attitude as required by the national curriculum

The exploratory module based on the constructivism concept and the problem is based on the actual games and locations in the theme park. This is again is in accordance with the cognitive theory. Learners can learn by drawing from prior knowledge in the short or long term memory

Fig. 8. Example of the indigenous content of the ME2 Package based on the Instructional and Cognitive Design Model

6.3   Unique Features of the Cognitive Architecture

The unique features of the Cognitive Architecture of the indigenous Malaysian multimedia packages include the following aspects:

i.   The overview of the knowledge to be taught. This is normally designed at the beginning of the modules using the montage or the morphing technique by adapting the Template pattern recognition theory.

ii.   The module and sub modules that are contained in the content are usually indicated to the learners earlier on with the intention of preparing or mind setting the learner so that he or she can plan his or her learning or pathways. This is in accordance with the feature pattern recognition theory. From the specific sub modules the learner can then explore the module in detail and able to see the link between previous modules and the module that he or she is going to work on. This is based on the structural pattern recognition theory.

iii.   The visual-text-sound technique found in one frame is a feature used in the cognitive architecture based on the Remulhart-Sperling theory. The theory states that the brain converts iconic or visual knowledge into text and sound for better perception and understanding. This allows the learner verbal rehearsal that is conducted by the system to help the learner understand the content and thus able to retain the knowledge in the short term and long term memory longer.

iv. Elements across the curriculum are closely aligned to the expectations of the Ministry of Education. The elements are the promotion of the subject matter skills across the curriculum, alignment of the courseware to curriculum specifications promotion of thinking, and compliance with cosmetic adequacy. The materials in the courseware will be cognitively challenging for higher order thinking: creative thinking, decision making, and problem solving.

v. The indigenous content in the digital multimedia packages include all of the resources, techniques, and activities necessary for students of mathematics and literacy to develop content knowledge,problem solving knowledge,epistemic knowledge and inquiry knowledge. These types of knowledge are developed through: teacher led instruction; group discussions; and, courseware materials that focus on developing concepts, solving problems, engaging students in simulations and performing co-operative learning activities based on the thematic or contextual approach.

vi. The indigenous content in the packages cover all skill areas that are important for success in using and applying mathematics and literacy. In particular, the materials emphasise creative and critical thinking skills, social skills, knowledge acquisition skills, scientific skills, generic skills, environmental skills, creative skills, and information technology skills. Some of the ways in which skills relate to important areas are detailed in the print screens.

7 Conclusion

The information era and the knowledge economy era is here to stay and along with it is the advancement of Computing and Communications Technologies[20]. The technologies will continue to improve further and nations have to grow with the advancement or they will be left behind. The indicators of the knowledge economy has shown how knowledge has become the most important resource in the present economy. The nation needs human resources who are not just skilled **but are also** knowledgeable in the various fields and profession they are in. Malaysia hopes to develop its own new citizens with the characteristics of the *k-Insan*. The ICTs and Multimedia technology has made many possibilities for e-learning environments and this certainly has direct implications to indigenous content development initiatives in the country. According to Frammingan [15]a Massachusettes-based International Data Corporation stated that 'online learning (CMC, VL and the like) market is currently generating US$600 million in annual receipts and will exceed US$ 10 billion by the year 2002. Almost half of the academic institutions in America is currently offering online learning (CMC, MMC or VL) as part of their curriculum delivery methods. A recent IDC market research report (2001) predicts that 85% of these educational institutions will have some form of online learning (CMC,MMC or VL) in place by the end of the year 2002. This all means that digital libraries and digital content initiatives are inevitable in order not to be obsolete[16];[17];[18];[19].

Malaysia still has a long and hard way ahead but the early initiatives with the creation of the Multimedia Super Corridor (MSC), the smart school project and other

ICT and multimedia application projects like ME, ME2 and MEL packages with the cognitive architecture to meet indigenous learners needs makes the scenario seems promising. Malaysia will certainly need to move more indigenous digital content initiatives. The holistic instructional and cognitive architecture model adopted in the packages mentioned has been tested in schools and also the smart schools in the country and have shown to help better probability of retention and recall levels .

References

1. Tengku Mohd Tengku Sembok, Halimah Badioze Zaman, M. Yusoff And A.R. Hamdan. 2001. ICT E-Learning Policy. Kuala Lumpur:MOE.
2. Cummings,L.E. 1995. Educational Technology : A Faculty resistence view, Educational Technology Review, 4, Autumn 1995.
3. Tengku Mohd Tengku Sembok, Halimah Badioze Zaman, Mohamed Yusoff, Abdul Razak Hamdan. 2001. Policy on ICT and Education. (Unpublished, written for the Ministry of Education, Malaysia).
4. Dick and Carey .2001. The Systematic Design of Instruction. New York: Longman.
5. Gagne, R.M and Briggs, L.J.1979. Principles of Instructional Design. New York: Holt, Reinhart and Winston.
6. Boyle, T.1997. Design for Multimedia Learning. London: Prentice Hall.
7. Byrnes, J.P. Cognitive Development And Learning.Second Edition. Boston: Allyn and Bacon.
8. Piaget, J. 1947. Psychology of Intelligence. Totowa, N.J.: Littlefield Adams.
9. Piaget, J. 1970. Piaget's Theory. In P.H. Mussen (ed) Carmichael's Manual of Child Psychology. Third edition. New Jersy: John Wiley.
10. Papert, S. 1993. Mindstorms: Children, computers and powerful ideas. New York: basic Books.
11. Reed, S.K. 2000. Cognition. Fifth edition California: Addison Wesley.
12. Sperling, G. 1967. Successive approximations to a model for short term memory, *Acta Pschologica,* 27: 285–295.
13. Remulhart, D.E. 1977. Attention and performance. London: Lawrence Erlbaum Associates.
14. Cunningham, D.J. Duffy T.M. and Knuth R. 1993. The textbook of the future. In C. Mcnight, A.Dillon, and J. Richardson (eds). Hypertext; A Psychological perspective. New jersey: Ellis Horwood.
15. Frammingan . 1999. Online Learning . Masschusettes : IDC.
16. Dowlin, K.E.1984. The Electronic Library . New York: Neal-Schuman.
17. Collier, M. 2002. Towards A General Theory of the Digital Library. *www.dl.ulis.ac.jp. /ISDL/proceeding/collier.html*
18. Collier, M. 1999. General Theory of the Digital Library. UK: De Monfort University.
19. International Data Corporation. 2001. Online Learning market survey. Massachusettes: IDC.
20. Hoffman, D.L. & Novak, T.P. 1995. Internet Use in the U.S. 1995. Baseline Estimates : preliminary market segments. Nashville: Vanderbilt University.
21. Wayne, A. 1996. Internet Business Primer. Naperville: Sourcebooks.
22. Ekelin, A. 2000. Networking for Women. *E-News, Alan @ connected.org*
23. Hartman, A. Sifonis, J and Kador J. (2000). Net Ready : Strategies for Success in the Economy. New York: Mc Graw Hill.
24. Mc Cluskey, A. 2000. Writing-A way to Knowledge and Empowerment *Alan @connected.org*

25. Tappscott, A. 1996. Digital Economy: Promise and Peril in the Age of the Networked Intelligence. London: McGraw-Hill.
26. Wayne, A. 1996. Internet Business Primer. Naperville: Sourcebooks.
27. Leahey, T.H. 2000. Learning and Cognition. Fifth edition. N.J, : Prentice Hall.
28. Dent, S.M. 1999. Partnering Intelligence: Creating Value for Your Business by Building Strong Alliances. California: Davies-Black Publishing.
29. Boyle, T. and Margetts, S. 1992. The CORE guided discovery approach to acquiring programming skills, *Computers and Education*, 18: 127–133.
30. Halimah Badioze Zaman, Tengku Mohd Tengku Sembok and Mohammed Yusoff .1996. Proposal on Teaching and Learning Materials (TLM) for Smart Schools. Submitted to MOE. Bangi: Universiti Kebangsaan Malaysia.
31. Halimah Badioze Zaman. 2003. Final Report IRPA 04-02-02-0038. BANGI: Universiti Kebangsaan Malaysia.
32. Halimah Badioze Zaman.2002. Final Report. IRPA 04-02-02-0008. BANGI: Universiti Kebangsaan Malaysia.

GridFS: A Web-Based Data Grid with P2P Concepts and Writable Replicas*

Qinghu Li, Jianmin Wang, Kwok Yan Lam, and Jiaguang Sun

School of Software, Tsinghua University, Beijing, China
liqinghu99@mails.tsinghua.edu.cn
{jimwang,sunjg}@tsinghua.edu.cn

Abstract. We merge concepts from P2P into Data Grid and present a web-based Data Grid, called GridFS, for the distributed sharing of educational resources. GridFS extends Data Grid by making replicas writable in practice. We propose a push-version-number consistency (PVNC) model and a writer/reader protocol to implement it. PVNC eliminates nearly all read latency and lessens the network utilization. We believe GridFS and PVNC would benefit hierarchical web cache systems and digital libraries.

1 Introduction

In order to manage education resource files as well as documents stored in digital libraries, we have launched an effort to build a writable, serverless Data Grid with large scale, high performance and high reliability [2]. We call it Grid File System (GridFS) to emphasize that it is an extension to Data Grid [1] constructed with P2P concepts over the web, and the files managed by it are writable as those managed by a traditional file system. Data replication is an important optimization technique applied in GridFS as a means of achieving shorter access times to data and fault tolerance. It results in consistency problems to make the file objects writable. In this work, we propose a push-version-number consistency (PVNC) model and a W/R locking protocol to implement it (For the detailed GridFS architecture, search algorithm and dynamic replication strategy, please refer to [2]).

2 PVNC Model and W/R Locking Protocol

We improve the performance of GridFS consistency by introducing a hybrid approach based on relaxing consistency for readers, while maintaining strong consistency semantics for writers. We present a push-version-number consistency (PVNC) model based on versions of files that are stable for the duration of an open/close session against a file. This model relaxes semantics so that write operation on particular

---

* Supported by the Ministry of Education P.R.C under contract 2001BA101A12-02 and the National Key Basic Research and Development Program of China (973 Program) under Grant No.2002CB312006.

T.M.T. Sembok et al. (Eds.): ICADL 2003, LNCS 2911, pp. 639–642, 2003.

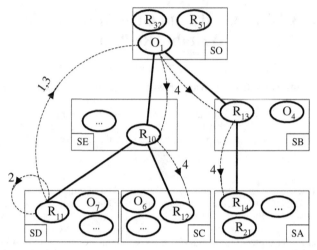

Fig. 1. Locking protocols for push-version-number consistency. *'S?'*: site; *'O_i'*: original file; *'R_{ij}'*: replica of O_i; *'1'*: acquire(W); *'2'*: write file; *'3'*: update(data); *'4'*: invalidate(new version)

replica and read operation on other replicas of the same file can be asynchronous and in parallel.

We capture PVNC in two locks: a writer lock (*W*) and a reader lock (*R*). Both the original and each replica can hold W lock, but W lock can be held by only one object at a time and must be acquired from the original. As illustrated in Fig. 1, Site *SO* contains the original O_1 which has two direct replicas: R_{10} on *SE* and R_{13} on *SB*. R_{11} on *SD* and R_{12} on *SC* are replicated not directly from O_1 but from R_{10}, and R_{14} on *SA* is replicated from R_{13}.

When an open operation on R_{11} for write is to be processed, *SD* first acquires the sole *W* lock from *SO*, and then write to R_{11}. Upon closing R_{11}, *SD* sends an explicit publish message to *SO*. *SO* replaces the old version of O_1 with the new one and then sends an invalidating message along with the new version number to *SE* and *SB*. *SE* immediately transmits this invalidating message to its direct replica container (site), *SD* and *SC*, so does *SB*. It is up to replica container to decide whether to acquire the updated version immediately or not according to its own consistency requirement. For example, if the replica is rarely accessed in the past, the replica container can acquire the new version until a new reader or writer comes to avoid useless re-acquiring.

The original container and each replica container manage the *R* locks on their own. During a read session of an object, which starts with an open operation and ends with the corresponding close operation, the reader sees data consistent with the end of a previous update session on the same container. To do so, we allow for multiple versions of the same object on the same container. Different versions must be open and then served concurrently. A newcome reader is arranged to open the latest version and its subsequent read operations are in the context of this version so that the container can bind requests to the appropriate data (If the latest version, indicated by the latest invalidation message, is not reacquired yet, the newcome reader will wait before it is reacquired.). Old versions are reclaimed by reference counting when no open instances remain.

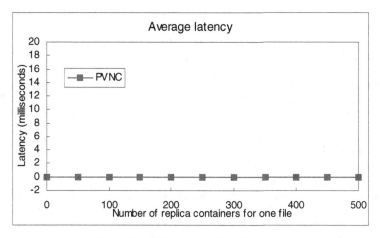

Fig. 2. Simulation results of read latency

3 Simulation

3.1 Simulation Methodology

We constructed an event simulation of the presented locking protocol to verify our design of W/R locking and understand performance of read operation in GridFS. Our simulator is constructed using PARSEC [3], which is a discrete event simulation tool to model events like file requests and data transfers.

To simplify the simulation, we focus on the latency associated with keeping a single file consistent.

GridFS is constructed over the web and a replica container (site) is a web server in practice. So we model the workload at reading site, corresponding to HTTP requests at Web servers, according to a heavy tailed distribution [4]. In [4], it is shown that heavy tailed distributions characterize well the bursty nature of traffic in the Internet. While desirable for their accuracy, heavy tailed distributions can lead to instabilities in simulation [5], so we also verified simulation results against more stable workloads, like Poisson read processes. For write workloads in GridFS, we chose to use data that are updated at fixed intervals.

3.2 Simulation Results

In the simulation, we chose to model file objects of 100K bytes which are updated at one minute intervals. Ten read operation per second are served at each replica container.

The latency results illustrated in Fig. 2 describe the time interval between an incoming read request and the file being available at the replica container. For PVNC, latency is negligible at all times. Since each replica container can maintain multiple versions of the same file, a reader always has data available even the latest version is not ready yet. That is to say, the replica container always holds at least one valid copy of a file to serve the newcome reader.

Previous research indicates that average latencies in the web are on the order of 100 to 200 milliseconds throughout the cache hierarchy [6]. So our PVNC reduces latency by at least 100 milliseconds. These latency results are for single files. As GridFS grows larger, savings become more significant on account of the effect of many files to be kept consistent.

4 Conclusion

We propose a consistency model named PVNC and implemented it in the W/R protocol. Based on versions of data that are stable for the duration of an open/close session against a file, PVNC eliminates nearly all read latency and lessens the network utilization. We believe hierarchical web cache systems and digital libraries would benefit from our GridFS and PVNC model.

References

1. A. Chervenak, I. Foster, C. Kesselman, C. Salisbury, and S. Tuecke. The Data Grid: Towards an architecture for the distributed management and analysis of large scientific datasets. Journal of Network and Computer Applications, 23:187–200, 2001.
2. L. Qinghu, W. Jianmin, K. Yanlam, S. Jiaguang. GridFS: A Web-based Data Grid for the Distributed Sharing of Educational Resource Files. The 2nd International Conference on Web-based Learning, 2003. Published by LNCS.
3. Parsec home page. http://pcl.cs.ucla.edu/projects/parsec.
4. M. E. Crovella and A. Bestavos. Self-similarity in World Wide Web traffic: Evidence and possible causes. Performance Evaluation Review, 24(1), 1996.
5. M. Crovella and L. Lipsky. Long-lasting transient conditions in simulations with heavy tailed workloads. In Proceedings of the 1997 Winter Simulation Conference, 1997.
6. J. Lin, L. Alvisi, M. Dahlin, and C. Lin. Hierarchical cache consistency in a WAN. In Proceedings of the 2nd USENIX Symposium on Internet Technologies, October 1999.

Hierarchical Classification of Chinese Documents Based on N-grams

Jihong Guan[1] and Shuigeng Zhou[2]

[1] School of Computer, Wuhan University,
Wuhan, 420079, China
jhguan@wtusm.edu.cn
[2] Department of Computer Science and Engineering, Fudan University,
200433, China
sgzhou@fudan.edu.cn

Abstract. This paper explores the techniques of utilizing N-gram information to categorize Chinese text documents hierarchically so that the classifier can shake off the burden of large dictionaries and complex segmentation processing, and subsequently be domain and time independent. A hierarchical Chinese text classifier is implemented. Experimental results show that hierarchically classifying Chinese text documents based N-grams can achieve satisfactory performance and outperforms the other traditional Chinese text classifiers.

1 Introduction

Text classification is a supervised learning process, defined as assigning category labels (pre-defined) to new documents based on the likelihood suggested by a training set of labeled documents. With the rapid growth of online information, text classification has become one of the key techniques for processing and organizing text data. And text classification technique has been used to classify news stories [1], to find interesting information on the Web [2], and to guide a user to search through hypertext [3].

Owing to the drastically growth of text information, topic hierarchies have been used as an efficient way to organize, view and explore large quantities of text documents that would otherwise be cumbersome. Topic hierarchy is a classification tree that consists of one root node, some internal nodes and some leaf nodes (leaves). The internal nodes and leaves represent concrete document classes. The *Yahoo* search engine system is an example of topic hierarchies that exist to make information more manageable. However, *Yahoo* makes use of manpower to classify Web pages into their hierarchy. And most classification methods described in the literature that ignore the hierarchical structure and treat the topics as separate classes are often inadequate in text classification where there is a large number of classes and a large number of relevant features needed to distinguish between them.

Traditional text classifiers are generally based on keywords in the documents, which means that the training and classifying processes need dictionaries support and efficient segmentation processing. As far as Chinese text documents classification is concerned [4-8], segmentation is a complex task. Current Chinese segmentation

T.M.T. Sembok et al. (Eds.): ICADL 2003, LNCS 2911, pp. 643–652, 2003.
© Springer-Verlag Berlin Heidelberg 2003

systems are generally large, and of low accuracy and efficiency [9]. Recalling that languages are domain-dependent and time-varying, the dictionaries and segmentation procedures used in the classifiers must be updated so that the classifiers are still effective and efficient in the changed language environment.

With these points above in mind, this paper explores the techniques of utilizing N-gram information to classify Chinese text documents hierarchically so that the classifier can shake off the burden of large dictionaries and complex segmentation processing, and subsequently be domain and time independent. Such a hierarchical Chinese text classifier is developed. Experimental results show that hierarchically classifying Chinese text documents based N-grams can achieve satisfactory performance and outperforms the other traditional Chinese text classifiers.

The reminder of this paper is organized as follows. First, in Section 2 we present an algorithm for Chinese N-grams extraction; then classification features selection approaches are discussed in Section 3, and in Section 4 we give a hierarchical classification method that considers training documents weighting, multiple classification paths and the situation of training documents locating at the internal nodes in the topic hierarchy; Following that, a hierarchical Chinese text classifier developed with the above-mentioned techniques is evaluated in Section 5; And finally, we conclude the paper in Section 6.

2   N-grams Extraction

2.1   Chinese N-grams and Chinese Text Classification

For a Chinese text document d of length L, if all punctuation marks and other symbols but Chinese characters are ignored, $i.e.$ the document is treated as a Chinese characters sequence of length L, then there are at most $L(L+1)/2$ N-gram items in d. In reality, a document cannot contain so many N-gram items. Usually, the documents are split by punctuation marks into series of sentences, and the N-grams are extracted from the sentences. Therefore, the longest N-grams are the longest sentences. Suppose the training documents collection D contains N_D documents, the average number of sentences in each document and the average length of sentences are N_s and L_s respectively, then there are at most $N_D N_s L_s (L_s+1)/2$ N-gram items in the training document collection D. Obviously, the number of N-gram items in the training collection will be substantially large, which reminds us of carefully selecting the N-grams while training classifiers. Furthermore, considering that text classification is a kind of semantic oriented operation, the selected N-grams should be able to express documents implication accurately as far as possible. However, the contribution of each N-gram item to classification performance is quite different, so how to select the proper N-grams for classification poses a key technical problem here.

The usefulness of a N-gram item for classification can be measured qualitatively by its occurrence *frequency*, *distribution* and *centralization*, which are defined as follows.

Definition 1. The *frequency* of N-gram item t occurring in document d is its occurrence count in d. We denote it *tf*.

Definition 2. The *distribution* of N-gram item t in document class c is the number of documents that contain t. We denote it *df*.

Definition 3. The *centralization* of N-gram item t in text collection D is defined to be the inversion of the number of classes that include t. We denote it *icf*.

Intuitively, a N-gram item with higher *tf*, *df* and *icf* is more useful to classification, *i.e.* it is more distinguishable. However, there is no simple mathematical approach to guide selection of the most distinguishable N-grams in terms of their *tf*, *df* and *icf*. In this paper, for the simplicity of processing and to reduce the chance of extracting N-grams with less distinguishing power, we specify three constraints as follows.

Constraint 1. Given a pre-specified minimum value of *tf*, being denoted as *min-tf*, a N-gram item t in document d is extracted only if its *tf* is no less than *min-tf*.

Constraint 2. Given a pre-specified minimum value of *df*, being denoted as *min-df*, a N-gram item t in class c is extracted only if its *df* is no less than *min-df*.

Constraint 3. Given a pre-specified minimum value of *icf*, being denoted as *min-icf*, a N-gram item t in collection D is extracted only if its *icf* is not less than *min-icf*.

Above, the thresholds *min-tf*, *min-df* and *min-icf* are selected by experiments over the training documents collection. Here, *tf*, *df* and *icf* are defined in a way of being independent of the training documents collection. Considering the fact that the length of different documents, the number of documents in different classes and the number of classes in different collections are quite different, it is more reasonable and practicable to define *tf*, *df* and *icf* with regard to the document length, the number of documents in the classes and the number of document classes in the training documents collection.

2.2 Chinese N-grams Extraction Algorithm

A naive algorithm for extracting Chinese N-grams from training documents collection is to scan the collection and obtain all Chinese N-grams conforming to *Constraint* 1, *Constraint* 2 and *Constraint* 3 in one pass. For small training collections, this way is effective and efficient. However, as the training collection becomes larger and larger, the number of N-gram items in the training collection will increase exponentially, and this naive algorithm cannot extract the required N-grams efficiently due to memory limit. Here we adopt a stepwise algorithm to extract the Chinese N-grams: Firstly, the 1-grams conforming to *Constraint* 1 and *Constraint* 2 are extracted by scanning the training documents; Then the candidates of 2-grams are created from the selected 1-grams, and the required 2-grams are obtained by filtering out the 2-grams not conforming to *Constraint* 1 and *Constraint* 2; In a similar fashion, the required 3-grams, 4-grams and so on are extracted. At last, the N-grams obtained from the above processing will be filtered again by applying *Constraint* 3 to get the final N-grams set. Before describing this algorithm in details, we present the following definition and lemma.

Definition 4. For *i*-gram item t_i and *j*-gram item t_j with $i{\geq}j$, if t_j is contained in t_i, than we say t_j is a sub-item of t_i, and denote $t_j \subseteq t_i$.

Lemma 1. If *i*-gram item t_i meets Constraint 1 and Constraint 2, then all the sub-items of t_i meet Constraint 1 and Constraint 2 too.

It is straightforward to prove *Lemma* 1 by applying Definition 1, 2 and 4. For the sake of space, the proof is omitted. Based on *Lemma* 1, we have a stepwise Chinese N-grams extraction algorithm. Owing to the limitation of space, we give no details of the algorithm.

2.3 Selection of the Maximum N

There is another problem to be solved: How much should the largest value of N be? Intuitively, the maximum N, *i.e. MAX-N*, should be such a value that the *i*-grams with $i{\leq}MAX{-}N$ can cover most of keywords in the training documents collection. According to the statistic analyses of Chinese documents [10], as far as occurrence frequency is concerned, in the Chinese documents, 1-chrarcter words make up the dominating part, and the next is 2-character words, then 3-character and 4-character words. Words with more than 4 characters are quite few and infrequent. So for any document, we can basically represent it with only the 1/2/3/4-character words. In other word, the largest value of N can be 4 because the 1/2/3/4-grams can cover all the 1/2/3/4-character words in Chinese documents.

3 Feature Selection

We take the extracted N-grams above as documents classification features, which are also referred to as *terms*. However, the number of the extracted N-grams is still very large, which will affect the performance and efficiency of classification. So a feature selection process is necessary over the extracted N-grams to get a relatively optimal and smaller subset of document features for classification. In what follows, the information gain approach that is popularly used to accomplish the selection task in machine learning is presented in the context of text classification. The following notation is used: C is the class variable; c denotes a specific class; f is an arbitrary term, and F is the whole set of terms used for features selection

Information gain measures the number of bits of information obtained for category prediction by knowing the presence or absence of a term in a document. The information gain of term f is defined to be:

$$IG(f) = \sum_{c \in C} (P(c, f) \log(\frac{p(c, f)}{P(c)P(f)}) + P(c, \bar{f}) \log(\frac{p(c, \bar{f})}{P(c)P(\bar{f})})). \quad (1)$$

The probabilities in the above equation are estimated with the following formula:

$$P(c) \approx \frac{N_c}{N},$$

$$P(c) \approx \frac{N_f}{N},$$ (2)

$$P(c,f) \approx \frac{N_{fc}}{N}.$$

Here, N_{fc} represents the occurrence count of term f in class c, and we have

$$N_c = \sum_{f \in F} N_{fc},$$

$$N_f = \sum_{c \in C} N_{fc}.$$ (3)

Furthermore, if $P(c,f) = 0$, then we let $P(c,f)\log(P(c,f)/(P(f)P(c)))$ and $\log(P(c,f)/(P(f)P(c)))$ be zero.

4 Hierarchically Text Classification

Hierarchical classification splits a huge classifier into a number of smaller and simpler classifiers by establishing classifiers separately at all nodes except the leaves in the topic hierarchy. For each smaller classifier, it deals with less classes and only a very small set of features are needed to cover the semantic variety of documents contained in the classes. As a result, the training processing is simplified relatively and better classification performance can be achieved as a whole.

It is a straightforward way to build classifiers at the nodes in the topic hierarchy by the Naive Bayesian method mentioned above. However, there are still some technical problems specific to hierarchical classification need to be handled, for which we give detailed discussions as follows.

4.1 Adding Virtual Nodes

In hierarchy classification, the training documents maybe distribute over all nodes except the root node of the topic hierarchy. That is to say, some training documents may be at the internal nodes. Such a case is popular in Web pages classification. For the convenience of classification, we move the training documents at internal nodes to leaves by introducing the concept of virtual nodes. Fig.1 illustrates this idea. N_{i-1} is an internal node owning some training documents locally. By adding a virtual sub-node n_{k+1} for N_{i-1} and moving the training documents at N_{i-1} to virtual node n_{k+1}, then there is no training document at internal node N_{i-1} any more. Virtual node n_{k+1} corresponds to a

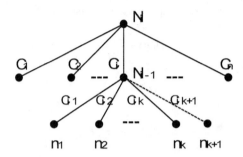

Fig. 1. Adding virtual nodes

virtual class C_{ik+1}. The same process can be performed over all other internal nodes that have training documents locally. Obviously, virtual nodes are essentially leaves.

At the classification stage, if a certain test document is classified to a virtual class, then we know that this document actually belongs to the father class of that virtual class. Again in Fig.1, if test document d is assigned to class C_{ik+1}, then d is in fact belongs to C_i. In the following discussion, we assume there is no training document at any internal node in the topic hierarchy.

4.2 Weighting Training Documents

Training documents for each class are collected from the training documents in the nodes corresponding to its subclasses. These nodes and consequently their training documents form a hierarchical structure that we map to a single set of training documents. Usually, a simple way is to ignore the hierarchical structure of the training documents and form a set of training documents as a union of all the training documents that appear in its sub-classes. The potential problem we see with this approach is that large sub-classes would completely cover smaller sub-classes even if those are in the higher levels of the hierarchy. To take into account the hierarchical structure of training documents, weight is assigned to each sub-class and it is used when propagating training documents to the higher level. The training documents are propagated through their probability distribution over features they contain. In Fig.1, suppose a classifier is to be established at node N_i, its sub-class C_i corresponds to node N_{i-1}, which has $k+1$ sub-classes (including a virtual class); t is a classification feature. By introducing the weighting mechanism, $P(t|C_i)$ is estimated as follows:

$$P(t \mid C_i) = \sum_{i=1}^{k+1} Weight(n_i) \times P(t \mid n_i). \tag{4}$$

This formula is used recursively starting from the node that represents the class in question. The recursion stops at the leaf nodes. The weight values are decided on the basis of the number of training documents at the corresponding nodes or the number of classification features included in the training documents that the nodes own. We use the following formula to calculate the weight values:

$$Weight(X) = \frac{\ln(1 + num(X))}{\sum_{i=1}^{k+1} \ln(1 + num(n_i))}. \tag{5}$$

Above, $num(.)$ is a function representing the number of training documents or the number of classification features included in the training documents.

4.3 Multiple Path Classification

Given a test document d, the goal is to find a leaf node (maybe virtual leaf node) corresponding to class c, of which the posterior $P(c|d)$ is maximized among all leaf classes. However, if an incorrect decision is made at any higher node in the hierarchy, then the final decision must be incorrect. A possible solution to this problem is to try on multiple classification paths at each node, and select the leaf node with the maximum posterior probability as the final result. Fig.2 shows a classification path.

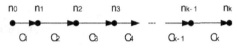

Fig. 2. A classification path

The classification path in Fig2 covers classes $c_1, c_2, \ldots, c_k$, it goes from the root node n_0 to a leaf node n_k. We denote the classification path $c = c_1 c_2 \text{ШШ}_k$. Given a test document d and a node in the path n_i (i=2~k), we have

$$P(c_i|d) = P(c_{i-1}|d) \times P(c_i|c_{i-1}, d)$$
$$(i = 2, \cdots, k) \tag{6}$$

Recursively using this formula, the following equation can be inferred:

$$P(c_k|d) = P(c_1|d) \times P(c_2|c_1, d) \times P(c_3|c_2, d) \times \cdots \times P(c_k|c_{k-1}, d). \tag{7}$$

The equation above manifests that the best classification performance can be achieveved by traversing the classification hierarchy to maximizes $P(c_k|d)$. If there are n leaf nodes in the topic hierarchy, then all the n classification paths should be tried for each test document. Such a greedy search would bring about serious efficient problem. The alternative is to select only a few outforward paths, say two, at each split point (or classification node). The two outforward paths correspond to these with the highest predicated posterior probability. Furthermore, considering a special case where the hierarchy height is k, and each classification path has similar length, that is k, then 2^k classification paths should be traversed. To calculate $P(c_i|c_{i-1}, d)$, the following formula is used:

$$P(c_i|c_{i-1}, d) = \frac{P(c_i|d)}{P(c_{i-1}|d)} = \frac{P(c_i|d)}{\sum_{j=1}^{|c_{i-1}|} P(c_j|d)}. \tag{8}$$

Above, $|c_{i-1}|$ is the number of sub-classes under nodes n_{i-1}.

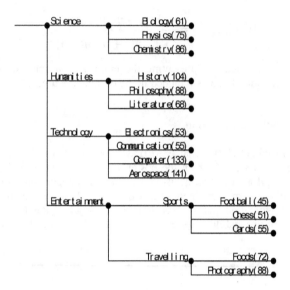

Fig. 3. Hierarchy of documents collection *DC*

5 Performance Evaluation

There are no commonly used Chinese documents collections for classification test available yet, such as the Reuters and OHSUMED collections for English classification test. Therefore, we have to collect training and test documents manually by ourselves. An experimental documents collection was established, which we denote *DC*, which was built specifically for hierarchical classification experiment. Documents in collection *DC* were downloaded from *Yahoo* China (Http: \\cn.yahoo.com) and the BBS of Wuhan University. Fig. 3 illustrates the topic hierarchy of collection *DC*, where the number in the parentheses after the name of each leaf class is the number of documents contained in the corresponding class. The topic hierarchy has three levels: the first level has 4 classes; the second level 12 classes, and the third 5 classes. So the sum of class-labels in the topic hierarchy is 21, in which 15 are leaf classes. Totally, there are 1155 documents in collection *DC*, and all documents are in the leaf classes. The largest leaf class (Aerospace) has 141 documents, and the smallest (Football) has only 45.

We developed a hierarchical Chinese classifier based on the techniques described above with VC++ 6.0 on the Windows 2000 platform. The system was trained and tested over collections G1. In the experiments, the documents collections are split into two parts in terms of a certain ratio over each class. One part is used for training, and the remaining for test. *Recall* and *Precision* are used to measure the system performance, which are abbreviated to *r* and *p* respectively. At first, *r* and *p* are computed separately for each class; then the final results are obtained by averaging the *r* and *p* values over all classes.

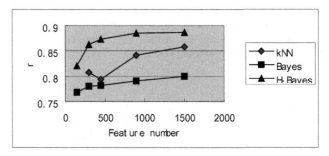

a) Recall *vs.* feature number

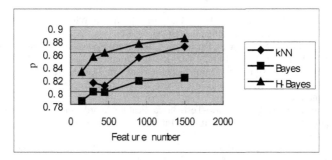

b) Precision *vs.* feature number

Fig. 4. Performance comparison between hierarchical classification and flat classification

Some typical experimental results are shown in Fig.4, in which performance comparison between flat classification (both Bayes method and kNN method) and hierarchical classification for different feature sizes on collection G1 is carried out. Obviously, as far as flat classification is concerned, kNN outperforms Bayes, especially when the number of classification features is large. However, It's worthy of our attention that even with 200 or 300 classification features, Bayes method can achieve good performance. And the important result is that hierarchical classification can achieve much better performance than flat classification.

6 Conclusion

In this paper, we have presented effective and efficient techniques to classify Chinese text documents hierarchically based on N-gram information. Owing to the using of N-grams for representing text documents, our classifier needs no dictionary support and segmentation processing, which make it more competitive in flexibility and practicability than the conventional Chinese text documents classifiers. Experiments demonstrate its satisfactory performance. However, we should point out that not all selected N-grams are necessarily semantically related to the document topics, so more powerful feature selection methods are necessary to eliminate irrelevant and redundant features. The method proposed in [11] may be helpful to enhance feature selection in our system, and the genetic algorithm which is a widely studied paradigm for optimal computation also can be another promising candidate for documents features selection in our future research [12-13].

References

[1]   Masand B. Classifying News Stories Using Memory-based Reasoning. International ACM SIGIR Conference on Research and Development in Information Retrieval. 1992:59–65.

[2]   Lang K. Newsweeder: Learning to Filter Netnews. International Conference on Machine Learning (ICML). 1995.

[3]   Joachims T. Webwatcher: a Tour Guide for the World Wide Web. International Joint Conference on Artificial Intelligence (IJCAI). 1997.

[4]   Huang X, Wu L. SVM based Document Classification System. Pattern Recognition and Artificial Intelligence. 1998,11(2): 147–153 (in Chinese).

[5]   Zou T. The Design and Implementation of an Automatic Chinese Documents Classification System., Journal of Chinese Information Processing, 1999, 13(3): 26–32 (in Chinese).

[6]   Li G. A Log-Likelihood-Ratio-Test-Based Feature Word Selection Approach in Text Categorization. Journal of Chinese Information Processing. 1999,13(4): 16–21 (in Chinese).

[7]   Zhan X. Hierarchical Method for Chinese Document Classification. Journal of Chinese Information Processing. 1999,13(6): 20–25 (in Chinese).

[8]   Diao Q. Term Weighting and Classification Algorithms. Journal of Chinese Information Processing. 2000,14(3): 25–29 (in Chinese).

[9]   Liu Y, Tan Q, Shen X. Modern Chinese Segmentation Specification and Automatic Segmentation Methods for Information Processing. Beijing: Tsinghua University Press, (in Chinese).

[10]   Zhao B, Xu L. Processing Chinese Information with Computer, Space Publisher House. 1988,2 (in Chinese).

[11]   Koller D, Sahami M. Toward Optimal Feature Selection. Machine Learning: Proc. of the 13th International Conference, Morgan Kaufman .1996.

[12]   Siedleck W, klansky J. A Note on Genetic Algorithms for Large-scale Feature Selection. IEEE Transactions on Computers. 1989,10:335–347.

[13]   Punch W. Further Research on Feature Selection and Classification Using Genetic Algorithms. Proceedings of the International Conference on Genetic Algorithms. Springer. 557–564

Evaluating the Effectiveness of Thesaurus and Stemming Methods in Retrieving Malay Translated Al-Quran Documents

Zainab Abu Bakar and Nurazzah Abdul Rahman

Faculty of Information Technology and Quantitative Sciences
Universiti Teknologi MARA, 40450 Shah Alam, Malaysia
{zainab,nurazzah}@tmsk.itm.edu.my

Abstract. Information Technology has enabled information in many forms such as text, image or sound, to be accessed widely using search terms via a computer. Due to this type of popularity and advancement in technology, there is an increase interest in searching Malay text to enable scholars and researchers to access databases on-line. Malay texts are scanned are stored in databases ready to be used for text retrieval systems that employ conflation methods to identify word variants from these databases. This paper evaluates the retrieval effectiveness of conflation methods; namely stemming and thesaurus to search and retrieve relevant Malay translated Al-Quran documents based on user natural query words. The Malay Translated Al-Quran texts are stored in an inverted file structure. The retrieved documents are weighted and ranked using Inverse Document Frequency (idf) function. The retrieval effectiveness (E) is measured using standard recall (R) and precision (P). Experiments performed on the Malay Translated Al-Quran documents show that combined search of stemming and thesaurus improve retrieval effectiveness (E) and recall (R) but decrease its precision (P).

1 Overview

Information technology has enable information to be captured, transmitted, stored, retrieved, manipulated or displayed [1] via a computer that is linked to the Internet. Information retrieval is a study on how to determine and retrieve from a corpus of stored information; the part that is relevant to particular information needs [2]. Information can be in form of texts, images, and sound. Nowadays, information can be retrieve with any combination form as mentioned. According to van Rijsbergen [2] a good information retrieval system should be able to retrieve only relevant topic based on the user query. The main function of information retrieval system is to provide the user with tools to perform searching effectively and efficiently. The popular statistical-based techniques have an important facility known as term conflation [3. It is the ability to retrieve words that are not exactly alike the query word from the database. Conflation is defined as a computational procedure that identifies word variants and reduced them to a single canonical form [4]. Word conflation performs two useful functions in information retrieval systems [4]. Firstly, the dictionary size is reduced since words are grouped and thus improve processing

T.M.T. Sembok et al. (Eds.): ICADL 2003, LNCS 2911, pp. 653–662, 2003.

time. Secondly, similar words retrieved generally have similar meanings and if conflation is carried out to both document and query words, the retrieval effectiveness may be increased. There is an increasing use of computational procedures that seek to conflate only those word variants that have minor differences in the character of the word [5]. There are many types of word variants that are encountered by searcher in the terms used for database indexing. The most common being spelling errors, alternative spellings, alternative forms of multi-word concepts, transliteration problems, the use affixes, and alternative forms of abbreviations [6].

2 Stemming Algorithms

One of well-known conflation algorithms, stemming, is only used to identify morphological variants. Stemming algorithms are language dependent. They have proven to be successful to reduce words with the same stem to a common form and are evidenced by the work of many researchers [7]. The developments of stemming algorithms for free-text retrieval purpose are carried out by Frakes [8]. Hafer and Weiss [9], Harman [10], Lennon[4], Lovins [11], Niedermair et al. [12], Porter [13], Ulmschneider and Doszkocs [14], Walker and Jones [15] and in many languages such as English [5, 4, 13] and also in Malay [16].

Conflation method on morphological variants can be accomplished by either manual or automated approaches [7]. Manual conflation is usually performed during the search by truncating the right-hand letters of the word. For example, the use of *stud** will retrieve all words that contain the same prefix such as *study, studies, studied, studying, student and studious*. Through extensive experience, the user will know the effective truncated word to use. A stemming algorithm is an automated procedure when it reduces words with the same stem to a common form, usually by removing derivational and inflectional suffixes from each word [11]. For example, the words *study, studies, studied, studying, student or studious* are reduced to the root word *study*. Grouping these words into common form will increase in retrieving relevant documents against a given query [10]. By stemming, the efficiency of document retrieval is increased since the size of index files is reduced by 50% as a result of grouping many morphological word variants into a single stem word [5].

Stemming algorithms can be very simple by just removing plurals, past and present particles to very complex techniques that include all morphological rules. Such complex procedures require either removal of the longest matching suffix once or interactively and specification of detailed context-sensitive rules in order to avoid significant error rate [4, 2, 7, 17]. The removals of suffixes by a stemmer to English and similar languages, Slovene and French, are found to be sufficient for the purpose of information retrieval [13]. This is not true in Malay language [18] and Arabic [19]. To stem Malay text effectively, not only suffixes but prefixes and infixes must be removed in proper order [16].

The stemming procedures in English and similar languages are generally unsuited to the conflation of all possible types of word variant and they show specific defects in chosen applications [6, 16]. In order to overcome certain defects, there are experiments combining stemming algorithms with n-gram matching method [3, 4, 15, 20, 21, 22, 23]. Results from these experiments agree that combining stemming and n-gram matching methods improve overall retrieval performances.

3 Thesaurus

Another language dependent conflation method is thesaurus. Its can build all types of relationship that exist between words, such as hierarchic, synonym, and morphological. The information retrieval thesaurus typically contains a list of terms, where a term is either a single word or phrase. The relationships between them are also included to assist in coordinating indexing and retrieval. However, the construction of a comprehensive thesaurus for a given subject domain requires a large amount of manual and highly trained effort.

According to Srinivasan [24], there are two methods in constructing thesaurus. There is either manual or automatic construction method. Process of manually constructing a thesaurus is very complex process. It is a long process that involves a group of individuals and variety of sources. First, one has to define the boundaries of subject area. Boundary definition includes identifying central subject areas and peripheral ones since it is likely that all topics included are of equal importance. Once this process is completed, the domain is generally partitioned into divisions or sub areas. Once the domain, with it sub areas, has been sufficiently defined, the thesaurus is more complex structurally than automatic ones, there are more decisions to be made.

Meanwhile, automatic construction method has three approaches. The first approach is designing thesaurus from document collection. Second is merging existing thesaurus and the third automatic approach, thesaurus is built using information obtained from users. In this third alternative, the objective is to capture thesaurus from the user's search. Rapizal [25] has constructed a thesaurus based on 36 natural language query words used in the Malay information retrieval.

4 Experimental Details

Before an information retrieval system can be used, document collection must be built, evaluated, and tested using identified conflation methods. In any information retrieval system test collection consists of document database, set of queries for the database, and relevance judgments that are formulated based on the queries are required [26]. Without the availability of the test collection the retrieval effectiveness and efficiency of various information retrieval algorithms cannot be compared and justified. A document database is usually in a textual form. It may contain images such as photographs, graphs, tables, maps, figures, patterns, and many more. A document identifier represents the texts in the document, thus the size of the database is reduced and will improve the time efficiency to search [5]. Robertson [27] describes document set as a unit of linguistic material. A document can also be represented by keywords that are considered to be significant [2].

4.1   Test Collection

Al-Quran consists of 114 chapters or surah where every chapter contains variable number of documents. Al-Quran test collection consists of Al-Quran documents, natural query words, relevance judgments, thesaurus list, stopword list, morphological rules, and dictionary of root words.

Al-Quran Documents. There are 6236 Al-Quran documents that are translated from the holy Quran. The Arabic texts are translated into the Malay language by Hamidy and Fachruddin [28]. Al-Quran documents are compiled by Fatimah [16]. Al-Quran documents have total number of 144310 correctly spelt words. The collection was stored into flat files and consists 6236 of documents. Every document was named uniquely. For instance chapter Ali-Imran: 197 will be named as q003197. The character 'q' means Quran, the first 3 digits referred to the chapter number and the last 3 digits referred to the verse number.

Query Words. Query is a formal statement of information need of the user. It is often expressed in short natural language question or statement. In this research, the query words are taken from Fatimah's collection [16]. She has obtained it by considering several guidelines put forward by Popovic [29], Salton [30], and Tague [31]. There are 36 natural language query words.

Relevance Judgment. In information retrieval experiments, the relevance of each document that is retrieved according to each query is assessed for its effectiveness. Even the best of information retrieval system has a limited recall; user may retrieve few relevant documents in response to his query, but almost never all the relevant documents.

On subjective points of view of relevancy, the knowledge of the user at the time of the search and other documents that the user knows will be considered. This will result in different documents being assigned to a given query. The difference in relevance judgments for these documents will not invalidate experiments using the test collections from which relevance assessments are made [2]. Fatimah [16], Popovic [27] have listed the process of obtaining relevance assessments.

The other component of Al-Quran test collection is a list of relevance judgments. Some examples are shown in Table 1. Fatimah [16] formulates the relevance judgment list with the assistance of Arab students from the Universiti Kebangsaan Malaysia by searching Al-Quran and referring to well-known Islamic books regarding the same subject matter based on the natural language queries. This relevance judgment table consists of document number that should be retrieved for every query.

Table 1. Relevance Judgment Documents Based on Natural Language Query

Natural Language Query Words	Relevant Documents
kelahiran nabi isa	q003045, q003046, q003047, q019019, q019023, q019024, q019025, q019026, q019027, q019028, q019029, q019030, q019031, q019032, q019033, q066012, q021091, q066012, q021091
tanda-tanda hari kiamat	q021096, q021097, q027082

Thesaurus List. The first construction of thesaurus vocabulary is based on the 36 natural language queries [25] and is used by Zaini [32] and Rosmadi [33] in their final year projects. These query keywords are obtained after all the stop words and duplicate words removed. The complete thesaurus obtained from Abdullah and Ainon [34] are scanned and compiled by BSc (Hons) (Information Technology) students. The newly compiled thesauruses are used in various experiments on different test collections. For this experiment the entries are sorted and their equivalent thesauruses are merged for the same entry. The number of entries is reduced from 11466 to 10780.

4.2   Processors

There are several processors to be performed in any information retrieval system. Initially, the query processor will process each natural language query words. The query word with hyphenation will be split into two words. For example the word '*tipu-daya*' will be split to word '*tipu*' and word '*daya*'. Stopwords are then removed from the query. If stemming method is chosen then the query words will be stemmed. If thesaurus is chosen then the thesauruses for each query word is added to query words. If both stemming and thesaurus are chosen then the query words and their thesauruses will be stemmed.

The retrieval processor will find an associate key in a key file that matches the query words. The key file contains key term, number of documents having the same key term, number of occurrences of the key term in the collection, the first and the last address of documents that have the key term. When the word and the key term match, weights using inverse document frequency (idf) functions (1) are added to the document [30]. This process will continue until the last word of the natural language query words is reached. The *idf* function is given by the following:

$$\text{weight}_{ik} = \text{tf} * \text{idf}$$

$$= \text{freq}_{ik} * \left[\log_2 \frac{n}{\text{docFreq}_k} + 1 \right] \tag{1}$$

The notation *tf* is the key term frequency and *idf* is the inverse document frequency. The total number of documents in the collection is *n*. $docFreq_k$ is the number of documents to which term k is assigned and $freq_{ik}$ is the frequency of term k in a given document i.

When all the words are processed, the weighted documents are ranked by the weights in descending order. The document that has the most number of words will certainly have more weights. The sorted documents are then used against relevance judgment list to evaluate their retrieval effectiveness.

4.3   Evaluation Process

There are many ways to evaluate information retrieval systems. It can be evaluated in terms of execution efficiency, storage efficiency, retrieval effectiveness, and the features they offer to user [5]. The retrieval effectiveness on Al-Quran is based on relevance judgments that are already available. The retrieval effectiveness (E) is measured using standard recall (R) and precision (P) [2].

$$R = \frac{\text{number of items retrieved and relevant}}{\text{total relevant from collection}} * 100 \qquad (2)$$

$$P = \frac{\text{number of items retrieved and relevant}}{\text{total retrieved from collection}} * 100 \qquad (3)$$

Recall relevance, R, is defined as the proportion of relevant material retrieved, while precision , P, is the proportion of retrieved material that is relevant.

$$E = 100 * \left[1 - \frac{\left(1 + \beta^2\right)PR}{\beta^2 P + R} \right] \qquad (4)$$

Retrieval effectiveness, E, is a weighted combination of recall and precision. β is in the range of 0 to infinity. It is used to reflect the relative importance of recall and precision. If $\beta = 1.0$, it reflects that there is equal importance of precision and recall, while if $\beta = 2.0$ reflects the importance of recall is twice to precision. In this experiment the value of $\beta = 2.0$ is used [20, 23].

5   Results and Discussion

The experimental results in Table 2 show recall (R), precision (P), and retrieval effectiveness (E) for retrieval options of exact match or non-conflation, stemming, thesaurus, and combination of thesaurus and stemming methods.

For natural language query 8 and 17, 100% of the retrieved and relevant documents for all methods are obtained from the total retrieved documents. However their efficiencies are very low and are less than 4% due to the large number of retrieved documents. Since the retrieved and relevant documents are twice important than the precision value, the retrieval effectiveness values are generally high which are greater than 80%.

Thesaurus method has successfully retrieved some relevant documents for query 9, 13, 20, 25, 33, and 35 as compared to exact match and stemming method. As can be observed the recall values of the queries and the averages of 32.58%, 42.18%, 48.07%, and 60.22% increase from exact match to stemming method to thesaurus to combined thesaurus with stemming methods, respectively.

Table 2. Recall, Precision, and Retrieval Effectiveness of Query Language on Conflation Methods

Q#	Recall (R)				Precision (P)				Effectiveness (E)			
	Ex	St	Th	Th+St	Ex	St	Th	Th+St	Ex	St	Th	Th+St
1	21.05	31.58	21.05	31.58	3.81	4.11	3.48	3.75	88.95	86.49	89.53	87.29
2	13.51	16.22	16.22	20.27	1.31	1.49	1.43	1.27	95.27	94.54	94.70	94.92
3	61.54	76.92	61.54	76.92	21.33	21.98	16.16	11.49	55.31	48.72	60.59	64.03
4	33.33	33.33	33.33	33.33	0.18	0.18	0.12	0.09	99.13	99.14	99.42	99.54
5	4.65	9.30	95.35	100.00	3.51	4.26	5.29	2.96	95.63	92.48	78.35	86.79
6	20.00	20.00	50.00	50.00	20.00	2.90	2.10	1.51	80.00	90.83	91.01	93.28
7	15.38	23.08	15.38	23.08	14.29	11.54	14.29	11.54	84.85	80.77	84.85	80.77
8	100.00	100.00	100.00	100.00	2.94	2.11	0.32	0.30	86.84	90.29	98.42	98.54
9	0.00	0.00	90.00	90.00	0.00	0.00	1.99	1.20	0.00	0.00	90.87	94.29
10	0.00	66.67	16.67	83.33	0.00	7.02	1.37	3.88	0.00	75.31	94.85	83.66
11	79.49	92.31	79.49	92.31	32.63	24.49	29.81	18.75	38.25	40.59	40.38	48.28
12	1.84	2.24	5.99	6.79	23.96	22.95	24.59	24.22	97.75	97.27	92.94	92.07
13	0.00	0.00	62.50	75.00	0.00	0.00	0.88	0.56	0.00	0.00	95.81	97.28
14	66.67	66.67	66.67	66.67	2.44	1.47	2.44	1.47	89.36	93.24	89.36	93.24
15	5.88	5.88	78.43	84.31	1.16	1.02	2.75	2.20	96.76	96.99	87.95	90.05
16	37.50	75.00	37.50	75.00	12.50	4.92	2.24	1.00	73.21	80.52	90.96	95.24
17	100.00	100.00	100.00	100.00	4.32	4.07	2.21	1.48	81.58	82.50	89.86	93.00
18	77.78	94.44	83.33	94.44	0.74	0.75	0.53	0.50	96.46	96.39	97.43	97.53
19	30.23	30.23	39.53	39.53	9.29	9.29	4.93	4.87	79.17	79.17	83.56	83.69
20	0.00	0.00	21.43	64.29	0.00	0.00	0.61	0.69	0.00	0.00	97.25	96.67
21	64.71	73.53	64.71	73.53	82.50	81.52	82.50	81.52	32.38	25.00	32.38	25.00
22	54.55	100.00	54.55	100.00	100.00	84.62	100.00	84.62	40.00	3.51	40.00	3.51
23	40.26	40.26	40.26	40.26	96.88	96.88	96.88	96.88	54.41	54.41	54.41	54.41
24	41.94	41.94	41.94	41.94	100.00	100.00	100.00	100.00	52.55	52.55	52.55	52.55
25	0.00	0.00	100.00	100.00	0.00	0.00	1.09	0.45	0.00	0.00	94.79	97.79
26	8.10	9.11	10.38	14.18	60.38	52.94	23.84	23.33	90.20	89.08	88.30	84.62
27	36.00	56.00	41.33	61.78	25.16	15.16	14.67	11.60	66.86	63.60	69.69	66.87
28	41.82	42.00	45.64	46.18	42.05	42.00	31.03	26.91	58.14	58.00	58.29	59.61
29	3.51	3.51	3.51	3.51	36.36	33.33	22.22	21.05	95.72	95.73	95.78	95.79
30	3.33	22.22	5.56	23.33	60.00	80.00	35.71	36.84	95.89	74.03	93.32	74.82
31	47.06	47.06	58.82	58.82	20.51	13.33	1.04	0.82	62.62	68.75	95.13	96.10
32	19.73	19.73	24.83	24.83	21.89	21.80	14.17	11.87	79.88	79.89	78.42	79.62
33	0.00	75.00	0.00	75.00	0.00	0.94	0.00	0.91	0.00	95.53	0.00	95.64
34	83.12	84.42	84.42	88.31	3.24	3.15	2.26	2.03	85.98	86.28	89.78	90.70
35	0.00	0.00	0.00	19.44	0.00	0.00	0.00	1.85	0.00	0.00	0.00	93.30
36	60.00	60.00	80.00	90.00	0.27	0.27	0.22	0.21	98.65	98.69	98.89	98.95
Avg	32.58	42.18	48.07	60.22	22.32	20.85	17.87	16.52	62.55	65.84	77.50	81.65

Note: Ex – Exact Match   St – Stemming Method   Th – Thesaurus Method

Query 24 seems to have 100% efficiency since the total retrieved documents are all relevant. However the recall value is 41.94% for all methods, as there are other relevant documents that are not retrieved. The precision average values of 22.32%, 20.85%, 17.87%, and 16.52% decrease from exact match to stemming method to thesaurus to combined thesaurus with stemming methods, respectively. This performance can be observed from the precision values for some queries.

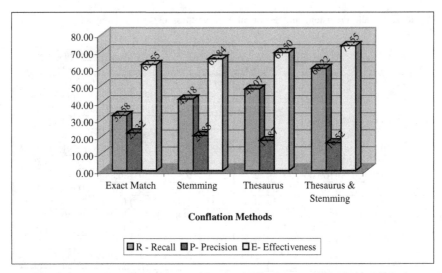

Fig. 1. Average Recall, Precision, and Retrieval Effectiveness of Conflation Methods

The average retrieval effectiveness values increase from 62.55% of exact match method to 65.84% of stemming method to 77.50% of thesaurus method to 81.65% for combination of thesaurus and stemming methods. The average results of retrieval effectiveness have the similar arrangement as the average values of recall but inverse to the average results of precision values. This can be observed from Figure 1 that shows the average values of recall, precision, and effectiveness of exact match, stemming method, thesaurus method, and combination thesaurus and stemming methods.

6 Conclusion

From the experiment, it is clear that combining thesaurus and stemming methods proves to be more effective in retrieving more relevant documents when compared to exact match, stemming, or the thesaurus. Although the combination appears to be the finest of all, the retrieve and relevant result is still low which is only 60.22%. This implies that that there are still key terms in Al-Quran documents that are not available in the thesaurus entries. The precision value is the lowest 16.52% due to the enormous number of documents retrieved while using this combination method. The thesauruses identified are found in many Al-Quran documents but these documents are not listed in the relevance judgment list.

The most obvious way of extending the work would be updating the thesaurus collection by removing and adding new words that relate to the Al-Quran texts.

References

1. Altar, S.: Information systems: a management perspective. 2nd edn. The Benjamin/Cummings Publishing, Inc, Menlo Park, California (1996)
2. van Rijsbergen, C.J.: Information Retrieval. 2nd edn. Butterworths, London (1979)
3. Ekmekcioglu, F.C., Lynch, M.F., Robertson, A.M., Sembok, T.M.T. & Willett, P.: Comparison of N-gram Matching and Stemming for Term Conflation in English, Malay, and Turkish Texts. The Journal of Computer Text Processing, Vol. 6:1. 1–14 (1996)
4. Lennon, M., Peirce, D.S., Tarry, B.D. & Willett, P.: An Evaluation of Some Conflation Algorithms for Information Retrieval. Journal of Information Science 3 (1981) 177–183
5. Frakes, W.B.: Stemming Algorithms. In Frakes, W.B. & Baeza-Yates, R. (ed.): Information Retrieval: Data Structures & Algorithms. Prentice Hall, Englewood Cliffs (1992b) 131–160
6. Freund, G.E. & Willett, P.: Online Identification of Word Variants and Arbitrary Truncation Searching Using a String Similarity Measure. Information Technology Research and Development, Vol. 1. (1982) 177–187
7. Popovic, M. & Willett, P.: The Effectiveness of Stemming for Natural-Language Access to Slovene Textual Data. Journal of the American Society for Information Science Vol. 43:5. (1992) 384–390
8. Frakes, W.B.: Term Conflation for Information Retrieval. In: van Rijsbergen, C.J. (ed.): Research and Development in Information Retrieval: Cambridge: CUP. (1984) 383–390
9. Hafer, M.A. & Weiss, S.F.: Word Segmentation by Letter Successor Varieties. Information Storage and Retrieval Vol. 10. (1974) 371–385
10. Harman, D.: How Effective is Suffixing? Journal of the American Society for Information Society for Information Science Vol. 42:1. (1991) 7–15
11. Lovins, J.B.: Development of a Stemming Algorithm. Mechanical Translation and Computational Linguistics Vol. 11. (1968) 22–31
12. Niedermair, G.T., Thurmair, G., & Buttel, I.: MARS A Retrieval Tool on the Basis of Morphological Analysis. In van Rijsbergen, C.J. (ed.): Research and Development in Information Retrieval, Cambridge, CUP (1985) 369–380
13. Porter, M.F.: An Algorithm for Suffix Stripping. Program, Vol. 14:3. (1980) 130–137
14. Ulmschneider, J.E. & Doszkocs, T.: A Practical Stemming Algorithm for Online Search Assistance. Online Review 7. (1983) 301–318
15. Walker, S. & Jones, R.M.: Improving Subject Retrieval in Online Cataloques. 1. Stemming, Automatic Spelling Correction and Cross-Reference Tables. British Library Research Paper 24, London (1987)
16. Fatimah Ahmad.: A Malay Language Document Retrieval System An Experimental Approach And Analysis. Ph.D. Thesis. Universiti Kebangsaan Malaysia (1995)
17. Savoy, J.: Stemming of French Words based on Grammatical Categories. Journal of the American Society for Information Science, Vol. 44:1. (1993) 1–9
18. Sembok, T.M.T, Yussoff, M. & Ahmad, F.: A Malay Stemming Algorithm for Information Retrieval. Proceedings of the 4th International Conference and Exhibition on Multi-lingual Computing (1994) 5.1.2.1–5.1.2.10
19. Al-Kharashi, I.A. & Evens, M.W.: Comparing Words, Stems and Roots as Index Terms in an Arabic Information Retrieval System. Journal of the American Society for Information Science 45:8. (1994) 548–560
20. Sembok, T.M.T. & Willett, P.: Experiments with N-gram String-Similarity Measure on Malay Texts. Technical Report, Universiti Kebangsaan Malaysia (1995)
21. Abu Bakar, Z., Sembok, T.M.T. & Yussoff, M.: Kajian Keberkesanan Algoritma Gabungan Dalam Capaian Maklumat atas Dokumen Melayu. Prosiding Simposium Kebangsaan Sains Matematik Vol.7. (1996) 260–266

22. Abu Bakar, Z., Sembok, T.M.T. & Yusoff, M.: Experiment on Conflation Algorithms on Malay Texts for Document Retrieval. Proceedings of the 15th IASTED International Conference (1997) 229–231
23. Abu Bakar, Z.: Evaluation Of Retrieval Efectiveness Of Conflation Methods On Malay Documents. Ph.D. Thesis, Universiti Kebangsaan Malaysia (1999)
24. Srinivasan P.: Thesaurus Construction. In: Frakes W.B, & Baeza-Yates R. (eds.): Information Retrieval: Data Structures and Algorithms. Prentice Hall, Eaglewood Cliffs (1992) 161–175
25. Rapizal Abd. Talib.: To Improve Malay Document Retrieval System Using Thesaurus Approach Base On User Query. B.Sc. Thesis. Universiti Teknologi MARA. (2000)
26. Frakes, W.B.: Introduction to Information Storage and Retrieval Systems. In Frakes, W.B. & Baeza-Yates, R.: (ed.): Information Retrieval:Data Structures & Algorithms. Prentice Hall, Englewood Cliffs (1992a) 1–12
27. Robertson, S.E.: The Methodology of Information Retrieval Experiment. In Sparck Jones, K. (ed.): Information Retrieval Experiment. London, Butterworths (1981) 9–13
28. Hamidy, H.Z. & Fachruddin, H.S.: Tafsir Quran. Translation. Klang Book Centre, Klang (1987)
29. Popovic, M.: Implementation of a Slovene Language-Based Free-Text Retrieval System. PhD. Thesis. University of Sheffield (1991)
30. Salton, G. & McGill, M.J.: Introduction to modern information retrieval. McGraw-Hill, New York: (1983)
31. Tague, J.M.: The pragmatics of information retrieval experimentation. In Sparck Jones, K. (ed.): Information Retrieval Experiment: London, Butterworths (1981) 59–102
32. Mohd Rosmadi Mokhtar.: Incorporating Stemming Algorithms in the Malay Information Retrieval that Employs Thesaurus Approach. B.Sc. Thesis. Universiti Teknologi MARA. (2001)
33. Mohd Zaini Mat Abas.: Image and Translated Al-Quran Verses Retrieval System Using Thesaurus Approach Base on Malay Query Words. B.Sc. Thesis. Universiti Teknologi MARA (2001)
34. Abdullah & Ainon.: Tesaurus Bahasa Melayu. Utusan Publication Sdn Bhd, Kuala Lumpur (1994)

Application of Latent Semantic Indexing on Malay-English Cross Language Information Retrieval

Muhamad Taufik Abdullah[1], Fatimah Ahmad[1], Ramlan Mahmod[1], and Tengku Mohd Tengku Sembok[2]

[1]Faculty of Computer Science and Information Technology,
Universiti Putra Malaysia, 43400 Serdang, Malaysia
{taufik,fatimah,ramlan}@fsktm.upm.edu.my
[2]Faculty of Information Science and Technology,
Universiti Kebangsaan Malaysia, 43600 Bangi, Malaysia
tmts@ftsm.ukm.my

Abstract. This paper concerns an application of latent semantic indexing on Malay and English cross language information retrieval system. The retrieval effectiveness was tested on the actual Quranic collection using latent semantic indexing model. The results show that average precision on cross language is higher than monolingual retrieval.

1 Introduction

As the Web becomes a universal repository of human knowledge and culture, which has allowed unprecedent sharing of ideas and information in a scale never seen before. This situation exacerbates the need to find ways of retrieving information across language boundaries, and to understand this information, once retrieved. Computer approaches to understanding foreign language texts range from rapid glossing system to full-fledged machine translation systems. But before these comprehension-aiding approaches are used, some selection must be made among all the documents to which they can be applied. Cross language information retrieval (CLIR) is a special case of information retrieval (IR). CLIR addresses this initial task of filtering, selecting and ranking documents that might be relevant to a query expressed in a different language.

Latent semantic indexing (LSI) is a variant of the vector-retrieval method. A central theme of LSI is that term-term inter-relationships can be automatically modeled and used to improved retrieval. LSI examines the similarity of the "contexts" in which word appear, and creates a reduced-dimension feature-space representation in which words that occur in similar contexts are near each other. The derived feature space reflects these inter-relationships. LSI uses singular value decomposition (SVD) to discover the important associative relationships. It is not necessary to use any external dictionaries to determine these word associations because they are derived from a numerical analysis of existing texts.

Research in the Malay language retrieval systems has been left lagging behind as compared to research that has been done on other languages such as English and other European languages. Although several reports are available on CLIR with European

T.M.T. Sembok et al. (Eds.): ICADL 2003, LNCS 2911, pp. 663–665, 2003.

Table 1. Average Recall and Precision values for mono and cross language retrieval

	Average Precision			
	Monolingual		Cross language	
Recall	Malay	English	Malay query	English query
0.0	0.330097	0.323781	0.363464	0.340485
0.1	0.195649	0.151428	0.231140	0.219489
0.2	0.155946	0.133413	0.177256	0.176118
0.3	0.136925	0.108503	0.151947	0.141188
0.4	0.107231	0.086562	0.125849	0.122306
0.5	0.095668	0.060751	0.104301	0.091794
0.6	0.069323	0.044725	0.080599	0.073668
0.7	0.057288	0.037614	0.065583	0.059694
0.8	0.042411	0.027447	0.048258	0.044904
0.9	0.025611	0.023210	0.028525	0.032133
1.0	0.019738	0.019884	0.020821	0.026283
Average	0.112353	0.092483	0.127068	0.120733

languages, no earlier research on Malay-English CLIR has so far been reported. The objectives of this research are to facilitate the end user reach to Malay textual documents and to enable end-user access to multilingual textual databases.

2 Experimental Results

We worked on the actual Malay Quranic collection and the actual English Quranic collection. These document collections contain 6236 documents in each language. The set of queries and relevance judgments adopted in this experiment was developed by Ahmad [1]. The technique used is LSI. The results of this experiment are analysed using recall and precision as measures of retrieval effectiveness.

Table 1 shows the average recall and precision values for 36 queries for Malay monolingual, English monolingual, cross language using Malay query, and cross language using English query. The recall-precision graphs pertaining to these average recall and precision values are shown in Figure 1.

From the table and figure shown above, it can be observed that Malay-English cross language retrieval performs better than monolingual retrieval. Cross language retrieval using Malay query achieves an average precision of 12.7%, while cross language retrieval using English query achieves an average precision of 12.1%. There is an improvement in performance of 13.1% from monolingual retrieval for Malay query and improvement of 30.5% for English query. These results indicate that the cross language retrieval is able to retrieve a higher percentage of relevant documents from a database than the monolingual retrieval using latent semantic indexing.

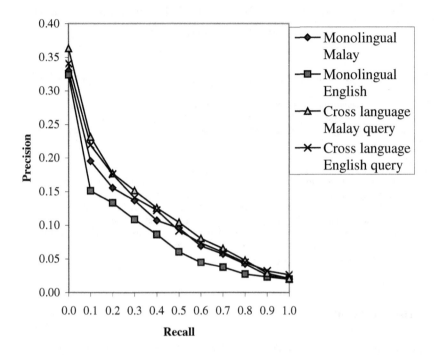

Fig. 1. Average Recall-Precision Graph for mono and cross language retrieval

3 Conclusions

These results have demonstrated that LSI technique could be applied to Malay language retrieval environment. The results of the cross language are quite impressive compared to monolingual results. In conclusion, latent semantic indexing works well for Malay-English cross language and monolingual information retrieval.

References

1. Ahmad, F.: *A Malay Language Document Retrieval System: An Experimental Approach and Analysis.* Tesis Ijazah Doktor Falsafah. Universiti Kebangsaan Malaysia (1995)

Identification of Font Styles and Typefaces in Printed Korean Documents

C.B. Jeong, H.K. Kwag, S.H. Kim, J.S. Kim, and S.C. Park

Department of Computer Science, Chonnam National University,
300 YongBong-dong, BukGu, Gwangju 500-757, Korea
{cbjeong,hkkwag,shkim,kimjisoo,sanchun}@iip.chonnam.ac.kr

Abstract. This paper proposes a system for the extraction of typographical attributes, such as font style and typeface, that can be used to improve the performance of OCR and keyword spotting technologies on printed Korean document images. Three typographical features have been devised and experimented with 7,200 Korean word images. The individual accuracies for font style identification and typeface identification are 97.2% and 99.1%, respectively.

1 Introduction

Optical font recognition (OFR) aims to recover typographical attributes with which texts have been printed [1, 2]. Due to its usefulness for both document and character recognition, OFR is currently considered to be a challenging problem to reduce the search space of word-to-word matching in keyword spotting and improve optical character recognition (OCR) performance [1-6]. Besides the improvement in document indexing and retrieval, OFR has many valuable applications. In this paper, we propose a system for classification of typographical attributes, font style (bold, italic, regular) and typeface (Serif, Sans-serif), that can be used to improve the performance of OCR and keyword spotting technologies on printed Korean documents. Our system first extracts the typographical property of font style and then finds the typeface property according to the style. We have devised three features, i.e. two for font style, and one for typeface, respectively. The effectiveness of each feature has been proven by an experiment with 7,200 word images.

2 Proposed System

2.1 Font Style Identification

Our concern of this paper is to detect the font style for each word, such as bold, italic, and regular. Two features are extracted to deal with three kinds of styles. The first feature is an average width of vertical strokes and the second one is the maximum difference between the neighboring vertical projection profiles. To identify the font style, a quadratic discriminant function (QDF) methodology is used.

T.M.T. Sembok et al. (Eds.): ICADL 2003, LNCS 2911, pp. 666–669, 2003.
© Springer-Verlag Berlin Heidelberg 2003

To compute the average width of vertical strokes, an array $H[i]$ is constructed so that it stores the number of horizontal runs whose length is i. if *most_freq* represents the most frequent run-lengths, then we set the value as

$$most\_freq = \arg\max_i H[i] \cdot \tag{1}$$

Three values in $H[i]$ including $H[most\_freq]$ are chosen to compute the average width of vertical strokes as $Eq(2)$. The feature F_1 is used for distinguishing bold style words from non-bold ones.

$$F_1 = \frac{1}{N}\sum_{i=most\_freq-1}^{most\_freq+1} H[i]\times i \text{, where } N = \sum_{i=most\_freq-1}^{most\_freq+1} H[i] \cdot \tag{2}$$

To obtain the second feature, a vertical projection profile is first constructed. Next the differences between neighboring values in the profile are computed. DVP_{max} is an adequate feature for distinguishing italic words from non-italic ones:

$$F_2 = DVP_{max} = \max\{|VP[i]-VP[i+1]|\} \text{ ,} \tag{3}$$

where $VP[i]$ is the vertical projection profile at the i-th column of the word image.

2.2 Font Typeface Identification

In Korean documents, Serif (Myungjo, Batang, Gungsuh) and Sans-serif fonts (Gothic, Gulim, Dotum) are the most popular classes. A remarkable distinction between Serif and Sans-serif fonts is in the serif. Serif fonts have a small decorative stroke at the beginning of vertical strokes, but Sans-serif fonts have no serif. Therefore, the beginning part of vertical stroke is first segmented and then its direction is computed as a feature. In the font typeface identification, a linear discriminant function (LDF) trained for a specific font style is used.

First, a thinning operation using vertical and horizontal run analysis is applied on the character image, and then vertical and horizontal stroke segments are obtained. A serif region exists around the beginning of a vertical segment, which does not meet with any horizontal segment. Fig. 1 shows the extraction of serif region, where the left image is a Korean character and the right one is its thinned version. When we consider two vertical segments S_1, S_2 in Fig. 1, the beginning part of S_2 meets with a horizontal segment, but that of S_1 does not contact any horizontal segment. Therefore we can extract a serif region from the segment S_1.

In the thinned image, we define a serif as a set of the first five connected skeletal pixels, as P_0, P_1, P_2, P_3 and P_4 in Fig. 2. Then four connected lines, P_0P_1, P_1P_2, P_2P_3 and P_3P_4, are formed and their directions are computed. Direction vector v_{ij}, defined as the vector from i-th pixel to j-th pixel, is computed as following:

$$v_{ij} = (x_j - x_i, y_j - y_i), (i = 0,...,3, j = i+1) \cdot \tag{4}$$

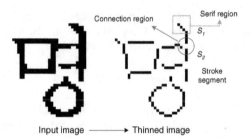

Fig. 1. Extraction of serif region in a Korean character

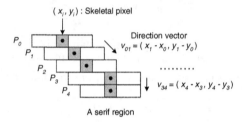

Fig. 2. Extraction of serif region in a Korean character

Assuming that D_{ij} is the position of the direction vector in a 36 sector plane, the final feature of the serif region is computed as an average:

$$F_3 = (\sum_{i=0}^{3} D_{ij})/(N-1), (j = i+1) \tag{5}$$

where N is the number of skeletal pixels in serif region. In fact, almost all feature values of Serif fonts are greater than 27 and that of Sans-serif fonts are less than 27.

3   Experimental Results

To evaluate the performance of the proposed system, we used 7,200 word images, where the two types of typographical attributes are combined. The 3,600 word images are used for testing, while the other words are used for training. Additionally, we use 3,000 character images, 1,500 Serif and 1,500 Sans-serif fonts, to evaluate usefulness of the feature in classifying two types of typefaces.

The accuracy for font style identification is 97.2% for Korean word images shown in a confusion matrix in Table 1. According to the table, a non-trivial number of confusions occur between bold and regular styles. The confusion happens when there is no vertical stroke in the input image and therefore the average width of vertical stroke F_1 is not discriminative. Once the font style of a word image is identified, its font typeface is classified depending on the style. The accuracy for typeface identification is 99.1%, as shown in Table 2. From the table, one can see that the difference between Serif and Sans-serif fonts is well represented by the stroke-based feature.

Table 1. Confusion matrix of style classification for Korean words

	Bold	Italic	Regular	Sum	Accuracy (%)
Bold	1,163		37	1,200	96.9
Italic		1,200		1,200	100
Regular	60	5	1,135	1,200	94.6
Total				3,600	97.2

Table 2. Recognition rates of typeface identification for Korean words(%)

	Bold	Italic	Regular	Average
Serif	98.3	99.1	97.7	98.4
Sans-serif	100	99.1	100	99.7
Total	99.2	99.1	98.9	99.1

4 Concluding Remarks

We have proposed a system for the extraction of typographical attributes, such as font style and typeface, in printed Korean document images. An experiment with 7,200 word and 3,000 character images shows that the proposed features are useful to detect typographical attributes. Our future work is to verify how the proposed system contributes to document indexing and retrieval as well as OCR applications.

Acknowledgement. This work was supported by grant No. R05-2003-000-10396-0 from the KOSEF.

References

1. Zramdini, A., Ingold, R. : Optical font recognition from projection profiles, Proc. Int. Conf. on Raster Imaging and Digital Typography, Darmstadt (1994) 249–260
2. Jung, M.C., Shin, Y.C., Srihari, S.N. : Multifont classification using typographical attributes. Proc. Int. Conf. Document Analysis and Recognition, Bangalore (1999) 353–356
3. Chaudhuri, B.B., Garain, U. : Automatic detection of italic, bold and all-capital words in document images, Proc. Int. Conf. Pattern Recognition, Brisbane (1998) 610–612
4. Garain, U., Chaudhuri, B.B. : Extraction of type style based meta-information from imaged documents, Proc. Int. Conf. Document Analysis and Recognition, Bangalore (1999) 341–344
5. Zhu, Y., Tan, T., Wang, Y. : Font recognition based on global texture analysis, Proc. Int Conf. Document Analysis and Recognition, Bangalore (1999) 349–352
6. Kim, S.H., Kim, S.S., Kwag, H.K., Lee, G.S. : Optical font recognition for printed Korean characters using serif pattern of strokes, Proc. Int. Conf. Circuits/Systems, Computers Communications, Phuket (2002) 916–919

A Domain Specific Ontology Driven to Semantic Document Modelling

Shahrul Azman Noah[1], Lailatulqadri Zakaria[1], Arifah Che Alhadi[1],
Tengku Mohd Tengku Sembok[1], Mohd Yusoff[2], Suhaila Zainuddin[2],
Maryati Mohd. Yusoff[2], and Nazlena Mohamad Ali[1]

[1] Department of Information Science, Faculty of Information Science & Technology,
Universiti Kebangsaan Malaysia, Bangi 43600 UKM Selangor Malaysia
[2] Department of Science and System Management, Faculty of Information Science &
Technology, Universiti Kebangsaan Malaysia, Bangi 43600 UKM Selangor Malaysia
{Samn,tmts,suhaila,mmy}@ftsm.ukm.my

Abstract. To support the realisation of semantic web – as well as digital library, the semantic information content of web documents need to be specified in order to make the tangled information more accessible to search engines and other applications. A number of efforts to support the semantic representation of web documents have been proposed. One such effort is the semantic document modelling of which existing web documents are classified and organised to form a semantic document model representing the contents of respective web documents. In this paper we propose a tool meant to assist in constructing semantic document models using natural language analysis technique and a domain specific ontology. Together with users involvement and participation the tool gradually construct the semantic document model which is represented as XML.

1 Introduction

Accessing and extracting semantic meanings or model from web documents is crucial for the realisation of the Semantic Web [1] particularly with more people, organisations and communities have turned to the web to distribute, share and exchange information. While the web offers the flexibility of making information easily available, it is considerably hard to find a fruitful way to organise, describe, classify and present this information with rich semantic contents [2]. Highly relying on librarians and domain experts during the tasks of document classification can often lead to delays and inconsistent results if such personnel are not available. What needed is a tool that can aid users to participate in the organisation and description of documents. The design and development of such a tool is a challenging task as the nature of human knowledge either explicit or implicit embedded within the web is in a textual form, unstructured and lack of semantics [3].

Few efforts in semantic document modelling is illustrated by the work of Brasethvik and Gulla [2,4,5] and Alani et al. [6]. Brasethvik and Gulla employ the natural language analysis technique and conceptual modelling to assist the task of semantic document classification and retrieval. In this case users construct their own

T.M.T. Sembok et al. (Eds.): ICADL 2003, LNCS 2911, pp. 670–675, 2003.

conceptual model by running a collection of documents from the same domain with the intention of extracting a set of candidate concepts. These concepts are then used by a committee (relevant to the domain) to manually create the desired conceptual model. The constructed conceptual model is then used to model, classify and retrieve documents. In this case, a document is semantically classified by selecting a fragment of the conceptual model that reflects the document's content. Natural language tools such as the WordSmith [7] toolkit and Lingosoft [8]toolset were used to analyse the text of the documents and propose relevant model fragments.

Alani et al. develop Artequakt which adopt an ontology driven approach to semantically model biography documents. The ontology used is from the domain of artists and artefacts which was constructed from part of the CIDOC Conceptual Reference Model and implemented in Protégé; a graphical ontology tool. Using the domain ontology, coupled with WordNet [9] (a general purpose lexical database) and GATE (a NLP tool for entity recognition), Artequakt extract the concepts and the relations between these concepts of the selected document and presented it as an XML reference file. Apart from the concepts and relations of concepts, the sentences and paragraphs describing the context of the concepts are also presented in the XML file.

In this paper, we report our on going research in developing a tool for semantic document modelling for web documents using natural language analysis (NLA) technique and a domain specific ontology. The idea is to build a domain specific corpus database containing semantic-rich document indexes which is meant to serve and integrate with a semantic document retrieval system within a project group or communities. The use of domain specific ontology is to reflect the users' "shared agreement" on the meaning of information [10]. In this approach a set of candidate concepts is extracted from web documents and instead of analysing all the sentences in the document, only those sentences related to the candidate concepts are analysed and compared with the domain ontology to construct the semantic document model. In this paper we use the MeSH [11] medical domain ontology and the generated semantic document model is in XML representation.

2 The Approach

Our approach to semantic document modelling and classification employs the natural language analysis (NLA) technique and a set of domain specific ontology (in this case the medical domain). Both are used to perform the task of textual analysis which results not only in the identification of important concepts represented by the documents but also the relationships between these concepts. Fig. 1 illustrates the overall process involved in constructing the semantic document model. As compared to Brasethvik and Gulla approach which relies on the conceptual model previously constructed by a selective of personnel, our approach utilise existing ontology of the chosen domain, i.e. the medical domain. A detail discussion of the process therefore follows.

Every HTML documents sent for processing will firstly be decoded to generate ASCII document files type that are free from any HTML tags. These documents will then undergo a word analysis process which involved document's filtering and words frequency calculation. In document's filtering, all stopwords will be eliminated and

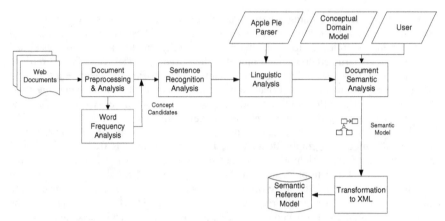

Fig. 1. Process in semantic document modelling

selected concepts will be stemmed to their root words. These concepts or words will be sorted according to the frequency of appearance within the document. The sentence analysis and recognition on the other hand will divide the documents into paragraphs, which are in turn broken down into sentences and stored in the document sentences repository. A set of concepts with high frequency previously obtained from the word analysis process will be matched with the sentences stored in the repository in order to select the candidate sentences to be used in the next NLA process. The results of the document analysis process, therefore, is a list of potential candidate concepts (for building the semantic document model) sorted according to the number of occurrences – as well as a list of document sentences in which the concepts were found.

The natural language analysis process can be divided into two subsequent stages: the morphology and syntactic analysis; and the semantic analysis. The morphology and syntactic analysis process will analyse the input sentences previously stored in the sentences repository into a description tree using the Apple Pie Parser [12].

The next challenging task is to perform the semantic analysis or to extract relationships between the selected concepts. This is perform either by the use of domain specific ontology or by exploiting the semantic structure of the analysed sentences with the help of the user. Noun phrase and verb phrase are good indications of concepts to be included in the documents domain model. Therefore, every noun phrases and verb phrases extracted from the analysed sentences are represented as concepts. These noun phrases will be analysed to filter determiners (such as *the*, *a* and *and*) that usually occur in word phrases.

All the extracted concepts will be first compared with the domain ontology in order to determine the relationships between each concept. If a pair of concepts found matched with the domain ontology, the relation of these concepts is automatically defined by referring to the domain ontology if such a relation existed. If a relation does no exist, a suggestion is provided based upon the syntactic sentence structure of the associated concepts, of which the user will define it manually. Similarly, for those concepts not presented in the domain ontology, the tool will first provide a list of concept candidates which can best be linked based upon the analysis of the chosen

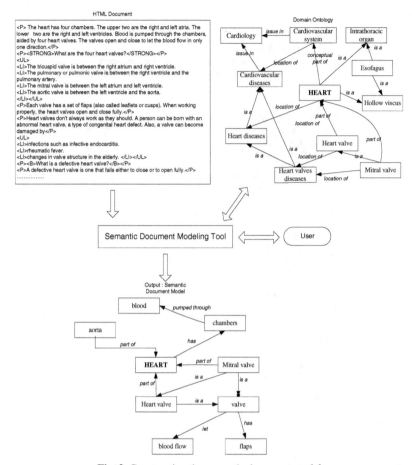

Fig. 2. Constructing the semantic document model

sentences. Once the desired concepts have been selected, the tool will provide the suggestion of possible relationships between these concepts.

Fig. 2 illustrates an example of a HTML document, a fraction of medical domain ontology and the output generated by the semantic document modelling tool. As can be seen from this example, the semantic relationships of "*mitral valve part-of heart*", "*heart valve part-of heart*" and "*mitral valve is-a heart*" are all extracted from the domain ontology whereas the other concepts and relationships are extracted by means of text analysis with the user's participation. The generated semantic document model is an XML representation of the concepts, relationships as well as the URL of the selected documents. Example below is part of the generated XML representation. This model is then stored in the Semantic Referent Model which will be used for semantic retrieval purposes.

```
<?xml version="1.0" encoding="UTF-8" ?>
  <DocumentInfo>
    <MetadataInfo>
      <Title>Heart Valves.htm</Title>
      <Keywords>heart valves, heart, four chambers, mitral valve, aorta, valve,</Keywords>
      <Url>http://www.americanheart.org/presenter.jhtml?identifier=4598</Url>
    </MetadataInfo>
    <Semantic_Content>
          <Concept>
            <Concept_Description>
              <String>blood</String>
            </Concept_Description>
            <Concept_relationship>
              <pumped_through>
                  <String> chamber <String>
              </pumped_through>
            </Concept_relationship>
          </Concept>
          <Concept>
            <Concept_Description>
              <String>chamber</String>
            </Concept_Description>
            <Concept_relationship>
              <part_of>
                <String> heart </string>
              <part_of>
            </Concept_relationship>
          </Concept>
          <Concept>
            <Concept_Description>
              <String>heart</String>
            </Concept_Description>
            <Concept_relationship>
            </Concept_relationship>
          </Concept>
    </Semantic_Content>
```

3 Discussion and Conclusion

Domain ontology plays an important role in supporting the tasks of document classification and organization. In this paper, we have presented how a domain ontology combined with a natural language analysis technique can be exploited not only to extract important concepts from documents but also to represent the semantic content of the documents. Although, controlled vocabulary has been used in information retrieval systems [5], the vocabulary tends to be a list of terms that are syntactically matched with terms in documents. The inherent meanings or structures of the terms in the vocabulary are not used to classify documents, and users are still left with a syntactic approach to information retrieval.

While ontologies for Semantic Web have been focus to support machines looking for information instead of human, semantic document model is intended to support human communication, which requires a human readable notation. In our case the constructed semantic document model is rather meant for later retrieval by human instead of machines or software agents. Our current research work is to develop a global semantic document model representing all the semantic contents stored in the database. Therefore, techniques from the field of data integration [13] and knowledge integration are necessary to support forming such a model. Therefore, searching and retrieval can be conducted by means of the global semantic document model and user can browse or expand the query using this model.

References

1. Berners-Lee, T. Hendler, J. and Lassila, O. The Semantic Web. Scientific American, May (2001) 35–43.
2. Brasethvik, T., and Gulla, J.A. Semantically accessing documents using conceptual model descriptions. ER Workshops (1999) 321–333
3. Mattia D., Luca, I. and Danielle, N. Knowledge representation techniques for information extraction on the web. Proceedings of the WebNet 98.
4. Brasethvik, T., and Gulla, J.A. A Conceptual Modelling Approach to Semantic Document Retrieval. Advanced Information Systems Engineering, 14th International Conference (2002) 167–182.
5. Brasethvik, T., and Gulla, J.A. Natural language analysis for semantic document modeling. Data and Knowledge Engineering (2001) 45–62.
6. Alani, H., Kim, S., Millard, D., Weal, M. Hall, W., Lewis, P. and Shadbolt, N. Automatic Ontology-Based Knowledge Extraction from Web Documents. IEEE Intelligent Systems 18(1) (2003)14–21.
7. Scott, M. WordSmith tools, at http://www.liv.ac.uk/~ms2928/wordsmiy.htm (accessed: October 2002).
8. Voutilainen, A. A short introduction to the NP tool, http://www.lingsoft.fi/doc/nptool/intro (accessed: October 2002)
9. Miller, G. WordNet: a lexical database for English. Communications of the ACM 38(11) (1996) 39–41.
10. Bannon, L. and Bodker, S. Constructing common information spaces. 5th European Conference on CSCW (1997)
11. Nelson S. Medical Subject Headings, at http://www.nlm.nih.gov/mesh/meshhome.html (accessed: 20 November 2002)
12. Sekine S. 2002. *Proteus Project – Apple Pie Parser (Corpus based Parser).* http://nlp.cs.nyu.edu/app (accessed on 15 September 2002)
13. Arens, Y. Chee, C.Y. Hsu, C. and Knoblosk, A. Retrieving and integrating data from multiple information sources. International Journal of Intelligent and Cooperative Information Systems, 2(2) (1993) 127–158.

The System of Registries: An Evaluation of User Feedback... A Year Later

Panayiota Polydoratou[1], Michael Pendleton[2], and David Nicholas[1]

[1] Centre for Information Behaviour and the Evaluation of Research (*ciber*)
City University, Department of Information Science London EC1V 0HB, UK
p.polydoratou@city.ac.uk
nick@soi.city.ac.uk
[2] United States Environmental Protection Agency, Office of Environmental Information
1200 Pennsylvania Avenue, NW, Mail Code 2822-T, Washington, DC 20460
pendleton.michael@epa.gov

Abstract. The U.S. Environmental Protection Agency's (EPA) System of Registries (SoR) is a metadata management tool that is critical to supporting EPA's efforts to manage and integrate environmental information. In March 2003, an SOR users conference was held to demonstrate new services and to promote the SoR's role in supporting various information integration and sharing initiatives currently underway, including the National Environmental Information Exchange Network (NEIEN). We developed an online questionnaire and asked conference attendees to provide feedback on how they use the SoR and what their future expectations are regarding services provided by the SoR. Sixteen of the forty-nine participants responded to questions on familiarity with registries, the types of information sought, and how they have used the information they've obtained in their work. Respondents also gave suggestions for existing services. Combined with results from web usage statistics over a 5-year period, we provide an assessment of SOR usage.

1 Introduction

The system of Registries (SoR) is a Web-based collection of metadata registries and repositories residing in the Environmental Protection Agency's (EPA) Office of Environmental Information (OEI). The registries that comprise the SoR provide identification information for objects of interest to EPA trading partners, including states and tribal entities, and the public. They described objects consist of data elements, XML tags, data standards, substances (chemicals, biological organisms, and physical properties), terms and definitions, facilities, regulations, and data sets that the Agency uses in its core business processes. These registries comprise a critical link in EPA's information architecture and are vital components to the Exchange Network being developed to facilitate data exchange with stakeholders through network nodes.

The System of Registries represents a 10-year effort to manage Agency information resources as strategic assets and an increasing recognition that environmentally sour decision-making must be based on accurate data and information. A concept paper in 1993, called for an incremental approach to building

T.M.T. Sembok et al. (Eds.): ICADL 2003, LNCS 2911, pp. 676–681, 2003.

a system of registries and data standards, which led to the initial implementation if the Environmental Data Registry in 1997. In 2003, the SoR became an integral component to the Agency architectural plans. Since its inception, the System of Registries has continued to evolve aiming to satisfy the needs of its users. The first users' conference held in January 2002 provided a wealth of input and additional functionality has been added as a direct result of input provided by conference participants.

Changes resulting from that conference included subsuming both the chemical and biological information related registries under one Substance Registry System, and the launch of one integrated search function across a number of the registries as part of a new user interface that acts as a "virtual gateway" to registry managed information were among the changes.

Following the successful first users' conference in January 2002, another registries oriented conference was held for users in March of 2003. That conference emphasized the SoR's new services and its role within several information integration and data-sharing initiates. This paper builds upon survey results regarding system use and functionality obtained from the first users' conference. We also examine usage trends indicated by the web logs transactions from the last 5 years.

2 Literature Review

The diversity of communities on the Internet and the information needs of each of those communities indicated the application of different metadata standards – sometimes simpler and sometimes more sophisticated – for the description of resources. Interest in metadata registries arose from the need to be able to search across diverse metadata standards. Leviston (2001) distinguishes between two different types of metadata registry systems. Systems that serve as reference points by listing URLs that point to Web sites of metadata initiatives and projects and systems, which are concerned with the management of the evolution of metadata standards over time and provide with mappings between element sets.

Some of the functions of metadata registry systems have been registered in the literature. Heery & Wagner (2002) described the working progress of three prototypes of the DCMI metadata registry and the role of the DCMI registry to facilitate semantic representation of resources. Nagamori and colleagues (2001) stress the importance of the re-use of metadata elements in different languages. Johnston (2002) defines the purpose of the MEG registry as a publication environment for developers, implementers and researchers to publish their schemes and disclose information on their usage. Heery (2002) also describes the CORES registry, its uses and role of more than a "dictionary" or metadata element sets.

Current prototypes indicate a variation of metadata registry systems functionality. The description of data elements, provision of guidelines for their use, mappings among elements of different metadata element sets and, for the case of DC registry, facilitation of multilingual searching are considered equally important for the registries' functionality. Consistent update of registry content is essential for validity and credibility.

3 Aims and Objectives/ Scope and Limitations

The aim of this paper is to further illuminate how the U.S. EPA's System of Registries is used by building on earlier survey findings pertaining to by examining additional survey results and by analyzing web usage statistics of from 1998 to 2002

Although we did not extensively survey SoR users,[1] we believe that these results, coupled with findings from the web usage statistics, do provide additional insight into user opinions. Our results should be viewed as suggestive rather than conclusive in light of the number of individuals surveyed. This fact notwithstanding, we do feel that those individuals surveyed are representative of the user base.

4 Methodology

We used an online questionnaire and analysed web logs transactions the years between 1998-2002.The online questionnaire was made available to SoR Conference attendees during the on the day of the conference, March 20th, 2003. Although sixty-five people attended the conference, only forty-nine could have completed the questionnaire due to the limited access to the computers. Of those forty-nine, sixteen (32.6%) completed a two-part questionnaire:

- Part 1: Indication of users area of interest, familiarity with SoR products and services provided, type of information sought and review of the application functionality.
- Part 2: General comments and feedback on the SoR.

In addition to the online questionnaire, web log transactions for 1998 to 2002 were analyzed to reveal EDR/SoR usage trends (increasing/decreasing).[2] We processed the available data using Microsoft Access and Excel. EPA was unable to provide us with access to the raw log files of the EDR/SoR; therefore our findings reflect analysis of less detailed data that is generally available to the public.[3]

5 Results

Similar to the first users' conference in January 2002, the March 2003 conference attracted attendees from a range of U.S. state and federal government organizations including Maine Department of Environmental Protection, Bureau of Labor Statistics, US Federal Aviation Administration - Representatives from private concerns were also in attendance from the Chemical Abstract Service and numerous consulting firm.

---

[1] We will augment survey these results with interviews from users within and outside of U.S. EPA.

[2] Although data were available from 1996, we chose 1998 as a starting point in response to changes in EPA's approach to web log measurement (from total requests to "counting" page requests,which reduced the numbers of "hits" were reduced significantly but provided better accuracy regarding which pages were actually being accessed and downloaded)

[3] The authors would like to thank Michael Pendleton, of the U.S. EPA, for his help on this issue and for providing sample reports of web usage statistics that allowed us to compare and validate our survey results.

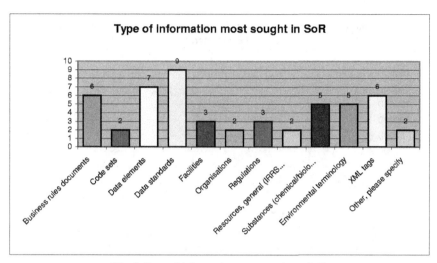

Fig. 1. Type of information most sought on SoR

According to a newsletter published immediately after the conference *"This year's conference put special emphasis on data standards implementation. Data standards are critical to the success of EPA's information integration initiatives, including the Enterprise Architecture and the Environmental Information Exchange Network"*[4]. Results from web usage statistics of the last five years show that EPA is not the sole user of the registries. Although it is one of the main users of the services, it appears to encounter a decline in its use after peaking in 1999 and 2000. The commercial and academic domains appear to be steady users throughout the years. Examples of universities that point their students to the information in EDR/SoR include the University of Virginia (USA) and the University of Liverpool (UK).

The EDR remains the most popular of the registries. The Facility Registry System (FRS) and the Substances Registry System (SRS) follow closely behind in usage. Once again, survey respondents indicated that data standards and their associated business rules represent the most sought after information on the SoR. The newly available XML tags are also quite popular (Figure 1).

Half of the respondents (8) indicated that locating information is the main reason for visiting the SoR. Few people have used the service to register an information resource (2), download information (2) and use information obtained in their work (4). Those who have searched and/or downloaded information from the SoR indicated a need to stay current with EPA information resources (8 people) or to download information on multiple standards at once (6 people). Data from the web logs transactions showed that the users of the SoR visit the services after either EPA, search engines or other sources direct them there. Other referrals include academic institutions, commercial websites and health and/or environmental organizations. The peak year for EPA referrals was 2001 and search engines and other referrers are showing a steady increase after year 2000 (Figure 2).

---

[4] System of Registries Conference. Registry Update, Spring 2003. Available at:
   http://www.epa.gov/sor/spring2003.pdf

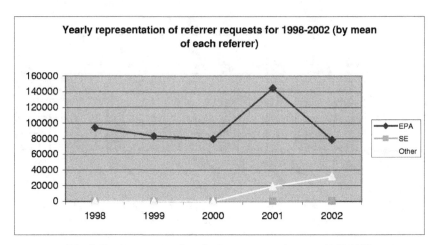

Fig. 2. Yearly representation of referrer requests between 1998-2002

5.1   General Comments and Suggestions (Strongest Features, Suggestions for Improvements, and How SoR Can Improve Current Work)

Respondents felt that one of the greatest strengths of the SoR was the enhanced search capability, which is a byproduct of feedback from last year's conference participants.

Most of the recommendations for improvement are for the Substance Registry System, indicating additions to current information, improvement of the "*domain lists of substances and physical measures*" and the search facility, which for some features remains slow. According to one respondent, there is a need for "better/simpler search and download".

One of the respondents suggested expanding the collaboration with other US organizations and even other countries. In particular, there was a suggestion to enhance information on the SoR with data sources from "*the European Chemicals Bureau or international organizations such as OECD*" in exchange of estimation techniques and QSARs.

6   Conclusions

Attendees indicated a variety of areas that they were interested in such as standards development, implementation, auditing, systems analysis, etc. Data from web usage statistics reveled that besides EPA, academic institutions consistently use SoR resources (particularly the Substances Registry System) and the commercial domain being one on rise.

Users of SoR search for data standards, XML tags, associated business rules documents, and metadata pertaining to individual data elements that explain usage and new features such as XML tags – available through EDR – appeared to be popular as well. Comments and suggestions on the SoR services were rich and representative of the interest in SoR. Expanding collaboration with other governmental organizations and countries, transfer of ideas and SoR processes into other organizations, data validation, exchange of information and avoidance of duplication of efforts were among those issue identified by users as key next steps. We believe that metadata registry systems are a vital part in the process of data standardization and metadata management. We feel that the results from our surveys and web usage statistics bring some light on the use of metadata registry systems and provide some indication of users' preferences and expectations. The next steps in our research are to conduct a series of interviews with current users of metadata registry systems.

References

1. EPA's Data Standards Process. *Standard Update Newsletter*, Vol. 1 No.2, Summer 1999. Available at http://www.epa.gov/edr/1033summer99.pdf (last visited on the 20/06/2003)
2. Heery, R. (2002) Functional Requirements for CORES schema creation and registration tool *UKOLN – CORES* http://www.cores-eu.net/registry/d22/funcreq.html 16/04/2003
3. Heery, Rachel and Harry Wagner (2002). A metadata registry for the semantic Web. D-Lib, Vol. 8, No. 5. Available at: http://www.dlib.org/dlib/may02/wagner/05wagner.html (last visited on the 20/06/2003)
4. Johnston, P. (2002) Functional Requirements for MEG registry *UKOLN – MEG* http://www.ukoln.ac.uk/metadata/education/regproj/funcreq/ (last visited on the 20/06/2003)
5. Leviston, Tony. (2001). Discussion Paper: Describing metadata registry requirements and realities. January 2001. Available at: http://www.dstc.edu.au/Research/Projects/Infoeco/publications/registry-discussion.pdf (last visited 27/06/2002)
6. Nagamori, M., et al. (2001). A multilingual metadata schema registry based on RDF schema. *DC-2001, International Conference on Dublin Core and Metadata Applications*, Japan.

OAI-Based Interoperable System for the Folk Music Digital Library

Qiaoying Zheng, Wei Zhu, and Zongying Yang

Shanghai Jiao Tong University Library,
1954 Hua Shan Road Shanghai, 200030, P.R.China
{zheng,wzhu}@mail.lib.sjtu.edu.cn
zyyang@mail.sjtu.edu.cn

Abstract. According to research of the International Digital Library Project (IDLP) – CMNet (Chinese Memory Net – US-Sino Collaborative Research Toward A Global Digital Library in Chinese Studies) founded by the America, this paper presents a part of the research result. Database structure and metadata standard of Chinese Folk Music DL (CFMDL) is described in it. We introduce the OAI-based metadata interoperation framework for Chinese folk music DL: OAI-based system framework for CMNet, OAI protocol for metadata harvesting, administration and value-added services of metadata harvesting for CFMDL. Tsinghua University, Peking University, and Shanghai Jiaotong University applied jointly for the major project, "Theories, Methods and Technical Research of the Globalization of the Chinese Culture Digital Library". Shanghai Jiaotong University mainly undertakes the research of key theories, methods and technologies for the Chinese folk music DL and the major content of the research are digitalization processing methods for the Chinese folk music, metadata standards and criteria, system interoperability, and visiting methods toward distributed, heterogeneous resources, all of which are crucial issues in DL technologies.[1] Chinese folk music database has three tables: musical_composition, musical_instrument and character. The instrument column in table musical_composition links to musical_instrument, while composer, executant and conductor columns in table musical_composition links to table character. Chinese folk music includes various types of musical works in every historical period of Chinese nations. The data collection of Chinese folk music database metadata gives priority to Chinese ancient music, also considers modern music, including musical works (composition), musical characters (e.g., composers, executants), musical instruments, etc. CFMDL system framework is based on OAI protocol. Data providers that own information repository are responsible for creating and publishing metadata, meanwhile organize the numerical objects in the information repository to produce structural metadata and make end-users or service providers can use and browse the information repository. Service providers send requests to data providers that publish the metadata to extract metadata, process and organize them, as well as build value-added services that are based on the metadata collected from data providers. A registration sever provides the registration interfaces for data providers and service providers, and the server also administers and organizes the data providers and service providers. Administration and Value-added Services of Metadata Harvesting for CFMDL system.

---

[1] This research was supported by the Chinese National Science Foundation, No 60221120145.

T.M.T. Sembok et al. (Eds.): ICADL 2003, LNCS 2911, pp. 682–683, 2003.

1. Information management of data providers
2. Administration of metadata harvesting
3. Administration and reorganization of metadata
4. Query module and Data browsing function

An XML-Based Query Generator for Multiple Boolean Search Systems on the Web

Christopher Khoo, Jin-Cheon Na, and Firdaus Bin Othman

Division of Information Studies, School of Communication and Information
Nanyang Technological University, Singapore
{assgkhoo,tjcna,efirdaus}@ntu.edu.sg

Many bibliographic retrieval systems, such as online library catalogs and databases of article abstracts, as well as full-text databases are accessible on the Web through Boolean search interfaces. Though they provide access to a wealth of information, they are difficult for end-users to search effectively because of variations in the query language syntax, field codes and user-interface structure. To search such systems effectively requires a substantial amount of searching skill and knowledge.

This project seeks to develop a query-translation system for multiple Boolean search systems using XML and XSLT (eXtensible Stylesheet Language-Transformations). The main objectives are to identify the characteristics of the Boolean search languages and user-interface structures used in various systems, to develop standard XML representations for query statements and for profiling the search systems, and to develop a method for query translation using XSLT.

The overall stages to process and translate a query statement from a user's input to a form suitable for querying a Boolean search system on the Web are shown in the figure. This is part of an ongoing effort to develop a knowledge-based search intermediary system or meta-search engine for searching multiple retrieval systems on the Web.

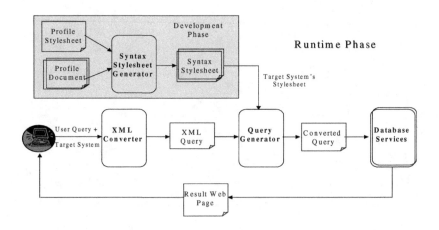

T.M.T. Sembok et al. (Eds.): ICADL 2003, LNCS 2911, p. 684, 2003.

Design and Implementation of a Content-Based Video Retrieval System Using Moving Objects Trajectories

Choon-Bo Shim and Jae-Woo Chang

Dept. of Computer Engineering,
Research Center of Industrial Technology, Engineering Research Institute
Chonbuk National University, Jeonju, Jeonbuk 561-756, South Korea
{cbsim,jwchang}@dblab.chonbuk.ac.kr

Abstract. In this paper, we design and implement a content-based video retrieval system using moving objects' trajectories. For this, we first present a spatio-temporal representation scheme which can efficiently deal with a single moving object as well as multiple moving objects. Secondly, we describe an efficient similar sub-trajectory retrieval scheme based on a new k-warping distance algorithm. Thirdly, we propose a new signature-based access method which can deal with a large amount of database and can support efficient retrieval on a user query based on moving objects' trajectories. To show the usefulness of applying our above schemes to a real video database application, we implement a content-based soccer video retrieval system, called CSVR, because the soccer video data have a lot of motion information based on a soccer ball being a salient object. The CSVR provides graphic user interfaces for both soccer video indexing and retrieval. Finally, we do the performance analysis of our similar sub-trajectory retrieval scheme based on our k-warping distance algorithm.

1 Introduction

Recently, a lot of interests in content-based (or similarity-based) retrieval have been increased in multimedia database applications. Unlike image data, the most important feature in video data is the trajectory of moving objects. The trajectory of a moving object can be represented as a spatio-temporal relationship which combines spatial properties between moving objects in each frame with temporal properties among a set of frames. It also plays an important role in video indexing for content-based retrieval. Thus, it is necessary to support content-based retrieval using a sequence of locations of moving objects.

T.M.T. Sembok et al. (Eds.): ICADL 2003, LNCS 2911, p. 685, 2003.

ACNET: The Genesis of Iranian Information Consortia and Its Impact on National Digital Library Development

Nader Naghshineh[1] and Fatima Fahimnia[2]

[1] School of Psychology and Educational Science, University of Tehran,
Tehran, Iran 14155-3993
Dialog@neda.net
[2] Department of Library and Information Sciences,
School of Psychology and Educational Science, University of Tehran, Tehran, Iran
fahimnia@ut.ac.ir

Abstract. The paper studies the evolution of collaborative information ventures in Iran, starting with the formation of the committee for Information cooperation in early 80's. It will then studies the background forces at play that prompted a number of Iranian academic libraries to lay the corner stone for ACNET. The progress had been hindered by the secondary effects stemming from the geopolitics of information such as information vendors' inclination towards a "captured market" model, de-diversification of supply channels, artificially-bloated pricing as well as limited negotiating options. The Bryson Model used for determining the strategic focus of ACNET indicates that any Information Consortia in Iran should operate along a business premise in order to ensure the versatility and flexibility necessary to safeguard the interests of its stake-holders. The ACNET has been reincorporated as an NGO in 2003(WWW.ACNET.OR.IR) Like any multi-agency initiative, ACNET presents an option for repackaging of solutions, that while primarily intended for an Academic clientele, could attract a larger group of stake-holders from other sectors. This is especially so when one considers the main impediment before launching a digital library access solution, is the fact that the business processes prevalent in the target environment (stake-holders, government agencies, and private concerns) are non-digital in nature. The essence of the problem is how to extend the solutions from an academic to a non-academic environment. This can be done in two ways. One method to envision an add-on module for an existing Digital Library system, specifically designed for non-academic clients. The module would provide a transparent back-processes that would ensure compliance of the resource sharing with the current standards and practices in digital rights management. It can include a template incorporating most adept at addressing the information seeking profile or habit of the non-academic target group. In some cases, it even includes an online accounting clearance system. The other method is to set up a pathfinder team for any sector that wishes to use the ACNET resources. An information Audit is carried out, whereby the client environment is assessed on the degree it can lend itself to digital library business processes. In essence what is done here is to help the client to set up its own digital resource that it could share as an asset. This asset could then be incorporated in the existing digital library holding. Information seeking models would imprinted within the interface software on a directional or multi-directional basis. This virtual digital library would in effect act as a colony construct. While it has an integrated appearance its internal relationships between parts could be designed to optimize the productivity based on client most prevalent information searching behavior.

T.M.T. Sembok et al. (Eds.): ICADL 2003, LNCS 2911, p. 686, 2003.
© Springer-Verlag Berlin Heidelberg 2003

Digesting Bilingual Web News via Mining Financial Activities and Events

Pik-Shan Cheung, Ruizhang Huang, and Wai Lam

Department of Systems Engineering and Engineering Management
The Chinese University of Hong Kong, Shatin, Hong Kong
{pscheung,rzhuang,wlam}@se.cuhk.edu.hk

We attempt to develop a financial knowledge management system, known as FAM (Financial Activity Mining), which is able to digest online multilingual news and conduct financial activity mining. FAM is able to present news on discovered activities or events. Our system is particularly helpful for tracking stock performance of a targeted company or an event, with all the related news collected. Clear presentation of relationships between related activities provides convenient environment for users to monitor the financial market.

FAM involves several components to mine financial activities and events. Financial news are fetched automatically from the Internet (e.g., BBC at www.bbc.com) and stored into a database. This step is done in real-time automatically so that the latest news can be obtained as soon as they are released. In the story preprocessing component, stop-words are filtered and remaining keywords are stemmed for English stories.

After the preprocessing step, metadata will be automatically generated. Metadata captures key attributes of the news including the source, release date, language, people names, geographical locations names, and organization names. Some attributes such as source and release date can be determined when the news is fetched. Those named entities, in particular, people names, geographical location names, and organization names are automatically extracted from the news content [1]. A transformation-based linguistic tagger [2] for each language, one for English and one for Chinese is employed to perform this named entity extraction task. This approach is based on a tagger which can tag different kinds of named entities and part-of-speech information according to a set of trained transformation rules. The training corpus contains manually assigned tags or annotations.

The financial activity mining task is done in the unsupervised learning component. There are two levels in the unsupervised learning procedure. At the lower level of the mining procedure, stories describing similar financial activities are grouped together to form activity clusters. Activity clusters are continuously updated when new story arrives. At a higher level, FAM can cluster related financial activities to form financial events. Through the generation of financial events, activities of companies or organizations can be monitored.

To handle multilingual news, FAM performs context-based gloss translation on Chinese stories. A bilingual dictionary is used. However, several translations will be retrieved for a Chinese word by the dictionary. Among all the translations, only some of them are appropriate. In order to conduct translation term disambiguation, we make use of co-occurrence statistics and mutual information.

T.M.T. Sembok et al. (Eds.): ICADL 2003, LNCS 2911, p. 687, 2003.

On Extracting Facial Expressions for the Virtual Image Masking

Kyong Sok Seo[1], Jin Ok Kim[2], and Chin Hyun Chung[1]

[1] Department of Information and Control Engineering, Kwangwoon University, 447-1, Wolgye-dong, Nowon-gu, Seoul, 139-701, Korea
chung@kw.ac.kr
[2] School of Information and Communication Engineering, Sungkyunkwan University, Suwon, Kyunggi-do, 440-746, Korea
jinny@ece3.skku.ac.kr

Abstract. Since PC camera based net-meeting and video chatting program have been introduced, users become to enjoy real-time communication with each other through PC as having face to face meeting. This paper proposes the virtual image masking for the net-meeting users on internet. Net-meeting users adapted by the virtual image masking can hide their face on the other party's monitor and show only their facial expressions instead of face, whose shapes could be a tiger or a spider-man. For implementation of the virtual image masking, we first detect a facial area to adapt skin color method with the standard of Asian's skin color. And we find positions of eyes on the facial area, then, extract the user's expression like winking or blinking. This virtual image masking would be useful to protect user's privacy on the open communication environment like internet.

Fig. 1. Labeled image

Results and Conclusion. In this paper, a face detection fully supported by the skin color method is not easily influenced background. Even though the color of the wall beside user is similar to user's skin color, the labeled image implemented by the proposed method in Fig. 1 shows good result. This labeled image would be switched to a virtual image. In extracting process of a user's expression, detecting the states of eyes is planed to confirm face detection an d to extract the states of eyes. For searching eyes, its edges are extracted by Sobel filter, and histogram equalization is adapted get good contrast of gray scale image for threshold of eyes' area. Searching eyes based on the geometrical analysis makes us find easier the states of eyes because eyes' area is only needed. After finding the eyes, extracting expression like wink and blinking is easier to be determined.

T.M.T. Sembok et al. (Eds.): ICADL 2003, LNCS 2911, p. 688, 2003.
© Springer-Verlag Berlin Heidelberg 2003

Variable Order Verification Use of Logic Representation

P. W. Chandana Prasad, M. Maria Dominic, and Ashutosh Kumar Singh

Faculty of Information and Science and Technology
Multimedia University, Jalan Ayer Keroh Lama, 75450, Melaka, Malaysia
{petatiyan.prasad,murugeson.dominic,ashutosh.kuman}@mmu.edu.my

Abstract. Boolean functions are fundamental to synthesis and verification of digital logic, and compact representations of Boolean functions have great practical significance. Conversion between those representations is common, especially when one is used to represent the input and another speeds up relevant algorithms. In the last 15 years, a number of applications based on efficient manipulation of Boolean functions gained industrial significance, notably in automated design and verification of logic circuits. The efficient representation and manipulation of Boolean functions is important for many algorithms in a wide variety of applications in particular, many problems in computer-aided design for digital circuits (CAD). The efficiency of the Boolean manipulation depends on the form of representation of the Boolean function. It is unavoidable and important problem to find a variable ordering which minimize the size of a BDD, since variable ordering has a great influence on the computation time and storage requirements for Boolean function manipulation number of times each variable takes part in the Logic operation to obtain the best possible the variable order. This paper describes a technique for finding the best variable ordering by analyzing the logic gate representation in the given Boolean function. Algorithm starts with initial variable ordering. The system will check each sub expression to find out the number times each variable takes part in each type of logic operations. The number of occurrences for each variable will be stored and then all the totals are arranged in descending order to identify the variable ordering for that Boolean function. If more than one input variables have the same total then a special criteria will be used to break the tie: We present graph-based evidence of the improvement obtained by using highly effective logical verification based variable ordering technique for BDDs. It is shown that the effectiveness of the Decision Diagram is mainly depending on the variable ordering selected. It is not practical to have any unique ordering for a given Boolean function and it can be selected among the number of best results, what will be more appropriate with the design. This new technique, easy to implement and automate, consistently creates high quality variable ordering for Boolean function.

T.M.T. Sembok et al. (Eds.): ICADL 2003, LNCS 2911, p. 689, 2003.
© Springer-Verlag Berlin Heidelberg 2003

A Korean-Japanese-Chinese Aligned Wordnet with Shared Semantic Hierarchy[*]

Key-Sun Choi and Hee-Sook Bae

Korterm, Computer Science Division, KAIST, 373-1 Guseong-dong
Yuseong-gu Daejeon 305-701 Korea
kschoi@cs.kaist.ac.kr
elle@world.kaist.ac.kr

A Korean-Japanese-Chinese aligned wordnet, "CoreNet" is introduced. For the purpose of this paper, the term "wordnet" refers to a network of words. It is constructed based on a shared semantic hierarchy that is originated from NTT *Goidaikei* (Lexical Hierarchical System). Korean wordnet was constructed through the semantic category assignment to every meaning of Korean words in a dictionary. Verbs and adjectives' word senses are assigned to the same semantic hierarchy as that of nouns. Each sense of verbs is investigated from corpora for their usage, and compared with Japanese translation. Chinese wordnet with the same semantic hierarchy was built up based on the comparison with Korean wordnet. Each sense of Chinese verb corresponds to Korean with its argument structure. The use of the same semantic hierarchy for nouns and predicates has several advantages. First, the surface forms of nouns and predicates share the similar one, especially in Chinese words. In case of Korean and Japanese, the typical formation is like "*do*+Noun" in English like "Noun+*suru*" in Japanese and "Noun+*hada*" in Korean. Second, the language generation from conceptual structures takes freedom to choose the surface form whether it chooses noun phrases or verb phrases. CoreNet has been constructed by the following principles: word sense mapping to concept, corpus-based, multi-lingualism, and single concept system for multi-languages. The overall flow of construction is based on dictionary-based bootstrapping, incremental similarity-based classification and manual post-editing. Among consideration points, the followings are introduced: multiple concept mapping, verbal noun, and concept splitting. For multiple concept mapping, a word is mapped into numerous concepts that comprise respective meanings of the word. For example, *school* is an "institution for the instruction of students." The word *school* is mapped into three concepts such as LOCATION, ORGANIZATION, and FACILITY. For verbal noun, a word that is a verb is assigned to concepts after it is transformed to a noun. For example, "*write*" is transformed to its noun form "*writing*" that is mapped into a concept WRITING falling under EVENT. For concept splitting, every time inconsistency among nodes of concepts is discovered, a node may be added. What differs between CoreNet and NTT Goidaikei is that CoreNet features mapping between word senses (not just words) and concepts. These works have lasted since 1994.

---

[*] This work has been supported by Ministry of Science and Technology in Korea. The result of this work is enhanced and distributed through Bank of Language Resources supported by grant No. R21-2003-000-10042-0 from Korea Science & Technology Foundation.

T.M.T. Sembok et al. (Eds.): ICADL 2003, LNCS 2911, p. 690, 2003.

A New Video Segmentation Method Using Variable Interval Frame Differencing for Digital Video Library Applications

Youngsung Soh

Dept. of Information Engineering, Myong Ji Univ., San 38-2, Namdong,
Yongin, Kyunggido, Korea
soh@mju.ac.kr

Automatic video segmentation is a necessary step before indexing the large amount of video data. Transitions in video can be divided into two types: abrupt transition and gradual transition. Abrupt transition is called "cut" and is formed when one shot is followed by another shot with totally different characteristic. Gradual transition is the one in which shot boundary is not clearly visible. Fade in/out, wipe, and dissolve are examples.

In this paper, we propose a new video segmentation method which can detect cut and dissolve in uncompressed monochrome video using variable interval frame differencing. For gradual changes, we focus only on dissolve since fade in/out is just a special case of dissolve. Thus we assume that other types of gradual changes are already known. We basically use histogram and edge features, but differencing is performed not just for contiguous frames but for distant frames.

Our method consists of four stages. They are Feature Computation(FC), Cut Detection(CD), Separation of given Sequence into Subsequences(SSS), and Dissolve Detection(DD). In FC, we use two features: Histogram Difference Metric and Edge Difference Metric. CD uses these two features to detect cuts. In SSS, we break given sequence into subsequences separated by cuts detected and other gradual changes assumed to be known. Finally in DD, we test above two features among variable intervals of frame and detect dissolves.

Many methods were proposed for the detection of cuts and dissolves. Among them are twin comparison method, K-means clustering based method, bitplane method, and statistical hypothesis testing method. We compared the proposed method with four conventional approaches and showed that the proposed performs better than all four. Movie, commercial, and sightseeing videos were used to assess the performance of each approach. The proposed method yielded highest hit ratio along with lowest miss and false positive ratios. This superiority seems to come from the flexible nature of our frame differencing interval. The proposed method assumes that gradual changes other than dissolve are known in advance. As mentioned earlier, fade in and fade out are special cases of dissolve, thus can be detected with a similar algorithm. However, a study is needed to detect wipe and camera work. This is intended for future research.

T.M.T. Sembok et al. (Eds.): ICADL 2003, LNCS 2911, p. 691, 2003.
© Springer-Verlag Berlin Heidelberg 2003

Towards Flexible and User-Friendly Management of Documents

Ilvio Bruder and Andre Zeitz

University of Rostock, Germany
{ilr,zeitz}@informatik.uni-rostock.de

1 Introduction

Managing a document as one object in an information system, such as a digital library, is quite simple. A differentiated approach to store a document, for example, with respect to the logical structure and to different media types, is more complicated. For managing many documents with different structures the data model has to be flexible and robust. Another problem is the efficient import of documents and collections. To import structures and attributes from a document a mapping from the document structure onto the data model has to be defined. There are two approaches for mapping documents onto models of an information system. In the first case, the mapping is very simple and user-friendly, the problem is that some useful map definitions are not applicable. In the second approach, the mapping is very complicated and wide-ranged map definitions are possible, but many users have problems to define such a mapping. Because of these problems, we will show a generic and flexible data model and a simple import and mapping language to handle multimedia documents in a digital library.

2 Mapping of Document Collections to the Generic Model

The ideal mapping from a source schema into the target schema would be a one-to-one mapping. But there are problems such as efficiency and complexity of such mappings. For best results, we suggest a manual mapping of the schemes as a basis for automatic mapping of the documents. It is possible to support the manual process by automatic preselection of mapping elements. In order to simplify the process of defining mapping rules, we try to find some mapping rules automatically. The manual mapping has to include definitions of mapping elements. Element attributes (especially from elements which are not mapped) can be also defined with respect to special search scenarios. These mapping elements and attributes can be indexed for fast access. The two mapping functions are sufficient for a simple mapping. Media types and media objects (full-text, images, etc.) are automatically mapped to the right internal data model, i.e., stored in special ways and in appropriate data stores, i.e., in a full-text system. It is also possible to define more complex mapping rules for customizing the document model which will be used internally. Excluding elements or attributes is possible, too.

T.M.T. Sembok et al. (Eds.): ICADL 2003, LNCS 2911, p. 692, 2003.
© Springer-Verlag Berlin Heidelberg 2003

Effective Design of E-learning Application Incorporating Multiple Intelligences

Kemalatha Krishnasamy[1], Sai Peck Lee[1], and Sellappan Palaniappan[2]

[1] Faculty of Computer Science and Information Technology
University of Malaya, 50603 Kuala Lumpur
kemalatha@perdana.um.edu.my
saipeck@um.edu.my
[2] Information Technology Department,
Malaysia University of Science and Technology,
47301 Petaling Jaya, Selangor
sell@must.edu.my

Abstract. Electronic learning (e-learning) is currently a common concept, and this is due to an attempt by many educational sectors to develop structures and systems that are more adaptable and responsive to changes. The real effectiveness of e-learning applications lies in the recognition by the educator and the learner that all people have learning strengths and weaknesses. Within the field of computer science in general and education in particular, there is not much emphasis on the importance of developing an effective electronic learning application that caters for all types of people. Therefore, there is a need to develop an electronic learning application that is not complicated and difficult to use but at the same time considering the various types of learners. This study reviews design strategies for an e-learning application in smart schools and discusses the two main perspectives on the education sector, that is, the focus on generative teaching or learning without incorporating Multiple Intelligences (MI) and the focus on teaching/learning based on Multiple Intelligences where various approaches of learners are considered. Students from selected smart schools in Malaysia participated in Multiple Intelligence assessment based on Dr. Howard Gardner's theory of Multiple Intelligences for determining basic intelligence. Students were also surveyed on their attitude towards electronic learning. Finally, correlation coefficients were computed to match online design of activities with their competencies and characteristics according to their intelligences. The findings of the survey indicate that students with visual/spatial and interpersonal intelligences use and benefit more from online learning and prefer them to traditional instructional strategies techniques when compared with students whose intelligences are verbal/linguistic, logical/mathematical, bodily kinesthetic and intrapersonal. Furthermore, the findings show that some online activities appear to be generic across all applications. The purpose of this study is to determine the success factors in using the Internet for the propagating of learning in Malaysian schools. A secondary purpose is to evaluate the appropriateness and effectiveness of using the online materials and activities prepared in accordance with Multiple Intelligences to enhance the process of teaching and learning at the secondary school level. These issues will form the basis of developing a set of criteria for the integration of the teaching/learning vision, measurement of goals, internal/external data collection, inventiveness and proactive implementation. Educational providers should not plan activities based solely upon popularity.

T.M.T. Sembok et al. (Eds.): ICADL 2003, LNCS 2911, pp. 693–694, 2003.
© Springer-Verlag Berlin Heidelberg 2003

Learning activities are likely to be most effective when the perceived preferred learning mode is combined with a variety of other activities associated with the learning style of an individual based on Multiple Intelligences. The incorporation of Multiple Intelligences in electronic learning strategies provides a degree of flexibility in the way students can undertake their learning and provide a collaborative and interactive environment.

Keywords: e-learning, online learning, Multiple Intelligences, effective design

Integrating Web Databases through Semantic Networks

Jeong-Oog Lee

Dept. Of Computer Science, Konkuk University,
322 Danwol-dong, Chungju-si, Chungcheongbuk-do, 380-701, Korea
ljo@kku.ac.kr

The amount of information which we can get from web environments, especially in the web databases, grew rapidly. And, many questions often can be answered using integrated information than using single web database. Therefore the need for integrating web databases became increasingly. In order to make multiple web databases to interoperate effectively, the integrated system must know where to find the relevant information which is concerned with a user's query on the web databases and which entities in the searched web databases meet the semantics in the user's query.

This paper suggests a method to integrate web databases[1]. Generally, with web interfaces, users can acquire information about what he wants, even though he does not know the detailed database schema information. That is, information in web databases can be provided to the users easily through web interfaces. With analyzing web interfaces, an information integration system can integrate web databases without concerning the underlying database structures. The basic idea is to create virtual database tables for the web databases using fields in web interfaces, which provides ease mechanism for integration regardless of underlying database models, DBMSs, and so forth. The integration system for web databases can integrate web databases easily using these virtual database tables, not needing to know all the actual database schema information.

Using WordNet and the descriptions of the database objects, a concept-based semantic network for each virtual database table can be created. A semantic network provides mappings between concepts in WordNet and information in a virtual database table. After construction of semantic networks for all the virtual database tables, a global semantic network can be created with the semantic relations in WordNet and the semantic networks. A global semantic network provides semantic knowledge about a distributed environment. Also, the proposed approach provides a semantic query language, SemQL, to capture the concepts about what users want, which enables users to issue queries to a large number of autonomous and heterogeneous web databases without knowledge of their schemas.

In the proposed approach, each information source can describe its domain knowledge and construct its own semantic network independent of other information sources, which guarantees the autonomy of each information source. Also, it enables a number of information sources to be merged into the information integration system, so that it gives good extensibility to the system.

---

[1] This paper was supported by Konkuk University in 2003.

T.M.T. Sembok et al. (Eds.): ICADL 2003, LNCS 2911, p. 695, 2003.
© Springer-Verlag Berlin Heidelberg 2003

Metadata++: A Scalable Hierarchical Framework for Digital Libraries[*]

Mathew Weaver[1], Lois Delcambre[1], and Timothy Tolle[2]

[1]Computer Science & Engineering, OGI School of Science & Engineering
Oregon Health & Science University
{mweaver,lmd}@cse.ogi.edu
[2]Resource Planning and Monitoring, Pacific Northwest Region
USDA Forest Service
ttolle@fs.fed.us

Abstract. Metadata++ is a digital library system that we are developing to serve the needs of the United States Department of Agriculture Forest Service, the United States Department of the Interior Bureau of Land Management, and the United States Department of the Interior Fish and Wildlife Service to support natural resource managers, scientists and publics as they analyze issues and make decisions. The system provides access to institutional knowledge consisting of formal and informal agency reports and documents – including Environmental Assessments, Decision Notices, Appeal Decisions, specialist reports, and so forth. Metadata++ uses a set of hierarchically structured controlled vocabularies – with synonyms and associations – as the primary organizational framework. Users browse the hierarchy to select search terms and see the search results directly in the context of the hierarchy. In order to be useful as a digital library infrastructure, this hierarchy must be implemented in an efficient and scalable manner. This paper introduces the Metadata++ system and evaluates the performance of four different approaches to managing the hierarchy. We present a novel approach that uses a common file system with an associated indexing engine to store terms as directories (with narrower terms as subdirectories) and show how we achieve both scalability and efficiency.

---

[*] This work is supported in part by the National Science Foundation, grant number EIA 9983518. Any opinions, findings, conclusions, or recommendations expressed here are those of the author(s) and do not necessarily reflect the views of the National Science Foundation.

T.M.T. Sembok et al. (Eds.): ICADL 2003, LNCS 2911, p. 696, 2003.

The Making of the PolyU Course Scheme Database as One of the Digitization Initiatives of the Pao Yue-kong Library of the Hong Kong Polytechnic University

Christina Chau

Head of Special Collections, Pao Yue-kong Library,
The Hong Kong Polytechnic University,
Hung Hom, Kowloon, Hong Kong.
lbcwchau@polyu.edu.hk

Abstract. Digitization enables increased availability and use of library materials through advances in digital imaging technology. The paper presents the design of the PolyU Course Scheme Database as one of the digitization initiatives of the Pao Yue-kong Library of the Hong Kong Polytechnic University, which is available for remote access starting from 2001. Functionalities of electronic books are added in database design to enhance document interactivity, navigation and retrieval, including provision of hyperlinks to link the Table of Contents to the beginning of chapters, availability of index lists, navigation buttons for moving back and forth among the pages, and full-text search capabilities, etc. In support of the initiative, an in-house database was developed using Microsoft Access which proved to be useful for profiling and management of the Course Scheme Collection by means of VBA codes, look up wizard, filtering, querying, form creation and report generation.

Further Development

The use of the CS Database in Microsoft Access proved to be useful for profiling and management of the Course Scheme Collection. To extend the use and access of the CS Database among staff members, it is planned to implement Active Server Pages (ASP) to link the web interface with the CS Database.

While information professionals are glad to have the opportunity to increase availability of library collections through digitization, we are very much aware of the fact that digital resources may slip away due to rapid changes in technology (Wiggins, 2001). Work has to be done on digital preservation before it is too late to ensure the long-term access to precious digital materials (Woodyard, 2002). Currently, efforts are being made to create backup copies of the data regularly, ensure there is sufficient documentation, and plan to migrate the data to current, compatible format (Deegan, 2002). Following implementation of the Theses Database using XML in the middle of this year, it is planned to migrate the data from Course Scheme Database to XML platform so as to facilitate search and retrieval across multiple collections.

T.M.T. Sembok et al. (Eds.): ICADL 2003, LNCS 2911, pp. 697–698, 2003.
© Springer-Verlag Berlin Heidelberg 2003

References

1. Connaway, Lynn Silipigni (2001) A web-based electronic book (e-book) library: the netLibrary model. *Library Hi Tech* Vol.19, No.4, 340–349.
2. Deegan, Marilyn and Tanner, Simon (2002) *Digital futures: strategies for the information age.* London: Library Association Publishing.
3. Feddema, Helen Bell (2002) *Microsoft Access version 2002 inside out.* Washington: Microsoft Press.
4. Hampson, Andrew, Pinfield, Stephen, and Upton, Ian. (1999) Digitisation of exam papers. *The Electronic Library*, Vol. 17, No. 4, 239–246.
5. Kenney, Anne R., Rieger, Oya Y. (2000) *Moving theory into practice: digital imaging for libraries and archives.* California: Research Libraries Group.
6. Landoni, R.,Wilson, R. and Gibb, F. (2000) From the Visual book to the WEB book: the importance of design. *The Electronic Library.* Vol. 18, No. 6, 407–419.
7. Lee, Stuart D. (2001) *Digital imaging: a practical handbook.* London: Library Association Publishing.
8. Wiggins, Richard. (2001) Digital preservation: paradox & promise. *Library Journal netConnect Supplement*, 12–15.
9. Woodyard, Deborah. (2002) Digital preservation at the British Library. *Library + Information Update* Vol.1, No. 2, 36–37.

Usage of Digital Library Services for the Medical Professionals

Raj Kumar

Institute of Medical Education & Research Sector-12,
Chandigarh – 160012 INDIA
rajkumar196@yahoo.co.in

Abstract. The present paper dwells upon the over-all usage of digital library services for the medical professionals. The medical professionals are in constant need of easy access to the latest information for better care of the patients and the research work. Earlier the access to Medical Information by the Doctor and researcher was difficult because of it being available in the print form only. Now, during the digital revolution, information technology has become too important for the library services to be ignored. Digital library provides rapid and convenient access to the health care information. The digital library services are based on existing Internet communication standards and the World Wide Web software technology to store, organize and disseminate information. The digital library offers the latest updated information about the new modalities of treatment to the medical professionals. The library and information science professionals should accept the challenges, fully explore and utilize the resources for the timely benefit to the medical professionals.

T.M.T. Sembok et al. (Eds.): ICADL 2003, LNCS 2911, p. 699, 2003.
© Springer-Verlag Berlin Heidelberg 2003

Author Index

Lecture Notes in Computer Science

For information about Vols. 1–2828
please contact your bookseller or Springer-Verlag

Vol. 2865: S. Pierre, M. Barbeau, E. Kranakis (Eds.), Ad-Hoc, Mobile, and Wireless Networks. Proceedings, 2003. X, 293 pages. 2003.

Vol. 2867: M. Brunner, A. Keller (Eds.), Self-Managing Distributed Systems. Proceedings, 2003. XIII, 274 pages. 2003.

Vol. 2868: P. Perner, R. Brause, H.-G. Holzhütter (Eds.), Medical Data Analysis. Proceedings, 2003. VIII, 127 pages. 2003.

Vol. 2869: A. Yazici, C. Şener (Eds.), Computer and Information Sciences – ISCIS 2003. Proceedings, 2003. XIX, 1110 pages. 2003.

Vol. 2870: D. Fensel, K. Sycara, J. Mylopoulos (Eds.), The Semantic Web - ISWC 2003. Proceedings, 2003. XV, 931 pages. 2003.

Vol. 2871: N. Zhong, Z.W. Raś, S. Tsumoto, E. Suzuki (Eds.), Foundations of Intelligent Systems. Proceedings, 2003. XV, 697 pages. 2003. (Subseries LNAI)

Vol. 2873: J. Lawry, J. Shanahan, A. Ralescu (Eds.), Modelling with Words. XIII, 229 pages. 2003. (Subseries LNAI)

Vol. 2874: C. Priami (Ed.), Global Computing. Proceedings, 2003. XIX, 255 pages. 2003.

Vol. 2875: E. Aarts, R. Collier, E. van Loenen, B. de Ruyter (Eds.), Ambient Intelligence. Proceedings, 2003. XI, 432 pages. 2003.

Vol. 2876: M. Schroeder, G. Wagner (Eds.), Rules and Rule Markup Languages for the Semantic Web. Proceedings, 2003. VII, 173 pages. 2003.

Vol. 2877: T. Böhme, G. Heyer, H. Unger (Eds.), Innovative Internet Community Systems. Proceedings, 2003. VIII, 263 pages. 2003.

Vol. 2878: R.E. Ellis, T.M. Peters (Eds.), Medical Image Computing and Computer-Assisted Intervention - MICCAI 2003. Part I. Proceedings, 2003. XXXIII, 819 pages. 2003.

Vol. 2879: R.E. Ellis, T.M. Peters (Eds.), Medical Image Computing and Computer-Assisted Intervention - MICCAI 2003. Part II. Proceedings, 2003. XXXIV, 1003 pages. 2003.

Vol. 2880: H.L. Bodlaender (Ed.), Graph-Theoretic Concepts in Computer Science. Proceedings, 2003. XI, 386 pages. 2003.

Vol. 2881: E. Horlait, T. Magedanz, R.H. Glitho (Eds.), Mobile Agents for Telecommunication Applications. Proceedings, 2003. IX, 297 pages. 2003.

Vol. 2882: D. Veit, Matchmaking in Electronic Markets. XV, 180 pages. 2003. (Subseries LNAI)

Vol. 2883: J. Schaeffer, M. Müller, Y. Björnsson (Eds.), Computers and Games. Proceedings, 2002. XI, 431 pages. 2003.

Vol. 2884: E. Najm, U. Nestmann, P. Stevens (Eds.), Formal Methods for Open Object-Based Distributed Systems. Proceedings, 2003. X, 293 pages. 2003.

Vol. 2885: J.S. Dong, J. Woodcock (Eds.), Formal Methods and Software Engineering. Proceedings, 2003. XI, 683 pages. 2003.

Vol. 2886: I. Nyström, G. Sanniti di Baja, S. Svensson (Eds.), Discrete Geometry for Computer Imagery. Proceedings, 2003. XII, 556 pages. 2003.

Vol. 2887: T. Johansson (Ed.), Fast Software Encryption. Proceedings, 2003. IX, 397 pages. 2003.

Vol. 2888: R. Meersman, Zahir Tari, D.C. Schmidt et al. (Eds.), On The Move to Meaningful Internet Systems 2003: CoopIS, DOA, and ODBASE. Proceedings, 2003. XXI, 1546 pages. 2003.

Vol. 2889: Robert Meersman, Zahir Tari et al. (Eds.), On The Move to Meaningful Internet Systems 2003: OTM 2003 Workshops. Proceedings, 2003. XXI, 1096 pages. 2003.

Vol. 2891: J. Lee, M. Barley (Eds.), Intelligent Agents and Multi-Agent Systems. Proceedings, 2003. X, 215 pages. 2003. (Subseries LNAI)

Vol. 2892: F. Dau, The Logic System of Concept Graphs with Negation. XI, 213 pages. 2003. (Subseries LNAI)

Vol. 2893: J.-B. Stefani, I. Demeure, D. Hagimont (Eds.), Distributed Applications and Interoperable Systems. Proceedings, 2003. XIII, 311 pages. 2003.

Vol. 2894: C.S. Laih (Ed.), Advances in Cryptology - ASIACRYPT 2003. Proceedings, 2003. XIII, 543 pages. 2003.

Vol. 2895: A. Ohori (Ed.), Programming Languages and Systems. Proceedings, 2003. XIII, 427 pages. 2003.

Vol. 2896: V.A. Saraswat (Ed.), Advances in Computing Science – ASIAN 2003. Proceedings, 2003. VIII, 305 pages. 2003.

Vol. 2897: O. Balet, G. Subsol, P. Torguet (Eds.), Virtual Storytelling. Proceedings, 2003. XI, 240 pages. 2003.

Vol. 2898: K.G. Paterson (Ed.), Cryptography and Coding. Proceedings, 2003. IX, 385 pages. 2003.

Vol. 2899: G. Ventre, R. Canonico (Eds.), Interactive Multimedia on Next Generation Networks. Proceedings, 2003. XIV, 420 pages. 2003.

Vol. 2901: F. Bry, N. Henze, J. Maluszyński (Eds.), Principles and Practice of Semantic Web Reasoning. Proceedings, 2003. X, 209 pages. 2003.

Vol. 2902: F. Moura Pires, S. Abreu (Eds.), Progress in Artificial Intelligence. Proceedings, 2003. XV, 504 pages. 2003. (Subseries LNAI).

Vol. 2903: T.D. Gedeon, L.C.C. Fung (Eds.), AI 2003: Advances in Artificial Intelligence. Proceedings, 2003. XVI, 1075 pages. 2003. (Subseries LNAI).

Vol. 2904: T. Johansson, S. Maitra (Eds.), Progress in Cryptology – INDOCRYPT 2003. Proceedings, 2003. XI, 431 pages. 2003.

Vol. 2905: A. Sanfeliu, J. Ruiz-Shulcloper (Eds.), Progress in Pattern Recognition, Speech and Image Analysis. Proceedings, 2003. XVII, 693 pages. 2003.

Vol. 2910: M.E. Orlowska, S. Weerawarana, M.P. Papazoglou, J. Yang (Eds.), Service-Oriented Computing – ICSOC 2003. Proceedings, 2003. XIV, 576 pages. 2003.

Vol. 2911: T.M.T. Sembok, H.B. Zaman, H. Chen, S.R. Urs, S.H.Myaeng (Eds.), Digital Libraries: Technology and Management of Indigenous Knowledge for Global Access. Proceedings, 2003. XX, 703 pages. 2003.

Vol. 2913: T.M. Pinkston, V.K. Prasanna (Eds.), High Performance Computing – HiPC 2003. Proceedings, 2003. XX, 512 pages. 2003.

Vol. 2914: P.K. Pandya, J. Radhakrishnan (Eds.), FST TCS 2003: Foundations of Software Technology and Theoretical Computer Science. Proceedings, 2003. XIII, 446 pages. 2003.

Vol. 2916: C. Palamidessi (Ed.), Logic Programming. Proceedings, 2003. XII, 520 pages. 2003.